Published by Willford Press,
118-35 Queens Blvd., Suite 400,
Forest Hills, NY 11375, USA

ISBN: 978-1-68285-754-0

Cataloging-in-Publication Data

Internet : services, challenges and applications / edited by Charlie Penn.
   p. cm.
Includes bibliographical references and index.
ISBN 978-1-68285-754-0
1. Internet. 2. Wide area networks (Computer networks). 3. Computer networks. I. Penn, Charlie.
TK5105.875.I57 I58 2019
004.678--dc23

For information on all Willford Press publications
visit our website at www.willfordpress.com

Contents

Permissions

List of Contributors

Index

Preface

The main aim of this book is to educate learners and enhance their research focus by presenting diverse topics covering this vast field. This is an advanced book which compiles significant studies by distinguished experts in the area of analysis. This book addresses successive solutions to the challenges arising in the area of application, along with it; the book provides scope for future developments.

Internet is a global system of interconnected computer networks, which use the Internet protocol suite (TCP/IP) for linking devices worldwide. It includes public, private, business, academic and government networks that are interconnected by an array of wireless, electronic and optical networking technologies. The Internet consists of a wide range of information services and information resources, such as hypertext documents, electronic mail, applications of the World Wide Web, telephony and file sharing. The Internet communications infrastructure comprises of a system of software layers and hardware components, which control various aspects of its architecture. The Internet is a tool of modern society enabling social interactions, associations and activities. This book brings forth some of the most innovative concepts and elucidates the challenges and applications of Internet services. The ever-growing need of advanced Internet services is the reason that has fueled the research in this field in recent times. This book is a complete source of knowledge on the present status of this important area of study.

It was a great honour to edit this book, though there were challenges, as it involved a lot of communication and networking between me and the editorial team. However, the end result was this all-inclusive book covering diverse themes in the field.

Finally, it is important to acknowledge the efforts of the contributors for their excellent chapters, through which a wide variety of issues have been addressed. I would also like to thank my colleagues for their valuable feedback during the making of this book.

Editor

SimAttack: private web search under fire

Albin Petit[1,2*], Thomas Cerqueus[1], Antoine Boutet[1], Sonia Ben Mokhtar[1], David Coquil[2], Lionel Brunie[1] and Harald Kosch[2]

Abstract

Web Search engines have become an indispensable online service to retrieve content on the Internet. However, using search engines raises serious privacy issues as the latter gather large amounts of data about individuals through their search queries. Two main techniques have been proposed to privately query search engines. A first category of approaches, called *unlinkability*, aims at disassociating the query and the identity of its requester. A second category of approaches, called *indistinguishability*, aims at hiding user's queries or user's interests by either obfuscating user's queries, or forging new fake queries. This paper presents a study of the level of protection offered by three popular solutions: Tor-based, TrackMeNot, and GooPIR. For this purpose, we present an efficient and scalable attack – SimAttack – leveraging a similarity metric to capture the distance between preliminary information about the users (i.e., history of query) and a new query. SimAttack de-anonymizes up to 36.7 % of queries protected by an unlinkability solution (i.e., Tor-based), and identifies up to 45.3 and 51.6 % of queries protected by indistinguishability solutions (i.e., TrackMeNot and GooPIR, respectively). In addition, SimAttack de-anonymizes 6.7 % more queries than state-of-the-art attacks and dramatically improves the performance of the attack on TrackMeNot by 23.6 %, while retaining an execution time faster by two orders of magnitude.

Keywords: Privacy, Web search, Unlinkability, Indistinguishability

1 Introduction

Search engines (e.g., Google, Bing, Yahoo!) have become the preferred way for users to find content on the Internet. However, by repetitively querying for a large number of topics and websites, users disclose a large amount of personal data to these search engines. Consequently, the latter are able to create accurate knowledge on users by extracting their personal interests from their queries. Even though all user queries are not related to sensitive topics, this automated data processing about individuals raises a serious privacy issue, as users cannot control the use of their personal data and have no right to be forgotten. To deal with this issue, many solutions have been proposed to enforce private Web search. These solutions can be mainly classified into two categories. The first one, called *unlinkability*, consists in hiding the user's identity from the search engine (typically her IP address). Anonymous communication protocols (e.g., Onion Routing [1], TOR [2], Dissent [3, 4], RAC [5]) are the main solutions enforcing this property. The second type of solutions, called

indistinguishability, aims at either altering the user's queries or hiding the user's interests. For instance, GooPIR [6] adds extra queries to the original query while TrackMeNot [7] sends periodically fake queries.

Despite these solutions improve the user privacy, a previous study [8] using a machine learning algorithm and preliminary information about the user (i.e., part of its query history) shows that an adversary is able to break both categories of solutions. However, this study was conducted using only 60 specific users (i.e., users who issued queries with a given number of keywords or queries considered as *sensitive* by the authors) and considering non-active users (called "other user" in the study). Consequently, it is not clear if an adversary is still able to break these unlinkability and indistinguishability solutions for active users. As active users can expose more information to the adversary, they represent the most difficult category of users to protect.

To better understand the limits of unlinkability and indistinguishability solutions on individual's privacy, we present in this paper a study of private Web search solutions focusing on active users. This study is conducted

---

*Correspondence: albin.petit@insa-lyon.fr
[1]Université de Lyon, CNRS, INSA-Lyon, LIRIS, UMR5205, F-69621 Lyon, France
[2]Universität Passau, Innstrasse 43, 94032 Passau, Germany

with SimAttack, an efficient attack that leverages a similarity metric to capture the distance between a query and user profiles. These user profiles gather preliminary information about the users collected by the adversary. While the original version of SimAttack [9] was designed for a specific target, this paper presents a generalization of this attack for unlinkability and indistinguishability solutions.

We exhaustively evaluated our new SimAttack on three popular solutions: Tor-based, TrackMeNot, and GooPIR. Our experiments used real world Web search datasets involving up to 15,000 users. We show that SimAttack scales particularly well with respect to the number of users considered in the system. More precisely, compared to the previous machine learning attacks, SimAttack divides by 158 and 100 the execution time considering respectively 1,000 users protected by an unlinkability solution and 100 users protected by TrackMeNot. Moreover, SimAttack succeeds to de-anonymize as many users queries as the machine learning attack for unlinkability solutions, and identify up to 45.3 % of initial queries for TrackMeNot.

Finally, the generic nature of SimAttack based on a similarity distance between pre-built user profiles and a query allows an adversary to design attacks for others private Web search solutions.

For instance, we leverage SimAttack to evaluate the privacy protection offered by GooPIR. We succeed to identify at least 50.6 % of initial queries protected by this solution even if they were protected by 7 fake queries. Last but not least, as we show in our study that the previous aforementioned solutions (i.e., Tor-based, TrackMeNot, and GooPIR) do not protect properly the user privacy, we also analyze hybrid private Web search solutions: GooPIR over an unlinkability solution and TrackMeNot over an unlinkability solution.

The remaining of the paper is organized as follows. In Section 2, we present the state-of-the-art approaches. In Section 3, we describe the considered adversary model. In Section 4, we detail SimAttack and how it is able to break unlinkability solutions, indistinguishability solutions and their combinations. We then present our experimental set-up in Section 5 before evaluating the robustness of unlinkability solutions, TrackMeNot, GooPIR and hybrid solutions in Section 6, 7, 8 and 9, respectively. Finally, Section 10 concludes the paper.

2 Related work
The main solutions to privately query search engines can be classified in two categories: (*i*) systems ensuring unlinkability between requesters and their queries, and (*ii*) systems guaranteeing indistinguishability of user interests. Privacy-aware mechanism can be also directly

implemented on the search engine side through Private Information Retrieval (PIR) protocols.

2.1 Unlinkability solutions
One approach to protect the user privacy from a too curious search engine is to prevent the latter from identifying the real identity of users. The identity of users is tracked through multiple techniques such as the IP address, quasi-identifiers (e.g., cookies), or fingerprints (e.g., HTTP headers, set of browser plugins [10]). While quasi-identifiers can be removed as suggested in [11], a basic solution to hide the IP address consists in leveraging a Proxy [12] or a VPN [13] server as relay. This distant server forwards user queries to the search engine on behalf of the user and returns results to the user. Unfortunately, this mechanism only shifts the privacy problem from the search engine to the relay which can collect and analyze queries from users.

Anonymous networks (e.g., Onion Routing [1], Tor [2], Dissent [3, 4], RAC [5]) represents a more complex approach to prevent a third party to map a user identity to a query. Indeed, anonymous network leverages onion routing and path forwarding to route user queries through multiple nodes before reaching the search engine. However, this approach relies on either a high number of cryptographic operations (e.g., Tor-based solutions), or all-to-all communication (e.g., RAC and Dissent) which generate a costly overhead in terms of latency and network traffic. These important overheads make anonymous networks impractical for interactive tasks such as Web search.

Other techniques try to achieve the same goal using a fully decentralized architecture. For instance, [14] and [15] proposed a protocol in which users exchange their queries in a privacy-preserving way (i.e., users do not know who issued which queries) and send them on behalf of each other. As the identity of the initial requester is unknown by the search engine and the other users, the results must be broadcasted to all the users. Therefore, these solutions generate significant overheads in terms of traffic and latency.

2.2 Indistinguishability solutions
Indistinguishability solutions consist in making the search engine only able to collect inaccurate users' queries and interests. Consequently, as the users' interests cannot be truly discovered, the privacy of users is preserved. A popular solution in this category, TrackMeNot [7], periodically sends fake queries on behalf the user. The challenge in this approach is to create fake queries that cannot be distinguished from the real ones. To do so, TrackMeNot (TMN) based the generation of fake queries on RSS feeds. However, as these RSS feeds are set up by default or manually by the user, an adversary could be able

to distinguish real queries from fake ones. For instance, in [16] authors present a simple clustering attack over small time windows that enables an adversary to retrieve fake queries. Besides, other solutions adopt a similar technique: Plausibly Deniable Search (PDS) [17] generates k plausibly deniable queries which are similar to previous user queries but on different topics. Optimized Query Forgery (OQF) [18] provides a theoretical approach to generate fake queries by measuring the Kullback-Leibler divergence between the user profile and the population distribution. Noise Injection for Search Privacy Protection (NISSP) [19] (another similar approach to OQF) gives a theoretical property that optimal fake queries should respect. However, these four solutions (TMN, PDS, OQF and NISSP) might overload the network by generating a large number of fake queries.

Another possibility to achieve indistinguishability is to modify the initial query. For instance, GooPIR [6] adds to the initial query $(k - 1)$ fake queries (generated using a dictionary) where all of these queries are separated by the logical OR operation in a new obfuscated query. As GooPIR's authors consider that an adversary has no background knowledge about the user, this adversary can only guess the initial query with a probability equal to $1/k$. However, we present in Section 4 an efficient attack that is able to retrieve the initial query with a high probability considering user profiles preliminary created with their past queries. Another technique called Query Scrambler (QS) [20] protects the user by sending, instead of the initial query, a set of new queries built by generalizing the concepts of the initial query. Then, by filtering all the results, QS retrieves potential results related to the initial query. However, despite similar queries and the filtering approach proposed, the accuracy of the results remains low compared to the results obtained by issuing the original query.

A new approach using multiple HTTP cookies has been proposed to protect the user privacy while keeping the search engine able to store information about the activity of users. In this solution, the search engine splits user queries in multiple group profiles according to cookie sent with the query. Nevertheless, this approach supposes that a search engine only uses cookies to identify users and does not take into consideration other elements such as the IP address, the HTTP header, or other fingerprints. Besides, by splitting queries in multiple user profiles, this method only decreases the disclosure of information.

2.3 Private information retrieval

Search engines can implement Private Information Retrieval (PIR) protocols to offer privacy preserving query service to users. For instance, [21] presents a system in which the query is broken down in multiple buckets of words and then, the user uses homomorphic encryption to retrieve search results without revealing her initial query. However, this scheme faces many limitations to be adopted in practice (i.e., costly homomorphic encryption and it requires specific implementation at the search engine side).

3 Adversary model

Users are more and more concerned about the privacy risks of querying search engines. In this paper, we analyze the robustness of popular private Web search solutions. We considered three categories of solutions: unlinkability solutions, indistinguishability solutions, and indistinguishability solutions over unlinkability solutions. In our approach, we assumed an adversary which aims to retrieve for each protected query, both the content of the initial query and the identity of the associated user. Moreover, we assumed an adversary which was able to collect preliminary information about the interests of each user in the system. This preliminary information are stored in user profile structures. Preliminary information of users can be collected in different manners, from their social networks activity, from their posts on blogs or discussions on forums [1]. In this paper, we considered as preliminary information a part of the history of query of users.

In practice, our adversary model can be seen as a search engine receiving protected queries from users who just start to adopt a private Web search solution. In this use case, the preliminary information represent the non-protected queries sent by the users to the search engine before the exploitation of a private Web search solution. Consequently, the most active users have exposed more preliminary information to the search engine through their past querying activity.

4 SimAttack

In this section, we present SimAttack, an attack against private Web search solutions. SimAttack computes a distance between an incoming query and the preliminary information collected by the adversary (i.e., user profiles). As consequence, according to this similarity distance, the adversary is able to de-anonymize the query or differentiate the fake queries from real ones. SimAttack is a user-centric attack which tries to compromise the privacy of each user independently. In this paper, we generalized the original version of SimAttack [9] for unlinkability and indistinguishability solutions.

Compared to existing attacks, SimAttack is generic and can be adapted against all types of private Web search solutions. Indeed, by defining the user profile and the considered similarity metric, an adversary can personalize SimAttack to any type of protections.

The next sections explain how the similarity between a user profile and a query is computed, and detail how SimAttack is able to break several types of protection mechanism based on unlinkability, indistinguishability, and indistinguishability over unlinkability.

4.1 Similarity metric between a query and a user profile

We create a similarity metric $sim(q, P_u)$ to characterize the proximity between a query q and a user profile P_u. As mentioned in [22], vector space model is widely used for text representation. Thus, we model the query q as a vector where each dimension corresponds to a separate term. For each dimension, the value of the vector is either 0 or 1 (i.e., 0 means that the keyword is not used in the query while 1 means that the keyword is used in the query). Let us define a user profile P_u as a set of queries (i.e., a set of word vectors). The similarity metric $sim(q, P_u)$ returns a value between 0 and 1 where greater values indicate that the query is close to the user's profile. It is computed as presented in Algorithm 1.

Algorithm 1: Similarity metric between a query and a user profile

input: q : a query,
$\quad\quad$ P_u : profile of user u (history of query issued by u),
$\quad\quad$ α : a smoothing factor.

1 **for** $q_i \in P_u$ **do**
2 $\quad$ $coef[i] \leftarrow 2 \cdot |q \cap q_i| \cdot \frac{1}{|q_i|+|q|}$;
3 $coef \leftarrow sort(coef)$;
4 $sim \leftarrow coef[0]$;
5 **for** $i \in [\![1, |P_u|]\!]$ **do**
6 $\quad$ $sim \leftarrow \alpha \cdot coef[i] + (1 - \alpha) \cdot sim$
7 **return** sim ;

It first computes the value $coef[i]$ corresponding to the Dice's coefficient [23] between the query q and the query q_i stored in P_u, the profile of user u (line 2). As defined in Section 3, this profile contains part of the history of query already issued by the user and preliminary collected by the adversary. The coefficients $coef[i]$ are then ranked in ascending order (line 3). The similarity metric $sim(q, P_u)$ is finally computed as the exponential smoothing of these coefficients (lines 4 to 6). Consequently, this similarity depends on the smoothing factor α that enables to change the weight given to the coefficients. This parameter α takes its value between 0 and 1. In practice, the value of α does not strongly impact the results as shown in Section 6.1. Furthermore, we consider the Dice's coefficient which gives slightly better results than other similarity metrics (e.g., cosine similarity [22], Jaccard index [24]). As shown in our evaluations, although SimAttack is faster than concurrent approaches, the time required to perform the attack must remain as short as possible. The

Dice's coefficient provides a good trade off between performance against execution time compared to edit-based and more complex token-based metrics [25].

4.2 Unlinkability attack

The de-anonymization attack consists in finding the identity of the requester of a specific query. Algorithm 2 describes this attack. For each user profile P_u previously collected by the adversary, it computes its similarity with the query q (line 3). It then returns the identity id corresponding to the profile with the highest similarity. If the highest similarity equals 0 (i.e., all similarities equal 0), the identity of the requester remains unknown and the attack is unsuccessful. Otherwise, the algorithm considers the user, id, as the issuer of the query q.

Algorithm 2: De-anonymization Solutions Attack

input: q : a query,
$\quad\quad$ U : set of users.

1 $id \leftarrow u_0$;
2 **for** $u_i \in U$ **do**
3 $\quad$ **if** $sim(q, P_{u_i}) > sim(q, P_{id})$ **then** $id \leftarrow u_i$
4 **if** $sim(q, P_{id}) > 0$ **then return** id **else return** $\emptyset$

4.3 Indistinguishability attack

The attack against indistinguishability solutions aims to identify initial queries among faked or obfuscated queries received by the search engine. Contrary to the previous attack, the adversary knows the identity of the user and thus tries to pinpoint fake queries by analyzing the similarity between queries and the user profile. The attack detailed in the Algorithm 3 proceeds as follow. It first determines which obfuscation mechanism is being used. More precisely, it checks if the obfuscated query q^+ contains several fakes queries separated by the logical OR operator (line 1) (i.e., behavior of GooPIR). It might appear that the logical OR operator was introduced by the user in her query (and not by the obfuscation mechanism). Nevertheless, as the user query and all fake queries have the same number of keywords, it is easy in most of cases to detect if the logical OR was introduced by the user or the obfuscation mechanism.

Let us consider the first case in which the query q^+ is composed of $k+1$ queries (i.e., the initial query and k fake queries). The algorithm extracts each aggregated query q_i from q^+ and computes the similarity metric between these aggregated queries q_i and the user profile P_u (lines 3 and 4). Then it stores the query with the highest similarity in the variable q'. If the similarity $sim(q', P_u)$ is different from 0, the algorithm returns q' as the initial request. Otherwise, the attack fails and the initial query is not retrieved as the $(k + 1)$ queries are not similar to any user profile.

On the second case (i.e., the query does not contain the logical OR operator), it distinguishes two cases: if the adversary has a prior knowledge about RSS feeds used by the user to generate the fake queries or not. If we consider first that the adversary does not have this external knowledge, it evaluates if the similarity between the query q^+ and the user profile P_u is greater than a given threshold δ. If so, then q^+ is considered as a real query, and is therefore returned (line 8). Otherwise, the query is considered to be a fake query (line 11).

Algorithm 3: Indistinguishability Solutions Attack

    input: q^+ : a query,
           P_u : a user profile,
           δ : a threshold,
           P_{FQ} : a profile of fake queries.

1 **if** $q^+ = q_0$ OR ... OR q_k **then**
    // q^+ contains fake queries (i.e.,
       GooPIR)
2     $q' \leftarrow q_0$;
3   **for** $q_i \in q^+$ **do**
4   **if** $sim(q_i, P_u) > sim(q', P_u)$ **then** $q' \leftarrow q_i$
5   **if** $sim(q', P_u) > 0$ **then return** q'
6 **else**
    // q^+ is either a fake query or a
       real query (i.e., TrackMeNot)
7   **if** $P_{FQ} = \emptyset$ **then**
8   **if** $sim(q^+, P_u) > \delta$ **then return** q^+
9   **else**
10   **if** $sim(q^+, P_u) > sim(q^+, P_{FQ})$ **then return** q^+
11 **return** $\emptyset$;
    // q^+ is a fake query

Conversely, if we consider the situation where the adversary knows the RSS feeds used by the user to generate the fake queries, the adversary generates fake queries using these predefined RSS feeds. These fake queries are stored in a profile P_{FQ} (same structure as a user profile P_u). Then, the adversary uses this external knowledge to distinguish fake queries (line 10). It first compares the similarity between the query q^+ and the user profile P_u (i.e., $sim(q^+, P_u)$) against the similarity between the query q^+ and the profile of fake queries P_{FQ} (i.e., $sim(q^+, P_{FQ})$). If $sim(q^+, P_u)$ is greater than $sim(q^+, P_{FQ})$, q^+ is closer to the user profile than the profile of fake queries. Consequently, q^+ is considered as a real query, and is then

returned. Otherwise, the query is considered to be a fake query (line 11).

4.4 Indistinguishability over an unlinkability solution attack

The attack that breaks an indistinguishability solution over an unlinkability solution combines the two previous attacks. The attack aims at identifying both the initial requester and the initial query. To achieve that, it follows the Algorithm 4. As the attack presented in Algorithm 3, the Algorithm 4 first determines which obfuscation mechanism is being used by looking for logical OR operators (line 1). In that case, it first extracts the $(k + 1)$ queries q_i from q^+ and then retrieves for each query q_i, its potential requester $id[i]$ by invoking Algorithm 2 (lines 2 to 3). Then, it removes queries which are not associated to a potential requester (lines 5 to 6), i.e. queries for which Algorithm 2 was unsuccessful. We denote the set of indexes corresponding to the remaining queries by I. Finally, if I contains one element a (i.e., only one query is associated to a potential requester), it returns the pair $(q_a, id[a])$ corresponding to the initial query q_a and to the initial requester $id[a]$ (lines 7 to 9).

However, if I contains at least two elements, it retrieves the pairs $(q_a, id[a])$ and $(q_b, id[b])$ which have the highest similarity over I and evaluates the difference between them (i.e., $sim(q_a, P_{id[a]}) - sim(q_b, P_{id[b]})$). To ensure a certain confidence in the results, if this difference is too small, the attack is thus unsuccessful, as the algorithm retrieves at least two pairs of query and requester, and it is not able to clearly identify the real one. However, if the difference is greater than a threshold (initialized at 0.01 by default), it returns the pair $(q_a, id[a])$ corresponding to the initial query q_a and to the initial requester $id[a]$ which maximizes $sim(q_a, P_{id[a]})$ over I (lines 10 to 14).

When queries do not contain OR operators, the algorithm first retrieves the potential requester id by calling the Algorithm 2 (line 16). If this id is not empty (i.e., if the attack made by the Algorithm 2 is successful), it distinguishes two cases depending if the adversary has a prior knowledge about RSS feeds used by the user. As mentioned in the previous section, if the adversary is able to generate fake queries, she creates a profile P_{FQ} (similar to user profile P_u) that contains a set of fake queries. Let us consider the first case in which the adversary does not have this knowledge (lines 18 to 19). The adversary is able to distinguish between fake queries and real ones by comparing the similarity between the query q^+ and the user profile P_{id} (i.e., $sim(q^+, P_{id})$) with the threshold δ. If $sim(q^+, P_{id})$ is greater than δ, the query is considered as a real query sent by the user id and thus, the pair (q^+, id) is returned.

Now, if we consider that the adversary is able to generate a set of fake queries (lines 20 to 22). The algorithm determines if the similarity distance between the query q^+ and the user profile P_{id} (i.e., $sim(q^+, P_{id})$) is greater than the similarity metric between the query q^+ and the profile of fake queries P_{FQ} (i.e., $sim(q^+, P_{FQ})$). In that case, the pair (q^+, id) is respectively considered as the initial query and the initial requester and returned by the algorithm. Otherwise, as no pair has been returned, the attack is either unsuccessful or the query is considered as a fake query (line 23).

Algorithm 4: Indistinguishability over unlinkability Attack

---

    input: q^+ : a query,
           U : set of users,
           δ : a threshold
           P_{FQ} : a profile of fake queries.
1 **if** $q^+ = q_0$ OR ... OR q_k **then**
      // q^+ contains fake queries
2   **for** $q_i \in q^+$ **do**
3       $id[\,i\,] \leftarrow$ Algorithm_2(q_i, U);
4    $I \leftarrow [\![0, k]\!]$;
5   **for** $i \in [\![0, k]\!]$ **do**
6   **if** $id[\,i\,] = \emptyset$ **then** $I \leftarrow I \backslash \{i\}$
7   **if** $|I| = 1$ **then**
8       $a \in I$;
9   **return** $(q_a, id[\,a\,])$;
10   **else if** $|I| > 1$ **then**
11      $a \leftarrow$ index s.t. $sim(q_a, P_{id[a]})$ is maximal over I;
12      $b \leftarrow$ index s.t. $sim(q_b, P_{id[b]})$ is maximal over $I \backslash \{a\}$;
13   **if** $sim(q_a, P_{id[a]}) - sim(q_b, P_{id[b]}) > 0.01$ **then**
14   **return** $(q_a, id[\,a\,])$;
15 **else**
      // q^+ does not contain fake queries
16   $id \leftarrow$ Algorithm_2(q^+, U);
17   **if** $id \neq \emptyset$ **then**
18   **if** $P_{FQ} = \emptyset$ **then**
19   **if** $sim(q^+, P_{id}) > \delta$ **then** **return** (q^+, id)
20   **else**
21   **if** $sim(q^+, P_{id}) > sim(q^+, P_{FQ})$ **then**
22   **return** (q^+, id)
23 **return** $\emptyset$; // the attack is unsuccessful or q^+ is a fake query

---

5 Experimental set-up

In this section, we provide the experimental set-up of our evaluation: the datasets, an overview of the considered indistinguishability solutions (i.e., TrackMeNot and GooPIR), and both the evaluation metrics and the concurrent approaches we use to assess the performance of SimAttack. All our experiments were conducted on a commodity desktop workstation with a 2.2 GHz quad core processor with 8 GB of memory.

5.1 Web search dataset

To evaluate the robustness of private Web search solutions, we use a real world Web search dataset from AOL Web search logs [26] published in 2006. AOL dataset contains approximately 21 million queries formulated by 650,000 users over three months (March, April and May of 2006). As this dataset contains many inactive users (i.e., users that issued too few queries), we first filtered the whole dataset to target active users. More precisely, we select users that: (*i*) sent queries on at least 45 different days (i.e., half of the dataset period), and (*ii*) issued queries on a period of at least 61 days (i.e., two-thirds of the dataset period). Finally, after this filtering phase, our dataset gathers 18,164 users who issued from 62 queries to 3,156 queries over the dataset period.

We then focus on the most active users as they are the most exposed to an adversary. We create 5 datasets containing different number of active users (from 100 to 1,000 users): AOL100, AOL200, AOL300, AOL500, AOL1000. To do that, we order the 18,164 users according to the number of queries they issued and then select the top 1,000 users to create the dataset AOL1000. We then generate the 4 other datasets as a subset of AOL1000. To retain similar statistical properties and ensure that users issued a significant number of queries, we generate these 4 datasets by choosing randomly (according to the distribution of the number of queries per user) the desired number of users (e.g., 100 users for AOL100). Figure 1 depicts the Cumulative Distribution Function (CDF) of

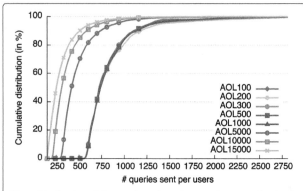

Fig. 1 Distribution of the number of queries issued per user for the different dataset

the number of queries issued by user in these 5 datasets. These CDF show that users part of these datasets issued at least 500 queries. We also note that each of these 5 datasets follows approximately the same distribution.

In addition, to assess private Web search solutions with a larger number of users, we create 3 extra datasets containing the top 5,000, 10,000 and 15,000 users: AOL5000, AOL10000 and AOL15000. Figure 1 shows that these 3 datasets do not follow the previous distribution of queries per user due to the lack of high active users in the AOL dataset. However, results obtained with these datasets give a lower bound as having more queries in the user profile would likely increases the efficiency of the attack.

Finally, we pre-process and filter the queries of users to remove the irrelevant keywords. To achieve that, we leverage the Stanford CoreNLP library [27]. Using the tokenizer, we split queries in string vectors and then remove stop words (i.e., articles and short function words) and irrelevant keywords. Irrelevant keywords are identified with the *Named Entity Tagger* and the *Part-Of-Speech Tagger*. The former enables the recognition of names or numerical and temporal entities while the latter recognizes the function of the word. As consequence, numbers, dates or pronouns are removed. Lastly, we stem each keyword by eliminating or replacing the suffix using Porter algorithm [28].

As mentioned in Section 3, we considered that the adversary has already built a user profile for each user. Consequently, we split each dataset in two parts: a training set used to build the user profiles, and a testing set used to assess the robustness of the considered privacy-preserving mechanism. We used two third of user queries to create the training set and the remaining third of queries to create the testing set. We used two third of user queries to create the training set, and the remaining third of queries to create the testing set.

5.2 TrackMeNot

TrackMeNot, called TMN in the rest of the paper, is a Firefox plugin which periodically generates fake queries to hide user queries in a stream of related queries. After the installation of TMN, the user can define different settings to select the desired level of protection. Two main parameters impact the user protection: the RSS feed lists and the delay between two fake queries. The RSS feeds list is composed by default of four RSS feeds coming from: cnn.com, nytimes.com, msnbc.com and theregister.co.uk. The user can modify this list to remove or add extra RSS feeds. Modifying this setting is crucial, as keeping the initial list might help an adversary to distinguish between real queries and fake ones. However, it is not trivial for users to find good RSS feeds, as they should find RSS feeds that cover all their ever changing interests. Moreover, the user can customize the

protection by choosing the time between two fake queries. TMN offers several possibilities: from 10 fake queries per minute to 1 fake query per hour. Consequently, the users are able to chose the quantity of noise they want to introduce in their queries. Also, the user could activate the "burst mode". In that case, when the user issues a query, TMN sends in the same time multiple fake queries to cover it.

To generate these fake queries, TMN transforms titles of articles listed in RSS feeds into queries. To do so, it randomly extracts keywords from a title and aggregate them into a fake query. The number of keywords is randomly chosen between 1 and 6. As a direct consequence, for a given title, this algorithm is able to create multiple fake queries and thus, two TMN users using the same RSS feeds do not systematically create the same fake queries.

Finally, to simulate users using TMN, we need to add fake queries to the datasets created in Section 5.1. To do that, we create our own implementation of TMN to generated the fake queries. We thus collected RSS feeds from the TMN default setting during one month and half (from August 28th, 2014 to October 9th, 2014), and we generate fake queries from the 13,878 news titles that we extracted. Additionally, we need to specify the number of fake queries that we want to generate. To do so, we consider that users used their computers 8 hours a day and have set up *60 queries per hour*. Consequently, we generate 14,880 fake queries per users (i.e., 60 queries × 8 hours × 31 days). We call TMN100 this new dataset that contains the queries of AOL100 plus 1,488,000 fake queries.

To ensure that the generated fake queries (built from RSS feeds captured in 2014) are using similar terms that users cared to look for in 2006, we compute the overlap between the words used in fake queries and the words used in the whole AOL dataset. We found out that 85.6 % of words used in fake queries are also contained in the AOL dataset (6,918 words out 8,082).

Furthermore, we also generate fake queries for the adversary (i.e., profile of fake queries P_{FQ} defined in Section 4.3). To do that, we generate the same number of fake queries for the adversary as for users (i.e., 14,880 fake queries).

5.3 GooPIR

GooPIR (Google Private Information Retrieval) is a Java program to query Google in a privacy-preserving way. This protection mechanism can also be used with other search engine but only Google is supported by the application. GooPIR obfuscates user queries by adding extra fake queries separated by the logical OR operation. GooPIR uses a dictionary to generate these fake queries. It can exploit any type of dictionary – in the current implementation news articles from WikiNews are used but GooPIR's authors mentioned that query logs can also be used. By default, GooPIR creates three fake queries but users can manually set up this number.

To generate k fake queries, GooPIR selects for each keyword of the initial query, k words using the dictionary. All these k selected words have a similar usage frequency than the keyword in the initial query. Consequently, if the initial query is composed of n keywords, GooPIR selects $k \times n$ words and then creates k fake queries of n words (i.e., fake queries and user's queries have the same number of keywords).

Query answers returned by Google contain results related to the initial query but also to the fake ones. As a consequence, GooPIR implements a filtering phase that tries to remove irrelevant results introduced by fake queries. This algorithm tests for each result if its title or its description contains keywords of the initial queries. If so, the result is displayed, it is discarded otherwise.

In our experiments, to implement the behavior of GooPIR, we created the dictionary from the AOL dataset by extracting all keywords and their usage frequency from the 20 million AOL Web search queries.

5.4 Evaluation metrics

To measure the efficiency of SimAttack, we consider the precision and the recall as defined below:

$$precision = \frac{1}{|U|} \sum_{u \in U} \frac{|A_u|}{|A_u| + |\overline{A_u}|}$$

$$recall = \frac{1}{|U|} \sum_{u \in U} \frac{|A_u|}{|Q_u|}$$

where U is the set of users in the system, Q_u is the set of queries sent by user u, A_u is the set of queries issued by user u and successfully retrieved by the adversary, and $\overline{A_u}$ is specific for each solution: (i) for unlinkability solutions, $\overline{A_u}$ is the set of queries not issued by the user u but considered by the attack as sent by u ; (ii) for TMN, $\overline{A_u}$ is the set of fake queries sent by u identified by the attack as real queries ; (iii) for GooPIR, $\overline{A_u}$ is the set of queries issued by u and not retrieved by the attack ; (iv) for TMN over an unlinkability solution, $\overline{A_u}$ is either the set of fake queries issued by u identified by the attack as real queries, or the set of queries not issued by u but considered by the attack as real queries sent by u ; (v) for GooPIR over an unlinkability solution, $\overline{A_u}$ is either the set of queries issued by u and not retrieved by the attack, or the set of not queries issued by u but considered by the attack as real queries sent by u.

To evaluate the trade off between the precision and the recall, we also consider the F-Measure as the harmonic mean of precision and recall:

$$F\text{-}Measure = 2 \cdot \frac{precision \cdot recall}{precision + recall}$$

5.5 Concurrent approach

To compare the performance of SimAttack, we consider a recent attack using machine learning algorithms [8] as comparison baseline. This attack targets both unlinkability solutions and TMN, and uses Weka [29] as machine learning framework. In both cases, this attack is based on two steps: it first builds and trains a model for each user from its query history (and for TMN, it builds and trains a model from fake queries), and then it leverages these models to de-anonymize anonymous queries or to distinguish fake queries from real ones.

To de-anonymize anonymous queries, the concurrent attack uses the Support Vector Machine (SVM) classifier. This choice is motivated by a previous study [30] that shows that SVM classifier gives better results for text classification. To implement this attack, we reproduce the same condition as reported by the authors: using LibSVM (i.e., an efficient implementation of SVM), the same algorithm (i.e., C-SVC), and the same type of kernel (i.e., linear). We also let the parameter Epsilon (i.e., tolerance of termination criterion) to its default value (i.e., 0.001). However, for parameter C (i.e., cost), Weka offers a specific option (`CVParameterSelection`) to find the value that maximizes the performance of the classification. Using this option, we found out that the best value for C is 1.1.

To distinguish fake queries from real ones, the concurrent attack considers several machine learning algorithms: Logistic Regression, Alternating Decision Trees, Random Forest, Random Tree and ZeroR. For the sake of simplicity, we only use the *Logistic Regression* classifier (reported by the authors of the attack as the classifier which produces the best performance), and the SVM classifier (which was not considered in the previous study).

6 Evaluation of unlinkability solutions

In this section, we evaluate the capacity of SimAttack to compromise the anonymity of users' queries protected by an unlinkability solutions. More precisely, we assess the sensitivity of SimAttack on unlinkability solutions over various parameters. Finally, we compare the performance provided by SimAttack against the performance of the concurrent machine learning approach.

6.1 Impact of smoothing factor α

As described in Section 4.1, the smoothing parameter α of SimAttack influences the similarity distance between a query and the user profile. To measure the impact of this parameter, we report on Fig. 2 the F-Measure returned by SimAttack for varying values of α on three different datasets: AOL100, AOL200, AOL300. We show that α has a limited impact on the performance of SimAttack to break the anonymity of users' queries for all datasets. For instance, for AOL100, the F-Measure only varies from

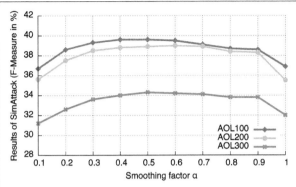

Fig. 2 The smoothing factor α has not a significant impact on the F-Measure of SimAttack

36.9 to 39.6 %. As the best F-Measure is observed for α at 0.5, we fixed the parameter α at 0.5 in the remaining evaluations.

6.2 Impact of the number of users in the system

The probability to associate a query with its correct requester is inversely proportional to the number of users in the system. Indeed, the more the users, the more the possibility to do a wrong mapping increases. To study the impact of the number of users in the system, Fig. 3 depicts both the recall and precision of SimAttack with different number of users. Results show that both recall and precision decrease when the number of users in the system increases. For instance, SimAttack de-anonymizes 36.7 % of queries with a precision of 42.9 % if we consider 100 users while it only de-anonymizes 11.9 % of queries with a precision of 17.7 % for 15,000 users. Nevertheless, this decrease is not linear and tends to stabilize as the number of users increases (around 10 % of recall for 15,000 users). As consequence, from a certain number of users, increasing this number does not offer a better protection.

6.3 Impact of targeting p users with the highest similarity instead of the highest one

In the previous sections, we consider that SimAttack succeeds if the attack returns the correct user. However, depending on the intentions of the adversary, this latter might consider that the attack succeeds if the initial user is among the 3, 5 or 10 most probable users. Consequently, we adapt SimAttack to link a query to the p most probable users. Results of this attack for different number of users in the system are illustrated in Fig. 4. Obviously, the number of de-anonymized queries increases according to the number of users considered by the adversary. However, this increase is rather small. For instance, the adversary de-anonymizes in average only 12.9 % more queries if the 10 most probable users are targeted compared to targeting the most probable one (i.e., $p = 10$ versus $p = 1$). In addition, if the adversary considers the 10 most probable users (i.e., $p = 10$) while the systems gather 100 users, the recall only reaches 52.8 %. This results is counter-intuitive, as the 10 most probable users represent 10 % of the dataset, this number is expected to be close to 100 % (as there is a high probability that an initial user is among the 10 most probable users). One possible explanation is that a large proportion of non-retrieved queries (74.8 % if we consider 100 users) was not retrieved because they do not contain keywords that has been already used in the previous queries of users. Therefore, these queries cannot be retrieved as their similarity with the user profile equals 0.

6.4 Impact of the number of user profiles

In the previous sections, we consider that the adversary has pre-built as many user profiles as the number of users in the system. However, in practice, the adversary might consider more user profiles than the number of users in the system. Consequently, we present on Fig. 5 the precision and the recall of SimAttack when the system gathers 100 users while the adversary considers from 100 to 1,000 user profiles. Results shows that increasing the number of

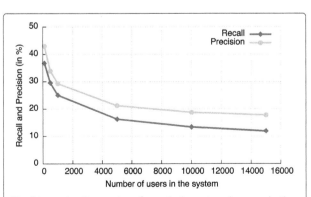

Fig. 3 Increasing the number of users in the system decreases both the recall and the precision of SimAttack

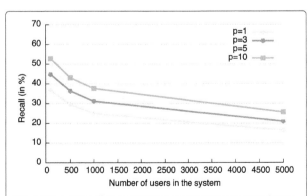

Fig. 4 The number of de-anonymized queries increases according to the number of probable users returned by SimAttack

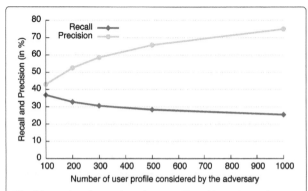

Fig. 5 Increasing the number of user profiles, with respect to the number of users in the system, decreases the precision while slightly reducing the recall

user profiles with the respect to the number of users in the system decreases the recall. For instance, adding 900 extra user profiles decreases the recall by 11.3 %. Indeed, the probability to correctly map queries from users to profile (i.e., the recall) increases as the number of possible user profiles decreases. On the contrary, the precision significantly increases according to the number of user profiles considered by the adversary. For instance, introducing 900 extra user profiles increases by 32 % the precision. Indeed, considering a larger number of user profiles reduces the number of misclassified queries between all the profiles and consequently, for a given user profile, the number of irrelevant queries (i.e., queries belonging to another user) decreases.

6.5 Impact of the size of the user profiles
The number of past queries of the users used to build the user profiles, and consequently the size of their profiles, impacts the efficiency of the unlinkability attack. To measure this impact, we depict on Fig. 6 the precision and the recall of SimAttack for AOL100 when the profile of users pre-built by the adversary only contains a sub part of their query history (from 0 to 100 %). Results show

that the efficiency of the attack decreases according to the proportion of queries considered in user profiles. Considering 100 % of past queries in user profiles provides 36.7 % of recall while considering only 5 % of queries drops this value to 16.9 %. This result illustrates that exploiting less accurate user profiles (i.e., preliminary information about the users) makes harder for the adversary to de-anonymization queries. Nevertheless, we note that the number of de-anonymized queries gently decreases (i.e., 8.7 %) when the proportion of queries considered in user profiles drops from 100 to 20 %. As a consequence, from a certain quantity of queries in a user profile, refining this profile does not significantly help the adversary to de-anonymize a higher number of queries.

6.6 Privacy protection
We now compare the performance of both SimAttack and the concurrent machine learning attack on unlinkability solutions. Figure 7 measures for both attacks the precision and the recall for different number of users in the system. Results show that both attacks have a similar recall and precision. For instance, for AOL200, SimAttack has a recall of 36.8 % and a precision of 41.4 % against 34.4 and 39.1 %, respectively, for the machine learning attack. Nevertheless, regardless the dataset, SimAttack is slightly better than the machine learning attack. In average, the F-Measure of SimAttack is 3 % higher than the F-Measure obtained with the concurrent attack.

6.7 Scalability
We then compare the performance in term of scalability of SimAttack against the concurrent machine learning approach. More precisely, we evaluate the execution time required by these two attacks when the number of users increases. Figure 8 compares the execution time of these attacks (using a logarithmic scale). The results show that the execution time for SimAttack increases linearly with respect to the number of users while this evolution is exponential for the machine learning attack. In addition,

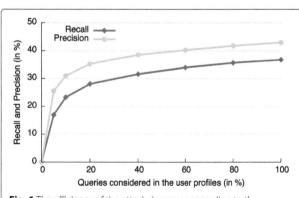

Fig. 6 The efficiency of the attack decreases according to the proportion of queries considered in user profiles

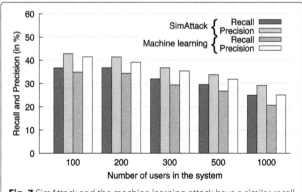

Fig. 7 SimAttack and the machine learning attack have a similar recall and precision

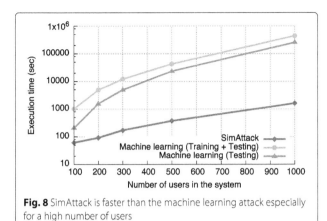

Fig. 8 SimAttack is faster than the machine learning attack especially for a high number of users

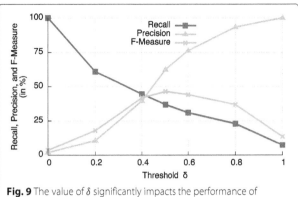

Fig. 9 The value of δ significantly impacts the performance of SimAttack

SimAttack is faster than the machine learning attack especially for a high number of users. For 1,000 users, the machine learning attack, including the time to train models, spends 434,322 *sec* while SimAttack spends 1,598 *sec*, 271 times faster. Without considering the time needed to train models (as the adversary might exploit the same models for multiple attacks), SimAttack remains faster than the machine learning (158 times faster).

6.8   Summary
SimAttack is able to de-anonymize a large number of queries protected by unlinkability solutions. Nevertheless, the SimAttack's capacity of de-anonymizing queries depends on the number of users in the system, and both the number and the quality of the preliminary user profiles collected by the adversary. While SimAttack provides similar performances than the concurrent machine learning attack, SimAttack is much more faster.

7   Evaluation of TrackMeNot
In this section, we evaluate the capacity of SimAttack to distinguish fake queries sent by TrackMeNot from the real queries sent by users. More precisely, we assess the sensitivity of SimAttack for TMN over various parameters. Finally, we compare the performance provided by SimAttack against the performance provided by the concurrent machine learning approach.

7.1   Impact of smoothing factor δ
As described in Section 4.3, the parameter δ is a threshold which controls if a query is considered as a fake query or not. Figure 9 presents the recall, the precision, and the F-Measure for several values of δ. In this attack, we consider an adversary which does not have any knowledge about the generation of fake queries (i.e., the RSS feeds used by the users). Results show that the value of δ significantly impacts the performance of SimAttack. The best results in term of F-Measure are obtained for a δ at 0.5. An adversary

considering $\delta = 0.5$ is able to identify 36.8 % of initial queries with a precision of 62.4 %. Nevertheless, while the value of δ can be adjusted to achieve a higher precision, it will be however at the cost of decreasing the recall.

7.2   Impact of the external knowledge
We now analyze the robustness of TMN when SimAttack uses prior knowledge about the RSS feeds of the users to distinguish fake queries from the users' queries (as explained in Section 4.3). Table 1 lists the performances of SimAttack in term of precision, recall, and F-Measure in that case. Results show that SimAttack is able to identify 45.3 % of initial results with a precision of 87.1 %. Compared to the results obtained by SimAttack when no prior knowledge are used (i.e., in the previous section), prior knowledge increases both the recall and the precision (45.3 % versus 36.8 % for the recall, and 87.1 % versus 62.4 % for the precision). Consequently, prior knowledge and the generation of fake queries helps the adversary to break the indistinguishability offered by TMN. Keeping the default list of RSS feeds of TMN is thus not safe and can compromise the privacy of user.

7.3   Impact of the number of fake queries
As discussed in Section 5.2, users can define the number of fake queries sent by TMN. To analyze the impact of this number, we analyze the robustness of TMN against SimAttack with varying numbers of fake queries (for 1, 10 and 30 fakes queries per hour while the default value being 60). These three different settings consist in adding 7,440, 2,480, and 248 fake queries per user, respectively. Figure 10 depicts the precision and the recall provided by

Table 1 Performance of SimAttack considering an adversary with prior knowledge about RSS feeds

Recall	Precision	F-Measure
45.3 %	87.1 %	61.0 %

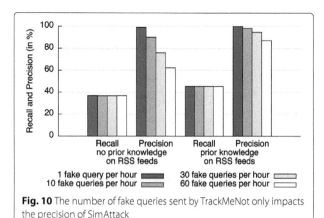

Fig. 10 The number of fake queries sent by TrackMeNot only impacts the precision of SimAttack

SimAttack for both with and without using prior knowledge. Results show that the recall remains unchanged regardless the number of fake queries (i.e., 36.8 and 45.3 % with and without using prior knowledge, respectively). Indeed, changing the number of fake queries does not affect the profile of users, and thus the same proportion of initial queries is retrieved. However, we show that the precision decreases as the number of fake queries increases. Indeed, increasing the number of fake queries increases accordingly the number of misclassified fake queries which reduces the precision. Consequently, sending too few fake queries helps the attacker to retrieve initial queries with a high precision (almost 100 % of precision for 1 fake query per hour).

7.4 Impact of the size of the user profiles

The number of queries stored in the user profiles impacts the efficiency of SimAttack. To measure this impact, we depict on Fig. 11 the precision and the recall of SimAttack for `TMN100` when the profile of users pre-built by the adversary only contains a sub part of their query history (from 0 to 100 %). Results show that exploiting smaller user profiles make harder the identification of user queries by SimAttack. For instance, if we consider

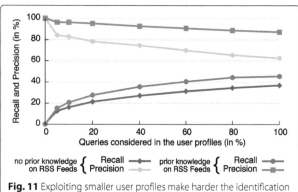

Fig. 11 Exploiting smaller user profiles make harder the identification of user queries by SimAttack

100 % of the user profiles, SimAttack identifies 36.8 % or 45.3 % of queries (depending on the exploitation or not of the prior knowledge) while this number drops to 12.6 % or 15.3 % if we consider only 5 % of the user profiles. However, the quality of the attack (i.e., the precision) increases. For instance, decreasing the number of queries considered in the user profiles from 100 to 5 % makes the precision increases from 21.7 to 92 %. Indeed, with less accurate user profiles, SimAttack does not have enough information to correctly retrieve the users. Consequently, increasing the size of user profiles increases the recall of SimAttack, but also decreases the precision as more queries get misclassified.

7.5 Privacy protection

We now compare the performance of both SimAttack and the concurrent machine learning attack on TrackMeNot using the TMN100 dataset. Firstly for the concurrent machine learning attack, Table 2 lists the precision, the recall, and the F-Measure with two different classifiers. We show that compared to the logistic regression classifier, the SVM classifier provides better performance in term of precision while achieving a slightly lower recall. Interesting enough, the SVM classifier performs better than the classifiers suggested in [8]. Secondly, as the machine learning attack requires prior knowledge on the RSS feeds, we also consider SimAttack using the same prior knowledge (results depict in Table 1). Results show that while the recall provided by SimAttack is lower than the recall provided by the machine learning attack with both classifiers, SimAttack outperforms the machine learning attacks in term of precision (87.1 % versus 29.8 % and 77.8 % for the logistic regression and the SVM, respectively). Finally, SimAttack provides better performance in term of F-Measure against the machine learning attack for both classifiers (61.0 % versus 37.4 % and 57.8 % for the logistic regression and the SVM, respectively).

7.6 Scalability

We finally compare the performance in term of scalability to conduct SimAttack on TMN against the concurrent machine learning approach. More precisely, we measure the execution time of both attacks (using prior knowledge on RSS feeds) on the TMN100 dataset. Results are reported in Fig. 12. We show that SimAttack is faster than the machine learning attack, especially for the logistic regression classifier. The training phase of the machine

Table 2 Performance of the machine learning classifiers on queries protected by TrackMeNot

Classifier	Recall	Precision	F-Measure
Logistic Regression	54.2 %	29.8 %	37.4 %
Support Vector Machine	46.0 %	77.8 %	57.8 %

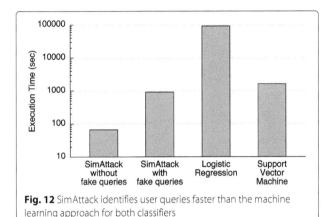

Fig. 12 SimAttack identifies user queries faster than the machine learning approach for both classifiers

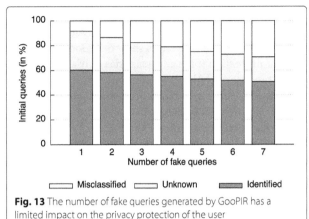

Fig. 13 The number of fake queries generated by GooPIR has a limited impact on the privacy protection of the user

learning attack is the main reason of this long execution time. Besides, using SimAttack without prior knowledge will sill reduce its execution time as SimAttack using prior knowledge spends additional time to build a profile composed of fake queries.

7.7 Summary

SimAttack succeeds to distinguish a high ratio of fake queries sent by TrackMeNot. Nevertheless, this ratio depends on the number of fake queries generated by TMN, and both the number and the quality of the preliminary user profiles collected by the adversary. Finally, SimAttack outperforms machine learning attacks and is faster.

8 Evaluation of GooPIR

In this section, we evaluate the capacity of SimAttack to distinguish fake queries generated by GooPIR. More precisely, we assess the sensitivity of SimAttack for GooPIR over different parameters.

8.1 Impact of the number of fake queries

As discussed in Section 5.3, users can define the number of fake queries generated by GooPIR. Figure 13 presents the performance of SimAttack for varying numbers of additional fake queries (from 1 to 7). Queries are classified in three categories: Identified, Misclassified and Unknown. *Identified* represents the proportion of obfuscated queries for which SimAttack retrieves the initial query (i.e., the recall), *Misclassified* represents the proportion of obfuscated queries for which SimAttack retrieves a fake query as initial query, and *Unknown* represents the proportion of obfuscated queries for which SimAttack is not able to classify any query as initial query. Results show that the number of fake queries generated by GooPIR has a limited impact on the privacy protection of the user: SimAttack retrieves 60.2 % of initial queries when only one additional fake query is generated while 50.6 % of initial queries are retrieved when 7 fake queries

are generated. Besides, regardless the number of fake queries, the percentage of queries retrieved by SimAttack remains relatively high (more than half of initial queries are identified).

We then study why some queries are not identified by SimAttack (i.e., *Misclassified* and *Unknown* queries on Fig. 13). Results show that the proportion of queries in the these two categories changes according to the number of fake queries. For instance, for 1 fake query, unknown queries represent 78.9 % of non-identified queries while misclassified queries represent 21.1 %. If we consider 7 fake queries, these percentages change to 40.8 and 59.2 %, respectively.

8.2 Impact of the size of the user profiles

Similarly to the other versions of SimAttack (i.e., applied to unlinkability solutions or TrackMeNot), the size of the user profiles impacts the efficiency of SimAttack on GooPIR. To measure this impact, we assess the performance of SimAttack when the user profiles contains only a limited part of the user query history (from 0 to 100 %). Figure 14 depicts for AOL100 dataset, the percentage of

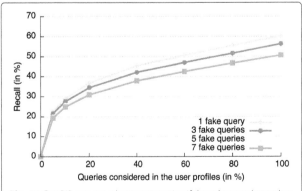

Fig. 14 GooPIR ensures a better protection if the adversary has only a smaller and inaccurate user profile

identified queries according to the ratio of the query history considered in the user profile for varying number of fake queries generated. Results show that GooPIR ensures a better protection if the adversary has only a smaller and inaccurate user profile. For instance, when 7 fake queries and only 5 % of the query history is considered in the user profiles, SimAttack retrieves 19.3 % of the initial query while this percentage increases to 50.6 % if 100 % of the query history is considered in the user profile. Indeed, SimAttack bases its identification exclusively on the user profile. Consequently, if this profile is less accurate, less user queries are identified.

Furthermore, changing the number of fake queries significantly impacts the percentage of identified queries only if the adversary considered enough queries in the user profiles. For instance, adding 6 fake queries decreases by 9.6 % the percentage of query identified when 100 % of the query history is taken into account in the user profile. This decrease drops to 3.4 % when only 10 % of the query history is considered.

8.3   Summary

SimAttack breaks GooPIR protection for more than half of the queries. In addition, the protection of the query of users is impacted by the number of fake queries: increasing the number of fake queries offers a better protection. Moreover, the size of the user profile have an impact on the performance as non-accurate user profiles make SimAttack less efficient.

9   Evaluation of indistinguishability over an unlinkability solution

As shown in the three previous sections, both unlinkability and indistinguishability approaches fail to properly protect user queries. Therefore, we carried out two further experiments which combine these two approaches (i.e., TrackMeNot and GooPIR over an unlinkability solution).

9.1   TrackMeNot over an unlinkability solution

In this section, we evaluate a solution composed of Track-MeNot over an unlinkability solution. Consequently, both queries of users and fake ones generated by TMN are sent anonymously. The remaining of this section presents a sensitivity analysis of the considered solution over various parameters.

9.1.1   Without prior knowledge on RSS feeds

We now analyze the robustness of TMN over an unlinkability solution if the adversary does not consider prior knowledge on RSS feeds of users. Figure 15 presents the recall, the precision, and the F-Measure for several values of δ on the TMN100 dataset. Results show that δ significantly impacts the performance of SimAttack: the

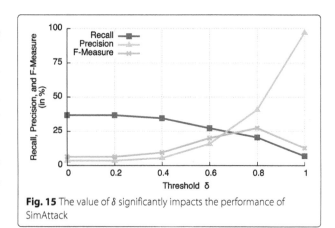

Fig. 15 The value of δ significantly impacts the performance of SimAttack

F-Measure varies from 6.4 to 27.3 % and gives it best value for δ equals 0.8. For this value, an adversary is able to identify 20.5 % of real queries with a precision of 40.7 %. Compared to the results obtained with Track-MeNot alone, adding the unlinkability solution decreases the recall and the precision (20.5 % versus 36.8 % for the recall, and 40.7 % versus 62.4 % for the precision). Indeed, as the adversary does not know the identity of the user, a lot of queries are now misclassified. In addition, compared to an unlinkability solutions alone (Section 6.2), combining TMN with an unlinkability solution decreases the percentage of queries de-anonymized by SimAttack from 36.7 to 20.5 %. Consequently, using TMN with an unlinkability solution protects 16.2 % more queries.

9.1.2   With prior knowledge on RSS feeds

We then analyze the performance of SimAttack when the adversary leverages prior knowledge on the RSS feeds of the users in order to distinguish fake queries to real queries. Table 3 lists the recall, the precision, and F-Measure obtained by the attack. Results show that SimAttack succeeds to identify 35.4 % of the queries of users with a precision of 14.7 %. Compared to the results of Track-MeNot alone, adding the unlinkability solution increases the protection of user's query, as 9.9 % more queries are not identified by SimAttack. However, the precision has significantly dropped: from 87.1 to 14.7 % without and with the unlinkability solution, respectively. Compared now to the precision obtained by SimAttack on an unlinkability solution alone (see Section 6.2), introducing the fake queries of TMN decreases the precision from 42.9 to 14.7 %. The decrease of precision is a direct result of the high ratio of fake queries misclassified.

Table 3 Performance of SimAttack considering an adversary with prior knowledge on RSS feeds

Recall	Precision	F-Measure
35.4 %	14.7 %	20.7 %

Furthermore, compared to the results obtained by SimAttack when no prior knowledge is considered (i.e., Section 9.1.1), SimAttack with prior knowledge increases by 14.9 % the recall but decreases by 16 % the precision. Overall, the F-Measure without prior knowledge is higher than the one with prior knowledge (27.3 versus 20.7 %). Interesting enough, SimAttack on TMN alone with prior knowledge provides higher performance than without prior knowledge (their F-Measures are 61.0 and 46.3 %, respectively).

9.1.3 Impact of the number of fake queries

We now evaluate the protection offered by TMN over an unlinkability solution according to the number of fake queries periodically sent by TMN. Figure 16 presents the recall and the precision for SimAttack with and without prior knowledge on RSS feeds. Results show that the number of fake queries does not change the recall (i.e., 20.5 and 35.4 % without and with using prior knowledge on RSS feeds, respectively). However, the precision strongly depends on the quantity of fake queries. Indeed, decreasing the number of fake queries from 60 to 1 fake query per hour, increases the precision by 31.4 and 32.5 % (for SimAttack without and with prior knowledge, respectively). Consequently, if the user wants a proper protection, TMN has to send a high number of fake queries.

9.1.4 Impact of the size of the user profiles

We finally evaluate how the size of the profile impacts the performance of SimAttack when TrackMeNot is combined with an unlinkability solution. Figure 17 depicts the recall and the precision of SimAttack with and without prior knowledge for a size of user profile changing from 0 to 100 %. Similarly to the other versions of SimAttack, smaller user profiles decreases the performance. For instance, decreasing the size of the user profiles from 100 to 5 % makes SimAttack able to identify 13.8 and 21.7 % less queries without and with prior knowledge on RSS

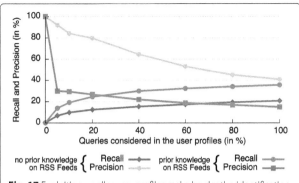

Fig. 17 Exploiting smaller user profiles make harder the identification of the user queries

feeds, respectively. In addition, results show that the precision decreases according to the size of the user profile. Nevertheless, considering from 100 to 5 % of the user profiles, the precision looses 51.2 and 15.0 %, respectively, for SimAttack with and without prior knowledge on RSS feeds of users. Furthermore, compared to the results obtained with TrackMeNot alone (Section 7.4), these results are only slightly lower, excepted for the precision of SimAttack with both prior knowledge and 5 % of the user profile, which drops from 96.3 to 14.7 %.

9.2 GooPIR over an unlinkability solution

In this section, we assess a solution combining the obfuscation of GooPIR and an unlinkability solution. The remaining of this section presents a sensitivity analysis of the considered solution over various parameters.

9.2.1 Impact of the number of fake queries

Firstly, we evaluate the impact of the number of fake queries generated by GooPIR. As the considered solution combines GooPIR and an unlinkability solution, SimAttack needs to retrieve the user query (among the $(k + 1)$ queries) but also the identity of the user who issued the protected query (among all users in the system). As explained in Section 4.4, SimAttack returns the most probable pair $(query, user)$. Figure 18 shows the percentage of queries retrieved by SimAttack and initially protected with a varying number of fake queries (from 1 to 7). Results shows that the number of fake queries has a limited impact on the protection of queries: changing from 1 to 7 fake queries protects only 9.2 % more queries. Besides, the percentage of queries retrieved by the SimAttack remains relatively high (i.e., a recall at 27.6 % for 7 fake queries) considering that queries are protected by two independent private Web search solutions. Furthermore, compared to the results of GooPIR alone (Section 8.1), the current percentage of initial queries identified is 23 % lower (for 7 fake queries) showing that adding the unlinkability solution has a huge impact on the user's protection.

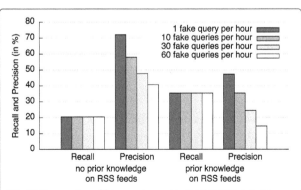

Fig. 16 The number of fake queries sent by TrackMeNot over an unlinkability solution does not change the recall but strongly impact the precision of SimAttack

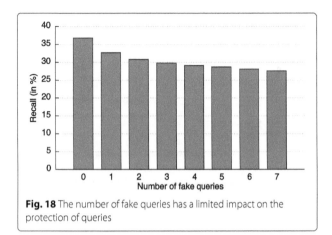

Fig. 18 The number of fake queries has a limited impact on the protection of queries

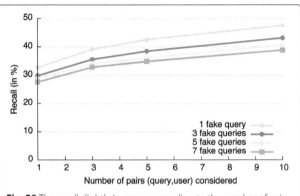

Fig. 20 The recall slightly increases according to the number of pairs (*query, user*) returned by SimAttack

9.2.2 Impact of the size of the user profiles

We then evaluate the impact of the size of the user profiles on the performance of SimAttack when GooPIR is combined with an unlinkability solution. Figure 19 presents the recall of SimAttack for different proportion of queries in the user profile (from 0 to 100 %). Results show that GooPIR over an unlinkability solution protects more strongly the queries of users if the adversary has smaller user profiles: for 1 fake query adding by GooPIR, SimAttack identifies 16.1 % of queries when 5 % of the user profile is considered, while 32.7 % of the queries are identified when 100 % of the profile is considered. Moreover, the linearity of the curve (considering the points between 5 to 100 %) means that the more information is own by the adversary, the more queries she is able to retrieve.

9.2.3 Impact of considering more than one pair (query,user)

In the previous sections, we consider that SimAttack succeeds if the attack returns the correct pair (*query, user*). However, an adversary can be interested to consider more probable pairs. We report on Fig. 20 the recall of SimAttack considering different number of pairs: from 1 to 10 pairs. Results show that the recall increases according to the number of pairs considered by the adversary. For

instance, considering 10 pairs instead on 1 makes the recall increases in average by 13.4 %. Nevertheless, this recall improvement remains relatively low.

9.3 Summary

Combining an indistinguishability technique (i.e., TrackMeNot or GooPIR) over an unlinkability solution gives a better protection to the queries of user, especially if the adversary is not able to collect a large quantity of information about the user or if the user configures its indistinguishability solution to sent a high number of fake queries. Nevertheless, in most of cases, the adversary is still able to retrieve a non-negligible proportion of user queries.

10 Conclusion

This paper presents SimAttack, a generic attack that targets popular private Web search solutions. SimAttack leverages a similarity metric to capture the distance between a query and pre-built user profiles gathering preliminary information about the user interests. We exhaustively evaluate SimAttack using a real world Web search dataset. We show that SimAttack succeeds to de-anonymize, or retrieve among fake queries a high ratio of initial queries from user.

Our analysis shows that neither unlinkability solutions, nor TrackMeNot and GooPIR protects properly the users. Besides, we study the combination of TrackMeNot and GooPIR over an unlinkability solution. The first combination (i.e., TrackMeNot over an unlinkability solution) gives a satisfactory protection when enough fake queries are periodically sent. However, this solution generates an important overhead in term of message on the network. The second combination (i.e., GooPIR over an unlinkability solution) still suffers from a high ratio of initial queries identified by SimAttack.

Dynamically evaluating protected queries in order to measure their level of protection over time represents an interesting research agenda for future works. For instance,

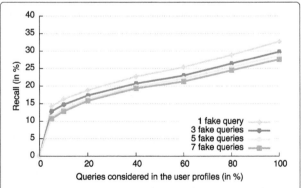

Fig. 19 Exploiting smaller user profiles make harder the identification of the user queries by SimAttack

thanks to this dynamic assessment, it will be possible to adapt the queries protection before sending them, and to reinforce the user awareness.

Endnote

[1]How the adversary collects preliminary information remains outside the scope of this paper.

Authors' contributions
AP designed and implemented SimAttack, carried out the evaluation and wrote the manuscript. TC and SBM participated in the design of SimAttack, contributed to the definition of the experiments and revised the manuscript. AB wrote and revised the manuscript. DC, LB and HK supervised and coordinated the work. All authors read and approved the final manuscript.

Acknowledgements
The presented work was supported by the EEXCESS project funded by the EU Seventh Framework Programme FP7/2007-2013 under grant agreement number 600601. Research reported in this publication has been carried out as part of the International Research and Innovation Centre in Intelligent Digital Systems (IRIXYS).

References
1. Goldschlag D, Reed M, Syverson P. Onion routing. Commun ACM. 1999;42(2):39–41.
2. Dingledine R, Mathewson N, Syverson P. Tor: The second-generation onion router. In: Proceedings of the 13th Conference on USENIX Security Symposium - Volume 13. San Diego, CA: USENIX Association; 2004. p. 21–1.
3. Corrigan-Gibbs H, Ford B. Dissent: accountable anonymous group messaging. In: Proceedings of the 17th ACM Conference on Computer and Communications Security. Chicago, Illinois, USA: ACM; 2010. p. 340–50.
4. Wolinsky DI, Corrigan-Gibbs H, Ford B. Dissent in numbers: Making strong anonymity scale. In: Proceedings of the 10th USENIX Conference on Operating Systems Design and Implementation. Hollywood, CA, USA: USENIX Association; 2012. p. 179–92.
5. Ben Mokhtar S, Berthou G, Diarra A, Quéma V, Shoker A. Rac: A freerider-resilient, scalable, anonymous communication protocol. In: Proceedings of the 33rd IEEE International Conference on Distributed Computing Systems. Philadelphia, PA, USA: IEEE Computer Society; 2013. p. 520–9.
6. Domingo-Ferrer J, Solanas A, Castellà-Roca J. h(k)-private information retrieval from privacy-uncooperative queryable databases. Online Inform Rev. 2009;33(4):720–44.
7. Toubiana V, Subramanian L, Nissenbaum H. Trackmenot: Enhancing the privacy of web search. CoRR. 2011. http://arxiv.org/abs/1109.4677.
8. Peddinti ST, Saxena N. Web search query privacy: Evaluating query obfuscation and anonymizing networks. J Comput Secur. 2014;22(1):155–99.
9. Petit A, Cerqueus T, Ben Mokhtar S, Brunie L, Kosch H. Peas: Private, efficient and accurate web search. In: Proceedings of the 14th IEEE International Conference on Trust, Security and Privacy in Computing and Communications. Helsinki, Finland: IEEE Computer Society; 2015. p. 571–80.
10. Eckersley P. How unique is your web browser? In: Proceedings of the 10th International Conference on Privacy Enhancing Technologies. Berlin, Germany: Springer-Verlag; 2010. p. 1–18.
11. Saint-Jean F, Johnson A, Boneh D, Feigenbaum J. Private web search. In: Proceedings of the 2007 ACM Workshop on Privacy in Electronic Society. Alexandria, VA, USA: ACM; 2007. p. 84–90.
12. Shapiro M. Structure and Encapsulation in Distributed Systems: the Proxy Principle. In: Proceedings of the IEEE 6th International Conference on Distributed Computing Systems. Cambridge, MA, USA: IEEE Computer Society; 1986. p. 198–204.
13. Seid HA, Lespagnol AL. Virtual private network. Google Patents. US Patent 5,768,271. 1998. https://www.google.com/patents/US5768271.
14. Castellà-Roca J, Viejo A, Herrera-Joancomartí J. Preserving user's privacy in web search engines. Comput Commun. 2009;32(13–14):1541–51.
15. Lindell Y, Waisbard E. Private web search with malicious adversaries. In: Proceedings of the 10th International Conference on Privacy Enhancing Technologies. Berlin, Germany: Springer-Verlag; 2010. p. 220–35.
16. Al-Rfou R, Jannen W, Patwardhan N. Trackmenot-so-good-after-all. arXiv preprint arXiv:1211.0320. 2012.
17. Murugesan M, Clifton C. Providing Privacy through Plausibly Deniable Search. Sparks, NV, USA: Society for Industrial and Applied Mathematics; 2009, pp. 768–79. Chap. 65.
18. Rebollo-Monedero D, Forné J. Optimized query forgery for private information retrieval. IEEE Trans Inf Theory. 2010;56(9):4631–42.
19. Ye S, Wu F, Pandey R, Chen H. Noise injection for search privacy protection. In: Proceedings of the IEEE 12th International Conference on Computational Science and Engineering. Vancouver, Canada: IEEE Computer Society; 2009. p. 1–8.
20. Arampatzis A, Efraimidis P, Drosatos G. A query scrambler for search privacy on the internet. Inform Retriev. 2013;16(6):657–79.
21. Pang H, Ding X, Xiao X. Embellishing text search queries to protect user privacy. VLDB'10. 2010;3(1–2):598–607.
22. Singhal A. Modern information retrieval: A brief overview. IEEE Data Eng Bull. 2001;24(4):35–43.
23. Dice LR. Measures of the amount of ecologic association between species. Ecology. 1945;26(3):297–302.
24. Jaccard P. The distribution of the flora in the alpine zone. New Phytologist. 1912;11(2):37–50.
25. Cohen W, Ravikumar P, Fienberg S. A comparison of string metrics for matching names and records. In: Proceedings of the KDD-03 Workshop on Data Cleaning and Object Consolidation. Washington, DC, USA: ACM; 2003. p. 73–8.
26. Pass G, Chowdhury A, Torgeson C. A picture of search. In: Proceedings of the 1st International Conference on Scalable Information Systems. Hong Kong: ACM; 2006. p. 1.
27. Manning CD, Surdeanu M, Bauer J, Finkel J, Bethard SJ, McClosky D. The Stanford CoreNLP natural language processing toolkit. In: Proceedings of the 52nd Annual Meeting of the Association for Computational Linguistics: System Demonstrations. Baltimore, MD, USA: Association for Computational Linguistics; 2014. p. 55–60.
28. Porter MF. An algorithm for suffix stripping. Program. 1980;14(3):130–7.
29. Hall M, Frank E, Holmes G, Pfahringer B, Reutemann P, Witten IH. The weka data mining software: an update. ACM SIGKDD Explor Newsletter. 2009;11(1):10–18.
30. Hearst MA, Dumais ST, Osman E, Platt J, Scholkopf B. Support vector machines. IEEE Intell Syst. 1998;13(4):18–28.

2

Recovering user-interactions of Rich Internet Applications through replaying of HTTP traces

Salman Hooshmand[1], Gregor V. Bochmann[1], Guy-Vincent Jourdan[1]* (iD), Russell Couturier[2] and Iosif-Viorel Onut[3]

Abstract

In this paper, we study the "Session Reconstruction" problem which is the reconstruction of user interactions from recorded request/response logs of a session. The reconstruction is especially useful when the only available information about the session is its HTTP trace, as could be the case during a forensic analysis of an attack on a website. Solutions to the reconstruction problem do exist for "traditional" Web applications. However, these solutions cannot handle modern "Rich Internet Applications" (RIAS). Our solution is implemented in the context of RIAs in a tool called D-ForenRIA. Our tool is made of a proxy and a set of browsers. Browsers are responsible for trying candidate actions on each DOM, and the proxy, which contains the observed HTTP trace, is responsible for responding to browsers' requests and validating attempted actions on each DOM. D-ForenRIA has a distributed architecture, a learning mechanism to guide the session reconstruction process efficiently, and can handle complex user-inputs, client-side randomness, and to some extents actions that do not generate any HTTP traffic. In addition, concurrent reconstruction makes the system scalable for real-world use. The results of our evaluation on several RIAs show that D-ForenRIA can efficiently reconstruct user-sessions in practice.

Keywords: User-interactions reconstruction, Rich Internet Applications, Traffic replay, HTTP traces

1 Introduction

Over the last decade the increasing use of new Web technologies such as "Asynchronous JavaScript and XML" (AJAX) [1], and "Document Object Model" (DOM) manipulation [2] have provided more responsive and smoother Web applications, sometimes called "Rich Internet Applications"(RIAs) [3] or "Single-page Applications" [4]. RIAs have become the norm for modern Web applications [5]. For example, Google has adopted RIA technologies to develop most of its major products (Gmail, Google Groups, Google Maps, etc.) In fact, an evaluation of the top 100 Web sites from alexa.com shows that 87 of them use AJAX to communicate with the server-side scripts[1].

Despite the benefits of RIAs, this shift in Web development technologies has created a lot of challenges; many previous methods for analyzing traditional Web

applications are not useful for RIAs anymore [6]. This is mainly due to the fact that AJAX fundamentally changes the concept of a web-page, which was the basis of a Web application. Among these challenges is the ability to analyze HTTP traffic of users' sessions.

When a user visits a website, user-browser interactions generate a set of HTTP requests and responses that are usually logged by the Web server. These logs can be used for example for "Session Reconstruction". We define the *Session Reconstruction Problem* as using *only* the logs to recover of an entire user-session, including the sequence of user-browser interactions during a user's visit, a reconstruction of the pages as they were presented to the user, the input values provided by the user and the elements of the page in which these inputs were provided. The reconstruction must not rely on prior instrumentation of the application, and must be performed completely offline (that is, without accessing the original application).

*Correspondence: gjourdan@uottawa.ca
[1]University of Ottawa, 800 King Edward Avenue, K1N 6N5 Ottawa, Canada
Full list of author information is available at the end of the article

Session reconstruction is specially important when the only information available from a previous session is the HTTP logs as could be the case during a forensic analysis of an attack on a website [7]. In addition, a session reconstruction tool may be used to understand users' navigation patterns in the website (in Web usage mining [8]) or to derive test-cases for the Web application [9].

The previous session reconstruction methods deal with traditional Web applications and cannot handle RIAs. Traditional web applications are composed of a set of web pages and users navigate the website by following hyperlinks. An assumption often made is that each user action navigates the application to a new page with a new URL. This URL is mentioned in the *href* property of the links (HTML anchors); therefore by simply considering links on each page and the next expected traffic, user actions of a traditional Web application can be extracted.

On the other hand, RIAs are event-based applications. Any HTML element, and not only links can potentially respond to actions of a user by an event-handler. These event-handlers can be assigned statically (using the attributes of an element), or dynamically by calling event-registration JavaScript functions. Detection of statically assigned handlers can be done by just scanning the DOM, however the algorithm needs a more advanced mechanism to keep track of dynamically assigned events. In addition, a session reconstruction tool for RIAs cannot tell which requests are going to be generated after triggering an action by simply looking at the target element of an action. The reason is that many of the requests are generated by script code running in the browser, and the response typically only contains a small amount of data which is used by the receiving script to partially update the current DOM (see Fig. 1 for an example). Therefore, extraction of candidate user actions at each state, and finding the source of a given HTTP request is challenging in RIAs. Consequently, when the Web application is a modern RIA, session reconstruction is not easy.

Although it is usually possible to recover user-client interactions by instrumenting the client or the application code, such instrumentation is not always desirable

or feasible (e.g., in the analysis of a previously happened security incident).

In this paper, we present an approach to reconstruct sessions of RIAs using HTTP traces as only input. Our method uses a proxy, which contains the trace, and a set of browsers to reconstruct the session; The proxy plays the roles of the server and browsers are responsible for trying candidate actions that change the client-state of the RIA. The browsers also capture some information about the client-state of the application after performing an action, such as the screen-shot and the DOM of each state. The approach has been implemented in a tool called *D-ForenRIA*[2]. To the best of our knowledge, *D-ForenRIA* is the first tool that can efficiently reconstruct user-browser interactions of a RIA from a given HTTP log. A companion site has been set up at http://ssrg.site.uottawa.ca/sr/demo.html where videos and further information is being made available.

D-ForenRIA is an improvement over a previous version of the tool [10]. The extensions are based on a new distributed architecture, adding the ability of detection of complex user-input actions and actions that do not generate any HTTP traffic, and proposing a more efficient way of ordering candidate actions. We also report our experiments on six different RIAs.

1.1 Demonstration scenario for D-ForenRIA

We have implemented our proposed session reconstruction algorithm in a tool called *D-ForenRIA*. In order to illustrate the capabilities of *D-ForenRIA*, we have created a sample attack scenario, using a vulnerable banking application created by IBM for demonstration and test purpose (Fig. 2). In our case study, the attacker visits the vulnerable web site (part 1 in Fig. 2), uses an SQL-injection vulnerability to gain access to private information (part 2 in Fig. 2) and transfers some money to her own account (part 3 in Fig. 2). She also uncovers a cross-site scripting vulnerability that she can exploit later against another user (part 4 in Fig. 2). This session creates the trace depicted in Fig. 3. *D-ForenRIA* can help to recover what the attacker has done during the session from this input log.

```
[{ "tid": 3,
"action": "DataProvider",
"method": "getNodeTypes",
"type": "rpc",
"result": [ {
    "nodeType": "6",
    "cls": "typo3-pagetree-topPanel-button",
    "html": "<span class=\"t3js-icon icon icon-size-small ...",
    "title": "Backend User Section",
    "tooltip": "Backend User Section"
}], "debug": "" } ]
```

Fig. 1 The body of a typical HTTP response in a RIA (Adapted from TYPO3 RIA [42])

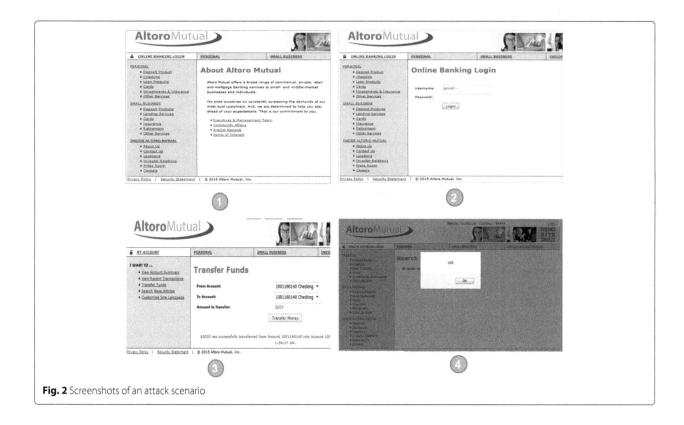

Fig. 2 Screenshots of an attack scenario

Figure 4 presents the user-interface of *D-ForenRIA*[3]. To reconstruct this session, the user provides the trace as an input to the *SR-Proxy* (region 1 in Fig. 4). The users can configure different settings such as the output folder (region 2 in Fig. 4) and observe some statistics about the progress of the reconstruction (region 3 in Fig. 4).

Given the full traces of this incident (Fig. 2), *D-ForenRIA* reconstructs the attack in a couple of seconds. The output includes screenshots of all pages seen by the hacker (region 4 in Fig. 4). To see the details of a recovered user action, a click on one of the thumbnails

opens a new window. For example, Fig. 5 presents the details of the step taken for unauthorized login including the inputs hacker exploited for SQL-injection attack. The full reconstructed DOM can also be accessed from that screen.

A forensic analysis of the attack would have been quite straightforward using *D-ForenRIA*, including the discovery of the cross-site scripting vulnerability. Comparatively, doing the same analysis without our tool would have taken much longer, and the cross-site scripting vulnerability would probably have been missed. A demonstration of this

Requests	Responses
•••	•••
GET http://testfire.net/ HTTP/1.1	HTTP/1.1 200 OK … <html> <body>…
GET http://testfire.net/style.css HTTP/1.1	HTTP/1.1 200 OK … body, table, td, p { …
•••	•••
GET http://testfire.net/default.aspx?content=business.htm HTTP/1.1	HTTP/1.1 200 OK … <html> <body>…
GET http://testfire.net/bank/login.aspx HTTP/1.1	HTTP/1.1 200 OK … <html> <body>…
POST http://testfire.net/bank/login.aspx HTTP/1.1	HTTP/1.1 200 OK …
•••	••••
GET http://testfire.net/search.aspx?txtSearch=%3Cscript%3Ealert%28%22XSS%22%29%3C%2Fscript%3E HTTP/1.1	HTTP/1.1 200 OK … { "ResultSet": { "totalResultsReturned": 2, ••••

Fig. 3 Portion of the HTTP log for an attack scenario

Fig. 4 Screenshot of the main window of *D-ForenRIA*

Fig. 5 Details of an SQL-Injection attack in *D-ForenRIA*

case study can be found on http://ssrg.site.uottawa.ca/sr/ demo.html. In the remaining sections of this paper we are going to explain the details of *D-ForenRIA* and different techniques that are used.

1.2 Organization

The rest of this paper is organized as follows: In Section 2, we first model the session reconstruction problem in the context of client/server applications, and then in Section 3 we discuss the session reconstruction problem in RIAs and present a detailed description of our session reconstruction approach. We present some evaluation results that highlight the effectiveness of *D-ForenRIA* in Section 4. Then we discuss the state of the art in Section 5. Finally, we present our concluding remarks and future directions in Section 6.

2 Session reconstruction problem

The session reconstruction problem can be defined for any application based on a "client/server" architecture (such as a Web application or many mobile applications). In this section, we first explain the general case of the session reconstruction problem for client/server applications, and present a solution for this general case. Then, in Section 3 we explain our particular approach to reconstruct sessions of RIAs.

Figure 6 represents the context of a session reconstruction tool. A user interacts with a client and each interaction may generate one or more requests to the server (Fig. 6 part a). The server in turn processes these requests and sends some responses back to the client. The set of exchanged request/responses can be logged by the server or by other tools on the network for further analysis. The goal of session reconstruction is to find the sequence of user-client interactions of a session using the log of that session (Fig. 6 part b).

If we assume that there have been n user-interactions during a session, the trace of the session can be presented as $< rs_1, rs_2, \ldots, rs_n >$, where rs_i is the sequence of requests/responses that have been exchanged after performing the ith interaction. rs_i can also be empty in the case that the interaction does not generate any requests/response. The goal of the session reconstruction tool is to find one (or more) sequence of interactions, that generate a sequence of requests/responses $< rs_1', rs_2' \ldots, rs_n' >$ that match the given trace. We are using a "Match" function and we are looking for a sequence of interactions such that $\forall_{1 \leq i \leq n}$ Match(rs_i, rs_i'). The *Match* function may be "strict", that is, two sequences match if they are equal. However, in practice, the *Match* function needs to be more flexible and ignore certain differences in the observed requests, rs_i', and the expected traffic rs_i. For each user interaction, the session reconstruction tool also extracts the type of the action, and all the required information to perform that action.

We also assume that the application can be modeled by a finite state machine. We define the FSM as a tuple (S, s_0, I, δ) where:

- S is a set of states. Each state corresponds to a client-side state of the application. In RIAs, the states represent DOM instances.
- s_0 is the initial state of the application, when the session starts.
- I is the set of possible user-browser interactions with the application.
- $\delta : S \times I \rightarrow S$ is the transition function, where $\delta(s_i, a_j)$ refers to the next state of the application after the execution of a_j in state s_i.

It should be noted that the aim of the session reconstruction is not to extract the full state machine of the

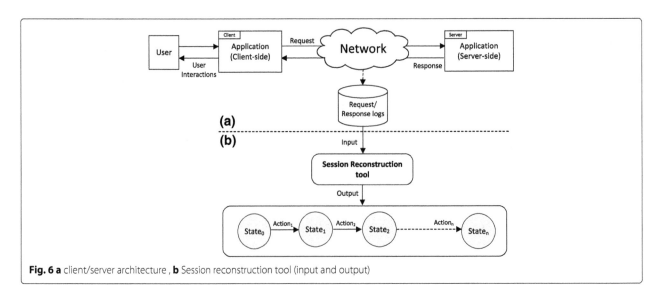

Fig. 6 a client/server architecture , **b** Session reconstruction tool (input and output)

application. Therefore, the reconstruction problem does not suffer from the "state explosion" problem that is seen e.g. in the crawling problem [6]. Indeed, reconstructing a user session is to find a simple path in the state machine of the application, a path which corresponds to the user interactions during a session. In fact, the extraction of the full state machine would be impossible for a session reconstruction tool, since that the tool is off-line during the reconstruction and just operates based on a given set of recorded trace. A state that was not reached by the user during the session cannot possibly be reconstructed.

In the case of RIAs, the client is a Web browser which communicates using HTTP with a server. From the given HTTP log, we want to produce the set of client-side states and user-browser interactions during the session. Each client-state is defined by the DOM built by the browser when on that state. The DOM represents the structure of an HTML page including the elements of the page and their attributes. The DOM is also used to generate a screenshot of the page as seen by the user. In

addition, the algorithm finds the XPath of the elements clicked, and the values that the user submits during the session.

Consider the example of Fig. 7. It shows a simple page of a RIA that displays a description of different products using AJAX (left), and a sequence of generated requests/responses during a session (right). Given the user-log of the session, $< Rb_1, Rb_2, Ra_1, Ra_2, Ra_3, Rc_1, Rc_2, Rc_3 >$, a working sequence of actions is $< Click(P_2), Click(P_1), Click(P_3) >$. This sequence of actions generates the given sequence of requests/responses.

Assumptions: To ensure the effectiveness of our session reconstruction method, the following assumptions are made about the target application, the input trace, and user-input actions.

- *Determinism*: It is assumed that the application is deterministic *from the viewpoint of the user*. It means that given a state and a given requests/responses sequence, the next client-state is uniquely defined[4]. If

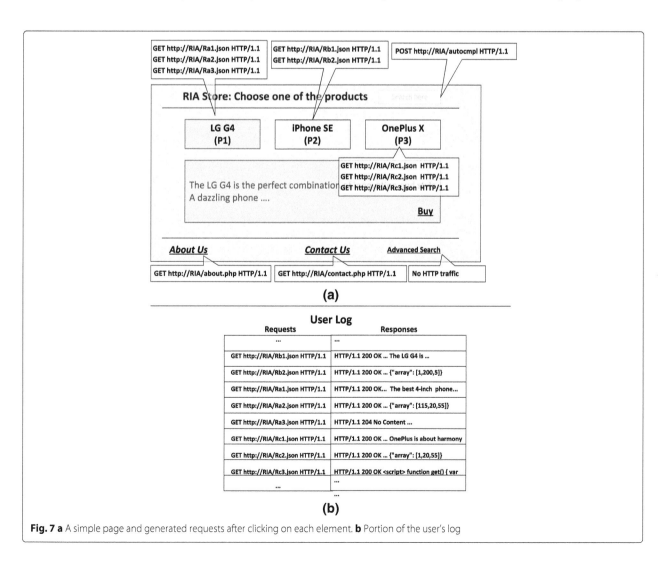

Fig. 7 a A simple page and generated requests after clicking on each element. **b** Portion of the user's log

the application is not deterministic from the viewpoint of the user, then when the session reconstruction tool tries an action that was actually performed by the user, it could reach a state that is not the state reached by the user. In this case, the tool will not be able to reconstruct the remaining actions. However, the application may still have randomness in the generated requests. This means that the execution of the same action from a given state, may generate a different sequences of requests and responses.

- *Input traces*: It is assumed that the session reconstruction tool has the log for a *single* user. Since the log on the server usually contains the trace for different users, the session reconstruction tool relies on other methods (such as [11]) to extract the traffic for a single user.

In addition, the tool can read the unencrypted requests/responses and can decrypt the logs if it is encrypted. This assumption is necessary since the tool needs to compare the generated request after performing an action with the input log. We also assume that the input log is "complete"; this means that there is no need to have the traffic from the previous session to reconstruct the current session, and the log is recorded from the start of the session.

- *Access to the application during reconstruction*: It is assumed that the reconstruction is done off-line. This means that during the reconstruction process there is no access to the server, and the tool only exploits previously collected HTTP traces. This assumption ensures that the tool remains effective even when the server is not available (for example, because of an attack or a bug in the application). Moreover, replaying the session off-line without accessing the server provides a sandboxed environment which is especially desirable during forensic analysis.

- *User-Input Actions*: Regarding the actions that include input values from users, we have made the following assumptions; first, it is assumed that the input values passed into the generated requests are not encoded in a non-standard way; otherwise, the session reconstruction tool cannot recover the *actual* values entered by the user; the second assumption is regarding the *domain* of user-input values. It is assumed that the tool can produce acceptable values for a user-input action, using some preset libraries of possible inputs. This is necessary to be able to automatically input values that will not be blocked by client-side validation. Note that this does not mean that the tool should somehow guess the correct user inputs values. These values will be found in the log. Instead the tool should be able to provide *some* inputs that will be usable to continue with the session.

2.1 A general session reconstruction approach

Here we present an algorithm for the session reconstruction of applications which are based on the client/server model. The algorithm uses three components that participate in the reconstruction of a session: The *Client*, that can list/execute possible actions on the current state; A *Robot* that simulates user-client interactions, and a *Proxy* that replaces the actual server and responds to the requests sent by the client.

Algorithm 1 A general session reconstruction algorithm

Input: An input user log R, switch to find first/all solution(s) *findAll*
Output: The sequence of user-interactions that generate the given log, *sol*

```
 1: Procedure Main()
 2:     sols ← {}
 3:     proxy ← InitProxy(R)
 4:     client ← InitClient(proxy)
 5:     robot ← InitRobot(client)
 6:     S0 ← client.GetState()
 7:     SR(S0, R, {})

 8: Procedure SR(State Sn, Trace R, ActionPath ap)
 9:  if R = {} then
10:     sols.add(ap)
11:     if not findAll then
12:         terminate()
13:     end if
14:  else
15:     A ← client.ExtractCandidateActions(Sn)
16:     for a ∈ A do
17:         Rs ← robot.Evaluate(a, Sn)
18:         if proxy.Match(Rs, begin(|Rs|, R)) then
19:             Sn+1 ← client.GetState()
20:             SR(Sn+1, R − Rs, ap + a)
21:         end if
22:     end for
23:  end if
```

The algorithm that is used to extract user-interactions, is shown in Algorithm 1. The *main* procedure takes care of initialization. The recursive session reconstruction procedure, SR, starts at line 8. In this approach, the algorithm extracts all possible candidate actions of the current state of the application S_n (line 15), and tries them one by one (line 17). Trying an action in S_n may change the state of the application to another state, S_{n+1}.

If the execution of action a generates a sequence of requests R_s which *Match* the requests/responses in the beginning of R (line 18), a is considered a possible correct action at the current state [5]. Since the requests can be generated in different orders, the order of elements in R_s does not matter for the *Match* function (line 18). The action is also accepted if it does not generate any requests (Such as clicking on the "Advanced Search" link in Fig. 7).

The algorithm then appends a to the currently found action sequence, and continues to find the rest of the actions in the remaining trace (line 20)[6]. The algorithm stops when all requests in the input trace are matched. The session reconstruction algorithm starts from the initial state of the algorithm (line 7). The output contains all solutions for the problem. Each solution includes a set of user-client actions (that matches the input trace). At each state, there may be several actions which are correct (line 18). In this case, the algorithm finds several correct solutions for the problem. However, in practice we can make the algorithm faster by adding a switch (parameter *findAll*) to stop the algorithm after finding the first solution (line 10).

During the execution of the algorithm, the *Client*, the *Robot*, and the *Proxy* collaborate to perform several tasks; the *Client* lists the possible actions on the current state (line 15), the *Robot* triggers the action on the current state (line 17) and the *Proxy*, responds to the requests generated during the executing the action by the client (line 17).

2.2 An improved session reconstruction algorithm

Although the general algorithm (Algorithm 1) is easy and straightforward, it should address different issues to be practical.

2.2.1 Signature-based ordering of candidate actions

Algorithm 1 blindly tries every action at each state to find the correct one (lines 16-17). However, in practice there may be a large number of candidate actions at a given state, so the algorithm needs a smarter way to order candidate actions from the most promising to the least promising. We propose to use a "Signature-based" ordering of candidate actions as follows.

In this technique, the algorithm uses the "Signature" of each action to sort the pool of candidate actions. The signature of an action is the traffic which has been generated when it was performed previously possibly from another state of the application (For example, in Fig. 7 the signature of clicking on P_2 is $\{Rb_1, Rb_2\}$). The signature of an action may also be discovered without the need to execute the action; for example, the signature of clicking on "contact-us" in Fig. 7 can be discovered by just looking at its *href* property in the DOM (Fig. 14). It is notable that the session reconstruction algorithm does not have the signature of all actions; the signature for an action is extracted once an action is evaluated for the first time.

To apply the signature-based ordering, the session reconstruction tool should be able to identify different instances of the same action at different states. We need to find an *id* such that this id remains the same in different states; therefore, in each state the session reconstruction tool calculates the id for each possible action and uses this id to find the signature of the action from previous states.

The signature-based ordering, assigns a priority-value $\in [0,1]$ to all candidate actions on the current state. This value is assigned based on how well the signature of the action, matches the next expected traffic; To this end, the *Match* function should return a value $\in [0,1]$, where a higher value means a higher match (e.g., 1 represents a full match and, 0 mean no match at all). When the signature of the action is not available (when the algorithm has not yet executed the action), the priority value of θ ($0 \leq \theta \leq 1$) is assigned to the action. As a consequence, the algorithm first tries actions in a decreasing order of match until the match value reaches the threshold θ. Then, the algorithm tries actions that do not have any signature, and finally the least promising actions are tried (actions that have lower match than the threshold). If two actions have the same match value (e.g. they both fully match the next expected trace), the action with the longest sequence of requests, will have a higher priority.

Example: Consider the simple example in Fig. 7a and the given trace of Fig. 7b. In this example, we assume that clicking on a product displays some information about the product, but does not add any new possible user actions to the page. The threshold value, θ, of 0.5 is used when we do not have a signature of an action.

To apply the "signature-based" ordering, the algorithm assigns priority-values to candidate actions. At the initial state, the priority for the two *href* elements is minimum since their initiating requests (*about.php* and *contactus.php*) do not match the next expected requests, $< Rb_1, Rb_2, ... >$.

The priority-value for the remaining actions is *0.5* because the algorithm has not tried any action yet. Assume that actions are tried in the order P_1, P_2, P_3. The algorithm will try clicking on P_1 and P_2 to discover the first interaction (i.e. $Click(P_2)$). In addition, it learns the signature of clicking on P_1 and P_2. At the next state, clicking on P_1 gets the priority of *1* since its signature $< Ra_1, Ra_2, Ra_3 >$ matches the remaining of traces , $< Ra_1, Ra_2, Ra_3, Rc_1, ... >$, clicking on P_2 gets priority of *0* since its signature does not match and *P3* gets *0.5* since we have not tried this action yet. So, the correct action $Click(P_1)$ is selected immediately. At the third state, also $Click(P_3)$ gets a priority of *0.5* while $Click(P_1)$ and $Click(P_2)$ are assigned priority of *0*. At this state the correct action is selected immediately. To sum up, the 3 actions are found after trying 4 actions on the current state.

2.2.2 Concurrent evaluation of candidate actions:

Algorithm 1 is sequential and single-threaded. At each state the algorithm extracts the list of candidate actions (line 17), and executes them one by one using the client (the **for** loop in lines 16-22). The client needs to carry out several tasks to execute an action; it needs to initiate several requests, processes the responses, and update its state. These tasks can take a long time for the client to finish.

Therefore the total runtime can often be decreased by using several clients. After extraction of candidate actions (line 17), the algorithm assigns each action to a client in a new thread. The algorithm does not need to wait for the client to finish the execution of the action, and assigns the next candidate action to the next client. In this approach, several actions can be evaluated concurrently, which potentially decreases the runtime of the algorithm.

2.2.3 Extracting action parameters

The approach needs to extract all candidate actions on each state. For each action, we need to extract all the information required to execute that action (we call such information the *parameters* of the action). For a *click* action, the only required parameter is the element that is the target of click. However, for actions that involve *user-inputs*, more parameters must be determined: First, the set of input elements, and second, the values that are assigned to these elements (value parameters). We assume that the *client* can provide us the list of input elements at each state. To detect value parameters of user-input actions, we propose the following approach:

1. At each state, the system performs each user-input action using an arbitrary set of values, x. These values are chosen from the domain of input elements in that user-input action. The system observes requests T after performing the user-input action.
2. If the next expected traffic is exactly the same as T but with different user-input values y instead of x, the system concludes that the user has performed the user-input action using y.

Example: The text-box on top of the example in the Fig. 7 is used to search in the sample site. To detect this user-input action, the algorithm fills the text-box using a predefined value (here "sampleText") and compares the generated request with the next expected request. Since these two requests (Fig. 8a, b) are quite similar, and the only difference is the submitted value, the algorithm determines that the user has performed this action using a different value, and resubmits the action using the correct value, namely "IPhone".

In this technique, the algorithm does not need to know anything about how the client-side formats the user input data, and it learns the format by trying an action and observing the generated traffic. However, this technique is only effective if the user-input data is passed as is; if there is any encoding of the submitted data, the actual data that has been used by the user cannot be extracted from the logs.

2.2.4 Handling randomness in requests

We have assumed that performing an action from the same state, may generate a sequence of requests/responses that includes some randomness. Both the client-side and the server-side of the application can contribute to this randomness. The client-side of the application can generate different *requests* after performing an action from the same state, and the server-side may respond with different *responses*.

The responses are served by the proxy by replaying a recorded trace. Therefore, there will be no randomness in the responses during the reconstruction. However, the session reconstruction algorithm still needs to handle randomness in the client-side generated requests.

If the execution of an action generates random requests, the algorithm cannot detect the correct action since executing the action generates requests which are different from the requests in input trace. The *Match* function (line 18 in Algorithm 1), needs to detect the existence of randomness and flexibly find the appropriate responses to the set of requests.

There are different forms and variations for the randomness in the generated requests; for example, the actual order of execution of a series of concurrent requests/responses can change. In this case, as we explained in Section 2.1, the *Match* function ignores the order of generated requests to find the matching responses. Requests in a client/server application usually contain some parameters (such as query-string parameters in a Web application); another form of randomness happens when the values of these parameters changes between two executions, for example when the value is dependent on the current time, or when the value is based

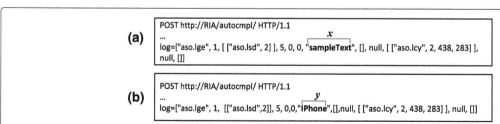

(a)
```
POST http://RIA/autocmpl/ HTTP/1.1
...                                              x
log=["aso.lge", 1, [ ["aso.lsd", 2] ], 5, 0, 0, "sampleText", [], null, [ ["aso.lcy", 2, 438, 283] ],
null, []]
```

(b)
```
POST http://RIA/autocmpl/ HTTP/1.1
...                                          y
log=["aso.lge", 1,  [["aso.lsd",2]], 5, 0,0,"iPhone",[],null, [ ["aso.lcy", 2, 438, 283] ], null, []]
```

Fig. 8 a The generated HTTP request after performing a user-input action using sample data. **b** the expected HTTP traffic in the trace. (x, y represent the sample and actual user-input values respectively)

on a randomly generated value. To handle randomness of this type, we use the following approach:

We say that two requests match *partially* if they have the same URL, the same set of parameters, but some of these parameters have different values. For example, the requests

req.php?language=EN&user=john&time=12345 and
req.php?language=FR&user=john&time=56745

match *partially* because they are both to *req.php*, they have the same three parameters *language*, *user* and *time*, but the values of parameters *language* and *time* are different.

Suppose that once the system executes action a from state S_n (line 17 in Algorithm 1), it observes that the generated requests have a *partial* match with the next expected traffic. This difference between parameter values can have two causes:

1. Two different actions may send requests containing the same parameter but with different values. For example in a news RIA if we have two actions, one for fetching the latest technology news sending requests to *fetch.aspx?cat=tech* and another action for fetching the business news requesting *fetch.asp?cat=business*, in this case, the parameter *cat* differentiates between two types of actions. We call the parameter *cat* in the previous example a "constant" parameter since its value differentiates between different actions and the value will be the same for the same action from the same state.

2. Requests for the same action, contain a parameter that has a changing value after each execution. For example, in a news RIA there may be an action to fetch the latest news that sends a request to *latest.aspx?last=12_15_20*. In this request, the value of parameter *last* represents the time of the last update fetched by the client and is changed *by the client* every time a request is sent. The next request might look like *latest.aspx?last=12_16_20*. We call parameter *last* of the previous example a "non-constant" parameter since its value changes at each execution of the same action from the same state.

When the session reconstruction tool observes that the value of a parameter in the log differs from the value of the same parameter in the generated request after execution of an action, it should categorize the parameter as constant or non-constant. If the parameter is constant it means that the action is incorrect (that is, this is not the action taken by the user at that level of the reconstruction). For example, it would be the case if the user had clicked to fetch latest technology news, but the session reconstruction tool had tried fetching business news at this state. However, if the parameter is actually a non-constant one, its value should be ignored during comparison. For example, the value of the *last* parameter in the previous example is a non-constant, therefore if the tool triggers an action which generates *latest.aspx?last=12_16_20* and we expect *latest.aspx?last=12_15_20* in the log, we have actually selected a correct action since the value of the parameter *last* is non-constant and should be ignored.

A naive approach to handle randomness in requests, would be to compare the generated request with a request in the user-log based on a similarity function [7]; if the similarity between two requests is more than a threshold, the requests are considered a match. However, this approximate matching may mistakenly match two requests and jeopardize the reconstruction. Therefore, our solution does not depend on a threshold and automatically verifies the randomness in requests' parameters as follows:

If session reconstruction tool tries action a, in order to verify that a actually generates a request with non-constant parameter values the system performs a from S_n again; if the system observes a change in the value of the same parameters, it concludes that the value of those parameters are variable. The *Match* function does not consider these changing values for checking the correctness of the action. In the example above, the actual value of the parameter *last* will be ignored by the *Match* function for that request.

Example: In Web applications, the requests are sent for a resource (with a URL), and each request can contain some parameters and their corresponding values (in the query string of a *GET* request, or in the body if a *POST* request). Two HTTP requests can be considered a *partial* match if they are sent to the same resource, have the same set of parameters, but the values for some parameters are different.

Figure 9 depicts an example of a request which contains a parameter, t, which gets a different value each time requested by the browser. By comparing the request received in the first execution (part a in Fig. 9) with the

---

(a) http://ubuntu/elfinder4L/php/connector.php?cmd=open&target=l1_Lw&t=_1430758719966_

(b) http://ubuntu/elfinder4L/php/connector.php?cmd=open&target=l1_Lw&t=_2836753719462_

Fig. 9 a,b: Two HTTP requests that include a parameter with a changing value

one received in the second execution (part b), the system detects that parameter t has changing values and ignores the value of t later during the reconstruction.

This technique works well if the randomness just happens in the values of request's parameters; however, there are some variation of randomness that cannot be easily handled by this approach; for example, when the number of requests that are generated after performing an action, or the number of parameters in a request are non-deterministic. Another important example of limitation is when the changes are slow, for example when the values are changed based on the date: it won't match the recorded traffic, but consecutive execution yields usually the same values.

2.2.5 Handling non-user initiated requests:

Requests that are exchanged between a server and a client can originate from different sources. In Algorithm 1, we have discussed user-initiated requests, however messages can also be sent without the user initiating a request first. These requests may originate from a *timer* on the client-side, or even from the server-side (such as Websockets[7] in RIAs). The general session reconstruction algorithm can be modified to handle these cases, as follows:

- *Timer initiated requests*: Timers can be detected based on the signature-based ordering of actions (Section 2.2.1); Timers are also one of the possible actions in the current state, so the algorithm first detects them on the current state (line 15 in algorithm 1) and evaluates each timer (line 17 in algorithm 1) to find the timer's signature. Later during the reconstruction, the algorithm triggers a timer when the signature of the timer matches the next expected traffic.
- *Server-initiated requests*: In client/server applications, sometimes the server needs to send some data to the client. In this case, the given trace to

the proxy contains both requests that originate from the client-side of the application, and requests that are sent from the server. The *proxy* in our general algorithm has to be changed to detect these server-initiated requests; When the proxy observes that the next expected traffic is server-initiated, it just *sends* these requests to the client.

3 D-ForenRIA: a session reconstruction tool for RIAs

In Sections 2.1 and 2.2, we presented a general and improved algorithm for the session reconstruction problem. In this section, we propose a session reconstruction approach for RIAs. This approach realizes the improved session reconstruction algorithm in the context of RIAs and addresses several challenges mentioned in the previous section.

Our solution is implemented in a tool called *D-ForenRIA*. In this section, we first present the most important components of *D-ForenRIA*, then we describe the messages exchanged between these components, and finally explain the details of each component.

3.1 Architecture of D-ForenRIA

Figure 10 presents the architecture of *D-ForenRIA* with two main components: A "Session Reconstruction Proxy" (SR-Proxy) and a set of "Session Reconstruction Browsers" (SR-Browsers). SR-Browsers are responsible for loading the DOM and identifying/triggering actions (they combine the role of "robot" and the role of "client" presented in Section 2.1). The SR-Proxy performs the role of the original Web server, and responds to SR-Browsers' requests from the given input HTTP trace (that is, the role of "proxy" in Section 2.1). This ensures that during reconstruction the SR-Proxy just uses a previously recorded trace and has no access to the server. Based on our session reconstruction algorithm, we infer which user-browser interactions are performed during the session.

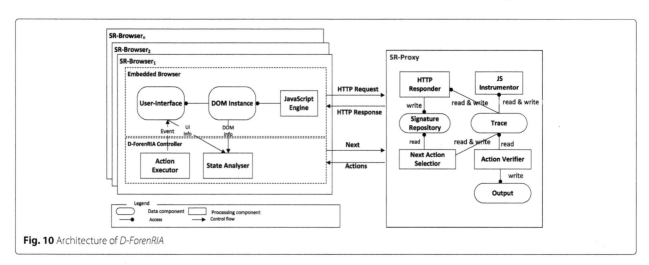

Fig. 10 Architecture of *D-ForenRIA*

D-ForenRIA works based on how Web applications work; during a session, the client does not know anything about the application, and user-interactions with the application generate a sequence of requests/responses that are accumulated in the browser. Therefore, during the replay, if the client is being fed with the same set of requests/responses by triggering the same user-interactions, we should be able to reconstruct the session.

In other words, we force the browser to issue the request related to the initial page in the trace; We feed the browser with the response for the initial page from the given trace. Through the natural rendering of this response, the browser will issue other requests (e.g. for images, JavaScript code) until the page loads completely. These requests are served by *D-ForenRIA*'s proxy from the given trace. During the reconstruction, the browser tries different actions and the SR-Proxy verifies the generated requests. When the requests generated after performing an action match the next unconsumed traffic, the SR-Proxy feeds the browser with the corresponding responses; this process continues until all HTTP traffic has been consumed.

3.1.1 Interactions between SR-Browser and SR-Proxy

We now present the communication chain between a *SR-Browser* and the *SR-Proxy*. Session reconstruction can be seen as a loop of interactions, where the *SR-Proxy* repeatedly assigns the next candidate action to the *SR-Browser* (see Fig. 11). We call this repetitive process *iteration*.

Figure 11 provides an illustration of the sequence of messages exchanged between the main components. The messages are exchanged in the following order:

1. At each iteration, the *SR-Browser* sends a *"Next"* message, asking the *SR-Proxy* the action to execute next.
2. The *SR-Proxy* asks the first *SR-Browser* reaching the current state to send the information about the state. This information includes list of all possible actions on the current DOM, and other information about the DOM such a screenshot of the rendered DOM.
3. The *SR-Browser* extracts the state information, and sends it to the *SR-Proxy*.
4. The *SR-Proxy* orders the list of candidate actions (using the signature-based ordering in Sections 2.2.1, 3.3).
5. After this, and while working on that same state, the *SR-Proxy* assigns a new candidate action to each *SR-Browser* that sends a *"Next"* message, along with all the required instructions to reach that state (using an *"ExecuteAction(actionlist)"* message).
6. As each *SR-Browser* executes known or new actions, they generate a stream of HTTP requests. The proxy responds to the generated requests using the recorded log ("HTTP Request" / "HTTP Response" loop).

This outer loop continues until all user actions are recovered.

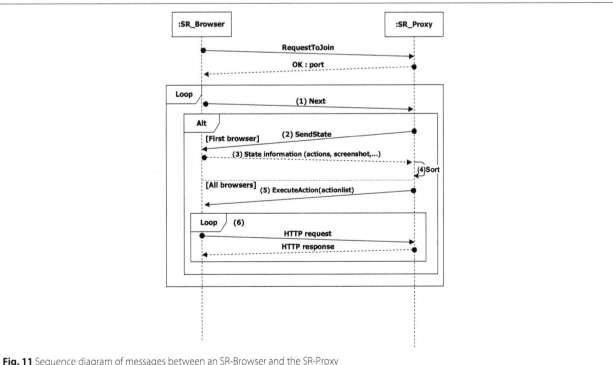

Fig. 11 Sequence diagram of messages between an SR-Browser and the SR-Proxy

3.1.2 SR-Browsers' and SR-Proxy's components

SR-Proxy and SR-Browsers have the following components which collaborate to reconstruct the session. In SR-Browsers, we have:

- The Embedded browser: A real Web browser (e.g., Firefox) which provides the ability to manipulate and access to the RIA's client states.
- The Controller: The controller is responsible for sending the "Next" messages to the SR-Proxy asking the action to be executed next.
  The controller also has the following components:

  - The Action Executor: Used to execute actions on the current state (e.g., clicks, form filling, timers). The execution is done by triggering an event of a DOM element; the corresponding event-handler is being executed and may use the JavaScript engine to complete the execution; The execution usually updates the user-interface of the embedded browser.
  - The State Analyzer: The analyzer is responsible for gathering information about the current DOM, such as the list of event handlers in the current DOM. In addition, it is used to extract information (such as the screenshots of the current DOM) when a new state is found. Furthermore, the analyzer checks whether the DOM has been updated completely after an action is being executed by the "Action Executor".

In the SR-Proxy, we have:

- The HTTP Responder: The HTTP responder replies to the stream of HTTP requests coming from embedded browsers. The previously recorded HTTP trace is given as an input to the SR-Proxy.
- The JS Instrumentor: The JS Instrumentor (JavaScript Instumentor) modifies the recorded responses before sending them back to the browser. This instrumentation is done to inject some JavaScript code to be executed on the embedded browsers to keep track of the event handlers in each state (Sections 3.2, 3.4).
- The Next Action Selector: This component keeps track of previously tried actions and uses this knowledge to choose which candidate action should be tried next.
- Signature Repository: The signature repository stores all detected signatures of actions once tried by an SR-Browser.
- The Action Verifier: This component confirms whether or not a performed action matches the

expected traffic in the log. If it is the case, it updates the output. The output contains all the required outputs of the session reconstruction process. This includes the precise sequence of user actions (e.g., clicks, selections), the user inputs provided during the session, DOMs of each visited page, and screenshots of the pages seen by the user.

D-ForenRIA is based on a set of SR-Browsers that can be dynamically added or removed during the reconstruction process. This architecture allows the concurrent execution of several actions at each RIA's state.

3.1.3 SR-Browsers' and SR-Proxy's algorithms

Based on this architecture, our simplified reconstruction algorithm executed by the SR-Browsers and SR-Proxy can be sketched as shown in Algorithms 2 and 3. We briefly overview the gist of the approach below, before providing details in the subsequent sections.

Algorithm 2 Sketch of the SR-Browser Algorithm

---

input: *SR-Proxy's address*
1: HandShake(*SR-Proxy*)
2: $e \leftarrow$ AskforNext(*SR-Proxy*)
3: **while** $e \neq$ finish **do**
4:    **if** e is "ExecuteAction" request **then**
5:       *ActionExecutor*.ExecuteAction(e);
6:       *StateAnalyzer*.WaitForStableCondition();
7:    **else if** e is "SendState" request **then**
8:       $s \leftarrow$ *StateAnalyzer*.GetStateInfo()
9:       Send(*SR-Proxy*, s)
10:   **end if**
11:   $e \leftarrow$ AskforNext(*SR-Proxy*)
12: **end while**

SR-Browser: Algorithm 2 specifies the steps executed by SR-Browsers. An SR-Browser first handshakes with the SR-Proxy. Then, there is a loop of interactions between the SR-Browser and the SR-Proxy; at each iteration, the SR-Browser asks the SR-Proxy what to do next (lines 2 and 11). The SR-Proxy can provide two answers. It either asks the SR-Browser to execute a set of actions, or it asks the SR-Browser to send back the state information. When the SR-Browser executes an action via the *Action Executor* (line 5) a stream of HTTP request/responses are exchanged between the *browser* and the SR-Proxy. The SR-Browser waits until all responses have been received, and makes sure that the DOM gets settled (line 6). In addition, when the SR-Browser discovers a correct action and a new state, the proxy requests the SR-Browser to send the state information to update the output (lines 14, 16). The state information includes the screenshot, the DOM, cookies of the current DOM and most importantly, the list of all candidate actions on the current DOM. The loop continues until all interactions are recovered.

Algorithm 3 Sketch of the SR-Proxy Algorithm

Input: set of logs *Traces*
Output: set of actions *output*

```
 1: Procedure MAIN()
 2:     output ← {}
 3:     while not finished do
 4:         SR-B ← HandShakeSRBrowser()
 5:         HandleSRBrowser(SR-B)
 6:     end while

 7: Procedure HandleSRBrowser(SR-B)
 8: while not finished do
 9:     req ← GetRequest(SR-B);
10:     if req is an "HTTP" message then
11:         HTTPResponsder.respondToHTTP(SR-B,req);
12:     else if req is a "Next" message then
13:         if ActionVerifier.Match(SR-B.lastRequests) then
14:             s ← SendState(SR-B)
15:             c ← SortCandidateActions(s, SignatureRepository)
16:             output.Add(SR-B.lastAssignedAction)
17:         else
18:             e ← NextActionSelector.ExtractNextCandidate
                    Action(SR-B, Traces, c)
19:             ExecuteAction(SR-B, e)
20:         end if
21:         SignatureRepository.record(SR-B.lastAssignedAction,
                SR-B.lastRequests)
22:     end if
23: end while
```

SR-Proxy: The algorithm used by the SR-Proxy is shown in Algorithm 3. The *main* procedure (lines 1-6) waits for SR-Browsers to send a handshake. Since *D-ForenRIA* has a distributed architecture, SR-Browsers can join at any moment during the reconstruction process. After joining of a new SR-Browser, the SR-Proxy spawns a new thread to execute the *HandleSRBrowser* method (lines 10-26). This method assigns a new port to the newly arrived SR-Browser and responds to SR-Browser's messages. If an SR-Browser sends a normal HTTP request (line 10), the *httpresponder* attempts to find that request in the traces. Otherwise, it is a *next* message and the SR-Proxy needs to decide what actions the SR-Browser will

do next. To do so, the SR-Proxy first verifies whether or not the last assigned action to this SR-Browser has generated requests/response that match the expected HTTP traffic (line 13). If it was the case, a new correct action and state have been recovered, and the SR-Proxy asks the SR-Browser to send its current state information (including the list of candidate actions) (line 14). The SR-Proxy then sorts these candidate actions from the most to the least promising based on the signature of the actions (line 15), and adds the newly discovered action to the output (line 16).

If the action executed by the SR-Browser did not generate the expected traffic (for example when the action were not triggered during the session), the *next action selector* chooses another action from the pool of candidates, and assigns it to the SR-Browser (lines 18-19). In all cases, the SR-Proxy also records the requests generated by an action in the *signature repository*. The information in the signature repository helps later when deciding if this action should be tried again (line 21). It is also notable that the SR-Proxy in *D-ForenRIA* is just used during the reconstruction and not for recording the traffic. The main steps of the session reconstruction procedure are explained below.

3.2 Extraction of candidate actions

In *D-ForenRIA*, after a state is discovered, the SR-Proxy assigns to the browser who executed the right action the task of extracting the candidate user-browser actions on the DOM. These actions are then assigned one-by-one to SR-Browsers by SR-Proxy, and tried concurrently by SR-Browsers until the correct action is found.

Event-handlers and Actions: To find candidate actions, *D-ForenRIA* needs to find "event-handlers" of DOM elements. Event-handlers are functions which define what should be executed when an event is fired. For example, in Fig. 12, *FetchData(0)* is the event-handler for the *onclick*

```
 1    var reqs =
 2    [ ["ra1.json", "ra2.json", "ra3.json"],
 3    ["rb1.json","rb2.json"],  ["rc1.json","rc2.json","rc3.json"]];
 4    //Attch handlers
 5    function attachHandler(){
 6    $("#p1").on("click", function(){ FetchData(0); });
 7    document.getElementById("p2").onclick = function(){ FetchData(1); }
 8    }
 9    //Fetching data
10    function FetchData(id){
11    $('#container').empty();
12    for (res of reqs[id]) {
13    $.get( res, function( data ,status ) {
14    $('#container').append(data); }, 'text'); }
15    }
```

Fig. 12 A simple JavaScript code snippet

event of P_1. The existence of this event-handler means that there is a candidate action "*Click P_1*" on the current DOM.

Event-handlers can be assigned statically to a DOM element, or dynamically during execution of a JavaScript code. To detect each type, we use the following techniques:

1. *Statically assigned event-handlers*: to find this type of handlers, it is enough to traverse the DOM and check the existence of attributes related to event-handlers (e.g. *onclick, onscroll,...*).

2. *Dynamically assigned handlers*:
   RIAs can also add event handlers dynamically, using some JavaScript code to assign handlers to HTML elements. JavaScript libraries (such as jQuery[8], Prototype and MooTools[9]) also provide their specific APIs to add event handlers[10]. One approach to find event listeners attached by these libraries is to parse the event information out of each JavaScript library. However, this approach requires calling the library's specific API to find the list of event handlers (such as calling the *retrieve("events")* method of an element in MooTools). This approach requires to know the API of the JavaScript libraries used in the reconstructed RIAs; since there are many such libraries used by RIAs this approach is not sustainable.
   A more effective approach for finding dynamic handlers is to account for the fact that no matter which libraries the RIA uses for assigning handlers, they all eventually call the JavaScript's *addEventListener* function [12] in the background. Therefore, by keeping track of *addEventListener* calls one can find every dynamically added event listeners. Since this approach is comprehensive, it is used in *D-ForenRIA*. As shown in Fig. 13, *D-ForenRIA* overrides the built-in *addEventListener* function such that each call of this function notifies *D-ForenRIA* about the call (line 3) and then calls the original *addEventListener* function (line 4). This technique is called hijacking [13] and is realized by the *JavaScript instrumentor* that injects the code in the responses sent to SR-browsers from the SR-Proxy (shown in Fig. 13). Note that because our code is

injected in a way to ensure that it will execute last, the hijacking will work even if the RIAs itself hijacks the same methods in the same way[11].

The Importance of Bubbling: DOM elements can also be nested inside each other and the parent node can be responsible for events triggered on child nodes via a mechanism called "Bubbling" [14]. In this case, there is a one-to-many relationship between a detected handler and possible actions and by finding an event-handler we do not always know the actual action which triggers that event. In some RIAs, for example, the *Body* element is responsible for all click events on the page. However, in practice, this event-handler is only responsible for a subset of the elements inside the body element. In this case, it is hard to find the elements which trigger the event and are handled by the parent's event handler. To alleviate this issue, elements with an assigned event-handler are tried first. Then, *D-ForenRIA* tries elements without any event-handler starting from the bottom of the tree assuming that leaf elements are more likely to be elements triggering the event.

3.3 Efficient ordering of candidate actions (SR-Proxy)

Web pages usually have hundreds of elements. So blindly trying every action on these elements to find the right one is impractical (see Section 4). *D-ForenRIA*, uses the signature-based ordering to order candidate actions at each state. As we discussed in Section 2.2, the signature based ordering is based on learning the signature of each action. In the case of RIAs, the signature of actions can be explicitly determined from the attributes of HTML elements that are involved in an action (such as the *href* attribute of a link), or determined once *D-ForenRIA* tries an action during the session reconstruction. *D-ForenRIA* assigns the signature-based scores to all elements on the current DOM. The SR-Proxy also remembers the signature of each action during the execution (line 21 in Algorithm 3).

In addition to signature-based ordering, *D-ForenRIA* also minimizes the priority of actions that involve elements with which users rarely interact; such as actions that involve elements that are invisible, have no event handler (Section 3.2), or have tags with which users usually do

```
1     var addEventListenerOrig = Element.prototype.addEventListener;
2     var EventListener=function(type,listener) {
3     notifyDynamicHandler(this, type, listener);
4     addEventListenerOrig.call(this, type,listener);
5     };
6     Element.prototype.addEventListener= EventListener;
```

Fig. 13 Hijacking the built-in JavaScript AddEventListener function to detect dynamically assigned handlers

not interact (e.g. *script, head*). For example, in the DOM of Fig. 14, the *meta, hr* and *body* elements have low impact tags and therefore clicking on them are given the lowest priority. Three *div* tags are also assigned a lower priority value because one is hidden and the other two have no handler attached, respectively.

3.4 Timeout-based AJAX calls

RIAs sometimes fetch data from the servers periodically (e.g., current exchange rate or live sports scores). There are different methods to fetch data from the server. One approach, which is called *polling*, periodically sends HTTP requests to the server using AJAX calls. There is usually a timer set with *setTimeout/setInterval* functions to make some AJAX calls when the timer fires. To keep track of such calls, *D-ForenRIA* takes a two-step approach:

1. *Timer Detection*: It detects all registered timers by overwriting the *setTimeout/setInterval* functions. The SR-Browser then executes these functions to let the SR-Proxy know about the signature of the timer.
2. *Timer Triggering*: Since *D-ForenRIA* knows the signature of timers, when it detects that the next expected HTTP request matches the signature of some timeout based function, it asks an SR-Browser to trigger that function.

However, there are two other approaches to implement periodic updates: *Long-Polling* which is based on keeping a connection between client and server open, and *Web-Sockets* which creates a bidirectional non-HTTP channel between the client and server. Currently, *D-ForenRIA* supports polling but not Web-Sockets or Long-Polling. This approach, however, has an important limitation; the technique assumes that the generated requests after triggering of the timer remain the same. Therefore, if the timer handler generates changing requests, the technique becomes ineffective.

Example: Assume that our example in Fig. 7 also has a timer which registers itself using a setInterval call to fetch the latest news from the server (Fig. 15). This timer has an interval of one minute and needs at least a minute to be triggered. During the reconstruction, the timer needs to be triggered at the right time to match the trace. To address this problem, as we described here, *D-ForenRIA* detects timer callbacks and calls them at the right moment.

Figure 16 presents a session of a user with our example. This session lasts two minutes and includes {Click P_1, Timer Callback, Click P_2, Click P_3, Timer CallBack} events. When *D-ForenRIA* loads the application, it detects the existence of the timer and executes the callback function to find its signature. After detection of "Click P_1", it finds that the next expected traffic matches the signature of the timer and asks the SR-Browser to trigger the callback function of the timer. The callback is called later again, after the detection of the next two actions (Click P_2 and Click P_3) as well.

3.5 Detection of user inputs (SR-Proxy)

User inputs are an essential part of any user session. There are two steps in each user input interaction: First, the user enters some values in one or more HTML inputs, and second, the application sends these values as an HTTP request to the server. The standard way to send user inputs is using HTML forms. In HTML forms [15], each input element has a *name* attribute and a value. The set of all name-value pairs represents all inputs provided by the user. To detect user inputs submitted using HTTP forms, *D-ForenRIA* takes the following approach: First,

```
1    <meta name="SSRG" content="Sample RIA">
2    <body onload = "attachHandler()">
3    <div style="visibility:hidden">SSRG 2016 </div>
4    <span>RIA Store:Choose one of the products</span>
5    <hr>
6    <span id='p1' >LG G4</span>
7    <span id='p2' >iPhone SE</span>
8    <span id='p3' onclick="FetchData(2)">OnePlus X</span>
9    <div id="container">--</div>
10   <hr>
11   <a href="about.php">About Us</a>
12   <a href="contactus.php">Contact Us</a>
13   <div id="news"></div>
14   <input type="text" id="srch" onkeypress='autocmpl(event);'>
15   <span>Advanced Search</span>
16   </body>
```

Fig. 14 A simple DOM instance

```
1    function updatenews() {
2    $.get( 'latestnews.json',
3    function( data ,status ) {
4    $('#news').html(data); }, 'text');
5    }
6    setInterval(updatenews, 60000);
```

Fig. 15 A timer registered using setInerval to fetch the latest news

when an SR-Browser is being asked to extract actions, it detects all form elements on the current DOM as candidate actions (Section 3.2). The SR-Proxy then compares the next expected HTTP request with the candidate form submission actions. If the next HTTP request contains a set of name-value pairs, and the set of names matches *name* of the elements inside the form, SR-Proxy identifies the user input action and asks the SR-Browser to fill the form using the set of corresponding values found in the log.

In addition to *forms*, in RIAs any input element can be used to gather and submit the data to the server. Furthermore, input data are usually submitted in JSON format, and there is no information about the input elements inside the submitted request. Therefore, by simply looking at an HTTP request, it is no longer possible to detect whether the request belongs to a user-input action or not.

To detect user input actions that are not submitted using forms, *D-ForenRIA* uses the method proposed in Section 2.2. SR-Browser considers all input fields (i.e., *input/select* tags) that have an event-handler attached, and are nested inside a *form/div* element as candidate user-input actions. The SR-Browser then needs to decide which values to put in input fields. For some input element types (such as *radio*, *select*) it is easy to choose appropriate input values since the element's attributes contain the set of possible valid inputs (such as *option* tags inside a *select* element). For some types of input elements (such as a text-box intended to accept an email address), putting a value which does not match the accepted pattern may prevent submission of user input values to the server (because of the client-side validation scripts). In this case, we assume that *D-ForenRIA* has a dictionary of correct sample values

for different input types. *D-ForenRIA*, also takes advantage of the new input elements introduced in HTML5 (elements such as *email*, *number* and *date*), to more easily assign correct values to input element.

3.6 Checking the stable condition (SR-Browser)

The SR-Browser usually needs to execute a series of actions as decided by the SR-Proxy in response to a "*Next*" message. After executing each action, an SR-Browser should wait until that action is completed and the application reaches what we call a "stable condition". In the stable condition, no more requests are going to be generated without new user interaction, and the DOM is fully updated. This condition must be met, otherwise the SR-Browser may try to execute the next action too early, an action that is not yet present on the DOM. To check the stable condition, an SR-Browser checks two things:

- *Receiving All Responses*: D-ForenRIA uses two techniques to be sure that the response for all generated requests have been received. First, SR-Browser waits for the *window.onload* event to be triggered. This event is being triggered when all resources have been received by the browser. However, this event is not triggered when a function requests a resource using AJAX.
  To keep track of AJAX requests, *D-ForenRIA* overrides the *XMLHttpRequest*'s *send* and *onreadystatechange* functions. The first function is called automatically when a request is being made and the second function can be used to detect when the browser fully receives a response.
- *Existence of the Action on DOM*: When there are no more pending requests, the system waits for the elements involved in the action to appear on the page. This check is required to let the browser consume all previously received resources and render the new DOM.

3.7 Loading the last known good state (SR-Browser and SR-Proxy)

When an SR-Browser performs an action on state *s*, and this execution does not generate the expected traffic, the SR-Browser needs to return back to some state (most

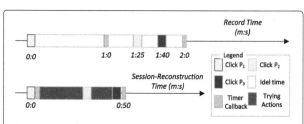

Fig. 16 A session with a timer: time flows from left to right along the axis (top) at Recording, and (bottom) at Session-Reconstruction time

probably *s*) as instructed by the SR-Proxy. *D-ForenRIA* uses a *reset* approach to transfer the client to a given state. To return back to the previous step, the SR-Proxy asks the SR-Browser to *reset* to the initial state and execute all previously detected actions [16].

As an alternative to the *reset* technique, there are approaches to *save/reload* the state of the browser. Saving/reloading the state, however, needs some information regarding the browser's internal implementation to get access to memory structures [17]. Therefore, save/load techniques are dependent on the browser's type, and there is no standard way to implement this idea. On the other hand, *D-ForenRIA*'s *reset* approach relies just on JavaScript execution and is supported by all browsers. However, one important limitation of the *reset* technique is that it can be time-consuming, particularly when there is a long sequence of previously detected actions.

3.8 Detection of actions that do not generate any HTTP request

When the reconstruction is done using only the previously recorded traffic as input, actions that do not generate any traffic can present a problem. In RIAs, actions may not generate any HTTP traffic because of caching or because the action just changes the DOM without requesting any resource from the server. To detect such actions, we use an auxiliary structure called "Action Graph". In this graph we define nodes and edges as follows:

- **Nodes**: Each node represents an action which is possible in some state of the RIA. Each node also contains some information about the set of HTTP requests/responses generated by the action.
- **Edges**: There is an edge between two nodes *a* and *b*, if there is a state from which *a* is possible and after performing *a*, *b* is available on the current state (probably a new state) of RIA.

Let node *C* be any currently enabled action; *D-ForenRIA* uses the following procedure to find the next action:

First, it checks all nodes of the graph to see if the signature of any action matches the next expected traffic. Suppose that we find such an action *D*. If *D* is present on the current DOM, we can immediately trigger that action. However, we may also accept *D* even if it is not present on the current DOM: This case happens when we find a path *CXD* from *C* to *D*, and we are sure that no action in *CX* generates any HTTP traffic. *D-ForenRIA* assumes that an action is not going to generate any traffic in two cases: first, if an action has not generated any traffic in a previous execution, and second, if all the generated requests in a previous execution contain HTTP headers that enable caching (such as *Cache-Control:public* headers [18]).

Example: Consider the example in Fig. 7. In this example, we have a node for each tried action during the reconstruction. Figure 17 presents the current state of the corresponding action graph. Suppose that action "Buy P_1" is enabled at the current state, and the next expected traffic is "*GET checkout.php*" which is the signature of clicking on the submit button when the user orders a product. Here the path: {Buy P_1, Submit} is valid since "Submit" matches the next expected request, and "Buy P_1" is known to not generate any traffic and it can be executed at the current state.

4 Experiments

To assess the effectiveness of the proposed session reconstruction system, we have conducted several experiments. These experiments are not exhaustive and are meant to evaluate the ability of *D-ForenRIA* to overcome the challenges detailed in the previous sections. As will be explained in Section 4.1, our test RIAs have been selected because they each present some of these challenges, and because they use a range of popular JavaScript libraries.

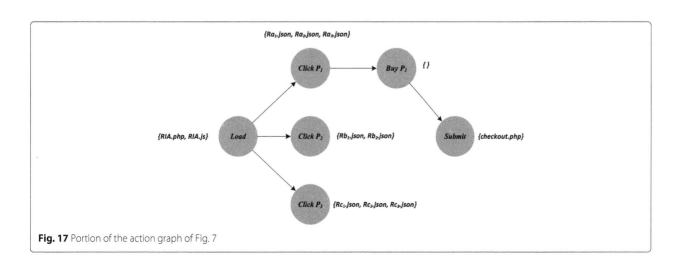

Fig. 17 Portion of the action graph of Fig. 7

Our research questions can be presented as follows.

- *RQ1*. Is *D-ForenRIA* able to reconstruct user-session efficiently?
- *RQ2*: Does distributed reconstruction have a positive influence on the performance and is there any limit on the number of browsers that should be added to reduce the execution time?
- *RQ3*: How effective are different techniques of ordering candidate actions on a given state?
- *RQ4*: What are the User-Log storage requirements in *D-ForenRIA*?

Our experimental data along with the videos are available for download[12].

4.1 Test applications

In this paper, we limit our test-cases to RIAs. We used sites with different technologies and from different domains. The reason to focus on RIAs is that other tools can already perform user-interaction reconstruction on non-AJAX Web applications (e.g. [7]). Table 1 presents characteristics of our test-cases.

The first site, C1, in our case study is a web-based open-source file manager, written in JavaScript using jQuery and jQuery UI. Our second case, C2, is an Ajaxified version of IBM's Altoro-mutual website. This is a demo banking website used by IBM for demonstration purposes. Our team has made this website fully AJAX-based where all user actions trigger AJAX requests to dynamically fetch pages. C3 is a fully AJAX-based periodic table and C5 is a Website developed by our team which represents a typical personal homepage. The more advanced website, C4, is a Web-based goal setting and performance management application built using Google Web toolkit, which has numerous clickables at each state. Finally, C6 is an open source project management tool, built using the Spring framework, and DWR (to handle AJAX). C6 has advanced user-input submission formats, and random values inside requests.

4.2 Experimental Setup

Experiments are performed on Linux-based computers with an Intel[6] Core™2 CPU at 3GHz and 3GB of RAM on a 100Mbps LAN. To implement the *D-ForenRIA*

SR-Browsers, we used Selenium. *D-ForenRIA*'s SR-Proxy is implemented as a Java application. For each test application, we recorded the full HTTP traffic of user interactions with the application using *Fiddler*[13].

To address RQ1, we captured a user-session for each of the subject applications and ran *D-ForenRIA* to reconstruct the session using the given traffic. We report "cost" and "time" of the reconstruction as measures for efficiency.

The "cost" counts how many events the SR-Browsers have to execute before successfully reconstructing all interactions. The following formula calculates the cost of session reconstruction:

$$n_e + \sum_{i=1}^{n_r} c(r_i) \tag{1}$$

where n_e is the number of actions in the user's session, and there are n_r resets (see Section 3.7) during reconstruction and the ith reset, r_i, has cost of $c(r_i)$. The cost of reset r_i is determined by how much progress have been made during the reconstruction; If r_i, happens when the algorithm has detected m user-actions, the algorithm needs to execute m previously detected actions again to perform a reset (See Section 3.7), therefore $c(r_i) = m$.

We emphasize that the *cost* provides a more reliable measure of efficiency than the total *time* of the session reconstruction. It is due to the fact that the *time* depends on factors that are out of the control of the session reconstruction tool (such as the hardware configuration and the networks speed). On the other hand, the *cost* only depends on the decisions made by the session reconstruction algorithm.

As a point of comparison, the results are also provided for the "basic solution" defined as follows:

The basic solution: Any system aiming at reconstructing user-interactions for RIAs needs to at least be able to handle user-inputs recovery, client-side randomness, sequence checks and be able to restore a previous state; otherwise the reconstruction may not be possible. In our experiments, we call such a system the "basic solution". It performs an exhaustive search for the elements of the DOM to find the next action and it does not use the proposed techniques in Section 3.3. To the best of our

Table 1 Subject applications and characteristics of the recorded user-sessions

ID	Name	#Requests	#Actions	URL
C1	Elfinder	175	150	https://github.com/Studio-42/elFinder
C2	AltoroMutual	204	50	http://www.altoromutual.com/
C3	PeriodicTable	94	45	http://ssrg.site.uottawa.ca/apr5/success1/
C4	Engage	164	25	http://engage.calibreapps.com/
C5	TestRIA	74	31	http://ssrg.eecs.uottawa.ca/testbeds.html
C6	Tudu Lists	80	30	https://sourceforge.net/projects/tudu/

knowledge at the time of writing, no other published solution provides such a basic solution; thus there is no other solution that can reconstruct RIA sessions, even inefficiently.

The Min-Time: If our session reconstruction algorithm can find all user-browser interactions without trying incorrect actions its execution time becomes minimum. In this case, the algorithm does not need to do any *reset*. We report the inferred time for this "no-reset" algorithm by measuring the total time required by *D-ForenRIA* to reconstruct the session minus the time spent during reloading the last known good state. This provides an "optimal" time for our tool.

To address RQ2, for each given user-session log, we ran *D-ForenRIA* with 1, 2, 4 and 8 browsers and report the cost and time of the reconstruction to measure the scalability of the system. To address RQ3, we ran *D-ForenRIA* using a single browser and measure how effective is applying each of the element/signature ordering. Finally, to answer RQ4 we report storage requirements for each action in the compressed format and the effect of pruning multimedia resources from traces.

4.3 Experimental results

Efficiency of D-ForenRIA (RQ1): Table 2 presents the time and cost of successful, full sessions reconstruction using *D-ForenRIA*, and the basic solution. In this experiment we use just a single SR-Browser. We report time measurement for several browsers in the next section. In all cases, the reconstructions are complete and successful, meaning that the complete set of user actions are correctly recovered.

D-ForenRIA outperforms the basic solution in all cases. If we look at the number of events that must be executed to discover the next action (column "#Events/Action" in Table 2), on average across all experiments it takes *D-ForenRIA* the execution of 34 events to find the next single user-browser interaction while the basic solution needs 1720 events to find the same thing. Regarding execution time, *D-ForenRIA* (even using a single browser) is orders of magnitudes faster than the basic solution. On average, over all experiments, *D-ForenRIA* needs 12.7 s

to detect an action while the basic solution needs around 8 min to detect an action.

Number of Resets per Action: Figure 18 presents a breakdown of the number of resets needed to detect a single user browser action in the test cases in *D-ForenRIA* and the basic solution. For *D-ForenRIA*, in all cases the majority of actions are identified without any reset. (The worst case happens in C4 where 32% of the actions need at least one reset to be found and 12% of these actions need more than 50 resets). On average in our test-cases, 83% of the actions are found immediately at the current state based on the ordering done by the SR-Browser and SR-Proxy. On the other hand, for the basic method (Fig. 18b), 52% of the actions need at least 25 resets. This figure also shows that the basic solution tries more than 50 actions to find 32% of actions.

Performance of the Distributed Architecture (RQ2): Figure 19 presents the execution time of the system when we add more browsers to reconstruct the sessions. The results are reported for 1, 2, 4 and 8 browsers. Since *D-ForenRIA* is concurrently trying different actions on each DOM we expected that adding more browsers would speedup the process as long as the system required *resets*. Specifically, if the algorithm needs nr_i resets to find the ith correct action, using up to nr_i browsers should decrease the execution time to find that action, while adding more browsers would not contribute any speedup. The results we obtained verified this argument. The best speedup happens in C3, C4 and C6 where we have the largest number of resets (See Fig. 18). For C5 adding more browsers is not as effective as C4 and C3 since many actions are found correctly without the need to try different actions (Ordering of actions detects the correct action as the most promising one (Section 3.3)). Sometimes, adding more browsers is not beneficial; for example in C1 and C2, we observed no improvement in the execution time after adding more browsers (from 2 to 8). This is because in these application many actions are found immediately by *D-ForenRIA*. However, concurrent trying of actions is the key to scalability when the signature based ordering cannot find the correct action at states.

Table 2 Time and cost of sucessfull reconstruction using *D-ForenRIA*, the basic solution, and Min-Time

ID	D-ForenRIA			Basic solution			Min-Time
	#Events	#Events/Action	Time (H:m:s)	#Events	#Events/Action	Time (H:m:s)	Time (H:m:s)
C1	183	1	0:02:44	102933	686	09:51:26	00:02:21
C2	52	1	0:02:25	34505	690	04:31:57	00:02:06
C3	1325	30	0:04:22	308548	6856	19:28:48	00:01:12
C4	3506	140	0:19:47	21518	861	02:12:01	00:01:36
C5	319	10	0:02:29	14847	478	00:48:29	00:00:39
C6	631	21	0:11:24	22529	751	02:32:39	00:05:21

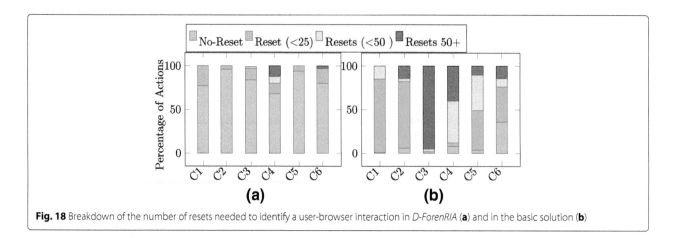

Fig. 18 Breakdown of the number of resets needed to identify a user-browser interaction in *D-ForenRIA* (**a**) and in the basic solution (**b**)

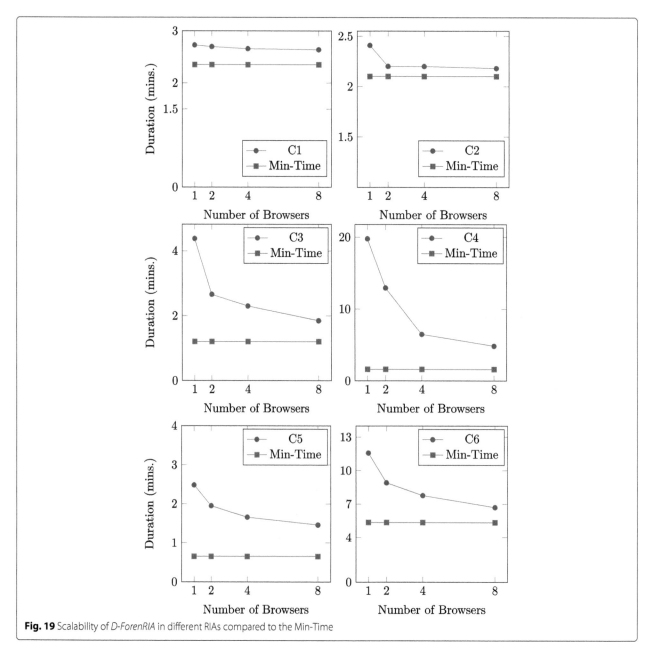

Fig. 19 Scalability of *D-ForenRIA* in different RIAs compared to the Min-Time

Efficiency of Candidate Actions Ordering Techniques (RQ3): As we discussed in Section 3.3, SR-Proxy and SR-Browsers in *D-ForenRIA* collaborate to find the most promising candidate actions on the current DOM. *D-ForenRIA* uses several techniques which we categorized as "Element-based" and "Signature-based". To understand the effectiveness of theses techniques we measured the characteristic of each DOM during reconstruction. For each DOM, we looked at the number of elements, number of visible elements, number of elements with a handler, number of leaf elements, and also the number of signatures that can be applied on the DOM. Table 3 presents the average of these measurements for all DOMS of the test cases.

In our experiments, ordering based on visibility helped us in finding correct actions sooner. We observed that in our test cases, all actions have been performed on visible elements on the page. On average, ordering based on visibility reduces the promising candidate actions by 18%. We also expected that the user-interactions happen with elements with an event-handler. The ordering based on event-handler was effective in all cases except C4. In all other RIAs, all the user-actions are performed on elements with an event handler; If we exclude C4, 76% of elements don't have any handler. In RIAs like C4 where there is a single handler to handle all events on the DOM, it is very challenging to find elements with actual event-handlers. As we suggested, *D-ForenRIA* gives high priority to leaf elements of the DOM (Section 3.3). However, there is still a considerable ratio of leaf nodes, 55% on the DOMs. Giving higher priority to leaf nodes helped us to find correct actions in less time, since in C4 all the actions were performed on leaf nodes.

To sum up, in websites similar to C4, it was insufficient to just apply "Element-based" ordering, however "Signature-based" was effective in all cases; Although we could only apply the signature-based ordering on a rather small portion of the actions in each page (on average 14% of actions on each DOM, since most of the actions have not been executed and have not shown a signature), it

could immediately detect the correct action on each DOM in 83% of cases (See Fig. 18).

HTTP-Log Storage Requirements (RQ4): One of the assumptions of the input user-log for *D-ForenRIA* is that it should contain both HTTP requests and responses. Since the input includes the body of requests and responses, one may be concerned about the size of the user-log. To investigate the storage requirements of "Full" HTTP traffic we measured some features of HTTP logs in our test cases (Table 4).

As expected the number of requests for each action is quite low. In our experiment the actions with the most number of requests are usually the first page of the application and the average number of requests per action is less than 3 requests. This low number of requests is expected because of AJAX calls for partial updates of the DOM which are common in RIAs. To measure the storage requirements, we calculated the compressed required space to store the "Full" HTTP request-responses of each action[14]. The required size per action varies from as low as 1.12 KBs to the high of 11.74 KBs for C4 and the average is 3.68 KBs. We also considered pruning multimedia resources from the log (i.e,. images and videos). These resources affect the appearance of the website, and usually do not affect the ability of the website to respond to user-interactions. Therefore, pruning multimedia resources usually does not jeopardize the reconstruction process. With pruning, the average required space for a single action dropped by 14% and reached about 3.19 KBs.

4.4 Discussion:

Recording HTTP traffic: The HTTP requests exchanged between a browser and the server can be logged at different places in the network; they can be logged on the server, in the proxy-server or even on the client-side. However, recording on the client-side requires additional configuration/installation of recording software which is not desired. HTTP servers (such as Apache[15] or IIS[16]) can be configured to record the full traffic. To use *D-ForenRIA*, there is no need to change the Web application or to instrument any code on the client side[17].

In addition, the traffic can also be captured while it goes through the network using other tools such as proxies.

Table 3 Characteristics of DOM elements and ratio of actions with signatures at each DOM

ID	#Elements	Visible(%)	Handlers(%)	DOM leaves(%)	Signs. applied(%)
C1	79	81	18	55	4
C2	108	98	29	47	12
C3	648	64	19	77	8
C4	268	85	0.3	43	20
C5	44	97	23	50	23
C6	148	68	32	59	19
Average	243	82	20	55	14

Table 4 Log size features for test cases

ID	Reqs./Action	Log Size/Action (KB)	Pruned Log Size/Action (KB)
C1	1.16	1.58	1.2
C2	1.36	1.41	0.41
C3	1.05	1.12	1.12
C4	6.56	11.47	9.96
C5	2.38	3.38	3.38
C6	2.66	3.16	3.12

Recording using proxies (or similar tools) is especially important in practice when a RIA sends requests to external servers since recording the traffic on external servers is inconvenient and usually not practical.

However, the recorded traffic using a proxy may be encrypted; the encrypted traffic may break our tool since the SR-Proxy cannot compare the generated requests with the log and verify the actions executed by SR-Browsers. In this case, the session reconstruction needs to take measures, such as a man-in-the-middle interception, to be able to read the unencrypted requests/responses.

SSL and recording HTTPS traffic: D-ForenRIA needs an access to the traffic in plain text format to perform the reconstruction. Nowadays, SSL/TLS [19] is widely used to encrypt the traffic between the client browser and server, making a network level direct access to the plain text of the traffic all but impossible. However, when the Web server receives an encrypted request, it must first decrypt it before processing it. Similarly, the response is first produced in plain text server-side before being encrypted and sent to the client. Therefore, HTTPS traffic is not actually a problem for session reconstruction if the logs from which the session is reconstructed are generated by the server hosting the application, which is in fact the normal situation: the reconstruction is carried out on behalf of the owner of the web server to investigate a security breach on that server. If access to the server logs are not possible, other methods are possible for HTTPS interception [20]; these methods are frequently used in industry to monitor an internal network, or by antivirus software for example, but they are more intrusive and require the installation of a certificate on the client. Nevertheless, such HTTPS interception system do provide perfectly adequate logging mechanism to allow session reconstruction on RIAs using HTTPS.

SSL-enabled sites do pose another issue for the session reconstruction process: the SR-Browsers communicate with the SR-Proxy as if the latter was the real server. Therefore, if the RIAs was using HTTPS, the reconstruction will use it as well, and the traffic should be encrypted based on the server's certificates which is not available to our tool. To solve this issue, *D-ForenRIA*'s SR-Proxy acts as man-in-the-middle [21]; we install our own certificate in SR-Browsers and then we just create and sign certificates with it.

User-input values encoded at client-side: We have assumed that the values used as sample data to detect user-input actions are going to be observed in the request generated after performing the action (Section 3.5). If the RIA applies some transformations on the input data before submitting it to the server, this can cause problems for the proposed technique. For example in C6, once a user selects a *true/false* value from a select element, the selected value is encoded as numerical values of *0/1*. To

alleviate this problem, our technique can be improved in the following way.

For each user-input action, each user-input element is being tried with all possible values for that element (For example the form that contains a select with *true/false* values will be submitted twice, once with *true* selected and once with *false* as the selected value). This shows how the RIA maps different user input values to values inside the HTTP requests. However, this approach is only effective when the set of possible values for a user-input element is predefined (such as *select*, *checkbox* or *radio* input elements). In case of a free form element (such as a *text-box*), it is impossible to try all possible input values and find the mapping. Anecdotally, we have not seen many RIAs that encode textual user inputs. This is probably because RIAs usually run over HTTPS and thus do not need to worry about the data being intercepted. Therefore, what *D-ForenRIA* supports is based on a widely utilized practice in modern RIAs. It would be possible to enhance *D-ForenRIA*'s ability to handle non-standard value encodings by adding library-specific decoding code if a commonly used JavaScript library was used to encode user-input in a non standard way. This kind of enhancement is however beyond the scope of this research.

Variations in an action's signature: The signature-based ordering assumes that an action would generate the same set of requests at different states. When this is true, it is possible to predict the behavior of an action in the current state, based on the action's behavior in previous states. Although this assumption holds in majority of cases in our experimental results (Fig. 18), there are a few cases where this assumption is not satisfied. In our test applications, only C5 exhibits this behavior: the list of different items (such as products, photos,...) are presented in paginated catalogs and there are next and previous buttons to navigate between pages. The next (and the previous) button, generates different sets of requests in different states. Therefore, using the signature-based ordering is not effective in this case. Consequently, when *D-ForenRIA* observes this variation in the generated requests of an action, it disables using the signature information to order the action.

Importance of multi-browser support: Selenium [22] is a set of tools that enable a program to instantiate a Web browser and trigger different events of a Web page. *D-ForenRIA* uses Selenium to implement the SR-Browsers. One important feature of Selenium is that it supports the most popular browsers. This feature enables us to use different browsers (for example Chrome or Firefox) during reconstruction. It is important for *D-ForenRIA* to use the browser that the user used while visiting the website. For example, in our applications, C4 could only be reconstructed using Firefox since the traces are generated using Firefox, and the website generates different traffic based on the user's browser[18].

Hijacking JavaScript functions: To keep track of events on each state, *D-ForenRIA* hijacks several corresponding JavaScript methods. This includes overriding methods such as *setTimeout, setInterval*, etc. One may wonder whether this overriding interferes with the RIA if the RIA itself hijacks these methods. To mitigate this issues, *D-ForenRIA*'s hijacking mechanism is executed after possible hijacking codes executed, and it includes the RIA's code for the hijacked method. In other words, *D-ForenRIA* first executes the application's code for the JavaScript event (such as setTimeout) and then instruments its required code. This approach guarantees execution of the RIA's code before the code required by *D-ForenRIA*.

Non-Deterministic RIAs: Many sites (such as news websites, web-based mail clients etc.) are not deterministic, and the next state of the application when a request is sent will depend on some other evolving conditions. Since we assumed that the RIA under reconstruction is deterministic, one may argue that this assumption limits the applicability of the tool in the real world. For example, loading the home page of a news website each time probably results in different content. However, in the session reconstruction context, we replace the server with a proxy; the proxy always replies to a request using previously recorded traffic. Since the response is always the same (which corresponds to the response logged during the actual session) the application becomes deterministic for that action (e.g. in the case of a news website, loading the homepage from a prerecorded log always returns the same set of news). This type of *server-side non-determinism* is not a problem for the session reconstruction problem.

Generalization of our testing results: We discuss in the following whether one can assume that our results remain valid for user-session reconstruction in general, for any RIA. There are several issues that may limit such a generalization.

One issue is about supporting all technical features of RIAs; several features need to be added to *D-ForenRIA*, to make the tool applicable to more RIAs. Some of these features can be easily added to the tool; for example, *D-ForenRIA* currently does not support user actions that involve a right-click or scrolling a list. However, the current techniques in *D-ForenRIA* can be easily extended to handle these events. On the other hand, adding features such as handling the traffic generated by Web sockets/long polling, or coping with incomplete input trace

that is recorded from the middle of a session, need more research and entirely new techniques.

A threat to the validity of our experiments is the generalization of the results to other test cases. To mitigate this issue, we used RIAs from different domains and test cases built using different JavaScript frameworks (Table 5). In addition, each of these applications is bringing new challenges for the session reconstruction tool. Table 6 presents the challenges we faced during reconstruction of the trace for each test case. We tackled these challenges one after the other starting from simpler cases such as C2, C3, C5 to more complex test cases C4 and C6. Although our session reconstruction approach is not an exhaustive one that handles every possible case, we have tried to solve a collection of difficult problems. However, there are more challenges to be addressed.

Another issue is regarding our input traces. We are using a single trace for each application which includes a limited number of user actions and is recorded by members of our research group. One may ask whether these traces are representative of the users of that application? We argue that the session reconstruction problem is similar to code testing, where people are trying to reach sufficient code coverage; each RIA consists of several different actions, but many of them trigger the same code. Here we are not trying to be representative because it is not meaningful in this case, what we are trying to do is to have a trace that covers the code of the application appropriately.

To measure the coverage of our traces, we measured the ratio of Javascript code executed during a session[19]. As Table 7 shows, the average code coverage is 82.7% with the minimum of 71.6% (for C5). In C2, all the possible actions have been performed during the session, and any other trace is just going to be a combination of these actions in a different order. In C1, C3 and C5, our traces do not include simple actions (such as actions that change the language of the RIA, or show a dialog). In C4 and C6 we have actions that encode user-input values, which are not supported by the current implementation of *D-ForenRIA*. Therefore, these actions are not included in our traces.

The characteristics of the RIA, can affect the performance of the signature based ordering. In the signature-based ordering, the assumption is that an action that is tried in a state will be present in other states of the RIA. If in a RIA performing an action generates an entirely new set of actions on the new state, the signature-based ordering will not be effective. However, based on the "partial updates" of the DOM in RIAs, usually performing an

Table 5 JavaScript frameworks of our test cases

Test case	C1	C2	C3	C4	C5	C6
JavaScript framework	jQuery/jQuery UI	Ajax	Ajax	GWT, Prototype	Ajax	DWR

Table 6 Challenges in our test cases

Challenge	Test case					
	C1	C2	C3	C4	C5	C6
Complex user-inputs	X	X		X		X
Changing values in Requests	X					X
Number of candidate actions			X	X		X
Bubbling				X		
Timers				X		X
Actions without HTTP traffic					X	X

action slightly changes the available actions on the page. Therefore, we believe that the signature-based ordering is effective in most RIAs.

5   Related works

Formerly, user-session reconstruction meant being able to find which pages a user had visited during a session from server logs. This task is often a preprocessing step for Web usage mining [23, 24]. In this paper, we assume that individual user-session have already been identified using one of these techniques [11, 25]. The previous session reconstruction approaches can be categorized as proactive and reactive methods [26].

Proactive methods record detailed information about actions during the actual session and usually do not deal with the recorded HTTP traffic. In proactive methods, the data about each user-browser action is collected during the actual session. Atterer [27], proposed to use a proxy which inspects HTTP responses from the server, and injects a specific user-tracking JavaScript code in the responses. Instead of using proxies, developers can also add user-tracking scripts to their code. The most popular example of these systems is Google Analytics [28]. The commercial products such as ClickTale [29] and ForeSee cxReplay [30] capture mouse and keyboard events in Web applications. The actions of the user can also be logged with browser add-ons. The Selenium IDE (implemented as a Firefox plug-in) [22] and iMacros for Chrome [31], or WaRR [32] record user actions and replay them later inside the browser. DynaRIA [33], ReAjax [34] also use an instrumented browser to capture all user interactions with an AJAX application. These tools provide several features to analyze the runtime behavior and structure of the application. In addition to using an instrumented browser, FireDetective [35] also instruments the server-side code of the application to capture a more accurate behavior

Table 7 Code coverage of our traces

Coverage	Test case					
	C1	C2	C3	C4	C5	C6
Trace Coverage (%)	89	100	75	88	71.6	73

of the application during a session. Rachna [36] reconstructs multi-tabbed user sessions using the recorded HTTP traffic, traces in lower layers of the network, and browser logs. Although a proactive session reconstruction approach can guarantee a complete reconstruction, they have deployment problems. These methods can also raise users' privacy concerns since they can track users' movements across the Web.

In reactive methods, the input of the session reconstruction is the previously captured HTTP traffic of a session. The reactive session reconstruction for traditional Web applications is a well-studied problem [25]. In this paper, our focus was on reactive session reconstruction method for RIAs. To the best of our knowledge, few works [10, 37] have been done for session reconstruction in RIAs. Here we briefly mention some of the previous reactive session reconstruction techniques. None of the previous methods handle complex RIAs, and their focus is on Web 1.0 applications.

A graph-based method, RCI tries to reconstruct user-browser interactions [7]. RCI first builds the referral graph, and then prunes the graph by removing the automatically generated requests during rendering a page. Then nodes of the graph, which represent visited pages, are compared with DOM elements to find a triggering element for each request [7, 38]. ClickMiner [7] reconstruct user session from HTTP traces recorded by a passive proxy. Their proposed approach focuses on actions that change the URL of the application. However, in RIAs many actions do not alter the URL but rather update the DOM of the page [39]. In addition, although there is some level of support for JavaScript, ClickMiner is lacking the specific capabilities that are required to handle RIAs (e.g., handling user-inputs, client-side randomness, restoring the previous state, sequence check). Our previous work, ForenRIA [10], proposes a forensics tool to perform automated and complete reconstruction of a user session in RIAs. However, ForenRIA is less effective and scalable than *D-ForenRIA* since it is implemented as a single-threaded system where a single client (i.e., browser) is responsible for executing all the possible actions on a given page. ForenRIA also did not have the ability to support complex user input actions, timers, and actions that do not generate any traffic.

In reactive session reconstruction methods, caching can present a problem [7]. The reason is that caching prevents the registration of all requests by the server, and thus blurs the picture of user behavior [11]. Therefore, the reconstruction algorithm should attempt to infer cached requests. ClickMiner uses referral relationship graphs to detect missing pages which are not present in the recorded traffic. A related problem, *Path completion*, has been discussed in Web mining research [40, 41]. Path completion refers to extraction of page visits that are not recorded in an access log due to caching. All previously proposed path completion methods use relationships between pages to address this problem. For example, Spiliopoulou et. al. proposed a path completion method using the referer and the site-topology. Li. et. al. also use referer information to solve this problem [40]. However, in RIAs the Web application has very few pages and the referer information is usually missing; Therefore, previous path completion methods do not work with RIAs. As far as we know, our idea of using the action-graph (Section 3.8) is the first path completion technique for RIAs.

6 Conclusions

Session reconstruction is much more challenging in RIAs than in traditional Web applications. In RIAs, simply looking at the data flowing between the browser and the server does not provide the necessary information to reconstruct user-interactions. In this paper, we proposed *D-ForenRIA*, a distributed tool to recover user-browser interactions from a given HTTP trace in RIAs. The main contributions are:

- Providing a formal definition of the session reconstruction problem in the context of client/server applications
- A general solution for the session reconstruction problem that has been implemented in the context of RIAs in a tool called *D-ForenRIA*
- Addressing several challenges for session reconstruction in RIAs including the identification of candidate user-browser interactions, efficient ordering of candidate actions, distributed reconstruction, detection of complex user-input interactions and actions that do not generate any HTTP traffic
- Experiments on six different websites showing promising improvement of performance and scalability

However, there are still several directions for improvements: first, the system must be tested on larger sets of RIAs. In addition, we need better algorithms to detect the most promising candidate actions where signature-based ordering is inapplicable. Moreover, the tool needs to be improved to handle cases where the log is incomplete, and when it is not recorded from the start of the session.

Exploring how *D-ForenRIA* can be used in a Web usage mining tool, or for the regression testing of RIAs by replaying the extracted user-actions, are other application domains for future work.

Endnotes

[1] The study performed in August 2016. Results are available at: http://ssrg.eecs.uottawa.ca/sr/alexaajax.html

[2] D-ForenRIA: Distributed Forensic session reconstruction for RIAs

[3] The user-interface was implemented by *Muhammad Faheem*.

[4] This does not prevent *server-side* non-determinism, where the response to a given request from a given client-state might be different at different time. This more common scenario is not a problem for session reconstruction since the responses are recorded and will this be deterministic in the replay.

[5] Here $|R_s|$ denotes the number of requests/responses in R_s, and *begin(n,b)* function returns the sequence of the first n elements of sequence b).

[6] Here $R - R_s$ refers the trace that contains elements in R minus the sequence of requests/responses that has been matched to R_s.

[7] https://www.websocket.org/aboutwebsocket.html

[8] https://jquery.com/

[9] https://mootools.net/

[10] For example, *on("event")* in jQuery or the *addEvent* method of Mootools.

[11] In this case, D-ForenRIA will hijack the hijacked code, and will call that hijacked code after having executed its own code.

[12] http://ssrg.site.uottawa.ca/sr/demo.html

[13] http://www.telerik.com/fiddler

[14] The compression was done using 7z algorithm

[15] https://httpd.apache.org/docs/2.4/mod/mod_dumpio.html

[16] https://msdn.microsoft.com/en-us/library/ms227673.aspx

[17] It is notable that the SR-Proxy in *D-ForenRIA* is just used during the reconstruction and not for recording the traffic.

[18] In our previous paper [10] we were using PhantomJS (PhantomJS.org) instead of Selenium. PhantomJS is much faster that Selenium and yields better reconstruction time, but only offers limited multi-browser support.

[19] The code coverage was measured using Chrome 59.0 devtools and we excluded the JavaScript code which can never be executed at run-time (dead code).

Acknowledgments
This work is supported by Center for Advanced Studies, IBM* Canada Lab and the Natural Sciences and Engineering Research Council of Canada (NSERC). A special thank to Muhammad Faheem and Sara Baghbanzadeh.

Authors' contributions
SH was the main researcher for this work during his Ph.D. studies. He has participated in the design of the algorithms, the implementation of the

D-ForenRIA, and in conducting the experiments. GVJ (the supervisor of SH),
GB, and IVO have made substantial contributions to the design of the
algorithms, the technical discussions and on the drafts of the manuscript. RC
shared his industrial insight and provided constant feedback on the suitability
of D-ForenRIA for real-world use. All authors have read and approved the final
version of the manuscript.

Author details
[1]University of Ottawa, 800 King Edward Avenue, K1N 6N5 Ottawa, Canada.
[2]IBM Security, Rogers St, MA 02140 Cambridge, USA. [3]IBM Centre for
Advanced Studies, Ottawa, Canada.

References
1. Garrett JJ, et al. Ajax: A new approach to web applications. 2005. Available at: http://adaptivepath.org/ideas/ajax-new-approach-web-applications/. Accessed Mar 2018.
2. Marini J. Document Object Model. New York: McGraw-Hill; 2002.
3. Fraternali P, Rossi G, Sánchez-Figueroa F, Vol. 14. Rich internet applications. New York: IEEE Internet Computing; 2010. pp. 9–12.
4. Mikowski MS, Powell JC. Single page web applications. 2013.
5. Nederlof A, Mesbah A, Deursen Av. Software engineering for the web: the state of the practice. In: Companion Proceedings of the 36th International Conference on Software Engineering. New York: ACM; 2014.
6. Mesbah A, Van Deursen A, Lenselink S. Crawling ajax-based web applications through dynamic analysis of user interface state changes. ACM Trans Web (TWEB). 2012;6(1):3.
7. Neasbitt C, Perdisci R, Li K, Nelms T. Clickminer: Towards forensic reconstruction of user-browser interactions from network traces. In: Proceedings of the 2014 ACM SIGSAC Conference on Computer and Communications Security. New York: ACM; 2014. p. 1244–1255.
8. Mobasher B. Data mining for web personalization. In: The Adaptive Web. Berlin, Heidelberg: Springer; 2007. p. 90–135.
9. Amalfitano D, Fasolino AR, Tramontana P. Rich internet application testing using execution trace data. In: Software Testing, Verification, and Validation Workshops (ICSTW), 2010 Third International Conference On. IEEE; 2010. p. 274–83.
10. Baghbanzadeh S, Hooshmand S, Bochmann G, Jourdan GV, Mirtaheri S, Faheem M, Onut IV. Reconstructing interactions with rich internet applications from http traces. In: IFIP International Conference on Digital Forensics. Springer; 2016. p. 147–64.
11. Spiliopoulou M, Mobasher B, Berendt B, Nakagawa M. A framework for the evaluation of session reconstruction heuristics in web-usage analysis. INFORMS J Comput. 2003;15(2):171–90.
12. addEventListener API, Mozilla Developers Network. https://developer.mozilla.org/en-US/docs/Web/API/EventTarget/addEventListener. Accessed 22 Mar 2017.
13. Chess B, O'Neil YT, West J. 2007. Available at: https://www.infopoint-security.de/open_downloads/alt/JavaScript_Hijacking.pdf. Accessed Mar 2018.
14. Bubbling and capturing in JavaScript. http://javascript.info/tutorial/bubbling-and-capturing. Accessed 22 Mar 2017.
15. W3C HTML5 recommendations. https://www.w3.org/TR/2014/REC-html5-20141028/forms.html#forms. Accessed 22 Mar 2017.
16. Oh J, Moon SM. Snapshot-based loading-time acceleration for web applications. In: Proceedings of the 13th Annual IEEE/ACM International Symposium on Code Generation and Optimization. IEEE Computer Society; 2015. p. 179–89.
17. Oh J, Kwon J-w, Park H, Moon SM. Migration of web applications with seamless execution. ACM SIGPLAN Not. 2015;50(7):173–85.
18. Caching in HTTP. https://www.w3.org/Protocols/rfc2616/rfc2616-sec13.html. Accessed 22 Mar 2017.
19. Freier A, Karlton P, Kocher P. The secure sockets layer (ssl) protocol version 3.0. 2011. Available at: https://tools.ietf.org/html/rfc6101. Accessed Jan 2018.
20. Carnavalet XCde, Mannan M. Killed by proxy: Analyzing client-end TLS interception software. In: Network and Distributed System Security Symposium. Internet Society; 2016.
21. Callegati F, Cerroni W, Ramilli M. Man-in-the-middle attack to the https protocol. IEEE Secur Priv. 2009;7(1):78–81.
22. Selenium: Web browser automation. http://www.seleniumhq.org/. Accessed 22 Mar 2017.
23. Srivastava J, Cooley R, Deshpande M, Tan P-N. Web usage mining: Discovery and applications of usage patterns from web data. SIGKDD Explorations. 2000;1(2).
24. Dell RF, Román PE, Velásquez JD. Web user session reconstruction with back button browsing. In: International Conference on Knowledge-Based and Intelligent Information and Engineering Systems. Berlin: Springer; 2009. p. 326–32.
25. Cooley R, Mobasher B, Srivastava J. Data preparation for mining world wide web browsing patterns. Knowl Inf Syst. 1999;1(1):5–32.
26. Dohare MPS, Arya P, Bajpai A. Novel web usage mining for web mining techniques. Int J Emerg Technol Adv Eng. 2012;2(1):253–62.
27. Atterer R. Logging usage of ajax applications with the "usaprox" http proxy. In: Proceedings of the WWW 2006 Workshop on Logging Traces of Web Activity: The Mechanics of Data Collection. ACM; 2006.
28. Clifton B. Advanced Web Metrics with Google Analytics. Indianapolis: John Wiley & Sons; 2012.
29. Clicktale: Light up the digital world. http://www.clicktale.com/. Accessed 22 Mar 2017.
30. Forsee: Web and mobile replay. http://www.foresee.com/products/web-mobile-replay/. Accessed 22 Mar 2017.
31. iMacros for Chrome. https://imacros.net/browser/cr/welcome/. Accessed 22 Mar 2017.
32. Andrica S, Candea G. Warr: A tool for high-fidelity web application record and replay. In: Dependable Systems & Networks (DSN), 2011 IEEE/IFIP 41st International Conference On. Los Alamitos: IEEE; 2011. p. 403–10.
33. Amalfitano D, Fasolino AR, Polcaro A, Tramontana P. The dynaria tool for the comprehension of ajax web applications by dynamic analysis. Innov Syst Softw Eng. 2014;10(1):41–57.
34. Marchetto A, Tonella P, Ricca F. Reajax: a reverse engineering tool for ajax web applications. IET Softw. 2012;6(1):33–49.
35. Zaidman A, Matthijssen N, Storey MA, Van Deursen A. Understanding ajax applications by connecting client and server-side execution traces. Empir Softw Eng. 2013;18(2):181–218.
36. Raghavan S, Raghavan S. Reconstructing tabbed browser sessions using metadata associations. In: IFIP International Conference on Digital Forensics. Switzerland: Springer; 2016. p. 165–88.
37. Hooshmand S, Mahmud A, Bochmann GV, Faheem M, Jourdan GV, Couturier R, Onut IV. D-forenria: Distributed reconstruction of user-interactions for rich internet applications. In: Proceedings of the 25th International Conference Companion on World Wide Web. International World Wide Web Conferences Steering Committee. New York: ACM; 2016. p. 211–4.
38. Xie G, Iliofotou M, Karagiannis T, Faloutsos M, Jin Y. Resurf: Reconstructing web-surfing activity from network traffic. In: IFIP Networking Conference, 2013. New York: IEEE; 2013. p. 1–9.
39. Mesbah A. Software analysis for the web: Achievements and prospects. In: Software Analysis, Evolution, and Reengineering (SANER), 2016 IEEE 23rd International Conference On, vol. 5. Los Alamitos: IEEE; 2016. p. 91–103.
40. Li Y, Feng B, Mao Q. Research on path completion technique in web usage mining. In: Computer Science and Computational Technology, 2008. ISCSCT'08. International Symposium On, vol. 1. Los Alamitos: IEEE; 2008. p. 554–9.
41. Munk M, Kapusta J, Švec P. Data preprocessing evaluation for web log mining: reconstruction of activities of a web visitor. Procedia Comput Sci. 2010;1(1):2273–280.
42. Typo3 CMS. http://cms-next.demo.typo3.org/typo3/. Accessed 22 Mar 2017.

3

Insights on the large-scale deployment of a curated Web-of-Trust: the Debian project's cryptographic keyring

Gunnar Wolf[1]* ⓘ and Víctor González Quiroga[2]

Abstract

The Debian project is one of the largest free software undertakings worldwide. It is geographically distributed, and participation in the project is done on a voluntary basis, without a single formal employee or directly funded person. As we will explain, due to the nature of the project, its authentication needs are very strict - User/password schemes are way surpassed, and centralized trust management schemes such as PKI are not compatible with its distributed and flat organization; fully decentralized schemes such as the OpenPGP Web of Trust are insufficient by themselves. The Debian project has solved this need by using what we termed a "curated Web of Trust".

We will explain some lessons learned from a massive key migration process that was triggered in 2014. We will present the social insight we have found from examining the relationships expressed as signatures in this curated Web of Trust, as well as a statistical study and forecast on aging, refreshment and survival of project participants stemming from an analysis on their key's activity within the keyring.

Keywords: Trust management, Cryptography, Keyring, Survival, Aging, Curated web of trust

1 Introduction

The Debian project is among the most veteran surviving free software projects; having been founded in August 1993 by Ian Murdock [1], it has grown to be one of the most popular Linux distributions by itself, as well as the technical base for literally hundreds of others. It is the only distribution that produces an integrated operating system capable of running on different operating system kernels - Although an overwhelming majority of Debian users use Linux, it has been *ported* to the FreeBSD and GNU HURD kernels as well [2–4].

But besides all of its technical characteristics, what makes Debian really stand out as a project is its social composition: it is, since its inception, a completely volunteer-driven, community-run project, with very big geographic dispersion [5–7]. Participants in the project have a shared set of emergent cultural values, some of which have been extensively documented [8].

Since Debian's early days, cryptographically strong identification was deemed necessary to guarantee the security guarantees Debian's users have; as the project grew, a viable trust management strategy had to be envised as well; we call it the *curated Web-of-Trust* model [9].

But cryptographic parameters that were deemed safe for long-term use in the mid nineties are now considered to be unsafe. By 2014, the Debian project underwent a large key migration to keep up with the security recommendations for the following years [10]. We described the full reasoning for this migration and an overview of the process and its numeric impact in the project in [9].

The aforementioned migration prompted a study of the direct metrics of the keyring's health, such as those detailed by [11], as well as a more transdisciplinary analysis of the keyring as a social network.

Throughout this work, we will present an overview of the *trust aging* that had started manifesting since around 2010, as well as its forceful re-convergence, and a statistical analysis on key survival expectations.

*Correspondence: gwolf@gwolf.org
[1]Instituto de Investigaciones Económicas, Universidad Nacional Autónoma de México, Mexico City, Mexico
Full list of author information is available at the end of the article

2   Background

In this section, we present background information needed for better understanding of what *prompted* our work, the process underwent by the Debian project that prompted for a fuller analysis to gain understanding of the keyring itself.

Throughout this section, a set of *Research Questions* (*RQs*) are presented, which guide the discussion that follows.

2.1   Trust models in public key cryptography

Besides encryption and signing, public key cryptography provides several models for identity assessment, called *trust models*. The most widespread model is the *Public Key Infrastructure* (PKI) model, a hierarchical model based on predetermined *roots of trust* and strictly vertical relationships (certificates) from *Certification Authorities* (CAs) to individuals. This model is mostly known for being the basis for the ssl and tls protocols, providing among others secure communication between Web browsers and servers using the https protocol.

As we have presented [9], the Debian project, being geographically distributed and with no organizational hierarchy, bases its trust management upon the *Web of Trust* (WoT) model, with an extra step we have termed *curatorship*. The WoT model has been an integral part of OpenPGP since its inception [12]. For this model, there is no formal distinction between nodes in the trust network: all nodes can both receive and generate certificates (or, as they are rather called in the WoT model, *signatures*) to and from any other node, and trust is established between any two nodes that need to assert it by following a *trust path* that hopefully links them in the desired direction and within the defined tolerable distance [11]. This leads to the first research question this work attempts to answer:

RQ1 Being Debian such a long-lived project, how does its trust model endure time? Does aging qualitatively challenge it?

Beside the aforementioned work, several other works have studied the information that can be gathered from the total keyring in the SKS keyserver network[1] [13]. The work we will present in this paper is restricted to a small subset thereof - As of December 2016, the SKS network holds over 4 million keys, while the active Debian keyrings hold only around 1500.

2.2   Cryptographic strength

Public key cryptography works by finding related values (typically, very large prime numbers). The relation between said numbers, thanks to mathematical problems that are *hard enough* to solve to be unfeasible to be attacked by brute force, translates to the strength of the value pair.

Over the years since the public invention and publication[2] of public key cryptography [14], several algorithms for finding and relating said numbers have been incorporated into the Digital Signature Standard [15]; currently, the most widely used are RSA (based on the *integer factorization problem*; [16]) and DSA (based on the *discrete logarithm* problem; [17]).

Said schemes' strength is directly related to the size of the numbers they build on. Back in the 1990s, when Internet connectivity boomed and they first became widely used [12], key sizes of 384 through 1024 bits were deemed enough; using longer keys demanded computing resources beyond what was practical at the time.

Of course, computers become more powerful constantly; cryptographic problems that were practically unsolvable 10 or 20 years ago are now within the reach of even small organizations ([10], p. 11). Cryptographic keys used for RSA and DSA algorithms should now be at least 2048 bits, with 4096 becoming the norm.

By 2009 (when the need to migrate to stronger keys was first widely discussed within the Debian project) the amount of 1024-bit keys was close to 90% of the total keyring; the upcoming need of migration was repeatedly discussed, and due to the threat of an attack becoming feasible for a medium-sized organization ([10], pp. 30,32), by July 2014 a hard cutoff line for expiring keys shorter than 2048 bits was set for January 2015, setting a six month period for key migration. We published a analysis on that migration process [9], which prompted the present work.

2.2.1   *Cryptographic certificates in the Debian project*

Not many free software projects started in the 1990s are still active today, but those that are tend to be very large and important. One such case is Debian; as mentioned in Section 1, the project was founded in 1993. Although the vast majority of its developers did not join until many years later, as we will explain in Section 5, many developers have been active for over a decade.

Being Debian a globally distributed project, where any project member is trusted to perform unsupervised uploads that will ultimately be installed and executed in millions of computers worldwide, the needed level of trust in a member's identity clearly surpasses what the traditional username-password pair offers; Debian Developers have used the cryptographic signature as their means of authentication to project services since its early days ([18], pp. 18–20).

Even more, *key signing parties* (KSPs, sessions where each participant verifies the other participants' identity, to later produce a cryptographic certificate or *signature* of the identity, thus strengthening the WoT, further studied in Section 3) ([18], p. 11) have been a long-standing tradition and are acknowledged as a social ties building event at developer conferences and gatherings.

Exchanging key signatures can be a challenging event for newcomers to a community, as can be seen following the exploration and proposal by [19]. Even within a community as tech-savvy as Debian is, we feel it important to understand how useful and how effective KSPs are. Thus the following research question:

RQ2 What is the actual effectivity of KSPs for Debian? Are they worth fostering and keeping, or should an alternative trust-building model be sought?

A long-time, socially active developer's key can often be signed by hundreds of people, and the more signing activity a given key has, the more *central* it becomes to the WoT (it becomes a *trust hub*).

While key migration pace did see a strong increase past July 2014, full project participation was effectively cut for 252 developers - that is, about a fourth of the project. Two and a half years later, there were still 167 keys marked as removed that have not been acted upon. We analyze this process at [9]; for the present work, suffice it to say that analyzing this migration process was instrumental in the analysis to be presented.

Our hypothesis is that, even considering the global dispersion of the project, the removed keys mostly belong to people who had already *drifted away* from their project engagement and were inactive; the upcoming Section 4 discusses how this can be understood (and even predicted) from the WoT, even analyzing it years before the migration took place; social practice in Debian makes it hard to determine when a developer is no longer active; although there is a formal process for following up seemingly-inactive developers, [20, 21] given the high amount of human work it requires, it has so far not reached enough coverage.

A process enhancement, automating a good part of the needed follow-up and providing a simple interface for inactive developers to signal they are effectively inactive, has been recently enabled [22]; this change is too recent to be accurately reported, but during the first month after its implementation, it has led to 20 developers to acknowledge they are no longer active in the project. Sixteen of them had 1024-bit keys, which means they had been inactive in most substantive project activities[3] for at least two and a half years already.

This process brings up yet another question: Given that both due to challenges brought up by advances regarding cryptographic strength, and by shifts in priorities or time availability in the lives of the members of the project will most likely continue to create fluctuations in each person's interactions with the project, can anything be learnt from past behaviour to help it cope with future fluctuations? Hence,

RQ3 From the data gathered, processed and presented as part of this work, what insights on future behaviour of the keyrings be found via statistical means?

2.3 Threats to validity

This article is based exclusively on the Debian Curated Web of Trust, it does not relate to or cover any other project's keyring. This is mainly because, to the best of our knowledge, *there just is no other project* which implements a CWoT in a similar fashion. As we explain in Section 2.2.1, the practice of exchanging key signatures is strongest in the Debian project, it does exist in other free software communities, but not with the same strength exhibited in Debian. Even just by sheer size, the footprint of @debian.org mail addresses in the SKS network is larger than most countries [13].

As for other groups that could be comparable, we could find the image of a community in several free software projects (such as Tor, Fedora, OpenBSD). However, said communities do not use a keyring as an integral part of their infrastructure. That is, there is no curation process to them, and access is not granted based on whether an individual presents a key that belongs to a given keyring.

It should be noted, the authors have started talking with a well recognized free software development project, which will possibly adopt curation and privilege-granting processes similar to Debian's. We do not want to commit them, so we have chosen not to name them.

We have been approached with questions regarding the analysis of the *keyring blobs* described in Section 4. Graphically interpreting a graph such as the ones prompting this study (Fig. 3) might not be meaningful; the shape of the *blob* itself could be an artifact of specific nodes ordering. In order to address this question, we tried reversing and randomizing the nodes in the *graphviz* source files, and found our observations to be sustained. We also switched the rendering engine to the JavaScript-based visjs, and found it to be stable. However, the analysis is still ocular; we have not performed any numerical analysis that can confirm our hypothesis.

As for Fig. 4, a similar question arises when considering overplotting: Are the colors we see a faithful representation, or is there hidden information underneath? Even more, is the color choice correct? As we mention in Section 4, some colors are more visible than others. For this question, we also compared the resulting plots to plots done with the edges presented in different order and with different colors; the results are coherent with what we present.

3 Measuring key signing parties (KSPs)

Given we are already using the developers' keyring to measure social engagement, connectedness and activity of individuals, it makes sense to study the KSPs. We will thus proceed to compare the size, progression and reach of the KSPs held at the Debian yearly developer's conference, *DebConf* (DC).

Before starting with this session's analysis, we must point out this section was written not only based on properties obtained from the data set, but with personal knowledge of one of the authors having been a participant and organizer of DebConf for most of its editions; we explain some observed trends based on insights of the Debian project community that cannot be supported by formal reference material.

Of course, KSPs are not only held at DC; a long-standing tradition is for developers to announce in the *debian-private* mailing list their travel plans, and it is customary for them to explicitly mention meeting their peers to exchange key signatures. There are also formal KSPs at different free software meetings. But for the purposes of our study, we decided to focus on the largest and more representative events.

We have analyzable data for the past twelve DC editions. Attendance to DC (and participation in its KSPs) varies by several factors, mainly the geographical location and the world (as well as each country's) economic conditions, but we will present some hypotheses as to some observed trends. The number of participants per each DC edition, as well as the proportion of its participants who were part of the KSP is shown in Fig. 1.

Part of the attendee and KSP participation data are quite natural, and are well known and discussed within the Debian community: throughout the years, the conferences with highest attendance are those held in locations closest to large concentrations of Debian developers - Table 1 shows the location where each of the DC conferences has been held since 2006, as well as the absolute numbers used for Fig. 1, sorted by its number of attendees.

We say this distribution is natural because the most attended DCs (15, 17 and 7) were held close to important developer density population centers, and the lowest

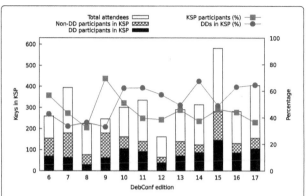

Fig. 1 Number of participants per each DebConf, showing the proportion (in black, as well as in the label) of those who were part of the key signing party

attendances (12, 8) were held in countries further away. Given the developer density in the United States, attendance for DC 10 and 14 rate seems low; this might be caused by several developers not willing travel there due to their ideological positions, or unable to do so, due to their national origin. We found it surprising to find only 246 people attended DC 9, held in Western Spain, in a region that between 2002 and 2013 pioneered free software development [23]; its number, however, is close enough to the following most attended, 6 and 16, to require further information to explain their relative sizes - Issues such as economic conditions on the relevant year ([24], p. 26) or even perceived ease to travel to the destination.

Not every attendee to the conference takes part in the KSP. Looking at the proportion of attendees who signed up to participate shows also an interesting picture. Only three times KSP participation has had over half of the attendees (DC 9, with 72.76%, 6, with 59.46%, and 10, with 53.49%). Other than those three occurrences, participation has remained in a fairly narrow 15% band, between 34 and 49%.

Not all participants in DC, nor in the KSP, are formal members of the Debian project (Debian Developers). Figure 1 captures this as well. We find some interesting patterns when looking at both relations; the match is not perfect: we counted each key as belonging to a DD if it had an identity with an *@debian.org* mail address. Some (few) DDs are known not to add this identity to their key material.

DC 9 was quite outstanding as it is by far the conference with least non-KSP participants, although it keeps a high proportion of non-DD participants. This can relate to the economic recession mentioned in ([24], p. 26): while fewer Debian Developers attended the conference than usual, it was held in a region with high free software involvement; looking at the list of participants, it contains a high number of local people affiliated with different Free Software projects.

Table 1 DebConf edition, location, number of attendees, number of KSP participants, and number DDs in the KSP for each DebConf since 2006, sorted by its number of attendees

DC	Location	Attendees	KSP	DDs
15	Heidelberg, Germany	581	282	145
17	Montreal, Canada	405	155	104
7	Edinburgh, Scotland	394	179	63
11	Banja Luka, Bosnia	335	139	91
14	Portland, United States	314	123	86
10	New York, United States	301	161	105
13	Vaumarcus, Switzerland	290	139	72
16	Cape Town, South Africa	282	130	85
6	Oaxtepec, Mexico	259	154	69
9	Cáceres, Spain	246	179	62
8	Mar del Plata, Argentina	223	76	29
12	Managua, Nicaragua	161	65	39

DC 7, 8 and 9 have the lowest percentage of DDs in the KSP. This can be caused by the aftereffects of the *Transnational Republic experiment* carried out in DC 6: a DD, well known and well connected to the WoT, presented a seemingly official ID document generated by a fictional non-government, the Transnational Republic experiment [25, 26]. This incident led to an important discussion within the project and a change in the way KSPs were held after said conference. As this clearly showed, this had the result of socially diluting the responsibility of verifying each other (that is, if everybody has checked somebody's identity, each participant does only a very cursory look on the documents. Given KSPs were already over 150 participants long, expecting thoroughness was clearly unrealistic.

Now, how significant are KSPs to the connectedness of their participants? Not everybody in a keyring cross-signs during a KSP. In fact, until the aforementioned incident in DC 6, the KSP *protocol* in Debian used to be for every participant to form two lines, having ID documents ready, and cross-check every other participant's identity.

From DC7 onwards, keysigning sessions are held in a *continuous KSP* fashion: after an initial session where a document stating the key for the full document with the keys of every participant is verified to be correct and the same for every KSP participant, attendees are encouraged to meet and have a relaxed talk and introduction with each other. Of course, the amount of cross-signatures every person will get is much smaller than with the two-line model, but they are also of greater significance.

After DC 9, the keyring maintenance team started raising awareness of the need to migrate to stronger keys, as explained in Section 2.2.1 and detailed at length in [9]; we infer that raised the need to reconnect newer, stronger keys into the keyring, as the high DD participation in KSPs starting at DC 10 shows.

Considering this, how effective are KSPs to build trust in keyrings? To this effect, we measured the ratio between total signatures and keys on each KSP's keyring (that is, the average percentage of the keyring each key is directly connected to), at the date of the KSP session itself, and weekly for the following 15 weeks; this can be seen in Fig. 2.

KSP effects are not immediate; participants are encouraged to print out a copy of the base document at home, from a computer system they ultimately trust; the first thing shown by Fig. 2 is how long does it usually take to KSP participants to sign, send, receive and upload the keys: while there is a big variation in the initial three weeks, changes quickly converge and change past said period is very minor.

As for the total connectedness for each of the KSP keyrings, the inner increment is quite sensible for all cases during the observed period; DC 7 shows the least

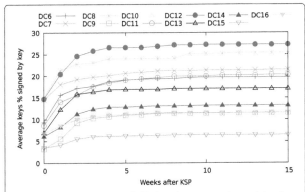

Fig. 2 Average percentage of KSP directly connected to each key by KSP at the KSP date, and weekly for the following 15 weeks

improvement, increasing the average percentage of keys signed directly from each key from 14.55 to 21.45 (a 47% increase). A hypothesis towards such a small increase could be that DC 7 was held in Scotland. The Debian-UK community, predominantly centered in Cambridge, is very large and tightly knit socially from the very early days of the project. The KSP started off with a very well connected keyring, and although this has been one of the largest conferences in the project history and the total participants in the KSP is the second highest, being this the first KSP after the *Transnational Republic experiment* mentioned above, it follows that many people would be reluctant to sign keys from people they weren't already familiar with.

Two years later, the KSP had the biggest increase: DC 9's keyring went from 3.20 to 11.55, a 261% increase. Do note that, although it was the smallest conference in Europe, Table 1 shows the absolute numbers for the KSP were coincidentally equal to DC 7's, and the proportion of DDs was almost equal. We think this might be explained because many of the DDs who attended DC 9 were *not* strongly connected to the project, in contrast with the mentioned situation of Debian-UK.

Table 2 compares the starting and ending points shown in Fig. 2. We find it striking that DC editions that would suggest very different settings are so close together - DC 7 and 8 are close to each others' antithesis; second largest and second smallest KSPs, DC7 in one of the DD-densest countries and DC8 in a very DD-sparse region; so are DC12 and DC15.

As mentioned at the beginning of the present Section, most of the explanations of phenomena depending on social interaction are just hypotheses; we have to acknowledge several data are within the range for uncertainty to play a heavy hand.

4 Trust aging and reestablishment

The work done for the described keyring migration, as well as the migration process itself, presented a great

Table 2 Increase of the average number of signatures 16 weeks after a KSP

DC	Partic.	DDs (%)	Begin	End	Increase	%
7	179	102 (57)	14.55	21.45	6.90	47
8	76	47 (62)	14.99	25.34	10.35	69
16	130	86 (66)	6.82	11.58	4.76	69
12	65	39 (60)	14.72	27.25	12.53	85
15	282	145 (51)	3.48	6.46	2.98	85
6	154	76 (49)	9.34	19.69	10.35	110
14	123	87 (71)	6.12	13.25	7.13	116
11	139	91 (65)	8.64	20.27	11.63	134
13	139	72 (52)	7.00	17.13	10.13	144
10	161	105 (65)	4.22	12.59	8.37	198
9	179	112 (63)	3.20	11.55	8.35	260

Table shows DebConf edition, absolute number of KSP participants, the portion of them that were DDs (as well as the percentage they are of the total), beginning and ending averages of directly connected keys in KSPs, with the proportion of increase seen in that KSP (absolute and percentage). The table is presented sorted by the increase percentage

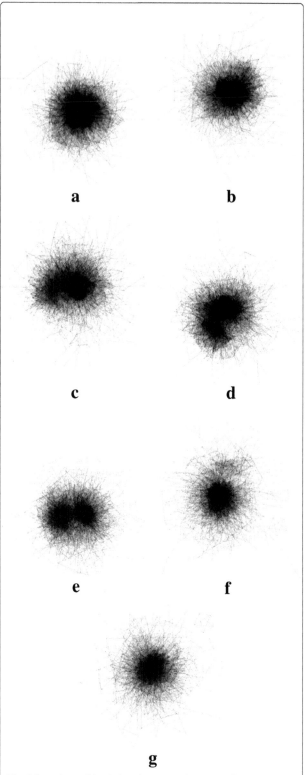

Fig. 3 Snapshots of the Debian keyring evolution at different points in time. **a** January 2009 **b** January 2010 **c** January 2011 **d** January 2012 **e** January 2014 **f** December 2014 **g** January 2015

opportunity to understand the key migration as a social phenomenon as well, using the keyring as a way to measure social cohesion and vitality.

We prepared graphic representations of the keyring at its various points in time, in the hope to learn from it patterns about its growth and evolution that can warn about future issues. For the trust-mapping graphs, we use directed graphs, where each key is represented by a node and each signature by an edge from the signer to the signee. For starters, we were interested in asserting whether the characteristics observed on the whole OpenPGP WoT [11] repeated in the subset of it represented by the Debian keyrings. Of course, said work was done as a static analysis on the keyring back in 2011; back then, the whole OpenPGP keyring stood at 2.7 million keys; at the time of this writing there are 4.5 million keys, growing by 100 to 400 keys every day [27].

Figure 3 presents seven snapshots of the main developers keyring, processed by *Graphviz* using the *neato* layout program, which implements the *spring* minimal energy model [28]. Of course, at the scale they are presented, each individual edge or node becomes irrelevant; there is too much density at the center, and the outlying nodes and edges appear as just noise. However, the *shape* of the strong set[4] does lend itself to analysis.

Figure 3a, b and g present a regular shape, approximately following Ulrich's observations, that the strong set of the WoT exhibits scale-freeness. Quoting ([11], Section 4.3),

Connectivity-wise, scale-free graphs are said to be robust against random removal of nodes, and vulnerable against the targeted removal of hubs (which leads to partitioning). This is usually explained by the hubs being the nodes that are primarily responsible for maintaining overall connectivity.

Ulrich notes that the WoT graph is *similar to a scale-free one and exhibits a hub structure, but is not scale-free in the strict sense*.

Something happened, however, in the course of 2010 that led to the WoT acquiring the shape shown in Fig. 3c by the end of the year - Instead of a seemingly uniform *blob*, there is a distinct protuberance. This horn grew throughout the following years, and by 2014, the keyring consisted of two roughly equivalent *blobs* somewhat weakly linked together, as Fig. 3d and e show.

We find this protuberance to be the portrait of a social migration: The project is often portrayed as unique among free software projects due to the close personal ties among developers; its yearly developers' conference, *DebConf*, has a very high repeating attendance rate. However, given the project has lived for over 20 years, it is understandable many of the original members have grown inactive and moved on to other life endeavors; formal retirement is requested from developers, but many people reduce their engagement gradually, and just never formally retire.

While the geographical dispersion makes it quite hard for some developers to meet others and obtain new certificates, as we already mentioned there is a tradition in Debian to announce travels in a (private, developers-only) mailing list, and active developers often will gladly meet people traveling to their region just for a key signature exchange.

Although the number of developers that by late 2010 had migrated to a stronger key was still quite small, the call for key migration was initially answered by those with most active key activity -hence, probably more conscious about the importance of this migration. Of course, although it was not a targeted removal, it was a socially self-selected one: trust hubs were among the first to migrate to stronger keys. And even though they attempted to re-build their WoT relationships and cross-sign with other developers at gatherings such as DebConf, the group of developers that -as explained in Section 4- had drifted away from project activity didn't reconnect with them.

While the migration to keys longer than 1024 bits took much longer than originally expected, the initial push was not bad: during 2010, it reached from practically zero to close to 10% of the keys - But many of those keys were *hubs*, people long involved in the project, with many social bonds, and thus very central keys. When those people migrated to newer keys, the signatures linking their long-known fellow developers to the project were usually not updated, and several old keys could have even *become islands*, gradually losing connectivity to the strong set.

Given Debian's longstanding practices, rather than isolated, many such keys started *drifting apart* as a block, growing separated from the center of mass. This explains why the migration started as a *lump* to later become two large, still somewhat strongly connected bodies, mostly stable over the years. Of course, as more developers migrated to strong keys, by late 2014 the remaining group started losing cohesion, and by December 2014 (before it was completely removed), it is barely noticeable - All of its real *hubs* had migrated to the new center of mass, with many previously connected keys becoming isolated, as Fig. 3f shows.

In order to prove this hypothesis, we generated again the same graphs, but factoring in the *trust aging*: if individual signatures are colored by their age, it is possible to visually identify if a significant portion of the group's trust is aging - That is, if social bonds as reflected by intra-key signatures are over a given edge. The seven subfigures of Fig. 4 correspond with those of Fig. 3, but with color-coded edges (according to the image caption)[5].

Surprisingly, even Fig. 4b shows a clear grouping of keys by signature age - But this grouping does not appear a year earlier, in Fig. 4a. This can, again, be indicative that the first people to migrate to stronger keys, even before it altered the overall shape of the WoT, migrated during 2009; by early 2010, they might constitute the tight, new (blue) group still in the periphery, that eventually became the core of the newer *blob*.

5 Statistical insights on the keyring history

Following from the same data set, we started a further statistical analysis; this section presents the preliminary results we gathered from applying survival analysis techniques.

The general focus of survival analysis is on the modeling the time it takes until a specific event occurs, in social sciences one often speaks of *event history* [29]. We have found interesting findings from studying how many people keeps participating in the Debian project throughout the time, that is, to model the time until departure from the Debian project. The main motivation comes from the need to understand keyring population along time and from the the implications of survival as reliability of subjects (it is more likely for someone to be trusted if they've been long enough in a community), thus arising a rough measure for trust. Our sampled data is defined by the keys that make up the curated WoT from the Debian Developers keyring [9].

The analyzed data is treated as a longitudinal study. We point out that intervals are not of the same length in time: each data point is a *tag* in the keyring's Git history,[6] and the period of analysis spans between July 2008 and July 2016. During said period, 124 tags were recorded, averaging to 23.96 days each, with a standard deviation

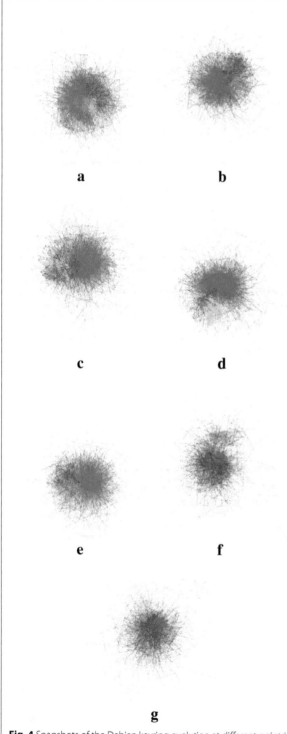

Fig. 4 Snapshots of the Debian keyring evolution at different points in time, showing signature age: blue, ≤ 1 year; green, between 1 and 2 years; yellow, between 2 and 3 years; orange, between 3 and 4 years; red, ≥ 4 years. Signature coloring is relative to each of the snapshots: blue edges in **a** represent signatures made throughout 2008. **a** January 2009 **b** January 2010 **c** January 2011 **d** January 2012 **e** January 2014 **f** December 2014 **g** January 2015

of 27.95, with a maximum of 69 days and a minimum of one day.

Given the way the keyring is structured, we used the *long key ID* (the lowest 64 bits of its fingerprint, in hexadecimal representation) as a unique identifier for each key. For each tag and key we counted the number of signatures made to that key by counting the number of non-zero entries in the corresponding key column of an adjacency matrix at a specified tag.

We identified people's participation in Debian using their key activity record (has the key stopped getting signatures?) and keyring membership (has the key stopped being part of the keyring of interest?) which codes our data as right-censored because no further information about keyring membership is known afterwards; right censoring scheme constitutes data where all that is known is that the individuals are still *alive* (the keys are still active) at a given time, [30].

For this analysis, in order to make a key-to-person correspondence, we considered key ownership using the following equivalence relation: keys are equivalent (i.e. they refer to the same person) if they have the same metadata. We considered that using the name as metadata was naturally appropiate to make a distinction among people.

We used the R programming language mainly leveraging routines from `survival` and `flexsurv` packages; unless otherwise stated, significance level is assumed to be 5%.

Our line of approach begins showing the proportion of remaining people in the keyring along time through the survival function, that is, keyring permanency. Then, using the accumulated hazard function, we get the expected exits per person that remains in the keyring until the end time (in perpetuity). And lastly, using the hazard rate function, we get the departure rate from the keyring.

For the non-parametric or observed curves we used the Kaplan-Meier product limit estimator for the survival function, [31], the Nelson-Aalen moments estimator for the accumulated hazard function [32], and the kernel density estimator for the hazard rate function, [33].

A parametric estimation to see the *mortality law* fitting our data was made using a Generalised Gamma distribution through maximum-likelihood estimation [34]. The motivation for using the Gen. Gamma model is due to the closeness and confidence band coverage it has to the observed hazard rate function obtained non-parametrically. Proper justification for said model comes from the fact that it minimizes Akaike's Information Criterion when compared to the other models, making it a better model in terms of information loss, [35], while also rejecting other models using a log-likelihood test of -1422.395 at 3 degrees of freedom, [36]. The estimated parameters found for our model were $\mu = 2.399$, $\sigma = $

0.2722, Q = 2.5594, with standard errors of 0.0719, 0.1432, 1.3519 respectively.

Finally to make inference about the effect of received signatures as a predictor for survival, we used a semi-parametric model using the Cox Proportional Hazards model [37] by taking the average number of signatures received by a person as a covariate. The estimated regressor for the avg. num. of signatures received was β = −0.00839, with a standard error of 0.0024 and a p-value of 0.0046. Proper verification for the proportional hazard assumption for the avg. num. of signatures received was done testing the Scaled Schoenfeld Residuals [38] against a Schoenfeld Individual Test which yielded a p-value of 0.1617. This means the average number of signatures received by someone has a statistically significant risk contribution at any given time [39].

In the non-parametric plot of Fig. 5, we observe downward steps when at least one people stops getting signatures. The crosses represent the followup time for censored observations (for which no further information is known and thus the proportion of keys remains). This plot does reflect the fact that many keys were dropped during the 1024-bits key removal (circa January 2015). Observed proportion of keys being above the theoretical model from year 3.5 to 6.5 years suggests that after three years the keys wouldn't be much likely to leave; at least not until after 6.5 years, where the probability of remaining afterwards is almost as the 50% chance of heads in a coin flip. It is remarkably that keyring permanency doesn't really go below 50%, showcasing good health in the keyring.

As we mentioned, due to the 1024-bit key migration, there is a clear skew that introduces a sharp drop around 6.5 years.

Figure 6 shows the people exits given one key in perpetual risk, that is, if it is to remain in the keyring for all its time span. The increasing steps from the non-parametric exits is natural being the accumulated sum per tag of the exits over remaining people ratios. The similarity from previous plot is expected since cumulated hazard is a logarithmic transformation from survival function. We see again that the observed plot lies below the theoretical model starting from year 3.5 through year 6.5 (about 3 years), quickly increasing afterwards more than expected. It is not until near year 3.5 that a someone is expected to be half-way to go, which is better when compared to the expected life of a subject being 5 years.

Figure 7 shows the departure rate is analogous to a *mortality* rate. The observed behaviour suggest that coming of age there's a sudden increase on the risk i. e. keys "wear out" to their age around year 5.5, certainly close to the expected life. Yet the parametric departure rate being under the non-parametric rate at the final years shows the dramatic effect from the 1024 removal. Another remarkably finding was that departure rate in general gives empirical evidence to say that 7 out of 100 keys will leave "any time now" (from the fact that hazard rate is the instantaneous probability of failure at a specified time; *failure* means, the probability of a key will completely cease activity after a given time of life) in a 8 year lapse.

From Fig. 8 we see that the average number of signatures received trend has a negative risk contribution. It is noteworthy that coming of age, the risk contribution starts to be positive by a bit, effectively showing the effect of the hazard rate at later ages. The resulting effect was that for each signature received by someone it reduces the baseline risk by 0.83% on average.

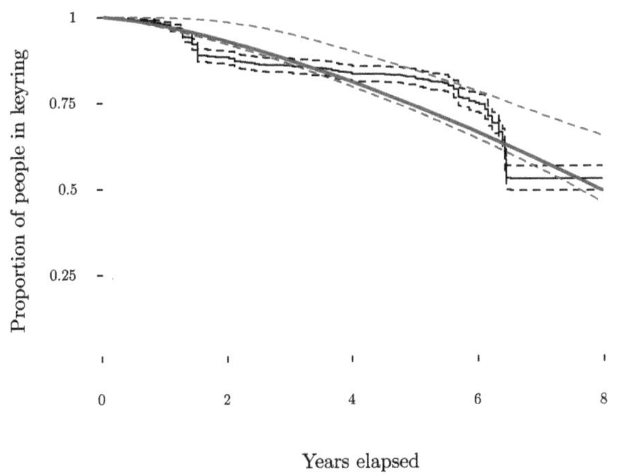

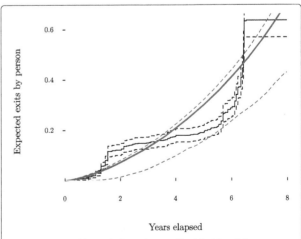

Fig. 5 Probability of people permanency. The black line follows observed (non-parametric) data from the keyring, with crosses representing the followup time for right-censored observations; the red line is the parametric estimation; dotted lines represent confidence bands

Fig. 6 Cumulated hazard of people exits. The black line follows observed (non-parametric) data from the keyring, with crosses representing the followup time for right-censored observations; the red line is the parametric estimation; dotted lines represent confidence bands

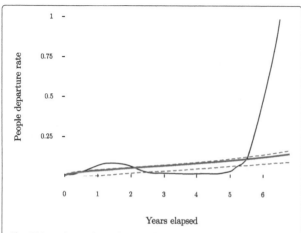

Fig. 7 Hazard rate of people exits. The black line follows observed (non-parametric) data from the keyring, the red line is the parametric estimation; dotted lines represent confidence bands

So how many signatures does someone needs to be almost failure-proof? We found a minimal average number of 358 signatures are required to make up for a failure risk statistically close enough to 0 (provided that the subject holds consistent and not by-chance interaction with the people from said 358 signatures).

As a comparison, the max recorded average of signatures received by a person was of 168.45 yielding an absolute failure risk reduction of about 75.67% from the baseline, and as expected, said person is indeed active; the mean average of signatures received was of 11.82 yielding an absolute failure risk reduction of about 9.45% from the baseline.

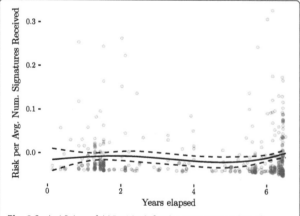

Fig. 8 Scaled Schoenfeld Residuals for the Average Number of Signatures Received. The black line follows the fitted trend for the risk contribution from the avg. signatures received, the red dots are observed risk contributions from the avg. signatures received at a specific time; dotted lines represent confidence bands; colored areas represent higher risk concentrations

In summary receiving 12 signatures (which is roughly the expected average number of signatures received) reduces the odds of exiting at any given time by 10% from the baseline risk. In general people in the project will constantly remain active for about 4.5 years, as long as they went through 1.5 years. It is just after six years where people effectively have an uncertain end unless they interacted meaningfully with other people: holding consistent relationship with at least 30% of people in the keyring can almost guarantee a lifetime membership.

6 Conclusions and future work

The Debian keyring is a very peculiar subset of the whole OpenPGP Web of Trust analyzed in [11]. The work we present here provides data empirically supporting the theoretical observations, particularly regarding the robustness of what he defines as the LSCC (Largest Strongly Connected Component). The migration away from 1024-bit keys provided an opportunity to follow the progression of the connectivity in our WoT after several of its hubs were removed.

The preliminary results for this work have been shared with a group of Debian developers. Historically, the usual practice for key signing has been to generate non-expiring signatures; people that have already cross-signed their keys don't have an incentive to refresh their trust. There is an ongoing discussion as to whether this practice should change towards time-limited signatures, better modeling ongoing social relationships, or to stick to current practice.

The resulting survival analysis can be used to generate an objective measure for trust; this study was done only on the *Debian Developers* keyring, it would be interesting to compare with the more loosely connected *Debian Maintainers* keyring. We also want to further explain the keyrings by stratification. The survival analysis showcases good health of the *Debian Developers* keyring (which makes up the mass of Debian's WoT).

Finally, the methodology followed for this study could be applied to other free software projects, aiming to correlate with events and trends spanning a wider population than Debian's; the applicability of our work to other projects, however, depends on having a proper data set to base the work off. As mentioned in Section 2.3, we are aware of only one large project interested in formally structuring a Curated Web-of-Trust keyring, but other data sets could be taken as inputs - several authors have performed studies based on the pattern of discussions in mailing lists [40]; most of the analysis we presented here is based on the observation of seven years of history, so it will take a long time before this can be applied over other data sets.

Endnotes

[1] For a WoT model to be able to scale beyond a small number of participants, *key servers* (systems that store and allow for retrieval of public key material) are needed. The *Synchronizing Key Server* (SKS) network is the largest network of OpenPGP key servers.

[2] While it is now known that public key cryptography was invented by the UK Government Communications Headquarters (GCHQ) in the early 1970s, it was kept as classified for over 25 years, which resulted in [14] being widely credited for its invention and publication.

[3] An active key is required for most regular activities a developer performs in Debian - Most notably, for uploading packages and for voting in general resolutions.

[4] The strong set is defined as the largest set of keys such that for any two keys in the set, there is a path from one to the other [41].

[5] Some care should be taken interpreting the presented graphs. Particularly, chosen colors are not equally strong and visible against white background; mid-range (orange, yellow) signatures appear weaker than red or blue ones. Also, the drawing algorithm overlays lines, and in high density areas, only the top ones prevail. Still, we believe our observations to hold despite these caveats.

[6] Version control systems handle the concept of *tags* in a repository: specific points of a project's development that are in some way relevant or significant; many projects use *tags* to mark their releases. This is the case of the Debian keyring maintainers' repository: tags mark each keyring version that was put in production. The team attempts to put a new version in production roughly once a month.

Acknowledgements
Jonathan McDowell and Daniel Kahn Gillmor, members of the Debian keyring maintenance team, for their input and explanations on the OpenPGP key format, specific semantics on signatures, and expert input on the direction of this research. GPLHost, for donating the computing resources needed for this work.

Funding
Not applicable.

Availability of data and materials
This study is based on data publicly available at the Debian keyring maintenance team's Git repository, available at https://anonscm.debian.org/git/keyring/keyring.git.
The scripts used to analyze the keyring are available at https://krstat.debian.net/acad/scripts.
Section 3 presents information from the *keysigning parties*, downloaded from their respective coordination pages, archived at https://people.debian.org/~anibal/.

Authors' contributions
VGQ is responsible for the analysis and subsequent explanation of Section 5. GW is responsible for the rest of the article. All authors read and approved the final manuscript.

Author details
[1] Instituto de Investigaciones Económicas, Universidad Nacional Autónoma de México, Mexico City, Mexico. [2] Facultad de Ciencias, Universidad Nacional Autónoma de México, Mexico City, Mexico.

References
1. Fernández-Sanguinoa J, et al. A Brief History of Debian1997–2015. https://www.debian.org/doc/manuals/project-history/. Accessed 22 Dec 2016.
2. Monga M. From Bazaar to Kibbutz: How freedom deals with coherence in the Debian project. In: Feller J, et al, editors. Collaboration, Conflict and Control: The 4th Workshop on Open Source Software Engeneering. Edinburgh: Association for Computing Machinery (ACM); 2004. p. 71–5. https://doi.org/10.1049/ic:20040268. http://homes.di.unimi.it/monga/lib/oss-icse04.pdf.
3. SPI, et al. Debian GNU/kFreeBSD1997–2016. https://www.debian.org/ports/kfreebsd-gnu/. Accessed 22 Dec 2016.
4. SPI, et al. Debian GNU/HURD1997–2016. https://www.debian.org/ports/kfreebsdgnu/. Accessed 22 Dec 2016.
5. Robles G, Gonzalez-Barahona JM, Michlmayr M. Evolution of volunteer participation in libre software projects: evidence from Debian. In: Proceedings of the 1st, International Conference on Open Source Systems. 2005. p. 100–7.
6. Robles G, Dueñas S, Gonzalez-Barahona JM, et al. In: Feller J, editor. Corporate Involvement of Libre Software: Study of Presence in Debian Code over Time. Boston: Springer US; 2007, pp. 121–32. https://doi.org/10.1007/978-0-387-72486-7_10. http://dx.doi.org/10.1007/978-0-387-72486-7_10.
7. Mateos-Garcia J, Steinmueller WE. The institutions of open source software: Examining the Debian community. In: Information Economics and Policy 20.4. *Empirical Issues in Open Source Software*; 2008. p. 333–44. https://doi.org/10.1016/j.infoecopol.2008.06.001. http://www.sciencedirect.com/science/article/pii/S0167624508000346.
8. Coleman EG. Coding freedom: The ethics and aesthetics of hacking. 2013. http://gabriellacoleman.org/Coleman-Coding-Freedom.pdf. (Visited on 01/13/2016).
9. Wolf G, Gallegos-García G. Strengthening a CuratedWeb of Trust in a Geographically Distributed Project. 2017. http://www.tandfonline.com/doi/full/10.1080/01611194.2016.1238421.
10. Smart N. ECRYPT II Yearly Report on Algorithms and Keysizes (2011-2012). *Tech. rep. 7th Framework Programme*. European Commission; 2012. http://www.ecrypt.eu.org/ecrypt2/documents/D.SPA.20.pdf. Accessed 14 Jan 2016.
11. Ulrich A, et al. Investigating the openPGP Web of Trust. In: Proceedings of the 16th European Conference on Research in Computer Security. ESORICS'11. Leuven: Springer-Verlag; 2011. p. 489–507. ISBN: 78-3-642-23821-5. http://dl.acm.org/citation.cfm?id=2041225.2041260.
12. Zimmerman PR. Why I Wrote PGP. 1991. https://www.philzimmermann.com/EN/essays/WhyIWrotePGP.html.
13. Cederlöf J. Dissecting the leaf of trust. 2004. http://www.lysator.liu.se/jc/wotsap/leaftrust.html.
14. Diffie WE, Hellman ME. New directions in cryptography. Inf Theory IEEE Trans. 1976;22(6):644–54.
15. PUB FIPS. 186. digital signature standard (DSS). In: National Institute of Standards and Technology (NIST) *(1994–2013)*. http://nvlpubs.nist.gov/nistpubs/FIPS/NIST.FIPS.186-4.pdf. Accessed 02 Feb 2016.
16. Rivest RL, Shamir A, Adleman L. A method for obtaining digital signatures and public-key cryptosystems. Commun ACM. 1978;21(2):120–6.
17. ElGamal T. A Public Key Cryptosystem and a Signature Scheme Based on Discrete Logarithms. 1985. http://link.springer.com/chapter/10.1007/3-540-39568-7_2. Accessed 02 Feb 2016.
18. Ferraro F, O'Mahony S. Managing the Boundaries of an "Open" Project. In: Padgett JF, Powell WW, editors. The Emergence of Organizations and Markets. *Chap. 18*. Princeton University Press; 2012. p. 545–65. http://www.umass.edu/digitalcenter/events/pdfs/OMahony_open_project.pdf. Accessed 13 Jan 2016.
19. Bichsel P, et al. Security and trust through electronic social network-based interactions. In: Computational Science and Engineering, 2009. CSE'09. International Conference on. *Vol. 4*. IEEE; 2009. p. 1002–7.

20. Debian Project. Teams/MIA2007–2014. https://wiki.debian.org/Teams/MIA. Accessed 07 Mar 2016.

21. Huber M, Debian MIA. Raiders of the "Lost" Maintainer. 2007. http://www.linux-magazine.com/Online/News/Debian-MIA-Raiders-of-the-Lost-Maintainer.

22. Zini E. Bits from the New Member Process. 2017. https://lists.debian.org/debian-devel-announce/2017/08/msg00009.html. Accessed 12 Sept 2017.

23. Aparicio FF. TIC y sociedad: salvando la brecha digital. El caso de Extremadura: los nuevos centros del conocimiento y el software libre. In: Revista Latinoamericana de, Tecnología Educativa-RELATEC 3.1. 2007. p. 29–44. http://relatec.unex.es/article/view/21.

24. DebConf organization. DebConf9 final report. 2009. https://media.debconf.org/dc9/report/.

25. Srivastava M. Please revoke your signatures from Martin Krafft's keys. 2006. http://lists.debconf.org/lurker/message/20060525.073637.78ce0660.en.html.

26. Krafft M. On the point of keysigning. 2008. http://madduck.net/blog/2008.01.28:on-the-point-of-keysigning/.

27. Synchronizing Key Servers. SKS OpenPGP Keyserver statistics; 2016. http://pool.sks-keyservers.net:11371/pks/lookup?op=stats. Accessed 31 Dec 2016.

28. Kamada T, Kawai S. An algorithm for drawing general undirected graphs. Inf Process Lett. 1989;31(1):7–15.

29. Tutz G, Schmid M. Modeling discrete time-to-event data. In: Springer Series Stat; 2016. https://doi.org/10.1007/978-3-319-28158--2.

30. Klein JP, Moeschberger ML. Survival analysis: statistical methods for censored and truncated data. New York: Springer-Verlag; 2003. https://doi.org/10.1007/b97377.

31. Kaplan EL, Meier P. Nonparametric estimation from incomplete observations. J Am Stat Assoc. 1958;53(282):457–81.

32. Aalen O. Nonparametric inference for a family of counting processes. Ann Stat. 1978;6(4):701–26.

33. Muller H-G, Wang J-L. Hazard rate estimation under random censoring with varying kernels and bandwidths. In: Biometrics. 1994. p. 61–76. https://doi.org/10.2307/2533197.

34. Prentice RL. A log gamma model and its maximum likelihood estimation. Biometrika. 1974;61(3):539–44.

35. Akaike H. A new look at the statistical model identification. IEEE Trans Automatic Control. 1974;19(6):716–23. https://doi.org/10.1109/TAC.1974.1100705.

36. Prentice RL. Discrimination among some parametric models. Biometrika. 1975;62(3):607–14.

37. Cox DR. Regression models and life-tables. J R Stat Soc Ser B Methodol. 1972;187–220.

38. Schoenfeld DA. The asymptotic properties of nonparametric tests for comparing survival distributions. Biometrika. 1981;68:316–9.

39. Grambsch PM, Therneau TM. Proportional hazard tests and diagnostics based on weighted residuals. Biometrika. 1994;81(3):515–26.

40. Poo-Camaño G, et al. Herding cats in a FOSS ecosystem: a tale of communication and coordination for release management. J Internet Serv Appl. 2017. https://doi.org/10.1186/s13174-017-0063-2.

41. Henk P. Penning. analysis of the strong set in the PGP web of trust. 2015. http://pgp.cs.uu.nl/plot/.

4

Using sentiment analysis to define twitter political users' classes and their homophily during the 2016 American presidential election

Josemar A. Caetano[*] (iD), Hélder S. Lima, Mateus F. Santos and Humberto T. Marques-Neto

Abstract

This paper proposes an analysis of political homophily among Twitter users during the 2016 American Presidential Election. We collected 4.9 million tweets of 18,450 users and their contact network from August 2016 to November 2016. We defined six user classes regarding their sentiment towards Donald Trump and Hillary Clinton: *whatever, Trump supporter, Hillary supporter, positive, neutral,* and *negative.* Next, we analyzed their political homophily in three scenarios. Firstly, we analyzed the Twitter *follow, mention* and *retweet* connections either unidirectional and reciprocal. In the second scenario, we analyzed multiplex connections, and in the third one, we analyzed friendships with similar speeches. Our results showed that *negative* users, users supporting Trump, and users supporting Hillary had homophily in all analyzed scenarios. We also found out that the homophily level increase when there are reciprocal connections, similar speeches, or multiplex connections.

Keywords: Internet, Online social networks, Sentiment analysis, Homophily

1 Introduction

The 2016 American Presidential Election was characterized by an intense competition, especially after the primaries of political parties that resulted in the dispute between Donald Trump, representing the Republican Party, and Hillary Clinton, representing the Democratic Party [34]. The political conflict between these two candidates was reflected in the discussions among users on online social networks like Twitter [27]. Although candidates' tweets can reach a large number of users, disputed debates in Twitter and in other social networks shows that not all users have the same sentiment regarding the candidates messages [38].

In this paper, we defined six Twitter user classes during the 2016 American Presidential Election that include sentiment variations that a user can have towards Donald Trump and Hillary Clinton. Figure 1 shows the division of Twitter users into politically engaged users and not politically engaged users. We named the first class as Whatever since its users did not engage in politics. A

politically engaged user can be either a supporter or a non-supporter. Thus, we named the second class as Trump Supporter and the third one as Hillary Supporter. We defined the three non-supporter classes Positive, Neutral, and Negative as classes that have users expressing positive, neutral, and negative sentiment towards both candidates, respectively. We collected 4.9 million tweets published by 18,450 users, their profiles and their relationships with other users.

After classifying the Twitter users, we analyzed how connected each user is with his/hers peers using homophily analysis. Homophily is the tendency of individuals to have characteristics and behavior similar to their peers'. This social phenomenon has been already perceived on online social networks [12]. The characteristics of peers (e.g., friends) can be immutable, such as ethnicity, or even mutable such as beliefs, professions [22], and sentiments towards a topic [40] or towards political candidates [6].

We analyzed homophily in three scenarios: (i) uniplex connections, (ii) multiplex connections, and (iii) friendship with a similar speech. A uniplex network is a network where there is only one type of connection between nodes; a multiplex network is a network with

*Correspondence: josemar.caetano@sga.pucminas.br
Department of Computer Science, Pontifical Catholic University of Minas
Gerais (PUC Minas), Belo Horizonte, MG, Brazil

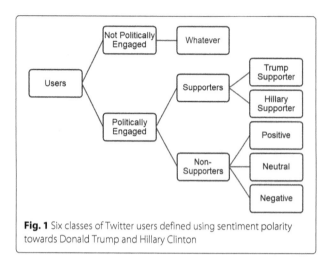

Fig. 1 Six classes of Twitter users defined using sentiment polarity towards Donald Trump and Hillary Clinton

more than one type of connection between nodes; friendship with a similar speech is a network where users follow each other and use hashtags and words in common. In this work, we considered the following Twitter user connections: follow (user A follows user B), mention (user A mentions user B), and retweet (user A retweets user B). These connections can be either unidirectional or reciprocal.

Our results revealed that, in all analyzed scenarios, Negative, Trump Supporter, and Hillary Supporter users had homophily. We also found out that the homophily level tends to increase when there are only reciprocal connections among users of those three classes. The level of homophily also increases when we analyzed the multiplex connections. Another circumstance that also increases homophily is when the users of those classes present similar speeches.

We hope that this work contributes to a better understanding of the political engagement of users in online social networks during the 2016 American Presidential Election. We also believe that the methodology proposed here is replicable on next elections in the US, and also in another country's political elections.

The paper is organized as follows. We first discuss the related work. Next we present our methodology divided into five: (i) collecting Twitter data; (ii) identifying political and non-political tweets; (iii) performing sentiment analysis in political and non-political tweets; (iv) identifying each user class; and (v) analyzing political homophily in Twitter. We then discuss the results for each scenario analysed, and then present our main conclusions and possible directions for future work.

2 Related work

Some papers have already proposed political homophily analysis on Twitter. In this section, we present some previous work related to the present paper. Colleoni,

E., Rozza, A., and Arvidsson, A [8] investigated the political homophily in an American Democratic and Republican voters database. They used machine learning and social network analysis approaches to classify users' party preference. The authors noticed that, the Democrats show a higher level of political homophily when comparing with the Republicans. They also found out that homophily levels are higher when reciprocal connections are considered. Additionally, they performed a second experiment with users that follow the official party accounts, and the Republicans political homophily also had higher rates than expected by chance and the Democrats had lower homophily than expected by chance.

Huber, G. A., and Malhotra, N [18] investigated the political homophily on online dating sites. Unlike the previous works, they did not use an algorithm for defining the political preference of the user, they did an analysis applying a questionary with questions such as "How do you think of yourself politically?" and "How would you describe yourself politically?". They found that people are more welcoming to other people that have similar political characteristics and are more welcome to reach them out. The political ideology homophily was half as extensive as racial homophily and higher than the educational homophily.

Halberstam, Y., and Knight, B. [17] investigated how political homophily influences the dissemination of information on social networks. The authors used a politically engaged Twitter users' database and identified that users linked to major political groups have more connections than users connected to minority political groups, they are exposed to more information than users connected to minority political groups and they receive the information faster than users connected to minority political groups.

Brady, W. J. et al.[4] researched how the propagation of polemic content happens over twitter social network. The authors did not focus on homophily itself although their findings are related to the present work. They found that polemic discourses are much more likely to be retweeted when analyzing the intra-group. This investigation used a network with retweet as edges and the user profiles as the nodes. They estimated each user's political ideology with an algorithm based on followers network proposed by Barberá, P. et al. [1].

Barberá, P. et al. [1] proposed a statistical model for political ideology estimation based on ideological positions. They suggested that ideological identification is a predictive feature of the following decision. They evaluated the model with 12 political and non-political subjects on a database of 150 million tweets. They found that explicitly political users are likely to share information that comes from similar ideological users than to share information with different ideological users. Conservatives are less likely than the liberals to take part in the heterogeneous dissemination of political and non-political information. They did not investigate the homophily of those groups, although this finding can also be related to a higher homophily once the groups are composed of more similar individuals than expected by chance.

Monti et al. [24] modeled the political disaffection on twitter, they randomly selected 50,000 Italian Twitter users, and collected their followers. The dataset analyzed contained 261,313 users and more than 35 million tweets from those users. The authors classified tweets as political (related to politics), negative (has negative sentiment expressed) and general (tweet do not mention any candidate). They considered as politically disaffected only tweets, political, negative, and general. They applied different classifiers to automatic identify political disaffection in tweets. Their results showed that Random Forest presented the best result on classification. They validated and compared their results with public opinion surveys regarding vote intentions and political topics. They found out a strong relationship between their classifier and the public opinion surveys. In the present work, we analyzed not only the disaffection but also the affection for one or both candidates. We considered only political tweets to classify users. Additionally, we investigated the homophily of each group to understand how much are they connected, and each user in those groups were classified based on the sentiment he/she expressed towards a candidate.

In a preliminary paper [6], we performed the political homophily analysis classifying users by the average sentiment expressed towards the candidates considering only follow connections. We analysed two homophily scenarios. In the first scenario, we defined four sentiment classes related to the candidates Donald Trump and Hillary Clinton and in the second scenario, we defined six sentiment classes. Our results showed that the existence of homophily among users that expressed negative sentiment towards Donald Trump and Hilary Clinton. The homophily was higher among users that had average negative sentiment towards Donald Trump. There was heterophylly among users that didn't publish tweets about

the candidates and among users with neutral average sentiment toward them. The main differences between the present work and [6] is the way we classify the users and the use of multiplex connections, we analyzed the retweet and mention features as possible connections in the uniplex connections, and we analyzed the similar speech homophily in Twitter using hashtags and the most important words given by the LDA algorithm [2].

These papers demonstrated that political homophily is a phenomenon present on Twitter, therefore in this paper, we perform a more comprehensive homophily analysis considering uniplex, multiplex connections, and similar speeches (as connections) among groups. Thus, we considered mentions, retweets, and similar speeches in Twitter as connections in addition to the usual following connections investigated in related works. Moreover, we perform the homophily analysis among six sentiment classes: Whatever, Neutral, Negative, Trump Supporter, Hillary Supporter, and Positive.

3   Methodology

Figure 2 shows the steps of the methodology followed in this work. In the first step, we have collected Twitter data. Section 3.1 describes the process of collecting timelines, connections among users, and Twitter user profiles. In the second step, we performed an analysis of each users' timeline to define which tweets are about politics and which tweets are not about politics. The details of this identification process are described in Section 3.2. In the third step of the proposed methodology, we performed the tweets' texts sentiment analysis which has two distinct approaches: one for political tweets that were about both candidates at the same time and another one for non-political tweets and political tweets that were about only one candidate.

The political users' timelines and sentiment analysis allowed us to classify each user. Thus, in the fourth step of the methodology, we arranged users into six different classes: *Whatever, Trump Supporter, Hillary Supporter, Positive, Neutral,* and *Negative*. The process used for classifying the users is explained in Section 3.4. Finally, in the fifth and last step of the proposed methodology, we analyzed the users' political homophily regarding their friendships, retweets, and the text features (hashtags and

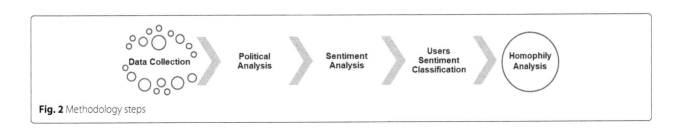

Fig. 2 Methodology steps

important words) of their tweets. We present the political homophily analysis in Section 3.5.

3.1 Data collection

In this section we begin presenting the Twitter social network, its features and nomeclatures and information about Donald Trump and Hillary Clinton use of Twitter. Finally, we discuss how we collected data from it.

3.1.1 Twitter and the 2016 american presidential election

Twitter is a social network that allows the publication of tweets - short messages, which, in 2016, were limited to 140 characters [16]. Released in 2006, it had about 328 million active users in 2017 and it was a very popular online social networks during the 2016 American Presidential Election [31].

On Twitter, when user A creates a link with user B, we say that A is following B, or that B has A as a follower. Unlike other social networks, on Twitter the connections between users are not necessarily reciprocal because when one user follows another one, not necesarily this one will follow his/her follower.

A Twitter user profile is composed of the following attributes: name, profile description, photo, and location. A timeline is the set of tweets that a Twitter user published. The republican candidate Donald Trump has a Twitter account identified by the username @realDonaldTrump and in November 2016 had about 17.1 million of followers. On the other hand, the democrat candidate Hillary Clinton, identified by the username @HillaryClinton, was followed by approximately 11.6 million users in November 2016.

A retweet is a tweet published by user A that has been shared by user B. Mention is a reference to a Twitter user in the tweet text. This reference starts with the character "@". One way to target a tweet to a specific user is putting a mention to him/her at the beginning of it. Thus, users mentioned at the beginning of a tweet are called targets.

3.1.2 Collecting data from twitter

We collected data on Twitter social network from August 1, 2016 to November 30, 2016 using the official Twitter API [36] to get tweets, user profiles, and their contact networks. It is noteworthy that the American Presidential Election occurred on November 8, 2016 and that televised debates between Donald Trump and Hillary Clinton happened on September 26, 2016, October 9, 2016, and October 19, 2016.

This API provides up to 200 tweets (per request) published by a user. Additionally, the API has a limit of 300 requests per 15 minutes time window. We started the data collection identifying *seed users*, that is, people who were publishing content about the American election on Twitter. We obtained this identification through the API's streaming method, which enables real-time collection of tweets. The objective of the real-time collection was to identify users who published tweets in English and did a retweet of a candidate's tweet. We based on the hypothesis that if a user retweeted a candidate tweet, then they read that tweet and made a reference to what the candidate said. Therefore, this user is probably using Twitter to discuss, or promote political discussions.

For each seed user, we collected their profile, timeline, and their contact network (followers and friends), that is, the network first hop. We also collected the same information from each user of seed user's contacts network (network second hop). In total, we collected data from 18,450 users (5284 seed users and 13,166 users from the first hop and second hop). Figure 3 shows the steps followed in the data collection.

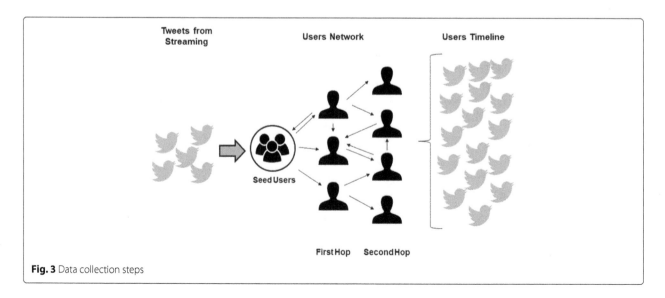

Fig. 3 Data collection steps

3.1.3 Dataset

Table 1 shows the total of tweets, user profiles, and relationships collected. We collected 4,935,128 tweets published by 18,450 users and 437,515 connections (follow relationship) among them. From the 437,515 relationships, 192,933 were unidirectional and 122,291 were reciprocal.

3.2 Political analysis

A prerequisite for analyzing tweets is to estimate the political bias of the users involved [39]. One way to extract a tweet political bias is through its syntactic and semantic features. Several papers have proposed this two analysis to find user communities and different tweet categories [11, 13, 23, 25, 32].

We performed a semantic analysis to identify which tweets had political content.Therefore considering mentions, targets and URLs occurrence in them. We defined the following conditions for the identification of political tweets:

- The tweet is a candidate's retweet;
- The tweet targets at least one candidate;
- The tweet mentions at least one candidate;
- The tweet has a candidate's proper name;

Whether one of these conditions was satisfied for one candidate, then that tweet was considered as a political tweet for her/him. If any of these conditions were satisfied for both candidates, then that tweet was considered as political for both of them. We considered as indicators of candidate targeting or mentioning, the Twitter username, the name, and the name abbreviation. Thus, for the candidate Donald Trump, we considered the words: "@realDonaldTrump", "Trump" and "DT". For the candidate Hillary Clinton, we considered the words: "@HillaryClinton", "Hillary", "HC". We performed the syntactic and semantic analysis with all tweet words converted to lower case to prevent words written in a different case from being ignored.

3.3 Sentiment analysis

After identifying the political and non-political tweets in each user timeline, we performed the sentiment analysis on each tweet text. We considered that if a political tweet is about a candidate A, then the tweet's sentiment is towards candidate A. Thus, a political tweet's sentiment is an opinion about a candidate A.

However, we observed in our dataset that political tweets that were about both candidates at the same time were a challenge for analyzing their political sentiment. Because a whole text sentiment analysis only takes into account what was the user's sentiment when he/she published a tweet, not his/her opinion about each subject in the tweet text.

Thus, whether a user expresses a very positive opinion about his/her favorite candidate and at the same time expresses a very negative opinion about the other candidate, then the sentiment analysis algorithm would consider the tweet them neutral since the very negative sentiment cancels the very positive sentiment. Furthermore, in these tweets, we were not able to correctly identify the user's opinion about each candidate either if his/her sentiment was positive or negative.

To address this problem, we divided the sentiment analysis into two approaches. In the first approach, we performed a sentiment analysis considering the whole tweet text. Thus, the text sentiment was assigned to a candidate if and only if the tweet was about that candidate. We used the same approach for nonpolitical tweets. In the second approach, we identified the words related to each candidate if and only if the tweet was about both candidates. Thus, we were able to perform a sentiment analysis considering just the related words to them.

Figure 4 presents a diagram with the two strategies followed in the tweet sentiment analysis.

3.3.1 Identifying words associated with both candidates

We identified the subjects and words associated with Hillary Clinton and Donald Trump in the same tweet using the Stanford Parser tool [20]. It allows the identification of subjects in a text and their associated words. Then we identified what subjects were related to each candidate considering the definitions presented in Section 3.2.

Furthermore, we considered words associated with pronouns possibly related to candidates in the analysis. That means, we defined the pronouns "he" and "him" as related to the candidate Donald Trump and the pronouns "she" and "her" as related to the candidate Hillary Clinton.

Table 1 Dataset

Collection	Total of documents
tweets	4935128
users	18450
relationships	437515

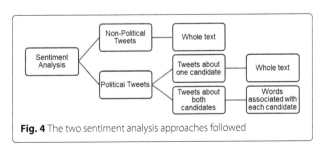

Fig. 4 The two sentiment analysis approaches followed

The words associated with the candidates' subjects and pronouns were used to build each candidate's bag of words. We performed a sentiment analysis in each candidate's bag of words to define the user's opinion towards the candidate.

The Stanford Parser library takes as its parameter a natural language parser model. The English-language parser template used in this work is called englishPCFG [19]. This template receives text as input and returns a list of tuples. Each tuple is a grammatical relation present in the text. The first position of a tuple is called *governor* and the second position of a tuple is called *dependency*. The tuple indicates that the word *governor* grammatically modifies the word *dependency*.

A grammatical relation can be a relation between subject and adjective, adjective and adverb, negation and adjective, etc. The library recognizes 50 grammatical relations. We selected the most relevant grammatical relations that would enable the identification of opinion words associated with each subject. We based the selection on the morphological classes covered by the SentiStrength lexeme dictionary [33].

3.3.2 Applying sentiment analysis in tweets
Some papers have proposed a sentiment analysis state of the art and practice strategies for different contexts and databases [16, 28, 30]. In [28], the authors presented a benchmark testing sentiment analysis tools in tweet databases. The results showed that SentiStrength tool [33] presented the best results.

Therefore, we performed the tweets' sentiment analysis using the SentiStrength tool. This tool uses a dictionary lexicon-based approach [16], that means, there is a dictionary of positive and negative words that are used to perform a text sentiment analysis.

SentiStrength analyzes the sentiment of each sentence in the text separately. At the beginning of the analysis, each sentence has a positive value α equal to 1 and a negative value β equal to -1. If the sentence contains words that belong to the word dictionary, then the values associated with those words are compared with α and β. If the word w sentiment value is greater than α, then α is updated to the w sentiment value. Similarly, if the w sentiment value is less than β, Then β is updated to the w sentiment value. A negative word has a value between -1 (slightly negative) and -5 (very negative). A positive word has a value between 1 (slightly positive) and 5 (very positive).

After analyzing each sentence, SentiStrength identifies the highest positive value α (max) and the smallest negative β value (min) of all sentences (whole text). The final sentiment analysis result is the difference (scale) between the values max and min. Therefore, the text sentiment can be between -4 (very negative) and 4 (very positive). The value 0 indicates a neutral sentiment.

SentiStrength dictionary consists of 700 words with a sentiment range from -5 (very negative) to 5 (very positive) [33]. In addition to the word dictionary, SentiStrength uses lists of emojis and boosting words (i.e., very, most, worst, best, etc.) to improve the sentiment analysis results [16].

3.4 Users sentiment classification
We calculated the average sentiment of each of the 18,450 users towards the candidates considering each user's political timeline (Section 3.2).

The process of averaging user sentiment towards candidates resulted in two scales, one referring to Donald Trump and the another to Hillary Clinton. The higher the value, the more positive the sentiment is, and the lower the value, more negative is the sentiment. Table 2 shows the average and standard deviation of the sentiment of the 18,450 users towards the candidates Donald Trump and Hillary Clinton.

In this paper, we assumed that a user has a positive sentiment towards a candidate when the average of the sentiment is greater than 0 and that a user has a negative sentiment towards a candidate when the average is less than 0. When the sentiment average has a 0 value, we considered that there is neutral sentiment towards the candidate. If a tweet is not political, then we considered as concealed sentiment (null value).

We assumed that there were at least six sentiment user classes in the 2016 American Presidential Election context acting on online social networks. Table 3 shows the name, description, and total of users of each one of the six classes defined. We assumed that each user from each class has more relationship with their peers and therefore, we wanted to analyze how similar a user is to his/her peers.

Figure 5 shows the total users of each class. The Whatever class contains 53.18% of users showing that more than half of the users did not publish any political tweets related to the candidates. Trump Supporter, Hillary Supporter, Positive, Neutral, and Negative classes have 5.43%, 19.00%, 0.55%, 12.35% and 9.49% of the total users, respectively.

3.5 Homophily analysis
To mathematically represent the homophily level of the kind i for each individual, Colleoni, Rozza and Arvidsson

Table 2 Average and standard deviation sentiments toward Donald Trump and Hillary Clinton observed in the dataset

	Donald Trump	Hillary Clinton
Mean	-0.130	-0.055
Standard Deviation	0.296	0.334

Table 3 Six classes of Twitter users definition

Class	Description
Whatever	Concealed sentiment towards both Donald Trump and Hillary Clinton
Trump Supporter	Positive sentiment towards Donald Trump and non positive sentiment towards Hillary Clinton; or negative sentiment towards Hillary Clinton and non negative sentiment towards Donald Trump
Hillary Supporter	Positive sentiment towards Hillary Clinton and non positive sentiment towards Donald Trump; or negative sentiment towards Donald Trump and non negative sentiment towards Hillary Clinton
Positive	Positive sentiment towards both Donald Trump and Hillary Clinton
Neutral	Neutral sentiment towards both Donald Trump and Hillary Clinton; or Neutral sentiment towards Donald Trump and concealed sentiment towards Hillary Clinton; or Concealed sentiment towards Donald Trump and neutral sentiment towards Hillary Clinton
Negative	Negative sentiment towards both Donald Trump and Hillary Clinton

[8] applied the following equation:

$$H_i = \frac{s_i}{s_i + d_i} \tag{1}$$

Where H_i is the homophily index, s_i represents the number of connections between i individuals (homogeneous connections), d_i represents the number of connections that bind individuals of kind i with individuals of other kinds (heterogeneous connections).

In this way, Currarini, Jackson and Pin [9] recommended to use inbreeding homophily index, developed by Coleman [7] to normalize the H_i. This measure is given by:

$$IH_i = \frac{H_i - w_i}{1 - w_i} \tag{2}$$

Where IH_i is the homophily index defined in Eq. 2 and w_i is the probability of the occurrence of i individuals. The w_i consists of the total of i individuals divided by the total number of individuals in a network.

Returning to the previous example, the IH_i value for groups A and B, is 0.2 and 0.96, respectively. This result demonstrates that the inbreeding homophily index can be used to compare relative homophily between different populations. The higher the value of IH_i, the stronger is the homophily occurrence.

The opposite of homophily is Heterophily since there is predominance of relationships among individuals of different kinds. When the IH_i is zero, it corresponds to the homophily baseline determinant. In this work, we defined the occurrence of homophily or heterophily using the following condition:

$$\begin{cases} IH_i > 0 \;\; homophily \\ IH_i < 0 \;\; heterophily \end{cases}$$

3.5.1 Multiplexity

McPherson, Smith-Lovin, and Cook [22] describe that people's social relationships are not entirely equal because there are different levels of closeness between individuals in society. For example, relationships between two people close to each other as marriage and friendship, or less close to each other as co-workers, schoolmates, neighbors, and acquaintances.

Multiplexity is the number of connection types linking two people [37]. Homophily patterns tend to be stronger when there are more types of relationships between people, that means, the higher the edges multiplexity, the higher the homophily level [22].

Fischer [15] was one of the pioneers in analyzing social networks with more than one kind of relationship. In that study, the authors investigated the differences in social relations between residents of small and large cities. They analyzed the impact of kinship ties, co-workers and neighborhood on people's social networks. An interesting finding was that, nonrelatives friends had a average

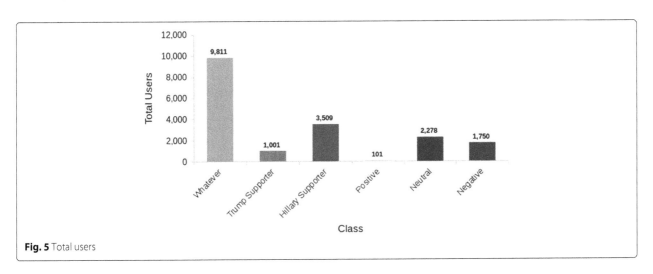

Fig. 5 Total users

age difference of 6 years, whereas among relatives, except siblings, the age difference was increased to 24 years. This example demonstrates that analyzing homophily by considering multiplexity assists in obtaining more refined information.

The term multiplex tie is commonly used to refer to occasions where there is an overlap of relationship types between two nodes in a network [14, 22, 37]. When there is only one kind of relationship between two nodes, one uses the term uniplex tie [14, 37] or simplex tie [22].

Figure 6 illustrates a Twitter user network containing multiplex ties. In this graph, the nodes correspond to the users and the edges are related to the interaction type among Twitter users (follow, retweet and mention). The relationships between node A and nodes B, C, and D are a uniplex tie since there is only one relationship among node A and other nodes. On the other hand, the relationship between nodes B and C is a multiplex tie, because there is more than one connection between them.

4   Experimental results

In this section, we first describe how we calculated the political homophily, next we present the user network considered for homophily analysis, then we present how we analyzed three different scenarios of political homophily on Twitter and their results.

We considered the following Twitter user connections in all scenarios: follow (user A follows user B), mention (user A mentions user B), and retweet (user A retweets user B). These connections can be either unidirectional or reciprocal. In each scenario, we measured homophily in two contexts: (i) considering only unidirectional edges and (ii) considering only reciprocal edges. The results obtained by [8] motivated our choice of using these two contexts. We present these scenarios results in Section 4.3.

In the first scenario, we calculated homophily considering only uniplex connections. In the second scenario, we analyzed homophily in a network only considering

multiplex connections. Our goal was to verify if the multiplexity interferes in the classes' homophily level. We have a hypothesis that if a user has multiple connections with another user, then the homophily level is higher than with only one type of connection (e.g., connections between users B and C in Fig. 6). We describe the results obtained in this scenario in Section 4.4.

We were also interested in understanding whether Twitter users tend to post similar content and whether homophily intensifies in this scenario. Thus, we decided to analyze the hashtags used in their tweets, and also the most important words in their timelines given by the LDA algorithm [2].

Thus, in one homophily analysis scenario, we considered only reciprocal follow connections among users who had hashtags co-occurrence in their timeline. We present the results obtained in this scenario in Section 4.6.

In the third scenario, we considered only the reciprocal follow connections among users who had at least three most important words in common (according to the LDA algorithm). The results obtained are presented in Section 4.5.

4.1   Performing homophily analysis

We calculated the homophily indexes for these classes considering the scenarios previously presented. We calculated the H_i (Eq. 1) for each one of the Twitter user classes and we also calculated the index IH_i (Eq. 2). The index IH_i is useful for comparing the homophily level among different classes when their number of users is different. For example, to compare whether homophily between Hillary Supporter users is greater than the homophily between Trump Supporter users.

Note that we considered the variable w_i as one of the parameters in the IH_i calculation for a class i, which corresponds to the probability of the occurrence of a user from class i in the network under analysis. Thus, w_i values were 0.5318, 0.1235, 0.0949, 0.0543, 0.1902, and 0.0055 in all scenarios that we analyzed for Whatever, Neutral, Negative, Trump Supporter, Hillary Supporter, and Positive, respectively.

4.2   Network description

We used a multiplex network, as presented in Section 3.5.1 to perform a more detailed homophily analysis considering the different interaction types among Twitter users. Thus, we defined the connection as: (i) follow, (ii) mention, and (iii) retweet. These connections represent the interaction among Twitter users. Figure 6 exemplifies the three connection types.

To perform the homophily analysis, we defined a network where the nodes represent users, and the edges represent the connections among them. This network contained 18,450 nodes and 795,986 edges. There is a

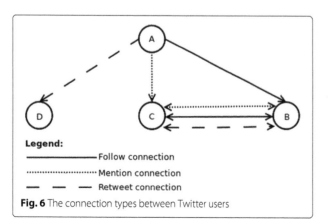

Legend:
——————— Follow connection
·················· Mention connection
— — — Retweet connection

Fig. 6 The connection types between Twitter users

unidirectional follow connection between two users when only one of them follows the other. There is unidirectional retweet connection between two users when only one of them retweets the other, and there is a unidirectional mention connection with two users when only one of them mentions the other. Therefore, there is a reciprocal follow connection with two users when both follow each other. There is reciprocal retweet connection between two users when both retweet each other, and there is reciprocal mention connection between two users when both mention each other.

The multiplex network contains 795,986 connections: 437,515 of them were follow connections, and 302,588 of them were retweet connections, and 55,883 were mention type connections. We did not consider auto loop connections, that means, we only considered connections that were not own retweets and were not own mentions. Figure 7 shows the three types of relationships among the user classes (inner and outer edges pattern).

The Whatever users are followed, retweeted, and mentioned more than they follow, retweet, and mention other users. They are among the users that most mentioned their peers. We noted that although the Whatever class had the highest number of nodes in the network, there were few follow connections and retweet connections among their peers. Neutral, Trump Supporter, and Positive users had few connections with other users. In all connection types, Negative users had the highest number of connections with Hillary Supporter users. These totals were even higher than among their peers, despite their higher number of connections among peers. Hillary Supporter users had the highest number of follow connections, retweet connections, and mention connections among peers. Although the Trump Supporter users had few connections with Hillary Supporter users, the Hillary

Supporter users retweeted and mentioned many users from Trump Supporter class.

The reciprocity in a relationship is a factor that indicates a higher level of proximity between users [8]. We carefully analyzed homophily in reciprocal relationship scenarios and noted that in our database there are 122,291 reciprocal follow connections, 4,030 reciprocal retweet connections, and 468 reciprocal mention connections. Therefore, the proportion of reciprocal follow connections is more meaningful than in other types of connections among users since there is 38.79% reciprocity and 1.35% retweet reciprocity and 0.84% mention reciprocity.

4.3 Homophily in uniplex connections scenarios

In this section, we present the homophily analysis considering the three connection types. Figure 8 shows the results obtained. Each chart refers to a specific connection type and the class' IH_i. For each class, we calculated two IH_i values: (i) considering only unidirectional connections and (ii) considering only reciprocal connections among users. In the following sections, we discuss the results obtained referring to follow connections, retweet connections, and mention connections. In Section 4.3.4 we analyze the homophily results considering the three different connection types.

4.3.1 Follow connections

In this scenario, we noted that there was homophily in Negative, Trump Supporter and in Hillary Supporter classes. The homophily level in these classes is even higher when analyzing only reciprocal connections that occur among users. We noted that Whatever class had strong heterophily, indicating that unlike the Negative users, Trump Supporter users, and Hillary Supporter users, they tend to follow users of others classes more frequently.

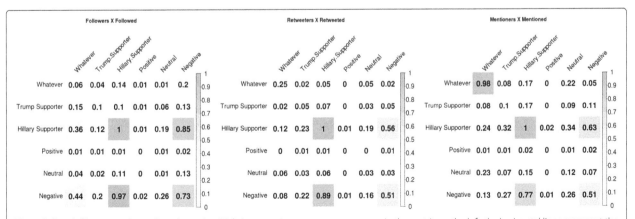

Fig. 7 Follow (left), retweet (center), and mention (right) connections among user groups. In the matrix on the left, the horizontal lines represent the followers, and the vertical lines represent the followed ones. In the matrix on the middle, the horizontal lines represent the retweeters, and the vertical lines represent the retweeted. In the matrix on the right, the horizontal lines represent the mentioners, and the vertical lines represent the mentioned ones. In all matrices, the cells contain the normalized total connections among classes

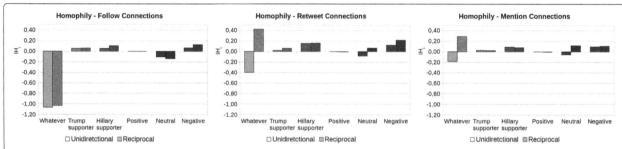

Fig. 8 Homophily in uniplex scenarios. Users classes' IH_i in three uniplex connection scenarios: follow connections (*left*), retweet connections (*center*) and mention connections (*right*). We considered the following analysis for each network: (i) only unidirectional connections and (ii) only reciprocal connections

The results also revealed that the Neutral and Positive classes had heterophily. However, the IH_i of Positive class is very close to zero (baseline that determines homophily), which demonstrates that Positive users tend to follow users from other classes as would be expected by chance in the network [22].

The highest IH_i occurred among Negative users. We also noted that 27.58% of the reciprocal Hillary Supporter users connections occurred among their peers (Table 4). Their IH_i is higher than the reciprocal follow connections of Negative class since 20.72% of the connections occurred among them. We noted that even though the Hillary Supporter class had the highest H_i value, the Negative class IH_i is higher than the Hillary Supporter class' IH_i. It occurs because Negative users total is almost half of the Hillary Supporter users total.

4.3.2 Retweet connections

In this scenario, all classes had homophily when analyzing only the reciprocal connections, except the Positive class. Negative, Trump Supporter, and Hillary Supporter classes had homophily either using unidirectional connections or reciprocal connections. The homophily was higher in the reciprocal connections among Negative and Trump supporter classes.

We noted that occurred a change from heterophily in unidirectional connections to homophily in reciprocal connections in Whatever class and Neutral class. Curiously the Whatever class had the lowest IH_i in unidirectional connections and the highest IH_i in reciprocal connections.

4.3.3 Mention connections

In this scenario, we analyzed homophily considering mention connection among users. We noticed that when analyzing the unidirectional links, there was homophily among the Negative users, Trump Supporter users, and Hillary Supporter users; heterophily close to the baseline among the Positive users and heterophily among the Whatever users and Neutral users.

Figure 8 shows unidirectional connections had a significant difference compared to the reciprocal connections of Whatever and Neutral classes. The results showed that the Whatever class had the lowest IH_i in unidirectional mentions. When considering just the reciprocal mentions, the IH_i reaches the highest value when compared with other classes. We also observed a similar phenomenon in the Neutral users. The Negative, Trump Supporter, and Hillary Supporter classes also had homophily in reciprocal connections. However, the homophily level increased only for Negative class when compared with the results in reciprocal connections. The Positive had homophily level close to the baseline in reciprocal connections.

Table 4 H_i of user classes represented like percentages

User class	Follow connections		Mention connections		Retweet connections	
	Unidirectional	Reciprocal	Unidirectional	Reciprocal	Unidirectional	Reciprocal
Whatever	3.25%	4.92%	44.41%	66.51%	34.59%	72.86%
Trump Supporter	10.37%	10.78%	7.62%	7.50%	7.39%	11.11%
Hillary Supporter	23.36%	27.58%	26.19%	25.13%	31.30%	31.77%
Positive	0.40%	0.37%	0.28%	0.00%	0.38%	0.00%
Neutral	2.79%	0.22%	7.10%	22.43%	4.93%	17.98%
Negative	15.30%	20.72%	18.05%	19.08%	20.14%	28.94%

The values represent the percentage of connections among users from the same class considering unidirectional connections and reciprocal connections referring to follow, mention and retweet types

4.3.4 Discussing uniplex connections results

After analyzing the homophily in scenarios involving follow, retweet, and mention connections, we found some general and specific characteristics that describe the different interaction types among Twitter users. A phenomenon that became evident is that for most connection types the homophily becomes stronger when we analyzed only the reciprocal connections, corroborating the work of Colleoni et al. [8] who also identified political homophily on Twitter. However, Colleoni et al. [8] considered only the follow connection type. Therefore, we demonstrated that mention and retweet interactions also exhibit the same behavior.

Another recurrent characteristic is that, in all analyzed scenarios, Negative, Trump Supporter, and Hillary Supporter classes had homophily. Among these classes, Trump Supporter is the class with lowest homophily level. Trump Supporter class had IH_i values ranging from 0.02 to 0.06 in the reciprocal connections, while Negative and Hillary Supporter classes had IH_i values ranging from 0.08 to 0.21 in the reciprocal connections.

The Whatever users and Neutral users connect in a diversified way when analyzing only unidirectional connections (Fig. 7). When analyzing both mention and retweet connection types of these two classes, we noted that heterophily occurred in unidirectional connections and homophily in reciprocal connections indicating that Whatever users and Neutral users have unidirectional interactions with users of different classes and more interactions among their peers (Table 4). We understand that the change of heterophily in the unidirectional connections for homophily in the reciprocal connections can be explained by non-political features, for example, company, city, personal preferences, and others. Although Whatever users and Neutral users mention and retweet more users with political engagement, the reciprocity of mention and retweet may indicate closer proximity among their peers.

The Positive class had heterophily close to baseline for all connection types. This feature can be related to the class definition since users that are positive towards both Donald Trump and Hillary Clinton are not common [35]. Thus, we believe Positive users do not characterize an organized community, which reflects the levels of homophily presented by them.

4.4 Multiplex homophily scenarios

After analyzing the results obtained in the uniplex connections scenarios, we noticed that the levels of homophily vary according to the connection type. This finding motivated us to investigate the pattern of homophily in a scenario considering multiplex connections. We considered the hypothesis that homophily is higher among friends who have more than one type of interaction with each other.

In Twitter, there is not friendship type interaction explicitly, as it exists on Facebook and in other online social networks. Kwak et al. [21] describes that Twitter users do not follow other users just to establish a friendship, but instead to track news channels and get information of their interest. This user behavior can explain why we detected only 39% reciprocal follow connections.

We assumed that the reciprocal follow connections represent friendship relationships among users [5, 10, 29]. Therefore, we verified that in situations where exists an overlap of a friendship connection with a reciprocal mention or retweet connections, the homophily is higher than the homophily in cases where there is only a friendship connection.

Figure 9 shows the values of IH_i in uniplex friendship connections, which represents the baseline of our analysis. We also presented IH_i in multiplex friendship connections, which corresponds to the homophily level in cases where there are a friendship connection and some other type of connection among users. The values of IH_i increase when analyzing only the multiplex connections of Negative users, Trump Supporter users, and Hillary Supporter users validating the hypothesis that homophily increases when multiplex ties are analyzed. The Positive class presents a heterophily near the baseline.

There was heterophily among Whatever users and among Neutral users in both uniplex and multiplex connections. This result differs from what was presented in Section 4.3.2 and Section 4.3.3, where high homophily occurred in cases of reciprocity in the retweet connection and mention connection scenarios, respectively. We have the hypothesis that many users who do not have political engagement usually mutually mention or retweet without necessarily being friends.

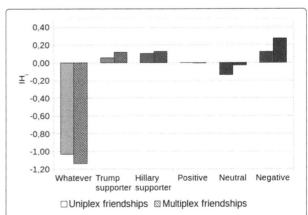

Fig. 9 Homophily in multiplex scenario. Values of IH_i for user classes in a scenario that compares homophily between a uniplex network and a multiplex network

The results of the homophily analysis in the uniplex and multiplex connections also validate the higher homophily among Negative users. It is important to note that the multiplex friendship connections represented only 525 cases, which corresponds to about 0.43% of the total number of friendships.

4.5 Homophily among users with similar speeches

In this section, we present the results obtained for scenarios that check homophily among users with similar speeches. In Section 4.6 we discuss results regarding friends who only used hashtags in common and in Section 4.7 we analyze homophily among friends who only used common important words (given by the LDA algorithm) in their tweets.

4.6 Enhancing friendship with hashtags usage

We found that 48,848 out of 122,291 friendships involve users who used some common hashtag in their timeline corresponding to about 40% of friendships. This result shows hashtags are indeed a prevalent feature on Twitter [11]. Figure 10 presents IH_i values of the friendships that have users who published some common hashtags and compares them with the friendships of users who did not have hashtags in common.

We found out that values of IH_i increase among Negative, Trump Supporter, and Hillary Supporter users when we analyzed only the friendships among users who used hashtags in common reinforcing the homogeneity observed in these groups.

The Positive IH_i values demonstrate that they had heterophily close to the baseline. The Whatever and Neutral classes had heterophily independently of having friends with hashtags in common or not.

4.7 Enhancing friendship with most important words in common

We applied the Latent Dirichlet Allocation (LDA) algorithm [3] in all user timelines to find out the main topic of each user and then we aggregated this words to obtain the most frequent words (according to the LDA algoritm) of each class. The LDA is a probabilistic model for topic detection that uses the Bayesian approach to learn the latent structure of topics that comprise a given text. We removed stop-words and lowercase letters, and then tokenized all tweets of each user. We ran the LDA algorithm using a Python library for topic modeling called `gensim` [26]. We choose $k = 1$ as the number of topics for the LDA algorithm, since we were interested to obtain the main topic of each user timeline. Each topic returned by the LDA algorithm contains words ordered by importance. Table 5 shows the five most frequent important words of each class.

The Whatever users did not have any most frequent words directly related to politics. The two Political Bots most frequent words were about politics. The word "trump" was the most frequent word in all politically engaged classes indicating that Donald Trump was frequently subject of discussion in these classes. The word "hillary" was the second most frequent word in Trump Supporter, Hillary Supporter, and Positive classes indicating that Hillary was also subject of discussions between those users but not as frequently discussed as Donald Trump.

We identified the 15 most important words of each user's timeline. Then, we defined that there is a connection between two users when both used at least three most important words in common. We considered the words in common occurrence as a homophily scenario because we have a hypothesis that if a user has a friendship with another user, then they probably use words in common and they are more related to each other. The same most important words can also indicate that they were talking about the same topic.

We found out that 34,791 out of 122,291 friends connections involve users who have most important words in common. This corresponds to about 28.5% of friendships between users. Figure 11 shows the IH_i values

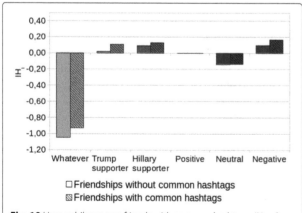

Fig. 10 Homophily among friends with common hashtags. IH_i values for user classes in a scenario that compares: (i) homophily among users who had friendships and did not publish hashtags in common to (ii) users who have friendships and published hashtags in common

Table 5 Most frequent words of each class

Whatever	Neutral	Negative	Trump Supporter	Hillary Supporter	Positive
today	trump	trump	trump	trump	trump
day	today	today	hillary	hillary	hillary
love	vote	vote	president	election	vote
time	good	good	obama	vote	president
life	love	love	america	president	america

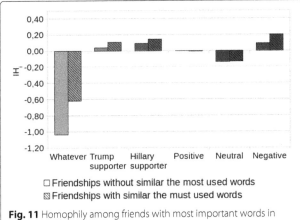

Fig. 11 Homophily among friends with most important words in common. The IH_i values for user classes in a scenario that considers the homophily among users that had at least three most important words in common

for friendships among users who used most important words in common and a comparison with friendships among users who did not use most important words in common.

We noted that the IH_i values increased among Negative users, Trump Supporter users, and among Hillary Supporter users when we analyzed only the friendships among users who had most important words in common corroborating the homogeneity observed in those groups.

In the Positive class, the IH_i values indicate an invariant homophily near the baseline. The Whatever and Neutral classes also demonstrated heterophily independently of their friends published tweets with most important words in common or not.

After analyzing the homophily among friends who published hashtags and among friends that had the most important words in common, we found that the homophily among the Negative, Trump Supporter, and Hillary Supporter reached the highest homophily levels observed in this work. Therefore, users with similar tweet text features (hashtags and important words) have more political homophily.

5 Threats to validity

We are aware one limitation of this work is the risk to have many tweets that contain sarcastic political content in our dataset since the SentiStrength does not ensure sarcasm recognition. Thus, some users that had a high average sentiment toward the candidates, in fact, had a low average sentiment toward them. However, detecting sarcasm is an open problem in the sentiment analysis research area [30].

6 Conclusion

In this paper, we used sentiment analysis to perform an analysis of the political homophily phenomenon on Twitter during the 2016 US presidential election. We collected

tweets, user profiles and contact networks over 122 days (08/01/2016 to 11/30/2016). We used sentiment analysis to identify six user classes on Twitter: Whatever, Neutral, Negative, Trump Supporter, Hillary Supporter, and Positive. Then, we analyzed the political homophily in these classes. We defined two types of networks to analyze homophily: uniplex and multiplex. A uniplex network is a network where there is only one type of connection among nodes, and a multiplex network is a network with more than one type of connection among nodes. We defined as Twitter user connections: follow (user A follows user B), mention (user A mentions user B), and retweet (user A retweets user B). These connections can be either unidirectional or reciprocal. We used the metric IH_i [7] to calculate the homophily in the identified groups. We analyzed homophily in three scenarios: (i) uniplex connections, (ii) multiplex connections and (iii) friendship with a similar speech.

In the first scenario, we analyzed the homophily for each type of connection in uniplex networks. We identified that there is homophily among user classes with political engagement (Negative, Trump Supporter, and Hillary Supporter) in all types of connections analyzed, whether for unidirectional or reciprocal connections. Therefore, users with political engagement are more connected and interact more frequently with other users from the same class. The Positive class presented heterophily close to the baseline for all types of connections. This demonstrates that Positive users, despite presenting political speeches, are not so connected with one another and do not build communities. The Whatever users and Neutral users had heterophily in all unidirectional connections and homophily in the retweet reciprocal connections and mention reciprocal connections. We understand that this change can be explained by non-political characteristics, such as company, location, personal preferences, etc.

In the second scenario, we compared homophily in uniplex connections with homophily in multiplex connections. Our goal was to check whether homophily among users who have more than one type of interaction is enhanced. To perform the analysis in these scenarios, we considered that two Twitter users have a friendly relationship when they follow each other. Thus, we considered that multiplex connection exists when in addition to the friendship relationship there is also a retweet or mention reciprocal relationship; and exists a uniplex connection when there is only friendship relationship between two users. The results showed that the IH_i in multiplex connections increased for Neutral, Negative, Trump Supporter, and Hillary Supporter classes when compared to the level of homophily obtained in uniplex connections. Positive users presented heterophily near the baseline for both uniplex connections and multiplex connections. The Whatever users had heterophily in both network types.

Therefore, we showed that homophily is enhanced for most classes when multiplex connections exist.

In the third scenario, we analyzed homophily among friends who had a common speech. We considered that the use of hashtags and the most important timeline words to determine their speech. We observed that there is homophily in Negative, Trump Supporter, and Hillary Supporter classes. We noted that, in both analyses, the heterophily among Whatever and Neutral users occurred when we analyzed the friends who had similar speeches. Positive users, as well as in most of the analyzed scenarios, maintained heterophily close to the baseline.

In most of the analyzed scenarios, Negative users had the highest homophily level. We concluded Negative users form a more homogeneous community, they are more engaged in the use of common hashtags, and they are mentioned and retweeted more often among peers.

As future work, we intend to characterize and analyze homophily involving other characteristics, such as day and time of the week with more frequency of messages. We also intend to analyze homophily by gender, age, and ethnicity through user profiles photos; perform a temporal political homophily analysis correlating it with external events that may have influenced the users sentiments. We also expect to enhance the user classification through data ming techniques to identify candidates' advocates, political bots, and other user classes.

Acknowledgements
We acknowledge colleagues of the Human Behavior and Software Engineering (HUB-SE) laboratory for their incentives and suggestions.

Funding
This work is supported by MASWeb (grant FAPEMIG/PRONEX APQ-01400-14), FAPEMIG (grant APQ-02924-16), PUC-Minas, CNPq, CAPES and STIC AmSud 18-STIC-07.

Authors' contributions
This work is the outcome of a research project at the Postgraduate Program of the PUC Minas developed by Josemar A. Caetano (JC), Hélder S. Lima (HL), and Mateus F. Santos (MS), and supervised by Humberto T. Marques-Neto (HM). JC and MS were responsible for collecting the Twitter data, for performing the political and sentiment analysis, and for classifying the Twitter users. HL and JC were responsible for performing the political homophily analysis. HM provided direction and guidance during all steps of the research. All authors read and approved the final manuscript.

References
1. Barberá P, Jost JT, Nagler J, Tucker JA, Bonneau R. Tweeting from left to right: Is online political communication more than an echo chamber? Psychol Sci. 2015;26(10):1531–42. https://doi.org/10.1177/0956797615594620. https://doi.org/10.1177/0956797615594620.
2. Blei DM, Ng AY, Jordan MI. Latent Dirichlet allocation. J Mach Learn Res. 2003;3(Jan):993–1022.
3. Blei DM, Ng AY, Jordan MI, Lafferty J. Latent dirichlet allocation. J Mach Learn Res. 2003;3:2003.
4. Brady WJ, Wills JA, Jost JT, Tucker JA, Van Bavel JJ. Emotion shapes the diffusion of moralized content in social networks. Proc Natl Acad Sci. 2017;114(28):7313–8. https://doi.org/10.1073/pnas.1618923114. http://dx.doi.org/10.1073/pnas.1618923114.
5. Brandt C, Leskovec J. Status and friendship: Mechanisms of social network evolution. In: Proceedings of the 23rd International Conference on World Wide Web, WWW '14 Companion. New York: ACM; 2014. p. 229–230. https://doi.org/10.1145/2567948.2577327. http://doi.acm.org/10.1145/2567948.2577327.
6. Caetano JA, Lima HS, dos Santos MF, Marques-Neto HT. Utilizando análise de sentimentos para definição da homofilia política dos usuários do twitter durante a eleição presidencial americana de 2016. In: VI Brazilian Workshop on Social Network Analysis and Mining, BraSNAM 2017. Brazil: SBC, Porto Alegre - RS; 2017.
7. Coleman J. Relational analysis: the study of social organizations with survey methods. Hum Organ. 1958;17(4):28–36.
8. Colleoni E, Rozza A, Arvidsson A. Echo chamber or public sphere? predicting political orientation and measuring political homophily in twitter using big data. J Commun. 2014;64(2):317–32.
9. Currarini S, Jackson MO, Pin P. An economic model of friendship: Homophily, minorities, and segregation. Econometrica. 2009;77(4):1003–45.
10. Davis Jr CA, Pappa GL, de Oliveira DRR, de L Arcanjo F. Inferring the location of twitter messages based on user relationships. Trans GIS. 2011;15(6):735–51.
11. DeMasi O, Mason D, Ma J. Understanding communities via hashtag engagement: A clustering based approach. In: ICWSM. Palo Alto: AAAI; 2016. p. 102–111.
12. Easley D, Kleinberg J. Networks, crowds, and markets: Reasoning about a highly connected world. New York: Cambridge University Press; 2010.
13. Ferrara E, Varol O, Davis C, Menczer F, Flammini A. The rise of social bots. Commun ACM. 2016;59(7):96–104. https://doi.org/10.1145/2818717. http://doi.acm.org/10.1145/2818717.
14. Ferriani S, Fonti F, Corrado R. The social and economic bases of network multiplexity: Exploring the emergence of multiplex ties. Strateg Organ. 2013;11(1):7–34.
15. Fischer CS. To dwell among friends: Personal networks in town and city. Chicago: University of chicago Press; 1982.
16. Giachanou A, Crestani F. Like it or not: A survey of twitter sentiment analysis methods. ACM Comput Surv. 2016;28(2):28:1–41. https://doi.org/10.1145/2938640. http://doi.acm.org/10.1145/2938640.
17. Halberstam Y, Knight B. Homophily, group size, and the diffusion of political information in social networks: Evidence from twitter. J Public Econ. 2016;143:73–88.
18. Huber GA, Malhotra N. Political homophily in social relationships: Evidence from online dating behavior. J Polit. 2017;79(1):269–83. https://doi.org/10.1086/687533. https://doi.org/10.1086/687533.
19. Klein D, Manning CD. Accurate unlexicalized parsing. In: Proceedings of the 41st Annual Meeting on Association for Computational Linguistics - Volume 1, ACL '03, pp. 423–430. Stroudsburg: Association for Computational Linguistics; 2003. https://doi.org/10.3115/1075096.1075150. https://doi.org/10.3115/1075096.1075150.
20. Klein D, Manning CD, et al. Fast exact inference with a factored model for natural language parsing. Advances in neural information processing systems. Marylebone: MIT Press; 2003, pp. 3–10.
21. Kwak H, Lee C, Park H, Moon S. What is twitter, a social network or a news media? In: Proceedings of the 19th International Conference on World Wide Web, WWW '10, pp. 591–600. New York: ACM; 2010. https://doi.org/10.1145/1772690.1772751. http://doi.acm.org/10.1145/1772690.1772751.
22. McPherson M, Smith-Lovin L, Cook JM. Birds of a feather: Homophily in social networks. Annu Rev Sociol. 2001;27:415–44.
23. Mitra T, Counts S, Pennebaker JW. Understanding anti-vaccination attitudes in social media. In: ICWSM. Palo Alto: AAAI; 2016. p. 269–278.
24. Monti C, Rozza A, Zappella G, Zignani M, Arvidsson A, Colleoni E. Modelling political disaffection from twitter data. In: Proceedings of the Second International Workshop on Issues of Sentiment Discovery and Opinion Mining, WISDOM '13, pp. 3:1–3:9. New York: ACM; 2013. https://doi.org/10.1145/2502069.2502072. http://doi.acm.org/10.1145/2502069.2502072.

25. Ranganath S, Hu X, Tang J, Liu H. Understanding and identifying advocates for political campaigns on social media. In: Proceedings of the Ninth ACM International Conference on Web Search and Data Mining, WSDM '16, pp. 43–52. New York: ACM; 2016. https://doi.org/10.1145/2835776.2835807. http://doi.acm.org/10.1145/2835776.2835807.

26. Řehůřek R, Sojka P. Software Framework for Topic Modelling with Large Corpora. In: Proceedings of the LREC 2010 Workshop on New Challenges for NLP Frameworks. Valletta: ELRA; 2010. p. 45–50. http://is.muni.cz/publication/884893/en.

27. Reuters. In breathless u.s. election, twitter generates buzz not cash. 2016. https://www.reuters.com/article/us-usa-election-twitter/in-breathless-u-s-election-twitter-generates-buzz-not-cash-idUSKCN12R2OV. Accessed 15 Dec 2017.

28. Ribeiro FN, Araújo M, Gonçalves P, André Gonçalves M, Benevenuto F. Sentibench - a benchmark comparison of state-of-the-practice sentiment analysis methods. EPJ Data Sci. 2016;5(1):23. https://doi.org/10.1140/epjds/s13688-016-0085-1. http://dx.doi.org/10.1140/epjds/s13688-016-0085-1.

29. Shin WY, Singh BC, Cho J, Everett AM. A new understanding of friendships in space: Complex networks meet twitter. J Inf Sci. 2015;41(6):751–64.

30. Silva NFFD, Coletta LFS, Hruschka ER. A survey and comparative study of tweet sentiment analysis via semi-supervised learning. ACM Comput Surv. 2016;49(1):15:1–26. https://doi.org/10.1145/2932708. http://doi.acm.org/10.1145/2932708.

31. statista. Most famous social network sites worldwide as of september 2017, ranked by number of active users (in millions). 2017. https://www.statista.com/statistics/272014/global-social-networks-ranked-by-number-of-users/. Accessed 15 Dec 2017.

32. Subrahmanian VS, Azaria A, Durst S, Kagan V, Galstyan A, Lerman K, Zhu L, Ferrara E, Flammini A, Menczer F. The darpa twitter bot challenge. Computer. 2016;49(6):38–46. https://doi.org/10.1109/MC.2016.183.

33. Thelwall M, Buckley K, Paltoglou G, Cai D, Kappas A. Sentiment in short strength detection informal text. J Am Soc Inf Sci Technol. 2010;61(12):2544–58. https://doi.org/10.1002/asi.v61:12. http://dx.doi.org/10.1002/asi.v61:12.

34. Times TNW. Some donald trump voters warn of revolution if hillary clinton wins. 2016. https://www.nytimes.com/2016/10/28/us/politics/donald-trump-voters.html. Accessed 15 Dec 2017.

35. Twitter. Clinton: Half of trump supporters 'basket of deplorables'. 2016. http://www.bbc.com/news/av/election-us-2016-37329812/clinton-half-of-trump-supporters-basket-of-deplorables. Accessed 15 Dec 2017.

36. Twitter. Twitter api docs. 2017. https://dev.twitter.com/overview/api. Accessed 15 Dec 2017.

37. Verbrugge LM. Multiplexity in adult friendships. Soc Forces. 1979;57(4):1286–309.

38. Vilares D, Thelwall M, Alonso MA. The megaphone of the people? spanish sentistrength for real-time analysis of political tweets. J Inf Sci. 2015;41(6):799–813. https://doi.org/10.1177/0165551515598926.

39. Wong FMF, Tan CW, Sen S, Chiang M. Quantifying political leaning from tweets, retweets, and retweeters. IEEE Trans Knowl Data Eng. 2016;28(8):2158–72. https://doi.org/10.1109/TKDE.2016.2553667.

40. Yuan G, Murukannaiah PK, Zhang Z, Singh MP. Exploiting sentiment homophily for link prediction. In: Proceedings of the 8th ACM Conference on Recommender Systems, RecSys '14, pp. 17–24. New York: ACM; 2014. https://doi.org/10.1145/2645710.2645734. http://doi.acm.org/10.1145/2645710.2645734.

5

Fog orchestration for the Internet of Everything: state-of-the-art and research challenges

Karima Velasquez[1], David Perez Abreu[1]* (ID), Marcio R. M. Assis[2], Carlos Senna[2], Diego F. Aranha[2], Luiz F. Bittencourt[2], Nuno Laranjeiro[1], Marilia Curado[1], Marco Vieira[1], Edmundo Monteiro[1] and Edmundo Madeira[2]

Abstract

Recent developments in telecommunications have allowed drawing new paradigms, including the Internet of Everything, to provide services by the interconnection of different physical devices enabling the exchange of data to enrich and automate people's daily activities; and Fog computing, which is an extension of the well-known Cloud computing, bringing tasks to the edge of the network exploiting characteristics such as lower latency, mobility support, and location awareness. Combining these paradigms opens a new set of possibilities for innovative services and applications; however, it also brings a new complex scenario that must be efficiently managed to properly fulfill the needs of the users. In this scenario, the Fog Orchestrator component is the key to coordinate the services in the middle of Cloud computing and Internet of Everything. In this paper, key challenges in the development of the Fog Orchestrator to support the Internet of Everything are identified, including how they affect the tasks that a Fog service Orchestrator should perform. Furthermore, different service Orchestrator architectures for the Fog are explored and analyzed in order to identify how the previously listed challenges are being tackled. Finally, a discussion about the open challenges, technological directions, and future of the research on this subject is presented.

Keywords: Fog, Cloud, Internet of Everything, Orchestration, Research challenges

1 Introduction

A new industrial revolution driven by digital data, computation, and automation is arriving. Human activities, industrial processes, and research lead to data collection and processing on an unprecedented scale, spurring new products, services, and applications, as well as new business processes and scientific methodologies [1].

The applications and services of the Internet of Everything (IoE) [2] can be the link between extremely complex Information and Communication Technology (ICT) network infrastructures and general activities of the whole society in general. These applications and services usually rely on the use of Cloud computing to achieve elasticity, on-demand self-service, resource pooling, among other

characteristics. However, new generation applications and services (e.g. IoE-based applications and services) have requirements that are only partially met by existing Cloud computing solutions [3].

In recent years there has been a paradigm shift to bring Cloud services towards the edge of the network. In this peripheral area, there is an abundance of heterogeneous IoE resource-constrained devices both generating and consuming data [4]. This represents an increment on the amount of data, that would lead to increased traffic and response time to transport to the Cloud and back. It is possible thus to place storage and processing devices at the rim of the network to help preprocess this data and alleviate the load sent towards the core network, while also reducing response times which benefits real-time applications particularly. This solution is known as Fog computing.

*Correspondence: dabreu@dei.uc.pt
[1]Department of Informatics Engineering, University of Coimbra, Polo II - Pinhal de Marrocos, 3030-290, Coimbra, Portugal
Full list of author information is available at the end of the article

Fog computing is an important paradigm to help address the requirements of the IoE that are not completely covered by the Cloud; nonetheless, the use of this technology creates new challenges. The Fog needs to support the orchestration of applications and services on demand, with adaptability, while providing flexible performance. In practice, traditional service orchestration approaches that were applied to Cloud services are not suitable for the large scale and dynamism of Fog services, since they can not effectively treat the prominent characteristics of the Fog's distributed infrastructure. It is crucial to clearly identify the challenges that differentiate the Fog from the Cloud, in order to create innovative orchestration solutions able to meet its required characteristics such as high mobility, high scalability, and performance in real-time. Some Fog orchestration architectures have already been proposed, but it is still not clear how well they meet the Fog's requirements.

This paper presents a review of the main Fog challenges that impair the migration of the orchestration mechanisms from the Cloud to the Fog. Furthermore, it shows a revision of different Fog service orchestration architectures (SORTS, SOAFI, ETSI IGS MEC, and CONCERT), in order to evaluate how these major challenges are being addressed.

The remainder of the paper is structured as follows. Section 2 presents the scope of the paper, the Internet of Everything, including the involved paradigms namely Internet of Things (IoT), Fog, and Cloud computing. Section 3 defines more thoroughly the Fog computing paradigm, what are the main differences between Cloud and Fog computing environments, to finish with some scenarios of applicability of Fog computing. Section 4 discusses some research challenges that a Fog Orchestrator must handle. Section 5 describes a set of Fog orchestration architectures, including how they deal with some of the previously identified Fog challenges. A comparative analysis of the reviewed architectures is presented in Section 6. Conclusions are drawn in Section 7.

2 The Internet of Everything

According to Byers and Wetterwald [5], about 50 billion of devices will be connected to the Internet by 2020. One consequence of this trend is the production of an unprecedented volume of data in the most diverse segments. Such data can be used to provide new services for the improvement of various areas of the society (e.g. transport, health, economy). In this context, *IoT*, *Fog*, and *Cloud* computing paradigms of service provision stand out.

The term IoT [6] is widely used, although still a blurry one, to refer to a vision of a future Internet where any object can communicate with other devices using Internet communication protocols. The IoT paradigm has been defined as a technology to connect objects that surround

us providing a reliable communication and making available the services provided by them. Additionally, the IoT brings ubiquity providing a new dimension to the ICT, known as "Any THING" communication involving interaction between computers, humans, and things to complement the previous "Any TIME" and "Any PLACE" communication paradigm presented in the ICT [7]. The IoT will ultimately comprise virtualized sensors, actuators, and platforms, which will result in a set of software "things" [8].

The Fog paradigm envisions a set of micro-data centers, placed at the edge of the network, with the following characteristics [9]: location awareness, mobility support, real-time interactions, low latency, geographical distribution, heterogeneity, interoperability, security, and privacy.

Cloud computing [10, 11] is a well-known paradigm to providing basic computing assets as a service. Cloud Services Providers (CSPs) offer specialized servers in data centers with large storage area, high computing capacity, and a powerful network infrastructure. According to NIST [12], CSPs must offer their customers the *on-demand self-services*, *broad network services access*, *resource pooling*, *rapid elasticity* and *measured services*.

Cisco Systems Inc. [13] describes IoE as a set of relationships derived from the connectivity between *people*, *processes*, *data* and *things*. According to Cisco, the IoE could generate $4.6 trillion in value for the global public sector in the next 15 years. In addition, there is an expectation of generating $14.4 trillion in the private sector over the same period. The IoE enables the emergence of new services based on the IoT, Fog, and Cloud computing paradigms to enhance the quality of life of citizens, creating a strong dependency on them [14]. The relation between these three main paradigms is depicted in Fig. 1. At the bottom level is the IoT, where reside different resource constrained devices (e.g. sensors and actuators) gathering data. Next, to the IoT layer comes the Fog computing level, where the data is aggregated and preprocessed. Finally, at the upper layer is the Cloud computing where the data can be stored and analyzed.

Out of the three paradigms involved in the IoE (IoT, Fog, and Cloud), Fog computing is the most recent and least explored in the research field. To clarify the concept and the new demands it imposes, the following section offers a description of the Fog, where it can be applied, and its new challenges that differentiate it from the Cloud.

3 The Fog computing paradigm

The frontier between the Cloud and the end devices is known as the Fog. The Fog is an environment with a plethora of heterogeneous devices that work in a ubiquitous and decentralized manner, communicating and cooperating among themselves [15]. Thus, the Fog emerges as an extension of the Cloud paradigm escalating from

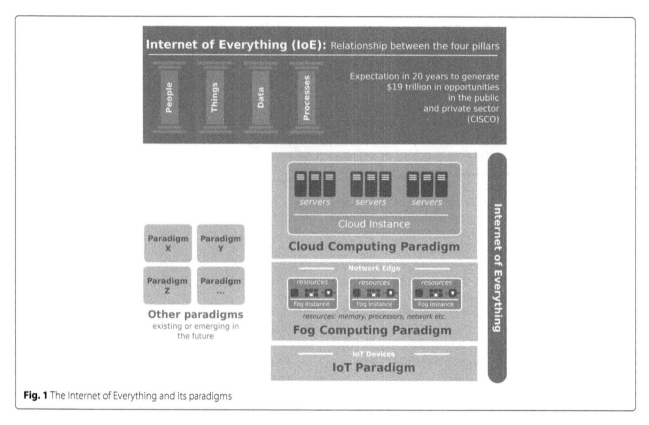

Fig. 1 The Internet of Everything and its paradigms

the core of the network towards its edge; it is comprised of a heavily virtualized platform able to perform storage, processing, and networking activities between the Cloud servers and the end devices [16, 17]. The Fog comes to support novel applications and services that are not completely fit for the Cloud, granting them ubiquity, high resilience, low latency, decentralized management, and cooperation [18, 19].

The OpenFog consortium [20] defines Fog as:

"A horizontal, system-level architecture that distributes computing, storage, control and networking functions closer to the users along a cloud-to-thing continuum".

A Cloudlet is an autonomous Fog instance domain that can maintain relationships with other domains. Cloudlets are typically used to offload applications when devices are not capable of executing them, but without incurring in the costs (both of time and monetary) of using a more specialized data center in the Cloud [21, 22].

The use of Cloudlets in the context of Fog environments has proven to provide several advantages in terms of response times and energy consumption, among other benefits [23]. Thus, most multi-layer architectures (that include Cloud and Fog) incorporate the concept of Cloudlets for the deployment of services and applications in order to improve response times, Quality of Service (QoS), and other factors.

The scenario at the edge of the Cloud is vastly different from the one at its core. Thus to fully understand their peculiarities, next subsection reviews the main aspects where Cloud and Fog diverge.

3.1 From Cloud to Fog computing

The Fog introduced a paradigm shift from the traditional concept where the core of the network is in charge of providing information that will be consumed at the edge of it. To address the challenges arising from Cloud to Fog computing, the latter has to fulfill the following key features [3, 15, 20, 24]:

- Heterogeneity and Interoperability, to deal with a broad diversity of physical and virtualized devices deployed in wide-ranging environments;
- Edge location, location awareness, and low latency, to guarantee that the most time-sensitive data is processed closest to who is requesting it;
- Wireless communication, to reach a variety of devices at the edge avoiding the installation of a fix communication network and contributing to reduce the amount of traffic in the core network;
- Real-time support, to satisfy services and applications with time-sensitive requirements;
- Mobility support, to allow continuity in the services provided to devices and final users.

In the Fog, final users (i.e. mobile devices and IoT sensors) generate ample quantities of data at the edge of the network making them producers and consumers at the same time. The treatment of this unprecedented quantity of data represents a challenge for traditional paradigms like Grid and Cloud computing; thus the Fog arises to overcome these limitations [3, 25].

Although Cloud and Fog computing share overlapping features, the Fog becomes a non-trivial extension of the Cloud that must deal with characteristics inherent to its placement in the overall network infrastructure, such as location awareness, geographical distribution, low latency, real-time, and mobility support [17, 26–28]. Another significant difference regarding the Cloud is that the Fog encompasses a huge set of heterogeneous devices, mostly wirelessly connected, that are more constrained in terms of resources in comparison with the servers that reside in the Cloud [29].

Fog computing provides to the Cloud an alternative to manipulate exabytes of data generated daily form the IoT [25]. With the ability to process the data near where it is generated and required, it is possible to tackle the challenges regarding data volume, interoperability, and time-sensitivity. By eliminating the round-trip time related to traveling to the Cloud and back, it is feasible to accelerate the awareness and response time of services and applications. Furthermore, by preventing the need to send the data to the Cloud, or at least by aggregating it first, capacity of the communication channel is saved by the reducing the amount of traffic in the core network.

The Fog and IoT paradigms are used together in different application scenarios, some of which are described in the next subsection.

3.2 Application scenarios

The combination of the Fog and IoT paradigms could be used in many scenarios to achieve and improve applications and services requirements. In this subsection some examples of the collaborative use of Fog and IoT are described within four specific areas: *Automation, Healthcare, Smart Cities,* and *Infotainment.*

3.2.1 Automation

One important scenario where the Fog could play a major role is related to Automation. These systems refer to the integration of cyber technologies that make devices Internet-enabled to implement services for different industrial tasks such as Internet-based diagnostics, maintenance, and efficient and cost-effective operation [30].

So far the common user interaction involves a person behind the vast majority of the endpoints connected to the data network. With the advent of the IoT the landscape becomes different, with many sensors and actuators communicating with them as end users. Thus, it is necessary

to adopt a *system view* instead of an *individual view* of the endpoints [26].

Other constraints for this environment include data and service security since many decentralized endpoints could lead to security disruptions; scalability, dealing with naming and addressing a huge amount of devices, and also with the heterogeneity of a massive amount of services and execution options [31]. Furthermore, minimizing latency and timing jitter are other crucial factors for this type of scenario. Many critical automation systems such as in-flight control systems, medical applications, and internal vehicle networking require stable real-time behavior [5].

Moreover, operators infrastructures can contain devices from multiple manufacturers communicating with different technologies, sometimes proprietary, creating additional problems regarding interoperability and service deployment that must rely on manual intervention by network managers [32]. This suggests the need of a management solution, possibly based on Software Defined Networking (SDN) and Network Function Virtualization (NFV) providing low-level abstractions that ease the configuration and administration tasks of the devices.

This clearly represents one scenario that benefits from the Fog characteristics; however, the Fog must have a management process able to communicate with such a heterogeneous environment with stringent requirements and provide it with the QoS needed to maintain these industrial systems running smoothly.

3.2.2 Healthcare

Another scenario of applicability of Fog computing is healthcare. Several wearable devices (e.g. Fitbit [33]) and platforms (e.g. Google Fit SDK [34] and IoS health API [35]) that let users collect and monitor their fitness and health data have been emerging in recent years. This growth has been promoted mainly by the advances in manufacturing technology and the emergence of interoperability standards (e.g. Bluetooth Low Energy -BLE- and Radio-Frequency Identification -RFID-). However, it is necessary to integrate these devices and the data they collect into a new health model [36, 37]. Such a model should allow the integration of physicians, health professionals, clinics, and the patients. Through the integration and analysis of this data, it will be possible to obtain more accurate diagnoses and improve the effectiveness of the treatment of diseases.

In this context, the processing of data generated by wearable devices requires low latency among other requirements related to the speed of events, such as interoperability, scalability, and security. This is due to the fact that in an emergency situation, such as an epileptic seizure [38], the processing and generation of alerts for the most diverse stakeholders (i.e. doctor, emergency unit, ambulance) must be the fastest in order to avoid undesirable situations (e.g. death or permanent sequelae). Fog computing brings processing to the edge of the network, significantly improving technical factors that allow shorter responses in emergency scenarios. Fog can also interface with other paradigms such as Cloud computing, allowing persistent data to be driven by the Clouds for permanent storage and performing tasks such as analytics.

Hosseine et al. [38] describe a layer-based framework for collecting, aggregating, and analyzing data for automatic and actual detection of epileptic seizures. In this solution, Fog computing is used as a middleware to perform real-time data processing, feature extraction and classification to feed machine learning and data caching mechanisms. A Fog-driven IoT interface, named as FIT is proposed in by Monteiro et al. [39]. The purpose of their solution is to enable the communication between IoT devices (e.g. smart watches) and the Cloud for the specific purpose of analyzing acoustic data to detect speech-language pathologists. To do this, Fog nodes are placed on the LAN-level in the network hierarchy. The Fog nodes are used to collect, store and process raw-data, before sending it to the Cloud for permanent storage.

3.2.3 Smart Cities

The Smart City paradigm emerged to describe the use of new technologies in everyday urban life, providing the management of its services (e.g. energy, transportation, lighting, public safety) using ICT. These technologies implement a logical/virtual infrastructure to control and orchestrate physical objects to accommodate the city services to the citizen needs [40].

In the context of Smart Cities, mobility is a key requirement that should be explored allowing devices and services to capture information about the environment and act in real-time. For example, a mobility scenario should take into consideration vehicles and pedestrians into the city providing them relevant information and services according to their location.

In this urban mobility scenario, inside the Smart City paradigm, a Fog Orchestrator faces major challenges, for example, consider the complexity of the resource management related to a Cloud-based traffic sensing and travel planning service/application.

The Orchestrator must be able to maintain low latencies, high resilience, and trustworthiness according to the applications and users expectations, even in times when the infrastructure is stressed under heavy loads of traffic. The key issue here is that such loads are intrinsically specific to a particular application and cannot be reutilized from other scenarios or domains; thus further research in this direction to achieve the requirements mentioned above is required.

3.2.4 Infotainment

For applications with stringent latency requirements, the Fog offers an attractive alternative to the Cloud. Many applications, such as Vehicle-to-Vehicle (V2V) and Vehicle-to-Roadside (V2R) communication, virtual reality applications, gaming applications, video streaming, financial trading applications among others, require very low latency levels (i.e. around tens of milliseconds) [18], thus rendering the Cloud services insufficient. The term *Infotainment* refers to a combination of Information and Entertainment served together [41], and is used in this subsection to group the applications mentioned above.

Infotainment applications are becoming more global every day with about 82% of the Internet traffic estimated for 2021 corresponding to video alone (both business and consumer), virtual and augmented reality traffic to increase 20-fold between 2016 and 2021, consumer Video-on-Demand (VoD) to be equivalent to 7.2 billion DVDs per month, and Internet gaming traffic to grow tenfold by 2021 (i.e. 4% of consumer Internet traffic) [25]. Furthermore, by 2021 the number of devices connected to IP networks will be more than three times the global population [25]. Many of these new connected devices will correspond to devices located at the IoT level.

With such an increment in the demand of traffic that additionally has rigorous demands regarding latency, the inclusion of Fog helps bringing the services closer to the users. To efficiently handle these services, new management functions at IoT and Fog level must be conceived to deal with the scenario requirements efficiently; for flexible connectivity in heterogeneous and highly mobile environments, with strong latency guarantees, network operators require innovative orchestration mechanisms that support dynamic multi-technology resource management [42].

To properly achieve the application scenarios described above, it is important to thoroughly recognize the characteristics of the environment, and the challenges they impose. Orchestration and resource management in Fog environment have to deal with different requirements and objectives. A selection of the challenges that a Fog Orchestrator must overcome is presented in the following section.

4 Research challenges in Fog orchestration

Fog computing brings challenges at many different levels. Looking from a broader perspective, one of the first challenging issues is the modeling of the orchestration element that needs to be able to perform the deployment of the Cloudlets [43, 44] and handle tasks inside the environment.

The combination of IoT, Fog, and Cloud embraces a complex scenario where in some cases it is not suitable to migrate or apply well-known solutions or mechanisms from other domains or paradigms. This statement is already considered by important Cloud providers, such as Amazon and Microsoft who have released new services (i.e. AWS Greengrass [45] and Azureus IoT Edge [46] respectively) focused on addressing the new requirements at the edge of the Cloud. Some aspects to take into consideration are:

- Resource Management, which requires the design and development of mechanisms that handle tasks such as *Scheduling, Path Computation, Discovery and Allocation*, and *Interoperability*;
- Performance that deals with *Latency, Resilience*, and *Prediction and Optimization* from the gauges, mechanisms, and algorithms point of view;
- Security Management that must include mechanisms and policies to cope with *Security and Privacy* and *Authentication, Access, and Account*.

Each task represents a challenge to be addressed by the Fog Orchestrator. These tasks are described in the following subsections.

4.1 Scheduling

Scheduling is one of the main tasks of an Orchestrator. In Fog environments, it is necessary to consider how to exploit the collaboration between nodes to offload applications efficiently. In general, the processing nodes should be managed by a resource broker in the Orchestrator to perform a smart scheduling of the resource taking into consideration the applications' workflows [47].

Capacity planning and Cloudlets positioning models can be derived from the cellular phone antenna placement problem. The additional challenge is to extend those models to look beyond the maximum number of users expected but also understanding applications behavior and load patterns. An ideal capacity planning would be able to avoid applications that require low delays to be offloaded to the Cloud, which can hinder applications functioning. On the other hand, it would also minimize Cloudlets size to avoid underutilization and reduce operating expenses.

As soon as Cloudlets are deployed, they bring many new interesting challenges to scheduling. Among those, we consider *application classification* and *user mobility* as two key aspects to be associated with scheduling in providing efficient resource management for the Fogs and their users.

Application classification must provide the scheduler with information about application requirements, which will allow the scheduler to prioritize the Cloudlet use and optimize other (potentially conflicting) objectives (e.g. reduce network usage, reduce Cloud costs). By making use of such information, a Fog scheduler can decide which application(s) should run in the Cloudlet and which

should run in the Cloud. Moreover, application classes could also allow a system-level scheduler to prioritize applications within a Cloudlet, allowing smaller granularity control over the delays observed by applications at each class.

User mobility is another challenging issue, as it can determine the amount of load in Cloudlets over time. Users data and processing are widely used to support mobile applications in smart devices. Thus, understanding user behavior and mobility patterns can improve resource management by better planning the scheduling of the application beforehand. This planning is of paramount importance to avoid application delays perceived by the users during mobility. For example, when two applications with different requirements are to be scheduled to the same Cloudlet, if a predictive mechanism can accurately determine when the less QoS-strict application can be migrated to the Cloud, the other application can experience lower delays since its arrival to the Cloudlet. Note that this planning can also involve data movement, depending on the application being migrated. In this case, planning should also consider the time taken to move data between parts (i.e. Cloudlets or Cloudlets–Cloud).

Although mobility can be reasonably predicted in general [48], prediction misses will eventually occur from lack of information or user unpredictable behavior. Prediction misses can incur in additional computing and networking costs: the same data/application movement will be needed to contour the incorrect prediction results. Scheduling strategies to deal with mobility prediction failure are also an interesting problem to be studied in the Fog computing context.

Scheduling in Fog computing environments should prioritize several factors. Three of them stand out: i) the diversity of workloads submitted, ii) the high degree of heterogeneity of the resources present in Cloudlets, and iii) a new class of mobility applications [49, 50]. Even though some solutions at Cloud level, such as Kubernetes [51], provide mechanisms for deployment, maintenance, and scaling application across multiples hosts; these should be rethought to achieve Fog requirements efficiently. In Cloud environments, application scheduling used to follow a centralized approach taking advantage of the global knowledge of the relatively small quantity of homogeneous data centers. Nonetheless, in the heavily distributed scenario of Fog where there is a large number of heterogeneous micro-data centers potentially located over large geographical areas, the legacy scheduling approaches are not suitable considering that it is necessary to achieve latency requirements.

Thus, new approaches to prediction and scheduling execution based on hybrid mechanisms are necessary to guarantee low latency and service-continuity during users' mobility. Local scheduling at Fog level following a choreography approach in combination with optimization mechanisms at the upper levels (i.e. Cloud level) to take advantage of a global view of all infrastructure, can be the next step to efficiently exploit the collaboration between all the nodes in a Cloud/Fog scenario and fulfill an end-to-end application awareness scheduling.

4.2 Path computation

Path computation is playing a key role on the Internet and has evolved to support new types of applications and services, as well as network structures. These demands tend to be heterogeneous since there is an increasing number of users accessing the Internet. In addition, path computation must consider the characteristics of entities connected to the Internet, new services and applications provided over the Internet, and communication platforms such as wireless technologies and Cloud/Fog systems.

The main objectives of path computation are: (1) *maintaining end-to-end connectivity*, how to find the best way of reaching a destination which is not directly connected to the source?; (2) *adapting to dynamic topologies*, how can the best new path be found?; (3) *Maximizing network and application traffic performance*, how can users be provided with a high level of QoS at the lowest possible cost, while providers obtain the highest profits possible with the lowest investment?; and (4) *providing network resilience*, how does the routing protocol behave when failures occur and what is its impact on traffic performance?

Path computation in Cloud, Fog and IoE environments plays a crucial role, since it goes beyond packet and flow based decisions, and involves supporting dynamic services. In particular, routing can provide information to support functions such as service placement by Orchestrator. This is especially important within the Fog computing paradigm where the aim is to ensure these services can be accessed with the lowest latency possible (see SubSection 4.5) as well as to reduce energy consumption [15, 52].

One key aspect of path computation in multi-hop wireless networks concerns the best way to characterize the links in the network. Although this was already a problem in wired networks, it has become of critical importance in wireless environments owing to the rapidly changing characteristics of the medium and topologies in IoT/IoE environments, the existence of multiple channels, and inter-flow interference. In view of this, it is critical to select metrics that, in addition to traffic load levels, depict the characteristics of the links and paths in the network [53–55].

Connectivity and routing in Fog is a challenge given the heterogeneous nature of its mostly wireless links, in comparison with other distributed systems such as the Cloud. Just take into consideration that it is necessary to maintain the connectivity between the services and devices deployed in an IoT large-scale scenario. Nevertheless, these challenges also provide new opportunities for cost-reduction and enlarging the network connectivity scope. For example, a multi-hop wireless network could be partitioned into different clusters due to the coverage of available resources in Fog nodes (i.e. Cloudlets, sink nodes, smartphones) to enhance the support of the services in the IoE. In this kind of scenarios, the SDN and virtualization approaches could be used to instantiate particular devices in real-time, and adapting routes to changing conditions.

4.3 Discovery and allocation

One important issue that must be addressed in a scenario as the one described so far is related to the discovery of the physical and virtual devices in the Fog, as well as the resources associated with them. The resource discovery is a process where different computational capacities (e.g. CPU memory, storage) can be reported to the management unit so it can account for the resources available in the overall system [56]. This process also refers to the associations of devices grouped, known as Cloudlets, that embody the Fog.

For the discovery process, a device could advertise its available capacities, or it could be sensed by the management entity. However, it is worth noticing that in a highly dynamic scenario (unlike the Cloud), this information might vary rapidly [57]. Thus, the time frame on which the information must be updated becomes a critical factor to guarantee the accuracy of the information reported.

The management entity in charge of the Fog is therefore responsible for the accounting of the resources available in the Fog, and then selecting the one that best fit for the service's requirements [58]. As for Cloud computing, at the Fog level the goal usually is to maximize the utilization of resources while the idle periods are minimized [59]. Nevertheless, according to the needs and the nature of the environment (e.g. high mobility), different policies can be used for the allocation process. Some examples are [49]: (1) *Concurrent*, requests are allocated to the receiving Cloudlet, regardless of usage or capacity; (2) *First come first served*, requests are served according to their arrival time; and (3) *Delay-priority*, applications requiring lower latency are prioritized.

Another thing to consider is the tradeoff between different (sometimes competing) optimization parameters. For instance, it could be required to minimize the energy consumption while also minimizing the latency [60]. These represent a multi-objective optimization problem that renders the allocation process into a non-trivial problem.

The management entity, using the data from the discovery process, should apply the preferred policy in order to achieve the applications' requirements. Both the discovery and allocation processes represent two challenges that must be addressed by an Orchestrator.

4.4 Interoperability

In a macro view, interoperability [61] is the ability that distributed system elements have to interact with each other [62]. Several factors influence the interoperability of a system, such as the heterogeneity of the elements present in it. Thus, in Fog computing environments where the set of Cloudlets have a high degree of heterogeneity, there are several challenges to maintain the interoperability between its elements [20].

Considering the similarities between Cloud and Fog paradigms, it is possible to derive the problem and the solutions to maintain the interoperability found in the Inter-Clouds for Fog environments. It is feasible to group the solutions to keep interoperability into: *translators*, *standard interfaces* and *ontologies*. Translators, or brokers [63], concentrate the communication protocols supported by the Orchestrator to perform the communication between the involved parties. It is a solution widely used by Inter-Clouds to achieve interoperability between Cloud providers. However, it may not be applicable by the Orchestrator when considering the low latency requirements of applications and services. The insertion of a new translation layer may increase the overhead to the process. Standard interfaces provide a straightforward and standardized way of communicating between elements of a distributed system. In addition, standardized interfaces [20] make the process of insertion and diffusion of new functionalities more controlled and homogeneous, since in most cases there are working groups or consortiums involved in the development of the interface.

On the other hand, heterogeneity causes certain interfaces to be accepted only by portions of the Cloudlets, also the problem of the *egg-and-chicken* may appear when considering new interfaces. The variability of standard interfaces can lead to the need for brokers, which may refer to problems arising from their use (e.g. overhead). Ontologies [64–67] are a representation of knowledge (e.g. W3C Semantic Web standard web ontology language [68]). They "hide" the technologies used by delegating the implementation to local contexts of Cloudlets. Implementing and maintaining an ontology increases the complexity of the Orchestrator, creating problems similar to those generated by brokers.

Providing interoperability is a problem inherent to distributed environments. Associations of multiple Clouds, as well as other distributed systems, have already faced this challenge and it is no different in the Fog. However, since the Fog intends to address the applications that have latency constraints and mobility support as main properties, the approach considered for interoperability is

an open challenge that must be addressed [15, 20]. The choice of a broker can serve interoperability but can insert an overhead that can lead to denial of applications with a certain latency requirement [69]. Added to this, the diversity of Cloudlets can lead to the maturity of several protocols by the broker. Already adopting standard interfaces can decrease the amount of Cloudlets available in the environment which can compromise the amount of applications that can be executed.

4.5 Latency

One of the characteristics of Fog environments is that they provide low levels of latency [15, 70]. This allows the deployment of a different kind of services with real-time and low latency restrictions that are not necessarily fit for the Cloud; but also requires a new set of mechanisms that guarantee that these low latency levels are met.

Smart routing and forwarding mechanisms should be designed, aiming at faster response time. A multipath approach [71] could be employed to achieve this goal, especially when dealing with huge bulks of data; however, for small but critical tasks, the use of redundant packets has proven to be efficient [72, 73].

Another possibility is designing intelligent service placement mechanisms [74, 75] for the Orchestrator. It is also important to take into consideration the mobile nature of the devices (e.g. sensors in cars), for which location awareness [76] and dynamism support [77, 78] must also be included.

Given that the tendency is shifting time-constrained services and applications towards the edge of the Cloud into the Fog, it is imperative to guarantee that the time restrictions are met [79]. The service orchestrator must incorporate novel mechanisms, different from those already available for other distributed systems such as Cloud, that are sensitive to time constraints, and that support other features such as mobility, dynamism, and geo-distribution [17].

Another issue to take in consideration is the more limited resources regarding the bandwidth of the links in comparison with Cloud systems, given their wireless nature and narrower capacity [80].

4.6 Resilience

In the complex and diverse environment where the IoE acts, a seamless interaction between all the actors that build the IoE paradigm, from the physical (e.g. sensors, actuator, smart objects) to the logical perspective (e.g. service, applications, protocols), is a critical aspect. Even more, in this kind of scenarios, the availability of the physical and logical devices and their services represent a key requirement, given that some critical applications such as assisted driving, augmented maps, and health monitoring require continuous availability while providing real-time feedback to users.

An improved connectivity between Cloud [81] services and devices in the IoT [82] is necessary to support the emerging applications enabled by the IoT Cloudification. To deal with disruptions in the IoE, it is required to have mechanisms that enhance its resilience both at infrastructure and service levels. Sterbenz et al. [83] defined resilience as the ability of the network to provide and maintain an acceptable level of service in the face of various faults and challenges to normal operation. Considering that the IoE includes components from the IoT to the Fog and the Cloud, the main resilience challenges emerge from the objects and communication point of view.

To increase the resilience of smart objects that enable the interaction with the physical world, replication and backup schemes must be implemented; however, how is it possible to adopt aforementioned schemes efficiently? One traditional approach is using a primary and backup model, where devices and services are duplicated for robustness purposes. This would not be adequate considering that this strategy could waste valuable resources in the already constrained Fog nodes in case no failure occurs. In this context, virtualization mechanisms have proven to be useful from the cost and operational perspectives. Emerging virtualization paradigms like Containers [84] and NFV [85] allow the improvement of the performance and availability of service and device components. Once mapped as a logical item, physical objects can be handled like any other piece of software, granting the possibility to apply migration, instantiation, and other well-known techniques over them. Thus, a failure concerning a service or device can be recovered by migrating or instantiating a logical object over a different physical device.

From the communication point of view, the traditional approach of distributed systems relies in trying to hide the distributed nature of the system to offer a perspective of a single machine. In Cloud environments, this "hiding" approach remains for the network layout considering that Cloud services just expose high-level information about their setup and distribution. On the other hand, in Fog scenarios it is essential to know about the network topology to take advantage of the geographical distribution which requires a more fine-grained topology abstraction. Thus, it is necessary to have an efficient and flexible way to control the route of the data and the topology of the communication infrastructure in the IoE.

Regarding the resilience at the communication infrastructure level, an approach in two phases could be applied using a detailed fine-grained topology abstraction at Cloud and Fog levels. In a first step, an offline mechanism to find disjoint paths between the components of the IoE could be executed to obtain backup paths that can be switched in case of failures. In a second stage, the detection of a failure and the migration of the data flows will be performed inline. To achieve this last task, the use of path-splitting and multipath routing strategies appears to be a feasible solution [86].

To guarantee a smooth work of the proposals mentioned above from the resilience perspective, an Orchestrator should be in charge of intelligent migration and instantiation of resources and services providing a global view of the status of the IoE. Furthermore, the interaction between federative Clouds and services represents an additional challenge, since the Orchestrator has to unify politics from different administrative entities smoothly.

4.7 Prediction and optimization

A proper management of resources and services in an IoE environment, where these are geographically distributed generating multi-dimensional data in enormous quantities, is only possible if the orchestration process takes into consideration prediction and optimization mechanisms of all overlapping and interconnected layers in the IoE [63]. Thus it is necessary that the Orchestrator has a global view of all the resources and services, from the edge of the infrastructure to the computation and storage place on the Cloud.

Although a global view of the infrastructure helps in the management process, an efficient orchestration at the Fog level remains a challenge. The service oriented computing model applied in Cloud environments is based on hiding implementations and runtime details to services and applications to ease its deployment. In the case of the Fog paradigm, geo-distribution, physical location, and the type of node/device actually matters. Thus, it is necessary to find a middle ground that exposes enough details about the distribution and physical location of the edge devices to take advantage of prediction and optimization.

To achieve successful results in prediction mechanisms, it is necessary to collect an enormous amount of resources', services', and users' data to feed the proper algorithms. Here, data analytics plays a vital role to extract useful information from the data gathered and perform prediction and optimization tasks. Taleb et al. [87] introduced the term Follow Me Cloud (FMC) to denote a framework that enables mobile Cloud services to follow their respective mobile users during their journeys by migrating all or portion of the services to optimal computational centers ensuring the best Quality of Experience (QoE). This new paradigm brings a huge challenge for the orchestration and management of resource in Cloud and Fog environments considering that in many cases prediction mechanisms should be used in order to guarantee the proper QoE.

Some efforts have been performed in prediction. Nadembega et al. [88] present a mobility-based service migration prediction for Cloud and Fog environments to ensure QoE to users while avoiding signaling messages and reducing the amount of data transferred between data centers and Cloudlets. The prediction mechanisms used in this research used three schemes: (1) a data transfer throughput estimation scheme that aims to estimate in advance the time required for data to travel from the computational nodes to users; (2) a service area handoff time estimation scheme to estimate that a user will remain inside a specific coverage area; (3) a service migration management scheme to split the requested service into offloading portion.

Patel et al. [89] measured the performance impact of prediction during live virtual machine migration using machine learning algorithms. Specifically, a time series prediction using historical analysis of past data relating dirty memory pages was performed using two prediction models; the first one using an autoregressive integrated moving average model, and the second one based on a learning model using the support vector regression technique.

For the researchers above, the prediction impact in the overall performance was remarkable; however, to achieve these results the datasets used for the machine learning algorithms played a key role pointing out the importance of their significance for prediction mechanisms. Thus prediction is still an open issue in the context of orchestration and resource management into Cloud and Fog environments.

The planning and continuous optimization of resource management such as the placement of virtual services and other components on physical resources have an enormous impact on the effectiveness and performance of Cloud and Fog solutions. To address these issues, an analytical framework able to provide a mathematical foundation for optimizing or finding a trade-off between the (possibly conflicting) objectives involved in the optimization problems, that the Cloud and Fog Orchestrator have solved, will be useful [90].

A valuable analytical framework for orchestration optimization could be based on queuing theory [91]. In this context, computational tasks can be modeled as clients, and resources can be modeled as queueing nodes. Clients move across the network of queues following a routing policy and are serviced by each node according to some scheduling policy decided by the Orchestrator. Thus, different performance metrics can be evaluated. For example, the service latency can be measured as the total time the corresponding to the movement of the client from the source node to the destination node, and resource utilization could be mapped to the usage of corresponding nodes.

The use of offline techniques and frameworks like the ones explained before should be combined with monitoring and inline optimization mechanisms that enable flexibility and self-configuration in order to guarantee users' QoS. These challenges from the orchestration point of view on Fog environments remain open for deeper research and contributions.

4.8 Security and privacy

Many benefits may arise from the decentralization of Cloud-based solutions through the distribution of computation, storage and communication responsibilities towards nodes closer to data sources.

From the point of view of security and privacy, there are mixed effects that must be taken into account. In the positive side, decentralization usually improves resilience, by simply removing central points of failure or compromise. Intermediate nodes have a better opportunity to detect and mitigate threats, filter malicious traffic and perform other security checkpoint activities. Distributed storage may also reduce the volume of a potential data breach or impact of government surveillance efforts, with clear improvements in privacy.

It is important to point out that the aforementioned benefits do not come without more complex deployment, policy, control and coordination requirements. The added complexity can reduce the overall security and privacy guarantees, as more components come under the influence of an *attacker*. Immediate and major challenges arising from decentralization are distributed infrastructure protection, identity lifecycle and cryptographic key management (i.e. secure generation, distribution, exchange, storage, use, and replacement of credentials and keys). These are rather classical problems, but they receive new undertones which may allow interesting trade-offs and novel solutions in the context of Fog computing.

Infrastructure protection includes many different types of threats, ranging from network security solutions to malware detection and elimination. When interest is restricted to applications of cryptography, secure routing protocols become of particular interest, since route manipulation is a relatively simple attack vector for performing denial of service attacks or simply deviating sensitive traffic towards nodes under control of an attacker [92]. There are several proposals available in the research literature for securing routing protocols [93], but surprisingly they have not been adopted or even considered for standardization.

The Fog computing model presents another opportunity for improving this situation, due to higher computing and storage resources typically available in routers and other pieces of modern network infrastructure. Additional challenges in the infrastructure protection space are to coordinate distributed detection of malicious code and traffic, potentially involving different service providers and manufacturers of infrastructure equipment [94, 95]. The fierce competition in these markets introduces additional privacy requirements, where threats must be detected in a privacy-preserving way without disclosing critical information.

Security mechanisms are not restricted to the basic networking level and can also be important at much higher abstractions, for example at the service provisioning level. As services become more distributed, information such as service type and interface, device hostname and ownership may be considered sensitive and require protection. Significant attention has been dedicated to the design of protocols for private (as in *privacy-preserving*) service discovery over the network [96]. Unfortunately, many of these protocols were proposed very recently and have not been thoroughly analyzed regarding security, performance or ease of deployment, what amounts to an interesting research challenge. These are important aspects that must be considered by a Fog Service Orchestrator.

In the scope of privacy, there are other relevant research goals beyond the service provisioning level. The Fog computing model transfers many Cloud-based functionalities to the infrastructure, such as data aggregation. In such a task, near-user edge devices combine partial observations about monitored metrics or characteristics to provide a complete view to the upper layers in the hierarchy, preferably by preserving the privacy of the lower-level users. It turns out that privacy-by-design mechanisms offer interesting solutions to this problem that can be efficiently implemented at these points using differential privacy techniques [97].

Despite the fact that solutions for security and privacy issues are well-studied in Cloud environments, not all of them are suitable for the Fog due to their different characteristics as well as the vast scale of devices at the edge of the network. From the privacy perspective, the main challenge lays into how to preserve the end user privacy since the Fog nodes are deployed near them collecting sensitive data concerning to identity and usage patterns. Regarding security, a significant challenge is how to deal with the massively distributed approach of the Fog to guarantee the proper authentication mechanisms and avoid massive distributed attacks. Thus, it is necessary to outline future research directions to cope with the challenges discussed in this subsection.

4.9 Authentication, access, and account

To perform activities related to application life cycle management (i.e. deployment, migration, application of policies) the Orchestrator interacts with the Cloudlets in the environment. However, due to the degree of heterogeneity of the Cloudlets in relation to the security aspects, new challenges arise when carrying out this interaction [98]. The interaction between the Orchestrator and each Cloudlet follows the steps described in the well-known Authentication, Access, and Account (AAA) framework. Authentication makes it possible to identify the Orchestrator in the Cloudlet by querying its credentials. Allocation allows the Orchestrator to perform a set of actions (e.g. access to selected resources and execution commands) after it is authenticated. Finally, the account records the amount and time of use of the resources by the Orchestrator.

Regarding Authentication, the Orchestrator must provide the means to handle the most diverse Cloudlet authentication approaches and protocols. Two challenges are inherent in this action, manage the authentications and the passage of credentials by the Orchestrator to Cloudlets over a network. Stojmenovic et al. [99] also emphasize the need for the Orchestrator to prevent malicious attacks that act on the authentication process, such as the Man-in-the-Middle attack [100]. The use of a cryptographic key distribution infrastructure [101, 102] can improve the authentication process in terms of security and control.

The Fog environment is oriented to low latency, which may lead to the use of symmetric keys because of its low complexity in relation to the asymmetric keys in the implementation of the key infrastructure for authentication. Nevertheless, this choice brings with it one of the main problems in using symmetric keys: the possibility of compromising the whole environment if a key is compromised (e.g. stealing). As mentioned by Dastjerdi et al. [101], another approach that can be used to "hide" credentials is Trusted Execution Environment (TEE) [103]. However, factors such as complexity and speed decrease also arise when using this approach. In addition to these solutions, it is possible to delegate the authentication and authorization process to Internal or External Identity Providers (IdP) [104]. IdPs are prepared to use standard protocols for these purposes (e.g. X.509 [105] and Security Assertion Markup Language [106]). In contrast, while addressing the heterogeneity problem, the insertion of a new layer in the process may increase the cost of the Orchestrator to perform authentication and authorization.

To use the resources and perform actions in the Cloudlets, it is necessary that the Orchestrator is authorized to do so. The set of actions and resources available to the Orchestrator is determined and disseminated by the Cloudlets. Consequently, it is required to design and develop mechanisms to ensure that this information matches the current state of the Cloudlets and that the information collected reflects the set of actions and resources to which the Orchestrator has access. This disclosure feeds a catalog that the Orchestrator uses to manage the applications. The discrepancy in the information can lead to the commitment of the orchestration plan consuming more time in an application deployment or migration. The role of the accounting process in this context is to help feed the catalog, accounting for the resources used and the resources that will be released after the migration or termination of an application.

Note that due to the dynamicity of the Fog environment, considering the Cloudlet and applications lifecycle, AAA-related processes can be executed several times in a short space of time which can cause overhead. Additionally, the diversity of Cloudlets can expose the environment to malicious attacks, compromising the orchestration. Thus, it is necessary to consider this factor and the consequent impacts on the orchestration of each approach employed for AAA.

The Fog requires a well-constructed Orchestrator able to deal with the full management function for this complex environment, and properly handle all the challenges previously described. Several efforts have been carried out towards this direction, and some of them are outlined below.

5 Fog orchestrator architectures

The OpenFog Reference Architecture (OpenFog RA) was designed by the OpenFog Consortium as a guide to help in the design and maintenance of hardware, software, and system elements that are needed for Fog computing environments [20]. The architecture is structured by a set of *pillars*, which represent key attributes needed to provide distribution of computing, storage, control, and networking functions in the vicinity of the data source (i.e. users, things). These pillars are:

- Security, which ensures that the deployment will offer a secure end-to-end environment;
- Scalability, which allows adaptation to workloads, system costs, performance, and other needs;
- Openness, which permits Fog nodes to exist anywhere, be pooled by discovery, and be dynamically created;
- Autonomy, which enables Fog nodes to continue functioning and delivering services in case of an external failure;
- Programmability, which provides highly adaptive deployments, like retasking a Fog node for accommodating operational dynamics automatically;
- Reliability, Availability, and Serviceability, which guarantees the delivery of expected functionality under normal and adverse operating conditions;
- Agility, which focuses on the transformation of massive amounts of data into manageable formats, and also deals with the highly dynamic nature of the Fog handling sudden changes;

- Hierarchy, which helps standardizing the organization of multiple Fog islands in a single or federated system.

The OpenFog RA provides guidelines for the features a proper Fog system should offer; however, it does not include instructions about the management or orchestration of the scenario and the actors playing key roles in it (e.g. devices, services, and applications).

The main focus of this research is on orchestration; thus all the architectures evaluated in this section specifically describe how to deal with orchestration functions in Fog environments. Given that the Fog paradigm is relatively recent, not much research is available on the topic of Fog service orchestration. In certain stages of new technologies, there is a moment where the concepts are diffuse and can be applied or restricted to more situations. In the case of Fog computing, there are divergences on the definition when considering other technologies with similar purposes.

For example, some authors describe Fog and Edge computing as distinct technologies [107, 108], while other authors interpret both as synonymous when considering Fog as a paradigm of computation [109, 110]. It is also possible to assume Mobile Edge Computing (MEC) [111] as an interpretation Fog environment but with a specific niche [16]: mobility. In MEC, Cloudlets are mobile devices that interact directly with an IoT or cellular layer. Such Cloudlets are orchestrated centrally in an upper layer (Cloud). Following this idea, this section presents some Fog-based architectures and some MEC-based architectures, to later on analyze them.

For the selection of the architectures to analyze, we reviewed existing Fog computing orchestration literature published between January 2008 and September 2017. The publications were located using keyword search on Google Scholar and other academic databases, such as ScienceDirect, Springer, IEEE Xplore, and ACM digital Library. The keywords we used included "Fog computing orchestration", "Cloud computing orchestration", "Edge computing orchestration", and "Mobile Edge computing orchestration".

The search performed left us around seventy-five papers published in the context of Cloud/Fog orchestration. From this subset, approximately twenty researches proposed Fog-enabled architectures regarding orchestration but just half of them (i.e. ten works) described in detail the modules inside the architecture and their roles. These works were published after 2014, confirming the novelty of the topic.

Finally, among the few works we were able to find regarding Fog orchestration or other environments that could be extrapolated (i.e. ten works), this section describes a subset including the ones with higher citation number (which reflects the impact that the publications generated in the scientific community), and more recent publication date (which covers the most contemporary research in Fog Orchestrators). Additionally, the works that did not address in enough detail at least half (five out of nine) of the research challenges identified in Section 4 were not included in this study because we considered they do not fulfill the minimum requirements of an end-to-end orchestration approach, or did not provide enough details on how to handle them, thus it could lead to an unbalanced analysis.

The four Fog service orchestration architectures selected to be discussed on this section are: SORTS, SOAFI, ETSI IGS MEC, and CONCERT; which cover at least half of the identified research challenges with enough detail so that they can be objectively compared.

5.1 SORTS

Velasquez et al. [112] proposed a hybrid approach for service orchestration in the Fog, framed in the SORTS

(Supporting the Orchestration of Resilient and Trustworthy Fog Services) project [113]. The infrastructure is divided by levels that are managed using both choreography and orchestration, according to the needs of the different levels. The architecture allows the use of different Orchestrator instances, corresponding to the optimization goals of various scenarios.

5.1.1 Logical network infrastructure

The SORTS infrastructure is divided into three levels, shown in Fig. 2 from bottom to top: (1) the IoT, (2) the Fog, and (3) the Cloud. The IoT level is composed of Virtual Clusters that represent a group of terminal communication devices (e.g. smartphones, vehicles); these devices can communicate with each other inside their Virtual Cluster or with neighboring Virtual Clusters, allowing mobility of the devices. At this level, a choreography approach is used, meaning that the devices cooperate among each other for managing purposes. This allows quicker response times in case of changes in the topology (e.g. shift from one Virtual

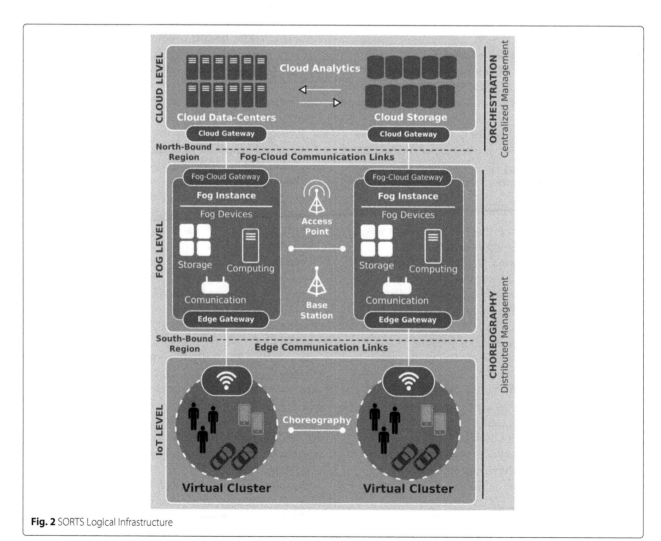

Fig. 2 SORTS Logical Infrastructure

Cluster to the next) thus increasing the resilience of the system.

The Fog level is divided into the South-Bound and the North-Bound regions. The South-Bound region, closer to the IoT, is composed of Fog computing devices, able to perform migration of services (code offloading); Fog communication devices, able to establish connections between the different levels of the infrastructure; and Fog storage devices, able to perform caching functions for the IoT users. These activities are controlled using choreography mechanisms.

The orchestration is used at the North-Bound region of the Fog level and the Cloud level (top level of the infrastructure). Fog/Cloud gateways and links are used to connect the Fog (North-Bound region) and Cloud levels. The Cloud level enables the use of a massive amount of resources for demanding storage and processing tasks. The hybrid approach (i.e. choreography plus orchestration) facilitates the achievement of a higher independence for the lower levels, granting them more dynamism and quicker response time in case of failures; at the same time, at the upper levels permits maintaining a global view that allows the implementation of optimization tasks involving the overall system.

5.1.2 SORTS orchestrator architecture

The architecture presented in Fig. 3 was designed to manage the resources and communication in the scenario previouly described. Overlapped instances of the architecture are to be replicated at different Fog Instances and Virtual Clusters allowing the use of the distributed choreography mechanisms; and also at the Cloud level, where a single instance is deployed for global orchestration.

The Orchestrator is composed of different modules. The *Communication Manager* handles the communication among the different Orchestrator instances; the

Resource Manager monitors the resource usage of the infrastructure; the *Service Discovery* enables the lookup of services available in the nearest location; the *Security Manager* provides different authentication and privacy mechanisms.

The *Status Monitor* oversees the activities in the system; the *Planner Mechanisms* schedule the processes in the system and the location where they will be placed; and the *Optimization Mechanisms* which are meant to be applied at the upper levels, are used to improve the performance of the system.

5.2 SOAFI

The Service Orchestrator Architecture for Fog-enable Infrastructure (SOAFI) is a reference architecture proposed by Brito et al. [98]. The development of this architecture was performed to demonstrate the importance of the Orchestrator in a Fog environment. In addition, the work is focused in the portability of concepts from other environments into building an Orchestrator in the context of Fog, such as the use of precepts of the TOSCA [114] and ETSI NFV MANO [115].

This architecture (see Fig. 4) consists of two main elements organized on a client-server model: *Fog Orchestrator* and *Fog Orchestration Agent*.

5.2.1 Fog orchestrator

The Fog Orchestrator (FO) is a centralized entity that organizes the Fog nodes into logical groups called Logical Infrastructure. Through this grouping, it is possible to create the hierarchy of capacity and objectives within the framework. The responsibilities of the FO are divided into *Infrastructure Management*, *Orchestration* itself, *Security*, and *Monitoring*.

- *Infrastructure Manager*, handles all resources present in the Fog, maintaining the tasks of discovery, allocation, and catalog of resources. Such information generated by infrastructure management components is used by the Orchestrator to perform its activities;
- *Orchestrator*, carries out the composition of resources to offer new services. After receiving a template with information about the characteristics of the service, the Orchestrator requests information from the Infrastructure Manager to create and execute an orchestration plan. Another component that the Orchestrator relates to is the Monitoring, from which obtains information to support its operations. The process can be performed manually, through an external request. It can also be performed automatically, responding to an internal request;
- *Security*, provides data security mechanisms. In addition, it performs authentication management activities that are required in a heterogeneous and dynamic environment such as the Fog;

Fig. 3 SORTS Orchestrator components

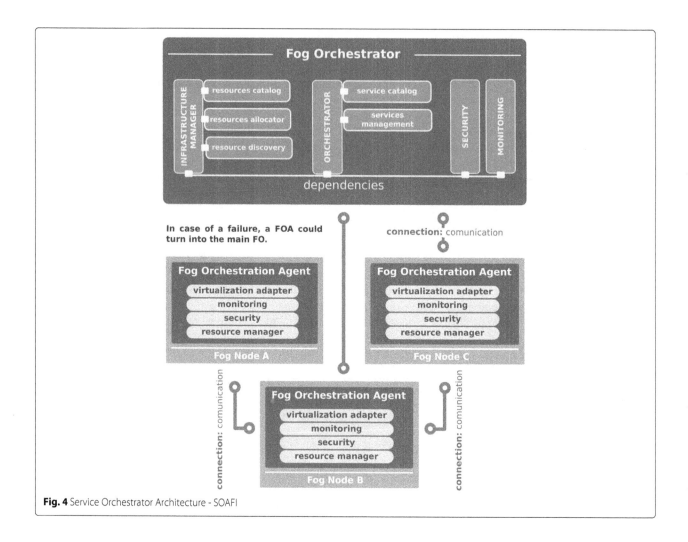

Fig. 4 Service Orchestrator Architecture - SOAFI

- *Monitoring*, interacts with the Cloudlets to obtain data about the system and create a global view of all Cloudlets.

5.2.2 Fog orchestration agent

Within SOAFI, each Cloudlet has a Fog Orchestration Agent (FOA) installed which is an interface with the Fog Orchestrator. The authors of the architecture describe that in addition to interfacing with the FO, the FOA has a set of responsibilities, such as:

- *Allocation*, manages resources present in the Cloudlet. The management activities are conditioned to the degree of authorization that FOA has in relation to the resources of interest;
- *Discovery*, detects the connection and disconnection of resources in a Cloudlet. Another related activity is the announcement that each Cloudlet makes regarding its presence to the rest of the Cloudlets present in the environment. This publication allows the FO to discover new Cloudlets;

- *Optimization*, locally manages the running services and enables the creation of a set of policies for the execution of virtualized environments;
- *Interoperability*, maintains the Machine to Machine (M2M) interoperability through a standardized communication way that considers different communication protocols. It also provides support for various virtualization approaches (e.g. Containers and VMs).

According to Section 3, Cloudlets are autonomous entities. Because of this behavior, Cloudlets may never communicate with the FO. This absence of communication can be derived from the absence of the FO in the environment or due to other reasons such as the impossibility of communication as results of problems in the network. In this situation, the architecture allows the FOA to temporarily become a FO, as long as it has the conditions to support all Fog Orchestrator responsibilities. With this, the FOA can temporarily perform the orchestration of its services in the Cloudlets.

5.3 ETSI IGS MEC

This subsection presents the reference architecture for Mobile Edge Computing ETSI GS MEC [116] described by the ETSI Industry Specification Group. In the reference architecture, the Cloudlets are the Mobile Edge Hosts (ME Hosts). The ME Hosts contain the resources (i.e. compute, storage and network) and available components within the architecture. In addition to the ME Hosts, the architecture contemplates more modules (see Fig. 5). Among them is the Orchestrator that is the component with the main function within the architecture.

5.3.1 Mobile edge orchestrator

The Mobile Edge Orchestrator (MEO) performs the planning, deploying and managing of the application's lifecycle. To achieve this, it communicates with other components of the architecture to obtain the state of the resources (available and used), the executing applications and the current capacity. These communications are described in the reference architecture by points of interaction that are channels of communication between components present in the architecture (see Fig. 5):

- *Mm1*, receives requests to start and/or terminate applications in the environment;
- *Mm3*, allows obtaining information about the state of the applications. It also enables the Orchestrator to maintain up-to-date service information and manage application-related policies;
- *Mm4*, maintains resource management and application deployment images by the respective ME Hosts. The information obtained in these interactions will help the Orchestrator to build a catalog of the resources;
- *Mm9*, handles the requests to migrate an application. This migration may be internal to the MEC domain, or external to another domain.

The architecture describes the need for the presence of several points discussed in Section 4 (i.e. *Scheduling, Discovery, Allocation, Optimization, Authentication, Access, and Account*). However, as it is a reference architecture, how these points will be implemented depends on the technology used and the needs of the niche to which the architecture will be applied. It is important to say that the

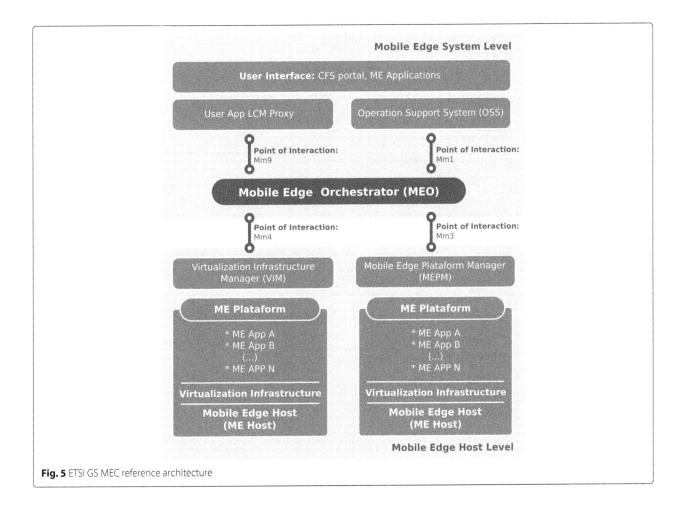

Fig. 5 ETSI GS MEC reference architecture

official documentation does not indicate clearly whether these tasks are performed by the Orchestrator.

5.4 CONCERT

CONCERT is a Cloud-based architecture for next-generation cellular systems proposed using two prominent approaches, decoupling the control and data plane and deploying services closer to users (at the edge of the network). In CONCERT, the data plane deals with different physical resources which are coordinated/orchestrated at the control plane to expose them as virtual resources to services and applications placed according to final users requirements. Thus, Liu et al. [91] proposed a converged edge infrastructure for cellular network communication and mobile edge computing services.

The CONCERT architecture is depicted in Fig. 6. From the bottom to the top the data plane encompasses different physical resources which are managed in an upper and decoupled control plane by the *Conductor entity*. The Conductor orchestrates and virtualizes all the data plane resources. On the top of the architecture, software-defined services are deployed using virtual resources.

The CONCERT data plane includes Radio Interfacing Equipments (RIEs), software-defined switches and computational resources. The RIEs deal with the signaling process between radio and digital domains besides taking care of radio resource slicing functions. These system's components provide the last-hop communication to final users. Conjointly with the base stations, it is possible to provide local servers at the edge of the network (Fog) to minimize the latency of applications and provide ubiquity to final users.

The software-defined switches interconnect the RIEs and the computational resources under the supervision of the Conductor, which is responsible for constructing and updating the forwarding tables of the switches enabling a smooth communication between all the data plane components.

The computational resources are in charge of all the data plane computation. These resources are distributed in different location taking into considerations their computational capabilities, for example, placing them next to the RIEs to achieve better response times as it was mentioned before. Another possibility is to aggregate the data by small regions in regional servers to decide which data could be processed locally and which one must be for-

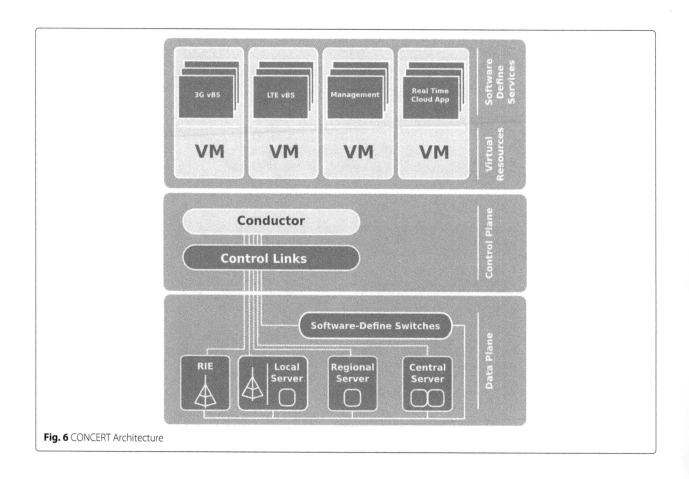

Fig. 6 CONCERT Architecture

warded to central servers in charge of hard demanding tasks.

The Conductor is the main component of the control plane, and its role is to orchestrate the physical resources available in the data plane and export them as virtual resources to the upper layers. The Conductor's mechanisms take care of the resource management and the communication infrastructure focusing on achieving applications' and users' requirements.

In Fig. 6, the mechanisms at the south-bound include radio interfacing management, networking management, and location-aware computing management; thus the data plane resources are orchestrated from the control plane. During the orchestration process, information about the state of the network infrastructure and the computational resource is gathered for optimization purposes.

The Conductor performs a variety of tasks via different mechanisms; for example, the Location-Aware Computing Management (LCM) mechanism is one of the most important given that it schedules computational tasks to computational resources. At this level, applications and services have different requirements, on the other hand, the computational resources may have different computational capabilities and are deployed in several locations. Thus the LCM has to decide the schedule strategies to fulfill applications' and users' requirements trying to find an optimal tradeoff among various objectives, such as low latency, resource utilization ratio, and resilience. In CONCERT, the Conductor can perform the tasks discussed above after collecting information about the deadlines, resource demands, location, and result destination of the applications and services in order to feed the proper mechanisms and algorithms embedded on it.

At the north-bound of the control plane, all the physical resources orchestrated are virtualized, creating a virtual infrastructure for the software-defined services.

At the top level of CONCERT, services are deployed following a software-defined approach taking advantage of the virtualization and orchestration performed by the Conductor in the control plane. Moreover, mobile edge Cloud services could be set up according to the user's requirements (e.g. low latency, high resilience) taking advantage of the LCM and other mechanisms provided by the Conductor.

In order to evaluate the reviewed architectures, a comparative analysis based on the challenges discussed in Section 4 is provided in the next section.

6 Discussion

A Fog Orchestrator requires a re-design of several mechanisms from well-known distributed systems (such as Cloud), in order to deal with the particular characteristics of the Fog. For instance, in the case of *Resource Management* (i.e. *Scheduling, Path Computation, Discovery and Allocation*, and *Interoperability*) it is important to consider the heterogeneity of the Fog, as well as the resource constraints of the devices at this level, which is very different from the reality in the Cloud.

Also, it is important to integrate solutions to handle the production of massive amounts of data at this level, which represents another shift in the previously known paradigm, and the heavy distributed nature of this scenario that also implies the need of keeping a precise knowledge of the devices and their locations.

In the case of *Performance* (i.e. *Latency, Resilience*, and *Prediction and Optimization*), new solutions are arising to deal with the high dynamism of the Fog and their mostly wireless links, using some knowledge of the edge environment. Also, to increase the performance, data is usually aggregated at the Fog level before being sent to the Cloud, thus the new solutions should consider data aggregation and preprocessing, diverging from mechanisms used on classic distributed systems.

Finally, for *Security Management* (i.e. *Security and Privacy* and *Authentication, Access, and Account*), it is important to handle the vastly distributed environment which enables more points of failure and the possibility of massive distributed attacks, and also consider the new threat regarding confidentiality of the sensitive data located in the proximity of the users.

The architectures reviewed in Section 5 are evaluated in this section considering how efficiently they handle these challenges. Table 1 summarizes the reviewed architectures, and how they deal with the challenges present in Fog environments, discussed in Section 4. For each challenge, Table 1 provides a short description on how the challenge is handled. In the case that an architecture does not provide information about the support for a particular challenge, N/A (Not Available) is listed in the table. Furthermore, since the ETSI IGS MEC architecture is just a reference, and no details are provided regarding the implementation, no more specifics are included in the table.

In general, the most addressed challenges are *Scheduling, Discovery and Allocation, Prediction and Optimization*. These challenges are the classic ones on distributed and Cloud environments; thus various mechanisms to deal with these challenges have been migrated to the Fog from its predecessors. On the other hand, the less natively included properties are *Path Computation* and *Interoperability*. This could be due to the majority of solutions use well-known external paradigms to deal with them. For *Path Computation*, SDN and NFV are commonly imported by Fog Orchestrators to deal with dynamic routing; meanwhile, standard description languages, such as ontologies, are utilized to achieve *Interoperability*.

For *Latency* and *Resilience*, the majority of the solutions are working towards embedded mechanisms. This

Table 1 Comparative analysis fog orchestrator architectures

Challenges	SORTS	SOAFI	ETSI IGS MEC	CONCERT
Scheduling	Planner mechanisms schedule processes and their locations	Service management and catalog done by the Orchestrator	Planning, deployment and management carried out by the MEO	LCM implements scheduling strategies, services deployed using a SDN approach
Path Computation	N/A	N/A	Indicated as needed but no further details provided	N/A
Discovery and Allocation	Service discovery mechanisms at the Orchestrator to enable lookup	Handled by infrastructure manager	Indicated as needed but no further details provided	Orchestrate physical resources into virtual ones, carried out by the Conductor
Interoperability	N/A	M2M interoperability through standard communication	N/A	N/A
Latency	Service placement mechanisms at the Orchestrator to minimize latency	N/A	N/A	Provide local servers at the Fog to minimize latency
Resilience	Survivability mechanisms at the Resource Manager	N/A	N/A	Use of resilience metrics for scheduling purposes
Prediction and Optimization	Global mechanisms to improve performance of the system	Set of policies for virtual environments	Indicated as needed but no further details provided	State of the network used for optimization mechanisms
Security and Privacy	Security manager provides different privacy mechanisms	Data security mechanisms as dependencies of the Orchestrator	N/A	N/A
Authentication, Access, and Account	Authentication mechanisms supported by its security manager	N/A	Indicated as needed but no further details provided	N/A

represents a currently active and challenging field of research, taking in consideration that they support important metrics for final users that heavily impact QoS and QoE. Thus, more research is needed in these areas to better support applications and services in the Fog, looking towards improving services performance and user satisfaction.

In the case of the ETSI IGS MEC architecture [116], since it refers to a reference architecture, it only mentions that the challenges should be addressed, but does not specify how it must be done. From this review, SORTS [112] is the architecture that supports the most challenges. An hybrid approach of choreography and orchestration was proposed in this research to enable Cloudlets and IoT islands to take decisions in a distributed way while at the Cloud level the Orchestrator can aggregate information from the lower layers to manage all the resources using a global view of the infrastructure allowing optimal decision-making over the entire system.

Overall, the reviewed architectures are still under development. The majority of them propose theoretical approaches to deal with the challenges present in Fog environments. Nevertheless, practical and experimental solutions are coming forward; once the research field becomes more mature, stronger solutions are to be expected.

7 Conclusions

In an Internet of Everything environment, smart devices communicate with each other and with the users through the Internet to gather, process, and analyze data, without much (or any) human intervention. This inevitably will enable the rise of new generation services and applications where unique and customized information will be processed for users on demand. This brings along different challenges that have to be addressed in order to guarantee their proper function while providing acceptable QoE for final users.

Fog Orchestration refers to the process of automating application workflows in the sense of providing dynamic policy-based lifecycle management of Fog infrastructure and services. The Orchestration includes the provisioning, management, and monitoring on a large number of Fog nodes (i.e. Cloudlets) with a broad range of capabilities that include computing (computer resources), routing (network) and distributed databases (storage). The Fog Orchestration system must manage heterogeneous, and distributed systems spread across a wide geographical area. This requires a hierarchical organization with effective policies integrated with the Cloud orchestration system via intelligent interfaces.

In this paper, a revision on the Fog paradigm and its challenges is provided, to later on introduce a set of Fog service Orchestrator architectures, and how these deal with the challenges of the Fog. A comparative analysis is provided on the different architectures.

Further research has to be carried out to come up with stronger and more efficient architectures that include mechanisms and processes to handle the identified challenges and other issues not covered in this research. Future works also include determining additional research challenges and proposing how to manage them.

Acknowledgements

Karima Velasquez and David Perez Abreu wish to acknowledge the Portuguese funding institution FCT - Foundation for Science and Technology for supporting their research under the Ph.D. grants ≪SFRH/BD/119392/2016≫ and ≪SFRH/BD/117538/2016≫ respectively. The work presented in this paper was partially carried out in the scope of the projects: ≪MobiWise: From mobile sensing to mobility advising≫ (P2020 SAICTPAC/0011/2015), co-financed by COMPETE 2020, Portugal 2020 - Operational Program for Competitiveness and Internationalization (POCI), European Union's ERDF (European Regional Development Fund), and the Portuguese Foundation for Science and Technology (FCT); and SORTS, financed by the the CAPES - Coordenção de Aperfeiçoamento de Pessoal de Nível Superior ≪CAPES-FCT/8572/14-3≫ and by the FCT - Foundation for Science and Technology ≪FCT/13263/4/8/2015/S≫. This work is part of the INCT of the Future Internet for Smart Cities ≪CNPq 465446/2014-0, CAPES 88887.136422/2017-00 and FAPESP 2014/50937-1≫.

Authors' contributions

KV, DPA, and MRM carried out the analysis of the State of the Art related with Internet of Everything, Fog and the Orchestration of resources in these environments; even more, they participated in the sequence alignment and drafted the manuscript. CS, DFA, LFB, and NL participated in the identification and description of the orchestration research challenges presented in Fog environments. MC, MV, EM[1], and EM[2] conceived and designed the study, besides reviewed the manuscript critically for important intellectual content. All authors read and approved the final manuscript.

Author details

[1]Department of Informatics Engineering, University of Coimbra, Polo II - Pinhal de Marrocos, 3030-290, Coimbra, Portugal. [2]Institute of Computing - University of Campinas, Av. Albert Einstein, 1251, Campinas - São Paulo, Brazil.

References

1. EU Commision. Communication from the Commision to the European Parliament, the Council, the European Economic and Social Committee and the Committee of the Regions. Towards a Thriving Data-Driven Economy. 2014. http://bit.ly/2wlVbVj. Accessed 21 Feb 2017.
2. Senna C, Batista DM, Soares Junior MA, Madeira ERM, Fonseca NLS. Experiments with a self-management system for virtual networks. In: Proceedings of the XXIX Brazilian Symposium on Computer Networks and Distributed Systems (SBRC 2011) - II Workshop de Pesquisa Experimental da Internet do Futuro (WPEIF 2011). Campo Grande: Brazilian Computer Society (SBC); 2011. p. 7–10.
3. Dastjerdi AV, Buyya R. Fog computing: Helping the internet of things realize its potential. Computer. 2016;49(8):112–6. https://doi.org/10.1109/MC.2016.245.
4. Kazmi A, Jan Z, Zappa A, Serrano M. Overcoming the heterogeneity in the internet of things for smart cities. In: Podnar Žarko I, Broering A, Soursos S, Serrano M, editors. Interoperability and Open-Source Solutions for the Internet of Things. Cham: Springer; 2017. p. 20–35.
5. Byers CC, Wetterwald P. Fog computing distributing data and intelligence for resiliency and scale necessary for iot: The internet of things (ubiquity symposium). Ubiquity. 2015;2015(November):4–1412. https://doi.org/10.1145/2822875.
6. Gubbi J, Buyya R, Marusic S, Palaniswami M. Internet of things (iot): A vision, architectural elements, and future directions. Future Gener Comput Syst. 2013;29(7):1645–1660. https://doi.org/10.1016/j.future.2013.01.010.
7. ITU-T. Overview ot the Internet of Things: ITU; 2012. http://www.itu.int/rec/T-REC-Y.2060-201206-I. Accessed 29 May 2017.
8. Minerva R, Biru A, Rotondi D. Towards a definition of the internet of things (iot): IEEE; 2015. http://bit.ly/2rMn5uS. Accessed 26 Jan 2017.
9. Kai K, Cong W, Tao L. Fog computing for vehicular ad-hoc networks: paradigms, scenarios, and issues. J China Univ Posts Telecommun. 2016;23(2):56–96. https://doi.org/10.1016/S1005-8885(16)60021-3.
10. Vaquero LM, Rodero-Merino L, Caceres J, Lindner M. A break in the clouds: towards a cloud definition. SIGCOMM Comput Commun Rev. 2008;39(1):50–5.
11. Geelan J, Klems M, Cohen R, Kaplan J, Gourlay D, Gaw P, Edwards D, de Haaff B, Kepes B, Sheynkman K, Sultan O, Hartig K, Pritzker J, Doerksen T, von Eicken T, Wallis P, Sheehan M, Dodge D, Ricadela A, Martin B, Kepes B, Berger IW. Twenty-one experts define cloud computing. Electron Mag. 2009. http://cloudcomputing.sys-con.com/node/612375. Accessed 05 Sept 2017.
12. Mell P, Grance T. The NIST definition of cloud computing. Technical report, National Institute of Standards and Technology, Information Technology Laboratory. 2009.
13. Bradley J, Loucks J, Macaulay J, Noronha A. Internet of everything (ioe) value index. Technical report, Cisco Systems Inc. 2013.
14. Atzori L, Iera A, Morabito G. The internet of things: A survey. Comput Netw. 2010;54(15):2787–805. https://doi.org/10.1016/j.comnet.2010.05.010.
15. Vaquero LM, Rodero-Merino L. Finding your way in the fog: Towards a comprehensive definition of fog computing. SIGCOMM Comput Commun Rev. 2014;44(5):27–32. https://doi.org/10.1145/2677046.2677052.
16. Yi S, Li C, Li Q. A survey of fog computing: Concepts, applications and issues. In: Proceedings of the 2015 Workshop on Mobile Big Data. Mobidata '15. New York: ACM; 2015. p. 37–42. https://doi.org/10.1145/2757384.2757397.
17. Yi S, Hao Z, Qin Z, Li Q. Fog computing: Platform and applications. In: 2015 Third IEEE Workshop on Hot Topics in Web Systems and Technologies (HotWeb); 2015. p. 73–8. https://doi.org/10.1109/HotWeb.2015.22.
18. Chiang M, Zhang T. Fog and iot: An overview of research opportunities. IEEE Internet Things J. 2016;3(6):854–64. https://doi.org/10.1109/JIOT.2016.2584538.
19. Hung SC, Hsu H, Lien SY, Chen KC. Architecture harmonization between cloud radio access networks and fog networks. IEEE Access. 2015;3:3019–34. https://doi.org/10.1109/ACCESS.2015.2509638.
20. Group OCAW. OpenFog Reference Architecture for Fog Computing. Technical report, OpenFog Consortium. 2017.

21. Verbelen T, Simoens P, De Turck F, Dhoedt B. Cloudlets: Bringing the cloud to the mobile user. In: Proceedings of the Third ACM Workshop on Mobile Cloud Computing and Services. MCS '12; 2012. p. 29–36. https://doi.org/10.1145/2307849.2307858.

22. Jararweh Y, Tawalbeh L, Ababneh F, Dosari F. Resource efficient mobile computing using cloudlet infrastructure. In: 2013 IEEE 9th International Conference on Mobile Ad-hoc and Sensor Networks; 2013. p. 373–7. https://doi.org/10.1109/MSN.2013.75.

23. Gao Y, Hu W, Ha K, Amos B, Pillai P, Satyanarayanan M. Are cloudlets necessary? Technical report, Carnegie Mellon University, School of Computer Science. 2015.

24. Cisco. Fog Computing and the Internet of Things: Extend the Cloud to Where the Things Are. Technical report, Cisco. 2015.

25. Cisco. The Zettabyte Era: Trends and Analysis. Technical report, Cisco. 2016.

26. Bonomi F, Milito R, Natarajan P, Zhu J. In: Bessis N, Dobre C, editors. Fog Computing: A Platform for Internet of Things and Analytics. Cham: Springer; 2014, pp. 169–86.

27. Bonomi F, Milito R, Zhu J, Addepalli S. Fog computing and its role in the internet of things. In: Proceedings of the First Edition of the MCC Workshop on Mobile Cloud Computing. MCC '12; 2012. p. 13–6.

28. Botta A, de Donato W, Persico V, Pescapé A. Integration of cloud computing and internet of things: A survey. Futur Gener Comput Syst. 2016;56:684–700. https://doi.org/10.1016/j.future.2015.09.021.

29. Varshney P, Simmhan Y. Demystifying fog computing: Characterizing architectures, applications and abstractions. In: 2017 IEEE 1st International Conference on Fog and Edge Computing (ICFEC). Madrid: IEEE; 2017. p. 115–24. https://doi.org/10.1109/ICFEC.2017.20.

30. Jazdi N. Cyber physical systems in the context of industry 4.0. In: 2014 IEEE International Conference on Automation, Quality and Testing, Robotics; 2014. p. 1–4. https://doi.org/10.1109/AQTR.2014.6857843.

31. Breivold HP, Sandström K. Internet of things for industrial automation – challenges and technical solutions. In: 2015 IEEE International Conference on Data Science and Data Intensive Systems; 2015. p. 532–9. https://doi.org/10.1109/DSDIS.2015.11.

32. Rotsos C, Farshad A, Hart N, Aguado A, Bidkar S, Sideris K, King D, Fawcett L, Bird J, Mauthe A, Race N, Hutchison D. Baguette: Towards end-to-end service orchestration in heterogeneous networks. In: 2016 15th International Conference on Ubiquitous Computing and Communications and 2016 International Symposium on Cyberspace and Security (IUCC-CSS); 2016. p. 196–203. https://doi.org/10.1109/IUCC-CSS.2016.035.

33. Fitbit, Inc. Fitbit. https://www.fitbit.com. Accessed 01 Aug 2017.

34. Alphabet Inc. Google Fit SDK. https://developers.google.com/fit. Accessed 30 Aug 2017.

35. Apple Technology Company. HealthKit. https://developer.apple.com/healthkit/. Accessed 29 Aug 2017.

36. Farahani B, Firouzi F, Chang V, Badaroglu M, Constant N, Mankodiya K. Towards fog-driven iot ehealth: Promises and challenges of iot in medicine and healthcare. Futur Gener Comput Syst. 2017.

37. Kraemer FA, Braten AE, Tamkittikhun N, Palma D. Fog computing in healthcare: A review and discussion. IEEE Access. 2017;5: 9206–22.

38. Hosseini MP, Hajisami A, Pompili D. Real-time epileptic seizure detection from eeg signals via random subspace ensemble learning. In: 2016 IEEE International Conference on Autonomic Computing (ICAC). Wurzburg: IEEE; 2016. p. 209–18. http://dx.doi.org/10.1109/ICAC.2016.57.

39. Monteiro A, Dubey H, Mahler L, Yang Q, Mankodiya K. Fit: A fog computing device for speech tele-treatments. In: 2016 IEEE International Conference on Smart Computing (SMARTCOMP). St. Louis: IEEE; 2016. p. 1–3. https://doi.org/10.1109/SMARTCOMP.2016.7501692.

40. Borgia E. The internet of things vision. Comput Commun. 2014;54(C): 1–31. https://doi.org/10.1016/j.comcom.2014.09.008.

41. Saini M, Alam KM, Guo H, Alelaiwi A, El Saddik A. Incloud: a cloud-based middleware for vehicular infotainment systems. Multimedia Tools Appl. 2017;76(9):11621–49. https://doi.org/10.1007/s11042-015-3158-4.

42. Rotsos C, King D, Farshad A, Bird J, Fawcett L, Georgalas N, Gunkel M, Shiomoto K, Wang A, Mauthe A, Race N, Hutchison D. Network service orchestration standardization: A technology survey. Comput Stand Interfaces. 2017;54:203–15. https://doi.org/10.1016/j.csi.2016.12.006. SI: Standardization SDN&NFV.

43. Chen M, Hao Y, Li Y, Lai C, Wu D. On the computation offloading at ad hoc cloudlet: architecture and service modes. IEEE Commun Mag. 2015;53(6):18–24. https://doi.org/10.1109/MCOM.2015.7120041.

44. Satyanarayanan M, Bahl P, Caceres R, Davies N. The case for vm-based cloudlets in mobile computing. IEEE Pervasive Comput. 2009;8(4):14–23. https://doi.org/10.1109/MPRV.2009.82.

45. Amazon, Inc. AWS Greengrass. https://aws.amazon.com/greengrass. Accessed 07 Feb 2018.

46. Microsoft. Microsoft Azure - IoT Edge. https://azure.microsoft.com/en-us/services/iot-edge. Accessed 07 Feb 2018.

47. Pham X-Q, Huh E-N. Towards task scheduling in a cloud-fog computing system. In: 2016 18th Asia-Pacific Network Operations and Management Symposium (APNOMS). Kanazawa: IEEE; 2016. p. 1–4. https://doi.org/10.1109/APNOMS.2016.7737240.

48. Song C, Qu Z, Blumm N, Barabási A-L. Limits of predictability in human mobility. Science. 2010;327(5968):1018–21. https://doi.org/10.1126/science.1177170.

49. Bittencourt L, Diaz-Montes J, Buyya R, Rana OF, Parashar M. Mobility-aware application scheduling in fog computing. IEEE Cloud Comput. 2017;4(2):26–35. https://doi.org/10.1109/MCC.2017.27.

50. Sun X, Ansari N. Edgeiot: Mobile edge computing for the internet of things. IEEE Commun Mag. 2016;54(12):22–9. https://doi.org/10.1109/MCOM.2016.1600492CM.

51. The Linux Foundation. Kubernetes. https://kubernetes.io. Accessed 18 Apr 2018.

52. Ooi BY, Chan HY, Cheah Y-N. Dynamic service placement and redundancy to ensure service availability during resource failures. In: 2010 International Symposium on Information Technology, vol. 2; 2010. p. 715–20. https://doi.org/10.1109/ITSIM.2010.5561605.

53. Campista MEM, Esposito PM, Moraes IM, k. Costa LHM, b. Duarte OCM, Passos DG, Albuquerque CVND, Saade DCM, Rubinstein MG. Routing metrics and protocols for wireless mesh networks. IEEE Netw. 2008;22(1): 6–12. https://doi.org/10.1109/MNET.2008.4435897.

54. Alotaibi E, Mukherjee B. Survey paper: A survey on routing algorithms for wireless ad-hoc and mesh networks. Comput Netw. 2012;56(2): 940–65. https://doi.org/10.1016/j.comnet.2011.10.011.

55. Paris S, Nita-Rotaru C, Martignon F, Capone A. Cross-layer metrics for reliable routing in wireless mesh networks. IEEE/ACM Trans Netw. 2013;21(3):1003–16. https://doi.org/10.1109/TNET.2012.2230337.

56. Marín-Tordera E, Masip-Bruin X, García-Almiñana J, Jukan A, Ren G-J, Zhu J. Do we all really know what a fog node is? current trends towards an open definition. Comput Commun. 2017;109:117–30. https://doi.org/10.1016/j.comcom.2017.05.013.

57. Marín-Tordera E, Masip-Bruin X, Almiñana JG, Jukan A, Ren G, Zhu J, Farre J. What is a fog node A tutorial on current concepts towards a common definition. CoRR. 2016;abs/1611.09193. http://arxiv.org/abs/1611.09193.

58. Masip-Bruin X, Marín-Tordera E, Tashakor G, Jukan A, Ren G-J. Foggy clouds and cloudy fogs: a real need for coordinated management of fog-to-cloud computing systems. IEEE Wireless Communications. 2016;23(5):120–28. https://doi.org/10.1109/MWC.2016.7721750.

59. Mahmud R, Buyya R. Fog computing: A taxonomy, survey and future directions. CoRR. 2016;abs/1611.05539. http://arxiv.org/abs/1611.05539.

60. Deng R, Lu R, Lai C, Luan TH, Liang H. Optimal workload allocation in fog-cloud computing toward balanced delay and power consumption. IEEE Internet Things J. 2016;3(6):1171–81. https://doi.org/10.1109/JIOT.2016.2565516.

61. Bernstein D, Ludvigson E, Sankar K, Diamond S, Morrow M. Blueprint for the intercloud - protocols and formats for cloud computing interoperability. In: Proceedings of the 2009 Fourth International Conference on Internet and Web Applications and Services. ICIW '09. Washington: IEEE Computer Society; 2009. p. 328–36.

62. Assis MRM, Bittencourt L, Tolosana-Calasanz R. Cloud federation: characterisation and conceptual model. In: 2014 IEEE/ACM 7th International Conference on Utility and Cloud Computing. London: IEEE; 2014. p. 585–90. https://doi.org/10.1109/UCC.2014.90.

63. Wen Z, Yang R, Garraghan P, Lin T, Xu J, Rovatsos M. Fog orchestration for internet of things services. IEEE Internet Comput. 2017;21(2):16–24. https://doi.org/10.1109/MIC.2017.36.

64. Barnaghi P, Wang W, Henson C, Taylor K. Semantics for the internet of things: Early progress and back to the future. Int J Semant Web Inf Syst. 2012;8(1):1–21.

65. Shin S, Seo S, Eom S, Jung J, Lee KH. A pub/sub-based fog computing architecture for internet-of-vehicles. In: 2016 IEEE International Conference on Cloud Computing Technology and Science (CloudCom). Luxembourg City: IEEE; 2016. p. 90–3. https://doi.org/10.1109/CloudCom.2016.0029.

66. Singh D, Tripathi G, Alberti AM, Jara A. Semantic edge computing and iot architecture for military health services in battlefield. In: 2017 14th IEEE Annual Consumer Communications Networking Conference (CCNC). Las Vegas: IEEE; 2017. p. 185–90. https://doi.org/10.1109/CCNC.2017.7983103.

67. Abreu DP, Velasquez K, Pinto AM, Curado M, Monteiro E. Describing the internet of things with an ontology: The suscity project case study. In: 2017 20th Conference on Innovations in Clouds, Internet and Networks (ICIN). Paris: IEEE; 2017. p. 294–9. https://doi.org/10.1109/ICIN.2017.7899427.

68. W3C. OWL 2. https://www.w3.org/TR/owl2-primer. Accessed 25 July 2017.

69. Pham X-Q, Man ND, Tri NDT, Thai NQ, Huh E-N. A cost- and performance-effective approach for task scheduling based on collaboration between cloud and fog computing. Int J Distrib Sens Netw. 2017;13(11):1–16. https://doi.org/10.1177/1550147717742073.

70. Velasquez K, Perez Abreu D, Curado M, Monteiro E. Service placement for latency reduction in the internet of things. Ann Telecommun. 2017;72:105–15. https://doi.org/10.1007/s12243-016-0524-9.

71. Chen Y-C, Lim Y-S, Gibbens RJ, Nahum EM, Khalili R, Towsley D. A measurement-based study of multipath tcp performance over wireless networks. In: Proceedings of the 2013 Conference on Internet Measurement Conference. IMC '13. New York: ACM; 2013. p. 455–68. https://doi.org/10.1145/2504730.2504751.

72. Vulimiri A, Michel O, Godfrey PB, Shenker S. More is less: Reducing latency via redundancy. In: Proceedings of the 11th ACM Workshop on Hot Topics in Networks. HotNets-XI. New York: ACM; 2012. p. 13–8. https://doi.org/10.1145/2390231.2390234.

73. Vulimiri A, Godfrey PB, Mittal R, Sherry J, Ratnasamy S, Shenker S. Low latency via redundancy. In: Proceedings of the Ninth ACM Conference on Emerging Networking Experiments and Technologies. CoNEXT '13. New York: ACM; 2013. p. 283–94. https://doi.org/10.1145/2535372.2535392.

74. Moens H, Hanssens B, Dhoedt B, Turck FD. Hierarchical network-aware placement of service oriented applications in clouds. In: 2014 IEEE Network Operations and Management Symposium (NOMS); 2014. p. 1–8. https://doi.org/10.1109/NOMS.2014.6838230.

75. Xiong G, Hu Y-X, Tian L, Lan J-L, Li J-F, Zhou Q. A virtual service placement approach based on improved quantum genetic algorithm. Front Inf Technol Electron Eng. 2016;17(7):661–71. https://doi.org/10.1631/FITEE.1500494.

76. Steiner M, Gaglianello BG, Gurbani V, Hilt V, Roome WD, Scharf M, Voith T. Network-aware service placement in a distributed cloud environment. In: Proceedings of the ACM SIGCOMM 2012 Conference on Applications, Technologies, Architectures, and Protocols for Computer Communication. SIGCOMM '12. New York: ACM; 2012. p. 73–74. https://doi.org/10.1145/2342356.2342366.

77. Zhang Q, Zhu Q, Zhani MF, Boutaba R, Hellerstein JL. Dynamic service placement in geographically distributed clouds. IEEE J Sel Areas Commun. 2013;31(12):762–72.

78. Wang S, Urgaonkar R, Chan K, He T, Zafer M, Leung KK. Dynamic service placement for mobile micro-clouds with predicted future costs. In: 2015 IEEE International Conference on Communications (ICC); 2015. p. 5504–10. https://doi.org/10.1109/ICC.2015.7249199.

79. Dolui K, Datta SK. Comparison of edge computing implementations: Fog computing, cloudlet and mobile edge computing. In: 2017 Global Internet of Things Summit (GIoTS); 2017. p. 1–6. https://doi.org/10.1109/GIOTS.2017.8016213.

80. Osanaiye O, Chen S, Yan Z, Lu R, Choo KKR, Dlodlo M. From cloud to fog computing: A review and a conceptual live vm migration framework. IEEE Access. 2017;5:8284–300. https://doi.org/10.1109/ACCESS.2017.2692960.

81. Fajjari I, Aitsaadi N, Pujolle G. Cloud networking: An overview of virtual network embedding strategies. In: Global Information Infrastructure Symposium - GIIS 2013; 2013. p. 1–7. https://doi.org/10.1109/GIIS.2013.6684379.

82. Xiao J, Boutaba R. Reconciling the overlay and underlay tussle. IEEE/ACM Trans Netw. 2014;22(5):1489–502. https://doi.org/10.1109/TNET.2013.2281276.

83. Sterbenz JPG, Çetinkaya EK, Hameed MA, Jabbar A, Qian S, Rohrer JP. Evaluation of network resilience, survivability, and disruption tolerance: analysis, topology generation, simulation, and experimentation. Telecommun Syst. 2013;52(2):705–36. https://doi.org/10.1007/s11235-011-9573-6.

84. Pahl C, Lee B. Containers and clusters for edge cloud architectures – a technology review. In: 2015 3rd International Conference on Future Internet of Things and Cloud; 2015. p. 379–86. https://doi.org/10.1109/FiCloud.2015.35.

85. Matias J, Garay J, Toledo N, Unzilla J, Jacob E. Toward an sdn-enabled nfv architecture. IEEE Commun Mag. 2015;53(4):187–193. https://doi.org/10.1109/MCOM.2015.7081093.

86. Perez Abreu D, Velasquez K, Curado M, Monteiro E. A resilient internet of things architecture for smart cities. Ann Telecommun. 2017;72:19–30. https://doi.org/10.1007/s12243-016-0530-y.

87. Taleb T, Ksentini A. Follow me cloud: interworking federated clouds and distributed mobile networks. IEEE Netw. 2013;27(5):12–9. https://doi.org/10.1109/MNET.2013.6616110.

88. Nadembega A, Hafid AS, Brisebois R. Mobility prediction model-based service migration procedure for follow me cloud to support qos and qoe. In: 2016 IEEE International Conference on Communications (ICC); 2016. p. 1–6. https://doi.org/10.1109/ICC.2016.7511148.

89. Patel M, Chaudhary S, Garg S. Machine learning based statistical prediction model for improving performance of live virtual machine migration. J Eng. 2016;2016:9. https://doi.org/10.1155/2016/3061674.

90. Amato F, Moscato F. Exploiting cloud and workflow patterns for the analysis of composite cloud services. Futur Gener Comput Syst. 2017;67:255–65. https://doi.org/10.1016/j.future.2016.06.035.

91. Liu J, Zhao T, Zhou S, Cheng Y, Niu Z. Concert: a cloud-based architecture for next-generation cellular systems. IEEE Wirel Commun. 2014;21(6):14–22.

92. Goldberg S. Why is it taking so long to secure internet routing? Commun ACM. 2014;57(10):56–63. https://doi.org/10.1145/2659899.

93. Butler KRB, Farley TR, McDaniel P, Rexford J. A survey of BGP security issues and solutions. Proc IEEE. 2010;98(1):100–22. https://doi.org/10.1109/JPROC.2009.2034031.

94. Oberheide J, Cooke E, Jahanian F. Cloudav: N-version antivirus in the network cloud. In: van Oorschot PC, editor. Proceedings of the 17th USENIX Security Symposium. Berkeley: USENIX Association; 2008. p. 91–106.

95. Krishnan S, Taylor T, Monrose F, McHugh J. Crossing the threshold: Detecting network malfeasance via sequential hypothesis testing. In: 43rd Annual IEEE/IFIP International Conference on Dependable Systems and Networks (DSN). Budapest: IEEE; 2013. p. 1–12. https://doi.org/10.1109/DSN.2013.6575364.

96. Wu DJ, Taly A, Shankar A, Boneh D. Privacy, discovery, and authentication for the internet of things. In: Askoxylakis IG, Ioannidis S, Katsikas SK, Meadows CA, editors. Proceedings of the 21st European Symposium on Research in Computer Security. Lecture Notes in Computer Science. vol 9879. Cham: Springer International Publishing; 2016. p. 301–19.

97. Dwork C. Differential privacy: A survey of results. In: Agrawal M, Du D, Duan Z, Li A, editors. Proceedings of the 5th International Conference on Theory and Applications of Models of Computation TAMC. Lecture Notes in Computer Science, vol. 4978. Berlin: Springer Berlin Heidelberg; 2008. p. 1–19.

98. de Brito MS, Hoque S, Magedanz T, Steinke R, Willner A, Nehls D, Keils O, Schreiner F. A service orchestration architecture for fog-enabled infrastructures. In: 2017 Second International Conference on Fog and Mobile Edge Computing (FMEC). Valencia: IEEE; 2017. p. 127–32. https://doi.org/10.1109/FMEC.2017.7946419.

99. Stojmenovic I, Wen S, Huang X, Luan H. An overview of fog computing and its security issues. Concurrency Comput Pract Experience. 2016;28(10):2991–3005.

100. Conti M, Dragoni N, Lesyk V. A survey of man in the middle attacks. IEEE Commun Surv Tutorials. 2016;18(3):2027–51.

101. Dastjerdi AV, Gupta H, Calheiros RN, Ghosh SK, Buyya R. Fog computing: Principles, architectures, and applications. CoRR. 2016;abs/1601.02752. http://arxiv.org/abs/1601.02752.

102. Misra P, Simmhan YL, Warrior J. Towards a practical architecture for the next generation internet of things. CoRR. 2015;abs/1502.00797. http://arxiv.org/abs/1502.00797.

103. Sabt M, Achemlal M, Bouabdallah A. Trusted execution environment: What it is, and what it is not. In: 2015 IEEE Trustcom/BigDataSE/ISPA, vol. 1. Helsinki: IEEE; 2015. p. 57–64. https://doi.org/10.1109/Trustcom.2015.357.

104. Celesti A, Tusa F, Villari M, Puliafito A. Evaluating a distributed identity provider trusted network with delegated authentications for cloud federation. In: CLOUD COMPUTING 2011, The Second International Conference on Cloud Computing, GRIDs, and Virtualization; 2011. p. 79–85.

105. ITU. X.509 : Information technology - Open Systems Interconnection. http://www.itu.int/rec/T-REC-X.509. Accessed 28 July 2017.

106. OASIS. SAML Version 2.0. http://saml.xml.org/saml-specifications. Accessed 29 July 2017.

107. Tran TX, Hajisami A, Pandey P, Pompili D. Collaborative mobile edge computing in 5g networks: New paradigms, scenarios, and challenges. IEEE Commun Mag. 2017;55(4):54–61. https://doi.org/10.1109/MCOM.2017.1600863.

108. Ahmed A, Ahmed E. A survey on mobile edge computing. In: 2016 10th International Conference on Intelligent Systems and Control (ISCO); 2016. p. 1–8. https://doi.org/10.1109/ISCO.2016.7727082.

109. Satyanarayanan M, Chen Z, Ha K, Hu W, Richter W, Pillai P. Cloudlets: at the leading edge of mobile-cloud convergence. In: 6th International Conference on Mobile Computing, Applications and Services; 2014. p. 1–9. https://doi.org/10.4108/icst.mobicase.2014.257757.

110. Ruay-Shiung-Chang, Gao J, Gruhn V, He J, Roussos G, Tsai W-T. Mobile cloud computing research - issues, challenges and needs. In: 2013 IEEE Seventh International Symposium on Service-Oriented System Engineering; 2013. p. 442–53. https://doi.org/10.1109/SOSE.2013.96.

111. ETSI, Vodafone, IBM, Huawei, Intel, Nokia Networks, NTT DOCOMO. Mobile-edge computing: Introductory technical white paper. Technical report, ETSI Industry Specification Group. 2014.

112. Velasquez K, Abreu DP, Gonçalves D., Bittencourt L, Curado M, Monteiro E, Madeira E. Service orchestration in fog environments. In: 2017 IEEE 5th International Conference on Future Internet of Things and Cloud (FiCloud); 2017. p. 329–36. https://doi.org/10.1109/FiCloud.2017.49.

113. Centre for Informatics and Systems - UC. FCT/ CAPES - SORTS: Supporting the Orchestration of Resilient and Trustworthy Fog Services. https://www.cisuc.uc.pt/projects/show/228. Accessed 29 Aug 2017.

114. TOSCA. Topology and Orchestration Specification for Cloud Applications (TOSCA) Version 1.0. 2013. http://docs.oasis-open.org/tosca/TOSCA/v1.0/os/TOSCA-v1.0-os.pdf. Accessed 17 Feb 2015.

115. Network Functions Virtualisation (NFV) ETSI Industry Specification Group (ISG). ETSI NFV Work Group. Network Functions Virtualisation (NFV); Management and Orchestration. http://bit.ly/2IJtqAR. Accessed 28 Apr 2017.

116. ETSI. Technical report, ETSI Industry Specification Group. 2016.

6

Model-driven development of user interfaces for IoT systems via domain-specific components and patterns

Marco Brambilla[1] ⓘ*, Eric Umuhoza[1] ⓘ and Roberto Acerbis[2]

Abstract

Internet of Things technologies and applications are evolving and continuously gaining traction in all fields and environments, including homes, cities, services, industry and commercial enterprises. However, still many problems need to be addressed. For instance, the IoT vision is mainly focused on the technological and infrastructure aspect, and on the management and analysis of the huge amount of generated data, while so far the development of front-end and user interfaces for IoT has not played a relevant role in research. On the contrary, user interfaces can play a key role in the acceptance of IoT solutions by final adopters. In this paper we discuss the requirements and usage scenarios covering the front end aspects of IoT systems and we present a model-driven approach to the design of such interfaces by: defining specific components and design patterns using a visual modeling language for IoT applications; describing an implementation of the solution that comprises also automatic code generation from models; and by showing the solution at work.

Keywords: Internet of things, Model-driven development, User interaction, Design pattern, Mobile applications, Modeling, User experience, Software engineering, IFML

1 Introduction

User interaction plays a crucial role in a large class of software and systems. This is true also for the Internet of Things (IoT) systems, although this aspect has been frequently neglected. Indeed, the current IoT vision is mainly focused on the technological and infrastructural aspect, and on the management and analysis of the huge amount of generated data [1–3]. So far, the development of the front-end of IoT applications and user interfaces for IoT has been covered by a very limited set of research [4–6]. On the other side, a lot of research has been focusing on scenarios related to industrial use of IoT (IIoT) [7, 8], and machine-to-machine (or sensor-to-sensor) communication [9–11]. Initiatives like the Industrial Internet Consortium (IIC)[1] demonstrate this trend and the growing awareness of the importance of this within the companies. However, IoT has gone far beyond the industrial plant context: IoT is (and will more and more be) a part of the everyday life of consumers too. Therefore, exactly as it has happened in other fields like the Web, mobile and wearable, user interfaces in the IoT ecosystem will play more and more a key role in the end user acceptance.

Indeed, the intelligent things connected together by the IoT paradigm can cooperate and exchange information, but their ultimate goal is to provide value to the people. Such value can be perceived only through appropriate user interfaces, which visualize information (through dashboard, reports, or infographics), let user navigate the information, and also interact with the devices, by setting properties or regulating their behavior.

In this paper we propose **a model-driven approach to the design of user interfaces of IoT systems**, by defining IoT-specific UI components and design patterns. In particular, we focus on the following research questions, phrased as research objectives:

- *RQ1*: Define the main domain-specific concepts for IoT and the typical use cases;
- *RQ2*: Define a (visual) modeling language for the development of the user interaction aspects of IoT applications;

*Correspondence: marco.brambilla@polimi.it
[1]Politecnico di Milano. Dipartimento di Elettronica, Informazione e Bioingegneria, Piazza L. Da Vinci 32, 20133 Milan, Italy
Full list of author information is available at the end of the article

- **RQ3**: Define a set of design practices that increase productivity and simplifies the design of IoT front-ends;
- **RQ4**: Implement model-driven tools covering the design, deployment, and execution phases of IoT applications.

In the rest of the paper we address these questions by defining solutions and demonstrating the feasibility of the proposed approaches with examples and use cases. In particular, the solutions we propose focus on extending the standard IFML language adopted by the Object Management Group (OMG) [12], together with methodological guidelines and tool support for implementation. The research has therefore addressed the following aspects:

1. Study of the IoT domain, adoption and its current applications (responding to **RQ1**);
2. Extraction of common use cases for the IoT (responding to **RQ1**). The use cases identified during this phase include: device management, device discovery (or search), interaction with devices, and information collection from devices;
3. Definition of a set of new IFML components allowing the modeling of the IoT user interactions (responding to **RQ2**);
4. Definition of a set of reusable design patterns (responding to **RQ3**);
5. Implementation of the proposed solution as an IoT management platform, design tools, and code generators (responding to **RQ4**).

The paper is organized as follows: Section 2 discusses the background on IFML language; Section 3 shows the common use cases of the IoT systems; Section 4 presents our extensions to IFML tailored to IoT-based applications; Section 5 introduces design patterns for the modeling of the user interactions with IoT systems; Section 6 shows an example; Section 7 summarizes our implementation; Section 8 describes three industrial cases where the approach has been applied and validate the advantages of the solution; Section 9 reviews the related work; and Section 10 concludes.

2 Background on IFML

The Interaction Flow Modeling Language (IFML) is designed for expressing the content, user interaction and control behavior of the front-end of software applications. Its metamodel uses the basic data types from the UML metamodel, specializes a number of UML metaclasses as the basis for IFML metaclasses, and presumes that the IFML Domain Model is represented in UML.

An IFML model supports the following design perspectives: (i) The *view structure specification*, which consists of the definition of view containers, their nesting relationships, their visibility, and their reachability; (ii) The *view content specification*, which consists of the definition

of `ViewComponents`, i.e., content and data entry elements contained within `ViewContainers`; (iii) The *events specification*, which consists of the definition of `Events` that may affect the state of the user interface. `Events` can be produced by the user's interaction, by the application, or by an external system; (iv) The *event transition specification*, which consists of the definition of the effect of an `Event` on the user interface; (v) The *parameter binding specification*, which consists of the definition of the input-output dependencies between `ViewComponents` and between `ViewComponents` and `Actions`; and (vi) The reference to `Actions` triggered by the user's events. The effect of an `Event` is represented by an `InteractionFlow` connection, which connects the event to the `ViewContainer` or `ViewComponent` affected by the `Event`. The `InteractionFlow` expresses a change of state of the user interface: the occurrence of the event causes a transition of state that produces a change in the user interface.

Figure 1 shows a simple example of IFML model, describing a user interface where the user can search for a product by entering some search criteria in the Product Search Form. The model consists of a `ViewContainer` *Products* (describing a screen or Web page) which contains two `ViewComponents` (visual widgets positioned in the screen), namely the *Product Search* `Form`, where the user can enter the search criteria, and the *ProductResultList* `List`, which displays the search results. Furthermore, a *Product Deletion* `Action` can be triggered when the user selects the *Delete* `Event` associated to *ProductResultList*. This example model conforms to the IFML metamodel, an excerpt of which is shown in Fig. 2.

2.1 Mobile IFML

Front-end design is a more complex task in mobile applications due mainly to: (i) the smallness of the screens of mobile devices. This constraint requires an extra effort in interaction design at the purpose of exploiting at the best the limited space available; (ii) Mobile apps interact with other software and hardware features installed on the device they are running on; and (iii) the user interaction which is basically done by performing precise gestures on the screen or by interacting with other sensors. These interactions often depend on the device, the operating system and the application itself. This section presents a mobile extension of IFML designed for expressing the content, user interaction, and control behaviour of the front-end of mobile applications [13]. An excerpt of those extensions, along with the IoT extensions presented in Section 4, is depicted in Fig. 3.

2.1.1 Containers and components

This section presents the concepts added to IFML in order to model the containers and components that characterize

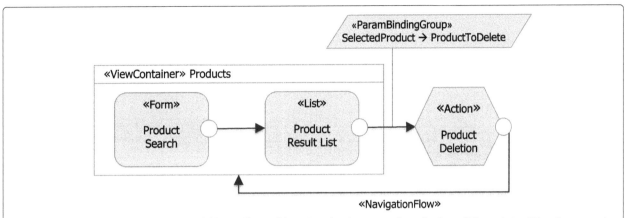

Fig. 1 IFML example: product search, listing and deletion. The model consists of a `ViewContainer` *Products* which contains two `ViewComponents` (*Product Search* form and *ProductResultList* `list`); and *Product Deletion* `Action` triggered once the user selects the *Delete* `Event` associated to *ProductResultList*

the mobile context. A new class called `Screen` has been defined to represent the screen of a mobile application. Since the screen is the main container of a mobile application, it extends the core class `ViewContainer` of the IFML standard. The class `ToolBar` represents a particular sub-container of the screen. It may contain other containers and may have on its boundary a list of events. It extends the core class `ViewContainer` of the IFML standard.

The class `MobileComponent` denotes the particular mobile view component such as button, image, and icon. A `MobileComponent` is subject to user events, described next.

A characteristic trait of mobile interfaces is the utilization of predefined `ViewContainers` devoted to specific functionalities that are provided at the operating system (including *Notifications* area and *Settings* panel). These system level containers provide economy of space and enforce a consistent usage of common features. The `MobileSystem` stereotype has been defined to distinguish these special `ViewContainers`. A `ViewContainer` stereotyped as `MobileSystem` denotes a fixed region of the interface, managed by mobile operating system or by another interface framework in a cross-application way. The `MobileSystem` stereotype can be applied also to A `ViewComponents` to highlight

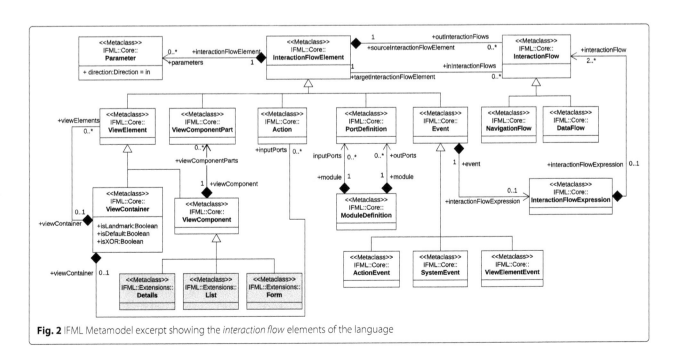

Fig. 2 IFML Metamodel excerpt showing the *interaction flow* elements of the language

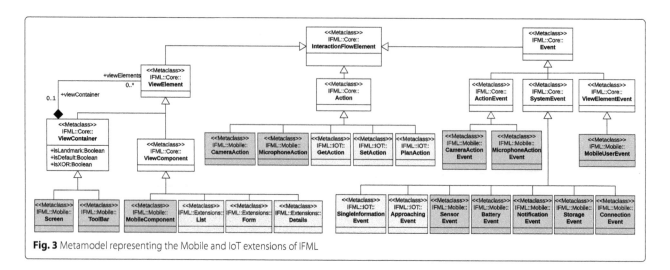

Fig. 3 Metamodel representing the Mobile and IoT extensions of IFML

that the interface uses the components of the system (as shown in Fig. 5).

2.1.2 Mobile context

The context is a runtime aspect of the system that determines how the user interface should be configured and the content that it may display. The context assumes a particular relevance in mobile applications, which must exploit all the available information to deliver the most efficient interface. Therefore, the context must gather all the dimensions that characterize the user's intent, the capacity of the access device and of the communication network, and the environment surrounding the user. A new class MobileContext extending the Context has been defined to express the mobile contextual features.

2.1.3 Events

In this section we describe the new event types that are defined within IFML for the mobile context. A new class MobileUserEvent allowing the modeling of the mobile user events have been defined. MobileUserEvent extends ViewElementEvent of the IFML. The MobileUserEvent is further extended to model the specific mobile user events. Its specific extensions include: DragDrop, DoubleTap, Touch, and LongPress. Each of them represents an event related to the gesture which triggers it.

The screens in Fig. 4a show an example of the usage of the LongPress gesture allowing the user to manage the selected list. Figure 4b shows a fragment of IFML model for lists management. When a user performs the LongPress gesture on one element of the list, a pop up containing information of the selected element is shown allowing her to edit or delete the list.

A new class MobileSystemEvent has been defined to express the mobile system events. It extends SystemEvent of the IFML. The following classes extend MobileSystemEvent for specific system events:

- SensorEvent, defining events related to the sensors of the device;
- BatteryEvent, describing the events related to the state of the battery;
- NotificationEvent, grouping the events related to the generic notifications handled by the operating system;
- StorageEvent, describing the events related to the archiving capacity; and
- ConnectionEvent, describing the events related to the connection state of the device.

MobileActionEvent class has been defined to model the events triggered by a mobile action. Among mobile actions, we have actions related to the photo camera such as the *Shoot* action and actions related to microphone. Figure 5 shows example of such events. A user takes a photo with the device's photo camera and the application displays the product corresponding to the taken photo if any. Once the photo is available, a screen asking the user if he wants to use or retake the photo is displayed. The *photo available* CameraActionEvent is associated to the CameraAction *shoot*.

3 Use cases

In this section we present the main use cases we identified for the IoT applications. Before proceeding with the use case specifications, we provide a quick summary of the IoT terminology used in the paper. In particular, we will make use of the following IoT concepts:

- *Device or Thing:* It denotes all types of devices which can generate information (about physical event or state) and initiate, modify, or maintain those events or states; or that can perform actions.
- *Category:* The IoT devices can be grouped into different *categories* based on some criterion such as type, features, and geographical location.

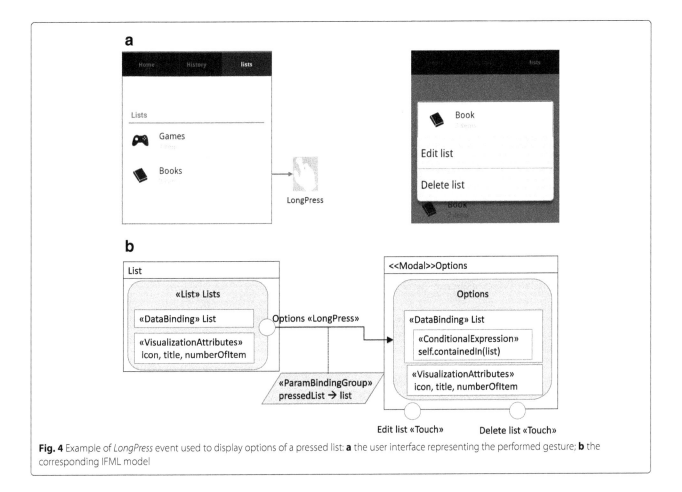

Fig. 4 Example of *LongPress* event used to display options of a pressed list: **a** the user interface representing the performed gesture; **b** the corresponding IFML model

- *Terminal:* A terminal is any device which can run an IoT application with a user interface which can control other devices through the network.
- *Communication:* The devices can communicate in different ways and can be connected with terminals and external systems. Several communication protocols for the IoT have been proposed around the IEEE 802.15.X standard.
- *External System:* With external system we refer to all the systems connected to a network in which the information of devices and terminals can be stored, processed and retrieved. Examples of the external

systems include enterprise management systems such as customer relationship management (CRM) and enterprise resource planning (ERP).

- *Intermediary:* It represents any device or system which acts as a gateway between the IoT device and the terminal in an indirect communication.

The use cases we identified for the IoT applications are based on our industrial experiences as well as on an extensive investigation on IoT applications available on the market and what is expected to be the user interface of the IoT applications in different areas of their application.

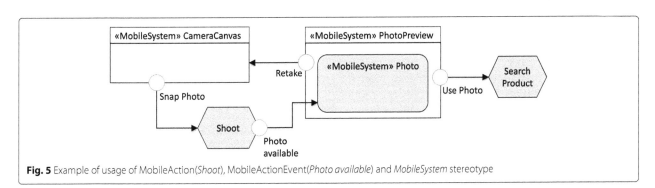

Fig. 5 Example of usage of MobileAction(*Shoot*), MobileActionEvent(*Photo available*) and *MobileSystem* stereotype

In particular, we rely on direct experience on scenarios in the fields of building monitoring (with sensors and actuators controlling the status of large venues used for public events), smart cities (covering the needs of monitoring people flow including pedestrians and vehicles, parking availability and public transportation), marketing and sales monitoring (for controlling interactions with store windows and artifacts), and massive sensor deployment on commercial goods for adaptive maintenance (large appliances). Furthermore, we investigated the possible uses of IoT equipped products for the consumer market, produced by famous vendors (Philips, bTicino, Vimar, and others). Out of this analysis we derived a set of abstract use cases that cover all these scenarios. We present those use cases using the following schema: for each use case we provide a *description*, *primary actor*, and *main tasks*. The detailed list of use cases is reported in Table 1.

The user of the IoT application could have different roles, defined as a set of allowed actions. The main roles are: *Administrator*, the user who has access rights to the whole system, including the external systems; *Performer*, the user who can manage and interact with the devices of the local network; and *Viewer*, the user who can display the information of the devices or the information about the environment monitored by those devices. The use cases reported in Table 1 essentially cover device and user management, IoT devices usage, and data management. The identified use cases are: Configure Access and Permission, Manage Devices, Interact with Devices, Manage Wait for Signal, Search Devices, Manage Notifications, Get Information from Devices, Visualize Information, Share Information, Store Information, Retrieve Stored Information. Their detailed characterization reported in Table 1 responds to **RQ1**.

4 Modeling language for IoT

In this section we address the specification of a domain-specific language for IoT UI design, thus responding to **RQ2**. The interactions between the user and the IoT systems, as shown in Fig. 6, can be logically divided in two phases: (i) **User ⇆ Terminal** communication. This phase represents the interactions between the user and the terminal used to access the IoT system; and (ii) **Terminal ⇆ IoT devices** communication. This phase represents the interactions between the terminal and the IoT devices. The first phase can be modeled using the IFML standard and its extensions, especially the Mobile IFML (introduced in Section 2.1). This section addresses the second phase of the interactions with the IoT system. It presents the new elements added to the IFML to model both the *events* and *actions* associated to the IoT devices.

4.1 Content model

This section presents the content model of an IoT system.

The designed model covers use cases presented in Section 3, with a multi-tenant and enterprise perspective. Indeed, the use cases described so far represent the perspective of a single IoT system. Based on this, we now aim at a platform that supports multiple IoT systems within and across enterprises. Therefore, the proposed model allows to define a unique infrastructure for a multi-tenant application platform that can serve multiple customers at the same time.

Figure 7 shows a piece of content model. The model comprehends the concepts needed for modeling the application's users and the structure of an organization and its customers and the concepts needed to define IoT services.

- *User*, it represents the physical user that access the application. The user can be either a *CustomerUser* or a *OrganizationUser* referring respectively to a customer or a company.
- *Tenant*, this concept defines an access domain for either an organization or a customer. The Tenant is characterized by its own configurations and graphical layout. It is the main partitioning condition for the data.
- *Organization*, it describes a company that offers a service to the customer. The organization produces and sells *Things* managed by the application. The organization belongs to a tenant or another organization.
- *Customer*, this concept describes a company that either bought or uses service from the organization. The customer has a reference to the organizations that sold the *Things* or provides technical assistance.
- *Branch*, it represents a sub organization unit belonging to a customer.
- *Location*, it represents a physical location owned by a Customer. The location is the place where a Thing is installed (e.g. office, store, and plant).
- *Thing*, this concept represents a generic object connected to Internet, able to send and receive data. The characteristics of a thing are defined by the corresponding *ThingDefinition* and it is bound to a specific *Location*.
- *ThingDefinition*, it represents the definition of a Thing. It describes the exposed *Metrics* and the supported *Command*.
- *Command*, it represents an instruction that can be executed by a Thing. A Command has a name and a set of *CommandParameter* characterized by a name and a type.
- *Metric*, this concept represents an observable characteristic of a Thing. It can be either a physical measure (e.g. temperature) or a value of an internal variable (e.g. number of prints and working hours). A metric

Table 1 IoT use cases

Use case	Description	Actor	Main tasks
Configure access and permissions	Allows the application owner or the administrator, to set the access rights for users, teams or roles.	Administrator	• Manage users, teams & roles • Access configuration • Permission configuration • Visualize information
Interact with devices	Allows the user to send a set of operations to the devices, which are in charge to perform them.	Administrator performer viewer	• Send operations • Manage routines
Manage devices	Allows the user to manage and configure the devices which belong to the system.	Administrator	• Include devices in the system • Remove devices from system • Manage categories • Include devices to categories • Assign a location
Manage wait for signal	Allows the user to connect the terminal to the network and start listening to the devices of that network.	Administrator performer viewer	• Activate wait for signal • Deactivate wait for signal
Manage notifications	Allows the user to receive the notifications coming from different devices directly or through an external system.	Administrator performer viewer	• Visualize notification • Save notification • Delete notification
Search devices	Allows the user to search for devices already registered to the system, belonging to the local or to external networks.	Administrator performer viewer	• Search a specific device • Search devices by category • Search devices by criteria
Store information	Defines how the system can store the information gathered by different devices about the environment or the state of the devices.	Administrator	• Store locally the information • Store externally the info • Store in a device the info
Retrieve stored information	Allows the user to retrieve information stored in the terminal or in an external system.	Administrator performer viewer	• Local information retrieval • External information retrieval
Get information from devices	Allows the user to request information to the devices of the network.	Administrator performer viewer	• Get information from devices associated to the application • Get information from devices associated to the external system • Get information from devices of the same network
Visualize information	Allow the user to visualize the information related to or produced by devices in different ways.	Administrator performer viewer	• Display information
Share information	Allow the user to share information through a communication channel with other users or systems.	Administrator performer viewer	• Share information

is characterized by a name, a measurement unit, and a type (e.g. integer, float, and boolean).

- *Measure*, it represents a value of a metric at a specific timestamp. A set of measures constitute time series. Things send measures to the server runtime system at regular intervals or when particular events occur.

4.2 Interaction model

In this section we present the new components which allow to refer to the IoT concepts during the modeling of the UI for IoT-based applications. Those concepts include the IoT-specific actions and the events from IoT devices.

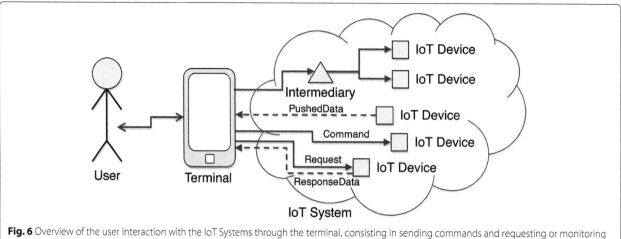

Fig. 6 Overview of the user interaction with the IoT Systems through the terminal, consisting in sending commands and requesting or monitoring data from the IoT devices (possibly through an intermediary)

4.2.1   IoT actions

This category comprehends the components describing the actions triggered when the user interacts with different IoT devices. Those actions can be grouped into two categories: *Device actions*, that represent the actions sent directly to the devices; and *Intermediary actions*, that represent the actions sent to the devices through an *Intermediary* (a component that manages the communication between the user and the devices). Each category can be further decomposed into two subcategories: *Set* and *Get* actions. Notice that the content model takes care of defining the concepts related to the data transfer,

through *Metric* and *Measure* (which actually contain all the metadata about data transfer formats, size and so on).

Set actions. This category contains the actions which permit the user to send to one or more devices, a series of identifiers of the operations or programs which those devices have to perform or execute. We assume that the operations are known a priori by the devices, thus when we send an identifier of an operation to a given device, the device knows how to perform the corresponding operation. The *Set* operations are mainly used to configure the devices (e.g.: change the range in which the sensors are

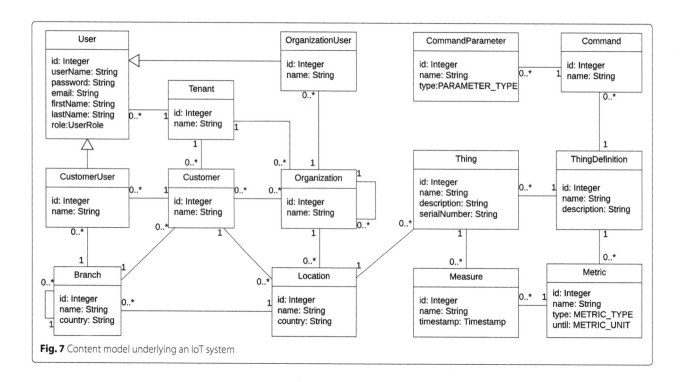

Fig. 7 Content model underlying an IoT system

activated) and to perform specific actions such as *turn on* and *turn off* the device. We have defined a new class, `SetAction`, that allows the modeling of those actions (see Fig. 3).

Get actions. The *Get* actions are mainly used to retrieve the information from devices, category of devices, a program or an operation. We have defined a new class, *GetAction*, that allows the modeling of those actions (see Fig. 3). The class `GetAction` has been further extended to represent the specific data to retrieve. Examples of those data include details and state of the device, information provided by the device and status of the operation assigned to the device.

Plan actions. For the previous actions, we assume that the devices execute specified operations once the user triggers the action. But there exist other cases in which the user wants to schedule the execution of a given action at a specific time. We have defined a specific action, called `PlanAction`, to model those operations which are not executed immediately by the devices but scheduled for execution (once or several times) in a subsequent moment. `PlanAction` is an asynchronous action that waits until the time scheduled for the execution of the operation. It inputs the targeted devices, execution time, operations, and optionally (for the repeating actions or operations) the number of repetitions.

4.2.2 IoT events
In this section we describe the new events defined as IFML extension for the IoT domain. Those events are grouped in: events from devices, and events associated to IoT actions.

Events from IoT devices. The IoT devices emit specific signals containing information about their status or about what they are monitoring. Those signals are captured by specific catching events and sent to the users (terminal) in form of notifications. Those events are grouped into two categories:

1. *Single Information Event.* It is an event which captures every single message from the device it is listening to. A new class `SingleInformationEvent` extending `SystemEvent` of the IFML standard has been defined to model those events.

   The usage of this event is exemplified in the Fig. 8. In this example, the information from the device is shown to the user only once the terminal is connected. To test the connectivity we use the `ActivationExpression`, a Boolean condition which determines whether the associated ViewElement is active or inactive, associated

to the event. The `ActivationExpression` *Context. ConnectivityType<>"NONE"* states that the `SingleInformationEvent` will be activated only when there is a network activated on the terminal.

2. *Approaching Event.* It is an event allowing to capture the first signal sent by the device to which is associated. This event is used when the data transmitted by the device must be shown to the user only once, i.e., each time the device is detected for the first time by the terminal.

   A new class, `ApproachingEvent`, extending `SystemEvent` has been defined to model the approaching events. The usage of this event is exemplified in Fig. 9. In this example, the information from the device is shown to the user once the user enters in the coverage area of the device transmitting via BLUETOOTH. The `ActivationExpression` "Context. ConnectivityType = "BLUETOOTH" states that user receives information from the device only when the BLUETOOTH connectivity is activated on his terminal.

Action events. This category groups two types of events: *Timer event*, denoting the time on which the associated action is scheduled for execution; and *Repeat event*, specifying the time on which the execution of the associated action will be repeated. We have defined a new class for each type of those events: `TimerEvent` and `RepeatEvent`.

5 Interaction patterns for IoT
In this section, we present the IoT interactions under a problem-oriented view, with the aim of showcasing some exemplary and reusable solutions to typical problems, thus responding to **RQ3**. We introduce a number of patterns that can be used to tackle typical problems in the design of the user interactions (UI) with the aim of showing the expressiveness of the designed IoT extensions. We show the matching between those patterns and the user interface patterns defined in the context of IFML [14]. We also present a set of alternative data synchronization patterns which can be relevant to different IoT solutions, and we analyze their compatibility with the UI patterns for IoT.

5.1 IoT patterns
The UI design patterns for the IoT systems can be grouped into three categories: *Set Patterns*, *Get Patterns*, and *Event-based Patterns*.

5.1.1 Set patterns
This category regroups patterns that allow the user to send to the device a set of operations to be executed.

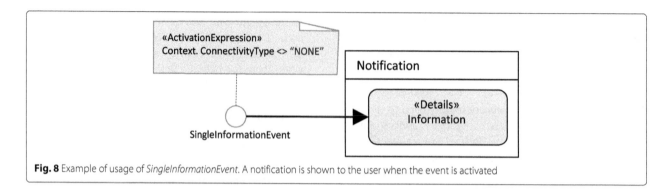

Fig. 8 Example of usage of *SingleInformationEvent*. A notification is shown to the user when the event is activated

Figure 10 exemplifies one pattern of this category, *One Device One Operation*, a pattern which allows the user to set an operation to be executed by one specific device. The user selects a device of interest from a list of the devices of the system. Then, he chooses the operation to be performed from a list of operations supported by the selected device.

Other patterns of this category are:

- One Device More Operations,
- More Devices One Operation,
- More Devices More Operations,
- One Device One Program, and
- One Category More Operations

described in Appendix (Table 6).

5.1.2   Get patterns

This category comprehends interaction patterns allowing to retrieve information from a device, category, program or operation. Figure 11 exemplifies one pattern of this category, *Get Details of a Device*, a pattern which allows the user to retrieve the general information about the device such as Id, name, description, and model. The user selects a device he is interested in from a list of devices.

Other patterns of this category are:

- Get State of the Device,
- Get Information from the Device,
- Get Information for One Category,
- Search Device, and
- Nearby Devices

described in Appendix (Table 7).

5.1.3   Event-based patterns

This category regroups patterns triggered by an occurrence of a specific events. Figure 12 exemplifies one pattern of this category, *Pull Information*. This pattern allows the user to check periodically availability of new data from devices. To save some resources like power, for the data that can be delayed for some amount of time without impacting on the outcome of the application, the user can decide to activate periodically the listening service and pull all the information from the devices.

Other patterns of this category are *Application Launch* and *Push Information*, described in Appendix (Table 8).

5.2   User interaction patterns

The work on [14] presents a set of design patterns that can be used to address typical issues (related to interface organization, content and navigation) of user interface modeling in general. We report in Table 2 a subset of patterns which are relevant, as building blocks, for the modeling of UI patterns for the IoT systems. Table 3 shows a matching between those UI patterns with the IoT patterns introduced in Section 5.1. As rows of Table 3, we list the IoT patterns, while as columns we have generic UI patterns. A checked cell (i×j) means that the *j*th UI pattern has been (can be) used to model the *i*th IoT pattern.

The work on [14] covered also the traditional database operations of creation, update and deletion of an object of a given entity—*CRUD Patterns*. In the IoT context, those patterns are used to configure an IoT system by adding, updating or removing an IoT object to the repository of

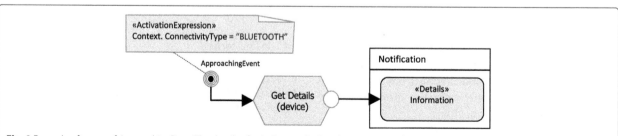

Fig. 9 Example of usage of *ApproachingEvent*. The details of a device are displayed to user as notification once he enters into the coverage area of that device

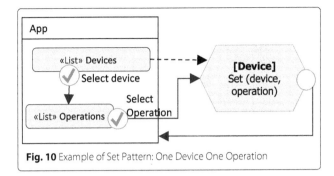

Fig. 10 Example of Set Pattern: One Device One Operation

the system. Those patterns are not explicitly considered in this section since they regard the static part of the IoT system.

Permission and Access configuration. Security is a key issue in IoT systems. In Section 3, we have reported the common roles in an IoT system. The configuration of permission and access rights is done by using the CRUD pattens on users, groups and by assigning the access rights to the group of users. Access control is then managed by the *Login* and *User management* patterns (see Table 2).

5.3 Data synchronization patterns

There are several factors to consider when trying building a model to describe data alignment. Data synchronization patterns have been widely studied in computer science. We report the patterns that can be applied in the context of IoT-based applications in Table 4, while a synthesis of the compatibility between those patterns and user interaction patterns for the IoT-based applications is reported in Table 5. The table lists the user interaction patterns for the IoT-based applications as rows and the data synchronization patterns as columns. A checked cell indicates a possible match in the adoption of the corresponding pair of patterns.

6 Example

To demonstrate the effectiveness of the designed extensions and usage of UI design patterns presented in

Section 5, we have modeled the interaction of *smart-home*, an application that allows a user to interact with different devices of a smart home system. The example is inspired by a real world project implemented by our approach and reported in Section 8.

Figure 13a contains a piece of the user interface of *smart-home* application. The UI in Fig. 13a is divided in three paths: (i) Manage cameras. When the user selects manage camera from the Home screen, a new screen *Cameras* showing a list of available cameras is displayed. The screen shows real-time images from the selected camera. The button *Details* associated to each camera allows the user to access to the details, state and current image, of the selected camera; (ii) Manage Lights. Once the user selects *Manage Lights* from the Home screen, a new screen called *Lights* is displayed. The screen *Lights*, contains a list of available lights with their current state (*ON* or *OFF*). The user can change the state of the selected light by pressing on/of button associated to each light; (iii) Manage Alarms. The path which allows the user to see the logs of recent alarms. Once the user selects manage alarm from the home screen, a new screen *Recent Alarms* containing a list of the recent alarms is displayed.

Figure 13c shows the IFML model describing the user interaction of the piece of *smart-home* application. The interaction model is obtained by combining the following IoT user interaction patterns:

- *Get Information from One Category*, used to retrieve the current status of the monitored lights;
- *Get State of the Device*, used to retrieve the current state of *Camera01*;
- *Get Information from the Device*, used to retrieve the information about the object monitored (image displayed on screen of *Camera 01*);
- *One Device One Operation*, used for instance to turn off the *Light01*;
- *Get Details of a Device*, used to access the details of the selected logLine of the alarms.
- *Store Information*, used to store the new alarm;
- *Push Information*, used to inform the user about the new alarm. In the exemplified case, the new alarm arrived (as a notification message) while the user was visualizing an updated list of Lights after turning off the Light01.

7 Implementation

Besides the formal definition of the IoT extensions to the IFML language and the modeling of UI design patterns for IoT, our research included the implementation of a platform for the development of mobile and web applications for interacting with IoT systems, with the aim of responding to *RQ4*. This has been achieved in collaboration with WebRatio[2], a company focusing on model-driven

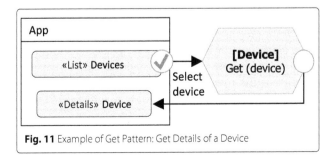

Fig. 11 Example of Get Pattern: Get Details of a Device

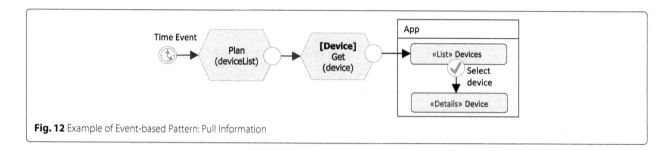

Fig. 12 Example of Event-based Pattern: Pull Information

development of UIs and now building a new offer for IoT[3]. The platform relies on a single, general-purpose static data model (introduced in Section 4.1) representing any infrastructure for managing IoT systems. Our implementation relied on WebRatio, a development environment supporting IFML that comprises several modeling perspectives and includes a code generation framework that automates the production of the software components in all the tiers of the application and the connection between the application and external APIs.

From architectural perspective, we can see the platform as a multitenant stateless server application and a set of thick client applications. Clients maintain the session of authenticated users and are responsible for the composition of the user graphical interface. No presentation logic is executed on the server. The backend serves data, either in pull or push fashion, and executes the business logic.

Table 2 User interaction patterns

Pattern	Description
Master details and multi-details	Present some items and a selection permits the user to access the details of one instance at a time.
Multi-level master details	Also called cascaded index, consists of a sequence of lists over distinct classes, such that each List specifies a change of focus from one object, selected from the index, to the set of objects related to it via an association role. In the end, a single object is shown.
Default selection	Simulates a user's choice at the initial access of a list, thus selecting a default instance.
Multi-field form	Form for submitting information through several fields.
Preloaded field	Variant of Multi-field Form where some fields are preloaded with existing values.
Pre-assigned selection field	Form where the value of a selection field is pre-selected.
Data lookup	Useful for data entry task that involves a complex form with choices among many options, such as in the case of form filling with large product catalogs.
Cascade selection fields	Useful for data entry task that involves entering a set of selections which have some kind of dependency between each others.
Basic search	Keyword search upon a collection of items.
Location-aware search	Enables search of items that are related and close to the current user position.
Login	Recognizes and checks for validity a user-provided identity.
User management	Shows and enables editing application-dependent information associated with the identity of an authenticated user.

7.1 Backend

The back-end architecture is composed by the following components: Microservices layer and API gateway.

7.1.1 Microservices layer

The microservices layer provides access to the data. A microservice is a standalone, independently deployable software system, which provides a specific and atomic functionality. The micro-services present in our architecture include: (i) *Identity*, which provides information for user management; (ii) *Network*, which groups the concepts related with the organizational structure of the actors; (iii) *Inventory*, which groups the concepts related to the definition of things; (iv) *Data*, which allows clients to access to the actual value gathered by the IoT sensors; and (v) *View*, which allows managing all the graphical resources used by the clients.

7.1.2 API gateway

The API gateway is a component that works as proxy toward the micro-services. It exposes the micro-services APIs to the clients.

7.2 Client architecture

The front-end architecture is based on standard Web technologies and hybrid containers. The clients are thick stateful applications. After the login, a client saves the identity of the user and uses it to sign the subsequent requests. The clients communicate only with the API gateway, and never directly with the micro-services. The client builds dynamically the user interface using the common resources retrieved by the service (on the proxy) together

Table 3 Synthesis of User Interaction Patterns used to model IoT Patterns

IoT patterns	User interaction patterns										
	Master details	Multi-level master details	Default selection	Multi-field form	Preloaded field	Data look up	Cascade selection fields	Basic search	Location-aware search	Login	User profile display
One device one operation					✓	✓	✓			✓	
One device more operations				✓	✓	✓	✓				
More devices one operation				✓	✓	✓	✓				
More devices more operations				✓	✓	✓	✓				
One device one program			✓		✓		✓				
One category more operations				✓	✓		✓				
Get details of a device	✓	✓						✓			
Get state of the device	✓							✓			
Get information from the device	✓	✓						✓			
Get information for one category	✓	✓						✓			
Search device								✓			
Nearby devices								✓	✓	✓	
Pull information	✓	✓	✓		✓		✓			✓	✓
Application launch			✓		✓					✓	✓
Pull information	✓	✓	✓		✓		✓			✓	✓

Table 4 Data Synchronization Patterns

Pattern	Description
Asynchronous data synchronizations	Managing a data synchronization event asynchronously and without blocking the user interface.
Synchronous data synchronization	Manage a data synchronization event synchronously; blocking the user interface while it occurs.
Partial storage	Synchronize and store data only as needed to optimize network bandwidth and storage space usage.
Complete storage	Synchronize and store data before it is needed so the application has better response or loading time.
Full transfer	On a synchronization event, the entire dataset is transferred between the mobile device and the remote system.
Timestamp transfer	On a synchronization event, only the parts of the dataset changed since the last synchronization are transferred between the mobile device and the remote system using a last-changed timestamp.
Mathematical transfer	On a synchronization event, only the parts of the dataset changed since the last synchronization are transferred between the mobile device and the remote system using a mathematical method.

with the templates specific for *things* and *metrics*, and the graphic elements owned by the correspondent *tenant*.

Figure 14 shows an example of an interaction between the client and the API Gateway in order to perform a request. Initially the client requests a token by using the */authenticate* endpoint. The API Gateway then queries the *Identity* microservice to verify the client credentials and generate a token. The client saves the token and use it for the subsequent requests. In the exemplified case, the client performs a request to retrieve all the *Things* belonging to its *Customer*.

Figure 15 reports a piece of the user interface of a Web application implemented for supporting a IoT-based scenario.

8   Experiences and validation

Thanks to the collaboration with the Semioty team of WebRatio, we had the possibility of validating our approach around ten real industrial cases. In this section we report our experience within three of them. They represent significant real-world cases to which we have applied our approach, and thus have been useful for validating our solution too.

8.1   Home automation system

A company specialized in consumer home automation solutions needed a mobile application for home automation systems management. The requirements of the application were:

- monitoring of various home appliances: HVAC (heating ventilation and air conditioning), lights, security system (cameras and alarms), watering system, and environmental sensors;
- visualization of the status of all the appliances and devices, filter devices, and highlight the active ones;
- Real time notification about consumption and states of appliances;
- Multi-platform (iOS, Android, and Windows) and multi-device (Smartphone and Tablet) implementation. In particular, the Tablet version shall allow the visualization of the house map with the things in their respective rooms;
- Remote configuration of the home automation system, by sending commands to devices like turning on/off the lights. The commands can be sent to a single device or a group of them.

8.2   Smart ovens for bakery industry

A company specialized in manufacturing of ovens for bakery industry, needed a tool allowing the configuration and monitoring of industrial ovens deployed on their customers' premises. The tool shall provides four different user interfaces:

1. The *Production Dashboard* for the final user of the oven. It shall visualize information related to the use of the oven. The information to visualize include: cooking sequences in temporal order and details (dates and times, completion percentage, carriage load, calculated energy consumption and temperature profile) of the cooking in progress and made. It shall also allow to send recipes to the oven.
2. The *Dashboard for Power Management*. It shall visualize the information regarding energy consumption of the oven, which include: (i) Current and previous consumption referenced by day, week, month and year; (ii) Calculation of energy consumption costs referring to day, week, month and year; and (iii) Energy consumption and average cost per recipe. For each, the consumption and the average cost of all cooking are displayed.
3. The *Dashboard for Maintenance* which shall allow to visualize and manage the status of various components of the oven.
4. The *Recipe Dashboard* shall allow to visualize, edit, add and delete recipes available for the oven.

8.3   Industrial printers management

A company specialized in printing technologies, wanted an application to monitor the smart printers deployed to their customers. The application shall allow the

Table 5 Synthesis of the compatibility between Data Synchronization Patterns and the IoT Patterns

IoT patterns	Data synchronization patterns						
	Async. data sync.	Sync. data sync.	Partial storage	Complete storage	Full transfer	Timestamp transfer	Math. transfer
One device one operation	✓		✓	✓		✓	✓
One device more operations	✓		✓	✓		✓	✓
More devices one operation	✓		✓	✓		✓	✓
More devices more operations	✓		✓	✓		✓	✓
One device one program	✓		✓	✓		✓	✓
One category more operations	✓		✓	✓		✓	✓
Get details of a device	✓	✓	✓	✓		✓	✓
Get state of the device	✓	✓	✓	✓		✓	✓
Get information from the device	✓	✓	✓	✓		✓	✓
Get information for one category	✓	✓	✓	✓		✓	✓
Search device	✓	✓	✓	✓		✓	✓
Nearby devices	✓	✓	✓	✓		✓	✓
Pull information	✓		✓	✓	✓	✓	✓
Application launch	✓	✓	✓	✓	✓	✓	✓
Push information	✓		✓	✓	✓	✓	✓

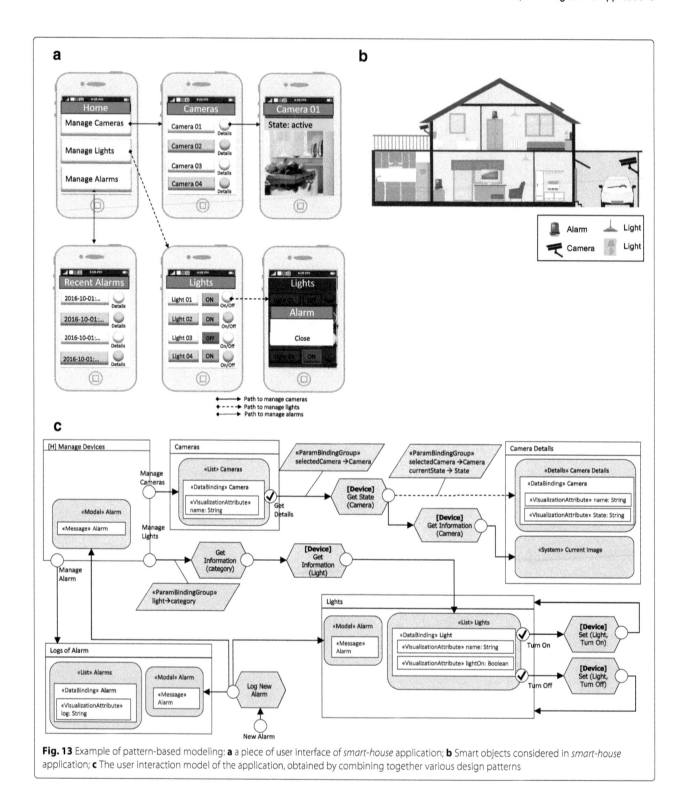

Fig. 13 Example of pattern-based modeling: **a** a piece of user interface of *smart-house* application; **b** Smart objects considered in *smart-house* application; **c** The user interaction model of the application, obtained by combining together various design patterns

monitoring of: (i) the different states assumed by the printer during a given interval of time; (ii) printing parameters (including velocity, number of prints, and quantity of ink); and (iii) overall equipment effectiveness statistics. The final aim of the system is to enable predictive maintenance and continuous monitoring of the devices, so as to increase the level of service for the customers.

8.4 Preliminary validation

In all the described scenarios we applied our approach and obtained the final version of the running applications

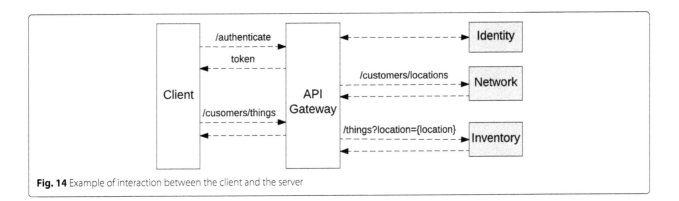

Fig. 14 Example of interaction between the client and the server

with satisfaction of the customer. The generated applications consisted in a cloud-based deployment of the server side of the system, plus (when needed) multi-platform mobile apps generated on Cordova PhoneGap distribution. In this stage, since the platform is not yet completely industrialized, due to the diversity of the customers we had to deploy one application per customer, as opposed to the multi-tenant solution devised in our conceptual framework.

Although we didn't run a comprehensive and detailed validation of the work, we report here the assessment of some quality metrics of our approach.

In terms of**adequacy of the modeling language**, we can report high satisfaction of the designers. Indeed the defined content model and user interaction components were completely covering all the requirements of all the applications. The only case that could not be covered completely automatically was the one of the design of the

map of the location with the position of the devices. To optimize the experience, this had to be manually implemented in Javascript.

In terms of **executability**, the generators and execution platform were covering the requirements too: all the general structure of the application, the navigation and the main contents of the pages have been generated automatically. The part of interfaces that could not be generated is basically the customization of the user interface style.

In terms of **coverage of the design patterns**, all the main behaviour could be covered and were subsumed by one or another pattern. Therefore the design of the basic application structure could be specified with a pattern-based approach. What could not be covered with this was the connection between patterns: this part required some manual design and refinement of the models for optimizing the experience in the move from a use case (i.e., pattern) to another.

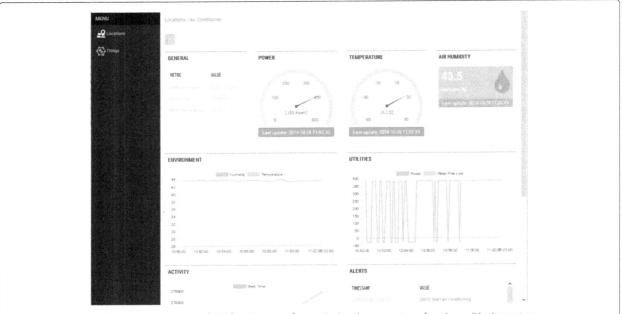

Fig. 15 Example of a real case implementation of a UI for IoT system, for monitoring the parameters of an air conditioning system

9   Related work

This work is related to a large corpus of researches that apply model-driven development (MDD) to specify the **user interaction for multi-device UI modeling**. Among them we can cite: UsiXML [15], TERESA [16], IFML [12], and MARIA [17]. These approaches deal with the specification of general purpose user interfaces and interaction and they are agnostic with respect to the technical platform or technology. Our approach instead focuses on the specifics of user interactions for IoT systems.

On the other side, the approaches that apply **MDD to the development of IoT-based applications do not specifically focus on user interfaces**; they can be grouped into two clusters.

The first cluster includes the works that target **executability for IoT**, i.e., produce executable code for the IoT-based applications. Among them we can cite: (i) FRASAD (Framework for sensor application development) [18], a node-centric, multi-layered software architecture which aims at filling the gap between applications and low-level systems of sensor nodes. It provides a *rule-based* programming model which allows to describe the local behaviors of the sensor node and a *domain specific language* for sensor-based applications modeling. The final application code is automatically generated from the initial models; (ii) Pankesh Patel and Damien Cassou [19] proposed a development methodology which consists on separating the IoT application development into different concerns: domain, functional, deployment, and platform. This separation allows stakeholders to deal with those concerns individually and reuse them. The framework integrates a set of modeling languages to specify each of which allowing to describe one of the above mentioned concerns of the IoT applications; (iii) Franck Fleurey et al. [20] proposed a MDD approach to generate efficient communication APIs to exchange messages with and between resource-constrained devices. This approach is based on ThingML (things modeling language) [21]; (iv) Mainetti et al. [22] proposed a conceptual model for IoT, the Web of Topics (WoX). WoX extends the concept of topic from the MQ Telemetry Transport (MQTT) publish-subscribe protocol [23] with the aim of filling the gap between the design and the solution domains in the IoT context. In WoX the generic IoT entity is seen as a set of couples Topic-Role. A WoX Role is expressed in terms of technological and collaborative dimensions; (v) Conzon et al. [24, 25] provided a model driven development toolkit based on the semantic discovery service, allowing to dynamically selecting and locating available resources or devices, and provides a graphical interface allowing developers to compose mashup applications. (vi) Ferry Pramudianto et al. [26] proposed a MDD approach which focuses on the separation of domain modeling from technological implementations. The framework allows domain experts to construct domain models by composing virtual objects and linking them to the implementation technologies. It allows automatic generation of a prototype code from the domain models and manual refinement of it. All these approaches have in common the main target, that is executability of IoT systems, while they differ on the development phases covered and the kind of support provided to the designer. In this sense, their main focus is to build APIs or middleware layers so as to mask access to diverse IoT devices, thus allowing discovery, integration and execution of device functions. Our work is targeting an orthogonal dimension, that is user interaction. As such, our approach could be used together with one of the approaches discussed above. They can provide the common access layer to the devices, and our solution can provide model-driven specification and execution of the application layer over them.

In the second cluster of MDD approaches we include works that apply **MDD to other aspects of IoT applications**. Among them we can mention a MDD approach for the analysis of IoT applications via simulation [27]. Prehofer and Chiarabini [28] compared the *model-based* and *mashup approaches*, considering tools and methodologies for the development of IoT applications, using UML and Paraimpu [29]. Again, our approach is working on orthogonal aspects with respect to these issues. However, it can integrate very well with them, thanks to the availability of formal semantics of IFML and of simulation solutions based on IFML [30]. Neither detailed formal specification nor simulation/validation tooling are needed for the proposed extensions for IoT, because we rely on existing resources and infrastructure about IFML. Viceversa, in our approach we concentrate on providing efficient design methods and executability.

10   Conclusions

In this paper we presented the IoT domain and use cases (*RQ1*), and we addressed them by defining a set of extensions of OMG's standard IFML for modeling the UI of the IoT-based applications (*RQ2*). We have presented a set of design patterns for the common user interactions for those applications (*RQ3*). Besides the formal definition of the IoT extensions to the IFML language and the modeling of UI design patterns for IoT, our research included the implementation of a code generator prototype tailored to IoT applications development (*RQ4*). The future works include the completion of code generators, the implementation of other real case scenarios in collaboration with the WebRatio customers, and the validation of the approach in terms of performance (both of the code generators and of the generated systems) as well as of acceptance by the final users of the generated solutions.

Appendix

Table 6 IoT User Interaction Patterns: Set Patterns

ID	Pattern	Description	Example
P1	One device one operation	This pattern allows the user to set an operation to be executed by one specific device. The user selects a device of interest from a list of the devices of the system. Then, he chooses the operation to be performed from a list of operations supported by the selected device.	
P2	One device more operations	This pattern allows the user to send to a single device a set of the operations to be performed. The interactions start with the selection of a device of interest. Then the user selects desired operations from a list of supported operations.	
P3	More devices one operation	This pattern allows the user to send to many devices one operation to be executed. The interactions start by selecting the devices of interest. Then the user selects an operation (from a list of the operations supported by the selected devices) to be executed by those devices.	
P4	More devices more operations	This pattern allows the user to send a set of operations to different devices. Those operations are not necessary the same for all devices, thus the operations must be binded to the devices which can perform them.	
P5	One device one program	This pattern allows the user to send the program (identifier) to the device which will execute it. A *program* is a set of operations which have to be executed in a precise order. We assume that the programs are already configured in the devices, thus, the user has only to send the program identifier to the device.	
P6	One category more operations	This pattern allows the user to set operations to different devices based on the groups they belong to, without needing to select one device at a time.	

Table 7 IoT User Interaction Patterns: Get Patterns

ID	Pattern	Description	Example
P7	Get details of a device	The user retrieves, the general information about the device such as Id, name, description, and model. The user selects a device he is interested in from a list of devices.	
P8	Get state of the device	This pattern allows the user to retrieve the current state a given device. The interactions start with the selection of the device for which the user needs tho know the state. Then, the corresponding state is displayed to the user.	

Table 7 IoT User Interaction Patterns: Get Patterns (*Continued*)

ID	Pattern	Description	Example
P9	Get information from the device	This pattern allows the user to retrieve the information provided by a device about the monitored object. The interactions start with the selection of the device for which the user needs tho know the information of the monitored object. Then, the requested information is displayed to the user.	
P10	Get Information for one category	This pattern allows the user to get the information from all devices of the same category.	
P11	Search device	This pattern allows the user to search a specific device. The search of the device can be done in different ways depending on the application and on the devices.	
P12	Nearby devices	This pattern allows the user to retrieve all the devices near to a given location. The location can be setted by the user or retrieved from the ContextDimension, Position, which represents the location information of the device used to access the application.	

Table 8 IoT User Interaction Patterns: Event-based Patterns

ID	Pattern	Description	Example
P13	Pull information	This pattern allows the user to check periodically availability of new data from devices. To save some resources like power, for the data that can be delayed for some amount of time without impacting on the outcome of the application, the user can decide to activate periodically the listening service and pull all the information from the devices.	
P14	Application launch	This pattern allows the user to retrieve the information sent by the devices when the application was not running or when he was offline. The launching event calls the external system and gets the notifications sent by all the devices when the user was offline.	
P15	Push information	This pattern allows the user to visualize the messages sent by an IoT device as a push notification.	

Endnotes

[1] http://www.iiconsortium.org/

[2] http://www.webratio.com

[3] http://www.semioty.com

Authors' contributions

Equal contribution. All authors read and approved the final manuscript.

Author details

[1] Politecnico di Milano. Dipartimento di Elettronica, Informazione e Bioingegneria, Piazza L. Da Vinci 32, 20133 Milan, Italy. [2] WebRatio s.r.l, Piazzale Cadorna, 10, 20123 Milan, Italy.

References

1. Koreshoff TL, Robertson T, Leong TW (2013) Internet of things: a review of literature and products. In: Proceedings of the 25th Australian Computer-Human Interaction Conference: Augmentation, Application, Innovation, Collaboration. OzCHI '13. ACM, New York. pp 335–44. doi:10.1145/2541016.2541048
2. Vatsa VR, Singh G (2015) A literature review on internet of things (iot). Int J Comput Syst (ISSN: 2394-1065) 2(08)
3. Atzori L, Iera A, Morabito G (2010) The internet of things: A survey. Comput Netw 54(15):2787–805. doi:10.1016/j.comnet.2010.05.010
4. Broll G, Rukzio E, Paolucci M, Wagner M, Schmidt A, Hussmann H (2009) Perci: Pervasive service interaction with the internet of things. IEEE Internet Comput 13(6):74–81
5. Kranz M, Holleis P, Schmidt A (2010) Embedded interaction: Interacting with the internet of things. IEEE Internet Comput 14(2):46–53
6. Shirehjini AAN, Semsar A (2017) Human interaction with IoT-based smart environments. Multimed Tools Appl 76(11):13343–65
7. Da Xu L, He W, Li S (2014) Internet of things in industries: A survey. IEEE Trans Ind Inf 10(4):2233–243
8. Capello F, Toja M, Trapani N (2016) A real-time monitoring service based on industrial internet of things to manage agrifood logistics. In: Proceedings of the 6th International Conference on Information Systems, Logistics and Supply Chain, Bordeaux, France, Available From: http://ils2016conference.com/wpcontent/uploads/2015/03/ILS2016_FB01_1.Pdf, Accessed. pp 10–21
9. Holler J (2014) From Machine-to-machine to the Internet of Things: Introduction to a New Age of Intelligence. Academic Press, Amsterdam. ISBN:978-0124076846
10. Vermesan O (2014) Internet of things - from research and innovation to market deployment. River Publishers, Aalborg. ISBN:9788793102941
11. Farooq M, Waseem M, Mazhar S, Khairi A, Kamal T (2015) A review on internet of things (iot). Int J Comput Appl 113(1):1–7
12. Brambilla M, Fraternali P, et al. (2014) The Interaction Flow Modeling Language (IFML), Version 1.0. Technical report, Object Management Group (OMG), http://www.ifml.org
13. Brambilla M, Mauri A, Umuhoza E (2014) Extending the Interaction Flow Modeling Language (IFML) for Model Driven Development of Mobile Applications Front End. In: Awan I, Younas M, Franch X, Quer C (eds). Mobile Web Information Systems: 11th International Conference, MobiWIS 2014. Proceedings. Springer International Publishing, Cham. pp 176–91. doi:10.1007/978-3-319-10359-4_15
14. Brambilla M, Fraternali P (2014) Interaction Flow Modeling Language: Model-Driven UI Engineering of Web and Mobile Apps with IFML. Morgan Kaufmann Publishers Inc., USA
15. Vanderdonckt J (2005) A MDA-compliant environment for developing user interfaces of information systems. In: Pastor O, Falcão e Cunha J (eds). Advanced Information Systems Engineering: 17th International Conference, CAiSE 2005. Proceedings. Springer Berlin Heidelberg, Berlin. pp 16–31. doi:10.1007/11431855_2
16. Berti S, Correani F, Mori G, Paternò F, Santoro C (2004) Teresa: a transformation-based environment for designing and developing multi-device interfaces. In: CHI '04 Extended Abstracts on Human Factors in Computing Systems, CHI EA '04. ACM, New York. pp 793–4. doi:10.1145/985921.985939
17. Paternò F, Santoro C, Spano LD (2009) Maria: A universal, declarative, multiple abstraction-level language for service-oriented applications in ubiquitous environments. ACM Trans Comput-Hum Interact 16(4):19:1–19:30. doi:10.1145/1614390.1614394
18. Nguyen XT, Tran HT, Baraki H, Geihs K (2015) Frasad: A framework for model-driven iot application development. In: 2015 IEEE 2nd World Forum on Internet of Things (WF-IoT). IEEE. pp 387–92. doi:10.1109/WF-IoT.2015.7389085
19. Patel P, Cassou D (2015) Enabling high-level application development for the internet of things. J Syst Softw 103:62–84
20. Fleurey F, Morin B, Solberg A, Barais O (2011) Mde to manage communications with and between resource-constrained systems. In: MODELS. Springer, Berlin. pp 349–63
21. Fleurey F, Morin B (2016) ThingML. http://thingml.org. Online; Accessed 6 Sept 2016
22. Mainetti L, Manco L, Patrono L, Sergi I, Vergallo R (2015) Web of topics: An iot-aware model-driven designing approach. In: 2nd IEEE World Forum on Internet of Things, WF-IoT 2015. IEEE, Milan. pp 46–51. doi:10.1109/WF-IoT.2015.7389025
23. Locke D (2016) MQ Telemetry Transport (MQTT) V3.1 Protocol Specification. https://www.ibm.com/developerworks/library/ws-mqtt/. Online. Accessed 6 Sept 2016
24. Conzon D, Brizzi P, Kasinathan P, Pastrone C, Pramudianto F, Cultrona P (2015) Industrial application development exploiting iot vision and model driven programming. In: Intelligence in Next Generation Networks (ICIN), 2015 18th International Conference On. IEEE. pp 168–75
25. (2016) Ebbits. http://www.ebbits-project.eu/news.php. Online. Accessed 6 Sept 2016
26. Pramudianto F, Indra IR, Jarke M (2013) Model driven development for internet of things application prototyping. In: The 25th International Conference on Software Engineering and Knowledge Engineering, Boston, MA, USA, June 27-29, 2013. pp 703–8. http://dblp.uni-trier.de/rec/bib/conf/seke/PramudiantoIJ13
27. Brumbulli M, Gaudin E (2016) Towards model-driven simulation of the internet of things. In: Complex Systems Design & Management Asia. Springer, Berlin. pp 17–29
28. Prehofer C, Chiarabini L (2015) From internet of things mashups to model-based development. In: Proceedings of the 2015 IEEE 39th Annual Computer Software and Applications Conference - Volume 03, COMPSAC '15. IEEE Computer Society, Washington. pp 499–504. doi:10.1109/COMPSAC.2015.263
29. Pintus A, Carboni D, Piras A (2012) Paraimpu: a platform for a social web of things. In: Proceedings of the 21st international conference on world wide web, WWW '12 Companion. ACM, New York. pp 401–4. doi:10.1145/2187980.2188059
30. Bernaschina C, Comai S, Fraternali P (2017) IFMLEdit.Org: Model Driven Rapid Prototyping of Mobile Apps. In: Proceedings of the 4th International Conference on Mobile Software Engineering and Systems, MOBILESoft '17. IEEE Press, Piscataway. pp 207–8. doi:10.1109/MOBILESoft.2017.15

7

High-performance IP lookup using Intel Xeon Phi: a Bloom filters based approach

Alexandre Lucchesi*, André C. Drummond and George Teodoro (iD)

Abstract

IP lookup is a core operation in packet forwarding, which is implemented using a Longest Prefix Matching (LPM) algorithm to find the next hop for an input address. This work proposes and evaluates the use of parallel processors to deploy an optimized IP lookup algorithm based on Bloom filters. We target the implementation on the Intel Xeon Phi (Intel Phi) many-core coprocessor and on multi-core CPUs, and also evaluate the cooperative execution using both computing devices with several optimizations. The experimental evaluation shows that we were able to attain high IP lookup throughputs of up to 182.7 Mlps (Million packets per second) for IPv6 packets on a single Intel Phi. This performance indicates that the Intel Phi is a very promising platform for deployment of IP lookup. We also compared the Bloom filters to an efficient approach based on the Multi-Index Hybrid Trie (MIHT) in which the Bloom filters was up to 5.1× faster. We also propose and evaluate the cooperative use of CPU and Intel Phi in the IP lookup, which resulted in an improvement of about 1.3× as compared to the execution using only the Intel Phi.

Keywords: Longest prefix matching, Software router, Intel Xeon Phi

1 Introduction

The use of software-based routers is motivated by their extensivity, programmability, and good cost-benefit. However, these routers need to attain high packet forwarding rates, which may be achieved with efficient algorithms and/or with the use of high-performance parallel computing devices. The next hop calculation for input packets is a core operation in the forwarding phase of routers, and is implemented via Longest Prefix Matching (LPM) since the development of CIDR (Classless Inter-Domain Routing).

In this work, we investigate the use of the Intel Xeon Phi processor as a platform for efficient execution of LPM algorithms for IP lookup. The Intel Phi is a highly parallel platform that supports up to 72 computing cores and 4-way hyperthreading. It is also equipped with 512-bit SIMD instructions and has a high-bandwidth memory. The Intel Phi may be attached as a coprocessor in a computer through PCIe or it can be deployed as an independent or standalone system in the newest Knights Landing (KNL) generation.

The design of the Intel Phi as a standalone system was a critical aspect that motivated its use in this work. The use of PCIe to connect coprocessors (Graphics Processing Unit (GPU) or Intel Phi) to the CPU has shown to be a major bottleneck for attaining high performance in data intensive applications, limiting the application throughput to that of the PCIe channel used. Previous work that used GPU for IP lookup reported this limitation [1, 2]. Thus, even though the number of computing cores of current Intel Phi processors is smaller than the one found in GPUs, the Intel Phi is likely to emerge as a major platform for the practical deployment of parallel and efficient IP lookup algorithms.

We have designed a parallel algorithm that uses Bloom filters (BFs) and hash tables (HTs) to efficiently find the LPM for both IPv4 and IPv6. Our implementation leverages the Intel Phi capabilities to mitigate the main drawback of the algorithm – the high costs of computing hash functions during lookup/store operations. This is achieved with the use of vectorization to reduce the costs of hashing computations and thread-level parallelism to increase throughput.

In order to evaluate our propositions, we have compared the BFs-based algorithm to a parallel version of the Multi-Index Hybrid Trie (MIHT). The MIHT is an efficient sequential IP lookup algorithm that has been shown

*Correspondence: lucchesi@aluno.unb.br
Department of Computer Science, University of Brasília, Brasília, Brazil

to attain better performance than well-known tree/trie-based algorithms commonly used for IP lookup: the Binary Trie, the Prefix Tree, the Priority Trie, the DTBM, the 4-MPT and the 4-PCMST [3]. The experimental evaluation has shown that our optimized BFs-based algorithm was able to outperform MIHT in both sequential and parallel settings on the Intel Phi. In a parallel execution using IPv4 and IPv6 prefix datasets, our BFs algorithm was, respectively, up to 3.8× and 5.1× faster than MIHT. The results show that, although the MIHT is a very memory-efficient algorithm, it benefits less from the Intel Phi. For instance, the use of vector SIMD instructions available in most of the modern device architectures can be used to improve the BFs approach, but it is not effective for MIHT because of the irregular nature of the data structures used.

The main contributions of this paper can be summarized as:

- We design and implement an optimized BFs-based LPM algorithm that fully exploits the Intel Phi and modern CPU capabilities, such as SIMD instructions. This algorithm performs better than MIHT even in a sequential executions, and attains higher scalability in a parallel setups.
- We propose a novel approach combining dynamic programming and Controlled Prefix Expansion [4] (DPCPE) to enhance the performance of IPv6 lookups. This optimization resulted in performance gains of up to 5.1× in our BFs-based algorithm.
- We propose and evaluate a cooperative execution model for IP lookup that uses Intel Phi and multi-core CPUs available in the system. After optimizing PCIe data transfers, we were able to achieve a speedup of about 1.33× vs. the execution using only the Intel Phi.
- We show that the most efficient sequential algorithm may not be the best solution in a parallel setting. The results also show that the Intel Phi is a promising platform for high-performance IP lookup. To the best of our knowledge, this is the first work to systematically evaluate the Intel Phi using multiple algorithms and device architectures for IP lookup.

This paper is built on top of our previous work [5], and has extended it with the introduction of techniques to cooperatively use the CPU and Intel Phi, a thorough evaluation using a larger number of datasets, the use of the new KNL Intel Phi that is faster and is deployed as a standalone processor, and a detailed description of the optimization approaches used.

The rest of this document is organized as follows. Section 2 describes the Intel Phi and related work. Section 3 presents the use of BFs to solve the IP lookup problem. Section 4 details of the Bloom Filters algorithm design, optimizations, parallelization strategies, and relevant implementation details. The MIHT algorithm used for comparison purposes is presented in Section 5. We experimentally evaluate our solution in Section 6, and we conclude and present future directions in Section 7.

2 Background and related work

This section describes the Intel Xeon Phi accelerator used to speedup the IP Lookup, and presents the closest related work in the IP lookup domain.

2.1 Intel Xeon Phi

The Intel Phi processor is based on the Intel Many Integrated Core (MIC) architecture, which consists of many simplified, power efficient, and in-order computing cores equipped with a 512-bit vector processing unit (SIMD unit). In this architecture, the computing cores are replicated to create multicore processors with up to 72 cores (model 7290), which are placed in a high performance bidirectional ring network with fully coherent L2 caches. The Intel Phi runs specific versions of the CentOS, SuSE, and RedHat Linux OSs.

The MIC architecture combines features of general-purpose CPUs and many-core processors or accelerators to provide an easy to program and high-performance computing environment [6]. It is based on the x86 instruction set and supports traditional parallel and communication programming models, such as OpenMP (Open Multi-Processing), Pthreads (POSIX Threads Programming), and MPI (Message Passing Interface).

The characteristics of the two Intel Phi used in this work are presented in Table 1. As shown, the 7250 is part of the newest KNL generation and, as a consequence, has better computing capability and memory bandwidth. The 7120P is only deployed as a coprocessor attached to the CPU through a PCIe channel. The 7250, on the other hand, is executed in a standalone mode in which it is the machines' bootable processor. The standalone mode brings improvements for data-intensive applications because it removes the communication overheads of the PCIe communication among CPU and coprocessors to offload computations, which exists in the 7120P and is still a major limitation with GPUs. The table also presents the prices for the processor. Although the 7250 is more

Table 1 Characteristics of the Intel Phi processors used

Processor	Name	Cores	Freq.	Mem. bandwidth	Exec. mode	Price ($)
7120P	KNC	61	1.33 GHz	352 GB/s (GDDR5)	Coprocessor	1500
7250	KNL	68	1.60 GHz	500 GB/s (MCDRAM)	Standalone	2400

expensive than the 7120P, the first one does not need to be deployed with a host machine — thus reducing the cost of the entire system.

2.2 Previous work

The trie/tree-based is a popular class of IP lookup algorithms [3, 11–13], and finding the LPM in these algorithms usually consists of sequentially traversing a sequence of tree nodes. Generally, these algorithms strive to reduce the number of required memory accesses as a means to speed up the lookup process. For instance, in order to achieve that, the Multi-Index Hybrid Trie (MIHT) [3] employs space-efficient data structures, such as B^+ trees and Priority Tries [14]. Recently, the use of compressed trie data structures have also been proposed [15, 16]. Nevertheless, trie/tree-based schemes commonly share the characteristic of being memory-intensive and irregular. Another class of algorithms for IP lookup is based on Bloom filters [17, 18]. These algorithms are more compute-intensive and may require many hash calculations during each lookup/store operation. Hashing is used within Bloom filters as a means to avoid unnecessary memory accesses to hash tables (where IP prefixes and next hop information are actually stored).

A wide range of hardware architectures have been used to implement IPv4 lookup algorithms, including CPU, FPGA, GPU and many-cores [7–10]. While some GPU-based implementations present, in specific configurations, high IP lookup rates, they suffer from a high lookup latency because of the required data transfers between host and GPU. Table 2 roughly compares the main characteristics of previous works using GPU accelerators. Although the authors have used different hardware, data, and testing methodologies, we have made our best effort to provide an overall comparison between them. The table presents the algorithm used in each work, the computing device employed, the maximum throughput attained for both IPv4 and IPv6 using randomize input querying

addresses (worst case scenario), and whether they consider the data transfers among CPU and coprocessor in the experiments.

As shown in the table, a variety of proposals exist for IP lookup using GPUs. The first two approaches have developed algorithms specifically for IPv4, whereas the other approaches can deal with both IPv4 and IPv6. However, in [1] different algorithms are used in each IP configuration. Among other algorithms, the Multi-bit Trie based solution presented in [9] attained by far the highest throughput. However, this solution does not consider the time spent in the data transfers among CPU and GPU, which makes the results attained unrealistic. The PCIe communication cost can not be ignored, because it may be the performance limiting factor. As compared to the remaining approaches [1, 10], it is noticeable that our approach is more efficient than [1], whereas the throughput of GAMT [10] is higher. However, the performance of GAMT is reached with the cost of transferring data through PCIe, which increases the delays in the packet forwarding. Also, the performance of GAMT may be higher because it employs a compacting scheme that greatly reduces the routing table, and could also be used in our solution because it is a preprocessing phase. In our approach with the Intel Phi 7250, the data transfers using the PCIe to offload computation to the coprocessor do not exist, because the 7250 is deployed as the bootable or standalone processor. However, the PCIe will still be used by the NIC to receive and transmit packets in a complete router solution. Therefore, although the PCIe may continue to be a bottleneck in the case of very high forwarding rates, it will saturate in higher forwarding rates for the 7250 as compared to other coprocessor based solutions. Further, with the increase in the number of computing cores of the Intel Phi, we expect that the computing capabilities of this processor will improve rapidly, and it may be able to attain similar performance to the best GPU algorithm and keep the advantage of not requiring PCIe data transfers.

Table 2 Comparison between previous work that employed accelerators in the IP lookup problem. We present the algorithm used, the processor, and the maximum performance for IPv4 and IPv6. Finally, we also shown if the performance collected considered the PCIe data transfers, which are not necessary on our algorithm when using the KNL Intel Phi

Algorithm	Computing device	IPv4 (Mlps)	IPv6 (Mlps)	Considers PCIe transfer?
Radix Tree [7]	GTX280	0.035	–	Yes
SAIL_L [8]	Tesla C2075	547	–	Yes
Multi-bit Trie [9]	Tesla C2075	2,900	3,600	No
DIR-24-8-BASIC (IPv4)	2x GTX480	76.17	74.22	Yes
Binary search (IPv6) [1]				Yes
GAMT [10]	Tesla C2075	1,072	658	Yes
Bloomfwd	Phi 7250	169.6	182.7	–

A Parallel Bloom Filter (PBF) was implemented in the Intel Phi [19]. PBF was proposed to reduce synchronization overhead and improve cache locality. However, the proposed implementation was not specialized for IP lookup and, as such, our approach is different both in the algorithmic and implementation levels. Our approach is built on top of [17] and includes several optimizations targeting efficient execution on the Intel Phi. As presented in the experimental evaluation, these optimizations are crucial to attain high performance.

Other interesting related work include Click [20], RouteBricks [21], and Open vSwitch [22]. Click proposes a modular architecture to deploy software routers. In Click, routers are built on top of fine-grain components chained along the processing path, which provides the ability to quickly implement extensions by creating new components and connecting them to the computation workflow. These components only have to implement a common interface. RouteBricks is a solution based on Click, which has been constructed with the goal of maximizing performance of software routers. It proposed a number of optimizations to minimize the costs of processing packets and has also employed parallelism. Such as Click, Open vSwitch is an interesting software-based switching platform, which we will investigate in our future effort as a target to integrate our Bloom Filters based approach into a complete software router solution, as discussed in Section 7.

3   Bloom filters for IP lookup

The use of BFs coupled with HTs for computing IP lookups has been proposed in [17]. The naïve algorithm uses 32 and 64 pairs of BFs and hash tables, respectively, for IPv4 and IPv6 lookups. Dharmapurikar et al. have also described the use of Counting Bloom Filters (CBFs) [23] to enable dynamic forwarding tables (FIBs) and Controlled Prefix Expansion (CPE) [4] to reduce the number of BFs and HTs pairs for IPv4 to 2 pairs and a direct lookup array (DLA). In Section 3.1, we present the naïve Bloom Filters based algorithm in detail, whereas Section 3.2 details the CPE and other optimizations for IPv4 that are incorporated into the Baseline version we use for performance comparisons.

3.1   The Naïve Bloom filters algorithm

A BF is a data structure for membership queries with tunable false positive errors [24] commonly used in web caching, intrusion detection, and LPM [17]. In essence, a BF is a bit-vector that represents a set of values. The BF is programmed by computing hash functions on each element it stores, and by setting the corresponding indices in the bit-vector. Further, to check if a value is in the set, the same hash functions are computed on the input value and

the bits in the bit-vector structure addressed by the hash values are verified. The value is said to be contained in the set with a given probability only if all bits addressed by the hash values are set. Note that the actual prefix values are stored in HTs, which are searched only when a match occurs on their associated BF. A CBF is a BF variant that adds a counter associated to each bit in the bit-vector, such that each counter is incremented or decremented when an element is added or removed, respectively.

The lookup operations in the naïve Bloom filters algorithm are executed within multiple sets of filters and hash tables — one for each possible IP prefix length. As network addresses in IPv4 are 32-bit long, they require the algorithm to employ 32 Bloom filters with their respective 32 hash tables. Each hash table stores their corresponding [prefix, next hop] pairs and any other relevant routing information, such as metric, interface, etc. If a default route exists, it is stored in a separate field in the forwarding table data structure. Let $F = \{(f_1, t_1), (f_2, t_2), \ldots, (f_{32}, t_{32})\}$ be the set of Bloom filters (f_i) and associated hash tables (t_i) that form an IPv4 forwarding table, where (f_1, t_1) corresponds to the data structures that store 1-bit long prefixes, (f_2, t_2) corresponds to the data structures that store 2-bit long prefixes, and so on. In addition, let $len(f_i)$ be the length of the bit-vector of the i-th Bloom filter, where $1 \leq i \leq 32$. The forwarding table construction is as follows. For every network prefix p of length l to be stored, k hash functions are computed, yielding k hash values: $H = \{h_1, h_2, \ldots h_k\}$. The algorithm uses H to set the k bits corresponding to the indices $I = \{h_i \bmod len(f_l) \mid 1 \leq i \leq 32\}$ in the bit-vector of the Bloom filter f_l. It also increments the corresponding counters in the array of counters of f_l.

Algorithm 1: STORE($FIB, prefix, nextHop$): Storing a network prefix in the Naïve BFs algorithm

---

Input: *FIB* {forwarding table}, *prefix* {network prefix}, *nextHop* {next hop address}.
Result: Updated FIB.

```
// FIB.BF - array of bit-vectors or Bloom filters.
// FIB.CT - array of counters.
// FIB.HF - array of sets of hash functions.
// FIB.HT - array of hash tables.
1  l := prefix.length

2  foreach h ← FIB.HF[l] do
3      i := h(prefix)
       // Ensure i is within BFs size.
4      i := i mod FIB.BF[l].size
5      FIB.BF[l][i] := True
       // Increment associated counter (CBF).
6      FIB.CT[l][i] ++
   // Store routing information in the hash table.
7  FIB.HT[l].store(prefix, nextHop)
```

The process of storing prefixes into the forwarding table data structure of the Bloom filters algorithm is detailed in Algorithm 1. The algorithm receives as input a triple

[*FIB, prefix, nextHop*], and iterates over the set of hash functions associated to the Bloom filter that stores prefixes whose length (*l*) is equal to that of the supplied prefix (Lines 2-6). Each hash function is applied to the prefix yielding indexes i used to set the corresponding bits in the associated Bloom Filter ($B[l][i]$ - Line 5) and to increment the counting Bloom Filter (Line 6). Finally, the prefix contents, including its next hop (*nextHop*) and any other relevant information, are stored in the associated hash table (Line 7).

The lookup process is carried out as follows. Given an input destination address *DA*, the algorithm first extracts its segments or prefixes. Let $S_{DA} = \{s_1, s_2, \ldots, s_{32}\}$ be the set of all the segments of a particular address *DA*, where s_i is the segment corresponding to the first $1 \leq i \leq 32$ bits of *DA*.

For each $s_i \in S_{DA}$, k hash functions are computed, yielding k hash values for each segment: $H = \{(h_1, h_2, \ldots h_k)_1, (h_1, h_2, \ldots h_k)_2, \ldots, (h_1, h_2, \ldots h_k)_{32}\}$. The element $H_i' \in H$ is used to query the Bloom filter $f_i \in F$. The algorithm checks the k bits in the bit-vector of f_i using the indices $I = \{h_j \bmod len(f_i) \mid h_j \in H_i', 1 \leq j \leq k$ and $1 \leq i \leq 32\}$. The result of this process is a *match vector* $M = \{m_1, m_2, \ldots, m_{32}\}$ containing the answers of each Bloom filter, i.e., each $m_i \in M$ indicates whether a match occurred or not in f_i. The match vector M is used to query the associated hash tables. The search begins by sequentially performing queries to the associated hash tables by traversing M backwards, i.e., starting in m_{32}. This is because we are interested in the LPM. If the algorithm finds the next hop (a true match) for a given *DA* in the pair (f_i, t_i), we have found the LPM and there is no need to continue looking into smaller prefix sizes. As Bloom filters may produce false-positives but never false negatives, when a filter does not match a segment, i.e., $m_i \in M$ indicates a mismatch, the algorithm can safely skip to the next Bloom filter f_{i-1} (if $i \geq 2$) without touching its associated hash table t_i. This process continues until the LPM is found or all pairs (f_i, t_i) are unsuccessfully searched. Please, note that false-positives will only lead to extra hash table searches, and the actual result of the algorithm will remain the same regardless of that ratio.

The actual lookup is presented in Algorithm 2. Starting from the Bloom filter associated to the largest address segment, the algorithm iterates on the filters backwards (Lines 2 to 13). Within an iteration, it extracts the most significant i bits of DA (Line 3), and checks whether that segment is in the corresponding Bloom filter (Lines 4 to 8). In this phase, a set of hash functions is applied to the segment p, and the resulting hash values are used to address the i-th BF (Line 7). If the value in the filter is false for any of the hash functions, then that particular segment is certainly not stored in the associated hash table and the

algorithm can leave this phase (Line 8) and continue to the next iteration checking for shorter segments of DA. When the filter responds that the segment is in the set, the search continues in the hash table associated (Line 10), which may or may not contain the searched routing information (e.g., it may be a false positive). Further, if the next hop address is not found in any hash table, the default route is returned (Line 14).

Algorithm 2: LOOKUP(*FIB, DA*): The lookup phase of Naïve IP lookup Bloom Filters algorithm

---

Input: *FIB* {forwarding table}, *DA* {destination address}.
Result: The next hop address.
```
// FIB.BF - array of bit-vectors or Bloom
   filters.
// FIB.HF - array of sets of hash functions.
// FIB.HT - array of hash tables.
// FIB.BF.n - Number of BFs/HTs (32 for IPv4).
// FIB.g - Default route.
```
1 $i := FIB.BF.n - 1$
2 **while** $i \geq 0$ **do**
       // Extract the most significant i bits of DA
          to p.
3      $p := DA[0:i]$
       // Loop on hash functions associated to i-th
          BF.
4   **foreach** $h \leftarrow FIB.HF[i]$ **do**
5          $j := h(p)$
           // Ensure i is within the BF size.
6          $j := j \bmod FIB.BF[i].size$
           // Check the j-th bit of i-th BF.
7   **if** $\neg FIB.BF[i][j]$ **then**
8 | break
       // If p is in associated Bloom Filter.
9   **if** $FIB.BF[i][j]$ **then**
           // Search hash table associated to i-th
              BF.
10         $nextHop := FIB.HT[i].lookup(p)$
           // Check if segment was found in HT.
11   **if** $nextHop \neq \emptyset$ **then**
12 | **return** *nextHop*
       // Try a shorter prefix.
13     $i := i - 1$
14 **return** *FIB.g*

3.2 Baseline Bloom filters algorithm

The Baseline Bloom Filters lookup algorithm we developed is built on top of the Naïve version and includes optimizations to (i) reduce the amount of memory used in each Bloom filters structure and to (ii) decrease the number of Bloom filters employed. The first optimization is implemented with the use of *asymmetric* Bloom filters [17], which implies that $len(f_i)$ may be different of $len(f_j)$, for $1 \leq i, j \leq 32$ and $i \neq j$. The goal of asymmetric Bloom filters is to optimally allocate memory for each data structure according to the expected number of elements to be stored. Also, for each distinct prefix length in the FIB, the algorithm allocates a CBF and a HT. As previously discussed, the CBF is intended to provide the ability of removing addresses from the Bloom filter.

The optimization CPE allows the expansion of shorter prefixes into multiple equivalent larger prefixes. Before building an IPv4 FIB, we use this technique to ensure there are only prefixes of length 20, 24, and 32. The first group is stored in a direct lookup array (DLA), while the other two are stored in separate sets consisting of one BF and one HT (G_1 and G_2, respectively). The DLA is a flat array with 2^{20} entries that stores the next hops associated to 20-bit prefixes. When using this structure, the lookup algorithm will sequentially search G_2 and G_1 (starting from G_2, since it stores the longest prefixes) and, if the LPM is not found, the next hop stored in the DLA position indexed by the first 20 bits of the input address is returned (it may be the default route).

For IPv6, previous work has reported that CPE was inefficient because of the longer "strides" between hierarchical boundaries of addresses, which would result in a very high memory use after expansion. It was suggested to use 64 sets of CBFs and HTs, one for each possible prefix length. However, even though most lengths in realistic IPv6 FIBs indeed are either empty or contain few prefixes, we have proposed an algorithm (DPCPE) that uses dynamic programming to group prefixes by length and perform the expansions with limited additional memory demands. The details of this algorithm are presented in Section 4.2.

4 Bloom filters optimizations and parallelization

This section describes the optimizations proposed in this work that are implemented on top of the baseline BFs IP lookup algorithm as well as its parallelization targeting the Intel Phi. The parallel CPU version employs similar parallelization strategies, but differs with respect to the instruction-level parallelism that used auto-vectorization. The baseline implementation on which our work is built incorporates the following optimizations: the use of CBF to allow FIB updates, asymmetric memory allocation proposed in [17], and CPE to reduce the number of required data structures.

4.1 Optimizing the hash calculations

Hashing is an important aspect of the algorithm because it impacts the efficiency of BFs and HTs. In the BFs, it affects both the false positive ratio (FPR) and the memory utilization. With respect to the associated HTs, the better the quality of the hash, the less collisions are likely to happen and, as a consequence, the lookup process will also be faster.

In order to improve the algorithm, we have (i) accelerated the hash calculations with the use of instruction-level parallelism or vectorization, as discussed in detail in Section 4.3; (ii) reduced the cost of hashing by combining the output of two hash calculations to generate more hashes; and (iii) implemented and evaluated the reuse of hash values between BFs and HTs to minimize the overall number of hash calculations. The reuse affects both the lookup and update operations. The generation of extra hashes was performed through the use of a well-known technique that employs a simple linear combination of the output of two hash functions $h_1(x)$ and $h_2(x)$ to derive additional hash functions in the form $g_i(x) = h_1(x) + i \times h_2(x)$. This technique results in faster hash calculations and can be effectively applied in the BFs and HTs without affecting the asymptotic false positive probabilities [25]. We have also proposed the reuse of one of the hashes calculated to search or store a key in the BF to address its associated HT, which avoids the calculation of another hash whenever a HT is visited. This is possible because we calculate the hash without taking into account the size of the BF. Thus, during the actual access to the BF or the HT, we compute the rest of the division of the hash value to the data structures size.

4.2 The new dynamic programming CPE (DPCPE)

Another crucial optimization we have implemented for IPv6 is the use of CPE to reduce the number of required sets of Bloom filters and hash tables in the algorithm. This technique consists of expanding every prefix of a shorter length to multiple, equivalent, prefixes of a greater length, so that the number of distinct prefix lengths and, consequently, filters and hash tables, is reduced. In IPv4, as previously discussed, we used CPE to expand prefixes into two groups: $G_1 \in [21–24]$ and $G_2 \in [25–32]$. After the CPE, G_1 has only 24-bit prefixes and G_2 has only 32-bit prefixes, and two sets of Bloom filters and hash tables are allocated to store these prefixes.

A Direct Lookup Array (DLA) is allocated to store the next hops of the remaining prefixes, whose lengths are ≤ 20 bits, using the prefixes themselves as the indices. In this way, we are able to bound the worst-case lookup scenario to two queries (G_1, G_2) and one memory access (DLA), as detailed in [17]. Note that the trade-off of CPE is faster search on the cost of increased memory footprint, as shown in Table 4. It was also mentioned that this technique also not viable for the IPv6 case [17], but, in this work, we proposed the DPCPE algorithm that builds the CPE for IPv6.

The DPCPE algorithm works as follows. Let $L = \{l_1, l_2, \dots, l_{64}\}$ be the prefix distribution of an IPv6 FIB, where l_i is the number of unique prefixes of length i (in bits). Given a desired number of expansion levels n (or target number of BFs), DPCPE uses dynamic programming to compute the set of lengths to be used so that the total number of prefixes in the resulting FIB is minimized. DPCPE always starts by picking the length 64, since it is the largest prefix length for IPv6 and, as such, its inclusion is required for correctness (i.e., every IPv6 prefix can, theoretically, be expanded to one or more 64-bit prefixes). Let $S = \{64\}$ represent the initial set of resulting lengths and $C = \{1, 2, \ldots, 63\}$ represent the initial set of candidate lengths. While $|S| < n$, the algorithm removes an element $l \in C$ and inserts it into S. In each iteration, the length l is selected by mapping a cost function f over all possible sets of lengths and choosing the length associated with the smaller cost. For instance, in the second iteration (assuming $n \geq 2$), f is mapped over the set $Q = \{\{l, 64\} \mid l \in C\}$ and the value l from the set that resulted in the minimum cost is selected. The cost function f takes as input L and a set of expansion levels $Q' \in Q$. It then computes the resulting number of prefixes after expanding L to Q'. The (maximum) number of prefixes, resulting from expanding a prefix of length $l_i \in L$ to $q \in Q'$ (such that, $i < q$), is defined as $2^{q-i} \times l_i$. Note that f does not take into account the problem of prefix capture [4], which happens whenever a prefix is expanded to one or more existing prefixes in the database. In this case, the existing longer prefix "captures" the expanded one, which is ignored. Therefore, although DPCPE is not guaranteed to return the optimal solution, it usually returns solutions that work better in practice for the BFs algorithm than directly using the database with no preprocessing (Section 6.6).

4.3 Parallelization

Our parallelization strategy employs both TLP and ILP to fully utilize the Intel Phi computing power. These parallelism strategies is described in the following sections.

4.3.1 Thread-level parallelism (TLP)

Due to its regular data structures, the Bloom filters algorithm exposes multiple opportunities for parallelism. For instance, in [17] it was suggested a parallel search over the two sets of Bloom filters/hash tables and the DLA (associated with the different prefix lengths) for a given input address, which is mentioned to be appropriate for hardware implementations. In this strategy, a final pass is performed to verify if a match occurs in any of these data structures and to select the next hop. The same approach could be used for a software-based parallelization by dispatching a thread to search each data structure. However, IPv4 prefix databases have the well-known characteristic that prefixes are not uniformly distributed in the range of valid prefix lengths and, as a consequence, it is more likely that a match occurs to prefixes within lengths that concentrate most of the addresses, i.e., the set of Bloom filter and hash table that stores 24-bit prefixes. Therefore, computing all Bloom filters in parallel may not be efficient because, most of the times, the results from the data structures associated with prefix lengths smaller or greater than 24 bits will not be used. Instead, it is more compute efficient to sequentially query the Bloom filters and the DLA. The other option for TLP, which is used in our approach, is to perform the parallel lookup computation for multiple addresses by assigning one or multiple addresses to each computing thread available. In this way, we can carry out the processing of each address using the compute efficient algorithm, while we are still able to improve the system throughput by computing the lookup for multiple addresses concurrently. This is possible because the processing of addresses is independent and, as such, there is no synchronization across the computation performed for different addresses. The implementation of the parallelization at this level employed the Open Multi-Processing API (OpenMP) [26], which was used to annotate the main algorithm loop that iterates over the input addresses to find their next hops. The specific OpenMP settings used, which led to the better results, were the *dynamic* scheduler with *chunk size* of one.

4.3.2 Instruction-level parallelism (ILP)

The use of ILP is important to take full advantage of the Intel Phi, which is equipped with a 512-bit vector processing unit (see Section 2.1). We used its SIMD instructions to efficiently compute the hash values for multiple input addresses at the same time. The ILP optimization focused on the hashing calculations because it is the most compute intensive stage of the algorithm. The original work [27] and previous implementations of algorithms employing Bloom filters to the LPM problem [18, 19] do not discuss their decisions and reasons on the hash functions used.

Thus, we have decided to implement, vectorize, and evaluate three hash functions: MurmurHash3 [28] (Murmur), Knuth's multiplicative method [29] (Knuth), and a hash function named to here as H2 [30]. Murmur is widely used in the context of Bloom filters, but its original version takes as input a variable-length string. In order to improve its efficiency, we have derived versions of it specialized to work on 32-bit (for IPv4) and 64-bit (for IPv6) integer keys. Knuth is a simple hash function of the form: $h(x) = x \times c \bmod 2^l$, where c should be a multiplier in the order of the hash size 2^l that has no common factors with it.

H2 takes as input a key and mixes its bits using a series of bitwise operations, as shown in Algorithm 3. Although simple, the H2 hash function has been shown to be effective in practice [30].

Algorithm 3: Definition of the H2 hash function

Input : x {A 32-bit unsigned integer key}.

Output: The computed hash value.

1 $x := ((x \gg 16 \oplus x) \times 0x45d9f3b$
2 $x := ((x \gg 16 \oplus x) \times 0x45d9f3b$
3 $x := ((x \gg 16 \oplus x)$
4 **return** x

The hash implementations employed the low-level Intel Intrinsics API [31] to perform a manual vectorization of all the hash functions. We have also evaluated the use of automatic vectorization available with the Intel C Compiler, but the manually generated code has proved to be more efficient.

4.4 Cooperative execution and efficient data transfers

In this section, we present a variant of our algorithm that cooperatively uses the CPU and Intel Phi when it is deployed as a coprocessor (7120P) attached to the PCIe. The use of hybrid machines equipped with CPUs and accelerators has raised quickly in the recent years [32]. However, utilizing these systems adequately may require the use of complex software stacks and scheduling strategies. As such, a number of works have already been developed to provide techniques that simplify the use of such machines [33–37].

In the case of IP lookup studied in this work, the IP addresses are stored in the host memory and are transferred in batches through the PCIe channel to the Intel Phi for processing. After the lookup algorithm is executed on the coprocessor, the computed next hops are copied back from the coprocessor device memory to the host. The data transfer times in this process may be significant to the overall execution, and strategies to reduce transfer costs should be used. Also, the availability of the CPU creates opportunities for leveraging this processor as an additional computing device to carry out IP lookups. These two optimizations are briefly described below. We argue that the cooperative execution would benefit any application domains in which the load on the router is higher than the throughput delivered by a single processor.

4.4.1 Efficient CPU-Intel Phi data transfers

The limited bandwidth between CPU and Intel Phi may represent a major bottleneck to the use of the coprocessor, especially for data intensive applications [32]. The data transfers necessary to run a computation in the Intel Phi are typically carried out synchronously (*sync*), by pipelining the input data transfer (host to device), the computation in the coprocessor, and the output data transfer (device to host).

A common approach used for reducing the impact of such transfer costs to performance is to overlap data transfer operations with the execution of other tasks. This technique receives the name of double buffering [38, 39] and has been used in several domains. In our problem, it can be used to reduce both the CPU and Intel Phi idle times during the transfers, and may be implemented using an asynchronous data transfer (*async*) mechanism available in the Phi. In this strategy, while the Intel Phi is in the computation stage of the sync pipeline, we concurrently launch the input data transfer of a batch of IP addresses while a second buffer is being processed in the Intel Phi. The same also occurs for the output data transfers. This will allow for the overlapping of computation and data transfers.

4.4.2 Cooperative execution on CPU and Intel Phi

To cooperatively use both devices, we divide the input IP addresses into two sets that are independently and concurrently processed by the CPU and Intel Phi. The work division must be computed in a way to minimize the load imbalance between them. Otherwise, a processor may take much longer to process its lookups, and this may offset the potential performance gains of this approach. In order to carry out this partitioning, we take into account the relative performance among the processors, which should be the same as the relative sizes of the sets of IP addresses assigned for computation with each of the devices. The relative performance is computed in a profiling phase before the execution. Additionally, in order to avoid the CPU threads computing IP lookups to interfere with the CPU thread responsible for managing the Intel Phi, an entire CPU physical core is allocated to the latter. As such, in our system configuration, 15 CPU cores are used for IP lookup computations and 30 threads are launched in these cores. Similar strategies to cooperatively use CPUs and coprocessors have been employed in other application domains [33, 40]. In this work, we use these techniques and demonstrate their performance in the IP lookup domain.

5 MIHT algorithm and implementation

This algorithm uses a data structure named Multi-Index Hybrid Trie (MIHT) [3]. The MIHT was built by combining the advantages of B^+ trees and priority tries [14] to design dynamic forwarding tables. It consists of one B^+ tree and multiple priority tries. A B^+ tree is a generalization of a binary search tree in that a node can have more than two children. A B^+ tree of order m is an ordered tree that satisfies the following properties: (i) each node has at most m children; (ii) each node, except the root, has at least $\frac{m}{2}$ children; (iii) the root has at least 2 children; (iv) all leaves occur on the same level; and (v) the satellite information is stored in the leaves and only keys and children pointers are stored in the internal nodes. Although priority tries may be used alone to build dynamic forwarding tables, MIHT uses them as auxiliary substructures to build a more efficient algorithm. A priority trie is similar to a binary trie in that each node has at most two children and the branch is based on the address bits. However, priority tries have two main advantages over binary tries in the context of IP lookup. First, in a priority trie, prefixes are reversely assigned, i.e., longer prefixes are associated with higher levels nodes and shorter prefixes are associated with lower level nodes, allowing the search to finish immediately whenever a match occurs (a binary trie always requires the traversal until a leaf). Second, as opposed to the binary trie, there are no empty internal nodes in a priority trie — every node stores routing information to improve memory usage.

5.1 Algorithm

In order to build the forwarding table in the MIHT, each network prefix is split into two parts: a prefix (the key) and a suffix. Let $p = p_0 p_1 \ldots p_{l-1}$ be a network prefix and $q = p_i p_{i+1} \ldots p_{l-1}$ for $0 \leq i \leq l-1$ be a suffix of p. The length of a prefix p is denoted $len(p)$. For example, $len(p_0 p_1 \ldots p_{l-1}^*) = l$. For an integer $k \leq l$, the k-prefix key of p, denoted $prefix\_key_k(p)$, is the value of $(p_0 p_1 \ldots p_{k-1})_2$. The k-suffix of p, denoted by $suffix_k(p)$, is defined as $suffix_k(p) = p_k p_{k+1} \ldots p_{l-1}$, where $0 \leq k \leq l$. For example, $prefix\_key_4(00010^*) = prefix\_key_4(00011^*) = (0001) = 1$ and $suffix_4(00010^*) = 0^*$ [3]. For all network prefix p whose $len(p) \geq k$, its k-prefix (or key) is stored in the B^+ tree and a priority trie is allocated. Remember that, in a B^+ tree, data are stored only in external nodes (or leafs). In MIHT, the data consist of pointers to priority tries. If the key already exists in the B^+ tree, the pointer to the associated priority trie, which was previously allocated, is retrieved and used instead. The k-suffixes of all prefixes, along with their corresponding next hops and other routing information, are stored in priority tries. Network prefixes whose length is less than k are "keyless", i.e., they are stored directly as suffixes in a separate priority trie, named $PT[-1]$. All the suffixes stored in a particular priority trie share the same prefix. The root of MIHT has two pointers: one to a B^+ tree and another one to $PT[-1]$.

To search for a destination address DA, the algorithm extracts its key by applying $prefix\_key_k(DA)$ and searches the B^+ tree in a top-down manner, starting from the root. A tree traversal from the root to a leaf is performed with a binary search using the key value to search each visited node. If a match occurs in a leaf, then the algorithm searches $suffix_k(DA)$ in the corresponding priority trie using the pointer stored in that node. If we find the best matching of $suffix_k(DA)$ in some priority trie, then it is the LPM, and the search is terminated. If the $prefix\_key_k(DA)$ is not found in the B^+ tree, the algorithm searches DA in $PT[-1]$.

IP lookup operations can be performed by associating each network prefix with a key value of length k in the MIHT. By associating each prefix with a key value, the problem of searching for the longest matching prefix was transformed into a problem of searching for a corresponding index. Based on this transformation, the height of the MIHT is less than W (the length of input addresses), which accelerates the lookup speed. There are two parameters that affect the MIHT's performance: the length k of

the keys and the order m of the B^+ tree. A (k, m)-MIHT is a data structure combining a B^+ tree of order m and priority tries, which contains two types of nodes: index nodes (i-node) and data nodes (d-node). An i-node can be either *internal* or *external*. An internal i-node is a node in which each child is also an i-node. An external i-node is a leaf node in the B^+ tree, which stores keys and pointers to d-nodes. Finally, a d-node is a priority trie which stores the next hops. It has been shown in [3] that the best lookup performance in IPv4 is obtained setting $k = m = 16$, which is used in our evaluations.

This algorithm is already highly optimized for implementation in software, as described into greater detail in [3]. Thus, our implementation of the baseline sequential algorithm incorporated the optimizations originally proposed by the algorithm as well as we developed a few optimizations targeting Phi. For instance, in order to optimize the throughput of memory, we have aligned all the B^+ tree nodes in addresses multiple of 64 bytes. Such optimization is useful because it leverages the fact that each node stores sixteen 32-bit integers, which matches exactly the coprocessor's word size. This allows an entire node to be fetched from memory in one memory access, accelerating the traversal of the structure. As suggested in the original algorithm, the sixteen keys in a node are ordered and we perform a binary search on each visited node in order to quickly find the next child or data node.

5.2 Parallelization

This section describes the parallelization of the MIHT for IP lookup.

5.2.1 Thread-Level Parallelism (TLP)

The MIHT is built out of tree-based data structures and the lookup process consists basically of traversing these structures. Therefore, similarly to the the Bloom filters approach, we have parallelized the execution of multiple address lookups in MIHT. The implementation of the parallelization at this level also employed the OpenMP programming interface, and each computing thread is responsible for independently processing one or multiple input messages.

5.2.2 Instruction-Level Parallelization (ILP)

The MIHT is built from tree data structures, which are irregular in nature and make the use of SIMD operations very challenging and inefficient. Our analysis of the algorithm shows an opportunity for using SIMD vector instructions in the search performed in each node of the B^+ tree. However, since this search is very quick because of the small number of elements in a node and the fact they are ordered, the MIHT performance was not improved with the use of vector instructions.

6 Performance evaluation

This section evaluates the performance of our optimized BFs algorithm both for IPv4 and IPv6. We perform the lookups using pseudo-random generated IP addresses and addresses from a real packet trace in the "CAIDA Anonymized Internet Traces 2016" dataset [41].

6.1 Experimental setup and databases

The CPU runs were performed in a machine equipped with a dual socket Intel Xeon E5-2640v3 CPU (16 CPU cores with Hyper-Threading), 64 GB of main memory, and CentOS 7. This machine also hosts the Intel Xeon Phi 7120P, and is deployed in a local machine in our laboratory. The source codes were developed using C11 and compiled with the Intel C Compiler 16.0.3 for both the CPU and the Intel Phi using the -O3 optimization level.

We have used 7 real prefix databases for IPv4, whose characteristics are summarized in Table 3. The databases AS65000 and SYDNEY were obtained from [42, 43], respectively. The remaining databases are from [44]. Table 3 presents the amount of addresses in each database and the total number of prefixes before and after performing the CPE to group them into sets of 24-bit and 32-bit long prefixes.

For IPv6, we use the AS65000-V6 [42], EQUINIX, LINX, and NWAX datasets. Because IPv6 is still not widely used, the available datasets have a small number of prefixes: AS65000-V6 has 31,645 unique prefixes distributed in 34 distinct prefix lengths; EQUINIX has 42,663 unique

prefixes distributed in 43 prefix lengths; LINX has 44,103 unique prefixes distributed in 45 prefix lengths; and NWAX has 42,227 unique prefixes distributed in 43 prefix lengths. Table 4 shows the effects of DPCPE on these datasets. The expansion with 3 levels was not possible because of the high memory requirements. Because the algorithm ignores the prefix capture problem (Section 4.2) when computing the levels, its estimates are half of the actual results for most of the configurations. We want to highlight that the main goal of the algorithm was not to provide an accurate estimate, but to reduce the number of filters instantiated and, as a consequence, improve the algorithm performance. Therefore, although not precise, the provided estimation will serve as a lower bound for the number of prefixes after expansion, and it can be used to decide whether it is worth computing the expansion.

The experimental results are organized as follows:

- From Sections 6.2 to 6.5, we evaluate the performance of the Bloomfwd as the hash configurations, input query data characteristics, and prefix dataset sizes are varied, and we compare our approach to the MIHT algorithm. These analyses are intended to stress the algorithm under different scenarios in order to understand the aspects that affect its performance. The experiments in this phase use the Intel Xeon CPU and Intel Phi 7120P processors only, because these processors are deployed in a local machine to which we have unlimited access.
- Further, in Section 6.6, we analyze the performance of the Bloomfwd and MIHT for multiple IPv4 and IPv6 prefix datasets in the Intel Phi. This evaluation uses the best parameters found in the previous experiments, and also compares the performance of the Intel Phi 7120P and 7250 devices. The 7250 Intel Phi used is part of the Stampede 2 supercomputer deployed in the Texas Advanced Computing Center (TACC), which we had access through the The Extreme Science and Engineering Discovery Environment (XSEDE) program.
- Finally, the benefits of cooperative execution using the CPU and Intel Phi 7120P are assessed in Section 6.7. This evaluation has not included the Intel Phi 7250 because it is a standalone bootable device and, as such, it is not attached to a CPU.

6.2 The effect of the hash function and false positive ratio

The false positive ratio (FPR or f) is a key aspect for the effectiveness of a Bloom filter because it affects the memory requirements and the number of hash calculations per lookup. We highlight that the FPR does not affect the results of the algorithm, but only the number of times that a value is informed to be in the associated hash

Table 3 Characteristics of the IPv4 prefix datasets used

Dataset	Location	Original		
		≤ 20	$21-24$	$25-32$
AS65000	-	104,283	516,699	1625
SYDNEY	Sydney	102,696	553,811	10,862
DE-CIX	Frankfurt	102,984	535,074	9287
LINX	London	100,331	519,503	354
MSK-IX	Moscow	102,555	528,728	9529
NYIIX	New York	102,085	528,455	3637
IX.br/SP	Sao Paulo	103,733	544,703	4095
		After CPE		
		≤ 20	$21-24$	$25-32$
AS65000	-	1,048,576	971,555	11,3397
SYDNEY	Sydney	1,048,576	1,037,247	67,397
DE-CIX	Frankfurt	1,048,576	1,007,513	209,488
LINX	London	1,048,576	982,940	19,863
MSK-IX	Moscow	1,048,576	1,004,073	203,360
NYIIX	New York	1,048,576	1,000,128	151,391
IX.br/SP	Sao Paulo	1,048,576	1,024,899	147,201

Table 4 Results of performing CPE in four real IPv6 prefix datasets collected from Routeviews [43]

Dataset	CPE level	Expansion levels suggested by algorithm	Estim. # of prefix. ×1000	Actual # of prefix. ×1000
AS65000-V6	CPE8	{24, 29, 33, 38, 40, 44, 48, 64}	61	60
	CPE7	{29, 33, 38, 40, 44, 48, 64}	77	76
	CPE6	{29, 33, 38, 44, 48, 64}	104	103
	CPE5	{33, 38, 44, 48, 64}	385	380
	CPE4	{33, 44, 48, 64}	1185	1166
	CPE3	{44, 48, 64}	650,417	—
EQUINIX	CPE8	{30, 35, 41, 45, 49, 51, 57, 64}	137	236
	CPE7	{30, 35, 41, 45, 51, 57, 64}	218	387
	CPE6	{30, 35, 41, 45, 51, 64}	368	648
	CPE5	{35, 41, 45, 51, 64}	962	1823
	CPE4	{35, 45, 51, 64}	1586	2702
	CPE3	{45, 51, 64}	672,373	—
LINX	CPE8	{17, 30, 33, 37, 43, 49, 57, 64}	194	216
	CPE7	{17, 33, 37, 43, 49, 57, 64}	271	367
	CPE6	{17, 33, 37, 43, 49, 64}	1079	942
	CPE5	{17, 37, 43, 49, 64}	2550	3818
	CPE4	{17, 37, 49, 64}	4301	6523
	CPE3	{17, 37, 64}	60,364,260	—
NWAX	CPE8	{30, 35, 41, 45, 49, 51, 57, 64}	137	235
	CPE7	{30, 35, 41, 45, 51, 57, 64}	217	386
	CPE6	{30, 35, 41, 45, 51, 64}	338	587
	CPE5	{35, 41, 45, 51, 64}	950	1763
	CPE4	{35, 45, 51, 64}	1574	2640
	CPE3	{45, 51, 64}	691,485	—

table by a Bloom filter without being. When this occurs, the algorithm will unsuccessfully search in the hash table. Probing a hash table consists in traversing a linked list, which may become expensive as the FPR increases. On the other hand, a very low FPR requires a larger number of hash calculations and a high memory utilization. The FPR is determined by three parameters: the number n of entries stored in the filter, the size m of the filter, and the number k of hash functions used to store/query the filters [24]. As detailed in [17], when FPR is minimized with respect to k, we get the following relationship:

$$k = \frac{m}{n} \ln 2 \qquad (1)$$

At this point, FPR is given by:

$$f = \left(\frac{1}{2}\right)^k \qquad (2)$$

For a desired false positive probability f, and knowing in advance the total number of prefixes n to be stored in the forwarding table for each prefix length, we compute the

size m of each Bloom filter using the following equation, derived by substituting 1 in 2.

$$m = \frac{n \lg \frac{1}{f}}{\ln 2} \qquad (3)$$

Then, we use m and n to calculate k from 1. Table 5 summarizes how these parameters are affected for each IPv4 prefix dataset presented in Table 3.

The trade-off between increasing the hash calculations and the application memory footprint in order to avoid the extra cost of a false positive is complex. Therefore, we have evaluated it experimentally by measuring the execution times for various FPRs and hash function configurations. Hash functions are used in the Bloom filters algorithms for querying the Bloom filters and to search the hash tables associated to each filter. As such, we are able to use combinations of hash functions to compute the multiple hashes within a Bloom filter or the single hash for a particular hash table. The hash functions used were presented in Section 4, and we employ the AS65000 prefix

Table 5 Bloom filters parameters as FPR is varied. Two bloom filters (G_1 and G_2) are created

f			1%	10%	30%	60%	90%
AS65000	G_1	m	9,312,412	4,656,206	2,434,631	1,032,974	213,057
		k	7	4	2	1	1
	G_2	m	1,086,917	543,459	284,163	120,566	24,868
		k	7	4	2	1	1
SYDNEY	G_1	m	9,942,074	4,971,037	2,599,250	1,102,819	227,463
		k	7	4	2	1	1
	G_2	m	646,005	323,003	168,891	71,658	14,780
		k	7	4	2	1	1
DE-CIX	G_1	m	9,657,071	4,828,536	2,524,739	1,071,205	220,942
		k	7	4	2	1	1
	G_2	m	2,007,955	1,003,978	524,959	2,22,732	45,940
		k	7	4	2	1	1
LINX	G_1	m	9,421,538	4,710,769	2,463,161	1,045,079	215,553
		k	7	4	2	1	1
	G_2	m	190,389	95,195	49,775	21,119	4356
		k	7	4	2	1	1
MSK-IX	G_1	m	9,624,099	4,812,050	2,516,119	1,067,548	220,188
		k	7	4	2	1	1
	G_2	m	1,949,218	974,609	509,603	216,216	44,596
		k	7	4	2	1	1
NYIIX	G_1	m	9,586,286	4,793,143	2,506,233	1,063,353	219,323
		k	7	4	2	1	1
	G_2	m	1,451,092	725,546	379,373	160,962	33,200
		k	7	4	2	1	1
IX.br/SP	G_1	m	9,823,717	4,911,859	2,568,307	1,089,690	224,755
		k	7	4	2	1	1
	G_2	m	1,410,931	705,466	368,873	156,507	32,281
		k	7	4	2	1	1

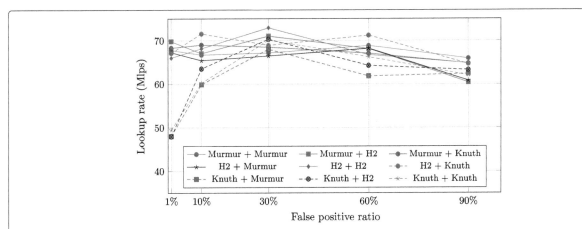

Fig. 1 Execution times for multiple hash functions and FPRs using 244 threads in the Intel Phi. The "Murmur + H2" entry means Murmur was used within the Bloom filters and H2 was used to address the hash tables

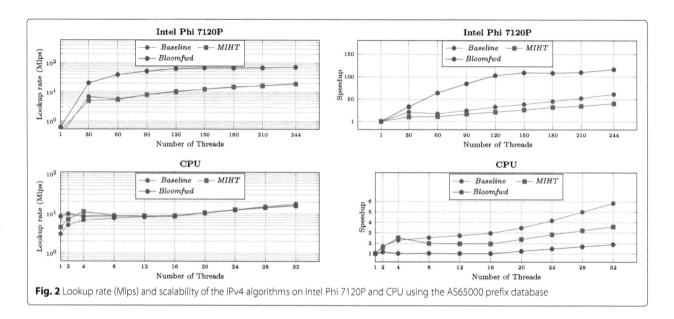

Fig. 2 Lookup rate (Mlps) and scalability of the IPv4 algorithms on Intel Phi 7120P and CPU using the AS65000 prefix database

database and an input IP address dataset with 2^{26} random IP addresses.

The results presented in Fig. 1 show that the performance of the application is affected by the FPR and hash functions. As presented, the use of Knuth resulted in a lower average performance as compared to other methods. The reason for the observed results is that this hash function preserves divisibility, e.g., if integer keys are all divisible by 2 or by 4, their hash values will also be. This is a problem in Bloom filters or hash tables in general, where many values will address the same bits in the bit-vector and only a half or a quarter of the buckets will end up being used, respectively.

On the other hand, Murmur and H2 are more sophisticated functions that provide a smaller number of collisions, hence all the configurations using any combination of them attained similar execution times. However, the best average performance was reached with 30% of FPR, where the results are less scattered for all hash functions. Furthermore, the best performance was attained when H2

was used in both stages of the algorithm. This occurs, in part, because we are able to reuse the hash calculated to probe the Bloom filter to address the hash table and, as a consequence, hash calculations are saved. Therefore, we use the configuration of 30% of FPR and H2 for both stages in the remaining experiments for IPv4. Because H2 only works for 32-bit unsigned integers and Murmur also resulted in good performance, we use 30% of FPR and MurmurHash3 (64 bits) for IPv6. As shown, the compromises of having a small or high FPR are complex. A small FPR will perform less hash calculations and use smaller data structures, whereas a high FPR will perform more hash computations and employ larger data structures. As such, the first is less expensive in the filter access, but may result in extra HT accesses, whereas the high FPR has an opposite compromise.

6.3 The scalability of BFs and MIHT

This section evaluates the optimized BFs algorithm for IPv4, which we refer here to as Bloomfwd, as the number

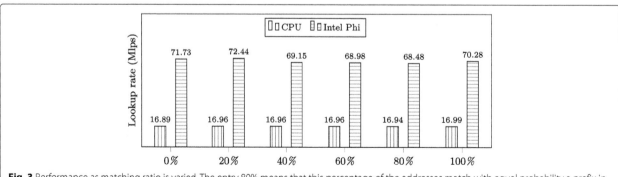

Fig. 3 Performance as matching ratio is varied. The entry 80% means that this percentage of the addresses match with equal probability a prefix in the forwarding table, while 20% of them end up in the default route

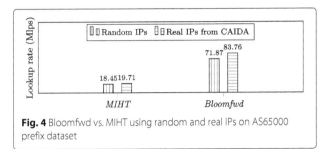

Fig. 4 Bloomfwd vs. MIHT using random and real IPs on AS65000 prefix dataset

of computing cores used is increased on the 7120P Intel Phi and on the CPU. We compare Bloomfwd to a Baseline implementation of the algorithm, introduced in Section 4.1, and to the MIHT. The difference between Baseline and Bloomfwd is on the hash functions, i.e., Baseline uses the standard C *rand()* function without vectorization [3, 17]. The MIHT is an algorithm that has outperformed several other IP lookup algorithms [18]. Our implementation of MIHT for IPv4 was tuned according to the original work for the (16,16)-MIHT. The speedups for the IPv6 dataset are similar and were omitted because of space constraints.

The lookup rates (in log scale) and speedups for both algorithms and processors are presented in Fig. 2. As shown, the performance of MIHT (≈ 0.46 Mlps) is better than Baseline (≈ 0.31 Mlps) for the sequential execution on the Intel Phi. However, as the number of computing threads used increases, the performance gap reduces quickly due to the better scalability of the BFs approach. For instance, the maximum speedup of Baseline as compared to its sequential counterpart is about $61\times$, whereas MIHT attains a speedup of only up to $40\times$ when compared to its sequential version. The Bloomfwd, on the other hand, is the fastest algorithm on a single core and is still able to attain better scalability on the Intel Phi ($116\times$). Also, it is at least $3.7\times$ faster than the other algorithms. The differences between the lookup rates of Bloomfwd and Baseline highlights the importance of the use of vectorization and the hash function choice to performance.

The analysis of the CPU results show that all algorithms attained very similar lookup rates at scale in a multi-threaded setup, though they attained different speedups.

We attribute the similar performance of the algorithms on the CPU to the fact that the memory bandwidth of this processor is much smaller than that of Intel Phi, which limits the scalability of the solutions [45]. Because the Bloomfwd is the fastest sequential algorithm, it reaches the memory bandwidth limits earlier as the number of cores used increases.

6.4 The impact of input address (queries) characteristics on performance

In order to investigate the effects of the input addresses on the performance, we performed the lookups using pseudo-random generated datasets containing 2^{26} IP addresses with different matching ratios and the AS65000 prefix database. We call *matching ratio* the relation between the number of addresses that matches at least one prefix in the database and the total number of addresses, thus a matching ratio of 80% implies that 20% of the input addresses do not match any prefix in the database and, as such, end up being forwarded to the default route. This evaluation intended to vary the characteristics of the input data and evaluate the algorithms under different configurations.

We ensure that a given address has the same probability to match any prefix stored in the database, and we also filter out all the IETF/IANA reserved IP addresses. Please note that a workload for forwarding could include other characteristics, such as the arrival of packets in bursts. We use random IP input addresses because it may be considered the worst-case scenario and it is the most commonly method used in previous works.

The lookup rates obtained for the Bloomfwd algorithm on both the CPU and on the Intel Phi are shown in Fig. 3.

As presented in Fig. 3, the matching ratio has little impact in the overall performance of the application. The reason for that is that the case of an address matching some prefix in the database *is not necessarily faster* than the case where the address end up in the default route, and vice-versa. For example, consider an address that does not match any prefix in the forwarding table. If no false positives occur, i.e., the two Bloom filters correctly answer not to look in their associated hash tables, the search quickly finishes with one additional memory access to the DLA.

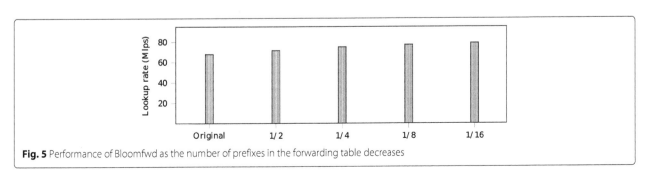

Fig. 5 Performance of Bloomfwd as the number of prefixes in the forwarding table decreases

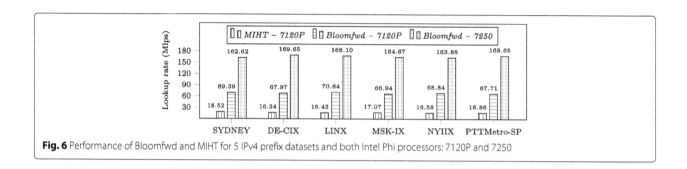

Fig. 6 Performance of Bloomfwd and MIHT for 5 IPv4 prefix datasets and both Intel Phi processors: 7120P and 7250

However, if for another prefix a false positive occurs in the first, but not in the second Bloom filter, or if there are plenty of values stored in the searched hash table buckets, then this case of matching will likely be *slower* than the former. As such, the speed and good statistical distribution of the hash function to control the FPR and also minimize the number of collisions in the hash tables is an important aspect to limit variations in performance as a result of dataset characteristics.

Further, in Fig. 4, we present the performance of Bloomfwd and MIHT for the AS65000 dataset using both random and real IP addresses from CAIDA traces. This comparison is interesting because it shows the impact, for instance, of the cache on performance. In the case of IPs from real trace, the same IP will be queried multiple times as a consequence, for instance, of a continuous communication flow among pairs of nodes. In the Bloomfwd case, the performance using the real IPs is about 1.16× higher than the case that uses random IPs.

6.5 The impact of the lookup table size to the performance

This section evaluates the impact of the lookup table size to the performance of our Bloomfwd algorithm into the 7120P Intel Phi processor. For sake of this analysis, we performed the lookups using pseudo-random generated datasets containing 2^{26} IP addresses and. Further, to evaluate different table sizes we have used the AS65000 prefix database as a reference (original) and have

randomly removed prefixes from this dataset to create smaller tables.

The experimental results are presented in Fig. 5. As expected, the performance of the algorithm improves as the size of the table used is reduced. In this evaluation, the lookup rate has increased from about 68 Mlps using the original dataset for about 79 Mlps (1.16×) when the number of prefixes is 1/16 of the original size.

6.6 The IP lookup performance for IPv4 and IPv6

This section evaluates the BFs algorithms on IPv4 and IPv6 prefix datasets in both 7120P and 7250. First, we discuss the performance for the 5 remaining IPv4 prefix databases presented in Table 3 using a querying input dataset with 2^{26} random IP addresses. The results, presented in Fig. 6, show that the performance gains of our Bloomfwd as compared to the MIHT is about 4× for 7120P, regardless of the dataset used. Further, we execute the Bloomfwd in the 7250 processor, and the algorithm attained an additional speedup of about 2.4× as compared to the execution in 7120P and a throughput of up to 169.65 Mlps. This significant performance gap between the processors could not be directly derived from their different characteristics, presented in Section 2.1. Therefore, we have benchmarked the processors using the STREAM benchmark (data-intensive application) and we have observed that, in practice, the 7250 attains a memory bandwidth that is about 2.7× higher than the 7120P, which explains the gains of the Bloomfwd with the 7120P.

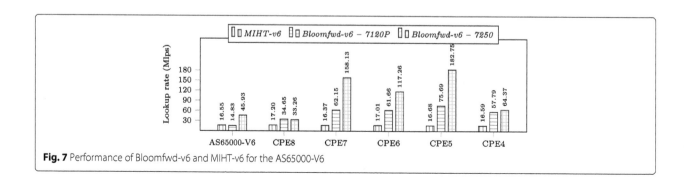

Fig. 7 Performance of Bloomfwd-v6 and MIHT-v6 for the AS65000-V6

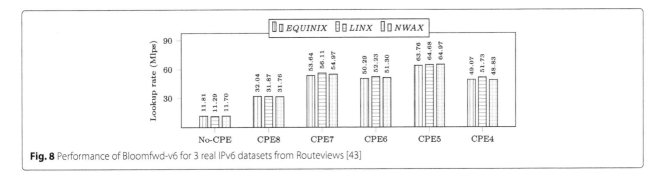

Fig. 8 Performance of Bloomfwd-v6 for 3 real IPv6 datasets from Routeviews [43]

We further evaluate the performance of the Bloom filters algorithm for IPv6 and the impact of using our DPCPE optimization. This experiment compares the lookup rates of our implementation (Bloomfwd-v6) with the corresponding version of MIHT for IPv6 (MIHT-v6 – the (32,32)-MIHT [18]).

Figure 7 shows the results for the AS65000-V6 with and without the use of DPCPE for multiple expansion levels and 2^{26} random input addresses. As presented, the performance of the Bloomfwd-v6 is greatly improved by the use of DPCPE, and the expansion with 5 levels is about 5.1× faster than the performance without CPE in the 7120P. This version is also 4.5× faster than the MIHT-v6 algorithm.

The performance of MIHT-v6 is similar in all cases because it groups routes by keys in Priority Tries (PTs), rather than prefix lengths (as in the Bloom filters approach). In other words, the number of distinct prefix lengths in the forwarding table does not directly affect the performance of MIHT. The Bloomfwd-v6 on the Intel Phi 7250 attained a throughput of up to 182.75 Mlps, and as presented there is a strong variation in performance as the number of CPE levels used is varied. The choice of the CPE levels is complex and involves many aspects such as caching capabilities and its effects on FPR, which requires an experimental evaluation for its adequate choice.

We have also evaluated the performance of MIHT-v6 and Bloomfwd-v6 using IP addresses from a real trace from CAIDA and the AS65000-V6 dataset. The MIHT-v6 and Bloomfwd-v6 achieved lookup rates of 19.7 Mlps and

83.76 Mlps, respectively, on the 7120P. We further executed the Bloomfwd-v6 in 7250 and it attained a lookup rate of 179.6 Mlps. These results are consistent with the ones using random queries and confirm the gains of our propositions. Finally, we executed the Bloomfwd-v6 in the Intel Phi 7120P for three other real IPv6 prefix datasets collected from Routeviews [43]. As depicted in Fig. 8, for each CPE configuration the algorithm attained similar lookup rates regardless of the prefix dataset. Furthermore, the performance pattern matches the one obtained for AS65000-V6 (Fig. 7), in which CPE5 was the best configuration.

6.7 Cooperative execution and data transfers strategies

This section evaluates the performance gains resulting from an implementation of Bloomfwd that employs an asynchronous strategy to fill and process two IP address buffers concurrently (double buffering) using the CPU and the Intel Xeon Phi 7120P cooperatively. The results from the synchronous execution were omitted because the performance of the asynchronous version was better in all cases, reaching speedups of up to 1.13× in comparison to the former. In order to exploit double buffering, the async strategy must choose an appropriate size for the buffers, which we have defined experimentally focusing on maximizing the IP lookup throughput. Figure 9 shows the impact of the buffer size on the performance of the application.

Figure 9 shows that the best performance is obtained using a 4M (*mebipackets*) buffer. However, despite the

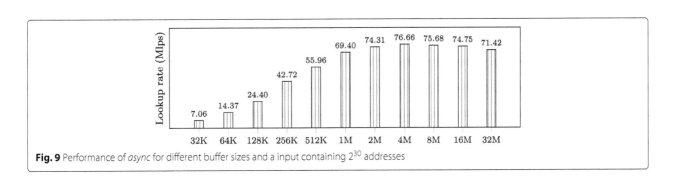

Fig. 9 Performance of *async* for different buffer sizes and a input containing 2^{30} addresses

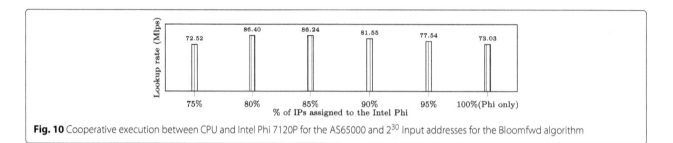

Fig. 10 Cooperative execution between CPU and Intel Phi 7120P for the AS65000 and 2^{30} input addresses for the Bloomfwd algorithm

throughput, another aspect that must be taken into consideration when choosing the buffer size is the trade-off between the buffer size and the average latency to compute lookups. Because the lookup rate attained with buffers of 2M was very close to the best performance (achieved with buffers of 4M), and considering that the time to process a 2M buffer (about 28ms including lookup and data transfers) is nearly $2\times$ smaller than the 4M case, we have chosen the 2M configuration in the next experiments, which evaluates the cooperative execution using the CPU and the Intel Phi 7120P to process 2^{30} random IPv4 addresses.

In the cooperative evaluation, the amount of work (% of IP addresses) assigned for computation in the coprocessor is varied. The rest of the IP addresses in each case are processed by the CPU. The previous experiments show that the Intel Phi is about to $4\times$ faster than the CPU execution. As such, our workload division strategy assigns about 80% of the IP addresses to the Intel Phi and the rest to the CPU. The results presented in Fig. 10 confirm that this is the best configuration, leading to a speedup of $1.18\times$ on top of the Intel Phi only execution. The combined gain with async and cooperative execution is about $1.33\times$ vs. the Intel Phi only execution.

7 Conclusions and future directions

In this work, we have designed, implemented, and evaluated the performance of efficient algorithms for IP lookup (MIHT and BFs approach) in multi-/many-core systems. The MIHT is known to be an efficient sequential algorithm [3]. However, it is also irregular, which typically leads to reduced opportunities for optimized execution on parallel systems. The baseline BFs algorithm, on the other hand, is a more compute intensive and regular algorithm with a less efficient sequential version. Nevertheless, it offers more opportunities for optimizations, for instance, due to SIMD instructions, and it is more scalable. As presented, the optimized BFs algorithm significantly outperformed the MIHT on the Intel Phi, and it was able to compute up to 169.6 Mlps (84.8 Gbps for 64B packets) and 182.7 Mlps (119.9 Gbps for 84B packets). The recent improvements in the Intel Phi, such as larger memory bandwidth, higher number of computing cores, and the possibility of its use as a standalone processor, makes

it a very attractive and promising platform for the development of high-performance software routers.

Finally, as a future work, we would like to evaluate the use of our Bloom filters based approach in Open Flow networks to perform Ethernet and TCP/UDP lookup (in addition to IP). We argue this is a promising approach because Bloom filters is capable of performing different kinds of pattern matching algorithms [46]. Further, we also want to integrate our accelerated lookup into a complete software router solution as DPDK [47] or ClickOS [20] running on top of Xeon Phi hardware to investigate the efficiency of a low cost solution.

Acknowledgments
The authors thank the anonymous reviewers for helpful comments that increased the quality of the article.

Funding
This work was supported in part by CNPq and CAPES/Brazil. This research used resources of the XSEDE Science Gateways program under grant TG-ASC130023.

Authors' contributions
Conceived and designed the experiments: AL, AD, and GT. Performed the experiments: AL. Analyzed the data: AL, AD, and GT. Wrote the manuscript: AL, AD, and GT. All authors read and approved the final manuscript.

References
1. Han S, Jang K, Park K, Moon S. PacketShader: a GPU-accelerated software router. ACM SIGCOMM Comput Commun Rev. 2011;41(4):195–206.
2. Kalia A, Zhou D, Kaminsky M, Andersen DG. Raising the Bar for Using GPUs in Software Packet Processing. In: NSDI. Washington, DC: IEEE; 2015. p. 409–23.
3. Lin CH, Hsu CY, Hsieh SY. A multi-index hybrid trie for lookup and updates. IEEE Trans Parallel Distributed Syst. 2014;25(10):2486–98.
4. Venkatachary S, Varghese G. Faster IP lookups using controlled prefix expansion. Perform Eval Rev. 1998;26:1–10.
5. Lucchesi A, Drummond A, Teodoro G. Parallel and Efficient IP Lookup using Bloom Filters on Intel® Xeon Phi™. In: Proceedings of the XXXV Brazilian Symposium on Computer Networks and Distributed Systems (SBRC). Porto Alegre: SBC; 2017. p. 229–42.
6. Jeffers J, Reinders J. Intel Xeon Phi Coprocessor High-performance Programming. Amsterdam, Boston (Mass.): Elsevier Waltham (Mass.); 2013.
7. Mu S, Zhang X, Zhang N, Lu J, Deng YS, Zhang S. IP Routing Processing with Graphic Processors. In: Proceedings of the Conference on Design, Automation and Test in Europe. Washington, DC: European Design and Automation Association; 2010. p. 93–8.

8. Yang T, Xie G, Li Y, Fu Q, Liu AX, Li Q, Mathy L. Guarantee IP lookup performance with FIB explosion. ACM SIGCOMM Comput Commun Rev. 2015;44(4):39–50.

9. Chu H-M, Li T-H, Wang P-C. IP Address Lookup by using GPU. IEEE Trans Emerg Top Comput. 2016;4:187–98.

10. Li Y, Zhang D, Liu AX, Zheng J. GAMT: A Fast and Scalable IP Lookup Engine for GPU-based Software Routers. In: Proceedings of the Ninth ACM/IEEE Symposium on Architectures for Networking and Communications Systems. Washington, DC: IEEE Press; 2013. p. 1–12.

11. Ruiz-Sanchez M, Biersack EW, Dabbous W, et al. Survey and Taxonomy of IP Address Lookup Algorithms. IEEE Netw. 2001;15(2):8–23.

12. Hsieh SY, Yang YC. A classified Multisuffix Trie for IP lookup and update. IEEE Trans Comput. 2012;61(5):726–31.

13. Sahni S, Lu H. Dynamic Tree Bitmap for IP Lookup and Update. In: Networking, 2007. ICN'07. Sixth International Conference On. Washington, DC: IEEE; 2007. p. 79–9.

14. Lim H, Yim C, Swartzlander Jr EE. Priority tries for IP address lookup. IEEE Trans Comput. 2010;59(6):784–94.

15. Rétvári G, Tapolcai J, Kőrösi A, Majdán A, Heszberger Z. Compressing IP Forwarding Tables: Towards Entropy Bounds and Beyond. In: ACM SIGCOMM Computer Communication Review, vol. 3. New York: ACM; 2013. p. 111–22.

16. Asai H, Ohara Y. Poptrie: a compressed trie with population count for fast and scalable software IP routing table lookup. In: ACM SIGCOMM Computer Communication Review, vol. 45. New York: ACM; 2015. p. 57–70.

17. Dharmapurikar S, Krishnamurthy P, Taylor DE. Longest Prefix Matching Using Bloom Filters. IEEE/ACM Trans Netw. 2006;14(2):397–409.

18. Lim H, Lim K, Lee N, Park KH. On Adding Bloom Filters to Longest Prefix Matching Algorithms. IEEE Trans Comput. 2014;63(2):411–23.

19. Ni S, Guo R, Liao X, Jin H. Parallel bloom filter on xeon phi many-core processors. In: International Conference on Algorithms and Architectures for Parallel Processing. Cham: Springer; 2015. p. 388–405.

20. Kohler E, Morris R, Chen B, Jannotti J, Kaashoek MF. The Click Modular Router. ACM Trans Comput Syst (TOCS). 2000;18(3):263–97.

21. Dobrescu M, Egi N, Argyraki K, Chun BG, Fall K, Iannaccone G, Knies A, Manesh M, Ratnasamy S. RouteBricks: Exploiting Parallelism to Scale Software Routers. In: Proc. of the ACM SIGOPS 22nd Symposium on Operating Systems Principles. New York: ACM; 2009. p. 15–28.

22. Open vSwitch: An Open Virtual Switch. 2017. http://openvswitch.org/. Accessed 25 Aug 2017.

23. Fan L, Cao P, Almeida J, Broder AZ. Summary Cache: A Scalable Wide-Area Web Cache Sharing Protocol. IEEE/ACM Trans Netw (TON). 2000;8(3):281–93.

24. Bloom BH. Space/time trade-offs in hash coding with allowable errors. Commun ACM. 1970;13(7):422–6.

25. Kirsch A, Mitzenmacher M. Less hashing, same performance: building a better bloom filter. Random Struct Algorithms. 2008;33(2):187–218.

26. OpenMP API for Parallel Programming, Version 4.0. 2016. http://openmp.org/. Accessed 25 Aug 2017.

27. Dharmapurikar S, Krishnamurthy P, Taylor DE. Longest prefix matching using bloom filters. In: Proceedings of the 2003 Conference on Applications, Technologies, Architectures, and Protocols for Computer Communications. New York: ACM; 2003. p. 201–12.

28. Appleby A. MurmurHash3 Hash Function. 2011. https://code.google.com/p/smhasher/wiki/MurmurHash3. Accessed 25 Aug 2017.

29. Knuth DE. The Art of Computer Programming: Sorting and Searching, vol. 3. Boston: Pearson Education; 1998.

30. Mueller T. H2 Database Engine. 2006. http://h2database.com. Accessed 25 Aug 2017.

31. Intel. Intel Intrinsics Guide. 2015. https://software.intel.com/sites/landingpage/IntrinsicsGuide/. Accessed 25 Aug 2017.

32. Sundaram N, Raghunathan A, Chakradhar ST. A framework for efficient and scalable execution of domain-specific templates on GPUs. In: IPDPS '09: Proceedings of the 2009 IEEE International Symposium on Parallel and Distributed Processing. Washington, DC: IEEE; 2009. p. 1–12. doi:10.1109/IPDPS.2009.5161039.

33. Luk CK, Hong S, Kim H. Qilin: exploiting parallelism on heterogeneous multiprocessors with adaptive mapping. In: 42nd International Symposium on Microarchitecture (MICRO). Washington, DC: IEEE; 2009.

34. Augonnet C, Thibault S, Namyst R, Wacrenier PA. StarPU: a unified platform for task scheduling on heterogeneous multicore architectures. In: Euro-Par '09: Proceedings of the 15th International Euro-Par Conference on Parallel Processing. Berlin: Springer-Verlag Publisher; 2009. p. 863–74. doi:10.1007/978-3-642-03869-3_80.

35. Teodoro G, Sachetto R, Sertel O, Gurcan MN, Meira W, Catalyurek U, Ferreira R. Coordinating the Use of GPU and CPU for Improving Performance of Compute Intensive Applications. In: IEEE International Conference on Cluster Computing and Workshops, 2009. CLUSTER'09. Washington, DC: IEEE; 2009. p. 1–10.

36. Duran A, Ayguadé E, Badia RM, Labarta J, Martinell L, Martorell X, Planas J. OmpSs: a proposal for programming heterogeneous multi-core architectures. Parallel Process Lett. 2011;21(02):173–93.

37. Teodoro G, Pan T, Kurc TM, Kong J, Cooper LA, Podhorszki N, Klasky S, Saltz JH. High-throughput analysis of large microscopy image datasets on CPU-GPU cluster platforms. In: 2013 IEEE 27th International Symposium on Parallel and Distributed Processing (IPDPS). Washington, DC: IEEE; 2013. p. 103–14.

38. Sancho JC, Kerbyson DJ. Analysis of Double Buffering on two Different Multicore Architectures: Quad-core Opteron and the Cell-BE. In: International Parallel and Distributed Processing Symposium (IPDPS). Washington, DC: IEEE; 2008.

39. Teodoro G, Kurc T, Kong J, Cooper L, Saltz J. Comparative Performance Analysis of Intel(R) Xeon Phi(tm), GPU, and CPU: a Case Study from Microscopy Image Analysis. In: 2014 IEEE 28th International Parallel and Distributed Processing Symposium. Washington, DC: IEEE; 2014. p. 1063–72.

40. Teodoro G, Kurc T, Andrade G, Kong J, Ferreira R, Saltz J. Application performance analysis and efficient execution on systems with multi-core CPUs, GPUs and MICs: a case study with microscopy image analysis. Int J High Perform Comput Appl. 2017;31(1):32–51.

41. The CAIDA UCSD Anonymized Internet Traces 2016. 2016. http://www.caida.org/data/passive/passive_2016_dataset.xml. Accessed 25 Aug 2017.

42. BGP Potaroo. 2016. http://bgp.potaroo.net/. Accessed 25 Aug 2017.

43. University of Oregon Route Views Project. 2017. http://www.routeviews.org/. Accessed 25 Aug 2017.

44. RIPE Network Coordination Centre. 2016. http://data.ris.ripe.net/. Accessed 25 Aug 2017.

45. Gomes JM, Teodoro G, de Melo A, Kong J, Kurc T, Saltz JH. Efficient irregular wavefront propagation algorithms on Intel (r) Xeon Phi (tm). In: 2015 27th International Symposium on Computer Architecture and High Performance Computing (SBAC-PAD). Washington, DC: IEEE; 2015. p. 25–32.

46. Broder A, Mitzenmacher M. Network applications of bloom filters: a survey. Internet Math. 2004;1(4):485–509.

47. DPDK. 2017. http://dpdk.org/. Accessed 25 Aug 2017.

8

EZ-AG: structure-free data aggregation in MANETs using push-assisted self-repelling random walks

V. Kulathumani[1*], M. Nakagawa[1] and A. Arora[2]

Abstract

This paper describes EZ-AG, a structure-free protocol for duplicate insensitive data aggregation in MANETs. The key idea in EZ-AG is to introduce a token that performs a self-repelling random walk in the network and aggregates information from nodes when they are visited for the first time. A self-repelling random walk of a token on a graph is one in which at each step, the token moves to a neighbor that has been visited least often. While self-repelling random walks visit all nodes in the network much faster than plain random walks, they tend to slow down when most of the nodes are already visited. In this paper, we show that a *single step push phase at each node* can significantly speed up the aggregation and eliminate this slow down. By doing so, EZ-AG achieves aggregation in only $O(N)$ time and messages. In terms of overhead, EZ-AG outperforms existing structure-free data aggregation by a factor of at least $log(N)$ and achieves the lower bound for aggregation message overhead. We demonstrate the scalability and robustness of EZ-AG using ns-3 simulations in networks ranging from 100 to 4000 nodes under different mobility models and node speeds. We also describe a hierarchical extension for EZ-AG that can produce multi-resolution aggregates at each node using only $O(NlogN)$ messages, which is a poly-logarithmic factor improvement over existing techniques.

Keywords: Mobile ad-hoc, Random walks, Scalable and robust data aggregation, Multi-resolution synopsis

1 Introduction

The focus of this paper is on computing order and duplicate insensitive data aggregates (also referred to as ODI-synopsis) and delivering them to every node in a mobile ad-hoc network (MANET) [1–4]. We are specifically motivated by data aggregation requirements in extremely large scale mobile sensor networks [5] such as networks of UAVs, military networks, network of mobile robots and dense vehicular networks, where the number of nodes are often several thousands.

In an order and duplicate insensitive (ODI) synopsis, the same data can be aggregated multiple times but the result is unaffected. MAX, MIN and BOOLEAN OR are natural examples of such duplicate insensitive data aggregation. These queries by themselves are quite common in many applications and some examples are provided below.

As one specific example, consider the application domain of intelligent transportation systems using dense vehicular ad-hoc networks (VANETs) [6]. VANETs are mobile networks supported by both vehicle to vehicle (V2V) and vehicle to road-side infrastructure (V2I) communication, which are in turn enabled by Dedicated Short Range Communication units (DSRC) on board each vehicle [7]. VANETs can be used for improving vehicular safety as well as efficiency by dynamically updating traffic maps and providing efficient re-routes [8]. For such applications, EZ-AG can be used to generate duplicate insensitive aggregates such as the maximum speed or minimum speed in a given area (that are indicative of congestion). It can be used to answer queries such as *is there any vehicle that exceeded a certain speed?*. It can be also used to answer V2I network management queries such as *is there at least one active infrastructure unit within a given area?*. VANETs are also often augmented with environmental sensors for tasks such as pollution monitoring [9]. In such applications, aggregation queries related to the sensors can be answered using EZ-AG.

*Correspondence: vinod.kulathumani@mail.wvu.edu
[1]Department of Computer Science and Electrical Engineering, West Virginia University, Morgantown WV 26505, USA
Full list of author information is available at the end of the article

EZ-AG can also be used for data aggregation in networks of drones, UAVs [10] and underwater robotic swarms [11]. For instance, EZ-AG can be used to answer queries such as *which is the drone with minimum or maximum battery level?* or *which robotic fish detects maximum pollution?* Aggregation queries resolved by EZ-AG can also be used for *consensus driven control applications.* For example, EZ-AG can be used to dynamically navigate networks of aerial vehicles towards the area with *minimum turbulence* [12] or to dynamically navigate a swarm of robotic fish [13] towards regions of higher vegetation.

Other duplicate sensitive statistical aggregates such as COUNT and AVERAGE can also be implemented with ODI synopsis using probabilistic techniques [4, 14]. Using these extensions, EZ-AG can be used to generate duplicate sensitive aggregates such as the number of vehicles in a road segment or average speed of vehicles in a road segment.

In static sensor networks and networks with stable links, data aggregation can be performed by routing along fixed structures such as trees or network backbones [15–18]. However, in MANETs, routing has proven to be quite challenging beyond scales of a few hundred nodes primarily because topology driven structures are unstable and are likely to incur a high communication overhead for maintenance in the presence of node mobility [19]. Therefore, structure-free techniques are more appropriate for data aggregation in MANETs. However, a simple technique like all to all flooding which involves dissemination of data from each node to every other node in the network is not scalable as it incurs an overall cost of $O\left(N^2\right)$, where N is the number of nodes in the network. Therefore, in this paper we explore the use of self-repelling random walks as a structure free method for data aggregation.

1.1 Overview of approach
Random walks are appropriate for data aggregation in mobile networks because they are inherently unaffected by node mobility. The idea is to introduce a token in the network that successively visits all nodes in the network using a random walk traversal and computes the overall aggregate. We say that a node is *visited* by a token when the node gets exclusive access to the token; the visitation period can be used by the node to add node-specific information into the token, resulting in data aggregation. Note that the concept of visiting all nodes individually differs from that of token dissemination [20, 21] over the entire network where it suffices for every node to simply hear at least one token, as opposed to getting exclusive access to a token.

Note, however that traditional random walks may be too slow in visiting all nodes in the network because they may get stuck in regions of already visited nodes. Hence, in this paper we consider self-repelling random walks [22].

A self-repelling random walk is one in which at each step the walk moves towards one of the neighbors that has been least visited [22] (with ties broken randomly). Self-repelling random walks were introduced in the 1980*s* and have been studied extensively in the physics literature. One of the striking properties of self-repelling random walks is the remarkable uniformity with which they visit nodes in a graph, i.e., without getting stuck in already visited regions.

Indeed, our results in this paper confirm that until about 85% coverage, duplicate visits are very rare with self-repelling random walks highlighting the efficiency with which a majority of nodes in the network can be visited without extra overhead. However, we observe a slow down when going towards 100% coverage because when most of the nodes are already visited, the token executing self-repelling random walk has to explore the graph to find the next unvisited node. To correct this shortcoming, we introduce a complementary *push* phase that speeds up the convergence of the random walk. The *push* phase consists of just one message from each node: before the random walk is started, each node announces its own state to all its neighbors. Note that the *push* consists of only a single hop broadcast from a node to its neighbors as opposed to a flood which consists of disseminating a node's state to all the nodes in the entire network. Thus, after the push phase, each node now carries information about all its neighbors. As a result, when the random walk executes, it does not have to visit all nodes to finish the aggregation. In fact, we show that the aggregation can finish *before* the slow down starts for the self-repelling random walk. As a result both the aggregation time and number of messages are now bounded by $O(N)$, as shown in our analysis.

1.2 Summary of contributions
- We introduce a novel structure-free technique for data aggregation in MANETs that exploits properties of self-repelling random walks and complements it with a push phase. We find that *a little push goes a long way* in speeding up aggregation and reducing message overhead. In fact, the push phase consists of just a single message from each node to its neighbors. By adding this push phase, we show that both the aggregation time and number of messages are bounded in EZ-AG by $O(N)$. In fact, we show that aggregation is completed in significantly less than N token transfers. The protocol is thus extremely simple, requires very little state maintenance (each nodes only remembers the number of times it has been visited), requires no network structures or clustering.
- We compare our results with structure-free techniques for ODI data aggregation such as gossiping and show a $log(N)$ factor improvement in

messages compared to existing gossip based techniques. We evaluate our protocol using simulations in ns-3 on networks ranging from 100 to 4000 nodes under various mobility models and node speeds. We also evaluate and compare our protocol with a prototype tree-based technique for data aggregation (i.e., structure based) and show that our protocol is better suited for MANETs and remains scalable under high mobility. In fact, *the performance of EZ-AG improves as node mobility increases.*

- Finally, we also provide an extension to EZ-AG which supplies multi-resolution aggregates to each node. In networks that are quite large, providing each node with only a single aggregate may not be sufficient. On the other hand, providing each node with information about every other node is not scalable. Hierarchical EZ-AG addresses this issue by providing each node with multiple aggregates of neighborhoods of increasing size around itself. Each node can thus have information from all parts of the network, but with a resolution that decays exponentially with distance. This idea is motivated by the fact that in many systems information about nearby regions is more relevant and important than far away regions with progressively increasing importance as distance decreases. Moreover, we also show that aggregates of nearby regions can be obtained at a progressively faster rate than farther regions. Hierarchical EZ-AG uses only $O(NlogN)$ messages and outperforms existing techniques for multi-resolution data aggregation by a factor of $log^{4.4}N$.

1.3 Outline of the paper
In Section 2, we describe related work and specifically compare our contributions with existing work in structured protocols, structure free protocols and random walks. In Section 3, we state the system model. In Section 4, we describe the EZ-AG protocol. In Section 5, we analytically characterize the bound on messages and time for EZ-AG. In Section 6, we describe a hierarchical extension for EZ-AG. In Section 7, we describe the results of our evaluation using ns-3 and compare EZ-AG with a prototype tree-based protocol for data aggregation. We conclude in Section 8.

2 Related work
2.1 Structure-based protocols
The problem of data aggregation and one-shot querying has been well studied in the context of static sensor networks. It has been shown that in-network aggregation techniques using spanning trees and network backbones are efficient and reliable solutions for the problem [15–18]. However, in the context of a mobile network, such fixed routing structures are likely to be unstable and

could potentially incur a high communication overhead for maintenance [19]. In this paper, we have systematically compared EZ-AG with a prototype tree-based technique for data aggregation and have shown that it outperforms the tree-based idea in mobile networks. We notice that the improvement gets progressively more significant as the average node speed increases.

2.2 Structure-free protocols
Flooding, neighborhood gossip and spatial gossip are three structure-free techniques that can be used for data aggregation. Note that flooding data from all nodes to every other node has a messaging cost of $O(N^2)$. Alternatively, one could use multiple rounds of neighborhood gossip where in each round a node averages the current state of all its neighbors and this procedure is repeated until convergence [23, 24]. However, this method requires several iterations and has also been shown to have a communication cost and completion time of $O(N^2)$ for convergence in grids or random geometric graphs, where connectivity is based on locality [25].

In [1, 2], a spatial gossip technique is described where each node chooses another node in the network (not just neighbors) at random and gossips its state. When this is repeated $O(log^{1+\epsilon}N)$ times, all nodes in the network learn about the aggregate state. Note that this scheme requires $O(N.polylog(N))$ messages. Our random walk based protocol, EZ-AG, requires only $O(N)$ messages. Note also that while all this prior work is on static networks, we demonstrate our results on mobile ad-hoc networks.

2.3 Random walks
Random walks and their cover times (time taken to visit all nodes) have been studied extensively for different types of *static* graphs [26, 27]. In this paper, we are specifically interested in time varying graphs that are relevant in the context of mobile networks.

Self-avoiding and self-repelling random walks are variants of random walks which bias the walk towards unvisited nodes [22]. The unformity in coverage of such random walks in 2-d lattices has been pointed in [28]. Our paper extends the analysis of self-repelling random walks presented in [28] for application in mobile ad-hoc networks that are modeled as time varying random geometric graphs. Further, we show that by complementing self-repelling random walks with a push phase, we can complete aggergation in $O(N)$ time and messages. The idea of locally biasing random walks and its impact in speeding up coverage has been pointed out in [29] for static networks. Self-repelling random walks are different than the local bias technique presented in [29]. Moreover, we show how to improve the convergence of self-repelling random walks using a complementary push-phase and demonstrate our results on mobile networks.

In a recent paper [30], we have addressed the problem of duplicate-sensitive aggregation using self-repelling random walks and in that solution we have used a gradient technique to speed up self-repelling random walks. The short temporary gradients introduced in [30] are used to *pull* the token towards unvisited nodes so that each node is visited at least once. The solution in [30] requires $O(N.log(N))$ messages. In this paper, we address duplicate insensitive aggregation and show that it can be achieved using self-repelling random walks with just $O(N)$ messages.

3 Model

3.1 Network model

We consider a mobile network of N nodes modeled as a geometric Markovian evolving graph [31]. Each node has a communication range R. We assume that the N nodes are independently and uniformly deployed over a square region of sides $\sqrt{A}$ resulting in a network density $\rho = N/A$ of the deployed nodes. Consider the region to be divided into square cells of sides $R/\sqrt{2}$. Thus the diagonal of each such cell is the communication range R. Let $R^2 > 2clog(N)/\rho$. It has been shown that there exists a constant $c > 1$ such that each such cell has $\theta(logN)$ nodes whp, i.e., the degree of each node is $\theta(logN)$ whp. Such graphs are referred to as geo-dense geometric graphs [29]. Denote $d = \theta(logN)$ as the degree of connectivity.

The objective of the protocol is to compute a duplicate insensitive aggregate of the state of nodes in a MANET. The aggregate could be initiated by any of the nodes in the MANET or by a special static node such as a base station that is connected to the rest of the nodes. The aggregate needs to be disseminated to all nodes in the network. The protocol could be invoked in a one-shot or periodic aggregation mode.

3.2 Mobility model

We consider 3 different mobility models for our evaluations.

- The first is a random direction mobility model (with reflection) [32, 33] for the nodes. This is a special case of the random walk mobility model [34]. In this mobility model, at each interval a node picks a random direction uniformly in the range $[0, 2\pi]$ and moves with a constant speed that is randomly chosen in the range $[v_l, v_h]$. At the end of each interval, a new direction and speed are calculated. If the node hits a boundary, the direction is reversed. Motion of the nodes is independent of each other. An important characteristic of this mobility model is that it preserves the uniformity of node distribution: given that at time $t = 0$ the position and orientation of users are independent and uniform, they remain

uniformly distributed for all times $t > 0$ provided the users move independently of each other [31, 33].
- The second is random waypoint mobility model. Here, each mobile node randomly selects one location in the simulation area and then travels towards this destination with constant velocity chosen randomly from $[v_l, v_h]$ [34]. Upon reaching the destination, the node stops for a duration defined by the *pause time*. After this duration, it again chooses another random destination and the process is repeated. We set the pause time to 2 s between successive changes.
- The third is Gauss Markov mobility model. In this model, the velocity of mobile node is assumed to be correlated over time and modeled as a Gauss-Markov stochastic process [34]. We set the temporal dependence parameter $\alpha = 0.75$. Velocity and direction are changed every 1 s in the Gauss Markov Model.

We consider node speeds in the range of 3 to 21 m/s. For the deployment density that we have chosen, a mapping between node speed and the average link changes per node per second is listed in Table 1. This table quantifies the link instability caused by node mobility at different node speeds. As seen in Table 1, because of high network density, the network structure is rapidly changing at the speeds chosen for evaluation.

While we have chosen the above mobility models for evaluation, we expect the results to hold even under other models such as motion on a Manhattan grid (suitable for vehicular networks). The crucial aspect of mobility that we capture in our evaluations is the high rate at which links change per second which is quantified in Table 1. Our results highlight that performance of EZ-AG actually improves with higher mobility speeds.

3.3 Metrics

A key metric that we are interested in is the number of times the token is transferred to already visited nodes. We present this in the form of *exploration overhead* which

Table 1 Mapping between speed and link changes per node per second (rounded off to integer)

Size	3 m/s	9 m/s	15 m/s	21 m/s
100	1	5	7	9
200	2	6	9	12
300	2	7	10	14
500	3	8	12	16
1000	3	9	14	18
2000	4	10	16	20
4000	4	12	18	23

is defined as the ratio of the number of token transfers to the number of unique nodes whose data has been aggregated into the token. We compute exploration overhead at different stages of coverage as the random walk progresses.

Typically, random walks are evaluated in terms of their *cover times*, which is defined as the time required to visit all nodes. For a standard random walk, the notion of physical time, messages and the number of steps are all equivalent. However, for the push assisted self-repelling random walks these are somewhat different. The total number of messages required to complete the data aggregation includes the push messages, the messages involved in the self-repelling random walk and the messages involved in disseminating the result to all the nodes using a flood. Moreover, each token transfer step itself consists of announcement, token request and token transfer messages. Thus, although proportional, the number of messages is different than the number of token transfer steps. Hence we separately characterize the number of messages during empirical evaluation.

Finally we note that since we study random walks on mobile networks, the notion of time is also related to node speed. Moreover, when dealing with wireless networks, time also involves messaging delays. Therefore, during empirical evaluation we separately characterize the actual convergence time (in seconds) along with the number of steps (i.e., number of token transfers).

4 Protocol

EZ-AG consists of 4 phases as shown in Fig. 1a. These phases are described below. The steps involved in the self-repelling random walk phase are shown in Fig. 1b. The communication cost in each of these phases is analyzed in Section 5.

Aggregation request phase: The node requesting the aggregate first initiates a flood in the network to notify all nodes about the interest in the aggregate. Note that each

node broadcasts this flood message exactly once. This results in N messages.

Push phase: Once a node receives this request, it *pushes* its state to its neighbors. Each node uses the data received from its neighbors to compute an aggregate of the state of all its neighbors. Note that the *push* consists of only a single hop broadcast from a node to all its neighbors. In contrast, a flood consists of disseminating a node's data to the entire network. Thus, the push phase also requires exactly N messages because each node broadcasts its data once.

Self-repelling random walk phase: Soon after the initiator sends out an aggregate request, it also initiates a token to perform a self-repelling random walk. A node that has the token broadcasts an *announce* message. Nodes that receive the announce message reply back with a token *request* message and include the number of times they have been visited by the token in this request. The node that holds the token selects the requesting node which has been visited least number of times (with ties broken randomly) and transfers the token to that node. This token transfer is repeated successively. Note that nodes which hear a token announcement schedule a token request at a random time t_r within a bounded interval, where t_r is proportional to the number of times that they have been visited. Thus nodes that have not been visited or visited fewer times send a request message earlier. When a node hears a request from a node that has been visited fewer or same number of times, it suppresses its request. Thus, the number of requests received for a token announcement remains fairly constant and irrespective of network density.

We note specifically that tokens do not grow in size when they visit successive nodes because they only carry the aggregated state. Determination of the next node to visit is done with the help of individual nodes which maintain a count of the number of times they have been

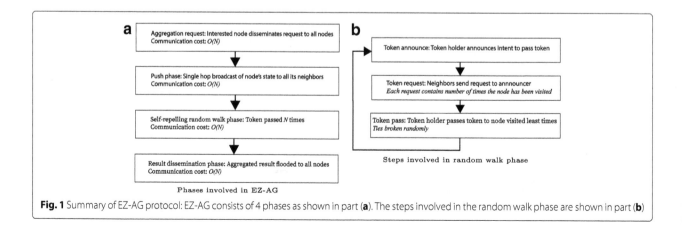

Fig. 1 Summary of EZ-AG protocol: EZ-AG consists of 4 phases as shown in part (**a**). The steps involved in the random walk phase are shown in part (**b**)

visited so far. This information is conveyed to the token holder after the *announce* message, which is then used to determine the next node to be visited. Thus, even at individual nodes, the state maintenance is minimal (each node only remembers the number of times it has been visited).

In the following section, we prove analytically that the aggregate can be computed from all nodes in the network whp in $O(N)$ token transfers. In the empirical evaluation, we show that the median number of token transfers is actually only kn, where $0 < k < 1$, and k is unaffected by network size. Thus, the median exploration overhead is less than 1. One can use this observation to terminate the self-repelling random walk after exactly N steps and whp one can expect that data from all the nodes has been aggregated.

Result dissemination phase: Once the aggregate has been computed, the result can simply be flooded back to all the nodes by the node that holds the result. This requires $O(N)$ messages. Another potential solution (when aggregate is only required at a base station) is to transmit the aggregated tokens using a long distance transmission link (such as cellular or satellite links) in hybrid MANETs where the *long links* are used for infrequent, high priority data.

The protocol is thus extremely simple, requires very little state maintenance, and requires no network structures or clustering.

4.1 Reliability of token transfer

The reliable transfer of tokens from one node to another is important for successful operation of EZ-AG. If a token is released by a node, but the intended recipient did not receive the token reply message, the token is lost. Reliability of token transfer can be imposed by requiring an acknowledgement from the node receiving the token and re-sending the token if an acknowledgement was not received. However, it is possible that the token was transferred correctly to a neighbor but the acknowledgement was lost or the recipient of the token moved away from the communication range of a sender. In this case, a duplicate token may be created by this process. But, since EZ-AG computes duplicate insensitive aggregates, the addition of a duplicate token will not impact the accuracy.

5 Analysis

In this section, we first show that the aggregation time and message overhead for push assisted self-repelling random walks is $O(N)$. We consider a static network for our analysis. In Section 7, we evaluate the protocol under different mobility models and verify that the results hold even in the presence of mobility.

First, we state the following claim regarding the uniformity in the distribution of visited nodes during the progression of a self-repelling random walk.

Proposition 1 *The distribution of visited nodes (and unvisited nodes) remains spatially uniform during the progression of a self-repelling random walk.*

Argument: Our claim is based on the analysis of uniformity in coverage of self-repelling random walks in [28] and in [35]. In [28], the variance in the number of visits per node of *self-repelling* random walks is shown to be tightly bounded, resulting in a uniform distribution of visited nodes across the network. More precisely, let $n_i(t, x)$ be the number of times a node i has been visited, starting from a node x. The quantity studied in [28] is the variance $(1/N) \left(\sum_i (n_i(t, x) - \mu)^2 \right)$, where $\mu = (1/N) \left(\sum_i n_i(t, x) \right)$. It is seen that this variance is bounded by values less than 1 even in lattices of dimensions 2048×2048. A detailed extension of this analysis for *mobile networks* is presented in Section 7.1 which shows the uniformity with which nodes are visited during a self-repelling random walk. We use this to infer that even after the walk started, the distribution of visited nodes (and by that token, unvisited nodes) remains uniform. The result shows that the self-repelling random walk is not stuck in regions of already visited nodes - instead, it spreads towards unvisited areas.

Theorem 1 *The required number of messages for data aggregation by EZ-AG in a connected, static network of N nodes with uniform distribution of node locations is $O(N)$.*

Proof We note that the aggregation request flood and the result dissemination flood require $O(N)$ messages. During the push phase, each node broadcasts its state once and this also requires only N messages. Now, we analyze the self-repelling random walk phase.

Consider the region to be divided into square cells of sides $R/\sqrt{2}$ (see Fig. 2). Thus the diagonal of each such cell is the communication range R. Recall from our system model that each such cell has $\theta(logN)$ nodes whp at all times and there are $O(N/log(N))$ such cells. Therefore, at the end of the push phase, each node has aggregated information about its $\theta(logN)$ cell neighbors. Also note that the network can be divided into $\theta(N/log(N))$ sets of nodes that each contain information about $\theta(log(N))$ nodes within their cell. Therefore, the self-repelling random walk has to visit at least one node in each cell to finish aggregating information from all nodes.

To analyze the number of token transfers required to visit at least one node in each cell, we use the analogous coupon collector problem (also known as the double dixie cup problem) which studies the expected number of coupons to be drawn from B categories so that at least

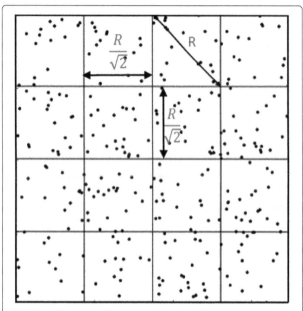

Fig. 2 Proof synopsis: Consider the region divided into square cells with diagonal size R. At the end of single step push phase, each node has information about all nodes in its cell. So it is sufficient for the token (performing a self-repelling random walk) to visit one node in each cell to finish aggregation

1 coupon is drawn from each category [36]. To ensure that at least 1 coupon is drawn from each category whp, the required number of draws is $O(B.log(B))$. Using this result and the fact that a self-repelling random walk traverses a network uniformly, we infer that $O((N/logN) * log(N/logN))$ token transfers are needed to visit at least 1 node in each of the $\theta(N/logN)$ cells.

Note that $log(N) > log(N/log(N))$. Hence, the required number of messages for the push assisted self-repelling random walk based aggregation protocol is $O(N/log(N) * log(N))$, i.e., $O(N)$.   □

Note that in the presence of mobility, the node locations with respect to cells may not be preserved during the push phase. Therefore the generation of $\theta(N/log(N))$ identical partitions of network state as described in the above analysis may not exactly hold. However, in Section 7 we empirically ascertain that kN token transfers (where $k < 1$) are still sufficient to aggregate data from all nodes even in the presence of mobility. In fact, we observe that *the required token transfers actually decrease with increasing speed*, indicating that data aggregation using self-repelling random walks is *actually helped by mobility*.

It follows from the above result that the total time for aggregation is also $O(N)$. The impact of network effects such as collisions on the message overhead and aggregation time (if any) will be evaluated in Section 7.

In terms of communication, for data aggregation to complete, we note that each node has to at least transmit its own data once. Thus, $O(N)$ is an absolute lower bound in terms of communication messages for data aggregation. We have thus shown that EZ-AG achieves this lower bound of $O(N)$ for data aggregation and therefore is indeed quite efficient in terms of communication. Moreover, we also show that the random walk phase terminates in exactly N token passes. Also during each transfer of the token, the number of requests for the token remain fairly constant and low (See Fig. 12). Thus, it is not the case that the constants of proportionality are high either.

By way of contrast, in a pure flooding based approach, each node will have to flood the data to every other node resulting in $O(N^2)$ cost. Instead, EZ-AG first aggregates the data using $O(N)$ cost and then floods the result in $O(N)$ cost, thus resulting in a total of only $O(N)$ communication cost. The impact of this order efficiency becomes increasingly significant as network size increases.

6 Extension for hierarchical aggregation

When a network is quite large, providing each node with only a single aggregate for the entire network may not be sufficient. On the other hand, providing each node with information about every other node is not scalable. We therefore pursue an extension to EZ-AG where each node can receive multi-resolution aggregates of neighborhoods with exponentially increasing sizes around itself. This way, each node can have information from all parts of the network but with a resolution that decays exponentially with distance. This idea is motivated by the fact that in many systems information about nearby regions is more relevant and important than far away regions with progressively increasing importance as distance decreases. In this section, we describe how EZ-AG can be extended to provide such multi-resolution synopsis of nodes in a network with only $O(NlogN)$ messages.

Existing techniques for such hierarchical aggregation require $O(Nlog^{5.4}N)$ messages [1]. Thus, EZ-AG offers a poly-logarithmic factor improvement in terms of number of messages for hierarchical aggregation. Moreover, EZ-AG can also be used to generate hierarchical aggregates that are distance-sensitive in refresh rate, where aggregates of nearby regions are supplied at a faster rate than farther neighborhoods.

6.1 Description

We divide the network into square cells at different levels (0, 1, .. P) of exponentially increasing sizes (shown in Fig. 3). At the lowest level (level 0), each cell is of sides $R/\sqrt{2}$. Recall from our system model that each such cell has $\theta(log(N))$ nodes whp. For simplicity, let us denote $\theta(log(N)$ by the symbol δ. Thus, there are N/δ cells at level 0. Note that 4 adjoining cells of level i constitute a cell of

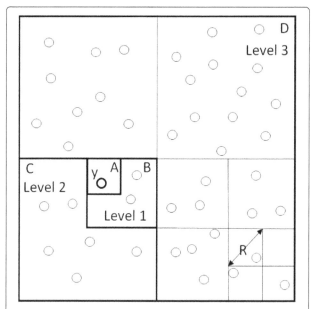

Fig. 3 Extension of EZ-AG to deliver multi-resolution aggregates: The network is partitioned into cells of increasing hierarchy where the cell at smallest level is of diagonal R. The node y shown in the figure would receive an aggregate corresponding to one cell at each level that it belongs to. In this case, it would receive aggregates for cells A, B, C and D. The largest cell D consists of the entire network

level $i + 1$. Thus, each cell at level j has $\delta 4^j$ nodes whp. At the highest level P, there is only one cell with all the N nodes. Note that $P = log_4(N/\delta)$. At any given time, a node belongs to one cell at each level.

To deliver multi-resolution aggregates, we introduce a token and execute EZ-AG at each cell at every level. A token for a given cell is only transferred to nodes within that cell and floods its aggregate to nodes within that cell. Thus, there are N/δ instances of EZ-AG at level 0 and each instance computes aggregates for δ nodes, i.e., $\theta(logN)$ nodes.

The computation and dissemination of aggregates by different instances of EZ-AG are not synchronized. Thus, a node may receive aggregates of different levels at different times. Also, since the nodes are mobile, an aggregate at level l received by a node at any given time corresponds to the cell of the same level l in which it resides at that instant.

6.2 Analysis

Theorem 2 *An ODI aggregate at level j can be computed using hierarchical EZ-AG in $O\left(4^j\delta\right)$ time and messages.*

Proof Note that each cell at level j contains $\theta\left(4^j\delta\right)$ nodes whp. Therefore, using Theorem 1, EZ-AG only requires $O\left(4^j\delta\right)$ time and messages to compute aggregate within the cell. □

We note from the above theorem that aggregates at level 0 can be published every $O(\delta)$ time, aggregates at level 1 can be published every $O(4\delta)$ time and so on. Thus, aggregates for cells at smaller levels can be published exponentially faster than those for larger cells. Thus, if the tokens repeatedly compute an aggregate and disseminate within their respective cells, EZ-AG can generate hierarchical aggregates that are distance-sensitive in refresh rate, where aggregates of nearby regions are supplied at a faster rate than farther neighborhoods.

Theorem 3 *Hierarchical EZ-AG can compute an ODI aggregate for all cells at all levels using $O(NlogN)$ messages.*

Proof Note that a cell at level 0 contains δ nodes and there are N/δ such cells. The aggregate for cells at level 0 can be computed using $O(\delta)$ messages.

In general, there are $N/4^j\delta$ cells at level j and aggregates for these cells can be computed using $O\left(4^j\delta\right)$ messages. Summing up from levels 0 to P, the total aggregation message cost (M) for hierarchical EZ-AG can be computed as follows.

$$M = \sum_{j=0}^{P} 4^j\delta\frac{N}{4^j\delta}$$
$$= \sum_{j=0}^{P} N$$
$$= O(NlogN)$$

Thus, hierarchical EZ-AG can compute an ODI aggregate for all cells at all levels using $O(NlogN)$ messages. □

6.3 Comparison of hierarchical EZ-AG with gossip techniques

In [1, 2], a spatial gossip technique is described where each node chooses another node in the network (not just neighbors) at random and gossips its state. When this is repeated $O(log^{1+\epsilon}(N))$ times (where $\epsilon > 1$), all nodes in the network learn about the aggregate state. Note that this scheme requires $O(N.polylog(N))$ messages. EZ-AG requires only $O(N)$ messages.

In [1], an extension to the spatial gossip technique is described which provides a multi-resolution synopsis of the network state at each node. The technique described in [1] requires $O\left(Nlog^{5.4}(N)\right)$ messages. The hierarchical extension of EZ-AG only requires $O(NlogN)$ messages.

7 Performance evaluation

In this section, we systematically evaluate the performance of EZ-AG using simulations in ns-3. We set up MANETs ranging from 100 to 4000 nodes using the network model described in Section 3. Nodes are deployed uniformly in the network with a deployment area and communication range such that $R^2 = 4log(N)/\rho$. Thus, the network is geo-dense with $c = 2$, i.e., each node has on average $2log(N)$ neighbors whp and the network is connected whp. We test such networks in our simulations with the following mobility models: 2-d random walk, random waypoint and Gauss-Markov (described in Section 3). The average node speeds range from 3 to 21 m/s. We also consider static networks as a special case.

First, we analyze the convergence characteristics of the push-assisted self-repelling random walk phase in EZ-AG and compare that with self-repelling random walks and plain random walks. Next, we analyze the total messages and time taken by EZ-AG. Finally, we compare EZ-AG with a prototype tree based protocol and with gossip based techniques.

7.1 Coverage uniformity

First, in Fig. 4a, b and c, we show the number of times each node is visited when the self-repelling random walk has finished visiting 50% of the nodes, 75% of the nodes and 85% of the nodes. We observe that most of the nodes are just visited once and this result holds even at 1000 nodes. These graphs *highlight the uniformity with which nodes are visited as self-repelling random walks progress.* The self-repelling random walk is not stuck in regions of already visited nodes - instead, it spreads towards unvisited areas. Otherwise, one would have observed more duplicate visits to the previously visited nodes.In Fig. 4d,

we analyze the distribution of number of visits at each node when 100% coverage is attained. Here, we see that most nodes are visited 2 or 3 times and the distribution falls off rapidly after that.

We then compare the uniformity in coverage with that of pure random walks. In Fig. 5, we plot the number of visits to each node until all nodes are visited at least once for a 500 node network. In comparison with self-repelling random walks (Fig. 5b), we observe that the tail of the distribution is much longer and the number of duplicate visits is much higher for pure random walks.

7.2 Convergence characteristics

Next, in Fig. 6, we show the exploration overhead of self-repelling random walk during different stages of coverage. As seen in Fig. 6, until about 85% coverage, self-repelling random walks have an exploration overhead of around 1 (irrespective of network size) but then the overhead starts to rise sharply. This is because, until this point self-repelling enables a token to find an unvisited node directly and there are very few wasted explorations. A slowdown for self-repelling random walk is noticed after this point. As a result, the exploration overhead at 100% coverage is close to 2 and moreover it increases with network size. This is what we aim to address using EZ-AG.

The exploration overhead at 100% coverage is shown in Fig. 7 for self-repelling random walks and EZ-AG (i.e., push-assisted self-repelling random walks). As seen in the figure, the exploration overhead for self-repelling random

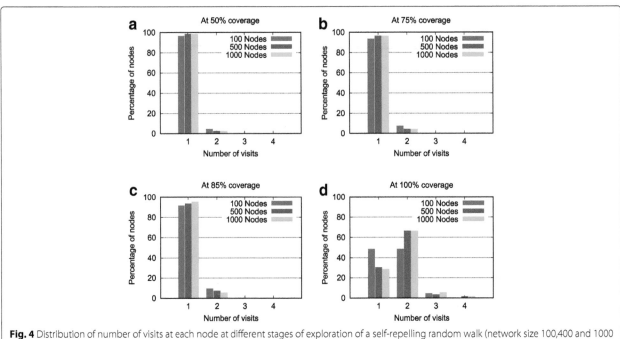

Fig. 4 Distribution of number of visits at each node at different stages of exploration of a self-repelling random walk (network size 100,400 and 1000 nodes). **a** 50% coverage, **b** 75% coverage, **c** 85% coverage, **d** 100% coverage

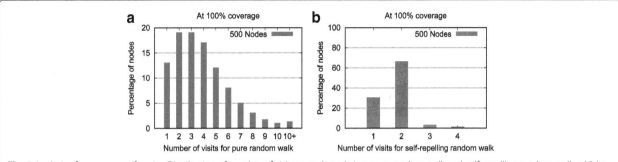

Fig. 5 Analysis of coverage uniformity: Distribution of number of visits at each node in a pure random walk and self-repelling random walk. **a** Visits distribution: Pure random walk, **b** Visits distribution: Self-repelling walk

walks grows with a logarithmic trend due to the wasted explorations towards the tail end of the random walk phase when most of the nodes are already visited. The push assisted self-repelling random walks remove these wasted explorations and as a result the median exploration overhead stays constant at all network sizes and is actually less than 1 (approximately 0.75 as seen in Fig. 7).

7.3 Impact of mobility and speed

In Fig. 8a and b, we evaluate the impact of mobility model and network speed on the exploration overhead of push assisted self-repelling random walks. We observe that even though random waypoint and Gauss Markov models do not preserve the uniform distribution of node locations, the exploration overhead exhibits a similar trend. As seen in Table 1, the network structure is rapidly changing at the speeds chosen for evaluation. Despite this, in

Fig. 8b, we observe that the exploration overhead actually starts decreasing with node speed (this is shown more clearly in Fig. 9 for networks with different sizes).

7.4 Variance and terminating condition

In Fig. 10, we show the variation in exploration overhead for EZ-AG over 50 different trials at different network sizes. We observe that irrespective of network size, for 97.5% of the trials, the exploration overhead is smaller than 1. We can use this to design a terminating condition for the random walk phase of the protocol. For example, we could terminate the random walk phase after exactly N steps, and then start the dissemination of the aggregate.

7.5 Messages and time

In Fig. 11a and b, we show the total number of messages and the total aggregation time as a function of network size for the aggregation protocol based on push-assisted self-repelling random walks. The total number

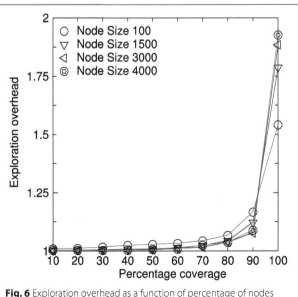

Fig. 6 Exploration overhead as a function of percentage of nodes visits for self-repelling random walks

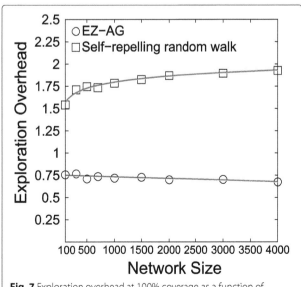

Fig. 7 Exploration overhead at 100% coverage as a function of network size

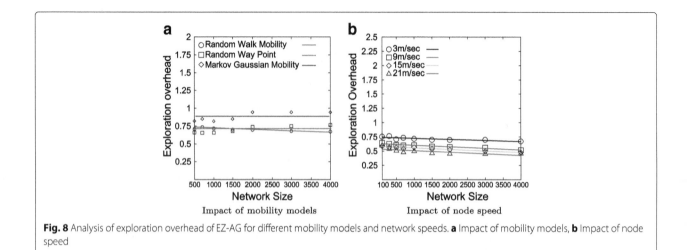

Fig. 8 Analysis of exploration overhead of EZ-AG for different mobility models and network speeds. **a** Impact of mobility models, **b** Impact of node speed

of messages required to complete the data aggregation includes the push messages, the messages involved in the self-repelling random walk phase and the messages involved in disseminating the result to all the nodes using a flood. Note that, each token transfer step itself consists of announcement, token request and token transfer messages. These are all included in Fig. 11a which shows that the messages grow linearly with network size.

An interesting aspect of the token transfer procedure is the number of requests generated for a token during each iteration. Note that the average number of neighbors increases as $\theta(logN)$ when the network size increases. However, from Fig. 12, the number of token requests per transfer is seen to be independent of the number of neighbors. From the box plot of Fig. 12, we observe that the average number of token requests in each trial is in the

range of $1 - 3$. This is because nodes that are visited less often send a request earlier than those that are visited more times. And, if a node hears a request from a node that has been visited less often than itself, it suppresses its request. Thus, irrespective of the neighborhood density, the number of token requests per node stay constant.

As seen in Fig. 11b, the total aggregation time also exhibits a linear trend. Note that the measurement of time is quite implementation specific and incorporates messaging latency in the wireless network. For instance, in our implementation each transaction (i.e., each iteration of token announcement, token requests and token passing) took on average 25 ms. But this number could be much smaller using methods such as [37] that use collaborative communication for estimating neighborhood sizes that satisfy given predicates.

7.6 Comparison with structured tree based protocol

In this section, we compare the performance of our protocol with a structured approach for one-shot duplicate

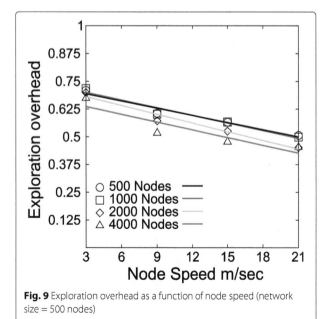

Fig. 9 Exploration overhead as a function of node speed (network size = 500 nodes)

Fig. 10 Variance in exploration overhead

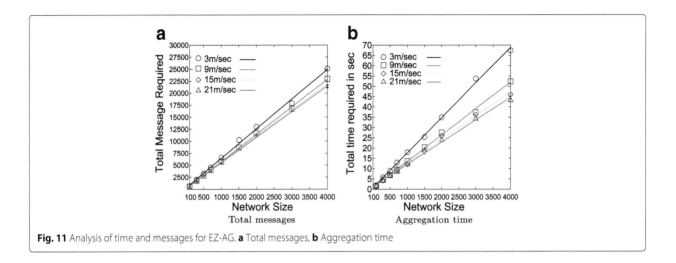

Fig. 11 Analysis of time and messages for EZ-AG. **a** Total messages, **b** Aggregation time

insensitive data aggregation that involves maintaining network structures such as spanning trees. For our comparison, we use a prototype tree-based protocol that we describe briefly. The idea is very similar to other tree-based aggregation protocols developed for static sensor networks [16, 17], but the key difference is that the tree is periodically refreshed to handle mobility as described below.

The initiating node maintains a tree structure rooted at itself by flooding a request message in the network. Each node maintains a *parent* variable. When a node hears a flood message for the first time, it marks the sending node as its *parent*. It then schedules a data transmission for its parent at a random time chosen within the next 25 ms. The message is successively forwarded through the tree structure until it reaches the root. During this process, a node also opportunistically aggregates multiple messages in its transmission queue before forwarding data to its parent. A message could be lost because a node's

parent has moved away or due to collisions. To handle message losses, a node repeats its data transmission to its parent until an acknowledgement is received from its parent. While this basic protocol is sufficient for a static network, the network structure is constantly evolving in a mobile network. Hence, the initiating node periodically refreshes the tree by broadcasting a new request every 2 s (with a monotonically increasing sequence number to allow nodes to reset their parents). The refreshing of the tree is stopped when data from all nodes has been received at the initiating node.

In Fig. 13a, we compare the total messages required for the tree-based protocol and the random walk based protocol at different node speeds. As seen in this figure, for static networks the tree based protocol is more efficient. However as the mobility increases, the random walk based protocol starts increasing in efficiency. In Fig. 13b we compare the total aggregation time which also exhibits a similar trend.

In Fig. 14 we compare the total number messages as a function of network size at an average speed of 9 m/s. Here we observe that the self-repelling random walk based protocol exhibits a linear trend while the tree based protocol exhibits a super-linear trend. This is due to the potentially large number of re-transmissions experienced by the tree-based protocol in a mobile network. This graph also shows that EZ-AG is far more scalable with network size under mobility than structure-based techniques for data aggregation.

8 Conclusions

In this paper, we have presented a scalable, robust and lightweight protocol for duplicate insensitive data aggregation in MANETs that exploits the simplicity and efficiency of self-repelling random walks. We showed that by complementing self-repelling random walks with a

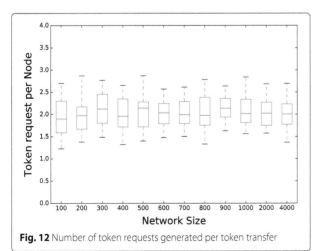

Fig. 12 Number of token requests generated per token transfer

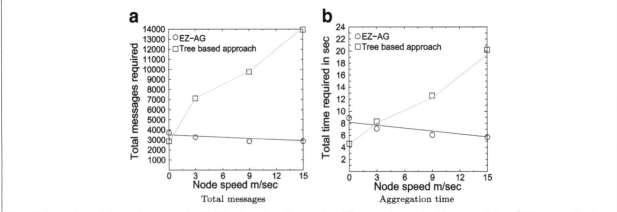

Fig. 13 Comparison of time and messages for EZ-AG and tree-based protocol at different node speeds with a network size of 500 nodes. **a** Total messages, **b** Aggregation time

single step push phase, our protocol can achieve data aggregation in $O(N)$ time and messages. In terms of message overhead, our protocol outperforms existing structure free gossip protocols by a factor of $log(N)$. We quantified the performance of our protocol using ns-3 simulations under different network sizes and mobility models. We also showed that our protocol outperforms structure based protocols in mobile networks and the improvement gets increasingly significant as average node speed increases.

We have shown that EZ-AG meets the lower bound of $O(N)$ in terms of communication requirements for aggregation. Also, each node only needs to store the number of times it has been visited. Thus, EZ-AG is lightweight in terms of both communication requirements and memory utilization. It also makes rather minimal assumptions of the underlying network. In particular, it does not assume knowledge of node addresses or locations, require a neighborhood discovery service or network topology information, or depend upon any particular routing or transport protocols such as TCP/IP.

We also described a hierarchical extension to EZ-AG that provides multi-resolution aggregates of the network state to each node. It outperforms existing technique by a factor of $O\left(log^{4.4}N\right)$ in terms of number of messages.

Note that EZ-AG uses only a single step push phase, i.e. a one hop broadcast from every node to its neighbors. Extending the push phase beyond a single hop may improve the speed of convergence, but at increased complexity. Requiring each neighbor to further push the data (i.e., a 2 hop push) essentially increases the communication cost by a factor equal to the degree of connectivity d. Pushing across the network diameter is essentially flooding with a cost of $O\left(N^2\right)$. A single step push, on the other hand, maintains the communication cost at $O(N)$, while significantly speeding up the aggregation.

Funding
This research was not supported by any external funding source.

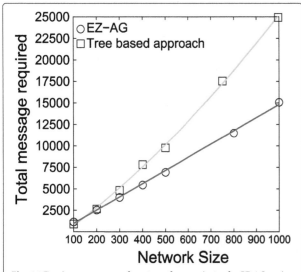

Fig. 14 Total messages as a function of network size for EZ-AG and tree based protocol (node speed = 9 m/s)

Authors' contributions
VK conceived the idea of introducing a push phase to speed up self=repelling random walks and worked on the analytic proofs. MN designed the algorithm and carried out experimental evaluations. AA contributed in the design and troubleshooting of the idea and also helped draft the manuscript. All authors read and approved the final manuscript.

Author details
[1]Department of Computer Science and Electrical Engineering, West Virginia University, Morgantown WV 26505, USA. [2]The Samraksh Company, Dublin OH 43017, USA.

References

1. Sarkar R, Zhu X, Gao J. Hierarchical spatial gossip for multiresolution representations in sensor networks. In: International Conference on Information Processing in Sensor Networks. New York: ACM; 2007. p. 311–319.
2. Kempe D, Kleinberg JM, Demers AJ. Spatial gossip and resource location protocols. In: ACM Symposium on Theory of Computing. New York: ACM; 2001. p. 163–172.
3. Kulathumani V, Arora A. Distance sensitive snapshots in wireless sensor networks. In: Principles of Distributed Systems (OPODIS), vol. 4878. New York: Springer; 2007. p. 143–158.
4. Nath S, Gibbons P, Seshan S, Anderson Z. Synopsis diffusion for robust aggregation in sensor networks. In: Proceedings of the 2Nd International Conference on Embedded Networked Sensor Systems, SenSys '04. New York: ACM; 2004. p. 250–262.
5. Wang Y. Mobile sensor networks: System hardware and dispatch software. ACM Comput Surv. 2014;47(1):12:1–12:36.
6. Dietzel S, Petit J, Kargl F, Scheuermann B. In-network aggregation for vehicular ad hoc networks. IEEE Commun Surv Tutor. 2014;16(4):1909–32.
7. Tahmasbi-Sarvestani A, Fallah YP, Kulathumani V. Network-aware double-layer distance-dependent broadcast protocol for vanets. IEEE Trans Veh Technol. 2015;64(12):5536–46.
8. Kim G, Ong YS, Cheong T, Tan PS. Solving the dynamic vehicle routing problem under traffic congestion. IEEE Trans Intell Transp Syst. 2016;17(8):2367–80.
9. Hu S, Wang Y, Huang C, Tseng Y. Measuring air quality in city areas by vehicular wireless sensor networks. J Syst Softw. 2011;84(11):2005–12.
10. Purohit A, Sun Z, Zhangi P. Sugarmap: Location-less coverage for micro-aerial sensing swarms. In: Proceedings of the 12th International Conference on Information Processing in Sensor Networks, IPSN '13. New York: ACM; 2013. p. 253–64.
11. Tan X. Autonomous robotic fish as mobile sensor platforms: Challenges and potential solutions. Mar Technol Soc J. 2011;45(4):31–40.
12. Kothari M, Postlethwaite I, Gu D. Uav path following in windy urban environments. J Intell Robot Syst. 2014;74(1):1013–28.
13. Yu H, Shen A, Peng L. A new autonomous underwater robotic fish designed for water quality monitoring. In: 2012 Proceedings of International Conference on Modelling, Identification and Control. Piscataway: IEEE; 2012. p. 561–6.
14. Considine J, Li F, Kollios G, Byers J. Approximate aggregation techniques for sensor databases. In: Proceedings of the 20th International Conference on Data Engineering, ICDE '04. Piscataway: IEEE; 2004.
15. Naik V, Arora A, Sinha P, Zhang H. Sprinkler: A Reliable and Energy Efficient Data Dissemination Service for Extreme Scale Wireless Networks of Embedded Devices. IEEE Trans Mob Comput. 2007;6(7):777–89.
16. Madden S, Franklin JM, Hellerstein J, Hong W. TAG: A Tiny AGgregation Service for Ad-hoc Sensor Networks. SIGOPS Oper Syst Rev. 2002;36(SI):131–46.
17. Gnawali O, Fonseca R, Jamieson K, Moss D, Levis P. Collection tree protocol. In: Proceedings of the 7th ACM Conference on Embedded Networked Sensor Systems, SenSys '09. New York: ACM; 2009. p. 1–14.
18. Intanogonwiwat C, Govindan R, Estrin D, Heidemann J, Silva F. Directed diffusion for wireless sensor networking. IEEE Trans Netw. 2003;11(1):2–16.
19. Kulathumani V, Arora A, Sridharan M, Parker K, Lemon B. On the repair time scaling wall for manets. IEEE Commun Lett. 2016;PP(99):1–4.
20. Chen Y, Shakkottai S, Andrews J. On the role of mobility on multi-message gossip. IEEE Trans Inf Theory. 2013;56(12):3953–70.
21. Levis P, Patel N, Shenker S, Culler D. Trickle: A self-regulating algorithm for code propagation and maintenance in wireless sensor networks. In: USENIX/ACM Symposium on Networked Systems Design and Implementation (NSDI). Berkeley: USENIX; 2004. p. 15–28.
22. Byrnes C, Guttman AJ. On self-repelling random walks. J Phys A Math Gen. 1984;17(17):3335–42.
23. Friedman R, Gavidia D, Rodrigues L, Viana A, Voulgaris S. Gossiping on manets: The beauty and the beast. SIGOPS Oper Syst Rev. 2007;41(5):67–74.

24. Boyd S, Ghosh A, Prabhakar B, Shah D. Randomized gossip algorithms. IEEE Trans Info Theory. 2006;52(6):2508–30.
25. Rabbat MG. On spatial gossip algorithms for average consensus. In: 2007 IEEE/SP 14th Workshop on Statistical Signal Processing. Los Alamitos: IEEE Computer Society; 2007. p. 705–9.
26. Lovascz L. Random walks on graphs: A survey. Combinatorics, Paul Erdos 80. 1993.
27. Ercal G, Avin C. On the cover time of random geometric graphs. Autom Lang Program. 2005;3580(1):677–89.
28. Feund H, Grassberger P. How a random walk covers a finite lattice. Physica. 1993;A(192):465–70.
29. Avin C, Krishnamachari B. The power of choice in random walks: An empirical study. In: Proceedings of the 9th ACM International Symposium on Modeling Analysis and Simulation of Wireless and Mobile Systems, MSWiM '06. New York: ACM; 2006. p. 219–28.
30. Kulathumani V, Arora A, Sridharan M, Parker K, Nakagawa M. Census: fast, scalable and robust data aggregation in manets. Springer Wirel Netw. 20171–18. Published online Feb 2017. https://doi.org/10.1007/s11276-017-1452-y.
31. Clementi A, Monti A, Pasquale F, Silvestri R. Information spreading in stationary markovian evolving graphs. IEEE Trans Parallel Distrib Syst. 2011;22(9):1425–32.
32. Le Boudec JY, Vojnovic M. Perfect simulation and stationarity of a class of mobility models. In: IEEE 24th Annual Joint Conference of the IEEE Computer and Communications Societies (INFOCOM), vol. 4. New York: IEEE; 2005. p. 2743–54.
33. Nain P, Towsley D, Liu B, Liu Z. Properties of random direction models. In: IEEE 24th Annual Joint Conference of the IEEE Computer and Communications Societies (INFOCOM), vol. 3. 2005. p. 1897–907.
34. Camp T, Boleng J, Davies V. A survey of mobility models for ad hoc network research. Wirel Commun Mob Comput (WCMC): Special Issue Mob Ad-hoc Netw. 2002;2:483–502.
35. Kulathumani V, Nakagawa M, Arora A. Coverage characteristics of self-repelling random walks in mobile ad-hoc networks. https://arxiv.org/pdf/1708.07049.pdf. Accessed Dec 2017.
36. Newman DJ, Shepp L. The double dixie cup problem. Am Math Mon. 1960;67(1):58–61.
37. Zeng W, Arora A, Srinivasan K. Low power counting via collaborative wireless communications. In: Proceedings of the 12th International Conference on Information Processing in Sensor Networks, IPSN '13. New York: ACM; 2013. p. 43–54.

9

Mapping the coverage of security controls in cyber insurance proposal forms

Daniel Woods[*], Ioannis Agrafiotis, Jason R. C. Nurse (iD) and Sadie Creese

Abstract

Policy discussions often assume that wider adoption of cyber insurance will promote information security best practice. However, this depends on the process that applicants need to go through to apply for cyber insurance. A typical process would require an applicant to fill out a proposal form, which is a self-assessed questionnaire. In this paper, we examine 24 proposal forms, offered by insurers based in the UK and the US, to determine which security controls are present in the forms. Our aim is to establish whether the collection of security controls mentioned in the analysed forms corresponds to the controls defined in ISO/IEC 27002 and the CIS Critical Security Controls; these two control sets are generally held to be best practice. This work contains a novel research direction as we are the first to systematically analyse cyber insurance proposal forms. Our contributions include evidence regarding the assumption that the insurance industry will promote security best practice. To address the problem of adverse selection, we suggest the number of controls that proposal forms should include to be in alignment with the two information security frameworks. Finally, we discuss the incentives that could lead to this disparity between insurance practice and information security best practice, emphasising the importance of information security economics in studying cyber insurance.

Keywords: Business security, Security controls, Cyber insurance, SANS20 controls, ISO/IEC 27000 series

1 Introduction

Insurers are taking on liability for ever more cyber risk; a 2015 report revealed that cyber insurance gross written premiums now stand at over $2 billion [1]. The same report reveals that demand for cyber insurance is expected to double by 2020. This is unsurprising given that company boards are beginning to better understand the nature of the risks that they face and realise the existence of gaps in traditional insurance coverage, as can been seen in a 2015 Cyber Risk Survey Report commissioned by Marsh [2]. For example, a 2015 study of 350 companies from 11 countries revealed the average cost of a data breach is $3.8 million [3]. While data breaches take the headlines, there are a multitude of other risks ranging from cyber extortion to unintended virus propagation, many of which can be covered by a range of new cyber insurance policies [4].

Despite soaring demand, underwriters are struggling to understand each consumer's cyber risk profile; a 2015

Cyber Liability Insurance Market Trend report showed the number one barrier to selling cyber policies is 'not understanding exposures' [1]. Getting this process wrong can be very costly. Target™ were reimbursed $90 million by their insurer following their 2013 data breach [5]. Traditional insurance techniques involve creating actuarial tables of loss histories across defined risk profiles. These are inapplicable for two reasons, the first being that insurers do not know the properties and attributes which delimit different risk profiles, while the second is that insurers do not have the loss history data to create the actuarial tables. In fact, relevant loss history may never exist given the dynamic nature of cyber risk. At present, all that insurers can rely on to quantify cyber risk is the information they collect in the assessment process. However, the evidence regarding the presence or not of specific security controls that insurers require in these assessment processes may have further consequences.

It is suggested that security decisions driven by insurers inform policy discussions in the US [6], the UK [7] and the EU [8]. Implicit in these discussions is the assumption that the insurance industry can have a meaningful

*Correspondence: daniel.woods@cybersecurity.ox.ac.uk
Department of Computer Science, University of Oxford, Oxford, UK

and positive impact on the management of cyber security. One argument in support of the assumption is that insurers have been successfully dealing in risk for hundreds of years. A more fine-grained view of the insurance industry reveals that there have been examples of insurers making systemic oversights. For example, the solicitors' professional indemnity market saw prominent insurers 'move away from the bottom of the market' during the 2010 crisis as the Irish insurer Quinn fell into administration [9]. With this in mind, the assumption that cyber insurance will have a positive impact on security posture of organisations requires further investigation.

The aim of this paper is to explore how well the current cyber insurance assessment process aligns with established network security best practice, as provided by the International Organization for Standardization and the International Electrotechnical Commission (ISO/IEC) 27002 and the Center for Internet Security (CIS) Critical Security Controls Version 6.0. Our approach investigates insurance proposal forms, a self-assessed questionnaire that applicants are expected to complete as an initial part of the cyber insurance application process. The key value of the results of our study is that they allow us to highlight neglected aspects of the assessment process. This can inform policy-makers by providing empirical evidence as to the success of cyber insurance in promoting established risk management standards. Further, it can help cyber insurers refine the assessment process grounded in security best practice.

Our paper is structured as follows: in Section 2 we outline how the insurance industry has developed, the coverage offered presently and the industry's method of assessment. Section 3 reviews related work on cyber insurance from a range of disciplines. Section 4 details our methodology, which focuses on one aspect of the assessment process and analysing self-assessed proposal forms. In Section 5, we compare the security controls that the insurance application process focuses on with the controls in the CIS Critical Security Controls and ISO 27002 frameworks. Section 6 provides a discussion of these results, and centres around lessons to be learned. Section 7 concludes with a discussion of how the assessment process will have to adapt to a changing market; particularly how an increase in demand from smaller businesses could lead to a greater reliance on the self-assessed forms analysed in this paper.

2 Cyber insurance industry

The first standalone Internet-based insurance policies were the hacker insurance policies of the late 1990s, in which an insurer partnered with a technology company to offer a policy covering the insured firm's first party loss [10]. As firms outside the technology industry became increasingly dependent on their networks, it became clear

that the coverage which traditional policies offered left significant gaps. For example, most business insurance policies used to cover tangible property often exclude liability relating to electronic data loss [11]. In response to this, insurance companies started to offer standalone cyber insurance policies. These policies are broken down into a number of sub-policies, with coverage offered for a specific set of risks. For example, First-Party Coverage covers the 'the cost of replacing or restoring lost data'. Table 1 includes the most common coverage and the risks that it provides liability for, it was chosen on the basis of studies of insurance policies [10, 12, 13]. The range of coverage found in Table 1 will form an *extensional definition* for cyber insurance.

The current market for standalone cyber insurance consists of insurers offering coverage to large companies. In the US, we find that 26% of companies with a revenue of $5 billion or more have cyber insurance, in stark contrast to less than 3% of those who return less than $500k [14]. In the UK, a 2015 report revealed that 2% of large companies use standalone cyber insurance while cyber insurance penetration is 'negligible' for smaller firms [15]. The demand for cyber insurance among smaller may increase. Smaller firms see a 'higher incidence of Cyber Crime' and the three biggest risks that smaller firms face are business interruption, privacy events and fraud [15]. Further, the current cyber insurance coverage offered, as detailed in Table 1, covers these risks.

There is a danger that a firm may apply for cyber insurance in the knowledge that they have little security infrastructure in place. This is the problem of adverse selection — which occurs when a more informed party engages in strategic behaviour at the expense of another party they are in contract with. Insurers address this issue

Table 1 Showing the range of coverage available

Coverage	What it covers
First-party coverage	Coverage for the cost of replacing or restoring lost data. Excludes
	intellectual property.
Data privacy and network	Coverage for liability claims of a third party like a data breach or
Security Liability	Unintentional transmission of a computer
Business interruption	Covers revenues lost as a result of network down time.
Cyber-extortion	Cover for investigation costs, sometimes the extortion demand.
Public relations	Fees for Public Relations firm to manage reputation in the event of a breach.
Multi-media liability	Costs relating to the content of a firm's website like copyright infringement.
Professional services	Liability relating to a service offer such as web hosting or internet service.

via extensive ex-ante assessment, which involves collecting information on an applicant, in order for an underwriter to classify the applicant into a given risk category and then set the insurance premium [16]. Much of this information is collected in a questionnaire filled out by an applicant, known as a proposal form. Table 2 contains a selection of the information that these forms seek to collect, along with the questions asked. For example, the insurer seeks information relating to the type of data collected by the applicant, via the question 'Do you store, process and/or transmit any Sensitive Data on Your Computer System (Tick all that apply)'. These were selected to give the reader an insight into the questions asked, a full picture can be found by investigating the forms presented in Table 3.

It is common practice to supplement this form with further assessment such as on-site audit and/or interviews with senior technology (IT) staff [17]. This supplementary assessment focuses on network security design and implementation, alongside organisational culture [16]. The aim of our paper is to assess the questions relating to the

Table 2 The type of information collected and questions asked in the ex-ante assessment

Information collected	Question in the form
Revenue	Gross Annual Revenue Last Year £
Type of Data Collected	Do you store, process and/or transmit any Sensitive Data
	on Your Computer System (Tick all that apply):
	Credit card info ☐ Customer info ☐ Money/Securities info ☐
	Healthcare info ☐ Trade secrets ☐ IP Assets ☐
Volume of data collected	Approximately how many private individuals do you hold sensitive data on:
Loss History	In the past 5 years has the company ever experienced
	any of the following events or incidents?:
	Sustained an unscheduled network outage that lasted over 24 hours Yes ☐ No ☐
	Portable media that was lost or stolen and was not encrypted Yes ☐ No ☐
Out Sourcing/Suppliers	Current Network and Technology Providers (if applicable):
	Internet Communication Services *Please Provide Information on.*
	Credit Card Processor(s) *Please Provide Information on.*
	Website Hosting *Please Provide Information on.*
	Anti-virus Software *Please Provide Information on.*
	Managed Security Services *Please Provide Information on.*

applicant's security controls in the self-assessed proposal forms. Our analysis will not consider more general information such as the applicant's financial situation, type of data collected or previous loss history. We believe that the self-assessed forms provide a scalable assessment process that could help meet increased demand from smaller businesses.

3 Related work

Cyber insurance has been part of academic discussion since Dan Geer first advocated for risk management techniques [18]. Bruce Schneier outlined his vision of cyber insurance detailing how security decisions are driven by an insurer's checklist and the corresponding insurance premium [19]. The benefits of such an approach have become consensus in the literature and it appears increasingly representative of the reality of industry. We draw a distinction between two bodies of academic work; the first tends to focus on the insurance market at large, the second is a multidisciplinary look at individual cyber insurance policies.

The first is a stream of literature of the field of Security Economics, which was founded upon the realisation that misplaced incentives play a part in explaining why many security systems fail [20]. In this vein, various works conclude that insurers offering reduced premiums provides incentives for security investment, which corroborates Schneier's early predictions [17, 21, 22]. There have been many attempts to model different aspects of the insurance market. A unifying framework is provided by Böhme et al. [23], which draws a distinction between two aspects of the market. First of all, the focus on how security investments accrue benefits to all parties in a system, not just the investor— particularly, how these positive externalities can reduce the risk an insurer faces [24–27]. Secondly, there have been various considerations of systemic risk, in which many firms make claims arising from the same event because of the interdependency of networks [28–30].

In addition, information asymmetries are considered in the context of principal-agent problems. Moral hazard, in which an agent engage in riskier behaviour because they know a principal protects them from the consequences, is explored by Shetty et al. [31]. Bandyopadhyay et al. consider the situation where the insured chooses not to report an incident because the amount of indemnity received is smaller than the costs relating to reputation damage [32]. The problem of adverse selection, which we discussed earlier, is examined in the literature. For example, if a firm knows they are relatively exposed to cyber risk they are more likely to seek cyber insurance [33]. It is suggested that this will lead to expensive premiums across the market [34]. Our work directly addresses the problem of adverse selection by analysing the information collected

Table 3 Forms included in our study and the insurer offering them

ACE Insured [43]	CFC Underwriting [56]	Philadelphia Insurance Companies [57]
ACE Privacy Protection [58]	CFC Underwriting [59]	PInsure [60]
ACE Privacy Protection [61]	Great American Insurance Group [42]	Risk placement Services [62]
AIG [40]	Hiscox [41]	Sutcliffe & Co Insurance Consultants [63]
Ascent Underwriting [64]	Lockton Companies [65]	Sybaris [66]
Beazley [67]	Markel International [68]	The Compass Group [69]
Business Insurance 24/7 [70]	Naturesave Insurance [71]	The Hartford [72]
CFC Underwriting [73]	OneBeacon Insurance [74]	TravelersJ [75]

that insurers use to determine the applicant's exposure to cyber risk.

The second body of work focuses on investigating cyber insurance policies. Parts of insurance literature provide an analysis of the insurability of cyber risks using the KARTEN framework [35] and the Berliner insurability framework [36]. This analysis reveals that 'Randomness of loss occurrence' and 'Information asymmetry' are problematic aspects of cyber insurance. As 'Information asymmetry' relates to adverse selection and moral hazard, this supports the results of the first body of literature. In addition, this stream of literature considers gaps in traditional policies [37]. Legal scholarship reflects on the issue of tangible property and data [11] and whether liability covers international cyber torts [38]. Business literature investigates the role of insurance within a risk management strategy [39], how insurers deal with moral hazard [16] and the type of coverage available [4]. There is further work analysing cyber insurance policies to understand coverage offered. Six policies are examined by Baer et al. [12], 14 are analysed by Marotta et al. [13] and Majuca et al. [10] focus on 7 different policies offered by AIG. We used these analyses of coverage to form our definition of cyber insurance.

We believe there is much to be gained from pooling the knowledge of these two bodies of work. The broad explanatory power of the Security Economics work can inform the empirical research undertaken in much of the second body of literature. Equally this second body can provide the empirical data to help refine the theory in the Security Economics literature. Our paper fits into the second body of work because we focus on the business processes of a cyber insurer. More specifically, we aim to analyse the effectiveness of the insurer's assessment, with a view to mitigating the adverse selection problem. We do this through the analysis of 24 different proposal forms. To our knowledge, this is the first time any such proposal forms have been systematically analysed in such a volume.

4 Methodology

In this paper we analyse 24 cyber insurance proposal forms, each corresponding to a different cyber insurance policy offered by a UK or a US insurance firm. These forms were chosen because they were publicly available, which provides an opportunity to investigate the initial part of the assessment process. The subsequent stages which involve processing and analysing the forms, as well as further assessment via on-site audit or telephone interview, require privileged access to much of what insurers consider intellectual property.

The proposal forms were all created between 2008 and 2016, with 20 of our forms being created in the last four years. Some examples of the forms considered include those from AIG [40], Hiscox [41], Great American Insurance Group [42], ACE Insured [43] and CFC Underwriting [44] and the full spectrum can be found in Table 3. These organisations fall into two categories; underwriters and brokers. An underwriter decides whether to offer the client a policy, receives the premium and takes on the responsibility of paying the insured's claims. A broker will represent one or more underwriters by brokering the deal between the insurer and the insured. The analysed forms are offered by a mixture of underwriters and brokers and consisted of 14 underwriters offering 16 policies and 8 brokers offering 8 policies.

The sample of proposal forms was collected by searching publicly indexed web page results. This search looked for variations upon, and not limited to, 'cyber security insurance proposal form'. These forms were collected using new search terms or more results for the same search term. The search ended when either of these stopped revealing new proposal forms. Forms not offered by a UK or US company, or forms that were offered outside the UK and US, were considered out of scope. Our rational being that these two countries are leading the cyber insurance market globaly [14, 15]. Many of the international forms were adaptations of the parent company's forms offered in the US or the UK. The forms were analysed using the ISO/IEC 27002 (ISO) and CIS Critical Security Controls frameworks.

The proposal forms were investigated using a form of content analysis known as deductive thematic analysis [45]. We selected a qualitative content analysis in order to build a conceptual model to describe the process of assessment in the insurance application process. This was chosen over a quantitative approach because we are trying to infer from the questions what information the forms seek to collect; a qualitative analysis can better capture these "meanings and intentions" [45]. While some have described content analysis as a "counting game" [46], others have identified its ability to "identify critical processes" [47]. A deductive approach was chosen because the themes, which are perceived as concepts by which models are structured, are provided by existing knowledge, avoiding issues related to their creation with other approaches [45].

ISO/IEC 27002 is an internationally recognised security management scheme [48]. It contains 19 sections, of which we focus on sections 6 to 18 as these contain actionable security controls. ISO/IEC 27002 was chosen over other standards in the 27000 series as it prescribes detailed controls, which are not applicable to a particular organization. This allows us to consider proposal forms without worrying about the specific organisations that they are intended for. The Center for Internet Security (CIS), led the development of the CIS Critical Security Controls (CSC). This involved a process of engagement with individuals, from a range of sectors and a range of roles, to ensure they are a 'prioritized, highly focused set of actions' [49]. We chose the CIS' CSC 20 Controls because they provide a more detailed perspective, as compared to ISO 27002, but can also be essential at identifying infrastructure vulnerability [50]. The version of CSC 20 that we used was version 6.0.

Both frameworks consist of broad controls with a number of sub-controls containing more detailed guidance. The content of the proposal forms will be referred to as questions in the rest of the paper. Our approach was to count for each sub-control the number of forms requesting information about that sub-control. The process of classifying units of analysis under themes is "one of the

most challenging aspects of the study" and "may be difficult to put into words" [45].

We illustrate this process by means of an example. In the CFC Underwriting's Esurance C&P proposal form [44], question 3.6 is 'Have your systems been subject to a third party security audit?' Considering the ISO framework, this question corresponds to sub-control '18.2: Information Security Reviews'. A similar rationale was applied throughout our analysis. This allowed a comparison between the information collected and the established best practice relating to network security.

A degree of subjectivity is inevitable; a handful of questions corresponded loosely to a sub-control and a judgement was made. For example, both the CSC sub-controls 5.7 and 16.2 mention passwords 'longer than 14 characters', which did not correspond to the question 'Does the company enforce passwords that are at least seven character...?' asked in ACE's Privacy Protection policy [43]. This method favoured controls phrased more generically because a higher degree of specificity means a given question is less likely to correspond to the control. This was done to maintain consistency throughout our analysis.

5 Results

In order to reason about the results of our qualittive analysis of the assessments, we devised two simple metrics. The first numbers the times that every sub-controls was refered to in all 24 assessment forms. This metric allows us to identify the most popular controls as well as those neglected by insurers. The second indicates the percentage of sub-controls referred in the forms for every control. The rationale being that in order for a security control to be effective the majority of the sub-controls are required to be in place. Therfore, a low percentage would indicate that the controls is not properly addressed. Figures 1 and 2 show the total number of sub-controls addressed per control for each of ISO/IEC 27002 and the

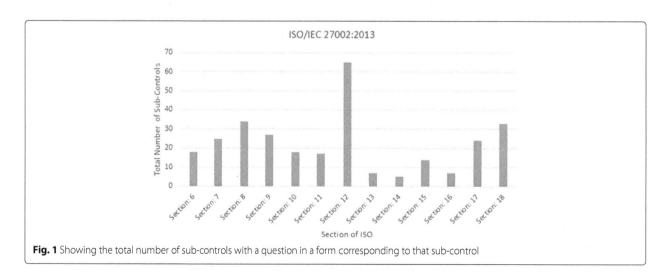

Fig. 1 Showing the total number of sub-controls with a question in a form corresponding to that sub-control

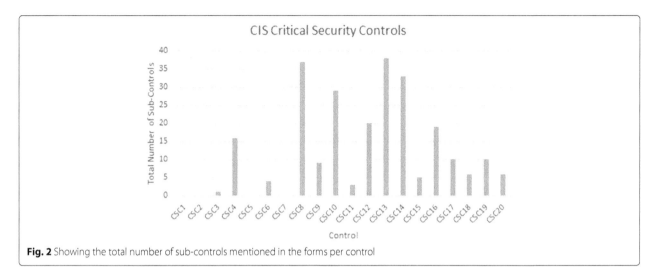

Fig. 2 Showing the total number of sub-controls mentioned in the forms per control

CIS CSC. This presents an overview of how the forms align with each of the frameworks. This is complemented by a more in-depth look at a select few controls. Due to space economy, we choose the three most and least addressed controls, exploring which specific sub-controls were and were not mentioned. Tables 4 and 5 detail the average percentage of sub-controls addressed per control, providing an insight into which sub-controls were not addressed.

5.1 ISO 27001

In this section, our analysis follows ISO/IEC 27002:2013. Figure 1 presents the number of sub-controls that were addressed by a given form and we then aggregate this information for all the forms and each control. The number of sub-controls in each section increases the maximum possible score. We note that every ISO control was addressed by at least one form. The three highest scoring controls were *Sections 8, 12* and *18* which relate to asset management, operational security and compliance respectively.

The sub-controls which were mentioned most often were *10.1 Cryptographic controls, 12.2 Protection from malware, 18.1 Compliance with legal and contractual requirements* and 1*2.3 Backup* with scores of 18, 23, 22 and 19 respectively. These scores correspond to the number of forms that ask about the sub-control. For example, 23 of the forms asked for information relating to the applicant's protection from malware.

Only two forms did not address a sub-control related to *18.1 Compliance with legal and contractual requirements,* which involves managing obligations to external authorities such as regulation regimes. Table 6 contains a number of these regulatory frameworks, along with the number of forms that it was mentioned in. Regulatory framework is used as an umbrella term to describe government regulation, compliance standards and security approaches.

Table 4 Percentage of sub-controls addressed per CSC control

Control	%
CSC 1: Inventory Authorized Devices and Unautorized Devices	0
CSC 2: Inventory Authorized Devices and Unautorized Software	0
CSC 3 : Secure Configurations for Hardware and Software on Mobile Devices, Laptops, Workstations, and Servers	0.58
CSC 4: Continuous Vulnerability Assessment and Remediation	8.33
CSC 5: Controlled Use of Administrative Privileges	0
CSC 6: Maintenance, Monitoring, and Analysis of Audit Logs	2.79
CSC 7: Email and Web Browser Protections	0
CSC 8: Malware Defenses	26.38
CSC 9: Limitation and Control of Network Ports, Protocols, and Services	5.54
CSC 10: Data Recovery Capability	29.17
CSC 11: Secure Configurations for Network Devices such as Firewalls, Routers, and Switches	1.79
CSC 12: Boundary Defense	9.17
CSC 13: Data Protection	4.11
CSC 14: Controlled Access Based on the Need to Know	17.13
CSC 15: Wireless Access Control	2.33
CSC 16: Account Monitoring and Control	5.04
CSC 17: Security Skills Assessment and Appropriate Training to Fill Gaps	10
CSC 18: Application Software Security Incident Response and Management	4.58
CSC 19: Incident Response and Management	6.54
CSC 20: Penetration Tests and Red Team Exercises	3.67

Table 5 Percentage of sub-controls addressed per control

ISO control	Percentage
Section 6: Organization of information security	37.50%
Section 7: Human resource security	34.70%
Section 8: Asset management	42.70%
Section 9: Access control	28.10%
Section 10: Cryptography	75%
Section 11: Physical and environmental security	35.40%
Section 12: Operations management	38.70%
Section 13 Communications security	14.60%
Section 14: System acquisition, development and maintenance	6.90%
Section 15: Supplier relationships	29.20%
Section 16: Info security incident management	16.70%
Section 17: Business continuity management	50%
Section 18: Compliance	68.80%

ISO 27001 and UK Cyber Essentials are included as they tended to be mentioned in the same section as formal regulation like HIPAA or GLBA.

Figure 1 demonstrates that the controls with the lowest scores were *Section 13: Communications security, Section 14: System acquisition, development and maintenance* and *Section 16: Information security incident management.* Section 13 contains two sub-controls, the first relates to secure networks and the second secure communication with third parties. The first was occasionally addressed through network segregation, which is mentioned in the sub-control. The second is addressed through non-disclosure agreements.

Section 14 relates to the development and procurement of products, particularly relating to security requirements. None of the forms addressed security requirements, though two US firms mentioned the use of open source code in development, which is relevant to the development process. Finally three forms asked about test procedures. Section 16 relates to incident response, which is mentioned in only eight forms; none of these forms mention insider threat. Since there is only one sub-control, however, this results in a relatively high score in Table 5.

Table 6 Compliance, regulation and standards

Regulatory approach	Questions
Payment Card Industry Data Security Standard (PCI DSS)	17
Health Insurance Portability and Accountability Act (HIPAA)	11
Gramm Leach Bliley Act (GLBA)	8
ISO 27001	7
UK Data Protection Act	5
UK Cyber Essentials	1

Table 5 shows, for each ISO control, the average percentage of sub-controls with at least one question relating to that sub-control in each form per control.

Only four sub-controls had no corresponding questions in any of the analysed forms. In ISO, *12.1* looks at controlling and documenting changes to operating responsibilities and procedures, *12.5* relates to controlling the installation of software, *12.7* looks at minimising the adverse effects of IT audits and *14.1* to specify security control requirements. All of these scored zero. Only one form contained a question relating to *14.2*, which looks at software/systems development processes. Only two forms contained questions corresponding to each of *13.2*, about policies and agreements regarding communications with third parties, and *9.3*, which relates to user's responsibilities including choosing strong passwords.

A low score in Table 5 suggests that many of the sub-controls have not been addressed, which suggests there is relevant information that has not been collected. It is unsurprising that Control 10, which relates to cryptography, scores well because there is only one sub-control and most of the forms mention cryptographic protocols. Similarly, Section 18 scores highly; this is because the first control relates to compliance and the second to external security audits, each of these sub-controls is well-represented in the proposal forms. This analysis reveals *Control 12: Operations Management* has much room for improvement, despite the sub-controls relating to malware control, backups and patching scoring highly. Control 12 contains some sub-controls which were entirely ignored such as *12.5 Control of operational software* and *14.1 Security requirements of information systems.*

5.2 CIS Top 20 security controls

In this section we detail our analysis of the forms based on the CIS Top 20 Critical Security Controls (CSC). Figure 2 uses the same methodology as Fig. 1, the difference being that the controls are provided by the CSC. Controls which have scored highly include: *CSC8: Malware Defenses, CSC10: Data Recovery Capability, CSC 13: Data Protection* and *CSC 14: Controlled Access Based on the Need to Know.* On the other hand, we note that *CSC1: Inventory of Authorized and Unauthorized Devices, CSC2: Inventory of Authorized and Unauthorized Software, CSC 5: Controlled Use of Administrative Privileges* and *CSC 7: Email and Web Browser Protections* had no corresponding questions in the proposal forms.

More specifically, *CSC8: Malware Defenses* scored highest in this analysis. Table 7 details the sub-controls of *CSC8: Malware Defenses* and the number of forms that ask a question relating to each sub-control. Table 7 reveals that 8.1 was the main factor for this high score, which asks for anti-virus and personal firewalls on all work stations. Control 8.2 was consistently mentioned in the

Table 7 Sub-controls for the malware defenses control

CSC 8: malware defenses	Questions
8.1 Automated tools to continuously monitor workstations	23
8.2 Employ software to automatically push regular AV updates	13
8.3 Limit use of removable devices outside approved business need	0
8.4 Enable anti-exploitation features	0
8.5 Identify executables in network traffic	0
8.6 Enables DNS query logging	0

forms; this sub-control relates to installing system updates to machines. However, the other six sub-controls were left completely unaddressed. For example, 8.4 relates to malware and removable media. Only two forms mention removable media outside of the context of encryption, both of which relate to downloading sensitive information, not malware defences. Similarly none of the forms mention searching for executables in network traffic, anti-exploitation features or DNS query logging.

CSC10: Data Recovery Capability consists of four sub-controls and we detail our analysis of this control in Table 8. Note that only one sub-control was not mentioned in the forms, compared to six in *CSC8: Malware Defenses*. Control 12.4 aims to ensure key systems have a back-up, which is not 'continuously addressable through operating system calls'. While some forms do ask if the back-up is housed off-site, this question does not fully comply with the sub-control, since a cloud provider could be housed off-site but still being continuously addressable through operating system calls.

Many controls had very low scores, such as *CSC17*, which relates to staff awareness and training. Only eight forms asked about delivering security training and two forms asked about periodic testing. The first two in terms of priority CSC controls relate to keeping an inventory of authorised software and hardware; yet none of the forms contain any of the followings words: inventory, authorised, unauthorised, blacklist or whitelist. One UK firm asks for 'approximate number of devices on network'; while this necessitates some form of crude inventory, it does not sufficiently address any of the sub-controls in *CSC1:*

Table 8 Sub-controls for the Data Recovery control

CSC10: data recovery	Questions
10.1 Each system is automatically backed every week	14
10.2 Perform test data restoration process regularly	5
10.3 Backups protected via physical security or encryption where stored	9
10.4 Key systems have a backup not continuously addressable via operating system calls	0

Inventory of Authorized and Unauthorized Devices. We will discuss whether keeping an inventory is implicit in other controls in Section 6.

Operating systems (OS) and applications were particularly under-addressed despite controls such as *CSC 18: Application Software Security*. Only three forms mentioned 'software' in a capacity beyond security software (such as AV or firewall) or patching. Two of these related to providing software to other firms — one of these related to supplying software using open source software. None of the following recommendations of *CSC2: Inventory of Authorized and Unauthorized Software* were mentioned: monitoring software installed on machines, software version installed or air-gapping high risk applications.

Further, only three forms mentioned operating systems; these related to standard configuration, the type of operating system (OS) in use and whether the OS continued to be supported by the manufacturer. The first falls under *CSC3: Secure Configurations for Hardware and Software* and was the only form to correspond to a sub-control under this control. CSC 5 outlines *The processes and tools used to track, control, prevent, correct the use, assignment, and configuration of administrative privileges on computers, networks, and applications.* Yet we found that only one of the form mentions administrative privileges, which was in connection with social media accounts.

CSC 7: Email and Web Browser Protections was a new addition to version 6.0 of the CSC; its sub-controls involve disabling unnecessary plugins, add-ons and scripting languages in all web browsers and clients, logging URL requests, maintaining network based URL filters, scanning and blocking email attachments with malicious code, among others. There are eight sub-controls comprising this control and none of the forms analysed contained a question corresponding to any of them.

As with the ISO analysis, Table 4 includes the average percentage of sub-controls addressed per control. The only factor affecting the scores relative to in Fig. 2 is the number of subcontrols, which range from 4 to 12. *CSC10: Data Recovery Capability* and *CSC 17: Security Skills Assessment* had very few sub-controls, consequently they score higher. While *CSC 12: Boundary Defense, CSC 13: Data Protection* and *CSC 16: Account Monitoring and Control* had many sub-controls, thus a lower score was asigned.

6 Discussion

Policy makers, organisations seeking insurance and insurers have different priorities and will interpret these results accordingly. Organisations can prioritise the controls in place before applying for insurance, policy makers may gain an insight into the extent to which insurance promotes security best practice, and insurers can address areas of cyber security they neglect to collect information about. We will discuss the specific lessons learnt in this section.

6.1 Organisations seeking insurance

The results presented in this paper provide organisations in the US and the UK that consider to apply for cyber insurance with a view of the minimum security controls that will be sought. While we do not know how the information collected translates to premium pricing, it is reasonable to assume that the controls mentioned will lead to a reduction. Further, implementing information security management schemes, such as ISO/IEC 27000 and the CSC, can be a challenge. This is particularly true for organisations operating under resource constraints, such as small and medium sized enterprises. Organisations must prioritise which controls to implement first, if at all. We suggest that the insurance industry could be used to help organisations prioritise which controls to implement. Insurers' exposure to multiple organisations with similar functionalities gives them a greater understanding of the risks that they hold. Consequently, insurers have a greater awareness of the financial losses that are occurring as a result of cyber attack and which controls are important to mitigate this loss.

With that in mind, the results suggest that cryptographic controls, malware protection, compliance with legal requirements and maintaining an effective back up, should be prioritised first, since these are the most commonly asked by insurers. This is in contrast to the CIS guidance that states "Controls CSC1 through CSC5 are essential to success and should be considered among the very first things to be done" [49]; these include keeping an inventory of devices and software, ensuring secure configurations on all devices, continuous vulnerability management and controlling administrative privileges.

This is a worrying discrepancy. One cause could be the difference in scope; the CSC are a set of "security actions" [49] and are restricted accordingly, meanwhile an insurer has no such restriction. This difference between organisational controls and security controls can account for some of the disparity. Measures such as the existence of a Chief Information Officer, maintaining a business continuity plan or being certified PCI compliant are not in the scope of the CSC. However, it does not explain why cryptographic controls and malware protection, which are covered in *CSC8: Malware Defenses* and *CSC10: Data Recovery Capability*, are mentioned so often, while the Critical Security Controls with a higher priority are not mentioned at all.

One possible explanation is that insurers consider these controls more effective at mitigating the risk they are liable for. It is important to remember that gaps in coverage mean that insurers have different incentives when assessing the effectiveness of controls. Another consideration is that compliance with legal requirements may address certain controls, so the forms need not. Additionally, insurers may seek more specific technical information in the interview process. Finally, the CSC are updated annually and some forms in our study were created before 2010. However, 20 of the forms were created in the last four years and although the CSC are updated, many of the controls remain constant throughout.

Refelcting on the recent incidents, the presence of the afforementioned controls might have mitigated the impact of the Wannacry attack in the NHS, where more than 40 hospital have been affected [51]. In these attacks, hackers used a well-known exloit to infect systems before encrypting all data and rendering them unavailable until a ransom is paid. As a consequence, many hospitals reverted to using paper and IT systems were discharged [52]. The presence of a back-up system as well as a malware defense system would have mitigated the impact of the attack and might have prevented the incident for happening. However, these controls mainly focus on mitigating the risk insurers are liable for and still allow room for the attack to take place.

6.2 Informing the insurance assessment process

Our results provide two distinct evaluations that can be used to improve the insurance process and address the problem of adverse selection. The first revolves around the results presented in Figs. 1 and 2 that present the absolute number of sub-controls mentioned in the forms. The second focuses on the analysis provided in Tables 4 and 5 which explains what additional information is required to adequately represent the specific control into question. Regarding the first evaluation, it gives an overview of which controls are in the proposal forms and which controls have been overlooked. This analysis suggests systems development and acquisition, communications management and incident management deemed of the highest priority.

However, this presentation of results may not be appropriate for all purposes. Figure 1 suggests that *ISO: Section 12* is well addressed. Yet Table 5 shows that there is a majority of sub-controls which are not accounted for. The first presentation may be appropriate for insurers with a relatively low maturity of assessment, where any additional information would help the underwriting process. Meanwhile, the second presentation of results is useful for high-maturity assessment seeking to collect information relating to all critical controls.

The results show that the information gathered by the forms is more aligned with the ISO/IEC 27002 framework. This is understandable given that the CSC relate to network security and many controls may be too detailed for the assessment process. In spite of this, there is still much we can learn from the CSC because appropriate network security is vital to mitigating many of the risks that cyber insurance covers. For example, the authors of the CSC deem *CSC5: Controlled Use of Administrative Privileges* to be of high priority. As a result, it was moved from being *CSC12* in Version 5.0 to *CSC5* in Version 6.0 of the CSC [49]. Yet none of the forms directly address any of the sub-controls pertaining to *CSC5*. Similarly, *CSC 7: Email and Web Browser Protections* relates to application security. However, none of the forms address the corresponding sub-controls, which is worrying given that applications are increasingly being considered as a "prime [attack] vector into an organisation" [53].

Addressing the lack of questions referring to *CSC1* and *CSC2* could provide valuable benefits for the insurer. An inventory of hardware and software could help the underwriting process by putting a value on the assets at risk. Further, it will help with forensic investigation and support other goals such as revoking access to devices once an employee has departed from the organisation. Here, our discussion touches upon the interdependence of security controls. One consideration is that the interdependence of controls mean that some controls are implicitly addressed. For example, some of the proposal forms ask for security software 'on all desktops, laptops and servers'. It could be argued that this necessitates an inventory of hardware, meaning there is no need to ask about *CSC1*.

Assessing the existence of controls alone provides a 'check-box compliance' view of network security. This has been raised as one criticism of regulation [54]. If the insurance industry is to evolve towards accurate risk assessment it must take a holistic and responsive view of risk management. We suggest that a wider coverage of the CSC sub-controls can provide provide guidance on how to manage the implementation of a control, rather than merely check of its existence. For example, many of the questions merely ask whether the firm is 'conducting regular penetration tests'. More alignment with the specific advice contained within *CSC20: Penetration Tests and Red Team Exercises* could provide a clearer view of the implementation of this control and help insurers better understand an applicant's network security practices. However, it is important to be aware of the tension between the need for more information and the ease of the application process, which is the second largest obstacle to selling cyber insurance according to a 2015 survey [1].

Reflecting on the afforementioned incident that crippled NHS services, it is evident that the controls offered by CIS would have not only mitigated the problem but might have prevented it from occurring in the first place. An inventory of hardware and software is a critical step in any business continuity plan and in the case of NHS systems were shout down because there was no clear indication of the software they were using [55].

Additioanlly, Microsoft had provided a patch for the exploit, however, most hospitals used obsolete operation systems and did not update their sytems due to the "complexity of keeping systems up to date" [55]. Having had inventories and system updates, three of the most important CIS controls, these atatcks may have been avoided. It is clear that there is an overlap but a small discrepancy as well between the controls suggested by best practice frameworks and those requested by the insurance community. Therefore, there should be further discussions between policy makers and the insurers on how to bridge this gap.

6.3 Implications for policy makers

In the introduction we discussed the public-private partnership for cyber insurance. One insurance contribution to the partnership is to 'promote established risk management standards', with the UK policy document naming ISO 27000 [48]. Our results provide some evidence verifying the adoption of ISO 27000. For instance, no section of ISO/IEC 27002 is entirely unaddressed. However, the results show that there are controls contained in ISO/IEC 27002 and the CSC which are not covered in the forms. This could be an issue for policy makers and we discuss potential reasons behind it.

One reason for the absence of ISO/IEC 27002 and CSC controls could be that insurers are focused on best practice from other lines of insurance. For example, 15 of the forms mention a business continuity plan, which does not form part of the CIS Security Controls framework. Note that this is an important control for mitigating the losses that would fall under business interruption coverage, which is traditionally offered by insurers.

Another reason could be that insurance contracts tend to only last a year. Consequently, the insurer has a financial incentive to prioritise controls that will have an immediate effect. Such controls include security products, maintaining back-ups and encrypting sensitive data. However, for some controls and procedures the length of time they have been in place becomes an important factor. For example, appointing a Chief Information Security Officer (CISO) will have little immediate affect but will pay off in the long term as changes in the structure of the organisation are being realised at a much later stage. This is also true for secure software engineering practices where the current policy is less important than the policy in place when the system was developed. Insurers are incentivised to focus on controls with an immediate effect.

Another factor to consider is that insurers may focus on the risks they are liable for as they do not cover all of the cyber risks that an organisation might face. Table 1, which details the range of coverage available, does not include reputation damage or intellectual property theft. For example, controls relating to data encryption or a functioning back up system, which mitigate the risk of data breach and data corruption respectively, scored very highly. Meanwhile, controlling administrative privileges was not mentioned, despite it comprising a whole Section of the CSC. One reason could be that it does not directly mitigate a risk the insurers are liable for.

A rational insurer is concerned with the controls which directly mitigate the risks that they are liable for, creating a question of misaligned incentives. In the literature, the insurer is assumed to be the victim of moral hazard. We suggest that where an applicant expects the insurer to manage their cyber risk exposure, the presence of gaps in coverage can lead the insurer to select security controls which expose the insured party to risks not covered by the policy. Such a case is an example of moral hazard in which the insured party is the victim and the insurer is the "guilty" party.

7 Conclusion and future work

We analysed 24 self-assessed proposal forms offered by UK and US insurers, using themes from two established information security frameworks. The analysis reveals that self-assessed proposal forms predominantly focus on a small range of controls related to malware defences, managing back-ups and use of encryption. Our results can inform the conscious evolution of the insurance application process. In particular, future proposal forms could include controls such as managing secure configuration, keeping an inventory of hardware and software, control of administrative privileges and application security. It is important to be conscious of the burden on the applicant, who must complete the proposal form.

Given insurer's understanding of risks, we suggest that our results could help inform organisation's security decisions. However, as insurers only ask for security controls which directly mitigate the risks that they bear financial responsibility for, misplaced incentives could lead to poor security decisions. It is important for organisations to bear these considerations in mind when purchasing cyber insurance and making investment decisions once insurance policies are purchased.

These incentives should be considered by policy makers given that they are not necessarily aligned with the public interest. Anderson et al. illustrate how misaligned incentives explain many security failures [20]. Forward thinking policy makers could anticipate misaligned incentives in the cyber insurance domain and try to correct these ahead of time to avoid failures in security. Further, our results support the assumption that cyber insurance will promote established risk management standards, particularly ISO/IEC 27002. This assumption requires further research as we have only looked at one part of the application process.

To our knowledge, this is the first systematic analysis of cyber insurance proposal forms. Consequently, there are many novel directions for the study of proposal forms. Our methodology is rooted in the themes provided by two information security frameworks. Yet cyber insurance covers areas distinct from information security. It would be interesting to see an analysis of the controls in place to mitigate Multi-Media Liability (outlined in Table 1) such as review by a qualified attorney. Especially in light of the different nature of risks such as international cyber torts [38]. Future work could use an inductive approach to capture controls not included in our analysis. Another direction could involve usability studies to investigate the trade offs between information collected and ease of the application process.

Proposal forms are but one piece of the puzzle. In future work we hope to interview key actors in the insurance industry to better understand how the telephone interviews and on-site audits fit into the rest of the insurance process. These interviews could also investigate why the controls that we have identified are lacking in their proposal forms. Further research could shed light upon the motivation of the insurance market for requesting information on certain controls. The relative importance of factors such as the nature of the claims made from insured organisations, the regulatory fines paid, the proposed legislation regarding security practices, the evolution of the threat intelligence community and the advices provided by security industry is still unclear and subject to further research.

Acknowledgements
The authors acknowledge that this work was inspired by research conducted with Novae Group plc, on a project aimed at Investigating the Relative Effectiveness of Risk Controls and the Value of Compliance.

Funding
This research was conducted primarily by a doctoral student; project funding considerations do not apply in this context.

Authors' contributions
This article is the product of project research at the University of Oxford by Daniel Woods (DW), supervised by Ioannis Agrafiotis (IA), Jason R. C. Nurse (JN) and Sadie Creese (SC). As a result, the core research and experimentation was conducted by DW, with IA, JN and SC providing direction and guidance during the research. All parties assisted in the journal manuscript drafting stage. All authors read and approved the final manuscript.

Authors' information
DW is a doctoral student in the Centre for Doctoral Training in Cyber Security; IA is a Research Fellow in Cyber Security; JN is a Research Fellow in Cyber

Security and a JR Fellow at Wolfson College; and SC is Professor of Cyber Security. All authors are based in the Department of Computer Science at the University of Oxford in the UK.

References

1. Advisen Ltd. Cyber Liability Insurance Market Trends: Survey Available. 2015. http://www.partnerre.com/opinions-research/cyber-liability-insurance-market-trends-2015-survey. Accessed 22 June 2017.
2. Marsh Insights. UK 2015 Cyber Risk Survey Report Available. 2015. http://uk.marsh.com/Portals/18/Documents/UK%202015%20Cyber%20Risk%20Survey%20Report-06-2015.pdf. Accessed 22 June 2017.
3. Ponemon Institute LLC. 2015 Cost of Data Breach Study: Global Analysis. 2015. Available: https://nhlearningsolutions.com/Portals/0/Documents/2015-Cost-of-Data-Breach-Study.PDF. Accessed 22 June 2017.
4. Siegel CA, Sagalow TR, Serritella P. Cyber-risk management: technical and insurance controls for enterprise-level security. Inf Syst Secur. 2002;11(4):33–49.
5. Manworren N, Letwat J, Daily O. Why you should care about the target data breach. Bus Horiz. 2016;59(3):257–66.
6. Department of Homeland Security. Cybersecurity Insurance Industry Readout Reports. 2014. Available: https://www.dhs.gov/publication/cybersecurity-insurance-reports. Accessed 22 June 2017.
7. HM Government & Marsh Ltd. UK Cyber security: The role of insurance in managing and mitigating the risk. 2015. Available: https://www.gov.uk/government/uploads/system/uploads/attachment_data/file/415354/UK_Cyber_Security_Report_Final.pdf. Accessed 22 June 2017.
8. The Lawyer. Incentives and barriers of the cyber insurance market in Europe. 2010. Available: https://www.thelawyer.com/issues/13-september-2010/as-professional-indemnity-crisis-rumbles-on-the-sra-consults/. Accessed 22 June 2017.
9. ENISA. As professional indemnity crisis rumbles on, the SRA consults. 2012. Available: https://www.enisa.europa.eu/publications/incentives-and-barriers-of-the-cyber-insurance-market-in-europe/at_download/fullReport. Accessed 22 June 2017.
10. Majuca RP, Yurcik W, Kesan JP. The evolution of cyberinsurance. Tech. Rep. CR/0601020, ACM Computing Research Repository. 2006. arXiv preprint cs/0601020.
11. Beh HG. Physicial losses in cyberspace. Conn Ins LJ. 2001;8:55.
12. Baer WS, Parkinson A. Cyberinsurance in it security management. IEEE Secur Priv. 2007;5(3):50–56.
13. Marotta A, Martinelli F, Nanni S, Yautsiukhin A. A Survey on Cyber-Insurance. 2015. Available: http://www.iit.cnr.it/en/node/36039. Accessed 22 June 2017.
14. Bradford J. Advisen Insight Cyber Insurance Market Update. 2015. http://www.advisenltd.com/2015/01/15/advisen-insight-cyber-insurance-market-update. Accessed 22 June 2017.
15. UK Cabinet Office. Cyber Security Insurance: New Steps to Make UK World Centre. 2015. Available: https://www.gov.uk/government/news/cyber-security-insurance-new-steps-to-make-uk-world-centre. Accessed 22 June 2017.
16. Kesan J, Majuca R, Yurcik W. Cyberinsurance as a market-based solution to the problem of cybersecurity: a case study. In: Proceedings of Workshop of Economic Information Security (WEIS) 2005; 2005.
17. Zahn N, Toregas C. Insurance for cyber attacks: The issue of setting premiums in context, Cyber Security Policy and Research Institute: George Washington University; 2014. http://static1.squarespace.com/static/53b2efd7e4b0018990a073c4/t/53c3daa5e4b056f825681c72/1405344421345/cyberinsurance_paper_pdf.pdf. Accessed 5 June 2017.
18. Geer D. Risk management is still where the money is. Computer. 2003;36(12):129–31.
19. Schneier B. Insurance and the computer industry. Commun ACM. 2001;44(3):114–4.
20. Anderson R. Why information security is hard-an economic perspective. In: Computer security applications conference, 2001. acsac 2001. proceedings 17th annual. IEEE; 2001. p. 358–365.
21. Baer W. Rewarding it security in the marketplace. Contemp Secur Policy. 2003;24(1):190–208.
22. Yurcik W, Doss D. Cyberinsurance: A market solution to the internet security market failure. In: Proceedings of Workshop of Economic Information Security (WEIS) 2002; 2002.
23. Böhme R, Schwartz G, et al. Modeling cyber-insurance: Towards a unifying framework. In: Proceedings of Workshop of Economic Information Security (WEIS) 2010; 2010.
24. Ogut H, Menon N, Raghunathan S. Cyber insurance and it security investment: Impact of interdependence risk. In: Proceedings of Workshop of Economic Information Security (WEIS) 2005; 2005.
25. Kunreuther H, Heal G. Interdependent security. J Risk Uncertain. 2003;26(2-3):231–49.
26. Bolot JC, Lelarge M. A new perspective on internet security using insurance. In: INFOCOM 2008. The 27th Conference on Computer Communications. IEEE. IEEE; 2008.
27. Zhao X, Xue L, Whinston AB. Managing interdependent information security risks: A study of cyberinsurance, managed security service and risk pooling. In: ICIS 2009 Proceedings; 2009. p. 49.
28. Böhme R, Kataria G. Models and measures for correlation in cyber-insurance. In: Proceedings of Workshop of Economic Information Security (WEIS) 2006; 2006.
29. Böhme R. Cyber-insurance revisited. In: Proceedings of Workshop of Economic Information Security (WEIS) 2005; 2005.
30. Herath HS, Herath TC. Cyber-insurance: Copula pricing framework and implication for risk management. In: Proceedings of Workshop of Economic Information Security (WEIS) 2007; 2007.
31. Shetty N, Schwartz G, Felegyhazi M, Walrand J. Competitive cyber-insurance and internet security. In: Proceedings of Workshop of Economic Information Security (WEIS) 2010; 2010. p. 229–47.
32. Bandyopadhyay T, Mookerjee VS, Rao RC. Why it managers don't go for cyber-insurance products. Commun ACM. 2009;52(11):68–73.
33. Schwartz G, Shetty N, Walrand J. Cyber-insurance: Missing market driven by user heterogeneity. 2010. Preparation. http://citeseerx.ist.psu.edu/viewdoc/citations;jsessionid=2B896C3184CEC6131A2155413CD27F1E?doi=10.1.1.476.7760.
34. Bandyopadhyay T, Mookerjee VS, Rao RC. Why it managers don't go for cyber-insurance products. Commun ACM. 2009;52(11):68–73.
35. Grzebiela T. Insurability of electronic commerce risks. In: System Sciences, 2002. HICSS. Proceedings of the 35th Annual Hawaii International Conference On. IEEE; 2002. p. 9.
36. Biener C, Eling M, Wirfs JH. Insurability of cyber risk: An empirical analysist. The Geneva Papers on Risk and Insurance-Issues and Practice. 2015;40(1):131–58.
37. Lee A. Why traditional insurance policies are not enough: The nature of potential e-commerce losses & (and) liabilities. Vand J Ent L Prac. 2001;3:84.
38. Crane M. International liability in cyberspace. Duke Law Technol Rev. 2001;1(1):23.
39. Gordon LA, Loeb MP, Sohail T. A framework for using insurance for cyber-risk management. Commun ACM. 2003;46(3):81–5.
40. AIG. CyberEdge Application Form. 2016. Available: https://www.aig.co.uk/content/dam/aig/emea/united-kingdom/documents/Financial-lines/Cyber/aig-cyberedge-application-form.pdf. Accessed 22 June 2017.
41. Hiscox. Privacy and Data Breach Protection. 2012. Available: http://www.hiscoxbroker.com/shared-documents/cyber-data-risks/10049_Privacy_and_Data_Breach_Protection_Mainform_Application.pdf. Accessed 22 June 2017.
42. Great American Insurance Group. Cyber (Net) Application. 2014. Available: http://www.greatamericaninsurancegroup.com/insurance/Specialty-Human-Services/Forms/Documents/F36223-Cyber-(NET)-Application.pdf. Accessed 22 June 2017.
43. ACE Insured. Cyber & Privacy Insurance Application Form. 2015. Available: https://www2.chubb.com/US-EN/_Assets/doc/Cyber-Privacy-Insurance-Application.pdf. Accessed 22 June 2017.
44. CFC Underwriting. Esurance Cyber & Privacy. 2008. Available: http://www.colemanambris.com/docs/documents/cyber-privacy-application.pdf. Accessed 22 June 2017.
45. Elo S, Kyngäs H. The qualitative content analysis process. J Adv Nurs. 2008;62(1):107–15.
46. Downe-Wamboldt B. Content analysis: method, applications, and issues. Health Care Women Int. 1992;13(3):313–21.

47. Lederman RP. Content analysis of word texts. MCN Am J Matern Child Nurs. 1991;16(3):169.

48. International Organization for Standardization (ISO). 2013. ISO/IEC 27002:2013 Available: http://www.iso.org/iso/catalogue_detail?csnumber=54533 Accessed 22 June 2017.

49. Center for Internet Security. CIS Critical Security Controls - Version 6.0. 2015. Available: https://www.sans.org/critical-security-controls. Accessed 22 June 2017.

50. Farnan OJ, Nurse JRC. Exploring a controls-based assessment of infrastructure vulnerability In: Lambrinoudakis C, Gabillon A, editors. Risks and Security of Internet and Systems: 10th International Conference, CRiSIS 2015, Revised Selected Papers. Lecture Notes in Computer Science. Cham: Springer; 2016. p. 144–59.

51. Wired. The NHS trusts and hospitals affected by the Wannacry cyberattack. 2017. Available: http://www.wired.co.uk/article/nhs-trusts-affected-by-cyber-attack. Accessed 22 June 2017.

52. Wired. WannaCry is back! Virus hits Australian traffic cameras and shuts down a Honda plant in Japan. 2017. Available: http://www.wired.co.uk/article/nhs-cyberattack-ransomware-security. Accessed 22 June 2017.

53. Ahmad D. The contemporary software security landscape. IEEE Secur Priv. 2007;5(3):75–7.

54. Siponen M, Willison R. Information security management standards: Problems and solutions. Inf Manag. 2009;46(5):267–70.

55. The Guardian. NHS seeks to recover from global cyber-attack as security concerns resurface. 2017. Available: https://www.theguardian.com/society/2017/may/12/hospitals-across-england-hit-by-large-scale-cyber-attack. Accessed 22 June 2017.

56. CFC Underwriting. Esurance Cyber & Privacy. 2008. Available: http://www.colemanambris.com/docs/documents/cyber-privacy-application.pdf. Accessed 22 June 2017.

57. Philadelphia Insurance Companies. Cyber Security Liability Application. 2010. Available: https://www.phly.com/Files/Application%20-%20Cyber%20Security%20Liability%20NY31-927.pdf. Accessed 22 June 2017.

58. Protection® AP. Cyber and Privacy Insurance. 2015. Available: https://www.scribd.com/document/249827931/Ace-Dataguard-Advantage-Application. Accessed 25 Oct 2016.

59. CFC Underwriting. Esurance CPM Application Form. 2013. Available: http://www.stgilesgroup.co.uk/storage/documents/Cyber%20Proposal%20Form.pdf. Accessed 22 June 2017.

60. Pinsure. Cyber Liability Proposal Form. 2014. Available: http://www.pinsure.co.uk/. Accessed 22 June 2017.

61. ACE Privacy Protection®. Cyber and Privacy Insurance. 2015. Available: https://www2.chubb.com/US-EN/_Assets/doc/Cyber-Privacy-Insurance-Application.pdf. Accessed 25 Oct 2016.

62. Risk placement Services Inc. Cyber Liability Premium Indication Form. 2014. Available: https://www.rpsins.com/media/1844/cyber_rps_02.pdf. Accessed 22 June 2017.

63. Sutcliffe & Co Insurance Consultants. Cyber Liability Insurance. 2013. Available: http://www.sutcliffeinsurance.co.uk/Portals/0/docs/cyber%20proposal%20form.pdf. Accessed 22 June 2017.

64. Ascent Underwriting. CyberPro Application. 2014. Available: http://www.ascentunderwriting.com/resources/docs/application.pdf. Accessed 25 Oct 2016.

65. Lockton Companies LLP. Professional Indemnity Insurance for Privacy Protection. 2013. Available: https://www.locktonsolicitors.co.uk/cmsUploads/quoteForm/files/LLP120920_Privacy_ProtectionProposalform.pdf. Accessed 22 June 2017.

66. Sybaris. Cyber Suite Insurance Proposal. 2016. Available: http://www.ip-insurance.com/uploads/1/4/6/2/14622220/ssr_2016_cyber_prop.pdf. Accessed 22 June 2017.

67. Beazley. Beazley Breach Response. 2014. Available: http://www.moagent.org/Products/SiteAssets/Pages/ForYourAgency/Cyber/default/CyberSecureFullApp.pdf. Accessed 25 Oct 2016.

68. Markel International. Cyber Insurance Proposal Form. 2015. Available: http://www.markelinternational.com/Documents/London%20Market/PFR/PI%20-%20Wordings/Intellectual%20Property/Cyber%20Insurance%20Proposal%20Form%2020110116.pdf. Accessed 22 June 2017.

69. The Compass Group Inc. Omniguard Cyber and Privacy Application. 2013. Available: http://www.bassunderwriters.com/Forms/Cyber%20Liability%20Program.pdf. Accessed 22 June 2017.

70. Business Insurance 24/7. Cyber/Privacy/Multimedia Liability Proposal Form. 2015. Available: http://www.cyber-liability-insurance.co.uk/docs/CYBER_PROP_2015.doc. Accessed 25 Oct 2016.

71. Naturesave Insurance. Available: http://www.naturesave.co.uk/download/Business-Insurance-Documents/Business-Proposal-Forms/Cyber%20Insurance%20Proposal%20Form.pdf. Accessed 22 June 2017. 2014.

72. The Hartford. Cyberchoice 2.09. 2011. Available http://www.thehartford.com/sites/thehartford/files/cyber-choice-application.pdf. Accessed 22 June 2017.

73. CFC Underwriting. Cyber, Privacy and Media Application Form. 2014. Available: http://www.swanmorss.com/usr/Pdfs/Cyber_App.pdf. Accessed 25 Oct 2016.

74. OneBeacoN Insurance. Professional @vantage for Financial Institutions. 2015. Available: http://www.onebeaconfs.com/sites/FinancialServices/documents/policydocuments/specialty/Cyber%20Liability%20Application%20SCB005%20ASIC%20FINAL.pdf. Accessed 25 Oct 2016.

75. TravelersJ. Cyber Risk Coverage Application. 2015. Available: http://www.travelerscanada.ca/brokers/application-forms/documents/CyberRisk%20Application.pdf. Accessed 25 Oct 2016.

10

Object-NoSQL Database Mappers: a benchmark study on the performance overhead

Vincent Reniers[*] [iD], Ansar Rafique, Dimitri Van Landuyt and Wouter Joosen

Abstract

In recent years, the hegemony of traditional relational database management systems (RDBMSs) has declined in favour of non-relational databases (NoSQL). These database technologies are better adapted to meet the requirements of large-scale (web) infrastructures handling Big Data by providing elastic and horizontal scalability. Each NoSQL technology however is suited for specific use cases and data models. As a consequence, NoSQL adopters are faced with tremendous heterogeneity in terms of data models, database capabilities and application programming interfaces (APIs). Opting for a specific NoSQL database poses the immediate problem of vendor or technology lock-in. A solution has been proposed in the shape of Object-NoSQL Database Mappers (ONDMs), which provide a uniform abstraction interface for different NoSQL technologies.

Such ONDMs however come at a cost of increased performance overhead, which may have a significant economic impact, especially in large distributed setups involving massive volumes of data.

In this paper, we present a benchmark study quantifying and comparing the performance overhead introduced by Object-NoSQL Database Mappers, for create, read, update and search operations. Our benchmarks involve five of the most promising and industry-ready ONDMs: Impetus Kundera, Apache Gora, EclipseLink, DataNucleus and Hibernate OGM, and are executed both on a single node and a 9-node cluster setup.

Our main findings are summarised as follows: (i) the introduced overhead is substantial for database operations in-memory, however on-disk operations and high network latency result in a negligible overhead, (ii) we found fundamental mismatches between standardised ONDM APIs and the technical capabilities of the NoSQL database, (iii) search performance overhead increases linearly with the number of results, (iv) DataNucleus and Hibernate OGM's search overhead is exceptionally high in comparison to the other ONDMs.

Keywords: Object-NoSQL Database Mappers, Performance evaluation, Performance overhead, MongoDB

1 Introduction

Online systems have evolved into the large-scale web and mobile applications we see today, such as Facebook and Twitter. These systems face a new set of problems when working with a large number of concurrent users and massive data sets. Traditionally, Internet applications are supported by a relational database management system (RDBMS). However, relational databases have shown key limitations in horizontal and elastic scalability [1–3]. Additionally, enterprises employing RDBMS in a distributed setup often come at a high licensing cost, and per CPU charge scheme, which makes scaling over multiple machines an expensive endeavour.

Many large Internet companies such as Facebook, Google, LinkedIn and Amazon identified these limitations [1, 4–6] and in-house alternatives were developed, which were later called non-relational or NoSQL databases. These provide support for elastic and horizontal scalability by relaxing the traditional consistency requirements (the ACID properties of database transactions), and offering a simplified set of operations [3, 7, 8]. Each NoSQL database is tailored for a specific use case and data model, and distinction is for example commonly made between column stores, document stores, graph stores, etc. [9].

*Correspondence: vincent.reniers@cs.kuleuven.be
Department of Computer Science, KU Leuven, Celestijnenlaan 200A, B-3001 Heverlee, Belgium

This is a deviation from the traditional "one-size-fits-all" paradigm of RDBMS [2], and leads to more diversity and heterogeneity in database technology. Due to their specific nature and their increased adoption, there has been a steep rise in the creation of new NoSQL databases. In 2009, there were around 50 NoSQL databases [10], whereas today we see over 200 different NoSQL technologies [11]. As a consequence, there is currently large heterogeneity in terms of interface, data model, architecture and even terminology across NoSQL databases [7, 12]. Picking a specific NoSQL database introduces the risk of vendor or technology lock-in, as the application code has to be written exclusively to its interface [7, 13]. Vendor lock-in hinders future database migrations, which in the still recent and volatile state of NoSQL is undesirable, and additionally makes the creation of hybrid and cross-technology or cross-provider storage configurations [14] more challenging.

Fortunately, a solution has been proposed in the shape of Object-NoSQL Database Mappers (ONDM) [7, 12, 13]. ONDMs provide a uniform interface and standardised data model for different NoSQL databases or even relational databases. Even multiple databases can be used interchangeably, a characteristic called as *polyglot* or *cross-database* persistence [13, 15]. These systems support translating a common data model and operations to the native database driver. Despite these benefits, several concerns come to mind with the adoption of such middleware, and the main drawback would be the additional performance overhead associated with mapping objects and translating APIs. The performance impact potentially has serious economic consequences as NoSQL databases tend to run in large cluster environments and involve massive volumes of data. As such, even the smallest increase in performance overhead on a per-object basis can have a significant economic cost.

In this paper, we present the results of an extensive and systematic study in which we benchmark the performance overhead of five different open-source Java-based ONDMs: Impetus Kundera [16], EclipseLink [17], Apache Gora [18], DataNucleus [19] and Hibernate OGM [20]. These were selected on the basis of industry relevance, rate of ongoing development activity and comparability. We benchmarked the main operations of write/insert, read, update and a set of six distinct search queries on MongoDB. MongoDB is currently one of the most widespread adopted, and mature NoSQL document databases, in addition it is the only mutually supported database by all five ONDMs. The benchmarks presented in this paper are obtained in a single-node MongoDB setup and in a distributed MongoDB cluster consisting of nine nodes.

The main contribution of this paper is that it quantifies the performance cost associated with ONDM adoption,

as such allowing practitioners and potential adopters to make informed trade-off decisions. In turn, our results inform ONDM technology providers and vendors about potential performance issues, allowing them to improve their offerings where necessary. In addition, this is to our knowledge the first study that involves an in-depth performance overhead comparison for search operations. We specifically focus on six distinct search queries of varying complexity.

In addition, the study is a partial replica study of an earlier performance study [21], which benchmarked three existing frameworks. We partially confirm the previous findings, yet in turn strengthen this study by: (i) adopting an improved measurement methodology, with the use of Yahoo!'s Cloud Serving Benchmark (YCSB) [3] —an established benchmark for NoSQL systems – and (ii) focusing on an updated set of promising ONDMs.

Our main findings first and foremost confirm that current ONMDs do introduce an additional performance overhead that may be considered substantial. As these ONDMs follow a similar design, the introduced overhead is roughly comparable: respectively the write, read and update overhead ranges between [4 − 14%], [4 − 21%] and [60 − 194%] (on a cluster setup). The overhead on update performance is significant due to *interface mismatches*, i.e. situations in which discrepancies between the uniform API and the NoSQL database capabilities negatively impact performance.

Regarding search, we found that query performance overhead can become substantial, especially for search queries involving many results, and secondly, that DataNucleus and Hibernate OGM's search overhead is exceptionally high in comparison to the other ONDMs.

The remainder of this paper is structured as follows: Section 2 discusses the current state and background of Object-NoSQL Database Mappers. Section 3 states the research questions of our study and Section 4 discusses the experimental setup and motivates the selection of ONDMs. Section 5 subsequently presents the results of our performance evaluation on write, read, and update operations, whereas Section 6 presents the performance results of search operations. Section 7 discusses the overall results, whereas Section 8 connects and contrasts our work to related studies. Finally, Section 9 concludes the paper and discusses our future work.

2   Object-NoSQL Database Mappers

This section provides an overview of the current state of Object-NoSQL Database Mappers (ONDMs) and motivates their relevance in the context of NoSQL technology.

2.1   Object-mapping frameworks for NoSQL

In general, object mapping frameworks convert in-memory data objects into database structures (e.g.

database rows) before persisting these objects in the database. In addition, such frameworks commonly provide a uniform, technology-independent programming interface and as such enable decoupling the application from database specifics, facilitating co-evolution of the application and the database, and supporting the migration towards other databases.

In the context of relational databases, such frameworks are commonly referred to as "Object-Relational Mapping" (ORM) tools [22], and these tools are used extensively in practice. In a NoSQL context, these frameworks are referred to as "Object-NoSQL Database Mapping" (ONDM) tools [12] or "Object-NoSQL Mapping (ONM)" tools [23].

In the context of NoSQL databases, data mapping frameworks are highly compelling because of the increased risk of vendor lock-in associated to NoSQL technology: without such platforms, the application has to be written for each specific NoSQL database and due to the heterogeneity in technology, programming interface and data model [7, 13], later migration becomes difficult. As shown in an earlier study, the use of ONDMs simplifies porting an application to another NoSQL significantly [21].

An additional benefit is the support for multiple databases, commonly referred to as database interoperability or cross-database and polyglot persistence [13, 15]. Cross-database persistence facilitates the use of multiple NoSQL technologies, each potentially optimised for specific requirements such as fast read or write performance. For example, static data such as logs can be stored in a database that provides very fast write performance, while cached data can be stored in an in-memory key-value database. Implementing such scenarios without an object-database mapper comes at the cost of increased application complexity.

However, ONDM technology only emerged fairly recently, and its adoption in industry is rather modest. Table 1 outlines the benefits and disadvantages of using ONDM middleware. The main argument against the adoption of ONDMs is the additional performance overhead. The study presented in this paper focuses on quantifying this overhead. In the following section, we outline the current state of ONDM middleware.

2.2   Current state of ONDMs

In this paper, we focus on object-database mappers that support application portability over multiple NoSQL databases. Examples are Hibernate OGM [20], EclipseLink [17], Impetus Kundera [16] and Apache Gora [18].

Table 2 provides an overview of the main features of several ONDMs such as: application programming interfaces (APIs), support for query languages and database support.

The API is the predominant characteristic as it determines the used data model and the features that are made accessible to application developers. A number of standardised persistence interfaces exist, such as the Java Persistence API (JPA) [24], Java Data Objects (JDO) [25] and the NPersistence API [26] for .NET. Some products such as Apache Gora [18] or offer custom, non-standardised development APIs.

Many of the currently-existing ODNMs (for Java) implement JPA. Examples are EclipseLink [17], DataNucleus [19] and Impetus Kundera [16]. Some of these products support multiple interfaces. For example, DataNucleus supports JPA, JDO and REST. JPA relies extensively on annotations. Classes and attributes are annotated to indicate that their instances should be persisted to a database. The annotations can cover aspects such as the relationships, actual column name, lazy fetching of objects, predefined query statements and embedding of entities.

Associated with JPA is its uniform query language called the Java Persistence Query Language (JPQL) [24]. It is a portable query language which works regardless of the underlying database. JPQL defines queries with complex search expressions on entities, including their relationships [24].

The uniform interface (e.g. JPA) and query language (e.g. JPQL) allow the user to abstract his/her application software from the specific database. However, this abstraction comes at a performance overhead cost, which stems from translating operations and data objects to the intended native operations and data structures and vice versa. For example, on write, the object is translated to the intended data structure of the underlying NoSQL database, while on read, the query operation is translated to the native query. Once the result is retrieved, the retrieved data structure is converted back into an object.

Table 1 Advantages and disadvantages of adopting ONDM middleware

Advantages	Disadvantages
Unified interface, query language and data model for multiple databases	Performance overhead incurred from translating the uniform interface and data model to its native counterparts
Increased application maintainability	
Cross-database persistence and database portability Third-party functionality (e.g. caching)	Potential loss of database-specific features due to the abstraction level of the ONDM

Table 2 Features and database support for the evaluated ONDMs

	Hibernate OGM	Kundera	Apache Gora	EclipseLink	DataNucleus
Evaluated Version	4.1.1 Final	2.15	0.6	2.5.2	5.0.0.M5
Interface	JPA	JPA, REST	Gora API	JPA	JPA, JDO, REST
Query Languages	JPQL, Native Queries	JPQL, Native Queries	Query interface	JPQL, Expressions, Native Queries	JPQL, JDOQL, Native Queries
RDBMS	✗	✓	✗	✓	✓
NoSQL Databases	*MongoDB*, Neo4j, Ehcache, CouchDB, Infinispan	*MongoDB*, Neo4j, CouchDB, Cassandra, ElasticSearch, HBase, Redis, Oracle NoSQL	*MongoDB*, HBase, Cassandra, Apache Solr, Apache Accumulo	*MongoDB*, JMS, XML, Oracle AQ, Oracle NoSQL,	*MongoDB*, HBase, Cassandra, Neo4j, JSON, XML, Amazon S3, GoogleStorage, NeoDatis

Database support for such mapping and translation operations varies widely. For example, EclipseLink is a mature ORM framework which has introduced NoSQL support only gradually over time, and it currently only supports Oracle NoSQL and MongoDB. While Kundera was intended specifically for NoSQL databases, it now also provides RDBMS support by using Hibernate ORM. Despite the heterogeneity between RDBMS and NoSQL, a combination of both can be used.

The following section introduces our main research questions, upon which we have built this benchmark study.

3   Research questions

Our study is tailored to address the following research questions:

RQ1 What is the overhead (absolute and relative) of a write, read and update operation in the selected ONDMs?

RQ2 What is the significance of the performance overhead in a realistic database deployment?

RQ3 What is the impact of the development API on the performance overhead?

RQ4 How does the performance overhead of a JPQL search query (search on primary key) compare to that of the JPA read operation (find on primary key)?

RQ5 What is the performance overhead of JPQL query translation, and does the nature/complexity of the query play a role?

Expectations and initial hypotheses.   We summarise our expectations and up-front hypotheses below:

- **RQ1:** Although earlier studies [21, 23] have yielded mixed results, in general, the performance overhead has been shown to be rather substantial: ranging between 10 and 70% depending on the operation for a single-node setup. DataNucleus in particular is shown to have tremendous overhead [23]. We expect

to confirm such results and thus increase confidence in these findings.

- **RQ2:** ONDMs are by design independent of the underlying database, and therefore, we expect the absolute overhead not to be affected by the setup or the complexity of the database itself. As a consequence, we expect the absolute overhead to potentially more significant (i.e. a higher relative overhead) for low-latency setups (e.g. a single node setup or an in-memory database), in comparison to setups featuring more network latency or disk I/O (e.g. a database cluster or a disk-intensive setup).

- **RQ3:** We expect to find that the programming interface does have a certain impact on performance. For example, the JPA standard relies heavily on code annotations, we expect the extensive use of reflection on these objects and their annotations within the ONDM middleware to substantially contribute to the overall performance overhead.

- **RQ4:** This is in fact an extension to **RQ3**, focusing on which development API incurs the highest performance overhead. On the one hand, JPA is costly due to its reliance on annotation-based reflection, while on the other hand, query translation can become costly as well. To our knowledge, this is the first benchmark study directly comparing the JPA and JPQL performance overhead over NoSQL search queries.

- **RQ5:** We expect complex queries to be more costly in query translation. Additionally, queries retrieving multiple results should have increased overhead as each result has to be mapped into an object.

The following section presents the design and setup of our benchmarks that are tailored to provide answers to the above questions.

4   Benchmark setup

This section discusses the main design decisions involved in the setup of our benchmark study. Section 4.1 first discusses the overall architecture of an ONDM frame-work, and then Section 4.2 discusses the measurement methodology for the performance overhead. Section 4.3 subsequently motivates our selection of Object-NoSQL Database Mapping (ONDM) platforms for this study, whereas Section 4.4 elaborates further on the benchmarks we have adopted and extended for our study. Next, Section 4.5 discusses the different deployment configurations in which we have executed these benchmarks. Finally, Section 4.6 summarises how our study is tailored to provide answers to the research questions introduced in the previous section.

4.1 ONDM Framework architecture

The left-hand side of Fig. 1 depicts the common architecture of Object-NoSQL Database Mappers (ONDMs) which is layered. As shown at the top of Fig. 1, an ONDM platform supports a `Uniform Data Model` in the application space. In the Java Persistence API (JPA) for example, these are the annotated classes. In Apache Gora however, mapping classes are generated from user specifications. An ONDM provides a `Uniform Interface` based on the `Uniform Data Model`. The `Middleware Engine` implements the operations of the `Uniform Interface` and delegates these operations to the correct `Database Mapper`.

The `Database Mapper` is a pluggable module that implements the native `Database Driver`'s API. Different `Database Mapper` modules are created for different NoSQL databases. The `Database Mapper` converts the uniform data object to the native data structure, and calls the corresponding native operation(s). The `Database Driver` executes these native operations and handles all communication with the database.

The right hand side of Fig. 1 illustrates the situation in which no ONDM framework is employed, and the

application directly uses the native client API to communicate with the database.

Comparing both alternatives in Fig. 1 clearly illustrates the cost of object mapping as a key contributor to the performance overhead introduced by ONDM platforms. Both write requests (which involve translating in-memory objects or API calls to native API calls) and read requests or search queries (which involve translating database objects to application objects) rely extensively on database mapping. Our benchmark study, therefore, focuses on measuring this additional performance overhead.

In addition, Fig. 1 clearly shows that an ONDM is designed to be maximally technology-agnostic: other than the `Database Mapper` which makes abstraction of a specific database technology, the inner workings of the ONDM do not take the specifics of the selected database technology into account.

4.2 Measurement methodology

In order to measure the overhead of ONDMs, we first measure t_{ONDM}, the total time it takes to perform a database operation (read, write, update, search), which is the sum of time spent by the ONDM components depicted on the left-hand side of Fig. 1.

In addition, we measure t_{DB}, the total time it takes to execute the exact same database operations using the native client API (right-hand side of Fig. 1). By subtracting both measurements, we can characterise the performance overhead introduced by the ODNM framework as $t_{Overhead} = t_{ONDM} - t_{DB}$. This is exactly the additional overhead incurred by deciding to adopt an ONDM framework instead of developing against the native client API.

To maintain comparability between different ODNMs, we must: (i) select a specific database and database version that is supported by the selected ONDM frameworks (our baseline for comparison), (ii) ensure that each ONDM framework uses the same database driver to communicate with the NoSQL database, (iii) run the exact same benchmarks in our different setups. These decisions are explained in the following sections.

4.3 ODNM selection

Our benchmark study includes the following five ONDMs: EclipseLink [17], Hibernate OGM [20], Impetus Kundera [16], DataNucleus [19] and Apache Gora [18]. Table 2 lists these ONDMs and summarises their main characteristics and features.

As mentioned above, to maintain comparability of our benchmark results, it is imperative to ensure that the selected ONDMs employ the exact same NoSQL database, and database driver version as our baseline. Driven by Table 2, we have selected MongoDB version 2.6 as the main baseline for comparison. In contrast to other

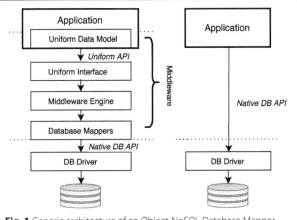

Fig. 1 Generic architecture of an Object-NoSQL Database Mapper (*left*), in comparison to a native client (*right*)

NoSQL technologies such as Cassandra for which many alternative client APIs and drivers are available, MongoDB provides only a single Java driver which is used by all of the selected frameworks. Furthermore, MongoDB can be used in various deployment configurations such as a single node or cluster setup, which will allow us to address **RQ2**.

In addition to MongoDB support as the primary selection criterion, we have also taken into account other comparability and industry relevance criteria: (i) JPA support, (ii) search support via JPQL, (iii) maturity and level of ongoing development activity. For example, we have deliberately excluded frameworks such as KO3-NoSQL [27] as their development seems to have been discontinued.

Although Apache Gora [18] is not JPA-compliant, it is included for the purpose of exploring the potential impact of the development API on the performance overhead introduced by these systems (**RQ3**).

4.4 Benchmark design

Our benchmarks are implemented and executed on top of the Yahoo! Cloud Serving Benchmark (YCSB) [3], an established benchmark framework initially developed to evaluate the performance of NoSQL databases. YCSB provides a number of facilities to accurately measure and control the benchmark execution of various workloads on NoSQL platforms.

Read, write, update. YCSB comes with a number of predefined workloads and is extensible, in the sense that different database client implementations can be added (by implementing the `com.yahoo.ycsb.DB` interface, which requires implementations for read, update, insert and delete (CRUD) operations on primary key).

Our implementation provides such extensions for the selected ONDMs (Hibernate OGM, DataNucleus EclipseLink, Kundera and Apache Gora). Especially the implementations for the JPA-compliant ONDMs are highly similar. To avoid skewing the results and to ensure comparability of the results, we did not make use of any performance optimization strategies offered by the ONDMs, such as caching, native queries and batch operations.

Furthermore, since implementations for NoSQL databases were already existing, we simply reused the client implementation for MongoDB for obtaining our baseline measurements.

Search. YCSB does not support benchmarking search queries out of the box. Therefore, we have defined a set of 6 read queries, which we execute on each platform in YCSB. These queries differ in both complexity and number of results. In support of these benchmarks, we populate our existing objects with more realistic values

such as `firstName` and `lastName`, instead of YCSB's default behavior which involves generating lenghty strings of random characters.

Note that we do not benchmark query performance for Apache Gora, since it has no support for JPQL and lacks support for basic query operators such as AND, OR[1].

4.5 Deployment setup

To address **RQ2** and assess the impact of the database deployment configuration on the performance overhead introduced by ONDMs, we have executed our benchmarks over different deployment configurations. Figure 2 depicts these different configurations graphically. The client node labeled YCSB Benchmark runs the ONDM framework or the native driver which are driven by the YCSB benchmarks discussed above.

The single-node setup (cf. Fig. 2a) involves two commodity machines, one executing the YCSB benchmark, and the other hosting a single MongoDB database instance.

The MongoDB cluster (cf. Fig. 2b) consists of a single router server, 3 configuration servers and 5 database shards. Each database is sharded and all of the inserted entities in each database are load balanced across all 5 database shards without replication.

Each node consists of a Dell Optiplex 755 (Intel® Core™ 2 Duo E6850 3.00GHz, 4GB DDR2, 250GB hard disk). In both cases, the benchmarks were executed in a local lab setting, and the average network latency between nodes in our lab setup is quite low: around $135\mu s$. As

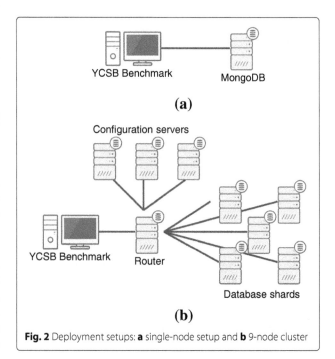

Fig. 2 Deployment setups: **a** single-node setup and **b** 9-node cluster

a consequence, our calculations of the relative overhead often represent the absolute worst case.

4.6 Setup: research questions

Below, we summarise how we address the individual research questions introduced in Section 3:

- **RQ1: Create, read, update.** We answer **RQ1** by running the benchmarks discussed above for the create, read and update operations. Our benchmarks are sequential: in the *load phase*, 20 million entities (20*GB*) are written to the database. In the *transaction phase*, the desired workload is executed on the data set (involving read and update). The inserted entity is a single object.
- **RQ2: Significance of performance overhead.** To put the absolute performance overhead measurements into perspective, we have executed our benchmarks in two different environments: (i) a remote single-node MongoDB instance, and (ii) a 9-node MongoDB cluster. These concrete setups are depicted in Fig. 2. In both cases, the actual execution of the benchmark is done on a separate machine to avoid CPU contention. The inserted data size consumes the entire memory pool of the single node and cluster shards. Read requests are not always able to find the intended record in-memory, resulting in lookup on disk. Based on the two types of responses we determine the general impact of ONDMs on overhead for deployments of varying data set sizes and memory resources.
- **RQ3: Impact of development API.** By comparing the results for the JPA middleware (Kundera, Hibernate ORM, DataNucleus and EclipseLink) to the results for Apache Gora (which offers custom, non-JPA compliant developer APIs), we can at least exploratively assess the potential performance impact of the interface.
- **RQ4: JPA vs JPQL.** To answer RQ5, we compare the basic JPA *find on primary key* (read lookup) to a JPQL *query on primary key*. By comparing both, we can assess the extra overhead cost of JPQL query translation.
- **RQ5: Search query performance overhead.** We have benchmarked queries on secondary indices in increasing order of query complexity for the ONDMs and compare the results to the benchmarks of the native MongoDB client API.

The next two sections present and discuss our findings in relation to these five research questions.

5 Write, read and update performance results

This section presents the results of our benchmarks that provide answers to questions **RQ1-3**. Research questions

RQ4-5 regarding search performance are discussed in Section 6.

The next sections first determine the overhead introduced by the selected ONDMs on the three operations (write, read, and update) in the context of the single remote node setup. In order to understand how the ONDMs introduce overhead, the default behaviour of MongoDB (our baseline for comparison) must be taken into account, which we discuss in the next Section 5.1.

5.1 Database behaviour

In our benchmarks, twenty million records (which corresponds to roughly 20GB) are inserted into the single node MongoDB database. Considering the machine only has 4GB RAM, it is clear that not all of the records will fit in-memory. As a consequence, read operations will read a record from memory around 5% of the time, but mainly require disk I/O. In-memory operations are, on average, 30 times as fast as operations requiring disk I/O. Similarly, the update operations will only be able to update a subset of objects in-memory. This, however, does not apply to the write operation: on write, the database regularly flushes records to disk, which also influences the baseline. Figure 3 shows the distribution in latency for each type of operation. We can clearly identify a bimodal distribution for read and update operations. Write operations are normally distributed, however skewed to the right, as expected.

The aim of this study is to identify the overhead introduced by ONDMs. However, the variance on latency for objects on-disk is quite high ($\pm 25ms$) and in this case, the behaviour of the ONDM frameworks may no longer be the contributing factor determining the overhead. Therefore, we have analysed the separate distributions of read and update. To alleviate this, we compare both data sets (in-memory versus on-disk) separately.

5.2 RQ1 Impact on write, read and update performance on a single node

Table 3 shows the overhead for write, read and update operations. Read and update operations are divided according to the overhead for objects in-memory and on-disk. We first discuss the results for operations in-memory. The write and read overhead of ONDMs ranges respectively between [9.9%, 36.5%] and [6.7%, 42.2%] and as such may be considered significant. However, the update operation is considerably slower and introduces twice as much latency for a single update operation in comparison to the native MongoDB driver[2]. The main reason for this is that update operations in the ODNMs frameworks first perform a read operation before actually updating a certain object. This is in contrast to the native database's capabilities: for example MongoDB can update records without requiring a read. Surprisingly

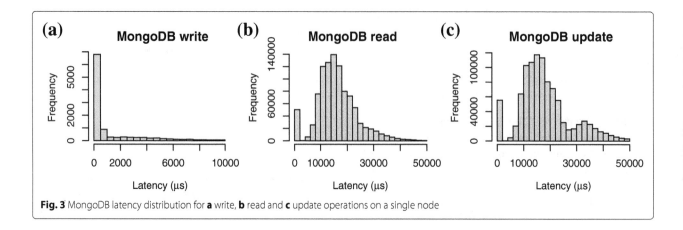

Fig. 3 MongoDB latency distribution for **a** write, **b** read and **c** update operations on a single node

enough, each of the observed frameworks require a read before update, resulting in the addition of read latency on update and thus significant overhead. Moreover, DataNucleus executes the read again, even though the object provided on update is already read, thus executing a read twice. This is a result of DataNucleus its mechanisms to ensure consistency, and local objects are verified against the database. The requirement of read on update in the ONDMs is a clear mismatch between the uniform interface and the native database's capabilities.

While operations on in-memory data structures show consistent overhead results, this is not the case for operations which trigger on-disk lookup. It may seem that the ONDM frameworks in some cases outperform the native database driver, but this is mainly due to the variance of database latency. The ordering in performance is not preserved for on-disk operations, and Kundera in particular experienced a higher latency. Considering the small overhead of around $[15\mu s, 300\mu s]$ which ONDMs introduce for operations in-memory, this is only a minimal contributor in the general time for on-disk operations. For example, MongoDB takes on average $15.9ms \pm 5.2ms$ for read on-disk. This is an increase in latency of 2 to 3 orders of magnitude. In other words, the relative overhead introduced by ONDMs is insignificant, when data needs to be searched for on-disk.

5.3 RQ2: Impact of the database topology

As shown for a single remote node, the overhead on write, read or update is significant for in-memory data. In case of the cluster, we expect the absolute overhead to be comparable to the single-node setup. Table 4 shows the results for write, read and update. As shown, the relative overhead percentages are substantially smaller in comparison to the single node. EclipseLink has only a minor write and read overhead of respectively 2.5 and 3.6%, which can be explained by considering that the absolute overhead remains more or less constant, while the baseline latency does increase. For example, EclipseLink's absolute read overhead is $15\mu s$ for the single node, and identically $15\mu s$ on the cluster. However, the write overhead decreases from $43\mu s$ to $29s$. This is attributed to the fact that MongoDB experienced more outliers, as its standard deviation for write is $12\mu s$ higher. The behaviour of each run is always slightly different, therefore the standard deviation, and thus behaviour of the database must be taken into account when interpreting these results. The ideal case is read in-memory, where the standard deviation is almost identical for all four frameworks and the native MongoDB driver. In general, the write and read overhead is still quite significant and ranges around [4%, 9%] for EclipseLink and Kundera, which are clearly more optimised than the other frameworks.

Table 3 Average latency and relative overhead for each platform on a single node

	Write		Read in-memory		Read on-disk		Update in-memory		Update on-disk	
Samples	$n = 20.000.000$		$n = 45.000$		$n = 750.000$		$n = 39.000$		$n = 750.000$	
Platform	Latency (μs)		Latency (μs)		Latency (ms)		Latency (μs)		Latency (ms)	
MongoDB	403 ± 110	-	217 ± 34	-	15.9 ± 5.2	-	298 ± 106	-	19.3 ± 9.1	-
EclipseLink	446 ± 105	10.8%	232 ± 41	6.7%	14.2 ± 5.0	−10.45%	579 ± 91	93.9%	16.9 ± 8.0	−12.0%
Kundera	442 ± 96	9.9%	256 ± 57	17.7%	17.1 ± 5.6	+8.0%	338 ± 56	13.3%	20.7 ± 9.8	+7.6%
Hibernate OGM	452 ± 72	12.3%	289 ± 42	32.8%	15.1 ± 6.5	−4.7%	620 ± 53	107.6%	16.8 ± 8.0	−12.8%
Apache Gora	495 ± 92	22.9%	282 ± 65	29.8%	14.5 ± 5.0	−8.5%	570 ± 108	91.0%	17.4 ± 8.2	−9.5%
DataNucleus	550 ± 76	36.5%	309 ± 64	42.2%	14.3 ± 5.0	−9.8%	882 ± 49	194.8%	17.7 ± 8.3	−8.0%

Table 4 Average latency and relative overhead for each platform on a cluster

Samples Platform	Write n = 20.000.000 Latency (μs)		Read in memory n = 360.000 Latency (μs)		Read on disk n = 610.000 Latency (ms)		Update in memory n = 300.000 Latency (μs)		Update on disk n = 600.000 Latency (ms)	
MongoDB	694 ± 90	-	434 ± 26	-	11.7 ± 3.8	-	534 ± 122	-	14.6 ± 6.7	-
EclipseLink	723 ± 78	4.1%	449 ± 27	3.6%	11.0 ± 3.5	−5.4%	1052 ± 72	97.1%	15.2 ± 6.8	3.6%
Kundera	725 ± 79	4.4%	471 ± 27	8.7%	11.2 ± 3.5	−4.2%	858 ± 57	60.8%	15.9 ± 7.4	8.9%
Hibernate OGM	764 ± 68	10.1%	505 ± 28	16.4%	11.2 ± 3.6	−3.6%	1083 ± 67	102.9%	14.9 ± 6.6	2.1%
Apache Gora	791 ± 62	14.0%	506 ± 26	16.7%	11.5 ± 3.7	−1.2%	1034 ± 75	93.7%	15.7 ± 7.2	7.5%
DataNucleus	788 ± 54	13.6%	526 ± 27	21.2%	11.4 ± 3.6	−2.2%	1567 ± 40	193.8%	15.4 ± 6.5	5.5%

In case of update, the frameworks again introduce a substantial overhead, because they perform a read operation before an update. The cost of the additional read is even higher in the cluster context, considering that a single read takes around $434\mu s$.

When operations occur on-disk, it may seem that the frameworks outperform the baseline. Once again, this is attributed to the general behaviour of the MongoDB cluster. The standard deviation for reading on-disk for the baseline is, for example, 10% higher than the frameworks. The results of each workload execution may also vary due to records being load balanced at run-time. However, the cluster allows for a more precise determination of the overhead as there are more memory resources available, which in turn results in less variable database behaviour such as on-disk lookups. In addition, the write performance is less affected by the regular flush operation of a single node.

5.4   RQ3: Impact of the interface on performance

In contrast to the four JPA-compliant frameworks, we now include Apache Gora in our benchmarks, which offers a non-standardised, REST-based programming interface.

Tables 3 and 4 presents the average latency of Apache Gora for write, read and update on the two database topologies. Even though the interface and data model is quite different from JPA, the overhead is very similar.

Surprisingly enough, we do not see a large difference in update performance. As we actually observe the same behaviour for Apache Gora's update operation: Apache Gora's API specifies no explicit update operation, but instead uses the same write method `put(K key, T object)` for updating records. As a result, the object has to be read before updating. If an object has not yet been read and needs to be updated, it may be best to perform an update query instead.

5.5   Conclusions

In summary, the following conclusions are made from the results regarding **RQ1-3** about the performance of ONDMs:

- The write, read and update performance overhead can be considered significant. Overheads are observed between [4%, 14%] for write, [4%, 21%] for read and [60%, 194%] for update, on the cluster.
- The relative overhead becomes insignificant as the database latency increases. Examples are cases which trigger on-disk lookups or even when a higher network latency is present.
- Interface mismatches can exist between the uniform interface and the native database's capabilities which decrease performance.

The next section discusses our benchmark results regarding the performance overhead introduced by the uniform query language JPQL for the JPA ONDMs.

6   JPQL search performance

Contrary to the name, NoSQL databases often do feature a query language. In addition, ONDMs provide a uniform SQL-like query language on top of these heterogeneous languages. For example, JPA-based object-data mappers provide a standardised query language called JPQL. We have evaluated the performance of JPQL for the JPA-based platforms: EclipseLink, Kundera, DataNucleus and Hibernate OGM.

While it is clear that there can be quite some overhead attached to a create, read or update operation, the question **RQ4** still remains whether or not the JPQL search overhead is similar to JPA read. Section 6.1 therefore first compares two different ways to retrieve a single object: using a JPQL search query, or with a JPA lookup.

Then, Section 6.2 addresses **RQ5** by considering how the performance overhead of a JPQL query is affected by its nature and complexity.

6.1   RQ4: Single object search in JPA and JPQL

We compare a read for a single object using the JPA interface, to the same read in JPQL query notation. This allows us to determine the exact difference in read overhead between JPA and JPQL for **RQ4**.

In order to be able to compare the results from the earlier JPA read to the JPQL search on the same object for **RQ4**, we have re-evaluated the read performance by inserting 1 million entities (roughly 1GB of data). The data set is completely in-memory for the single-node and cluster setup, allowing for a consistent measurement of the performance overhead. More specifically, our benchmarks compare the performance overhead incurred by `Query A` (JPA code) with the overhead incurred by `Query B` (JPQL equivalent code) in Listing 1.

Listing 1 JPQL and JPA search on primary key

```
A)  entityManager.find(Person.class, id);

B)  SELECT * FROM Person p WHERE p.id = :id
```

Table 5 shows the average latency for a find in JPA and a search in JPQL for the same object. We can clearly see that in general, a query in JPQL comes at a higher performance overhead cost (**RQ4**). Additional observations:

- Kundera and EclipseLink both perform similarly in JPA and JPQL single entity search performance.
- Interestingly, DataNucleus and Hibernate OGM are drastically slower for JPQL queries.

In DataNucleus the additional JPQL overhead stems from the translation of the query to a generic expression tree, which is then translated to the native MongoDB query.

Additionally, DataNucleus makes use of a lazy query loading approach to avoid memory conflicts. As a result, it executes a second read call to verify if there are any records remaining.

Code inspection in Hibernate OGM revealed that this platform extensively re-uses components from the Hibernate ORM engine, which may result in additional overhead due to architectural legacy.

JPQL provides more advanced search functionality than JPA's single find on primary key. The next section discusses the performance benchmark results on a number of JPQL queries of increasing complexity.

Table 5 The average latency on single object search in JPA, JPQL, and MongoDB's native read

Native driver	1-node read		9-node read	
MongoDB	197μs		434μs	
Platform	JPA Latency	JPQL Latency	JPA s Latency	JPQL Latency
Kundera	243μs	285μs	478μs	520μs
EclipseLink	218μs	291μs	448μs	520μs
Hibernate OGM	270μs	1.804μs	521μs	2.098μs
DataNucleus	288μs	811μs	492μs	1.236μs

6.2 RQ5: Relation between the nature and complexity of the query and its overhead

This section discusses the results of our search benchmarks, and more specifically how the overhead of a search query is related to the complexity of the query for **RQ5**. Queries which retrieve multiple results incur more performance overhead, as all the results have to be mapped to objects.

The benchmarked search queries are presented in Listing 2. The respective queries are implemented in JPQL and executed in the context of all four ONDM platforms. Our baseline measurement is the equivalent MongoDB native query. The actual search arguments are chosen randomly at runtime by YCSB and are marked as `:variable`.

The queries are ordered according to the average results retrieved per query. `Query C` is a query on secondary indices using the `AND` operator and always retrieves a single result. By comparison to `Query B`, which retrieves a single object on the primary key, we can determine the impact of a more complex query text translation.

In contrast, `Queries D, E` and `F` retrieve respectively on average 1.35, 94 and 2864 objects. When we compare the performance of Queries D,E and F, we can assess what impact the amount of results have on the overhead. First, we evaluate the case where we retrieve a single result with a more complex query.

Listing 2 JPQL search queries

```
C)  SELECT p FROM Person p WHERE
(p.email = :email) AND
(p.personalnumber = :personalnumber)

D)  SELECT p FROM Person p WHERE
p.email = :email

E)  SELECT p FROM Person p WHERE
(p.personalnumber < :upperBound) AND
(p.personalnumber > :lowerBound)

F)  SELECT p FROM Person p WHERE
(p.firstName = :firstName) OR
(p.lastName = :lastName)
```

6.2.1 JPQL search using the AND operator

Table 6 presents the results for `Query C`, the JPQL search using AND on secondary indices. The query always returns a single object in our experiment. In comparison to the results from JPQL search on a primary key in Table 5, we observe an increase in baseline latency due to the use of secondary indices and the AND operator.

Additionally for the ONDMs, we observe an increase in read overhead for the more complex query on the single node for Kundera and Eclipselink. As it turns out EclipseLink is less efficient than Kundera in handling the more complex query. Furthermore, DataNucleus shows a higher increase in performance overhead, as the query is

Table 6 The average latency and overhead for Query C, which retrieves a single object

Native driver	1-node		9-node	
	Latency	Overhead	Latency	Overhead
MongoDB	$281\mu s$	-	$621\mu s$	-
Platform				
Kundera	$408\mu s$	$127\mu s$	$743\mu s$	$122\mu s$
EclipseLink	$453\mu s$	$172\mu s$	$783\mu s$	$162\mu s$
Hibernate OGM	$590\mu s$	$309\mu s$	$921\mu s$	$301\mu s$
DataNucleus	$1.010\mu s$	$729\mu s$	$1.581\mu s$	$960\mu s$

Table 8 The average latency and overhead for Query E, which retrieves on average 94 objects

Native driver	1-node		9-node	
	Latency	Overhead	Latency	Overhead
MongoDB	$943\mu s$	-	$1.901\mu s$	-
Platform				
Kundera	$1.396\mu s$	$453\mu s$	$2.374\mu s$	$473\mu s$
EclipseLink	$1.556\mu s$	$613\mu s$	$2.550\mu s$	$649\mu s$
Hibernate OGM	$4.558\mu s$	$3.615\mu s$	$5.889\mu s$	$3.988\mu s$
DataNucleus	$3.831\mu s$	$2.888\mu s$	$4.786\mu s$	$2.885\mu s$

translated to a more complex expression tree first, and secondly due to the additional read from its lazy loading approach.

Surprisingly, Hibernate OGM's absolute overhead on the remote node is $309\mu s$ for the more complex Query C, while for the simple search (Query B) on primary key this was $1.607\mu s$. Clearly, Hibernate OGM has some inefficiencies regarding its query performance.

6.2.2 JPQL search on a secondary index
Query D is a simple search on a secondary index of a person. The query retrieves on average 1.35 objects. Therefore, multiple records can be retrieved on search which have to be mapped into objects.

Table 7 shows the average latency and relative overhead of Query D for the four JPA platforms, as for the similar query implemented in MongoDB's native query language.

Again, we conclude that Kundera and EclipseLink are most efficient at handling the query.

6.2.3 JPQL search on a range of values
Table 8 shows the average latency for the JPQL search Query E. The performance overhead introduced by the ONDM platforms increases as on average 94 results have to be mapped into objects, and ranges between $[453\mu s, 3.615\mu s]$ on the single node, and $[473\mu s, 3.988\mu s]$ on the cluster.

6.2.4 JPQL search using the OR operator
The average latency of Query F is presented in Table 9. Again, the performance overhead introduced by the ONDMs increases as this query involves retrieval of on average 2.864 records, to the range of $[7.6ms, 56.6ms]$ and $[10.2ms, 42ms]$ on the respective database topologies. These results allow us to highlight the specific object-mapping cost of each ONDM. Kundera seems to have significantly more efficient object-mapping than EclipseLink. The average overhead for each object retrieved ranges between $[3\mu s, 17\mu s]$.

6.3 Search performance conclusion
In summary, several conclusions can be made from the results regarding **RQ4-5** about the query search performance of ONDMs:

- JPQL search on a primary key has a higher overhead than JPA's find for the same object (**RQ4**).
- The performance overhead of a JPQL query is closely related to the complexity of its translation and the amount of results retrieved (**RQ5**) and there are large differences between the ONDM in terms of the performance cost associated to search queries. Finally, the additional performance overhead per search result in general decreases for queries

Table 7 The average latency and overhead for Query D, which retrieves on average 1.35 objects

Native driver	1-node		9-node	
	Latency	Overhead	Latency	Overhead
MongoDB	$250\mu s$	-	$576\mu s$	-
Platform				
Kundera	$347\mu s$	$97\mu s$	$677\mu s$	$100\mu s$
EclipseLink	$396\mu s$	$146\mu s$	$729\mu s$	$152\mu s$
Hibernate OGM	$553\mu s$	$304\mu s$	$883\mu s$	$306\mu s$
DataNucleus	$957\mu s$	$707\mu s$	$1.520\mu s$	$944\mu s$

Table 9 The average latency and overhead for Query F, which retrieves on average 2.864 objects

Native driver	1-node		9-node	
	Latency	Overhead	Latency	Overhead
MongoDB	$20.226\mu s$	-	$39.689\mu s$	-
Platform				
Kundera	$27.989\mu s$	$7.763\mu s$	$49.889\mu s$	$10.210\mu s$
EclipseLink	$33.640\mu s$	$13.414\mu s$	$56.059\mu s$	$16.370\mu s$
Hibernate OGM	$58.806\mu s$	$38.580\mu s$	$75.234\mu s$	$35.545\mu s$
DataNucleus	$77.093\mu s$	$56.587\mu s$	$81.628\mu s$	$41.993\mu s$

involving large amounts of results, which motivates the use of JPQL for large result sets.

The next section discusses our benchmark results in further detail.

7   Discussion

First, Section 7.1 discusses the main threats to validity. Then, we provide a more in-depth discussion about some of the more surprising results of our benchmarks, more specifically about Kundera's fast update performance (Section 7.2), and the observed mismatch between standards such as JPA and NoSQL technology (Section 7.3). Finally, we discuss the significant overhead in search performance for Hibernate OGM and DataNucleus (Section 7.4).

7.1   Threats to validity

As with any benchmark study, a number of threats to validity apply. We outline the most notable topics below.

Internal validity   We discuss a number of threats:

- **Throughput rate control.** A possible threat to validity is related to the method of measurement. Although YCSB allows specifying a fixed throughput rate, we did not make use of this function. Limiting the throughput ensures that no platform is constrained by the resources of the server or client. For example, the MongoDB native database driver can process create, read and update operations at a faster rate than the ONDMs, as shown. In such a case, the MongoDB driver may reach its threshold of maximum performance, as dictated by its deployment constraints. In contrast, the ONDMs work at a slower rate and are less likely to reach this threshold. Consequentially, the computing resources of the MongoDB node will not be as much of an issue. When applying throughput rate control, the possibility of reaching this threshold is excluded, and the average latency would be a more truthful depiction of the individual performance.
  To increase our confidence in the obtained results, we did run a smaller-scale additional evaluation in which we applied throughput rate control (limited to 10.000 operations per write, read and update) and did not notice any deviations from our earlier results. Furthermore, during our main experiment we have measured CPU usage, I/O wait time and memory usage. From these measurements[3] we gather that no cluster node used more than 10% CPU usage on average. Although the single-node database setup experienced the heaviest load, during workload execution, it was still idling 50% of the time.

As such, we conclude that the MongoDB cluster and single-node setup did not reach their limits during our benchmarks.

- **Choice of the baseline.** In this study, we implicitly assume that the choice for MongoDB as the back-end database has no significant impact on the performance overhead of ONDMs, because we subtract the MongoDB latency in our performance overhead calculations. Furthermore, the database-specific mapper is a modularly pluggable module which is independent of the core middleware engine responsible for data mapping. Each database-specific implementation only varies in its implementation of these engine interfaces. These arguments lead us to believe that there will be minimal variation in overhead between NoSQL technologies. We can confirm this by referring to a previous study on the performance overhead [21], in which Cassandra and MongoDB were used as the baseline for comparison. The study shows similar relative overheads despite using a different database technology as the baseline for comparison.

External validity.   There is a number of ways in which the results may deviate from realistic deployments of ONDM systems. Specifically, our benchmark is designed to quantify the worst-case performance overhead in a number of ways.

- **Entity relationships.** For simplicity, we chose to work with single entities containing no relationships. There are a number of different ways relationships can be persisted in NoSQL databases: denormalizing to a single entity, storing them as separate entities, etc. This may have a drastic effect on the object-data mapper's performance. A single entity containing no relationships allows us to monitor the overhead of each platform without unnecessary complexity. The performance overhead of an application that relies extensively on associations between entities may vary from the results obtained in our study.
- **Optimization strategies.** The studied ONDMs offer various caching strategies and transaction control mechanisms. EclipseLink even supports cross-application cache coordination, which may improve performance significantly. As already discussed in Section 4.4, to maximally ensure comparability of our results, we disabled these mechanisms in our benchmarks. In the case of Object-Relational Mappers (ORMs), the impact of performance optimizations has already been studied [28, 29]. A similar study can prove useful for ONDMs and should be considered future work.
- **Database deployment.** We have shown that although these frameworks introduce more or less a

constant absolute performance overhead, the significance of this performance overhead may depend highly on the nature and complexity of the overall database setup and the application case. For example, in the context of an in-memory database featuring a high-bandwidth and low-latency connection, the introduced overhead may be deemed significant. In contrast, general database deployments often read from disk and feature a higher network latency, and in such a context, the introduced overhead may be considered minimal or negligible.

It is therefore important to stress that for the above reasons, different and in many cases, better performance characteristics can be expected in realistic ONDM deployments.

7.2 Kundera's update performance

Looking at the update performance results of Impetus Kundera in Tables 3 and 4, one might conclude that Kundera significantly outperforms EclipseLink and Hibernate OGM when it comes to updating. However, upon closer inspection, we discovered that in the tested version of Kundera an implementation mistake was made.

More specifically, Kundera's implementation does not make use of the MongoDB property `WriteConcern.ACKNOWLEDGED`, which forces the client to actively wait until MongoDB acknowledges issued update requests (a default property in MongoDB since version 2.6 [30]). By not implementing this, Kundera's implementation gains an unfair advantage since some of the network latency is not included in the measurement.

We have reported this bug in the Kundera bug reporting system [31].

7.3 JPA-NoSQL interface mismatch

One remarkable result is the observation that update operations consistently introduce more performance overhead when compared to read or write operations (cf. Table 3). The main cause for this is that the JPA standard imposes that updates can only be done on *managed* entities, i.e. it forces the ONDM to read the object prior to update. This causes the update operation to be significantly costlier than a read operation[4]. As pointed out by [21], similar drawbacks are associated to delete operations (which were not benchmarked in this study).

In the context of Object-Relational Mappers (ORMs), this problem is commonly referred to as the *object-relational impedance mismatch* [32], and one may argue that in a NoSQL context, such mismatch problems may be more significant due to the technological heterogeneity among NoSQL systems and the wide range of features and data models supported in NoSQL.

Similar drawbacks apply to JPQL search operations, especially when there is a discrepancy between the native search capabilities and the features assumed by JPQL.

Future work is required to determine whether other existing standardised interfaces such as REST-based APIs, Java Data Objects (JDO) are better suited, and more in-depth research is required toward dedicated, NoSQL-specific abstraction interfaces that can further reduce the cost inherent to database abstraction.

7.4 JPQL search performance

When comparing the results of our query benchmarks (cf. Section 6), it becomes clear that the performance overhead results for DataNucleus and Hibernate OGM are drastically worse than those of EclipseLink and Impetus Kundera: in some cases, Hibernate OGM introduces up to 383% overhead whereas the overhead introduced by the other two ONDMs never exceeds 66%.

According to the Hibernate OGM Reference Guide [20], the search implementation is a direct port of the search implementation of Hibernate's Object-Relational Mapper (ORM). Architectural legacy could therefore be one potential explanation for these surprising results.

Similarly to Hibernate OGM, DataNucleus shows a more consistent overhead of around 300%. In this case, the overhead is mainly attributed to the fact that it executes additional and unnecessary reads. Furthermore, the queries are translated first into a more generic expression tree, and then to the native database query. Various optimization strategies are provided to cache these query compilations, which might in turn provide more optimal performance. However, it is clear that the compilation of queries to generic expression trees, independent of the data store, takes a toll on performance.

8 Related work

This section addresses three domains of related work: (i) performance studies on Object-relational Mapper (ORM) frameworks, (ii) academic prototypes of Object-NoSQL Database Mappers and (iii) (performance) studies on ONDMs.

8.1 Performance studies on ORM frameworks

In the Object-relational Mapper (ORM) space, several studies have evaluated the performance of ORM frameworks, mainly focused on a direct comparison between frameworks [33–37]. Performance studies were mainly conducted on Java-based ORM frameworks, however, some studies also evaluated ORM in .NET based frameworks [38, 39]. However, few studies actually focused on the overhead, but more on the differences between the frameworks. The benchmark studies of Sembera [40] and Kalotra [35] suggest that EclipseLink is slower than Hibernate. However, a study by ObjectDB actually lists

EclipseLink as faster than Hibernate OGM [41]. The methods used in each study differ and the results are not directly applicable to NoSQL. Since none of these studies quantify the exact overhead of these ORM systems, comparison to our results is difficult.

The studies by Van Zyl et al. [42] and Kopteff [34] compare the performance of Java ORM-frameworks to the performance of Object-databases. These studies evaluate whether object databases can be used instead of ORM tools and traditional relational databases, reducing the mapping cost.

Although executed in a different technological context (.NET), the studies of Gruca et al. [38] and Cvetkovic et al. [39] seem to indicate that there is less overhead associated to translating abstraction query languages (such as Entity SQL, LINQ or Hibernate HQL) to SQL in the context of relational databases, when compared to our results. The relatively high search overhead in our results is caused by the larger abstraction gap between NoSQL query interfaces and JPQL (which is a SQL-inspired query language by origin).

8.2 Academic prototypes

Our study focused mainly on Object-NoSQL Database Mappers (ONDMs) with a certain degree of maturity and industry-readiness. Apart from these systems, a number of academic prototypes exist that provide a uniform API for NoSQL data stores. This is a very wide range of systems, and not all of them perform object-data mapping. ODBAPI, presented by Sellami et al. [13], provides a unified REST API for relational and NoSQL data stores. Dharmasiri et al. [43] have researched a uniform query implementation for NoSQL. Atzeni et al. [7] and Cabibbo [12] have presented Object-NoSQL Database Mappers which employ object entities as the uniform data model. Cabibbo [12] is the first to coin the term "Object-NoSQL Datastore Mapper".

We have excluded such systems as most of these implementations are proof-of-concepts, and few of them are readily available.

8.3 Studies on ONDMs

Three existing studies have already performed an evaluation and comparison of Object-NoSQL Database Mappers. Wolf et al. [44] extended Hibernate, the ORM framework, to support RIAK, a NoSQL Key-Value data store. In support of this endeavour, they evaluated the performance and compared it with the performance of Hibernate ORM configured to use with MySQL. The study provides valuable insights as to how NoSQL technology can be integrated into object-relational mapping frameworks.

Störl et al. [23] conducted a comparison and performance evaluation of Object-NoSQL Database Mappers

(ONDMs). However, the study does not quantify the overhead directly, making a comparison difficult. Moreover, these benchmarks were obtained on a single node, and as a consequence, the results may be affected by CPU contention. Highly surprising in their results is the read performance of DataNucleus, which is shown to be at least 40 times as slow EclipseLink. We only measured similar results when *entity enhancement* was left enabled at-runtime, which recompiles entity classes to a meta model on each read. As a result, this may indicate fundamental flaws in the study's measurement methodology.

Finally, our study is a replica study of an earlier performance study by Rafique et al. [21], and we confirm many of these results. Our study differs in the sense that: (i) we adopted an improved measurement methodology, providing more insight on the correlation between the overhead and the database's behaviour and setup. Secondly, (ii) we conducted our evaluation using YCSB (an established NoSQL benchmark), (iii) we focus on a more mature set of ONDMs which have less overhead, and finally (iv) we evaluated the performance impact of ONDMs over search operations.

9 Conclusions and future work

Object-NoSQL Database Mapper (ONDM) systems have large potential: firstly, they allow NoSQL adopters to make abstraction of heterogeneous storage technology by making source code independent of specific NoSQL client APIs, and enable them to port their applications relatively easy to different storage technologies. In addition, they are key enablers for novel trends such as federated storage systems in which the storage tier of the application is composed of a combination of different heterogeneous storage technologies, potentially even hosted by different providers (cross-cloud and federated storage solutions).

There are however a number of caveats, such as the potential loss of NoSQL-specific features (due to the mismatch between APIs), and most notably, the additional performance overhead introduced by ONDM systems. The performance benchmarks presented in this paper have quantified this overhead for a standardised NoSQL benchmark, the Yahoo! Cloud Serving Benchmark (YCSB), specifically for create, read and update, and most notably search operations. In addition, we have explored the effect of a number of dimensions on the overhead: the storage architecture deployment setup, the amount of operations involved and the impact of the development API on performance.

Future work however is necessary for a survey study or gap analysis on existing ORM and ONDM framework with support for NoSQL and its features, specifically in the context of e.g. security and cross-database persistence. Additionally, we identify the need for a NoSQL search benchmark, as we have seen YCSB used for these purposes, although it is not supported by default. In addition, we aim to provide an extended empirical validation of our results on top of additional NoSQL platform(s).

The results obtained in this study inform potential adopters of ONDM technology about the cost associated to such systems, and provides some indications as to the maturity of these technologies. Especially in the area of search, we have observed large differences among ONDMs in terms of the performance cost.

This work fits in our ongoing research on policy-based middleware for multi-storage architectures in which these ONDMs represent a core layer.

Endnotes

[1] Furthermore, Apache Gora implements most query functionality based on client-side filtering, which can be assumed quite slow.

[2] The results indicate that this is however not the case for Kundera, which is attributable to an implementation mistake in Kundera's update mechanism (see Section 7.2)

[3] Our resource measurements indicate that factors such as I/O and CPU play a negligible role in the results. For example, the utilization of ONDM platforms required only limited additional CPU usage at the client side for read (Additional file 1).

[4] Kundera's update strategy is slightly different: the `merge( object )` update operation in Kundera reads the object only when it is unmanaged, whereas in the other platforms this is explicitly done by the developer. The solution in Kundera therefore avoids the cost of mapping the result of the read operation to an object.

Acknowledgements

This research is partially funded by the Research Fund KU Leuven (project GOA/14/003 - ADDIS) and the DeCoMAdS project, which is supported by VLAIO (government agency for Innovation by Science and Technology).

Authors' contributions

VR conducted the main part of this research with guidance from AR, who has done earlier research in this domain. DVL supervised the research and contents of the paper, and WJ conducted a final supervision. All authors read and approved the final manuscript.

Authors' information

The authors are researchers of imec-DistriNet-KU Leuven at the Department of Computer Science, KU Leuven, 3001 Heverlee, Belgium.

References

1. Bắzăr C, Iosif CS, et al. The transition from rdbms to nosql. a comparative analysis of three popular non-relational solutions: Cassandra, mongodb and couchbase. Database Syst J. 2014;5(2):49–59.
2. Stonebraker M, Madden S, Abadi DJ, Harizopoulos S, Hachem N, Helland P. The end of an architectural era:(it's time for a complete rewrite). In: Proceedings of the 33rd International Conference on Very Large Data Bases. Vienna: VLDB Endowment; 2007. p. 1150–1160. http://dl.acm.org/citation.cfm?id=1325851.1325981.
3. Cooper BF, Silberstein A, Tam E, Ramakrishnan R, Sears R. Benchmarking cloud serving systems with YCSB. In: Proceedings of the 1st ACM symposium on Cloud computing - SoCC '10. Association for Computing Machinery (ACM); 2010. p. 143–154. doi:10.1145/1807128.1807152. http://dx.doi.org/10.1145/1807128.1807152.
4. Lakshman A, Malik P. Cassandra: a decentralized structured storage system. ACM SIGOPS Oper Syst Rev. 2010;44(2):35–40.
5. Chang F, Dean J, Ghemawat S, Hsieh WC, Wallach DA, Burrows M, Chandra T, Fikes A, Gruber RE. Bigtable: A distributed storage system for structured data. ACM Trans Comput Syst (TOCS). 2008;26(2):4.
6. DeCandia G, Hastorun D, Jampani M, Kakulapati G, Lakshman A, Pilchin A, Sivasubramanian S, Vosshall P, Vogels W. Dynamo. ACM SIGOPS Operating Systems Review. 2007;41(6):205–220. doi:10.1145/1323293.1294281. http://dx.doi.org/10.1145/1323293.1294281.
7. Atzeni P, Bugiotti F, Rossi L. Uniform access to nosql systems. Inform Syst. 2014;43:117–133.
8. Stonebraker M. Sql databases v. nosql databases. Commun ACM. 2010;53(4):10–11. doi:10.1145/1721654.1721659.
9. Cattell R. Scalable sql and nosql data stores. ACM SIGMOD Rec. 2011;39(4): 12–27.
10. Stonebraker M. Stonebraker on nosql and enterprises. Commun ACM. 2011;54(8):10–11.
11. NoSQL databases. http://www.nosql-database.org. Accessed 22 Feb 2016.
12. Cabibbo L. Ondm: an object-nosql datastore mapper: Faculty of Engineering, Roma Tre University; 2013. Retrieved June 15th. http://cabibbo.dia.uniroma3.it/pub/ondm-demo-draft.pdf.
13. Sellami R, Bhiri S, Defude B. Odbapi: a unified rest API for relational and NoSQL data stores. In: 2014 IEEE International Congress on Big Data. IEEE; 2014. p. 653–660. doi:10.1109/bigdata.congress.2014.98. http://dx.doi.org/10.1109/bigdata.congress.2014.98.
14. Rafique A, Landuyt DV, Lagaisse B, Joosen W. Policy-driven data management middleware for multi-cloud storage in multi-tenant saas. In: 2015 IEEE/ACM 2nd International Symposium on Big Data Computing (BDC); 2015. p. 78–84. doi:10.1109/BDC.2015.39.
15. Fowler M. Polyglot Persistence. 2015. http://martinfowler.com/bliki/PolyglotPersistence.html. Accessed 22 Feb 2016.
16. Impetus: Kundera Documentation. https://github.com/impetus-opensource/Kundera/wiki. Accessed 28 May 2016.
17. Eclipselink: Understanding EclipseLink 2.6. 2016. https://www.eclipse.org/eclipselink/documentation/2.6/concepts/toc.htm. Accessed 27 May 2016.
18. Apache Gora: Apache Gora. http://gora.apache.org/. Accessed 28 May 2016.
19. DataNucleus: DataNucleus AccessPlatform. 2016. http://www.datanucleus.org/products/accessplatform_5_0/index.html. Accessed 28 May 2016.
20. Red Hat: Hibernate OGM Reference Guide. 2016. http://docs.jboss.org/hibernate/ogm/5.0/reference/en-US/pdf/hibernate_ogm_reference.pdf. Accessed 28-05-2016.
21. Rafique A, Landuyt DV, Lagaisse B, Joosen W. On the Performance Impact of Data Access Middleware for NoSQL Data Stores. IEEE Transactions on Cloud Computing. 2016;PP(99):1–1. doi:10.1109/TCC.2015.2511756.
22. Barnes JM. Object-relational mapping as a persistence mechanism for object-oriented applications: PhD thesis, Macalester College; 2007.
23. Störl U, Hauf T, Klettke M, Scherzinger S, Regensburg O. Schemaless nosql data stores-object-nosql mappers to the rescue? In: BTW; 2015. p. 579–599. http://www.informatik.uni-rostock.de/~meike/publications/stoerl_btw_2015.pdf.
24. Oracle Corporation: The Java EE6 Tutorial. 2016. http://docs.oracle.com/javaee/6/tutorial/doc/. Accessed 22 Feb 2016.

25. Apache JDO: Apache JDO. https://db.apache.org/jdo/. Accessed 22 Feb 2016.
26. NET Persistence API. http://www.npersistence.org/. Accessed 22 Feb 2016.
27. Curtis N. KO3-NoSQL. 2007. https://github.com/nichcurtis/KO3-NoSQL. Accessed 22 Feb 2016.
28. van Zyl P, Kourie DG, Coetzee L, Boake A. The influence of optimisations on the performance of an object relational mapping tool. 2009150–159. doi:10.1145/1632149.1632169.
29. Wu Q, Hu Y, Wang Y. Research on data persistence layer based on hibernate framework. 20101–4. doi:10.1109/IWISA.2010.5473662.
30. MongoDB: MongoDB Documentation. 2016. https://docs.mongodb.com/v2.6/. Accessed 22 Feb 2016.
31. Kundera bug regarding MongoDB's WriteConcern. https://github.com/impetus-opensource/Kundera/issues/830. Accessed 22 Feb 2016.
32. Ireland C, Bowers D, Newton M, Waugh K. A classification of object-relational impedance mismatch. In: Advances in Databases, Knowledge, and Data Applications, 2009. DBKDA '09. First International Conference On; 2009. p. 36–43. doi:10.1109/DBKDA.2009.11.
33. Higgins KR. An evaluation of the performance and database access strategies of java object-relational mapping frameworks. ProQuest Dissertations and Theses. 82. http://gradworks.umi.com/14/47/1447026.html.
34. Kopteff M. The Usage and Performance of Object Databases compared with ORM tools in a Java environment. Citeseer. 2008. http://citeseerx.ist.psu.edu/viewdoc/summary?doi=10.1.1.205.8271&rank=1&q=kopteff&osm=&ossid=.
35. Kalotra M, Kaur K. Performance analysis of reusable software systems. 2014773–778. doi:10.1109/CONFLUENCE.2014.6949308.
36. Ghandeharizadeh S, Mutha A. An evaluation of the hibernate object-relational mapping for processing interactive social networking actions. 201464–70. doi:10.1145/2684200.2684285.
37. Yousaf H. Performance evaluation of java object-relational mapping tools. Georgia: University of Georgia; 2012.
38. Gruca A, Podsiadło P. Beyond databases, architectures, and structures: 10th international conference, bdas 2014, ustron, poland, may 27–30, 2014. proceedings. 201440–49. Chap. Performance Analysis of .NET Based Object–Relational Mapping Frameworks. doi:10.1007/978-3-319-06932-6_5.
39. Cvetković S, Janković D. Objects and databases: Third international conference, icoodb 2010, frankfurt/main, germany, september 28–30, 2010. proceedings. 2010147–158. Chap. A Comparative Study of the Features and Performance of ORM Tools in a .NET Environment. doi:10.1007/978-3-642-16092-9_14.
40. Šembera L. Comparison of jpa providers and issues with migration. Masarykova univerzita, Fakulta informatiky. 2012. http://is.muni.cz/th/365414/fi_m/.
41. JPA Performance Benchmark (JPAB). http://www.jpab.org/. Accessed 22 Feb 2016.
42. Van Zyl P, Kourie DG, Boake A. Comparing the performance of object databases and ORM tools. In: Proceedings of the 2006 annual research conference of the South African institute of computer scientists and information technologists on IT research in developing couunties - SAICSIT '06; 2006. p. 1–11. doi:10.1145/1216262.1216263.
43. Dharmasiri HML, Goonetillake MDJS. A federated approach on heterogeneous nosql data stores. 2013234–23. doi:10.1109/ICTer.2013.6761184.
44. Wolf F, Betz H, Gropengießer F, Sattler KU. Hibernating in the cloud-implementation and evaluation of object-nosql-mapping. Citeseer.

A QoS-configurable failure detection service for internet applications

Rogério C. Turchetti[1,3][†], Elias P. Duarte Jr.[1][*][†], Luciana Arantes[2] and Pierre Sens[2]

Abstract

Unreliable failure detectors are a basic building block of reliable distributed systems. Failure detectors are used to monitor processes of any application and provide process state information. This work presents an Internet Failure Detector Service (IFDS) for processes running in the Internet on multiple autonomous systems. The failure detection service is adaptive, and can be easily integrated into applications that require configurable QoS guarantees. The service is based on monitors which are capable of providing global process state information through a SNMP MIB. Monitors at different networks communicate across the Internet using Web Services. The system was implemented and evaluated for monitored processes running both on single LAN and on PlanetLab. Experimental results are presented, showing the performance of the detector, in particular the advantages of using the self-tuning strategies to address the requirements of multiple concurrent applications running on a dynamic environment.

Keywords: Internet process monitoring, Unreliable failure detectors, Distributed systems, Fault-tolerance, SNMP

1   Introduction

Consensus [1] and other equivalent problems, such as atomic broadcast and group membership are used to implement dependable distributed systems [2, 3]. However, given the FLP impossibility [4], i.e., consensus can not be solved deterministically in asynchronous distributed systems in which even a single process can fail by crashing, deploying high-available distributed systems on the Internet is a challenge. In order to circumvent the impossibility of solving consensus in asynchronous distributed systems, Chandra and Toueg introduced failure detectors based on timeouts [5–7].

Failure detectors are used to monitor processes of any application running on a network. Failure detectors provide process state information. In this way, failure detectors are described as distributed "oracles" that supply information about the state of processes. Each application that needs process state information accesses the failure detector as a local module. Failure detectors can make mistakes, i.e., report that a fault-free process has failed or vice-versa and, therefore are said to be unreliable. It is impossible to implement a failure detector that always

provides the precise information, e.g. consider that a monitored process that is correct suddenly crashes; until the crash is perceived, the failure detector will report that the monitored process is correct. Chen, Toueg and Aguilera [8] defined a set of criteria to evaluate the quality of the service (QoS) of failure detectors. The authors defined a set of metrics to quantify the speed (e.g. how fast a process crash is detected) as well as the accuracy (e.g. how well it avoids mistakes) of failure detectors.

In this work we describe an Internet Failure Detection Service (IFDS) that can be used by applications that consist of processes running on independent autonomous systems of the Internet. IFDS reconfigures itself to provide the QoS level required by the applications. Chen et al. [8] and Bertier et al. [9] have investigated how to configure QoS parameters according to the network performance and the application needs. The parameters include the upper bounds on the detection time and mistake duration, and the lower bound on the average mistake recurrence time. Bertier et al. extended that approach by computing a dynamic safety margin which is used to compute the timeout. The main contribution of the present work is that IFDS handles multiple concurrent applications, each with different QoS requirements. In this way, two or more applications with different QoS requirements can

*Correspondence: elias@inf.ufpr.br
[†]Equal contributors
[1]Department Informatics, Federal University of Parana, UFPR, Curitiba, Brazil
Full list of author information is available at the end of the article

use the detector to monitor their processes, and IFDS reconfigures itself so that all requirements are satisfied.

IFDS was implemented using SNMP (Simple Network Management Protocol) [10]. Processes of a distributed application access the failure detector through a SNMP interface. In the proposed service, monitors execute on each LAN where processes are monitored. The monitor is implemented as a SNMP agent that keeps state information of both local and remote processes. The implementation of the service is based on a SNMP MIB (Management Information Base) called *fdMIB* (failure detector MIB), which can be easily integrated to distributed applications. The implementation also employs Web Services [11] that enable the transparent communication between processes running on different Autonomous Systems (AS). As Web Services are used as gateways for SNMP entities, they are transparent to the applications. Experimental results are presented for distributed applications with monitored processes executing both on a single LAN and in the PlanetLab [12], the worldwide research testbed. Results include an evaluation of the overhead incurred by the failure detector as the QoS parameters vary, the failure detection time, and average mistake rate.

The rest of the paper is organized as follows. Section 2 is a short introduction to failure detector and also presents an overview of related work. In Section 3 IFSD is specified, in particular we describe how the service dynamically adapts to network conditions and multiple concurrent application requirements. The architecture of the proposed failure detector service is described in Section 4. The implementation and experimental results are described in Sections 5 and 6, respectively. Section 7 concludes the work.

2 Failure detectors and related work

Consensus is a basic building block of fault-tolerant distributed computing [3, 13]. Informally, processes execute a consensus algorithm when they need to agree on a given value, which depends on an initial set of proposed values. The problem can be easily solved if the system is synchronous, i.e., there are known bounds on the time it takes to communicate messages and on how fast (or slow) processes execute tasks. On the other hand, if those time limits are unknown, i.e., the system is asynchronous, and processes can fail by crashing, then consensus becomes impossible to solve. This is a well-known result proved by Fischer, Lynch, and Paterson in 1985 and also known as the *FLP impossibility* [4]. Note that this impossibility assumes the most "benign" type of fault, the crash fault, in which one process simply stops to produce any output given any input.

As consensus is such an important problem and time limits for sending messages and executing tasks in real systems, such as the Internet, are unknown, the FLP impossibility represents a challenge for developing practical fault-tolerant distributed systems. Furthermore, it has been proved that several other important problems are equivalent to consensus so that they are also impossible to solve under the same assumptions. These include atomic broadcast, leader election, and group membership, among others [14].

Unreliable failure detectors were proposed by Chandra and Toueg [5] as an abstraction that, depending on its properties, can be used to solve consensus in asynchronous systems with crash faults. In this sense, a failure detector is a distributed oracle that can be accessed by a process to obtain information about the state of the other processes of the distributed system. Each process accesses a local module implementing the failure detector, which basically outputs a list of processes suspected of having failed. In a broad sense failure detectors can be used to monitor processes of any application running on a network. Furthermore, the failure detector must have a well-known interface through which it provides process state information.

The root of the FLP impossibility is that it is difficult to determine in an asynchronous system whether a process has crashed or is only slow. This problem also affects failure detectors: in asynchronous systems they can make mistakes. For example, fault-free but slow processes can be erroneously added to the list of failed processes. Thus, failure detectors are said to be unreliable, and instead of indicating which processes have failed, they indicate which processes are *suspected* to have failed. Chandra and Toueg in [5] give a classification of unreliable failure detectors in terms of two properties: completeness and accuracy. Completeness characterizes the ability of the failure detector to suspect faulty processes, while accuracy restricts the mistakes that the detector can make. Completeness is said to be strong if every process that crashes is permanently suspected by all correct processes. Otherwise, if at least one correct process suspects every process that has crashed, then completeness is weak. Accuracy is classified as strong if no process is suspected before it crashes, and weak if some correct process is never suspected. Both completeness and accuracy are *eventual* if they only hold after a finite but unknown time interval.

The most common approach to implement failure detectors is to employ heartbeat messages, which are sent periodically by every monitored process. Based on the observed message arrival pattern, the failure detector computes a timeout interval. If a heartbeat message is not received within this timeout interval, the monitored process is suspected to have crashed. A key decision to implement failure detectors is the choice of algorithm to compute a precise timeout interval. If the timeout interval is too short, crashes are quickly detected, but the likeliness of wrong suspicions is higher. Conversely, if the timeout interval is too long, wrong suspicions will be rare, but this comes at the expense of long detection times [15]. An adaptive failure detector can automatically update the timeout intervals and for this reason it is generally chosen to implement failure detectors on real networks [16].

In [8], Chen, Toueg, and Aguilera specify criteria to evaluate quality of service (QoS) provided by failure detectors. They define a set of metrics that quantify both the failure detector speed (how fast crashes are detected) and accuracy (how well it avoids mistakes). Three basic metrics (see Fig. 1) are defined as described below.

- **Detection time (T_D):** represents the time interval from the instant process p has crashed to the instant at which the failure detector starts to suspect p permanently.
- **Mistake recurrence time (T_{MR}):** this metric corresponds to the time interval between two consecutive mistakes, i.e., it represents how frequently the failure detector makes mistakes.
- **Mistake duration (T_M):** represents the time it takes for the failure detector to correct a mistake.

Other metrics are derived from those above; such as the **Query accuracy probability** (P_A) which corresponds to the probability that the output of the failure detector is correct at a random instant of time. Besides defining the above metrics, Chen et al. also propose a failure detector algorithm that adapts itself according to how metrics are configured and the characteristics of the network on which it is running, including the message loss probability (p_L), the expected message delay ($E(D)$) and message delay variance ($V(D)$).

Bertier et al. [9] extend the approach proposed by Chen et al. by implementing a failure detector in two layers: an adaption layer runs on top of a traditional heartbeat-based failure detector. The adaptation layer configures the Quality of Service (QoS) of the failure detector according to application needs. The purpose is also to minimize both network and processor overhead. While Chen's failure detector computes the timeout interval based on the expected arrival time of the next message, Berthier's also uses a safety margin which is continuously updated according to Jacobson's TCP (Transmission Control Protocol) timeout algorithm.

Another work that extends the original approach of Chen et al. was [17] proposed by Dixit and Casimiro. The authors define an alternative way to configure the QoS parameters, which is based on the stochastic properties of the underlying system. Initially, the user must provide a specification of the average mistake recurrence time (T_{MR} defined above) and the minimum coverage (C^L), which corresponds to a lower bound on the probability that heartbeat messages are received before the timeout interval expires. These parameters are used by a configurator which relies on another system called Adaptare that is a middleware that computes the timeout by estimating distributions based on the stochastic properties of the system on which the failure detector is running. The system was evaluated and presented sound results, especially in terms of the average mistake recurrence time and coverage.

In [16], Bondavalli and Falai present an extensive comparison of a large number of failure detectors executed on a wide area network. They conclude that no failure detector presents at the same time high speed and high accuracy. In particular, they show that using a more accurate predictor to compute the timeout interval does not necessarily imply on better QoS. The authors conclude that a perfect solution for the failure detection problem does not exist.

Tomsic et al. [18] introduced a failure detection algorithm that provides QoS and adapts to sudden changes in unstable network scenarios. The failure detector is called Two Windows Failure Detector (2W-FD) and it uses two sliding windows: a small window (to react rapidly to changes in network conditions) and a larger window (to make better estimations when the network conditions change gradually). The authors show that their algorithm presents better QoS when compared to others running on networks under unstable conditions.

In [19] the authors design an autonomic failure detector that is capable of self-configuration in order to provide the required QoS. In [20] a failure detector that is capable of self-configuration is applied to a cloud computing environment.

Network monitoring systems based on the Internet Simple Network Management Protocol (SNMP) have been used to feed system information to failure detectors. Lima and Macedo in [21] explore artificial neural networks in order to implement failure detectors that dynamically adapt themselves to communication load conditions. The training patterns used to feed the neural network were

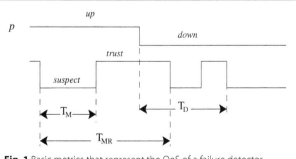

Fig. 1 Basic metrics that represent the QoS of a failure detector

obtained from a network monitoring system based on SNMP.

Wiesmann, Urban, and Défago present in [22] the SNMP-FD framework, a SNMP-based failure detector service that can be executed on a single LAN. Several MIBs are defined to keep information such as identifiers of hosts running monitors, identifiers and state of each monitored process, heartbeat intervals, heartbeat counters, among others.

In [23], a failure detector service for Internet-based distributed systems that span multiple autonomous systems (AS) is proposed. The service is based on monitors which are capable of providing global process state information through a SNMP interface. The system is based both on SNMP and Web services, which allow the communication of processes across multiple AS's.

To the best of our knowledge, the present work is the first that proposes a SNMP-based failure detector service with self-configurable Quality of Service. Given the requirements of multiple simultaneous applications, we present two strategies that allow the detector to self-configure. With respect to previous SNMP-based implementations of failure detectors, the major benefit of our proposed service is that it allows the user to specify QoS requirements for each application that is monitored, including: the failure detection time, mistake recurrence time and mistake duration. Given this input, and the perceived network conditions, our service configures and continuously adapt the failure detector parameters, including the heartbeat rate. Furthermore, as mentioned above, the proposed service can take into consideration the QoS requirements for multiple simultaneous applications to configure the system. Other SNMP-based implementations of failure detectors do not support QoS parameters to be input to the system, thus the user must manually configure the system and, worse, keep reconfiguring the system manually as network conditions and requirements change. Furthermore, IFDS introduces a novel implementation strategy in which SNMP objects themselves execute process monitoring – other works employ a separate daemon for that purpose.

3   IFDS: failure detection and QoS configuration

In this section, IFDS is described and specified. Initially, the system model is presented. Next, we give details on how IFDS computes adaptive timeout intervals, and then describe the configuration of IFDS parameters which are based both on network conditions and on applications QoS requirements. Besides showing how parameters are configured to monitor a single application process, two strategies are proposed to configure IFDS when multiple processes are monitored with different QoS requirements. The first strategy is called η_{max} and it maximizes monitoring parameters to encompass the needs of all

processes; the second strategy is called η_{GCD} and it computes the greatest common divisor of the corresponding parameters.

3.1   System model

We assume a distributed system $S = \{p_1, p_2, \ldots, p_n,\}$ that consists of n units that are called processes but also correspond to hosts. The system is asynchronous but augmented with the proposed failure detector, i.e. we assume a partially synchronous system. Processes communicate by sending and receiving messages. Every pair of processes is connected by a communication channel, i.e. the system can be represented by a complete graph. Processes fail by crashing, i.e., by prematurely halting. Every process in S has access to IFDS as a local failure detector module. IFDS returns process state information: correct or suspected. Monitored processes periodically send heartbeat messages. Timeouts are used to estimate whether processes have crashed.

3.2   IFDS adaptive timeout computation

Arguably, the most important feature of a failure detector is how precisely the timeout interval is computed. Remember that if a message is expected from a monitored process and it does not arrive before the timeout interval expires, then the process is suspected to have failed. A timeout interval that is too long increases the failure detection time, and a timeout interval that is too short increases the number of mistakes, i.e., correct processes can be frequently suspected to have crashed. Given the Internet characteristics in time and space, as well as different applications requirements, it is impossible to employ constant, predefined timeouts. Practical failure detectors must employ dynamic timeouts that are adaptive in the sense that they are reconfigured according to changing network conditions and application requirements.

IFDS computes the timeout interval (τ) for the next expected message using information about the arrival times of recently received messages. Note that for a given monitored host, multiple processes running on that host can be monitored, each with different QoS requirements. A single message is periodically expected from the host conveying information about the status of all its processes. IFDS computes the timeout with a strategy inspired on the works of Chen et al. [8] and Bertier et al. [9]. Chen's failure detector allows the configuration of QoS parameters according to network performance and the application needs. Bertier et al. extend that approach by also considering a dynamic safety margin to compute the timeout.

Chen et al. [8] compute an estimation of the arrival time (EA) of the next message based on the arrival times of previously received messages. That estimation plus a constant safety margin (α) are the basis for calculating the next timeout. Bertier et al. extend that approach by dynamically estimating α (the safety margin) using Jacobson's TCP timeout algorithm [24]. *EA* is computed as the weighted average of the n last message arrival intervals, where n is the window size for keeping historical records.

IFDS thus computes the timeout interval (τ) for monitoring a process based on an estimation of the next heartbeat arrival time (*EA*) plus a dynamic safety margin (α). Let's consider two processes: p and q, p monitors q. Every η time units, q sends a heartbeat to p. Let $m_1, m_2, \ldots, m_k$ be the k most recent heartbeat messages received by p. Let T_i be the time interval that each heartbeat took to be received by p, i.e. the time interval that elapsed since heartbeat $i-1$ had been received until heartbeat i is received, measured with the local clock. *EA* can be estimated as follows:

$$EA_{k+1} = \frac{1}{k}\left(\sum_{i=1}^{k} T_i - \eta\right) + (k+1)\eta \qquad (1)$$

EA_{k+1} is the expected time instant at which the next message (the $k + 1$-*th* message) will arrive. The next timeout will expire at:

$$\tau_{(k+1)} = EA_{(k+1)} + \alpha_{(k+1)} \qquad (2)$$

The safety margin α is computed based on Jacobson's TCP algorithm and is used to correct the error of the estimation for the arrival of the next message. Let A_i be the arrival time of heartbeat i, $error_{(k)}$ represent the error of the k-*th* message computed as follows:

$$error_{(k)} = A_k - EA_k - delay_{(k)} \qquad (3)$$

In the expression (4), $delay_{(k+1)}$ is the estimated delay of next message which is computed in terms of the $error_{(k)}$. γ represents the weight of the new measure, Jacobson suggests $\gamma = 0.1$:

$$delay_{(k+1)} = delay_{(k)} + \gamma.error_{(k)} \qquad (4)$$

$var_{(k+1)}$ represents the error variation, and it computed from first iteration; initially $var_{(k)}$ is set to zero.

$$var_{(k+1)} = var_{(k)} + \gamma.(|error_{(k)} - delay_{(k+1)}|) \qquad (5)$$

The safety margin $\alpha_{(k+1)}$ is then computed as shown below, where β and ϕ are constant weights for which we used $\beta = 1, \phi = 4$ and $\gamma = 0.1$.

$$\alpha_{(k+1)} = \beta.delay_{(k+1)} + \phi.var_{(k+1)} \qquad (6)$$

The timeout interval τ is thus adjusted after each heartbeat message arrives.

3.3 Configurig the failure detector service based on QoS parameters

In this subsection, we initially describe how IFDS is configured based on the QoS requirements of a single

application. Then the strategy is extended to handle multiple concurrent applications, each with different QoS requirements. Notice that even if two applications use the detector to monitor the same process, they may still have different QoS requirements. In this case, based on the different QoS requirements, a single heartbeat interval is chosen to monitor the process, i.e., the one that satisfies all requirements. On the other hand, the detection time used by the service for each application may be different. For example, one application may need a short detection time while the other can cope with a larger interval. If the heartbeat message is delayed and arrives after the shorter detection time but before the larger detection time, only the first application is informed that a false suspicion occurred.

As shown in Fig. 2, the detector receives as input from an application the following parameters:

- T_D^U: an upper bound on the detection time;
- T_M^U: an upper bound on the average mistake duration;
- T_{MR}^L: a lower bound on the average mistake recurrence time

Thereafter, the failure detector processes the input data and seeks a suitable value for η, as shown next.

3.3.1 QoS configuration for a single application
In Fig. 2, IFDS receives the QoS parameters from an application. The part of the Failure Detector devoted to the configuration of QoS parameter consists of two modules: Estimator and Configurator. Given the messages (heartbeats) received from a monitored process, the Estimator computes three parameters: the message loss probability (p_L), the message delay variance ($V(D)$), and the estimation for the arrival time of the next message (*EA*). The message loss probability is computed as $p_L = L/k$ where

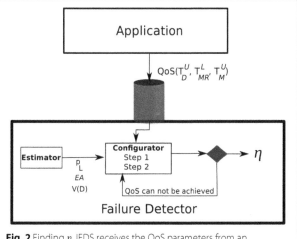

Fig. 2 Finding η. IFDS receives the QoS parameters from an application

k is the total number of messages that have been sent and L is the number of messages that were lost. $V(D)$ is computed from the observations of the message arrival times.

The configurator module runs Algorithm 1 adapted from [8, 9] to compute η, i.e., the heartbeat interval to be used by a monitored process in order to keep the quality of service required by the application. Algorithm 1 is described next.

Algorithm 1: Computing the heartbeat interval

---

1 /* T_D^U: upper bound on the detection time
2 T_M^U: upper bound on the average mistake duration
3 T_{MR}^L: lower bound on the mistake recurrence time
4 θ: reflects the failure detection probability
5 p_L: message loss probability
6 $V(D)$:   delay variance
7 η_{max}:   is set to min $\left(\theta * T_M^U, T_D^U\right)$
8 η: heartbeat interval */
9
10 **Step1** $\left(T_D^U, T_M^U, T_{MR}^L\right)$ ▷ input data
11
12   $\theta := (1 - p_L)\left(T_D^U\right)^2 / \left(V(D) + \left(T_D^U\right)^2\right);$
13
14   **if** $\left((\theta > 0)\ and\ \left(T_D^U > 0\right)\ and\ \left(T_M^U > 0\right)\right)$ **then**
15   **if** $\left((\theta * T_M^U) > T_D^U\right)$ **then**
16           $\quad\eta_{max} := T_D^U;$
17   **else**
18           $\quad\eta_{max} := \theta * T_M^U;$
19   **run** Step2$\left(T_D^U, T_{MR}^L, \eta_{max}\right)$
20   **else**
21   **return** ("QoS cannot be achieved");
22 **Step2** $\left(T_D^U, T_{MR}^L, \eta_{max}\right)$
23
24   $\eta := \eta_{max};$
25   **while** $\left(f(\eta) < T_{MR}^L\right)$ **do**
26       $\quad\eta := \eta - (\eta * 0.01);$
27   **return** (η);   ▷ output data
28 **Function** $f(\eta)$
29   **return** $\left(\eta * \Pi_{j=1}^{\lceil T_D^U/\eta\rceil -1} \dfrac{V(D)+(T_D^U-j\eta)^2}{V(D)+(p_L(T_D^U-j\eta)^2}\right);$

Algorithm 1 consists of two steps. The main purpose of **Step1** is to compute an upper bound for the heartbeat interval η_{max}, given the input values provided by the application: the upper bound on the detection time (T_D^U), upper bound on the average mistake duration (T_M^U), and lower bound on the average mistake recurrence time

(T_{MR}^L). First, θ is computed (line 12) which reflects the failure detection probability, based on both the probability that a message is received ($1 - p_L$), the message delay variance ($V(D)$), and the required detection time (T_D^U). Now remember that η_{max} must be chosen to meet the required upper bounds on the detection time and mistake duration time. Thus η_{max} is set to the minimum of the upper bound of the detection time (T_D^U) or the detection probability times the upper bound of the mistake duration rate ($\theta * T_M^U$).

Note that if either $\theta = 0$ or $T_D^U = 0$ or $T_M^U = 0$ then the maximum heartbeat interval is zero; this means that there is no heartbeat interval that is able to guarantee the QoS requirements. In this case, Step 2 is not executed.

The main purpose of Step 2 of the algorithm is to find the smallest η that respects the third QoS parameter: T_{MR}^L, the mistake recurrence time. **Step2** computes η as follows. η is initially equal to η_{max}. Then η is reduced by 1 % at each iteration until $f(\eta)\ geq\ T_{MR}^L$. This reduction factor (1 %) was chosen experimentally as it gives precise results, close to T_{MR}^L – if we use 10 % the precision is lost we can get a value that is acceptable but too distant from T_{MR}^L. As proved in [8], for each value of $\eta, f(\eta)$ computes the probability that the required mistake recurrence time (T_{MR}^L) is satisfied. Note that if η decreases $f(\eta)$ increases, the opposite is also true. For this reason, we always reduce the value of η until $f(\eta) \geq T_{MR}^L$. When this condition holds, the largest η that satisfies T_{MR}^L has been computed.

Next we give an example of the computation of η by Algorithm 1.

An application (App_1) specifies the following QoS requirements: $T_D^U = 30\,s$ (i.e., a crash failure is detected within 30 s), $T_M^U = 60\,s$ (i.e., the failure detector corrects its mistakes within 60 s), and $T_{MR}^L = 432000s$ (i.e., the failure detector makes at most one mistake each 5 days). Furthermore, the message loss probability is $p_L = 0.0$ and the delay variance is $V(D) = 0.01$. The algorithm in **Step1** computes $\gamma = 0.99$ and $\eta_{max} = min(30, 59.99)$. In **Step2**, the input values are processed initializing η equal to 30.00. After that, the algorithm continuously reduces the value of η until $f(\eta) \geq 432, 000$. The final value is $\eta = 14.6\,s$, which is employed by monitored processes to periodically send heartbeat messages to meet the QoS requirements of App_1.

Actually, the final value of η found in *Step2* is the largest interval that satisfies the QoS requirements. Thus, a shorter interval, $0 < \eta \leq 14.6$, can also be used for the example.

3.3.2 QoS configuration for multiple applications

When several applications are monitoring multiple processes with IFDS, each can have different QoS requirements. IFDS computes a heartbeat interval (η) for the monitored processes that simultaneously satisfies the QoS requirements of all applications. In order to understand why this can save monitoring messages consider a simple example in which 100 hosts connected on a single LAN each of which executes 100 processes that are be monitored. To make the example as simple as possible assume that all processes employ the same heartbeat interval. If one uses a separate FD service to monitor each process than 10,000 heartbeat messages are sent per interval. Using our shared/simultaneous monitoring strategy this number reduces to only 100 messages, each host employs one heartbeat message for all its processes.

In this work we assume that the different processes can need different heartbeat intervals to satisfy their QoS requirements. In order to determine a common heartbeat interval to be used by all processes, two different approaches are proposed: η_{max} and η_{GCD}, described below.

The η_{max} approach to adapt η to all application requests computes $\eta_{max} = min\left(\gamma T_{M1}^{U}, T_{D1}^{U}, \gamma T_{M2}^{U}, T_{D2}^{U}, \ldots, \gamma T_{Mn}^{U}, T_{Dn}^{U}\right)$, where $i = 1 \ldots n$, T_{Mi}^{U} and T_{Di}^{U} are the QoS requirements of application i. Algorithm 1 can be then used after this modification is introduced.

The other proposed approach is called η_{GCD} and in this case we compute the GCD (Greatest Common Divisor) among all η_i, $i = 1 \ldots m$, m is the number of QoS requirements. The idea is that if a process sends heartbeats every x units of time, and if x divides y, it also sends heartbeats every y units of time. Each η_i is first transformed to a new η'_i as follows: $\eta'_i = 2^n$ so that $2^n < \eta_i$ and $\eta'_i \in \mathbb{Z}^+$. The final $\eta_{GCD} = GCD(\eta'_i, \ldots, \eta'_n)$. Note that η_{GCD} must be > 0, otherwise it is impossible to apply this approach.

Note that η_{max} gives the largest possible heartbeat interval that satisfieds the QoS requirements. Thus in order to have a safety margin it is recommended to use an interval shorter than that, such as given by ηgcd. η_{GCD} is always smaller than η_{max} for a given system. For this reason, using the η_{GCD} approach produces a larger number of messages on the network than η_{max}. On the other hand, it has advantages such as a reduction of the failure detection time (T_D) and improvement of the query accuracy probability (P_A).

Consider an extension of the example given above for one application (App_1) where a second application (App_2) runs on the same host as App_1. App_2 QoS requirements are as follows: $T_D^{U} = 15$ s (i.e., a crash failure is detected within 15 seconds), $T_M^{U} = 30$ s (i.e., the failure detector corrects its mistakes within 30 seconds) and $T_{MR}^{L} = 864000$ s (i.e., the failure detector makes at most one mistake each 10 days). We assume that the message loss probability is $p_L = 0.0$ and the delay variance is $V(D) = 0.01$. First consider the η_{max} approach. In **Step1** of the algorithm $\eta_{max} = min((30, 59.99)_{app_1}, (29.99, 15.00)_{app_2}) = 15.00$. In **Step2**, the final value is computed as $\eta=7.2$ s,

then the algorithm uses this value to ensure the QoS parameters for both applications (App_1 and App_2).

On the other hand, if we use the η_{GCD} approach we have: App_1: $\eta_1 = 14.6 \rightarrow \eta'_1 = 8$; App_2: $\eta_2 = 7.2 \rightarrow \eta'_2 = 4$; $\eta_{GCD} = GCD(4, 8) \rightarrow 4$. Thus, $\eta_{GCD} = 4$ s. As mentioned above, we can notice that η_{GCD} is smaller than η_{max}.

Our implementation is capable of self-adapting to QoS violations caused by network conditions. If IFDS detects that the network cannot sustain the minimum QoS requirements, it readjusts η by increasing its value. For instance, in the example above, η can be readjusted to another value as long as it complies with the following condition: $\eta \leq 14.6$. Hence, Algorithm 1 is used to find a value of η that satisfies QoS requirements of as many applications as possible under the current network conditions.

4 IFDS: architecture

In this section we describe the architecture of the proposed Internet failure detection service. Figure 3 shows IFDS monitoring processes on two LAN's: A and B. These two LANs are geographically distributed and connected through the Internet. The number of monitored networks can be greater than two. For each network, there is both a Monitor Host and Monitored Hosts. As the names denote, a Monitored Host runs the processes that are monitored. The Monitor Host runs applications that are responsible for monitoring processes. Applications and other Monitors can subscribe to receive state information about specific processes.

Initially, every application that needs to obtain information about the states of monitored processes configures the quality of service (QoS) it expects from IFDS. Then, the detection service computes the heartbeat interval (η) that must be applied in order to provide the required QoS. The Monitor Host then configures η on every Monitored Host, so that periodically at an η interval, the monitored host will send back a heartbeat message to the Monitor Host.

As we shall see in Section 5, SNMP (Simple Network Management Protocol) is used by the Monitor and Monitored Hosts to exchange messages on a LAN. Each Monitored Host is registered on a SNMP MIB (Management Information Base). If the Monitor and Monitored hosts are located on different networks and must communicate across the Internet, they employ Web Services. In this case, a SNMP message is encapsulated with and transmitted using SOAP (Simple Object Access Protocol).

Note that all monitoring is done locally on each domain. Monitors on different domains communicate to obtain process state information. This communication is implemented in two ways. Either the local Monitor queries the remote Monitor to obtain process state information, or, alternatively, the Monitor can register at a remote monitor

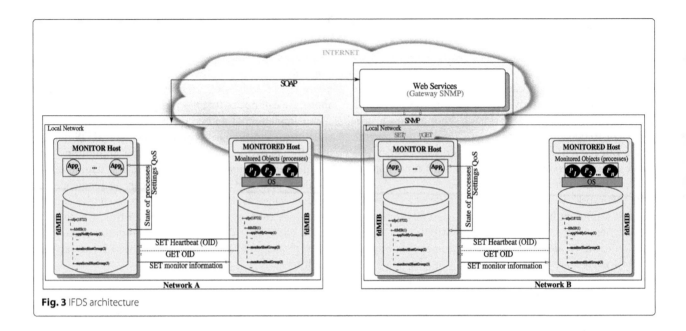

Fig. 3 IFDS architecture

to receive notifications whenever the state of remote monitored processes changes. In this case, a SNMP message is encapsulated with and transmitted using SOAP (Simple Object Access Protocol).

Web Services are thus used as a gateway for entities that implement SNMP to communicate remotely across the Internet. The use of Web Services is transparent to the user application, which employs only SNMP as the interface to access the failure detector. There are situations in which Web Services are not involved, i.e., when all the communication occurs on a local LAN. When a Monitor issues a query to another monitor running remotely, a virtual connection is open (using Web Services), and a remote procedure is executed that provides the required information.

When an application needs to communicate with a Monitor running remotely, it has an option to do that directly using Web Services. For example, consider the system in Fig. 3, suppose that the application process (App_1) on Network A needs to learn information about the status of a process running on Network B. In this case, App_1 invokes the corresponding Web Services that in turn executes the SNMP operation on Network B.

When the Monitor Host detects that the state of a monitored process on the same LAN has changed, it updates the corresponding entry and sends the new state information to all applications and other Monitors that have subscribed to receive information about that particular process.

All information about the state of processes is stored in a MIB called *fdMIB* (failure detector MIB). In Section 5 we present detailed information about this MIB and its implementation.

5   IFDS: implementation

As mentioned in the previous section, IFDS was implemented with SNMP and Web Services. SNMP is used by the Monitor and Monitored Hosts to exchange messages and each Monitored Host must be registered on the *fdMIB*, shown in Fig. 4. *fdMIB* consists of three groups: the Monitor Host Group, Monitored Host Group, and Application Notify Group. These three object groups are described below. Note that we propose a single MIB that maintains information about all IFDS modules.

The **Application Notify Group (appNotifyGroup)** keeps information about QoS parameters. Each application that is supposed to receive state information about a process must give the following parameters to *fdMIB*: the upper bound on the detection time (TD_U), the mistake duration time (TM_U), and the lower bound on the average mistake recurrence time (TMR_L). These parameters are described in Section 3. We also described how IFDS computes the heartbeat interval η, given the application parameters.

Another object of the appNotifyGroup is receiveHB (see Fig. 4) which is used to receive heartbeat messages from a monitored process. Every time a heartbeat message arrives, *fdMIB* updates the corresponding process state object in the monitorHostGroup table.

In order to receive notifications, an application subscribes at the Monitor Host to receive SNMP traps (notifyTrap) with process state information. The application will be notified whenever the Monitor detects a change of the state of the monitored process. Object statusChange is also updated to store 0, if the monitored process is correct, and 1 otherwise. Note that besides receiving traps (alarms) the application can at any

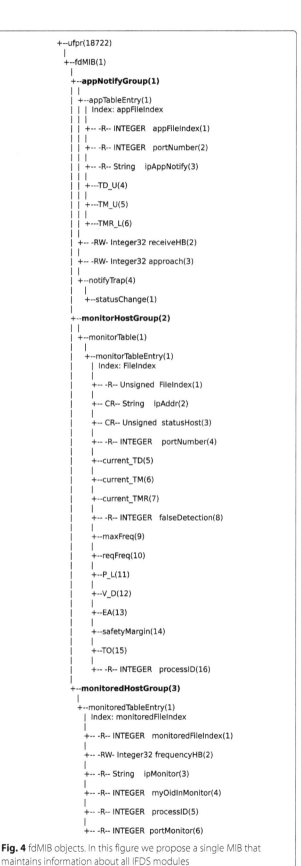

Fig. 4 fdMIB objects. In this figure we propose a single MIB that maintains information about all IFDS modules

time check the state of any monitored process by querying the corresponding MIB object.

The **Monitor Host Group** (`monitorHostGroup`) stores information about monitored processes, including IP addresses (`ipAddr`), port numbers (`portNumber`), process IDs (`processID`), state (`statusHost`), number of false detections (`falseDetection`), heartbeat interval required (`reqFreq`), an estimation of the probabilistic behavior of message delays (`V_D`), message loss probability (`P_L`), QoS parameters (`current_TD`, `current_TM` and `current_TMR`) these parameters are continuously updated and are used to check whether any QoS requirement has been broken (e.g., `current_TD > TD_U`), among others. Objects of the `monitorHostGroup` trigger and execute process monitoring. For instance, they can start threads that receive heartbeat messages and compute timeouts.

The **Monitored Host Group (`monitoredHost-Group`)** is responsible for sending heartbeat messages. It is executed on a host that is monitored. In order to communicate with the Monitor, the following objects are maintained: Monitor IP address (`ipMonitor`), Monitor port (`portMonitor`), monitored process OID (`myOidInMonitor`, an Object Identifier is a name used to identify the monitored process in the MIB), heartbeat interval (`frequencyHB`), and the process identifier in the local host (`processID`).

6 IFDS: experimental results

In this section we report results of several experiments executed in order to evaluate the proposed failure detection service. Experiments were conducted on both an Ethernet LAN and PlanetLab [12]. Three independent applications were used each with different QoS requirements, as shown in Table 1. All applications run on the same host. For instance, App_1 requires that the time to detect failures to be at most 8 seconds, i.e., $T_D^U = 8$ s. On average the failure detector corrects its mistakes within one minute, i.e., $T_M^U = 60$ s. Finally, the failure detector makes at most one mistake per month, i.e., $T_{MR}^L = 30$ days (2592000000 in ms). In the experiments, we assumed $p_L = 0.01$ and $V(D) = 0.02$, the sliding window (W) size is defined individually for each experiment.

IFDS configuration can be simply done using the regular *snmpset* command; for instance the command below is executed to configure the monitorHostGroup table

Table 1 QoS requirements

Applications	T_D^U (s)	T_M^U (s)	T_{MR}^L (days)
App_1	8	60	30
App_2	14	120	30
App_3	16	240	30

with the required QoS parameters (Fig. 4). In this example, App_1 monitors a process on a host with IP address 192.168.1.1, the port is 80, and the QoS parameters are those shown in Table 1.

snmpset -v1 -c private localhost .1.3.6.1.4.1.18722.1. 2.1.1.2.1 s 192.168.1.1:8:80:60:2592000000

The `snmpset` command shown above is used to update the value of a SNMP object. This command uses the following parameters: host address on which the MIB is deployed (localhost), the id of the object to be updated (.1.3.6.1.4.1.18722.1.2.1.1.2.1) and the data that is to be written on the object (192.168.1.1:8:80:60:2592000000).

Using Algorithm 1 (presented in Section 3.3) to compute the heartbeat interval for the three applications shown in Table 1, we get $\eta_{max} = min(1.954467, 3.901890, 4.694764)$. Thus, in this case the value of η is 1.954467 (enough to meet the QoS requirements of all three applications). If instead we use the η_{GCD} strategy on the same data in Table 1, we get $GCD = min(1, 2, 4)$. Thus $\eta = 1$ again enough to monitor $App_1, App_2,$ and App_3.

6.1 Experimental results: LAN

The LAN experiments were executed on two hosts: the monitor host was based on an Intel Core i5 2.50 GHz processor, with 4 GB of RAM, running Linux Ubuntu 12.04 with kernel 3.2.0-58; the monitored host was an Intel Core i5 CPU 3.20 GHz, with 4 GB RAM running Linux Ubuntu 13.10 with kernel 3.2.0-58. The hosts were on a 100 Mbps Ethernet LAN. The *fdMIB* was implemented using Net-SNMP version 5.4.4.

The first experiment was executed to evaluate how IFDS adapts to changes in the heartbeat frequency. How does the failure detector react and reconfigures itself? Figure 5 shows the expected arrival time (EA curve) and timeout (Timeout curve) computed by IFDS as the monitored host sends 200 heartbeat messages to the monitor host. The figure also shows the measured RTT (RTT curve). From the beginning to the 50th heartbeat message the interval between two messages (the Heartbeat Freq curve) is 1 s. Then from the 51st message to the 150th message this interval grows to 5 s, after that the frequency reduces to 1 s again.

The Figure shows that initially (first 10 messages) the timeout takes a while to stabilize. Then when the heartbeat frequency changes from 1 to 5 s, the EA and timeout curves show that after a short while IFDS could clearly adapt the timeout interval to the new heartbeat frequency. During that short while (after the 50th message) the Timeout curve remains below the Heartbeat Freq curve: during this time IFDS incurs in false suspicions. After a couple of messages the timeout grows enough to correct the mistakes. The Figure also shows how IFDS reacts when the heartbeat frequency reduces back to 1 second (from the 150th message). The EA and Timeout curves show that after a few messages IFDS readapts itself to the new situation.

Next we show – for the same experiment – both the QoS requirements (given by the application), as well as the current value of the QoS parameters computed by IFDS from the actual monitoring. The objective of this experiment

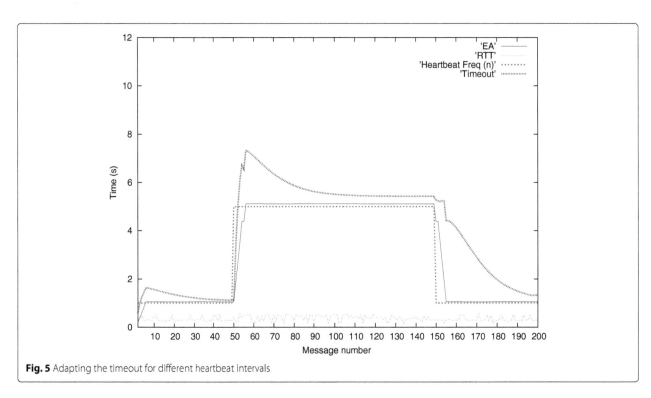

Fig. 5 Adapting the timeout for different heartbeat intervals

is to show that the applications' QoS requirements are not violated. Figure 6a and b show the QoS parameters for the same experiment described in Fig. 5. Besides the EA, Heartbeat Freq and RTT curves that also appeared in Fig. 5, these Figures also show the detection time (TD curve), the mistake duration time (TM curve), the detection times required by the applications: App1 TDU, App2 TDU, and App3 TDU curves.

In Fig. 6a we can observe 6 false detections (TM curve), notice that the QoS requirements (Table 1) are never violated. In the same Figure, the detection time T_D is always less than App1 TDU, App2 TDU and App3 TDU. This means that the false suspicions shown in Fig. 6a remain transparent to the applications, i.e. they are not noticed by any of the applications, even when the heartbeat frequency grows to 5 s. Note that after message 50 the TD curve gets very close to but does not grow above App1 TDU.

A similar situation can be seen in Fig. 6b, in which the mistake recurrence rate is checked. Note that the lower limit of the T_{MR} QoS parameter required by the applications is 30 days (Table 1). Curve TMR shows the average T_{MR} taking into account the false suspicions that occurred (TM curve). If we compute the average for the whole time the experiment was executed, it is 13, 086 ms, which is below the required value for this QoS metric. However, the real IFDS T_{MR} does not take into account the false suspicions that are not reported to the applications. As discussed, none of the false suspicions was ever reported to the applications, thus there was no mistake and mistake recurrence time and there is no QoS violation.

Next we describe an experiment designed to compare the two strategies proposed for monitoring multiple processes simultaneously: η_{max} and η_{GCD}. The experiment duration time was 60 min. The results for this experiment are shown in Table 2. This table shows: the heartbeat interval η (in seconds), the detection time T_D, the mistake duration time T_M, and the mistake recurrence time T_{MR}, the P_A metric (described below) plus the number of heartbeat messages sent during the experiment, and the number of false detections. During the experiment we simulated two false suspicions by omitting heartbeat messages. The P_A metric corresponds to the probability that the application will make a query about a given monitored process and that the reply is correct, in the sense that it reflects the real state of the monitored process. This metric was described in Section 2 and can be computed as follows:

$$P_A = 1 - \frac{E(T_M)}{E(T_{MR})} \tag{7}$$

The results in Table 2 show that the heartbeat interval computed by η_{max} is 1.95 s, while for η_{GCD} it is equal to 1 s. The next results are a consequence of these intervals. Remember that a higher heartbeat interval means that less messages are sent, and thus the overhead of η_{max} (1754 messages) is lower than the overhead of η_{GCD} (3551 messages). On the hand, the opposite happens to the detection time T_D: as η_{GCD}'s heartbeat interval is shorter, its detection time T_D is also shorter (1.32 s) while for η_{max} it grows to 2.46 s. The same happens to the mistake duration time (T_M) and P_A: the shorter the heartbeat interval, the shorter the mistake duration and the higher the probability that IFDS replies the correct state. Although the time recurrence time (T_{MR}) also reduces for a shorter heartbeat interval, the variation is lower than for the other parameters.

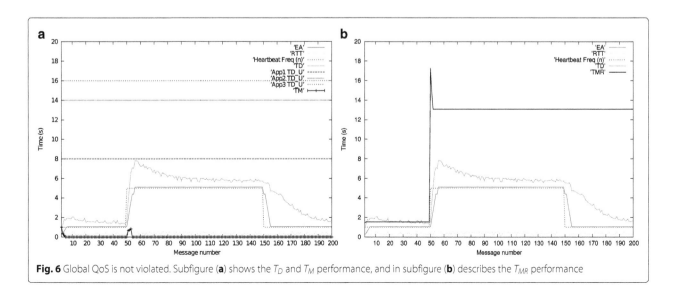

Fig. 6 Global QoS is not violated. Subfigure (**a**) shows the T_D and T_M performance, and in subfigure (**b**) describes the T_{MR} performance

Table 2 Comparing the two strategies: η_{max} and GCD

	η (s)	T_D (s)	T_M (s)	T_{MR} (s)	P_A	Num. of HB message	Num. of false detections
η_{max}	1.95	2.45	1.77	61.19	0.9711	1754	2
η_{GCD}	1.00	1.32	0.69	60.59	0.9998	3551	2

A discussion on these results leads to the conclusion that there is a trade-off. While η_{max} proves is the best strategy for applications that do not require a small detection time (which is the case for instance for monitoring remote processes via the Internet) η_{GCD} presents a shorter detection time and the best results for the P_A metric. This strategy is thus the better suited to monitor processes on a single LAN, where the applications generally do not tolerate long delays.

Next we evaluate the amount of resources required by IFDS. Figure 7 shows CPU and memory usage. We gradually increased the number of monitored objects. For each measure 10 samples were collected and the service was run for 60 min. The experiment comprises both the registration of each object in the *fdMIB* (which corresponds to setting the information about monitored processes such as IP address and port) and the transmission of heartbeat messages. A very short heartbeat interval of 1 millisecond was chosen to stress the system. As shown in Fig. 7a, memory usage grows linearly but remains low: it never reaches 0.2 %. In Fig. 7b we can see that up to 100 objects, there is a consistent increase in CPU usage. After that (100 objects), although peak values do increase, the average CPU usage remains stable around 7 %. CPU usage can be considered low enough. For example, the SNMP-based implementation of a failure detector by Wiesmann, Urban and Defago [22] reaches up to 11 % CPU utilization for 1 millisecond heartbeat interval.

6.2 Experimental results: PlanetLab

The last experiment was executed to investigate the time overhead of using Web Services for communicating across the Internet. In particular we were interested in comparing the time to report an event using a pure SNMP solution with one that also uses Web Services. We executed IFDS to monitor processes running on PlanetLab nodes located in the five continents: South America (Brazil), North America (Canada), Europe (Italy), Asia (Russia) and Oceania (New Zealand). PlanetLab hosts exchange information in two ways: using SNMP and Web Services. The time was computed using a monitor and a monitored process running in Brazil. After the monitor detects a failure it notifies yet another monitor. Then, we measured the time interval from the instant a fault was injected up to the instant the second monitor is notified. In other words, the time to report an event is the sum of the detection time plus the time to notify the event. In Fig. 8, we compare the time using SNMP only and Web services. As expected, WS takes longer to report an event: on average of 14.44 % more than SNMP, which we consider an acceptable overhead.

From the results in Fig. 8 it is also possible to see that the notification time respects the physical distance between hosts. The process that is the closest to the monitor (running on the Brazilian host) presents a notification time of approximately 1.31 s. As the physical distance between hosts increases, the notification time

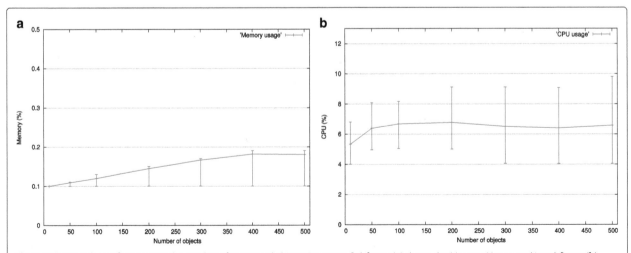

Fig. 7 Evaluating the performance as the number of monitored objects increases. Subfigure (**a**) shows the Memory Usage, and in subfigure (**b**) shows the CPU Usage

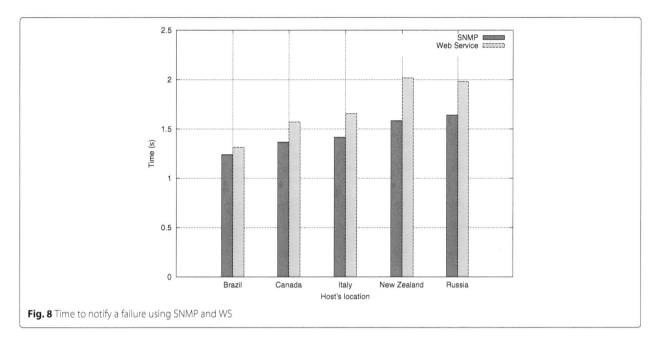

Fig. 8 Time to notify a failure using SNMP and WS

also increases, reaching up to approximately 2.01 s for the monitored process that runs on the New Zealand host. From these observations one can conclude that an application may take location also into account in order to determine the level of QoS that can be obtainable from each process – for example, the detection time of a process that is close by will be certainly lower than that of a process that is on another continent.

7 Conclusion

In this paper, we described the architecture and implementation of the Internet Failure Detection Service (IFDS). IFDS configures itself to meet the QoS requirements of multiple simultaneous applications as well as network conditions. Two strategies (η_{max} and η_{GCD}) were proposed to compute the interval (η) on which monitored processes send heartbeats. IFDS was implemented using SNMP and Web Services for enabling communication among applications across the Internet. Experimental results were presented, in which the failure detector service ran both on a single LAN and on PlanetLab. In this case, monitored processes run on hosts of five continents. The results show the effectiveness of the adaptive timeout with different intervals of heartbeat messages. On the one hand, the η_{max} strategy is more suitable for monitoring remote processes where applications can tolerate longer delays. On the other hand, the η_{GCD} strategy is better suited for monitoring processes running on a LAN.

Future work includes developing reliable distributed applications on top of the proposed IFDS, including State Machine Replication, as well an atomic broadcast service, both of which also rely on consensus. Making the link between an FD that provides QoS and consensus is certainly a relevant topic for future research. How can the QoS parameters have an influence on the execution of a consensus algorithm? How to specify the required QoS levels, taking into account features of the consensus algorithm as well as multiple process features – including location, for instance.

Acknowledgements
This work was partially supported by grants 309143/2012-8 and 141714/2014-0 from the Brazilian Research Agency (CNPq).

Authors' contributions
RCT carried out the implementation and ran the experiments; together with the other authors he also participated in writing this paper. EPD Jr. supervised the definition of the proposed architecture, supervised the implementation and experiments, and wrote the paper. PS and LA proposed the strategies for monitoring multiple processes that represents the main scientific contribution of this paper, they revised the architecture as it was proposed and also revised the written paper. All authors read and approved the final manuscript.

Competing interests
We confirm that I have read SpringerOpen's guidance on competing interests and have included a statement indicating that none of the authors have any competing interests in the manuscript.

Author details
[1]Department Informatics, Federal University of Parana, UFPR, Curitiba, Brazil.
[2]Sorbonne Université, UPMC Univ. Paris 06, CNRS, Inria, LIP6, Paris, France.
[3]CTISM, Federal University of Santa Maria, UFSM, Santa Maria, Brazil.

References
1. Turek J, Shasha D. The Many Faces of Consensus in Distributed Systems. IEEE Comput. 1992;25(6):8–17.
2. Guerraoui R, Rodrigues L. Introduction to Reliable Distributed Programming. Berlin: Springer; 2006.
3. Charron-Bost B, Pedone F, Schiper A, (eds). Replication: Theory and Practice. Berlin: Springer; 2010.

4. Fischer MJ, Lynch NA, Paterson MS. Impossibility of distributed consensus with one faulty process. J ACM. 1985;32(2):374–82.

5. Chandra TD, Toueg S. Unreliable failure detectors for reliable distributed systems. J ACM. 1996;43(2):225–67.

6. Freiling FC, Guerraoui R, Kuznetsov P. The failure detector abstraction. ACM Comput Surv. 2011;43(2):1–40.

7. Delporte-Gallet C, Fauconnier H, Raynal M. Fair synchronization in the presence of process crashes and its weakest failure detector. In: 33rd IEEE International Symposium on Reliable Distributed Systems (SRDS'14). Japan: IEEE Computer Society, Nara; 2014.

8. Chen W, Toueg S, Aguilera MK. On the quality of service of failure detectors. In: International Conference on Dependable Systems and Networks (DSN'00). New York: IEEE Computer Society; 2000.

9. Bertier M, Marin O, Sens P. Performance analysis of a hierarchical failure detector. In: International Conference on Dependable Systems and Networks (DSN'03). San Francisco, USA: IEEE Computer Society; 2003.

10. Harrington D, Presuhn R, Wijnen B. An Architecture for Describing Simple Network Management Protocol (SNMP) Management Frameworks. In: Request for Comments 3411 (RFC3411). United States: RFC Editor; 2002.

11. Christensen E, Curbera F, Meredith G, Weerawarana S. Web Services Description Language(WSDL) Version 1.1. http://www.w3.org/TR/wsdl. Access Feb 2016.

12. An open platform for developing, deploying, and accessing planetaryscale services. http://www.planet-lab.org/. Access May 2015.

13. Turek J, Shasha D. The many faces of consensus in distributed systems. IEEE Comput. 1992;25(6):8–17.

14. Cachin C, Guerraoui R, Rodrigues L. Introduction to Reliable and Secure Distributed Programming 2nd edn. Berlin: Springer; 2011.

15. Hayashibara N, Defago X, Katayama T. Two-ways adaptive failure detection with the ϕ-failure detector. In: International Workshop on Adaptive Distributed Systems. Italy: Sorrento; 2003.

16. Falai L, Bondavalli A. Experimental evaluation of the qos of failure detectors on wide area network. In: International Conference on Dependable Systems and Networks (DSN'05). Yokohama: IEEE Computer Society; 2005.

17. Dixit M, Casimiro A. Adaptare-fd: A dependability-oriented adaptive failure detector. In: 29th IEEE Symposium on Reliable Distributed Systems (SRDS'10). Delhi: IEEE Symposium; 2010.

18. Tomsic A, Sens P, Garcia J, Arantes L, Sopena J. 2w-fd: A failure detector algorithm with qos. In: IEEE International Parallel and Distributed Processing Symposium (IPDPS'15). Washington: IEEE Computer Society; 2015.

19. de Sá AS, de Araújo Macêdo RJ. Qos self-configuring failure detectors for distributed systems. In: Distributed Applications and Interoperable Systems (DAIS) 2010. Amsterdam, The Netherlands: Springer Berlin Heidelberg; 2010.

20. Xiong N, Vasilakos AV, Wu J, Yang YR, Rindos AJ, ZHOU Y, Song WZ, Pan Y. A self-tuning failure detection scheme for cloud computing service. In: The 26th IEEE International Parallel & Distributed Processing Symposium (IPDPS) 2012. Shanghai: IEEE Computer Society; 2012.

21. Lima F, Macêdo R. Adapting failure detectors to communication network load fluctuations using snmp and artificial neural nets. In: Dependable Computing, Second Latin-American Symposium (LADC'05). Salvador: Springer Berlin Heidelberg; 2005.

22. Wiesmann M, Urbán P, Défago X. An SNMP based failure detection service. In: 25th IEEE Symposium on Reliable Distributed Systems (SRDS'06). Leeds: IEEE Computer Society; 2006.

23. Moraes DM, Duarte Jr EP. A failure detection service for internet-based multi-as distributed systems. In: 17th IEEE International Conference on Parallel and Distributed Systems (ICPADS'11). Tainan: IEEE Computer Society; 2011.

24. Jacobson V. Congestion avoidance and control. In: Symposium Proceedings on Communications Architectures and Protocols (SIGCOMM'88). USA: ACM, Stanford; 1988.

12

Hitch Hiker 2.0: a binding model with flexible data aggregation for the Internet-of-Things

Gowri Sankar Ramachandran[1*], José Proença[1,3], Wilfried Daniels[1], Mario Pickavet[2], Dimitri Staessens[2], Christophe Huygens[1], Wouter Joosen[1] and Danny Hughes[1]

Abstract

Wireless communication plays a critical role in determining the lifetime of Internet-of-Things (IoT) systems. Data aggregation approaches have been widely used to enhance the performance of IoT applications. Such approaches reduce the number of packets that are transmitted by combining multiple packets into one transmission unit, thereby minimising energy consumption, collisions and congestion. However, current data aggregation schemes restrict developers to a specific network structure or cannot handle multi-hop data aggregation. In this paper, we propose *Hitch Hiker 2.0*, a component binding model that provides support for multi-hop data aggregation. Hitch Hiker uses component meta-data to discover remote component bindings and to construct a multi-hop overlay network within the free payload space of existing traffic flows. Hitch Hiker 2.0 provides end-to-end routing of low-priority traffic while using only a small fraction of the energy of standard communication. This paper extends upon our previous work by incorporating new mechanisms for decentralised route discovery and providing additional application case studies and evaluation. We have developed a prototype implementation of Hitch Hiker for the LooCI component model. Our evaluation shows that Hitch Hiker consumes minimal resources and that using Hitch Hiker to deliver low-priority traffic reduces energy consumption by up to 32 %.

Keywords: Data aggregation, Binding model, Component-based software engineering, Low energy, Component meta data, Middleware, IoT

1 Introduction

Internet-of-Things (IoT) devices must operate for long periods on limited power supplies and research has shown that wireless communication is the primary source of energy consumption in IoT devices [1]. The lifetime of IoT applications can therefore be increased by minimising radio communication. *Data aggregation* has been widely applied to tackle this problem [2–4]. Data aggregation is a technique in which multiple messages are combined in to a single datagram, thus reducing radio transmissions and hence the energy consumption of IoT devices. Furthermore in CSMA networks, less frequent transmissions result in fewer collisions and

therefore retransmissions. This significantly improves the performance of IoT devices.

This paper focuses on lossless data aggregation, through the efficient merging of application traffic flows, rather than algebraic in-network aggregation. Contemporary approaches to lossless data aggregation may be classified as either *application dependent* or *application independent* [5]. Application dependent approaches [6–8] support the creation of optimal network-wide data aggregation structures, but restrict the topology of the distributed application. In contrast, application independent approaches [6, 9] embed generic aggregation functionality in the underlying network stack, but do not consider the application, and therefore do not achieve optimal performance.

A new approach is needed that allows developers to build custom application communication structures, while providing support for efficient data aggregation. To

---

*Correspondence: gowrisankar.ramachandran@cs.kuleuven.be
[1]iMinds-DistriNet, KU Leuven, 3001 Leuven, Belgium
Full list of author information is available at the end of the article

tackle this problem, this paper introduces *Hitch Hiker*, a lightweight remote *binding model* with support for *multi-hop data aggregation*. Hitch Hiker uses the same semantics to configure aggregate data flows as standard bindings, reducing development overhead.

A component binding model specifies how remote software components communicate. Well known examples include Remote Procedure Call (RPC) [10, 11] and event-based communication [12, 13]. Hitch Hiker extends binding models to distinguish between *high-* and *low-priority* bindings. Low-priority bindings use a *multi-hop data aggregation overlay network*, built from the free payload space of high-priority bindings, and therefore avoid additional radio transmissions between remote components. Using component meta-data, Hitch Hiker constructs a multi-hop *data aggregation overlay*. The Hitch Hiker binding model allows developers to specify *high-priority* remote bindings that generate radio transmissions, or *low-priority* remote bindings which communicate exclusively using the data aggregation overlay and therefore result in no additional transmissions. By routing low-priority traffic over this data aggregation overlay, Hitch Hiker significantly reduces energy consumption. Furthermore, low-priority bindings provide developers with an elegant way of configuring data aggregation. To the best of our knowledge, Hitch Hiker is the first binding model that provides built-in support for data aggregation.

Our previous short paper on this topic [14] introduced a centralised version of Hitch Hiker, in which multi-hop data aggregation is managed by a single network entity. This paper extends Hitch Hiker [14] by allowing the user to choose between centralised Hitch Hiker or Ad-hoc Hitch Hiker. The Ad-hoc variant of Hitch Hiker eliminates the dependency on the network manager, thereby allowing Hitch Hiker to operate in a fully distributed manner. This allows for the use of multiple meta-managers as supported by LooCI. Ad-hoc Hitch Hiker uses an approach inspired by the well-known Adhoc On-Demand Distance Vector (AODV) [15] routing approach on top of the aggregation overlay for discovering data aggregation routes.

A prototype of Hitch Hiker has been implemented for the LooCI component model [13] running on the Contiki OS [16] and for the OMNeT++ [17] simulator. Our evaluation using two real-world case studies show that: (i.) the resource consumption of Hitch Hiker is minimal and (ii.) by using Hitch Hiker to transmit low-priority traffic, energy consumption is significantly reduced.

The remainder of this paper is structured as follows. Section 2 reviews related work. Section 3 introduces the Hitch Hiker-2.0 binding model. Section 4 explains the route discovery process of infrastructure Hitch Hiker. The ad-hoc mode of Hitch Hiker is explained in Section 5. Section 6 discusses the route maintenance schemes of Hitch Hiker. Section 7 describes our case study

applications. Section 8 introduces and evaluates prototype implementations of Hitch Hiker-2.0. Finally Section 9 concludes and discusses directions for future work.

2   Related work

We draw upon two streams of prior work. Section 2.1 discusses related work in the area of data aggregation. Section 2.2 discusses contemporary component and binding models. We then discuss opportunities for applying data aggregation in component bindings in Section 2.3.

2.1   Data aggregation schemes

He et al. [5] describe two classes of data aggregation approach: Application Dependent Data Aggregation (ADDA), which requires knowledge of application-level traffic flows and Application Independent Data Aggregation (AIDA) which performs aggregation in a generic fashion without application-specific information. We discuss both classes of aggregation in Sections 2.1.1 and 2.1.2, respectively.

2.1.1   *Application dependent data aggregation*

ADDA approaches use network-wide application information to optimise the manner in which information is collected and routed across the network. These efforts focus upon the network and application layers of the communication stack.

At the *Network Layer*, Intanagonwiwat et al. introduce Directed Diffusion [6], which provides data-centric routing, in-network caching and aggregation. To realise these features, Directed Diffusion provides a common data representation. Entities that request data register an *interest* in a particular data type at a certain network location, which causes a conceptual *gradient* to be established between sources and requesters, data is then *drawn* down these gradients from sources to requesters. As data travels down these routes, it is aggregated and cached.

At the *Application Layer*, Madden et al. contribute the Tiny AGgregation (TAG) [7] service, which allows users to specify SQL-like queries, which are multicast to relevant sensor nodes using a tree that is rooted at the base-station. As responses travel towards the root, developer-specified aggregation functions may be applied to data at each hop. Heinzelman et al. contribute the Low-Energy Adaptive Clustering Hierarchy (LEACH) protocol [8], which creates a clustered network structure that provides inherent support for aggregation and energy balancing during data collection. SPEED [18] and SPIN [19] extend application layer aggregation approaches to consider current energy levels when configuring aggregation and routing functionality. Asemani et al. [20] contribute LAG, which aims to create a data aggregation route towards the sink by taking into account the energy levels of nodes and their hop depth in the network. LAG uses learning automata to update the route as the energy levels of the nodes change during run-time.

Network-flow based data aggregation protocols [21, 22] take an orthogonal approach, modelling the sensor network as a graph and, based upon application-level traffic flows, calculating and configuring an optimal aggregation structure. Kapakis et al. [21] contribute MDLA, a network-flow based approach to achieving maximum network lifetime using linear programming and constraints. Xue et al. [22] contribute MaxLife, a commodities-inspired algorithm, wherein a commodity models the data that is generated by a sensor node and delivered to a base station. MaxLife is capable of calculating optimal data aggregation structures and thereby extending network lifetime. Voulkidis et al. [23] contribute a game-theoretic approach to reduce the number of transmissions. This approach estimate the spatial correlation of the sensor data and optimises the transmissions based on the spatial relationship. Xiang et al. [24] contribute a data aggregation approach based on compressed sensing, which uses diffusion wavelets to account for the spatial and temporal correlations. Network-flow based approaches offer efficient calculation of an optimal data aggregation structure, for static networks where network-wide data flows are known, but these approaches are unsuitable for dynamic networks which support runtime reconfiguration.

From the above application dependent data aggregation approaches, it can be seen that contemporary approaches are either inherently static as in network flow models [6], or otherwise restrict developers to a single application interaction model [7] or routing topology [21, 22]. In contrast, application-independent approaches provide a more *generic* aggregation approach, discussed below in Section 2.1.2.

2.1.2 Application independent data aggregation

AIDA schemes provide a one size fits all approach to data aggregation that is independent of application requirements. These approaches typically operate at the network and data link layer.

At the *Network Layer*, well known approaches to aggregation include the Shortest Path Tree (SPT), wherein a single, network-wide aggregation tree is centrally calculated and configured and the Greedy Incremental Tree (GIT) which approximates a shortest path tree, but is constructed in an incremental and decentralised fashion [25]. However, these approaches are poorly suited to Wireless Sensor Networks (WSN) scenarios where energy resources are unevenly distributed. Aonishi et al. contribute Adaptive GIT [9] to address this problem. Intanagonwiwat et al. contribute the Centre at the Nearest Source (CNS) [6] scheme, wherein the responsibility for

data aggregation is assigned to the node which is a source of that data type and closest to the destination.

Leandro et al. [26] contribute DRINA, a lightweight and reliable routing approach for in-network aggregation. DRINA follows a cluster-based approach and builds a shortest path tree to sink. Nodes in each cluster forward the sensed data to the cluster head, which then relays the data to the sink. This solution relies on a dedicated node to perform data aggregation, which means all nodes in the cluster must transmit the sensed data to the cluster head. Jongsoo et al. [27] propose Lump to perform Quality-of-Service aware aggregation for heterogeneous traffic. Lump prioritises packet based on the latency requirements. Lump maintains a queue for each next-hop address, where it stores the packets. Lump uses a periodic send-timer, which raises the priority level of the packets on each timer event. Whenever the priority is raised to the highest level, all packets in the queue are aggregated and transmitted.

At the *Data Link Layer*, He et al. contribute AIDA [5], which takes advantage of queuing delay and the broadcast nature of wireless media to implement application independent data aggregation. AIDA aggregates multiple packets into single frames prior to transmission, resulting in significant savings in terms of energy and latency. While AIDA uses data from the network layer, it treats the application layer as a black box and therefore cannot exploit patterns in application traffic flows. Furthermore, as AIDA operates at the data link layer, it is unable to perform multi-hop data aggregation.

2.2 Remote component binding models

Hitch Hiker combines aggregation with a lightweight remote binding model. In this section, we review component binding models and discuss opportunities for aggregation. Contemporary remote binding models typically offer either event-based or Remote Procedure Call (RPC) semantics.

RPC-based binding models allow remote functionality to be called using the same semantics as local procedures, thus lowering the overhead on component developers. RPC-based models are request-reply and therefore bidirectional in nature. In the case of resource-rich sensing systems, Remote Method Invocation (RMI) [10] has been used to provide reliable RPC-based bindings for Java component models such as OSGi [28] and RUNES [29]. In a WSN context, May et al. [11] extend NesC [30] with support for unicast and anycast RPC calls, wherein exactly one neighbouring node responds to the call. Where component models support remote reconfiguration, bindings may be modified at runtime.

Event-based binding models provide simple unidirectional communication between software modules. Event-based approaches are attractive in resource-constrained scenarios, as they are lightweight and do not cause software modules to block while waiting for responses as in RPC. The Active Messages [12] protocol provides remote bindings for the NesC [30] component model. A unique reference to an application handler is embedded in each active message and is used to dispatch incoming messages to the appropriate handler component. As NesC does not allow for runtime reconfiguration, bindings are fixed at development time. The LooCI binding model [13] provides unreliable event-based binding using a decentralised publish-subscribe *event bus* communication medium. In contrast to Active Messages, LooCI supports multi-model bindings allowing for the modelling of one-to-one, one-to-many, many-to-one and many-to-many relationships. Additionally, unlike Active Messages, LooCI bindings may be remotely modified at runtime in order to enact reconfiguration.

Considering opportunities for cross-layer optimisation, all of the binding models discussed above [10, 30] provide explicit meta-data that can be used to determine traffic flows and therefore optimise aggregation functionality. Despite this opportunity, current component models typically treat the network layer and below as a black box, resulting in suboptimal communication.

2.3   Opportunities for data aggregation

There are a number of advantages to embedding data aggregation support in a component binding model:

Flexible Network Topologies: ADDA approaches to data aggregation such as TAG [7] and Directed Diffusion [6] enforce a single network topology, which may be suboptimal for some application scenarios. In contrast, components can be remotely bound together to form distributed component graphs with flexible network topologies.

Support for Multiple Applications: WSN are increasingly required to simultaneously support multiple applications. Contemporary ADDA approaches are poorly suited to multi-application scenarios as they enforce a single routing structure across multiple applications with different networking requirements. In contrast, component bindings can be used to create a specific network topology for each application.

Appropriate Separation of Concerns: ADDA approaches require that the lower layers of the network stack be concerned with application-level data flows [5]. This means that aggregation protocols must be updated whenever new data types are introduced. In contrast, components provide externally visible meta-data that describes data flows via bindings. This allows aggregation functionality to evolve along with the application components during software reconfiguration.

Application-Optimised Aggregation: AIDA approaches such as CNS [6] and AIDA [5] are unaware of application data flows and therefore would be expected to perform sub-optimally in comparison to application dependent approaches. In contrast, component-binding meta-data provides a means to optimise generic aggregation functionality to suit a specific application.

By using component binding meta-data to build a multi-hop aggregation network, Hitch Hiker combines the key benefits of application dependent aggregation (i.e. an optimised aggregation approach) with those of application independent aggregation (i.e. flexible networking and a more appropriate separation of concerns). The following section describes the Hitch Hiker binding model.

3   The Hitch Hiker 2.0 binding model

Hitch Hiker 2.0 extends the previous version of Hitch Hiker, which is reported in [14]. In Hitch Hiker, the bindings are classified as either high or low priority bindings. This classification allows Hitch Hiker to support data aggregation by appending low-priority data in the overlay network created using the unused payload space of high-priority transmissions. Hitch Hiker uses meta data provided by component bindings to create a multi-hop data aggregation overlay. To support end-to-end routing of low-priority traffic, Hitch Hiker performs route discovery on multi-hop overlay network using a central meta-manager.

Hitch Hiker 2.0 expands the previous version of Hitch Hiker [14] with Ad-hoc Hitch Hiker, which does not rely on central meta-manager to discover the data aggregation overlay. Ad-hoc Hitch Hiker uses an approach inspired by AODV for route discovery.

This section describes the design of the Hitch Hiker binding model and its associated network stack. Section 3.1 provide background on LooCI, which is extended with Hitch Hiker. Section 3.2 introduces prioritised bindings. Section 3.3 describes how route information is extracted from bindings. Sections 3.4 and 3.5 describe the Hitch Hiker network stack.

3.1   The loosely-coupled component infrastructure

The Loosely-coupled Component Infrastructure (LooCI) [13] is a platform-independent component model and supporting middleware targeting networked embedded systems. The LooCI middleware is open-source and ports are available for embedded operating systems such as Contiki [16], Squawk [31] and Android. LooCI is a representative example of a runtime reconfigurable component model for the IoT, with which we have extensive experience. Hitch Hiker extends the basic LooCI component model to support priority-based multi-hop data aggregation. The remainder of this subsection provides a basic overview of the relevant features of LooCI.

Components LooCI components are individually deployable units of functionality. They are managed by creating an instance of the basic LooCI meta-model, described in [13], using a simple component declaration and communication API consisting of required and provided interfaces. LooCI is language-agnostic and components may be implemented in C or Java, allowing developers to exploit language-specific features while providing standardised encapsulation, discovery and lifecycle management. All messages that travel across component interfaces are hierarchically typed as described in [32]. Components may also declare properties that allow for inspection and customisation of component behaviour through externally accessible name/value tuples.

Communication All LooCI components communicate over a fully distributed 'event bus' spanning the entire network. The event-bus is an asynchronous event-based communication medium that follows a decentralised topic-based publish-subscribe model. Local and remote bindings are established by creating new subscription relationships, supporting one-to-one, many-to-one, and one-to-many bindings (as specified in [13]). Hitch Hiker extends the binding model of LooCI with support for data aggregation. Hitch Hiker classifies LooCI bindings as high-priority and low-priority, and this classification allows Hitch Hiker to support data aggregation by appending low-priority data in the overlay network created using the unused payload space of high-priority transmissions.

Reconfiguration LooCI components are connected to the middleware runtime installed on every device. Each component declares its human-readable name, its required interfaces (i.e. services) and provided interfaces (i.e. dependencies). A reconfiguration engine manages the basic meta-model and supports reflective operations using both local or remote API calls.

Meta Manager LooCI applications are deployed, inspected, and configured by *manager* nodes. In principle, any LooCI node may serve as a manager and a network may have multiple managers. The manager interacts with the nodes by using the reflection API to inspect and reconfigure LooCI's meta-model. Hitch Hiker uses a single meta manager in infrastructure mode for the creation of data aggregation overlay, which is a major

restriction. Hitch Hiker 2.0 supports Ad-hoc Hitch Hiker, which operates with either multiple or no manager at all.

3.2 Prioritised bindings

Figure 1 shows a small part of the *smart building* case study, evaluated later in this paper. Here, a temperature component, deployed on sensor node N_1, samples temperature data once every 30 s and sends the data to the comfort level component. The comfort level component on N_2, analyses sensor data, and sends the result to a manager located on N_3 every 30 s. These three components communicate via standard bindings, depicted as ─O─. For the remainder of this paper, we refer the standard bindings as *high-priority bindings*. LooCI provides bindTo and bindFrom calls to create high-priority bindings.

Hitch Hiker introduces the concept of *low-priority bindings*, depicted as ··O··· in Fig. 1. Low-priority bindings are used by non-critical applications, the definition of which is left to the developer. In principle, the developer should use low-priority bindings for traffic that can tolerate long latencies. Hitch Hiker provides bindHHTo and bindHHFrom calls to create low-priority bindings. In our example, a node monitor component deployed on N_1 is connected to a node alert component deployed on N_3 via a low-priority binding. The use of a low-priority binding indicates that the developer is willing to trade communication performance for energy efficiency. Low-priority bindings are realised in Hitch Hiker by routing messages via the data aggregation overlay network, referred to as *Hitch Hiker network*.

High-Priority Bindings Hitch Hiker extends the event-based LooCI binding model described in Section 3.1. LooCI bindings are: event-based, unidirectional, and unreliable. Conceptually, a LooCI binding is a connection between a source and a destination component, with an associated data type and a reference to the network *link* that connects the nodes hosting the two components. Table 1 shows the list of well-known LooCI binding types and their payload sizes.

Definition 1 (Binding). *A binding is a tuple b = $\langle C_s, C_d, Type, Link \rangle$, where C_s is the source component, C_d is the destination component, Type is the type of the events sent through the binding, and Link is the remote connection*

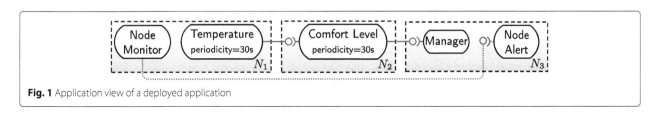

Fig. 1 Application view of a deployed application

Table 1 List of LooCI binding types and their payload sizes

Components	Binding type	Payload size (in bytes)
Temperature sensor	TEMP	5
Light sensor	LIGHT	3
Moisture sensor	MOISTURE	3
Air quality sensor	AIRQUALITY	8
PIR sensor	PIR	4
RFID reader	RFID	8
Door sensor	DOOR	3
Buzzer	BUZZER	3

between the nodes where the binding is deployed, defined below.

Definition 2 (Remote Connection). *A remote connection is a tuple* $\ell = \langle N_s, N_d, MTU, Bw, D \rangle$ *describing the communication channel between two network nodes, where N_s is the source node, N_d is the destination node, MTU is the maximum transmission unit between N_s and N_d, Bw is the bandwidth of the remote connection, and D is the expected delay of the remote connection.*

A LooCI binding is realised as an *outgoing binding* entry on the sending node and an *incoming binding* entry on the receiving node, which is established by issuing `bindTo` and `bindFrom` calls to the sender and receiver, respectively. These bindings are stored in a *binding table* which is used to dispatch events. LooCI bindings are created at runtime after the deployment of the involved components. High-priority binding is mediated by the transmission of a event using the network stack of the host operating system.

The binding from the temperature component is formally represented as ⟨Temperature,Comfort Level,Temp,ℓ⟩, where the associated remote connection $\ell = \langle N_1, N_2, 127\,B, 250\,kbps, 0.1\,s \rangle$.

Low-Priority Bindings   Hitch Hiker introduces the concept of a *low-priority* binding, depicted as ⋯○⋯ in Fig. 1. In our example, a *node monitor* component gathers the local node status and transmits this data to a *node alert* component running on a server. We selected node monitoring as an example of a low-priority application because this functionality is less important than the core WSN mission of gathering environmental data and this application data can tolerate delay. However, it should be noted that developers are free to define which components are high-priority and low-priority in their application context. In our example (Fig. 1), the low priority binding that connects the *node*

monitor to the *node alert* component is formally represented as ⟨Node Monitor, Node Alert, Status, ℓ_{status}⟩, where Status is the event type containing node status information and ℓ_{status} is the remote connection of the overlay network.

High-priority and low-priority bindings have an identical set of artefacts: a source component, destination component, data type (Definition 1) and a remote connection (Definition 2). Low-priority bindings are realised in LooCI by adding a separate set of *binding tables* to each node.

The overlay routes necessary to support low-priority bindings are established reactively, as it required to support low-priority bindings.

3.3 Component model probe extracts network data

The component model *probe* extracts data from the high-priority application to create the remote connections of the Hitch Hiker network. It *intercepts binding acknowledgment* messages containing the source component C_s, the source node N_s, the destination node N_d, and the binding *Type*, and builds a remote connection for the Hitch Hiker network. Recall that a remote connection is formally a tuple $\langle N_s, N_d, MTU, Bw, D \rangle$ (Definition 2). The *MTU* is calculated based on the event type, which has an associated payload size, as shown in Table 1. Hitch Hiker extracts periodicity information by querying source components for their *periodicity* property using the standard LooCI API. Hitch Hiker distinguishes between *periodic* and *non-periodic* components: the former send values at a fixed rate (e.g., a temperature reading every 10 s), and the latter exhibit unpredictable behaviour (e.g., an alert generated when a window is opened).

Formally, we write $\Pi(C)$ to denote the periodicity of a component C, defined below, which returns the special symbol $\perp$ when C is non-periodic.

$$\Pi(C) = \begin{cases} r & \text{if } C \text{ is periodic with rate } r; \\ \perp & \text{otherwise.} \end{cases}$$

Based upon the information intercepted in the binding acknowledgment—the source component C_s, the source node N_s, the destination node N_d, and the source *Type*—and the periodicity $\Pi(C_s)$, the probe calculates the remote connection for the Hitch Hiker network as follows.

1. Get the payload size *ps* associated with the *Type*.
2. Get the *MTU* *m* of the remote connection between the source (N_s) and destination (N_d).
3. Define *hd* to be the size of the headers used by the data-link, network and transport layers of the host protocol stack.
4. Define MTU_{HH} to be the unused payload size, calculated as $m - ps - hd$.

5. If $\Pi(C_s) = \bot$ then return the remote connection $\langle N_s, N_d, MTU_{HH}, \bot, \bot \rangle$, otherwise return the remote connection
$\langle N_s, N_d, MTU_{HH}, MTU_{HH}/\Pi(C_s), \Pi(C_s) \rangle$.

The component model probe reveals the remote connection between a source node N_s and a destination node N_d with a free payload space of MTU_{HH}. The probe also reveals the delay or the time-interval between two successive transmissions as $\Pi(C_s)$. For the example application shown in Fig. 1, the remote connection between node N_1 and N_2 has a free payload space of 75 B (excluding the temperature data and the overhead added by the other layers) with a delay of 30 s. This connection meta data is used for the configuration of Hiker routing protocol and it is discussed in Section 3.5.

3.4 Hitch medium access control (MAC) protocol

Figure 2 shows the Hitch Hiker network stack for a single embedded sensor node, with each layer numbered according to the 5-layer Tanenbaum reference model [33]. The Hitch Hiker protocol stack is composed of two protocols the *Hitch* MAC protocol and the *Hiker* routing protocol. The former is described below and the latter in the following subsection.

Hitch is a virtual MAC protocol that manages and provides access to the data aggregation overlay links. The Hitch MAC protocol is implemented as an independent module, which allows Hitch to be used with third-party routing protocols at the aggregation overlay level.

Link Data Structures Hitch manages the set of virtual data links that are available on each sensor node. Each virtual data link maps to a remote overlay connection (Definition 2) that may be multi-hop and is composed of: a destination address, MTU, delay and bandwidth. Virtual links are created by the *probe* and may be accessed through the HitchAPI, available online: http://goo.gl/7m2nwN.

A First In First Out (FIFO) queue is maintained per link where packets are buffered until they can be aggregated with high-priority traffic and dispatched. If the buffer reaches its capacity, the oldest frame in the queue is discarded, resulting in packet loss. Hitch is a best-effort protocol, which provides no reliability guarantees. Where reliability is required, it should be implemented by the upper layers.

Aggregation The Hitch protocol intercepts outgoing packets as they are passed to the host MAC protocol, and this protocol does not violate the security requirements of the host MAC protocol. If the virtual link queue associated with the destination of an intercepted packet is not empty, the available payload size is filled with packets from the queue, until either the available payload space is exhausted or the buffer is empty. The modified

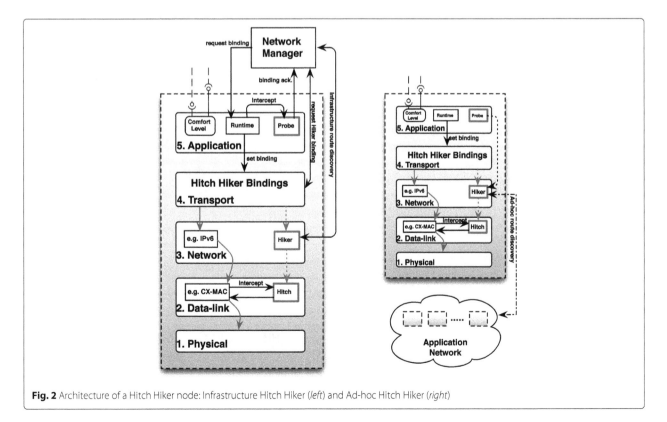

Fig. 2 Architecture of a Hitch Hiker node: Infrastructure Hitch Hiker (*left*) and Ad-hoc Hitch Hiker (*right*)

packet is then returned to the host MAC protocol to be transmitted.

Disaggregation The Hitch protocol intercepts incoming frames in the host MAC protocol, and disaggregates all encapsulated Hitch packets. The disaggregated packets are then passed to the network layer, while the original frame is passed back to the host data link protocol. And, it operates within boundary of the host MAC protocol.

3.5 Hiker network protocol

Hiker is a multi-hop routing protocol that operates efficiently with the Hitch data link protocol.

Route Data Structures Hiker maintains a minimalist *routing table* on each node. This routing table begins empty, and routes are reactively configured by the network manager to support low-priority bindings. Each route is comprised of a *remote destination*, the *virtual link* that represents the next hop on the route to this address and a *route-MTU* which denotes the maximum packet size that can traverse the complete route.

Routing When an incoming Hiker packet is received, the destination field of the packet is checked. If the destination is the local sensor node, it is passed to the transport layer. If the destination matches a known route, it is transmitted on the appropriate link using the `transmit(frame,link)` method of Hitch. If no route is known, the packet is discarded. Sections 4 and 5 explains the route discovery process of Hitch Hiker in infrastructure and ad-hoc mode, respectively.

Definition 3 (Route). *A route is a multi-hop remote connection (Definition 2) obtained by composing a non-empty sequence of remote connections, such that for every consecutive remote connections ℓ and ℓ' the destination node of ℓ matches the source node of ℓ'. Given a sequence of n remote connections:*

$$\langle N_{s,1}, N_{d,1}, MTU_1, Bw_1, D_1 \rangle, \ldots,$$
$$\langle N_{s,n}, N_{d,n}, MTU_n, Bw_n, D_n \rangle$$

its composition yields the route $\langle N_s, N_d, MTU, Bw, D \rangle$, *where*

$$N_s = N_{s,1} \quad MTU = \min_{i=1}^{n} MTU_i \quad D = \sum_{i=1}^{n} D_i.$$
$$N_d = N_{d,n} \quad Bw = \min_{i=1}^{n} Bw_i$$

Hiker Packet Encapsulation Figure 3 shows a host packet that is aggregated with multiple Hitch Hiker (HH) packets. Each encapsulated HH packet has a *2a+1* byte header, where *a* is the length of a network address. One additional byte is used to represent the length of the payload that follows. We use 6LowPAN IPv6 address shortening [34], resulting in 2 B addresses in our case-studies.

4 Infrastructure Hitch Hiker

In *infrastructure mode*, Hiker assumes that a single LooCI *network manager* is running for the entire network, as shown in Fig. 2. This network manager enacts all management and reconfiguration. This information is exploited to create the data aggregation overlay network as follows:

1. Overlay links are discovered based upon extended binding acknowledgements. This information is provided by the component model probe as described in Section 3.3.
2. The network manager assembles discovered overlay links to form a network graph, wherein each link is labelled with its associated delay, MTU and bandwidth.
3. When the user requests the establishment of a low-priority binding b:

   (a) The graph is pruned to remove all links which have an insufficient MTU to support the specified data type.
   (b) The Dijkstra algorithm is used to calculate the *shortest path* between the source and destination, using either delay or bandwidth as the link cost. Our evaluation uses delay as the link cost.
   (c) The network manager configures the *shortest path* overlay route, or responds with an exception where no overlay route is possible.
   (d) Finally, the network manager configures the route required by the low-priority binding b, by sending route-creation messages to all involved nodes.

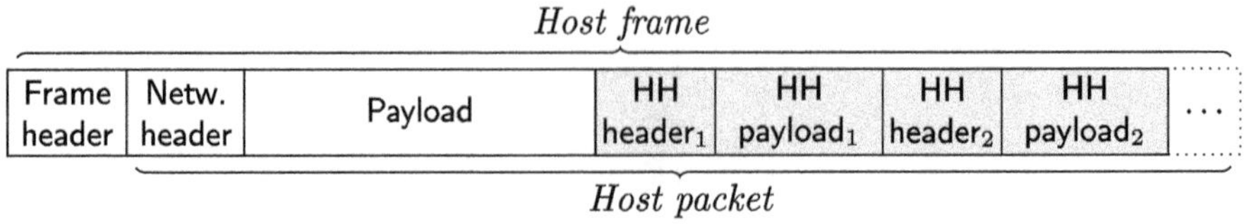

Host frame							
Frame header	Netw. header	Payload	HH header$_1$	HH payload$_1$	HH header$_2$	HH payload$_2$	...

Host packet

Fig. 3 Hiker packet; darker background captures the low-priority aggregated data

Figure 4 shows the networked interactions that are required to create both the high-priority and low-priority bindings for the running example shown in Fig. 1. In the interests of clarity and brevity, binding and route data shows only the network end-points.

Steps (1)–(5) The network manager receives a request to establish high-priority bindings to connect the Temperature, Comfort Level, and Manager components. The network manager then enacts this request by issuing standard LooCI `bindTo` and `bindFrom` commands that establish the required binding table entries. The associated binding acknowledgements inform the network manager of newly available overlay routes.

Steps (6)–(8) The network manager receives a request to establish a low-priority binding to connect the Node Monitor and the Node Alert components. To support this binding, Hitch Hiker configures an overlay *route* between the nodes N_1 and N_3 (Definition 3).

Steps (9)–(10) The network manager establishes the low-priority binding by issuing the required `bindHHTo` and `bindHHFrom` method calls, which establish the necessary entries in the Hitch Hiker wiring tables.

Since this mode of Hitch Hiker operate with a single network manager, the creation of Hitch Hiker bindings require binding meta data from the entire application network. In principle, any Hitch Hiker node in the network can create or remove bindings. In order to increase the flexibility of Hitch Hiker and to allow Hitch Hiker to operate with either multiple managers or no managers, we extend Hitch Hiker with support for decentralised route discovery, which is explained in Section 5.

5 Ad-hoc Hitch Hiker

In *ad-hoc mode*, Hiker routes are discovered in a fully decentralised manner. This allows Hiker to operate in networks with multiple managers or no managers at all, as shown in Fig. 2. The binding request can come from any node in the application network, and the Hiker of the source node self-discovers a overlay route, unlike

Infrastructure Hitch Hiker. To realise this, Hiker reimagines the well-known Ad-hoc On-Demand Distance Vector (AODV) routing approach [15]. To find overlay routes on top of bindings as opposed to at the network layer. In this mode, Hiker discovers the route as follows:

1. When the user requests the establishment of a low-priority binding b, a route-discovery message is flooded across the data aggregation overlay as shown in Fig. 5.
2. The source node broadcasts a discovery message containing the destination address, required MTU, a sequence number and a Time to Live (TTL) on all links provided by the Hitch MAC protocol, as indicated in Fig. 5. And, the source node waits for NET_TRAVERSAL_TIME seconds for route-creation message. If the route-creation message is not received within NET_TRAVERSAL_TIME, then the source node notifies the developer that there is no route between the source and destination, and the low-priority binding is not accepted. Section 6 explains the error handling schemes of Hitch Hiker.
3. All nodes receiving a route-discovery message decrement the TTL, add the sequence number and source link to their cache and re-broadcast the discovery message, discarding the message when the TTL reaches zero, or the available MTU is insufficient, or if the sequence number was previously observed.
4. When the destination node receives the route-discovery message as presented in Fig. 5, it establishes a route r by responding with a route-creation message as follows:

   (a) The first route-discovery message received by the destination denotes the shortest path between the source and the destination nodes. The destination node forwards a route-creation message back to the link on which the discovery message was received. This message contains the matching sequence number and the address of the destination node.

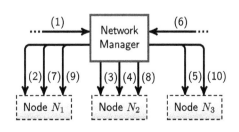

(1) Request HP bindings
(2) `bindTo` $N_1 \rightarrow N_2$
(3) `bindFrom` $N_1 \rightarrow N_2$
(4) `bindTo` $N_2 \rightarrow N_3$
(5) `bindFrom` $N_2 \rightarrow N_3$
(6) Request LP bindings
(7) `addHHRoute` $N_1 \rightarrow N_2$
(8) `addHHRoute` $N_2 \rightarrow N_3$
(9) `bindHHTo` $N_1 \rightarrow N_3$
(10) `bindHHFrom` $N_1 \rightarrow N_3$

Fig. 4 Network view - configuration of bindings and routes for Infrastructure Hitch Hiker

(b) On receipt of a route-creation message, each intermediate node adds a routing table entry mapping the specified destination address to the link on which the route-creation message was received.

(c) Following the creation of a routing table entry, the intermediate node checks its cache and forwards the route creation message on the link via which the original route-discovery was received. Step 2 repeats until the route is fully established.

As can be seen from the process described above, in ad-hoc mode, Hitch Hiker requires no supporting infrastructure. However, the use of flooding increases the overhead and latency of route discovery in comparison to infrastructure mode. Figure 5 shows the networked interactions that are required to create low-priority bindings for the running example shown in Fig. 1 using AODV routing approach.

6 Route errors and maintenance

Whenever a user creates a Hitch Hiker binding as described in Section 3, route discovery executes as described in Sections 4 and 5. If a low priority route was successfully created, Hitch Hiker returns *true* together with the performance properties of the route as listed in Definition 3, i.e. route MTU, latency and bandwidth. If the route was not created, Hitch Hiker returns *false* and the performance properties of the best available route, if one exists. Based upon this information, the developer may choose to (i.) abandon the binding, (ii.) modify the binding to work within available Hitch Hiker network capacity or (iii.) establish a high-priority binding.

6.1 Impact of reconfiguration

Hitch Hiker-2.0 builds on top of LooCI component model, which provides support for run-time reconfiguration of application. Such run-time reconfigurations may result in deployment of new components or the removal of existing components. In addition, the reconfiguration may also change the existing bindings in the application network. These reconfigurations disrupts the existing data aggregation overlay and might invalidate the existing routes of low-priority bindings.

In *infrastructure mode*, when the manager receives a reconfiguration command that invalidates a route, it removes the old route and then execute the route discovery process to find a replacement route. If no replacement route exists, an exception is generated. In *adhoc mode*, a mote that receives a reconfiguration command, which impacts a Hitch Hiker route will flood a *route-remove* message with the sequence number of the matching route. All motes that receive this message will remove the route, causing the source node to re-run the route discovery process.

7 Case study applications

We validate the performance of Hitch Hiker-2.0 in two representative application scenarios that are realised using the LooCI component model and prioritised bindings. Section 7.1 describes a low data rate multi-hop static *smart office* sensor network, while Section 7.2 describes a high data rate one-hop *mobile robot* sensor network.

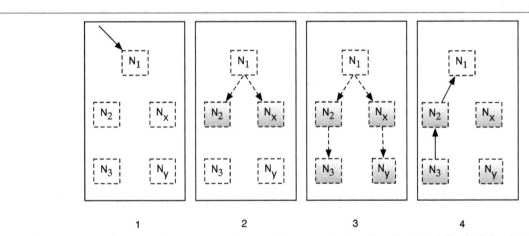

Fig. 5 Network topology of the application presented in Fig. 1. Each box represents the node in the network. The shaded nodes are new recipients. The dashed lines show possible reverse routes, while the solid lines show the discovered route. **1** Node N1 receives a low-priority binding request. **2** N1 broadcasts a route discovery message, N2 and Nx receive it. **3** N2 and Nx are not the intended destination. N2 and Nx make an entry in their node and forwards the request to their neighbours. **4** The intended destination N3 has been found. N3 sends out a route reply message along the reversed path of the request. This route reply message configures all the intermediate nodes and the source node

The mobile robot application provides the greatest opportunities for data aggregation due to its high data rate and one-hop network structure, while the smart office application is more challenging. In reality, we expect the characteristics of most WSN applications to fall somewhere between those of these two applications. The smart office and the mobile robots applications are overlaid with a non-critical *node health monitoring* application, which uses low-priority Hitch Hiker bindings, described in Section 7.3.

7.1 Smart office application

The *smart office* application aims to ensure employee comfort, while reducing energy consumption by sensing environmental conditions and controlling relevant appliances. Sensor nodes (N_2, N_3 and N_4) monitor: temperature, light and whether the window is open or closed every 30 s. This sensor data is transmitted to a comfort level component running on the cluster-head node (N_1) which aggregates the sensor information and forwards the aggregated data to a manager component running on a server (N_0), once every 30 s. Based upon the observed sensor data and configured comfort levels, a management component running on the server (N_0) issues commands to a control component running on the cluster-heads (N_1), which then activate or deactivate relay switches running on nodes N_2 to N_4 that control: lighting, ventilation and an audio alarm, which indicates that the window should be closed. The smart office application is realised using high-priority (i.e. standard) LooCI bindings. The payload size of all sensor data is **4 bytes**, the payload size of aggregated data is **12 bytes** and the payload size of relay control commands is **4 bytes**.

Figure 6 shows the application composition and all relevant binding and properties information. In terms of network topology, the scenario is comprised of 25 offices.

Each office contains three sensor nodes, and a cluster-head node. Sensor nodes communicate with cluster heads, which in turn communicate with a single server for management of comfort level. This approximates a 101-node tree topology rooted at the server.

7.2 Mobile robot application

The *mobile robot* application coordinates a set of mobile robots to detect chemical spills. Each robot (N_1 to N_{100}) runs a chemical sensor and a location sensor which sample every 10 s and transmit the data to a coordination component running on the server (N_0). The coordination component then calculates a set of navigation instructions every 10 s and transmits these to the navigation component running on each mobile robot (N_1 to N_{100}). The mobile robot application is realised using standard LooCI bindings. The payload size of location data is **6 bytes**, the payload size of chemical sensor data is **4 bytes** and the payload size of navigation commands is **5 bytes**. Figure 6 shows the application composition and all relevant binding and properties data. In terms of network topology, the scenario contains 100 mobile robots, all of which communicate directly with the coordinating server. This approximates a 101-node star topology.

7.3 Node health monitoring application

The *node health monitoring* application [35] is a low-priority application, inspired from real world deployments such as Great Duck Island [36]. We consider it low-priority because it adds value, but (i.) the data is not critical and (ii.) it should not reduce the lifetime of the base application. This component monitors battery level, memory use and the radio link quality. The application consists of a health monitor component that runs on all sensor nodes (N_1 to N_n) and sends node health information to an alert component running on

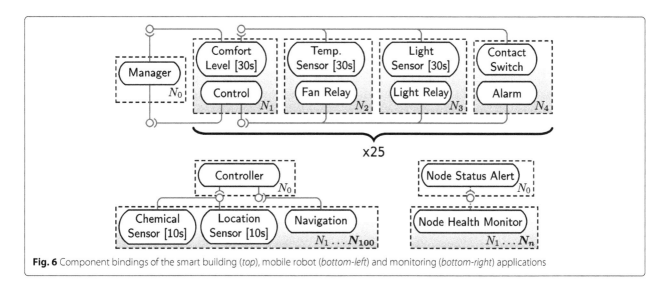

Fig. 6 Component bindings of the smart building (*top*), mobile robot (*bottom-left*) and monitoring (*bottom-right*) applications

the server node (N_0). Node health monitoring is overlaid on the smart building and mobile robot application using low-priority bindings. The payload size of node health monitor data is 18 B. The composition is shown in Fig. 6.

8 Implementation and evaluation

We have developed prototypes of Hitch Hiker-2.0 for the OMNeT++ simulator [17] and the Zigduino mote [37]. Simulation is used to study the performance of the three case-study applications described in Section 7. The Zigduino implementation validates node-local memory and energy characteristics for a concrete hardware/software stack.

OMNeT++ settings: The physical layer is a CC2420 IEEE 802.15.4 radio [38]. We use B-MAC [39] as a representative Low Power Listening (LPL) protocol. Simulation settings are based on prior experiments by Polastre et al. [39]. Table 2 shows the configuration settings of OMNeT++.

Zigduino configuration: Zigduino is an Arduino-compatible mote based on the ATmega128RFA1 [40], which offers a 16 MHz MCU, 16 KB of RAM, 128 KB of Flash and an IEEE 802.15.4 radio. We use ContikiOS v2.6, Contiki X-MAC (CX-MAC) [41] and LooCI v2.0 [13] extended with Hitch Hiker 2.0. The parameterisation of CX-MAC uses the default Contiki values. In the case of the mobile robot case-study the Zigduino is extended with a ShieldBot mobile robot base [42]. Table 2 shows the configuration settings of Zigduino. We compare Hitch Hiker against (i.) transmission of standard messages (referred as Standard binding) and (ii.) an optimally configured one-hop data aggregation scheme using an optimal aggregation buffer size of 3 (referred as One-hop aggregation). Values reported below represent averages taken over one week.

All source code and simulation material are available at: http://goo.gl/7m2nwN.

8.1 OMNET++ simulation results

Latency Figure 7 shows the results of our latency simulation. The x-axis shows the sampling frequency of the node health monitoring app, which was set to a consistent fraction of the case study application frequency (from left to right from 10 to 50 % of the base app frequency). The y-axis shows the latency of message transmission in seconds

for low-priority Hitch Hiker bindings, standard bindings and one-hop data aggregation.

As expected, the node health monitoring app exhibited a higher latency when using low-priority bindings than with standard bindings due to packets waiting for aggregation at each hop. However, the latency of low-priority bindings is lower than the one-hop aggregation scheme due to the exploitation of multi-hop routes. For the *mobile robot app* (right of Fig. 7) the latency of Hitch Hiker falls as high-priority traffic is transmitted at a higher rate and thus, there are increased opportunities for aggregation.

Energy Figure 8 shows the results of our energy simulation. As with our latency experiments, the sampling frequency of the node health monitoring app was set to 10 to 50 % of the base application frequency. The y-axis shows the power consumption low-priority Hitch Hiker bindings, standard bindings and one-hop data aggregation.

The results shown in Fig. 8 confirm the expected savings when using Hitch Hiker to route low-priority traffic. Energy consumption is reduced by up to 15 % in the smart building scenario and up to 32 % in the mobile robot scenario compared to standard bindings. The energy consumption of Hitch Hiker is also lower than that of one-hop data aggregation. The greatest savings are achieved for the mobile robot application as more low-priority transmissions are aggregated.

8.2 Zigduino/Contiki implementation results

This section reports the performance timings of route configuration and message transmission as well as energy consumption and memory overhead for the Contiki/Zigduino implementation. Configuration timings are dependent upon the type of route being configured. We therefore report average timings based upon the smart building application, as this has the most complex routing structure.

Route Creation The Hitch Hiker 2.0 provides two approaches for route creation. Infrastructure Hitch Hiker requires approximately 86 ms to configure a single low-priority binding. Each additional hop that must be configured adds 30 ms to the configuration overhead. Route configuration is thus lightweight; creating all of the Hitch Hiker bindings required for the smart building takes less than 3 s. However, this generates three transmissions per Hitch Hiker binding, which costs 36.5 mJ.

In contrast, Ad-hoc Hitch Hiker, takes more time to configure a route since it uses data aggregation overlay itself to flood route discovery messages. For the smart building application, in the worst case, Ad-hoc Hitch Hiker requires 65 s to configure a single low priority binding. Each additional hop that must be configured adds 30 s

Table 2 Configuration of the OMNeT++ simulation and the Zigduino implementation

Radio	OMNet	Zigduino	MAC protocol	OMNet	Zigduino
Transmit current	17 mA	18.6 mA	Check interval	0.1 s	0.125 s
Receive current	16.2 mA	16.6 mA	Slot duration	1.0 s	2.0 s
Sleep current	0.02 mA	4.1 mA	Queue length	10	15

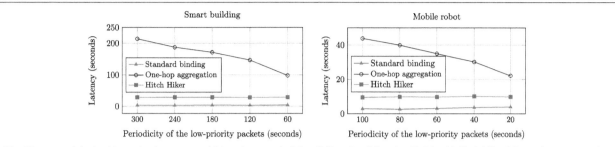

Fig. 7 Latency of the health monitoring app. overlaid on the smart building (*left*) and mobile robot (*right*), with Hitch Hiker-2.0, one hop aggregation and standard bindings

to the configuration time, and the complete smart building app takes less than an hour to configure. However, Ad-hoc Hitch Hiker generates only two transmissions per Hitch Hiker binding, which costs 23 mJ – significantly less than infrastructure mode.

Message Transmission Enqueueing, dequeueing and encapsulating a single Hitch Hiker packet within a host frame requires on average of 12.27 mJ, while a standard frame transmission using CX-MAC requires 21.41 mJ, a saving of 57.4 % compared to standard transmission.

Memory Hitch Hiker introduces minimal memory overhead in comparison to the basic LooCI component model. As shown in Table 3, the implementation of Infrastructure Hitch Hiker adds 3 % of ROM and 8 % of RAM to the LooCI component model. This implementation consists of component model probe along with Hitch and Hiker protocols, as presented in Section 3.

For Ad-hoc Hitch Hiker, the ROM and RAM overhead is approximately 6 and 8 % respectively. Ad-hoc Hitch Hiker consumes more memory than Infrastructure mode as each node must embed route discovery logic. Each routing table entry uses an additional 6 B of memory. We believe that this low overhead is reasonable in light of the energy savings reported in Section 8.1.

9 Conclusions and future work

This paper introduced *Hitch Hiker 2.0*, a novel remote binding model for IoT which supports prioritised bindings and multi-hop data aggregation. This prioritised binding model provides developers with a low-effort mechanism to manage data aggregation. Unlike prior work in the area of aggregation, Hitch Hiker uses component binding meta-data to construct a multi-hop overlay network for data aggregation. Hitch Hiker provides support for routing on multi-hop overlay network. To the best of our knowledge, Hitch Hiker is both the first *generic and yet application aware* data aggregation approach. Furthermore, Hitch Hiker is the first remote binding model to provide built-in support for data aggregation.

Hitch Hiker 2.0 extended our previous work [14] and provides a decentralised routing approach. Hitch Hiker 2.0 allows the user to choose between centralised and decentralised routing approach, making it a flexible binding model.

We have simulated the Hitch Hiker protocol in OMNeT++ for two case-study application scenarios. Our results show that using Hitch Hiker to route low-priority traffic reduces energy consumption and, for applications with a high data rate, latency. We also implemented a prototype of Hitch Hiker for the LooCI component model running on the Contiki OS and the Zigduino mote. Our evaluation of the prototype implementation shows that Hitch Hiker consumes minimal memory, introduces limited overhead and that transmitting

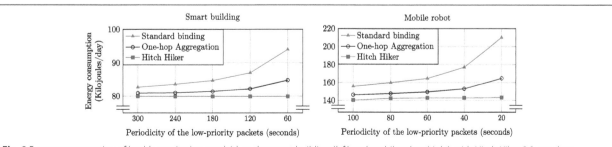

Fig. 8 Energy consumption of health monitoring overlaid on the smart building (*left*) and mobile robot (*right*), with Hitch Hiker-2.0, one-hop aggregation and standard bindings

Table 3 Memory overhead of Hitch Hiker-2.0 (HH)

Memory	LooCI	Infrastructure HH	Ad-Hoc HH
ROM	56534 B	1882 B (+3.3 %)	3244 B (+5.7 %)
RAM	8998 B	722 B (+8.0 %)	756 B (+8.4 %)

Authors' contributions
GSR worked on the design, implementation and the evaluation of Hitch Hiker. JP worked on the design and modeling. WD helped with the implementation on Zigduino hardware platform. MP,DS,CH and WJ were involved in the discussions during the design phase. DH supervised and played a critical role in the entire work. In addition, all authors read and approved the work.

messages with Hitch Hiker consumes a small fraction of the energy that is required for a standard radio transmission.

Our future work will focus on four fronts: improving the performance of Hitch Hiker for non-periodic components, adding support for virtual circuits, extending Hitch Hiker to support variable component payloads and realising a RPC version of the Hitch Hiker binding model.

Non-periodic components: The current design of Hitch Hiker tends to avoid aggregation with non-periodic bindings, where the source component not specify the *rate* property, due to the unpredictability performance of those links. This is a potential source of inefficiency in cases where non-periodic components transmit frequently. We plan to address this inefficiency by extending the *Component Model Probe* with support for monitoring the transmission timings of non-periodic components and extracting timing data.

Virtual circuits: In the current model, it is possible for the Hitch Hiker overlay to become congested and for buffers to overflow. In our future work, we will explore how resource reservation can be used to create virtual circuits on top of the Hitch Hiker overlay with associated Quality of Service assurances. We envisage that this could be achieved by extending the role of the network manager to include remote configuration of Hitch buffer sizes and admission control on low-priority bindings.

Variable component payloads: The current design of Hitch Hiker supports only fixed sized data types. While we believe that this covers the vast majority of WSN traffic, it is interesting to explore how Hitch Hiker could be extended to support variable sized payloads such as compressed images or microphone captures. As with non-periodic components this would necessitate extension of the *Component Model Probe* to support the monitoring of previous transmissions and maintenance of historic payload size data.

Remote Procedure Call: As Hitch Hiker extends LooCI, it supports only unidirectional event-based bindings. It would be interesting to extend Hitch Hiker with support for Remote Procedure Call (RPC) bindings. As RPC method calls are inherently request-reply and therefore bidirectional, this would result in a much more densely connected data aggregation overlay and therefore improved performance for Hitch Hiker.

Acknowledgements
This research is partially supported by the Research Fund, KU Leuven and iMinds (a research institute founded by the Flemish government), and by the Portuguese FCT grant SFRH/BPD/91908/2012. The research is conducted in the context of FWO-RINAiSense project.

Author details
[1]iMinds-DistriNet, KU Leuven, 3001 Leuven, Belgium. [2]iMinds-IBCN, Ghent University, 9000 Gent, Belgium. [3]HASLab/INESC TEC, Universidade do Minho, Braga, Portugal.

References
1. Raghunathan V, Schurgers C, Park S, Srivastava M, Shaw B. Energy-aware wireless microsensor networks. In: IEEE Signal Processing Magazine. IEEE; 2002. p. 40–50.
2. Rajagopalan R, Varshney PK. Data-aggregation techniques in sensor networks: A survey. IEEE Commun Surv Tutor. 2006;8(4):48–63. doi:10.1109/COMST.2006.283821.
3. Tan HO, Körpeoğlu I. Power efficient data gathering and aggregation in wireless sensor networks. SIGMOD Rec. 2003;32(4):66–71. doi:10.1145/959060.959072.
4. Kalpakis K, Dasgupta K, Namjoshi P. Efficient algorithms for maximum lifetime data gathering and aggregation in wireless sensor networks. Comput Netw. 2003;42(6):697–716. doi:10.1016/S1389-1286(03)00212-3.
5. He T, Blum BM, Stankovic JA, Abdelzaher T. Aida: Adaptive application-independent data aggregation in wireless sensor networks. ACM Trans Embed Comput Syst. 2004426–457. doi:10.1145/993396.993406.
6. Intanagonwiwat C, Govindan R, Estfin D, Heidemann J, Silva F. Directed diffusion for wireless sensor networking. IEEE/ACM Trans Networking. 2003;11:2–16.
7. Madden S, Franklin MJ, Hellerstein JM, Hong W. Tag: A tiny aggregation service for ad-hoc sensor networks. SIGOPS Oper Syst Rev. 2002131–146. doi:10.1145/844128.844142.
8. Heinzelman WR, Chandrakasan A, Balakrishnan H. Energy-efficient communication protocol for wireless microsensor networks. In: 33rd Annual Hawaii Int. Conf. on System Sciences; 2000. p. 10. doi:10.1109/HICSS.2000.926982.
9. Aonishi T, Matsuda T, Mikami S, Kawaguchi H, Ohta C, Yoshimoto M. Impact of aggregation efficiency on git routing for wireless sensor networks. In: Int. Conf. on Parallel Processing Workshops; 2006. p. 8–158. doi:10.1109/ICPPW.2006.41.
10. Birrell AD, Nelson BJ. Implementing remote procedure calls. ACM Trans Comput Syst. 1984. 39–59. doi:10.1145/2080.357392.
11. May TD, Dunning SH, Dowding GA, Hallstrom JO. An RPC design for wireless sensor networks. Int J Pervasive Comput Commun. 2007;2(4): 384–397.
12. von Eicken T, Culler DE, Goldstein SC, Schauser KE. Active messages: A mechanism for integrated communication and computation. In: 19th Annual Int. Symposium on Computer Architecture; 1992. p. 256–266. doi:10.1145/139669.140382.
13. Hughes D, Thoelen K, Maerien J, Matthys N, Del Cid J, Horre W, Huygens C, Michiels S, Joosen W. Looci: The loosely-coupled component infrastructure. In: IEEE Symposium on Network Computing and Applications; 2012. p. 236–243. doi:10.1109/NCA.2012.30.
14. Ramachandran GS, Daniels W, Proença J, Michiels S, Joosen W, Hughes D, Porter B. Hitch hiker: A remote binding model with priority based data

aggregation for wireless sensor networks. In: Proceedings of the 18th International ACM SIGSOFT Symposium on Component-Based Software Engineering. CBSE '15. New York: ACM; 2015. p. 43–48. doi:10.1145/2737166.2737179. http://doi.acm.org/10.1145/2737166.2737179.

15. Perkins CE, Royer EM. Ad-hoc on-demand distance vector routing. In: Mobile Computing Systems and Applications; 1999. p. 90–100. doi:10.1109/MCSA.1999.749281.

16. Dunkels A, Gronvall B, Voigt T. Contiki - a lightweight and flexible operating system for tiny networked sensors. In: 29th Annual IEEE Int. Conf. on Local Computer Networks; 2004. p. 455–462. doi:10.1109/LCN.2004.38.

17. Chen K. Performance Evaluation by Simulation and Analysis with Applications to Computer Networks. NJ, USA: Wiley; 2015.

18. He T, Stankovic JA, Lu C, Abdelzaher T. Speed: a stateless protocol for real-time communication in sensor networks. In: Distributed Computing Systems, 2003. Proceedings. 23rd Int. Conf. On; 2003. p. 46–55. doi:10.1109/ICDCS.2003.1203451.

19. Heinzelman WR, Kulik J, Balakrishnan H. Adaptive protocols for information dissemination in wireless sensor networks. In: 5th Annual ACM/IEEE Int. Conf. on Mobile Computing and Networking. New York: ACM; 1999. p. 174–185. doi:10.1145/313451.313529.

20. Asemani M, Esnaashari M. Learning automata based energy efficient data aggregation in wireless sensor networks. Wirel Netw. 2015;21(6):2035–2053. doi:10.1007/s11276-015-0894-3.

21. Kalpakis K, Dasgupta K, Namjoshi P. Efficient algorithms for maximum lifetime data gathering and aggregation in wireless sensor networks. Comput Netw. 2003;42(6):697–716. doi:10.1016/S1389-1286(03) 00212-3.

22. Xue Y, Cui Y, Nahrstedt K. Maximizing lifetime for data aggregation in wireless sensor networks. Mob Netw Appl. 2005;10(6):853–864. doi:10.1007/s11036-005-4443-7.

23. Voulkidis AC, Anastasopoulos MP, Cottis PG. Energy efficiency in wireless sensor networks: A game-theoretic approach based on coalition formation. ACM Trans Sen Netw. 2013;9(4):43–14327. doi:10.1145/2489253. 2489260.

24. Xiang L, Luo J, Rosenberg C. Compressed data aggregation: Energy-efficient and high-fidelity data collection. IEEE/ACM Trans Netw. 2013;21(6):1722–1735. doi:10.1109/TNET.2012.2229716.

25. Krishnamachari B, Estrin D, Wicker S. The impact of data aggregation in wireless sensor networks. In: 22nd Int. Conf. on Distributed Computing Systems Workshops; 2002. p. 575–578. doi:10.1109/ICDCSW.2002.1030829.

26. Villas LA, Boukerche A, Ramos HS, de Oliveira HABF, de Araujo RB, Loureiro AAF. Drina: A lightweight and reliable routing approach for in-network aggregation in wireless sensor networks. IEEE Trans Comput. 2013;62(4):676–689. doi:10.1109/TC.2012.31.

27. Jeong J, Kim J, Cha W, Kim H, Kim S, Mah P. A qos-aware data aggregation in wireless sensor networks. In: Advanced Communication Technology (ICACT), 2010 The 12th International Conference On. IEEE; 2010. p. 156–161.

28. Tavares ALC, Valente MT. A gentle introduction to OSGi. SIGSOFT Softw Eng Notes. 2008;33(5):8–185. doi:10.1145/1402521.1402526.

29. Costa P, Coulson G, Mascolo C, Picco GP, Zachariadis S. The runes middleware: a reconfigurable component-based approach to networked embedded systems. In: IEEE 16th Int. Symposium on Personal, Indoor and Mobile Radio Communications; 2005. p. 806–8102. doi:10.1109/PIMRC.2005. 1651554.

30. Gay D, Levis P, von Behren R, Welsh M, Brewer E, Culler D. The nesc language: A holistic approach to networked embedded systems. In: ACM Conf. on Programming Language Design and Implementation; 2003. p. 1–11. doi:10.1145/781131.781133.

31. Simon D, Cifuentes C. The squawk virtual machine: Java™ on the bare metal. In: Companion to the 20th Annual ACM SIGPLAN Conference on Object-oriented Programming, Systems, Languages, and Applications. OOPSLA '05. New York: ACM; 2005. p. 150–151. doi:10.1145/1094855.1094908. http://doi.acm.org/10.1145/1094855. 1094908.

32. Thoelen K, Preuveneers D, Michiels S, Joosen W, Hughes D. Types in their prime: Sub-typing of data in resource constrained environments In: Stojmenovic I, Cheng Z, Guo S, editors. Mobile and Ubiquitous Systems: Computing, Networking, and Services. Lecture Notes of the Institute for Computer Sciences, Social Informatics and Telecommunications Engineering. New York: Springer; 2014. p. 250–261.

33. Tanenbaum AS. Computer Networks (4. Ed.) NJ, USA, Prentice Hall; 2002. pp. –1891.

34. Shelby Z, Bormann C. 6LoWPAN: The Wireless Embedded Internet. NJ, USA: Wiley Publishing; 2010.

35. Werner-Allen G, Lorincz K, Ruiz M, Marcillo O, Johnson J, Lees J, Welsh M. Deploying a wireless sensor network on an active volcano. IEEE Internet Comput. 2006;10(2):18–25. doi:10.1109/MIC.2006.26.

36. Szewczyk R, Mainwaring A, Polastre J, Anderson J, Culler D. An analysis of a large scale habitat monitoring application. In: 2nd Int. Conf. on Embedded Networked Sensor Systems. SenSys '04; 2004. p. 214–226. doi:10.1145/1031495.1031521.

37. Logos Electromechanical. Zigduino Manual. 2014. Logos Electromechanical. Rev. 2. http://www.logoselectro.com/documentation/.

38. Texas Instruments. CC2420 Datasheet. 2014. Texas Instruments. http://www.ti.com/product/CC2420.

39. Polastre J, Hill J, Culler D. Versatile low power media access for wireless sensor networks. In: 2nd Int. Conf. on Embedded Networked Sensor Systems. SenSys '04. New York: ACM; 2004. p. 95–107. doi:10.1145/1031495.1031508.

40. Atmel Corporation. ATmega128RFA1 Datasheet. 2012. Atmel Corporation. http://www.atmel.com/devices/atmega1284.aspx.

41. Buettner M, Yee GV, Anderson E, Han R. X-MAC: A short preamble MAC protocol for duty-cycled wireless sensor networks. In: 4th Int. Conf. on Embedded Networked Sensor Systems; 2006. p. 307–320. doi:10.1145/1182807.1182838.

42. Seeedstudio. Shield Bot. 2014. Seeedstudio. http://www.seeedstudio.com/wiki/Shield_Bot.

13

A framework for searching encrypted databases

Pedro G. M. R. Alves[*] [iD] and Diego F. Aranha

Abstract

Cloud computing is a ubiquitous paradigm responsible for a fundamental change in the way distributed computing is performed. The possibility to outsource the installation, maintenance and scalability of servers, added to competitive prices, makes this platform highly attractive to the computing industry. Despite this, privacy guarantees are still insufficient for data processed in the cloud, since the data owner has no real control over the processing hardware. This work proposes a framework for database encryption that preserves data secrecy on an untrusted environment and retains searching and updating capabilities. It employs order-revealing encryption to perform selection with time complexity in $\Theta(\log n)$, and homomorphic encryption to enable computation over ciphertexts. When compared to the current state of the art, our approach provides higher security and flexibility. A proof-of-concept implementation on top of the MongoDB system is offered and applied in the implementation of some of the main predicates required by the winning solution to Netflix Grand Prize.

Keywords: Cryptography, Functional encryption, Homomorphic encryption, Order revealing encryption, Searchable encryption, Databases

1   Introduction

The massive adoption of cloud computing is responsible for a fundamental change in the way distributed computing is performed. The possibility to outsource the installation, maintenance and scalability of servers, added to competitive prices, makes this service highly attractive [1, 2]. From mobile to scientific computing, the industry increasingly embraces cloud services and takes advantage of their potential to improve availability and reduce operational costs [3, 4]. However, the cloud cannot be blindly trusted. Malicious parties may acquire full access to the servers and consequently to data. Among the threats there are external entities exploiting vulnerabilities, intrusive governments requesting information, competitors seeking unfair advantages, and even possibly malicious system administrators. The data owner has no real control over the processing hardware and therefore

cannot guarantee the secrecy of data [5]. The risk of confidentiality breaches caused by inadequate and insecure use of cloud computing is real and tangible.

The importance of privacy preservation is frequently underestimated, as well as the damage its failure represents to society, as the unfolding of a privacy breach may be completely unpredictable. A report from Javelin Advisory Services found a distressing correlation between individuals who were victims of data breaches and later victims of financial fraud. About 75% of total fraud losses in 2016 had this characteristic, corresponding to U\$ 12 billion [6]. This could be avoided with the use of strong encryption at the user side, never revealing data even to the application or the cloud.

The problem of using standard encryption in an entire database is that it eliminates the capability of selecting records or evaluating arbitrary functions without the cryptographic keys, reducing the cloud to a complex and huge storage service. For this reason, alternatives have been proposed to solve this problem, starting from anonymization and heuristic operational measures which do not provide formal privacy guarantees. Encryption schemes tailored for databases such as searchable encryption are a promising solution with perhaps more

*Correspondence: pedro.alves@ic.unicamp.br

This is the extended version of a paper by the same name that appeared in XVI Brazilian Symposium on Information and Computational Systems Security in November, 2016.

Institute of Computing, University of Campinas, Albert Einstein Ave. 1251, 13083-852 Campinas/SP, Brazil

clear benefits [7–10]. Searchable encryption enables the cloud to manipulate encrypted data on behalf of a client without learning information. Hence, it solves both of aforementioned problems, keeping confidentiality in regard to the cloud but retaining some of its interesting features.

1.1 The frustration of data anonymization
In 2006, Netflix shared their interest in improving the recommendation system offered to their users with the academic community. This synergy was directed to an open competition during 3 rounds which offered financial prizes for the best recommendation algorithms. An important feature of Netflix's commercial model is to efficiently and assertively guide subscribers in finding content compatible to their interests. Doing this correctly may reinforce the importance of the product for leisure activities, consolidate Netflix's commercial position, and ensure clients' loyalty [11].

The participants of the contest received a training set with anonymized movie ratings collected from Netflix subscribers between 1999 and 2005. There are approximately half million customers and about 17 thousands movies classified in the set, totalling over 100 million ratings. This dataset is composed by movie titles, the timestamp when the rating was created, the rating itself, and an identification number for relating same-user records. No other information about customers was shared, such as name, address or gender. The objective of the participants was to predict with good accuracy how much someone would enjoy a movie based on their previously observed behavior in the platform.

In the same year, America Online (AOL) took a similar approach and released millions of search queries made by 658,000 of its users with the goal of contributing to the scientific community by enabling statistical work over real data [12]. As Netflix, AOL applied efforts on anonymizing the data before publishing. All the obviously sensitive data, such as usernames and IP addresses, were suppressed, being replaced by unique identification numbers.

The ability to understand user's interests and predict their behavior based on collected data is desirable in several commercial models and consequently a hot topic in the scientific literature [13–15]. However, the importance of privacy-preserving practices is still underestimated, a challenge to overcome. For instance, despite the anonymization efforts of Netflix, Narayanan and Shmatikov brilliantly demonstrated how to break anonymity of the Netflix's dataset by cross-referencing information with public knowledge bases, as those provided by the Internet Movie Database (IMDB) [16]. Using a similar approach, New York Times' reporters were capable of relating a subset of queries to a particular person by joining apparently innocent queries to non-anonymous real state public databases [17].

1.2 "Unexpected" leaks
These events raised a still unsolved discussion about how to safely collect and use data without undermining user privacy. As remarked by Narayanan and Felten, "data privacy is a hard problem" [18]. Even when data holders choose the most conservative practice and never share data, system breaches may happen.

In 2013, a large-scale surveillance program of the USA government was revealed by Edward Snowden, a former NSA employee. Named PRISM, it was structured as a massive data interception effort to collect information for posterior analysis. Their techniques arguably had support of the US legal system and were frequently applicable even without knowledge of the data-owner companies [19, 20].

Two years later, in 2015, stolen personal data of millions of users of the website Ashley Madison was leaked by malicious parties exploiting security vulnerabilities [21]. As consequence, several reports of extortion and even a suicide, illustrating how increasingly sensitive data breaches are becoming.

In the same year, the Sweden's Transport Agency decided to outsource its IT operations to IBM. To fulfill the contract, the latter chose sites in Eastern Europe to place these operations. This resulted in Swedish confidential data being stored in foreign data centers, in particular Czech Republic, Serbia and Romania. As expected, this decision led to a massive data leak, containing information about all vehicles throughout Sweden, including police and military vehicles. Thus, names, photos and home addresses of millions of Swedish citizens, military personal, people under the witness relocation program, were exposed [22].

In 2016, Yahoo confirmed that a massive data breach, possibly the largest known, affected about 500 million accounts and revealed to the world a dataset full of names, addresses, and telephone numbers [23].

These occurrences take us to the disturbing feeling that, despise all efforts, the risk of data deanonymization increases in worrying ways following how much of it is made available [24, 25]. Hence, a seemingly obvious strategy to avoid such issue is to simply stop any kind of dataset collection.

1.3 Privacy by renouncing knowledge
History has proven that the task of collecting and storing data from third parties should be treated as risky. The chance of compromising user privacy by accident is too big and possibly with extreme consequences. This way, the concept of security by renouncing knowledge has attracted adepts, as the search engine DuckDuckGo that states in a blog post that "the only truly anonymised data

is no data", and because of that claims to forego the right to store their users' data [26, 27].

A more financial-realistic approach for dealing with this issue is not to give up completely of knowledge but reduce the entities with access by keeping it encrypted during all its lifespan: transportation, storage, and processing, staying secret to the application and the cloud. Thus, a new security fence is set, tying data secrecy to formal guarantees.

1.4 Our contributions

This work follows the state of the art and proposes directives to the modeling of a searchable encrypted database [28]. We detect the main primitives of a relational algebra necessary to keep the database functional, while adding enhanced privacy-preserving properties. A set of cryptographic tools is used to construct each of these primitives. It is composed by order-revealing encryption to enable data selection, homomorphic encryption for evaluation of arbitrary functions, and a standard symmetric scheme to protect and add flexibility to the handling of general data. In particular, our proposed selection primitive achieves time complexity of $\Theta(\log n)$ on the dataset size. Moreover, we provide a security analysis and performance evaluation to estimate the impact on execution time and space consumption, and a conceptual implementation that validates the framework. It works on top of MongoDB, a popular document-based database, and is implemented as a wrapper over its Python driver. The source code was made available to the community under a GNU GPLv3 license [29].

When compared to CryptDB [7], our proposal provides stronger security since it is able to keep confidentiality even in the case of a compromise of the database and application servers. Since CryptDB delegates to the application server the capability to derive users' cryptographic keys, it is not able to provide such security guarantees. Furthermore, our work is database-agnostic, it is not limited to SQL but can be applied on different key-value databases.

This work is structured as follows. Section 2 describes the cryptographic building blocks required for building our proposed solution. Sections 3 and 4 define searchable encryption, discuss related threats, and present existing implementations. Section 5 proposes our framework, while Section 6 discusses its suitability in a recommendation system for Netflix. Our experimental validation results are presented in Sections 7 and 8 concludes the paper.

2 Building blocks

The two main classes of cryptosystems are known as symmetric and asymmetric (or public-key) and defined by how users exchange cryptographic keys. Symmetric schemes use the same secret key for encryption and decryption, or equivalently can efficiently compute one from the other, while asymmetric schemes generate a pair of keys composed by public and private keys. The former is distributed openly and is the sole information needed to encrypt a message to the key owner, while the latter should be kept secret and used for decryption.

Besides this, cryptosystems that produce always the same ciphertext for the same message-key input pair are known as deterministic. The opposite, when randomness is used during encryption, are known as probabilistic. We next recall basic security notions and special properties that make a cryptosystem suitable to a certain application. Later, we shall make use of these concepts to analyze the security of our proposal.

2.1 Security notions

Ciphertext indistinguishability is a useful property to analyze the security of a cryptosystem. Two scenarios are considered, when an adversary has and does not have access to an oracle that provides decryption capabilities. Usually these are evaluated through a game in which an adversary tries to acquire information from ciphertexts generated by a challenger [30].

Indistinguishability under chosen plaintext attack – IND-CPA In the IND-CPA game the challenger generates a pair (PK, SK) of cryptographic keys, makes PK public and keeps SK secret. An adversary has as objective to recognize a ciphertext created from a randomly chosen message from a known two-element message set. A polynomially bounded number of operations is allowed, including encryption (but not decryption), over PK and the ciphertexts. A cryptosystem is indistinguishable under chosen plaintext attack if no adversary is able to achieve the objective with non-negligible probability.

Indistinguishability under chosen ciphertext attack and adaptive chosen ciphertext attack – IND-CCA1 and IND-CCA2 This type of indistinguishability differs from IND-CPA due to the adversary having access to a decryption oracle. In this game the challenge is again to recognize a ciphertext as described before, but now the adversary is able to use decryption results. This new game has two versions, non-adaptive and adaptive. In the non-adaptive version, IND-CCA1, the adversary may use the decryption oracle until it receives the challenge ciphertext. On the other hand, in the adaptive version he is allowed to use the decryption oracle even after that event. For obvious reasons, the adversary cannot send the challenge ciphertext to the decryption oracle. A cryptosystem is indistinguishable under chosen ciphertext attack/adaptive chosen ciphertext attack if no adversary is able to achieve the objective with non-negligible probability.

Indistinguishability under chosen keyword attack and adaptive chosen keyword attack – IND-CKA and IND-CKA2 This security notion is specific to the context of keyword-based searchable encryption [31]. It considers a scenario in which a challenger builds an index with keyword sets from some documents. This index enables someone to use a value $\mathcal{T}_w$, called trapdoor, to verify if a document contains the word w. This game imposes that no information should be leaked from the remotely stored files or index beyond the outcome and the search pattern of the queries. The adversary has access to an oracle that provides the related trapdoor for any word. His objective is to use this oracle as training to apply the acquired knowledge and break the secrecy of unknown encrypted keywords. As well as in the IND-CCA1/IND-CCA2 game, the non-adaptive version, IND-CKA, of this game forbids the adversary to use the trapdoor oracle once the challenge trapdoor is sent by the challenger. On the other hand, the adaptive version allows the use of the trapdoor oracle even after this event.

A cryptosystem is indistinguishable under chosen keyword attack if every adversary has only a negligible advantage over random guessing.

Indistinguishability under an ordered chosen plaintext attack – IND-OCPA Introduced by Boldyreva et al., this notion supposes that an adversary is capable of retrieving two sequences of ciphertexts resulting of the encryption of any two sequences of messages [32]. Furthermore, he knows that both sequences have identical ordering. The objective of this adversary is to distinguish between these ciphertexts. A cryptosystem is indistinguishable under an ordered chosen plaintext attack if no adversary is able to achieve the objective with non-negligible probability.

2.2 Functional encryption

Cryptographic schemes deemed "functional" receive such name because they support one or more operations over the produced ciphertexts, hence becoming useful not only for secure storage.

Order-revealing encryption (ORE) Order-revealing encryption schemes are characterized by having, in addition to the usual set of cryptographic functions like *keygen* and *encrypt*, a function capable of comparing ciphertexts and returning the order of the original plaintexts, as shown by Definition 1.

Definition 1 (ORE) *Let E be an encryption function, C be a comparison function, and m_1 and m_2 be plaintexts from the message space. The pair (E, C) is defined as an encryption scheme with the order-revealing property if:*

$$C(E(m_1), E(m_2)) = \begin{cases} \text{LOWER}, & \text{if } m_1 < m_2, \\ \text{EQUAL}, & \text{if } m_1 = m_2, \\ \text{GREATER}, & \text{otherwise.} \end{cases}$$

This is a generalization of order-preserving encryption (OPE), that fixes C to a simple numerical comparison [33].

Security As argued by Lewi and Wu, the "best-possible" notion of security for ORE is IND-OCPA, which means that it is possible to achieve indistinguishability of ciphertexts and with a much stronger security guarantee than OPE schemes can have [34]. Furthermore, differently from OPE, ORE is not inherently deterministic [35]. For example, Chenette et al. propose an ORE scheme that applies a pseudo-random function over an OPE scheme, while Lewi and Wu propose an ORE scheme completely built upon symmetric primitives, capable of limiting the use of the comparison function and reducing the leakage inherent to this routine [34, 36]. Their solution works by defining ciphertexts composed by pairs (ct_L, ct_R). To compare ciphertexts ct_A and ct_B, it requires ct_{A_L} and ct_{B_R}. This way, the data owner is capable of storing only one side of those pairs in a remote database being certain that no one will be able to make comparisons between those elements. Nevertheless, any scheme that reveals numerical order of plaintexts through ciphertexts is vulnerable to inference attacks and frequency analysis, as those described by Naveed et al. over relational databases encrypted using deterministic and OPE schemes [37]. Although ORE does not completely discard the possibility of such attacks, it offers stronger defenses.

Homomorphic encryption (HE) Homomorphic encryption schemes have the property of conserving some plaintext structure during the encryption process, allowing the evaluation of certain functions over ciphertexts and obtaining, after decryption, a result equivalent to the same computation applied over plaintexts. Definition 2 presents this property in a more formal way.

Definition 2 (HE) *Let E and D be a pair of encryption and decryption functions, and m_1 and m_2 be plaintexts. The pair (E, D) forms an encryption scheme with the homomorphic property for some operator $\diamond$ if and only if the following holds:*

$$E(m_1) \circ E(m_2) \equiv E(m_1 \diamond m_2).$$

The operation $\circ$ in the ciphertext domain is equivalent to $\diamond$ in the plaintext domain.

Homomorphic cryptosystems are classified according to the supported operations and their limitations. *Partially homomorphic encryption* schemes (PHE) hold on Definition 2 for either addition or multiplication operations, while *fully homomorphic encryption* schemes (FHE) support both addition and multiplication operations.

PHE cryptosystems have been known for decades [38, 39]. However, the most common data processing applications, as those arising from statistics, machine learning or genomics processing, frequently require support for both addition and multiplication operations simultaneously. This way, such schemes are not suitable for general computation.

Nowadays, FHE performance is prohibitive, so weaker variants, such as SHE[1] and LHE[2], have the stage for solving computational problems of moderate complexity [40, 41].

Security In terms of security, homomorphic encryption schemes achieve at most IND-CCA1, which means that the scheme is not secure against an attacker with arbitrary access to a decryption oracle [30]. This is a natural consequence of the design requirements, since these cryptosystems allow any entity to manipulate ciphertexts. Most of current proposals, however, reach at most IND-CPA and stay secure against attackers without access to a decryption oracle [42].

3   Searchable encryption

We now formally define the problem of searching over encrypted data. We present three state-of-the-art implementations of solutions to this problem, namely the CryptDB, Arx, and Seabed database systems.

3.1   The problem

Suppose a scenario where Alice keeps a set of documents in untrusted storage maintained by an also untrusted entity Bob. She would like to keep this data encrypted because, as defined, Bob cannot be trusted. Alice also would like to occasionally retrieve a subset of documents accordingly to a predicate without revealing any sensitive information to Bob. Thus, sharing the decryption key is not an option. The problem lies in the fact that communication between Alice and Bob may (and probably will) be constrained. Hence, a naive solution consisting of Bob sending all documents to Alice and letting her decrypt and select whatever she wants may not be feasible. Alice must then implement some mechanism to protect her encrypted data so that Bob will be able to identify the desired documents without knowing their contents or the selection criteria [43].

An approach that Alice can take is to create an encrypted index as in Definition 3.

Definition 3 (Encrypted indexing) *Suppose a dataset* $\mathcal{DB} = (m_1, \dots, m_n)$ *and a list* $\mathcal{W} = (W_1, \dots, W_n)$ *of sets of keywords such that* W_i *contains keywords for* m_i*. The*

following routines are required to build and search on an encrypted index:

BUILDINDEX$_K(\mathcal{DB}, \mathcal{W})$**:** *The list* $\mathcal{W}$ *is encrypted using a searchable scheme under a key K and results in a searchable encrypted index* $\mathcal{I}$*. This process may not be reversible (e.g., if a hash function is used). The routine outputs* $\mathcal{I}$*.*

TRAPDOOR$_K(\mathcal{F})$**:** *This function receives a predicate* $\mathcal{F}$ *and outputs a trapdoor* $\mathcal{T}$*. The latter is defined as the information needed to search* $\mathcal{I}$ *and find records that satisfy* $\mathcal{F}$*.*

SEARCH$_\mathcal{I}(\mathcal{T})$**:** *It iterates through* $\mathcal{I}$ *applying the trapdoor* $\mathcal{T}$ *and outputs every record that returns* TRUE *for the input trapdoor.*

This way, if the searchable cryptosystem used is IND-CKA then Alice is able to keep her data with Bob and remain capable of selecting subsets of it without revealing information [28].

3.2   Threat modeling

The development of efficient and secure solutions for management of datasets depends on the awareness of the threats we intend to mitigate. For such, this work follows Grubbs' definitions of adversaries for a database [44].

Active attacker The worst case scenario is when the attacker acquires full control over the server, being capable of performing arbitrary operations. Thus, he is not committed to follow any protocol.

Snapshot attacker The adversary obtains a snapshot of the dataset containing the primary data and indexes but no information about issued queries and how they access the encrypted data.

Persistent passive attacker Another possibility is a scenario in which the attack cannot interfere with the server functionality but can observe all of its operations. We do not consider only attackers that inspect issued queries in real-time, but also those that are able to recover them later. As demonstrated by Grubbs, the data contained in a real-world database goes far beyond the primary dataset (names, addresses, ...). It also includes logs, caches, and auxiliary tables (as MySQL's diagnostic tables) used, for instance, to guarantee *ACID*[3] and enable the server to undo incomplete queries after a power-break. It is very likely that an attacker competent to subjugate the security protocols of the system will be capable to also recover these secondary datasets.

The idea of a *snapshot attacker* is very popular among solutions and researchers intended to develop encrypted databases. Nevertheless, it underestimates the attacker and the many side-attacks a motivated adversary can execute. As Rogaway remarks, we cannot make the mistake to reduce the adversary to the lazy and abstract Bob, but we must remember that it can go far beyond that and take the form of a military-industrial-surveillance program with a billionaire budget and capability to surpass the obvious [45].

4   Related work

The management of a dataset is made by a database management system (DBMS). It is composed by several layers responsible for coordinating read and write operations, guarantee data consistency and integrity, and user access. The engineering of such a system is a complex task and requires smart optimizations to be able to store data, process queries and return the outcome with minimum latency and good scalability.

This way, searchable encryption solutions usually are implemented not inside but on top of these systems as a middleware to translate encrypted queries to the DBMS without revealing plaintext data and decrypt the outcome, as shown in Fig. 1. This strategy enables the use of decades of optimizations incorporated in nowadays DBMSs and portable to encrypted data. It is important to state that, ideally, security features should be designed in conjunction with the underlying database. Long-term solutions are expected to assimilate those strategies internally in the DBMS core.

4.1   CryptDB

CryptDB is a software layer that provides capabilities to store data in a remote SQL database and query over it without revealing sensitive information to the DBMS. It introduces a proxy layer responsible to encrypt and adjust queries to the database and decrypt the outcome [7].

The context in which CryptDB stands is a typical structure of database-backed applications, consisting of a DBMS server and a separate application server. To query a database, a predicate is generated by the application and processed by the proxy before it is sent to the DBMS server. The user interacts exclusively with the application server and is responsible for keeping his password secret. This is provided on login to the proxy (via application) that derives all the cryptographic keys required to interact with the database. When the user logs out, it is expected that the proxy deletes its keys.

Data encryption is done through the concept of "onions", which consist of layers of encryption that are combined to provide different functionalities, as shown in Fig. 2. Such layers are revealed as necessary to process the queries being performed. Modeling a database involves evaluating the meaning of each attribute and predicting the operations it must support. In particular, keyword-searching as described in Definition 3 is implemented as proposed in Song's work [43]. The performance overhead over MySQL measured by the authors is up to 30%.

Two types of threats are treated in CryptDB: curious database administrators who try to snoop and acquire information about client's data but respect the established protocols (a *persistent passive attacker*); and an adversary that gains complete control of application and DBMS servers (an *active attacker*). The authors state that the first threat is mitigated through the encryption of stored data and the ability to query it without

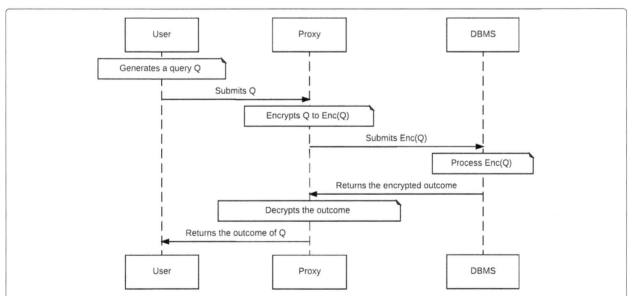

Fig. 1 Sequence diagram representing the process of generating and processing an encrypted query. The proxy is positioned between the user and the DBMS in a trusted environment. Its responsibility is to receive a plaintext query, apply an encryption protocol, submit the encrypted query to the DBMS, and decrypt the outcome

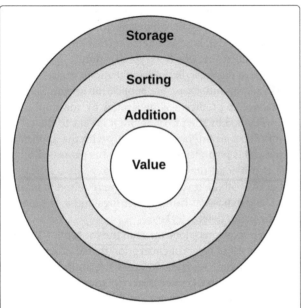

Fig. 2 Representation of the data format used by CryptDB. The current value to be protected lies in the center, and a new encryption layer is overlapped to it according to the need of a particular functionality

any decryption or knowledge about its content; while the second applies only to logged-in clients. In the considered scenario, the cryptographic keys relative to data in the database are handled by the application server. Thus, if the application server is compromised, all the keys it possesses at that moment (that are expected to be only from logged-in users) are leaked to the attacker. Such arguments were revisited after works by Naveed and Grubbs et al. demonstrated how to explore several weaknesses of the construction, such as the application of OPE [46, 47].

4.2 Arx

Arx is a database system implemented on top of MongoDB [8]. It targets much stronger security properties and claims to protect the database with the same level of regular AES-based encryption[4], achieving IND-CPA security. This is a direct consequence of the almost exclusively use of AES to construct selection operators, even on range queries, and not only brings strong security but also good performance due to efficiency of symmetric primitives, sometimes even benefiting from hardware implementations. The authors report a performance overhead of approximately 10% when used to replace the database of ShareLatex. The building blocks used for searching follow those described in Definition 3. Furthermore, they apply a different AES key for each keyword when generating the trapdoor, requiring the client to store counters, as explained in the next paragraph.

At its core, Arx introduces two database indexes, ARX-RANGE for range and order-by-limit queries and ARX-EQ for equality queries, both built on top of AES and using chained garbled circuits. The former uses an obfuscation strategy to protect data, while enabling searches in logarithmic time. The latter embeds a counter into each repeating value. This ensures that the encryption of both are different, protecting them against frequency analysis. Using a token provided by the client, the database is able to expand it in many search tokens and return all the occurrences desired, allowing an index to be built over encrypted data.

The context in which Arx stands is similar to CryptDB. However, the authors consider the data owner as the application itself. This way, it simplifies the security measures and considers the responsibility to keep the application server secure outside of its scope.

4.3 Seabed

Seabed was developed by Papadimitriou et al. and aims at Business Intelligence (BI) applications interested in keeping data secure on the cloud [48]. As well as CryptDB and Arx, Seabed was built consisting of a client-side query translator (to SQL), a query planner, and a proxy that connects to a Apache Spark instance [49]. Its main foundations are two new cryptographic constructions, *additively symmetric homomorphic encryption* (ASHE) and *Splayed ASHE* (SPLASHE). The former is used to replace Paillier as the additively homomorphic encryption scheme, stating that their construction is up to three orders of magnitude faster. The latter is used to protect the database against inference attacks [37].

SPLASHE works by splitting sensitive data into multiple attributes, obscuring the low-entropy of deterministic encryption. Formally, let C be a sensitive attribute of a dataset that can be filled with d possible discrete values. The approach taken by SPLASHE is to replace this attribute in the encrypted database by $\{C_1, C_2, \cdots, C_d\}$ such that $C_v = 1$ and $C_t = 0$ for $t \neq v$ if $C = v$. When encrypted by ASHE the ciphertexts will look random to the adversary.

Seabed's authors argue that SPLASHE is strong enough to mitigate frequency analysis, enabling the use of deterministic encryption whenever it is required in the database model. However, Grubbs states that SPLASHE's protection may be deflected through the auxiliary data stored by the database [44]. Their work demonstrates how state-of-the-art databases store metadata that can be used to reconstruct issued queries and, this way, recognize access patterns on the attributes. Such patterns leak the information that SPLASHE intended to hide. Considering this, the only threat really mitigated by SPLASHE against the deterministic encryption of Seabed is from a *snapshot attacker*.

5 Proposed framework

The goal of the proposed framework is to develop a database model capable of storing encrypted records and applying relational algebra primitives on it without the knowledge of any cryptographic keys or the need for decryption. A trade-off between performance and security is desirable, however we completely discard deterministic encryption whenever possible for security reasons. The only exception are contexts with unique records, which avoid by definition weaknesses intrinsic to deterministic encryption. The applicability of this framework goes beyond SQL databases. Besides the relational algebra hereby used to describe the framework, it can be extended to key-value, document-oriented, full text and several other databases classes that keep the same attribute structure.

The three main operations needed to build a useful database are insertion, selection and update. Once data is loaded, being able to select only those pieces that correspond to an arbitrary predicate is the basic block to construct more complex operations, such as grouping and equality joins. This functionality is fundamental when there is a physical separation between the database and the data owner, otherwise high demand for bandwidth is incurred to transmit large fractions of the database records. Furthermore, real data is frequently mutable and thus the database must support updates to remain useful.

We define as *secure* a system model that guarantees that the data owner is the only entity capable of revealing data, which can be achieved by his exclusive possession of the cryptographic keys. Thus, a fundamental aspect of our proposal is the scenario in which the database and the application server handle data with minimum knowledge.

Lastly, the framework does not ensure integrity, freshness or completeness of results returned to the application or the user, since an adversary that compromises the database in some way can delete or alter records. We consider this threat to be outside the scope of this framework.

5.1 Classes of attributes

Records in an encrypted database are composed by attributes. These consist of a name and a value, that can be an integer, float, string or even a binary blob. Values of attributes are classified according to their purpose:

static An immutable value only used for storage. It is not expected to be evaluated with any function, so there is no special requirement for its encryption.

index Used for building a single or multivalued searchable index. It should enable one to verify if an arbitrary term is contained in a set without the need to acquire knowledge of its content.

computable A mutable value. It supports the evaluation with arithmetic circuits and ensures obtaining, after decryption, a result equivalent to the same circuit applied over plaintexts.

The implementation of each attribute must satisfy the requirements without leaking any vital information beyond those related directly with the attribute objective (e.g.: order for *index* attributes). Since the name of an attribute reveals information, it may need to be protected as well. However, the acknowledgement of an attribute is done using its name, so even anonymous attributes must be traceable in a query. An option for anonymizing the attribute name is to treat it as an *index*.

The aforementioned cryptosystems are natural suggestions to be applied within these classes. Since *static* is a class for storage only, which has no other requirements, any scheme with appropriate security level and performance may be used, as AES. On the other hand, *index* and *computable* attributes are immediate applications of ORE and HE schemes. Particularly, the latter defines the HE scheme according to the required operations. Attributes that require only one operation can be implemented with a PHE scheme, which provides good performance; while those that require arbitrary additions and multiplications must use FHE and deal with the performance issues.

Definition 4 (Secure ORE) *Let E and C be, respectively, an encryption and a comparison function. The pair (E, C) forms an encryption scheme with the order-revealing property defined as "secure" if and only if it satisfies Definition 1; the encryption of a message m can be written as $E(m) = (c_L, c_R) = (E_L(m), E_R(m))$, where E_L and E_R are complementary encryption functions; and the comparison between two ciphertexts c_1 and c_2 is done by $C(c_{L1}, c_{R2})$. This way, C may be applied without the complete knowledge of the ciphertexts.*

In order to build a secure and efficient *index*, an ORE scheme that corresponds to Definition 4 should be used. We define the search framework as in Definition 5.

Definition 5 (Encrypted search framework) *Let S be a set of words, sk a secret key, and an ORE scheme (ENC, CMP) that satisfies Definition 4. The operations required for an encrypted search over S are defined as follows:*

BUILDINDEX$_{sk}(S)$: *Outputs the set*

$$S^* = \{c_R \mid (c_L, c_R) = \text{ENC}_{sk}(w), \forall w \in S\}.$$

TRAPDOOR$_{sk}(w)$: *Outputs the trapdoor*

$$\mathcal{T}_w = (c_L \mid (c_L, c_R) = \text{ENC}_{sk}(w)).$$

SEARCH$_{S^*,r}(\mathcal{T}_w)$: *To select all records in S^* with the relation $r \in \{$LOWER, EQUAL, GREATER$\}$ to word w, one computes the trapdoor $\mathcal{T}_w$ and iterates through S^* looking for the records $w^* \in S^*$ that satisfy*

$$\text{CMP}\left(\mathcal{T}_w, w^*\right) = r.$$

The set $\hat{S}$ with all the elements in S^* that satisfy this equation is returned.

5.2 Database operations

Let us consider a model composed by an encrypted dataset stored in a remote server and a user that possesses the secret cryptographic keys. The latter would like to perform queries on data without revealing sensitive information to the server, as defined in Section 3.1.

In 1970, Codd proposed the use of a relational algebra as a model for SQL [50]. This consists of a small set of operators that can be combined to execute complex queries over the data.

Through the functions defined in Definition 5, a relational algebra for encrypted database operations can be built. The basic operators for such algebra are defined as follows.

1. **Projection** (π_A): Returns a subset A of attributes from selected records. This subset may be defined by attribute names that may or may not be encrypted.

   (a) *encrypted*: If encrypted, a deterministic scheme is used or they are treated as *index* values.
   deterministic scheme: The user computes $A^* = \{Enc_{Det}(a)|a \in A\}$. A^* is sent to the server, which picks the projected attributes using a standard algorithm.
   index attributes: The user computes $A^* = \{Trapdoor_{sk}(a)|a \in A\}$. A^* is sent to the server, which picks the projected attributes using SEARCH.

   (b) *unencrypted*: Unencrypted selectors are sent to and selected by the server using a standard algorithm.

2. **Selection** (σ_φ): Given a predicate φ, returns only the records satisfying it.

   - Handles exclusively *index*, hence φ must be equivalent to a combination of comparative operators supported by SEARCH.
   - Let $w \diamond x \leftarrow \varphi$, where $\diamond$ is a compatible comparative operator, w an *index* attribute, and x the operand to be compared (e.g.: $\sigma_{age>30}$ signals for records which the attribute named "age" value is greater than 30). The trapdoor

$\mathcal{T}_\varphi = Trapdoor_{sk}(\varphi)$ is sent to the server that executes SEARCH.

3. **Cartesian product** ($\times$): The Cartesian product of two datasets is executed using a standard algorithm.

4. **Difference** ($-$): The difference between two datasets A and B encrypted with the same keys is defined as $A - B = \{x \mid x \in A \text{ and } x \notin B\}$.

5. **Union** ($\cup$): The union of two datasets A and B encrypted with the same keys is defined as $A \cup B = \{x \mid x \in A \text{ or } x \in B\}$.

Union and difference are defined over datasets with the same set of attributes. The opposite is expected for Cartesian product, so that no attribute may be shared between operands.

Ramakrishnan calls these "basic operators" in the sense that they are essential and sufficient to execute relational operations [51]. Additional useful operators can be built over those. For instance: rename, join-like, and division. The same observation applies in the encrypted domain, and complex operators can be constructed given basic operators defined over the encrypted domain.

6. **Rename** ($\rho_{a,b}$): Renames attributes. Their names may or may not be encrypted.

   (a) *encrypted*: Encryption shall be executed using a deterministic cryptosystem or names treated as *index* values.

   deterministic scheme: Let a be an attribute name to be replaced by b. The user computes $a^* \leftarrow Enc_{Det}(a)$ and $b^* \leftarrow Enc_{Det}(b)$, and sends the output to the server, which applies a standard replacement algorithm.

   index attributes: Let a be an attribute name to be replaced by b. The user computes $a^* \leftarrow Trapdoor(a)$ and $b^* \leftarrow c_R \mid (c_L, c_R) = Enc_{index}(b)$ and sends the output to to the server, which selects attributes related to a^* as EQUAL through the operation SEARCH and renames the result to b^*.

   (b) *unencrypted*: Unencrypted attribute names may be renamed by the server using a standard algorithm.

7. **Natural join** ($\bowtie$): Let A and B be datasets with a common subset of attributes. The natural join between A and B is defined as the selection of all elements that lies in A and B and match all the values in those attributes. More formally, let $c_1, c_2, \dots, c_n$ be attributes common to A and B; $x_1, x_2, \dots, x_n$ attributes not contained in A or in B; $a_1, a_2, \dots, a_m$

be attributes unique to A; $b_1, b_2, \ldots, b_k$ be attributes unique to B; and $\mathbb{K} = \mathbb{N}_{n+1}^*$. We have that,

$$A \bowtie B \equiv \sigma_{c_i = x_i} \left(\rho_{(c_i, x_i)}(A) \times B \right), \forall i \in \mathbb{K}.$$

8. **Equi-join** ($\bowtie_\theta$): Let A and B be datasets. The equi-join between A and B is defined as the selection of all elements that lie in A and B and satisfy a condition θ. More formally, $A \bowtie B = \sigma_\theta (A \times B)$.
9. **Division** ($/$): Let A and B be datasets and C the subset of attributes unique to A. The division operator joins the operands by common attributes but projects only those unique to the dividend. Hence, $A/B = \pi_C (A \bowtie B)$.

Finally, it is important to define data insertion and update despite these cannot be properly defined as relational operators.

- **Insert**: Encrypted data is provided and inserted into the database using a standard algorithm.
- **Update**: An update operation is defined as a selection followed by the evaluation of a *computable* attribute by a supported homomorphic operation.

This set of operators enables operating over an encrypted database without the knowledge of cryptographic keys or acquiring sensitive information from user queries.

5.3 Security analysis

We assume the scenario in which the data owner has exclusive possession of cryptographic keys. This way, insertions to the database must be locally encrypted before being sent to the server. The database or the application never deal with plaintext data. Our framework thus has the advantage over CryptDB of preserving privacy even in the outcome of a compromised database or application server.

Despite being conceptually similar to OPE, ORE is able to address several of its security limitations. ORE does not necessarily generate ciphertexts that reveal their order by design, but allows someone to protect this information by only revealing it through specific functions. ORE is able to achieve the IND-OCPA security notion and adds randomization to ciphertexts. Those characteristics make it much safer against inference attacks [37]. The proposal of Lewi and Wu goes even beyond that and is capable of limiting the use of the comparison function [34]. Their scheme generates a ciphertext that can be decomposed into left and right components such that a comparison between two ciphertexts requires only a left component of one ciphertext and the right component of the other. This way, the authors argue that robustness against such attacks is ensured since the database dump may only contain the

right component, that is encrypted using semantically-secure encryption. Their scheme satisfies our notion of a *Secure ORE* and, therefore, provides strong defenses against *Snapshot attackers*.

An eavesdropper (*Active* or *Persistent passive attacker*) is not capable of executing comparisons by himself in a *Secure ORE*. However he may learn the result of these and recognize repeated queries by observing the outcome of a selection. This weakness may still be used for inference attacks, that can breach confidentiality from related attributes. This issue can get worse if the trapdoor is deterministic, when there is no other solution than implementing a key refreshment algorithm. Besides that, the knowledge of the numerical order between every pair of elements in a sequence may leak information depending on the application. This problem manifests itself in our proposal on the σ primitive if it uses a weak index structure, like a naive sequential index. A balanced-tree-based structure, on the other hand, obscures the numerical order of elements in different branches. This way, an attacker is capable of recovering the order of up to $O(\log n)$ database elements and infer about the others, in a database with n elements.

Schemes used with *computable* attributes are limited to IND-CCA1, and typically reach only IND-CPA. Moreover, homomorphic ciphertexts are malleable by design. Thus, an attacker that acquires knowledge about a ciphertext can use it to predictably manipulate others.

Finally, BUILDINDEX is not able to hide the quantity of records that share the same index. This way, one is able to make inferences about those by the number of records. There is also no built-in protection for the number of entries in the database. A workaround is to fix the size of each *static* attribute value and round the quantity of records in the database using padding. This approach increases secrecy but also the storage overhead.

5.4 Performance analysis

The application of ORE as the main approach to build a database index provides an extremely important contribution to selection queries. SEARCH does not require walking through all the records testing a trapdoor, but only a logarithmic subset of it when implemented over an optimal index structure, such as an AVL tree or B-tree based structure [52]. This characteristic is highlighted on union, intersection and difference operations, which work by comparing and selecting elements in different groups. Moreover, current proposals in the state of the art of ORE enjoy good performance provided by symmetric primitives and does not require more expensive approaches such as public-key cryptography [33, 34, 36]. In particular, although fully homomorphic cryptosystems promise to fulfill this task and progress has been made with new cryptographic constructions [53], it is still prohibitively expensive for real-world deployments [54].

Space consumption is also affected. Ciphertexts are computed as a combination of the plaintext with random data. This way, a non-trivial expansion rate is expected. Differently from speed overheads which are affected by a single attribute type, all attributes suffer with the expansion rate of encryption.

5.5 Capabilities and limitations

Our framework is capable of providing an always-encrypted database that preserves secrecy as long as the data owner keeps the cryptographic keys secure. One is able to select records through *index* and apply arbitrary operations on attributes defined as *computable*. Furthermore, it increases the security of data but maintaining the computational complexity of standard relational primitives, achieving a fair trade-off between security and performance.

Although the framework has no constraints about attributes classified as both *index* and *computable*, there is no known encryption scheme in the literature capable of satisfying all the requirements. This way, the relational model of the database must be as precise as possible when assigning attributes to each class, specially because the costs of a model refactor can be prohibitive.

Some scenarios appear to be more compatible with an encrypted database as described than others. An e-mail service, for example, can be trivially adapted. The e-mails received by a user are stored in encrypted form as *static* and some heuristic is applied on its content to generate a set of keywords to be used on BUILDINDEX. This heuristic may use all unique words in the e-mail, for example. The sender address may be an important value for querying as well, so it may be stored as an *index*. To optimize common queries, a secondary collection of records may be instantiated with, for example, counters. The quantity of e-mails received from a particular sender, how often a term appears or how many messages are received in a time

frame. Storing this metadata information in a secondary data collection avoids some of the high costs of searching in the main dataset.

However, our proposal fails when the user wants to search for something that was not previously expected. For example, regular expressions. Suppose a query that searches for all the sentences that start with "Attack" and end with "dawn", or all the e-mails on the domain "mail.com". If these patterns were not foreseen when the keyword index was built, then no one will be able to correctly execute this selection without the decryption of the entire database. Since the format of the strings is lost on encryption, this kind of search is impossible in our proposal.

Lastly, relational integrity is a desired property for a relational database. It connects two or more sets using same-value attributes in both sets (e.g.: every value of a column in a table *A* exists in a column in table *B*), and establishes a *primary-foreign* key relationship. This way, the existence of a record in an attribute classified as *foreign* key depends on the existence of the related record on the other set, in which the *primary* key is equal to that *foreign* key. To implement such feature one must provide to the DBMS capabilities to reinforce relational integrity rules. In other words, the server must be able to recognize such a relationship to guarantee it will be respected by issued queries.

An example of the applicability of this concept is an e-commerce database. Best practices dictate that user data should be stored separately from products and orders. Thus, one may model it as in Fig. 3. When a new order arrives, it is clear that a user chose some product and informed the store about his intent to buy it. Users and products are concrete elements. However, a sale is an abstract object and cannot happen without a buyer and a product. This way, to maintain the consistency of the database the DBMS must assure that no sale record will exist without relating user and product. This can be achieved by constructing the sales table such

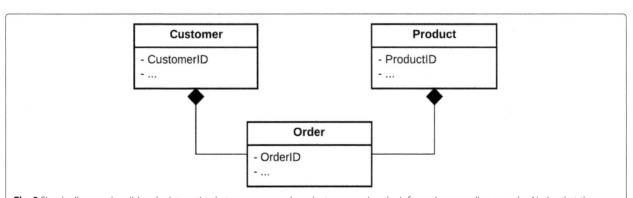

Fig. 3 Simple diagram describing the interaction between users and products composing the information regarding an order. Notice that the existence of users and products is independent, but there is a dependence for orders

that records contain *foreign* keys for the user and product tables (implying that these contain attributes classified as *primary* keys). By definition this feature imposes an inherent requirement that the DBMS has knowledge about this relationship between records on different tables. Any approach to protect the attributes against third parties will affect the DBMS itself and will never really achieve the needed protection. Thus, any effort on implementing secure relational integrity is at best security through obscurity[5].

6 The winner solution of Netflix's prize

The winner of Netflix Grand Prize was BellKor's Pragmatic Chaos team, who built a solution over the progress achieved in the 2007 and 2008 Progress Prizes [55]. Several machine learning predictors were combined in the final solution with the objective of anticipating the suitability of Netflix content for some user considering previous behavior in the platform. The foundation used for this considered diverse factors, such as:

- What is the general behavior of users when rating? What is the average rating?
- How critic is a user and how this changes over time?
- Does the user demonstrate preference for a specific movie or gender?
- Does the user demonstrate preference for blockbusters or non-mainstream content?
- What property of a movie affects the rating? Is there a correlation between the rating of a user and the presence of a particular actor in a particular gender?

The strategy used to combine these factors (and many others) escapes the scope of this work. We should attend only to the necessity of extracting data from the dataset to feed the learning model.

6.1 Searching the encrypted Netflix's database

An interesting application of our framework is enabling an entity to maintain an encrypted database on third party hardware with a similar structure of Netflix's dataset and being able to implement a prediction algorithm with minimum data leakage to the DBMS. The database should be capable of answering the requested predicates regarding user behavior.

Two scenarios must be considered: the recommendation system running on Netflix's infrastructure, and the dataset becoming public. The former offers an execution environment apparently honest (no one would share data with an openly malicious party) but that can be compromised at some point. To mitigate the damage, the data owner can implement different strategies to reduce the usefulness of any leakage that might happen. Thus, data being handled exclusively in encrypted form on the server is a natural option, since security breaches would reveal nothing but incomprehensible ciphertexts. This is the best case scenario since the data owner has as much control of the execution machine as possible, so our framework proposal can be applied in its full capacity.

As an example of the latter, an important feature required for running the Netflix's prize is the capability of in-dataset comparisons. This time any security solution should find the balance between protecting data secrecy and offering conditions for experimentation. Moreover, we must consider that the execution environment cannot be considered honest anymore. This way, the suitability of our framework depends on the relaxation of the indexing method. *index* values must be published to enable comparisons. For instance, both sides of Lewi-Wu's ciphertexts should be published, or even an OPE scheme may be used on the encryption of the index. From the perspective of the secrecy of ciphertexts, if a IND-OCPA scheme is used then there will be no security reduction beyond what the corresponding threat model expects, as discussed in Section 2.1. The adversary learns the ciphertext order but has restricted ability to make inferences using information acquired from public databases. The only strategy that can be applied uses the data distribution in the dataset (that can be retrieved by enabling comparisons), which puts an attacker in this scenario in a very similar position than the persistent passive attacker.

Given the boundary conditions for privacy preservation, we cannot precisely state the robustness of our framework in the context of the Netflix prize. It clearly increases the hardness against an inference attack, since the adversary is unable to observe the plaintext, but the distribution leaked will give him hints about its content. For instance, the correlation of age groups and most watched (or better rated) movies. It is a fact that all these are expressed as ciphertexts, but as previously stated, a motivated adversary may be able to combine such hints and defeat our security barriers.

Our framework performs much better in the more conservative scenario, where a production server provides recommendations to users with comparisons controlled by the data owner through the two-sided *index* attributes. The impossibility for arbitrary comparisons makes snapshot attacks completely infeasible.

As previously discussed, a motivated adversary with access to the database may be able to also retrieve logs and auxiliary collections. Consequently, previous queries may leak the second side of *index* ciphertexts and recall the danger of persistent passive attacks. So, an important feature for future work is the development of a key refreshment algorithm to nullify the usefulness of such information.

6.2 Data structure

The dataset shared by Netflix is composed by more than 100 million real movie ratings from 480,000 users about 17,000 movies, made between 1999 and 2005, and formatted as a training test set [11, 55]. It contains a subset of 4.2 million of those ratings, with up to 9 ratings per user. It consists of:

- *CustomerID:* A unique identification number per user,
- *MovieID:* A unique identification number per movie,
- *Title:* The English title of the movie,
- *YearOfRelease:* The year the movie was released,
- *Rating:* The rating itself,
- *Date:* The timestamp informing when the rating happened.

6.3 Constructing queries of interest over encrypted data

Following we rewrite some of the main predicates required for BellKor's solution using the relational algebra of Section 5.2, thus enabling their execution over an encrypted dataset.

Let

- $\mathcal{DB}$ be a dataset as described in Section 6.2,
- AID be the CustomerID related to a particular user (that we shall call Alice),
- BID be the CustomerID related to a particular user different to Alice (that we shall call Bob),
- MID be the MovieID related to an arbitrary movie in the dataset (that we should refer as $\mathcal{M}$),
- $\mathcal{T} = (\mathcal{T}_{\text{start}}, \mathcal{T}_{\text{end}})$ be a time interval of interest,
- $\mathcal{T}_{\text{first-alice}}$ be the timestamp of the first rating Alice ever made,
- $\mathcal{C}()$ be a function that receives a set and returns the quantity of items contained,
- r_{H} and r_{L} be thresholds for extreme ratings characterizing users that hated or loved a movie,
- $\sigma_{Date\in\mathcal{T}}(\mathcal{DB}) \equiv \sigma_{Date\,\geq\,\mathcal{T}_{\text{start}}}(\mathcal{DB}) + \sigma_{Date\,<\,\mathcal{T}_{\text{end}}}(\mathcal{DB})$,
- $f(X) = \frac{\sum_{x\in X}\pi_{Rating}(x)}{\mathcal{C}(X)}$.

Then, some of the required predicates for BellKor's solution are:

- **Movies rated by Alice:** Returns all movies that received some rating from Alice. For

$$U(X) = \sigma_{CustomerID=X}(\mathcal{DB}),$$

we have the query

$$\pi_{\text{MovieID}}(U(\text{AID})). \tag{1}$$

- **Users who rated M:** Returns all users that sent some rating for MID. For

$$M(X) = \sigma_{MovieID=\text{MID}}(\mathcal{DB}),$$

we have the query

$$\pi_{CustomerID}(M(\text{MID})). \tag{2}$$

- **Average of Alice's ratings over time:** Computes the average of all rates sent by Alice during a particular time interval $\mathcal{T}$. For

$$\mathcal{A}_{\text{AID},\mathcal{T}} = \sigma_{Date\in\mathcal{T}}(U(\text{AID})),$$

we have that

$$\text{avg}(\text{AID}, \mathcal{T}) = \begin{cases} f(\mathcal{A}_{\text{AID},\mathcal{T}}) \text{ if } \mathcal{C}(\mathcal{A}_{\text{AID},\mathcal{T}}) > 0, \\ 0, \text{otherwise.} \end{cases} \tag{3}$$

- **Average of ratings for a particular movie M in a timeset:** Computes the average of all rates sent by all users during a particular time interval $\mathcal{T}$ for a movie $\mathcal{M}$. For

$$\mathcal{M}_{\text{MID},\mathcal{T}} = \sigma_{Date\in\mathcal{T}}(M(\text{MID}))$$

we have that

$$\text{avg}(\text{MID}, \mathcal{T}) = \begin{cases} f(\mathcal{M}_{\text{MID},\mathcal{T}}) \text{ if } \mathcal{C}(\mathcal{M}_{\text{MID},\mathcal{T}}) > 0, \\ 0, \text{otherwise.} \end{cases} \tag{4}$$

- **Number of days since Alice's first rating:** Computes how many days have been since the Alice submitted the first rating of movie, relative to a moment $\mathcal{I}$.

$$\text{dsf}(\text{AID}, \mathcal{I}) = \mathcal{I} - \pi_{Date}(\sigma_{min(Date)}(U(\text{AID}))). \tag{5}$$

- **Quantity of users who hated $\mathcal{M}$:** Counts the quantity of very bad ratings $\mathcal{M}$ received since its release.

$$\mathcal{C}_H(\mathcal{M}) = \mathcal{C}\left(\sigma_{\text{MovieID}=\text{MID}}(\sigma_{Rating\leq r_H}(\mathcal{DB}))\right). \tag{6}$$

- **Quantity of users who loved $\mathcal{M}$:** Counts the quantity of very good ratings $\mathcal{M}$ received since its release.

$$\mathcal{C}_L(\mathcal{M}) = \mathcal{C}\left(\sigma_{\text{MovieID}=\text{MID}}(\sigma_{Rating\geq r_L}(\mathcal{DB}))\right). \tag{7}$$

- **Users that are similar to Alice:** The similarity assessment between users require the derivation of a specific metric according to the boundary-conditions. The winning solution developed a sophisticated strategy, building a graph of neighborhoods considering similar movies and users and computing a weighted mean of the ratings. For simplicity, we shall condense two factors that can be used for this objective: the set of common rated movies, and how close the ratings are. To query the movies rated both by Alice and Bob, let

$$\alpha_{\text{AID}} = \pi_{\text{MovieID,RatingA}}\left(\rho_{Rating,RatingA}(U(\text{AID}))\right)$$

and

$$\beta_{\text{BID}} = \pi_{\text{MovieID,RatingB}}(\rho_{\text{Rating,RatingB}}(U(\text{BID}))).$$

Then

$$\text{SIMILARITYSET (AID, BID)} = \alpha_{AID} \bowtie \beta_{BID} \quad (8)$$

returns a sequence of tuples of ratings made by Alice and Bob. A simple approach for evaluating proximity is to compute the average of the difference of ratings for each movie returned by Eq. 8, as shown in Eq. 9.

$$\frac{\sum_{\text{SIMILARITYSET(AID,BID)}} |\text{RatingA} - \text{RatingB}|}{\mathcal{C}(\text{SIMILARITYSET (AID, BID)})} \quad (9)$$

7 Implementation

A proof-of-concept implementation of the proposed framework was developed and made available to the community under a *GNU GPLv3* license [29]. It runs upon the popular document-based database MongoDB and was designed as a wrapper over its Python driver [56]. Hence, we are able to evaluate its competence as a search framework as well as the compatibility with a state-of-the-art DBMS. Moreover, running as a wrapper makes it database-agnostic and restricts the server to dealing with encrypted data. We choose to implement our wrapper over a NoSQL database so we could avoid dealing with the SQL interpreter and thus reduce the implementation complexity. However, our solution should be easily portable to any SQL database because of its strong roots in relational algebra. Table 1 provides the schemes used for each attribute class, the parameter size and its security level.

Lewi-Wu's ORE scheme relies on symmetric primitives and achieves IND-OCPA. The authors claim that this is more secure than all existing OPE and ORE schemes which are practical [34]. Finally, Paillier and ElGamal are well-known public-key schemes. Both achieve IND-CPA and are based on the hardness of solving integer factorization and discrete logarithm problems, respectively. Paillier supports homomorphic addition, while ElGamal provides homomorphic multiplication. Both are classified as PHE schemes [38, 39]. The implementation of AES was provided by the *pycrypto* toolkit [57]; we wrote a Python binding over the implementation of Lewi-Wu provided by the authors [58]; and we implemented Paillier and ElGamal

schemes. An AVL tree was used as the index structure. It is important to notice that performance was not the main focus in this proof-of-concept implementation.

The machines used to run our experiments are described in Tables 2 and 3. The former specifies the machine used to host the MongoDB server, and latter describes the one used to run the client. Both machines were connected by a Gigabit local network connection.

While it was trivial to index the plaintext dataset natively, it was not so simple with the encrypted version. MongoDB is not friendly to custom index structures or comparators, so we decided to construct the structure with Python code and then insert it into the database using pointers based on MongoDB's native identity codes. Walking through the index tree depends on a database-external operation at Python-side, calling MongoDB's FIND method to localize documents related to left/right pointers starting from the tree root. Such limitation brings a major performance overhead that especially affects range queries.

7.1 Netflix's prize dataset

We used the Netflix's dataset to measure the computational costs of managing an encrypted database.

We consider the two threat scenarios discussed in Section 6.1, a recommendation system running in production, and the disclosure of a real ratings dataset. Both require the ability of running all queries presented in Section 6.3, differing only in the content that must be inserted in the encrypted dataset (for instance, how much of the *index* ciphertexts may be stored). Hence, to demonstrate the suitability of our framework as a strategy to fulfill the development and execution of a good predictor in such contexts, and being capable of mitigating damages to user privacy, we implemented those queries in an encrypted instance of the dataset.

As shown in Table 4, the four attributes chosen are classified as *static*, which use the faster encryption and decryption available. *Rating* is tagged *computable* for addition and multiplication, thus being compatible with Eqs. 3 and 4. We use *CustomerID*, *MovieID*, and *Date* for indexing. Encrypting the document structure takes $540\mu s$ per record.

There is no way to implement integer division over Paillier ciphertexts. Thus, the predictor may be adapted to

Table 1 Chosen cryptosystems for each attribute presented in Section 5

Attribute	Cryptosystem	Parameters	Sec. level
static	AES	128 bits	128 bits
index	Lewi-Wu	128 bits	128 bits
computable (+)	Paillier	3072 bits	128 bits
computable (×)	ElGamal	3072 bits	128 bits

Table 2 Specifications of the machine used for running the MongoDB instance

CPU	2 x Intel Xeon E5-2670 v1 @ 2.60GH
OS	CentOS 7.3
Memory	16 x DDR3 DIMM 8192MB @ 1600MHz
Disk	7200RPM Western Digital HDD (SATA)

Table 3 Specifications of the machine used for running the queries described in this document

CPU	2 x Intel Xeon E5-2640 v2 @ 2.60GH
OS	Ubuntu 16.04.2
Memory	4 x DDR3 DIMM 8192MB @ 1600MHz
Disk	7200RPM Western Digital HDD (SATA)

use the non-divided result on Eqs. 3 and 4. Otherwise, a division oracle must be provided, to which one could submit their homomorphically added values and ask for a ciphertext equivalent to its division by an arbitrary integer. This approach does not reduce security for an IND-CPA homomorphic scheme.

Handling such a large dataset was not an easy task. The ciphertext expansion factor caused by AES, Paillier and ElGamal cryptosystems was relatively small, but the Lewi-Wu implementation is very inefficient in this regard, having an expansion of about $400\times$. This directly affects the index building and motivated us to explore different strategies to encrypt and load the dataset to a MongoDB instance in reasonable time.

Again, MongoDB is not friendly for custom indexing. A contribution by Grim, Wiersma and Turkmen to our code enables us to manage the AVL tree inside the database through JavaScript code stored inside MongoDB's engine (the only way to execute arbitrary code in MongoDB) [59]. Thus, our primary approach to feed the DBMS with the dataset was quite simple: encrypt each record in our wrapper, insert in the database, and update the index and balance the tree inside the DBMS. The two first operations suffered from an extremely high memory consumption and by far surpassed our available RAM capacity. However, an even worse problem we faced was to build the AVL tree. For the first thousand records we could do the node insertion and tree balancing with a transfer rate of about 600 documents per second, but it dropped quickly as the tree height increases, reaching less than 1 document per second before insertion of the 10,000th record.

We found out that the initial insertions required a novel approach. We completely decoupled the *index* from the *static* data encryption and chose to first feed the database with the *static* ciphertexts, constructing the entire AVL tree using the plaintext on client-sided memory, and then

Table 4 Attribute structure of elements in the Netflix's prize dataset

Name	Value type	Class
CustomerID	integer	*index, static*
MovieID	integer	*index, static*
Rating	integer	*static, computable*
Date	integer	*index, static*

inserting it in the database. Moreover, to speed up the index construction we followed Algorithms 1 and 2 to construct the AVL tree. It takes a sorted list of inputs and builds the tree with time complexity of $O(n)$ on the list size. As a result of this approach we were able to build the encrypted database and the index by 3000 documents per second during the entire procedure.

Algorithm 1 Build an AVL tree using an array of documents

1: **procedure** BUILD_INDEX(docs)
2:     $docs_{sort} \leftarrow sort(docs)$;
3:     $docs_{group} \leftarrow group(docs_{sort})$;   ▷ Combine equal elements
4:     return $build\_aux(docs_{group}, 0, lenght(docs_{group}) - 1)$;
5: **end procedure**

Algorithm 2 Recursively builds an AVL tree with a sorted array of documents without repeated elements. Receives the array itself, and the indexes for the leftmost and rightmost elements to be handled in each recursive call

1: **procedure** BUILD_AUX(docs, L, R)
2:     **if** $L = R$ **then**
3:         return $new\_node(docs\,[L])$;
4:     **else if** $L + 1 = R$ **then**
5:         $left\_node \leftarrow new\_node(docs\,[L])$;
6:         $right\_node \leftarrow new\_node(docs\,[R])$;
7:         $left\_node.right = right\_node$;
8:         $left\_node.height = 1$;
9:         return $left\_node$;
10:     **else**
11:         $M \leftarrow L + \lfloor (R - L)/2 \rfloor$;
12:         $middle\_node \leftarrow new\_node(docs\,[M])$;
13:         $middle\_node.left \leftarrow build\_aux(docs, L, M-1)$;
14:         $middle\_node.right \leftarrow build\_aux(docs, M+1, R)$;
15:         $lh \leftarrow middle\_node.left.height$;
16:         $rh \leftarrow middle\_node.right.height$;
17:         $middle\_node.height = 1 + \max(lh, rh)$;
18:         return $middle\_node$;
19:     **end if**
20: **end procedure**

Table 5 shows the latency of each step we observed during the construction of the AVL tree-based indexes. The total time to build those 3 indexes was 40 min.

The queries we derived in Section 6.3 were ported to our encrypted database, and the latency for each one can be seen in Table 6. The parameters used for each Equation were arbitrarily selected. The *CustomerID*s for Alice and

Table 5 Latency for each step in the construction of an AVL tree following Algorithm 1 for each *index* attribute specified in 4

Attribute	Sort (s)	Group (s)	Build_index (s)
CustomerID	329	459	129
MovieID	270	161	2
Date	187	197	5

Bob (AID and BID) were 1061110 and 2486445 respectively, while MID was fixed as 6287. The time interval used was 01/01/2003 to 01/01/2004. Lastly, we defined a "loved" rating as those greater than 3, and "hated" rating as those lower than 3. We applied some efforts in optimizing the execution, however these results can still be improved.

As it can be seen, complex queries composed by range selections, as well as those with numerous outcomes, suffered from the slow communication between server and the client. The latter influenced even the plaintext results. The outcome of Eq. 1 is quite small, requiring much less time to return than the outcome of Eq. 2 (the number of movies rated by a user is much smaller than the number of users that rated a movie).

The time interval selection in Eqs. 3 and 4 required our implementation to visit many nodes in the index tree for *Date*. Because each iteration requires a back and forth between the server and the client, this dramatically impacted the performance. The latencies for Eqs. 1 and 5 were only 1.4 times higher in the encrypted database, however it reached 710 times for Eq. 3. Lastly, Eqs. 6 and 7 depend on Paillier's homomorphic additions. This implied in a factor-12 slowdown.

The implementation of queries based on Eqs. 3 and 4 took the previous suggestion and skipped the final division. We believe this does not undermine any procedure that eventually consumes this outcome.

Table 6 Execution times for implementations of the equations presented in Section 6.3 on an encrypted MongoDB collection and an equivalent plaintext version

Equation	Encrypted	Plaintext
1	16.6 ms	11.9 ms
2	2 s	850 ms
3	2.7 s	3.8 ms
4	2.7 s	1.0 s
5	16.8 ms	11.8 ms
6 and 7	12 ms	1.0 ms
9	603 ms	200 ms

Each row contains the latency for the entire circuit required by the respective Equation and returning the outcome to the client. Times are computed as the average for 100 independent executions. The machine and parameters used in each cryptosystem follow those defined in Section 7

The optimal implementation of Eqs. 6 and 7 requires indexing of *MovieID* and *Rating* attributes. However, due to limitations in our implementation, rather than indexing the latter we use linear search over the outcome of the movie selection on client-side. Our approach for building indexes use the set data structure of MongoDB documents. Yet, in the most recent release such structure holds up to 16MB of data, much smaller than the required for indexing the entire dataset for *Rating* with our strategy.

Lastly, Eq. 8 was implemented aiming at the joining of data regarding two users, Alice and Bob. We let the evaluation of such information by a similarity-evaluation function as future work.

8 Conclusion

We presented the problem of searching in encrypted data and a proposal of a framework that guides the modeling of a database with support to this functionality. This is achieved by combining different cryptographic concepts and using different cryptosystems to satisfy the requirements of each attribute, like order-revealing encryption and homomorphic encryption. Over this approach, a relational algebra was built to support encrypted data composed by: projection, selection, Cartesian product, difference, union, rename, and join-like operators.

An overview of the security provided is discussed, as well as a performance analysis about the impact in a realistic database. As a case study we explored the Netflix prize, which published an anonymized dataset with real-world information about user behavior which was later deanonymized through correlation attacks involving public databases.

We offered a proof-of-concept implementation in Python over the document-based database MongoDB. To demonstrate its functionality, we selected and ran some of the main predicates required by the winning solution of the Netflix Grand Prize and measured the performance impact of the execution in a encrypted version of the dataset. We conclude that our proposal offers robustness against a compromised server and we discuss how it would help to avoid the deanonymization of the Netflix dataset. In comparison with CryptDB, our proposal provides higher security, since it delegates exclusively to the data owner the responsibility of encrypting and decrypting data. This way, privacy holds even in a scenario of database or application compromise.

As future research objectives we can mention:

- *Extend the scope to associative arrays*: Despite being powerful on SQL, Codd's relational algebra is not completely applicable for non-relational databases. For instance, NoSQL and NewSQL databases lack the concept of joining. A more convenient foundation for such context is algebra of associative arrays [60].

Hence, the formalization of our primitives in such algebra would be an interesting work.

- *Reduce the leakage of index construction in the database*: Our proposal leaks both sides of *index* ciphertexts to enable the index construction. At this moment, an eavesdropper monitoring queries would learn all information required to freely compare the exposed ciphertexts. As discussed in this document, such capability must be restricted, under risk of enabling an inference attack.

- *Key refreshment algorithm*: A persistent passive attacker is capable of learning the required information to perform comparisons through the entire database, just by observing issued queries and its outcome. Thus, the framework primitives must be improved to support an algorithm capable of avoid any damage caused by the knowledge of such information.

- *Hide repeated queries*: Even with encrypted queries and outcomes, the access pattern in a database may indicate repeated queries and the associated records. A technique such as ORAM could be useful to protect such information [61].

- *Explore different databases*: As stated, MongoDB is a very popular NoSQL database. However, it is not friendly to custom indexing or third party code running in its engine. Thus, to replace it by a more appropriate database could provide a more productive system.

- *Improve performance of our implementation*: Our implementation had as objective to be a proof-of-concept and demonstrate how the proposal works. The development of a space and speed-optimized versions is an important next step.

Endnotes

[1] SHE stands for "Somewhat homomorphic encryption".

[2] LHE stands for "Leveled fully homomorphic encryption".

[3] Relative to a set of desirable properties for a database. Acronym to "Atomicity, Consistency, Isolation, Durability".

[4] The Advanced Encryption Standard (AES) is a well-established symmetric block cipher enabling high performance implementation in hardware and software [62].

[5] When the security of a system relies only in the lack of knowledge by adversaries about its implementation details and flaws.

Acknowledgements

A prior version of this paper was presented at the XVI Brazilian Symposium on Information and Computational Systems Security (SBSeg16) [63].
The authors thank Proof. André Santanchè for the initial opportunity to develop this work, the Multidisciplinary High Performance Computing Lab (LMCAD) for providing the required infrastructure, and the anonymous reviewers that helped improving this work.

Funding

This research was partially founded by CNPq and the Google Research Awards Latin America.

Authors' contributions

The first author developed the study design, carried out the implementation efforts and wrote most the paper. The second author contributed with discussions about the proposal and its validation with the case study. Both authors read and approved the final manuscript.

References

1. Vecchiola C, Pandey S, Buyya R. High-Performance Cloud Computing: A View of Scientific Applications. In: Pervasive Systems, Algorithms, and Networks (ISPAN), 2009 10th International Symposium On. Kaohsiung: IEEE. 2009. p. 4–16.
2. Buyya R. Market-Oriented Cloud Computing: Vision, Hype, and Reality of Delivering Computing As the 5th Utility. In: Proceedings of the 2009 9th IEEE/ACM International Symposium on Cluster Computing and the Grid, CCGRID '09. Washington: IEEE Computer Society. 2009.
3. Hoffa C, Mehta G, Freeman T, Deelman E, Keahey K, Berriman B, Good J. On the Use of Cloud Computing for Scientific Workflows. In: eScience 08. IEEE Fourth International Conference On. Indianapolis: IEEE. 2008. p. 640–5.
4. Dinh HT, Lee C, Niyato D, Wang P. A survey of mobile cloud computing: architecture, applications, and approaches. Wirel Commun Mob Comput. 2013;13(18):1587–611.
5. Xiao Z, Xiao Y. Security and Privacy in Cloud Computing. IEEE Commun Surv Tutor. 2013;15(2):843–59.
6. Pascual A. 2017 Data Breach Fraud Impact Report: Going Undercover and Recovering Data. Technical report: Javelin Advisory Services; 2017.
7. Popa RA, Redfield CMS, Zeldovich N, Balakrishnan H. Cryptdb: Protecting confidentiality with encrypted query processing. In: Proceedings of the Twenty-Third ACM Symposium on Operating Systems Principles. SOSP '11. New York: ACM. 2011. p. 85–100.
8. Poddar R, Boelter T, Popa RA. Arx: A Strongly Encrypted Database System: Cryptology ePrint Archive, Report 2016/591; 2016.
9. Arasu A, Eguro K, Kaushik R, Kossmann D, Ramamurthy R, Venkatesan R. A secure coprocessor for database applications. In: 2013 23rd International Conference on Field programmable Logic and Applications. 2013. p. 1–8. doi:10.1109/FPL.2013.6645524.
10. Tu S, Kaashoek MF, Madden S, Zeldovich N. Processing analytical queries over encrypted data. Proc VLDB Endow. 2013;6(5):289–300.
11. Bennett J, Lanning S, et al. The netflix prize. In: Proceedings of KDD Cup and Workshop. New York. 2007. p. 35.
12. Arrington M. AOL Proudly Releases Massive Amounts of Private Data. 2006. https://techcrunch.com/2006/08/06/aol-proudly-releases-massive-amounts-of-user-search-data/ Accessed 24 July 2017.
13. Said A, Bellogín A. Comparative recommender system evaluation: benchmarking recommendation frameworks. In: Proceedings of the 8th ACM Conference on Recommender Systems. New York: ACM. 2014. p. 129–36.
14. Wang Z, Liao J, Cao Q, Qi H, Wang Z. Friendbook: a semantic-based friend recommendation system for social networks. IEEE Trans Mob Comput. 2015;14(3):538–51.
15. Pazzani MJ, Billsus D. Content-based recommendation systems. In: Brusilovsky P, Kobsa A, Nejdl W, editors. The Adaptive Web: Methods and Strategies of Web Personalization. Berlin: Springer. 2007. p. 325–41.
16. Narayanan A, Shmatikov V. Robust de-anonymization of large sparse datasets. In: Proceedings of the 2008 IEEE Symposium on Security and Privacy. SP '08. Washington: IEEE Computer Society. 2008. p. 111–25.
17. Barbaro M, Zeller T. A Face Is Exposed for AOL Searcher No. 4417749: The New York Times; 2006. Accessed 05 Apr 2017.
18. Narayanan A, Felten EW. No silver bullet: De-identification still doesn't work: White Paper; 2014. Manuscript. http://randomwalker.info/publications/no-silver-bullet-de-identification.pdf.

19. Greenwald G, MacAskill E. NSA Prism program taps in to user data of Apple, Google and others: The Guardian; 2013. https://www.theguardian.com/world/2013/jun/06/us-tech-giants-nsa-data.

20. Weber H. How the NSA & FBI made Facebook the perfect mass surveillance tool: Venture Beat; 2014. https://www.theguardian.com/world/2013/jun/06/us-tech-giants-nsa-data.

21. Thomsen S. Extramarital affair website Ashley Madison has been hacked and attackers are threatening to leak data online: Business Insider; 2015. Accessed 25 May 2016.

22. Magnusson N, Rolander N. Sweden Tries to Stem Fallout of Security Breach in IBM Contract: Bloomberg; 2017.

23. BBC News. Yahoo 'state' hackers stole data from 500 million users. 2016. Accessed 23 Sept 2016.

24. Sweeney L. Simple Demographics Often Identify People Uniquely. 2000. http://dataprivacylab.org/projects/identifiability/.

25. Golle P. Revisiting the uniqueness of simple demographics in the us population. In: Proceedings of the 5th ACM Workshop on Privacy in Electronic Society. WPES '06. New York: ACM. 2006. p. 77–80.

26. DuckDuckGo. Privacy Mythbusting #3: Anonymized data is safe, right? (Er, no.) https://spreadprivacy.com/dataanonymization-e1e2b3105f3c. Accessed 24 July 2017.

27. Schneier B. Data is a toxic asset. 2016. http://edition.cnn.com/2016/03/01/opinions/data-is-a-toxic-asset-opinion-schneier/index.html.

28. Bösch C, Hartel P, Jonker W, Peter A. A survey of provably secure searchable encryption. ACM Comput Surv. 2014;47(2):18–11851.

29. Alves P. A proof-of-concept searchable encryption backend for mongodb. 2016. https://github.com/pdroalves/encrypted-mongodb. Accessed July 2017.

30. Bellare M, Desai A, Pointcheval D, Rogaway P. Relations among notions of security for public-key encryption schemes. In: Advances in Cryptology — CRYPTO '98: 18th Annual International Cryptology Conference Santa Barbara, California, USA August 23–27, 1998 Proceedings. Berlin: Springer. 1998. p. 26–45.

31. Curtmola R, Garay J, Kamara S, Ostrovsky R. Searchable symmetric encryption: Improved definitions and efficient constructions. J Comput Secur. 2011;19(5):895–934.

32. Boldyreva A, Chenette N, Lee Y, O'Neill A. Order-preserving symmetric encryption. Lect Notes Comput Sci. 2009;5479:224–41.

33. Boneh D, Lewi K, Raykova M, Sahai A, Zhandry M, Zimmerman J. Semantically Secure Order-Revealing Encryption: Multi-input Functional Encryption Without Obfuscation. Berlin: Springer. 2015. p. 563–94.

34. Lewi K, Wu DJ. Order-Revealing Encryption: New Constructions, Applications, and Lower Bounds: Cryptology ePrint Archive; 2016. Report 2016/612.

35. Kolesnikov V, Shikfa A. On the limits of privacy provided by Order-Preserving Encryption. Bell Labs Tech J. 2012.

36. Chenette N, Lewi K, Weis SA, Wu DJ. Practical Order-Revealing Encryption with Limited Leakage. In: FSE. Bochum: Springer. 2016.

37. Naveed M, Kamara S, Wright CV. Inference attacks on property-preserving encrypted databases. In: Proceedings of the 22Nd ACM SIGSAC Conference on Computer and Communications Security. CCS '15. New York: ACM. 2015. p. 644–55.

38. Paillier P. Public-Key Cryptosystems Based on Composite Degree Residuosity Classes. In: Proceedings of the 17th International Conference on Theory and Application of Cryptographic Techniques, EUROCRYPT'99. Berlin: Springer. 1999. p. 223–38. http://dl.acm.org/citation.cfm?id=1756123.1756146.

39. El Gamal T. A public key cryptosystem and a signature scheme based on discrete logarithms. In: Proceedings of CRYPTO 84 on Advances in Cryptology. New York: Springer. 1985. p. 10–18. http://dl.acm.org/citation.cfm?id=19478.19480.

40. Gentry C. Computing Arbitrary Functions of Encrypted Data. Commun ACM. 2010;53(3):97–105.

41. Brakerski Z, Gentry C, Vaikuntanathan V. (leveled) fully homomorphic encryption without bootstrapping. In: Proceedings of the 3rd Innovations in Theoretical Computer Science Conference. ITCS '12. New York: ACM. 2012. p. 309–25.

42. Loftus J, May A, Smart NP, Vercauteren F. On CCA-Secure Somewhat Homomorphic Encryption. In: Proceedings of the 18th International Conference on Selected Areas in Cryptography. SAC'11. Berlin: Springer. 2012. p. 55–72.

43. Song DX, Wagner D, Perrig A, Perrig A. Practical techniques for searches on encrypted data. In: Proc 2000 IEEE Symp Secur Privacy. S&P 2000. Berkeley: IEEE. 2000. p. 44–55.

44. Grubbs P, Ristenpart T, Shmatikov V. Why Your Encrypted Database Is Not Secure: Cryptology ePrint Archive; 2017. Report 2017/468. http://eprint.iacr.org/2017/468.

45. Rogaway P. The moral character of cryptographic work.: Cryptology ePrint Archive, IACR; 2015, p. 1162.

46. Naveed M, Kamara S, Wright CV. Inference attacks on property-preserving encrypted databases. In: Proceedings of the 22Nd ACM SIGSAC Conference on Computer and Communications Security. CCS '15. New York: ACM. 2015. p. 644–55.

47. Grubbs P, McPherson R, Naveed M, Ristenpart T, Shmatikov V. Breaking web applications built on top of encrypted data. In: Proceedings of the 2016 ACM SIGSAC Conference on Computer and Communications Security. CCS '16. New York: ACM. 2016. p. 1353–64.

48. Papadimitriou A, Bhagwan R, Chandran N, Ramjee R, Haeberlen A, Singh H, Modi A, Badrinarayanan S. Big data analytics over encrypted datasets with seabed. In: Proceedings of the 12th USENIX Conference on Operating Systems Design and Implementation. OSDI'16. Berkeley: USENIX Association. 2016. p. 587–602. http://dl.acm.org/citation.cfm?id=3026877.3026922.

49. Shoro AG, Soomro TR. Big data analysis: Apache spark perspective. Global J Comput Sci Technol. 2015;15(1).

50. Codd EF. A relational model of data for large shared data banks. Commun. ACM 26. 1983;6:64–69.

51. Ramakrishnan R, Gehrke J. Database Management Systems, 3rd edn. New York: McGraw-Hill, Inc.; 2003.

52. Sedgewick R, Wayne K. Algorithms, 4th edn: Addison-Wesley Professional; 2011.

53. Doröz Y, Hoffstein J, Pipher J, Silverman JH, Sunar B, Whyte W, Zhang Z. Fully Homomorphic Encryption from the Finite Field Isomorphism Problem: Cryptology ePrint Archive; 2017. Report 2017/548.

54. Boneh D, Gentry C, Halevi S, Wang F, Wu DJ. Private database queries using somewhat homomorphic encryption. In: Proceedings of the 11th International Conference on Applied Cryptography and Network Security. ACNS'13. Berlin: Springer. 2013. p. 102–18.

55. Töscher A, Jahrer M, Bell RM. The BigChaos Solution to the Netflix Grand Prize. 2009. http://citeseerx.ist.psu.edu/viewdoc/download?doi=10.1.1.178.1356&rep=rep1&type=pdf.

56. Chodorow K, Dirolf M. MongoDB: The Definitive Guide, 1st edn. USA: O'Reilly Media, Inc.; 2010.

57. Litzenberger D. Python Cryptography Toolkit. 2016. http://www.pycrypto.org/. Accessed 3 July 2016.

58. Wu DJ, Lewi K. FastORE. 2016. https://github.com/kevinlewi/fastore. Accessed July 2017.

59. Grim MW, Wiersma AT, Turkmen F. Security and Performance Analysis of Encrypted NoSQL Databases. Technical report: University of Amsterdam; 2017. http://www.delaat.net/rp/2016-2017/p37/report.pdf.

60. Kepner J, Gadepally V, Hutchison D, Jananthan H, Mattson TG, Samsi S, Reuther A. Associative array model of sql, nosql, and newsql databases. Waltham: IEEE. 2016.

61. Stefanov E, Van Dijk M, Shi E, Fletcher C, Ren L, Yu X, Devadas S. Path oram: an extremely simple oblivious ram protocol. In: Proceedings of the 2013 ACM SIGSAC Conference on Computer & Communications Security. Berlin: ACM. 2013. p. 299–310.

62. Daemen J, Rijmen V. The design of Rijndael: AES-the advanced encryption standard. Springer Science & Business Media. 2013.

63. Alves PGMR, Aranha DF. A framework for searching encrypted databases. In: Proceedings of the XVI Brazilian Symposium on Information and Computational Systems Security. Niterói: SBC. 2016.

64. Netflix Prize Data Set; 2009. http://academictorrents.com/details/9b13183dc4d60676b773c9e2cd6de5e5542cee9a. Accessed July 2017.

14

A context-aware framework for dynamic composition of process fragments in the internet of services

Antonio Bucchiarone[*] [iD], Annapaola Marconi, Marco Pistore and Heorhi Raik

Abstract

In the last decade, many approaches to automated service composition have been proposed. However, most of them do not fully exploit the opportunities offered by the Internet of Services (IoS). In this article, we focus on the dynamicity of the execution environment, that is, any change occurring at run-time that might affect the system, such as changes in service availability, service behavior, or characteristics of the execution context. We indicate that any IoS-based application strongly requires a composition framework that supports for the automation of all the phases of the composition life cycle, from requirements derivation, to synthesis, deployment and execution. Our solution to this ambitious problem is an AI planning-based composition framework that features abstract composition requirements and context-awareness. In the proposed approach most human-dependent tasks can be accomplished at design time and the few human intervention required at run time do not affect the system execution. To demonstrate our approach in action and evaluate it, we exploit the ASTRO-CAptEvo framework, simulating the operation of a fully automated IoS-based car logistics scenario in the Bremerhaven harbor.

Keywords: Internet of services, Dynamic service composition, Process fragment, Context-aware, AI planning

1 Introduction

Service composition is one of the cornerstone technologies within service-oriented computing. It consists in reusing existing services as building blocks for new services (applications) with higher-level functionality. Service composition allows for extremely rapid software development and high re-usability of development results.

Despite all the advantages service composition brings to software engineers, when performed manually, it is still a very complex, time-consuming and error-prone task. The point is that composition requirements and service specifications usually contain numerous easy-to-miss technical details that have to be properly reflected in the composition. This becomes critical when composition has to be exploited in *complex and dynamic* application domains, requiring frequent revision of providers (i.e., component services), changes in existing offered functionalities (i.e. component services behavior), and adjustment of business policies and objectives (i.e., composition requirements).

This is the case for IoS-based application domains, where the execution environment is so dynamic, that service composition is considered to be a kind of every-minute routine activity.

We can mention at least two important examples of such IoS-based domains. The first one are *pervasive systems*, which are mobile systems operating in close connection with their context. Once service composition is exploited in this setting, it has to be flexibly and quickly adapted to the rapidly changing environment. For instance, let us imagine there is a car that has to regularly perform some activity implemented through composition of surrounding near-field communication services (e.g., car parking assisted by various parking services). Depending on the current surrounding environment (i.e., on the set of available services and on the context state) the solution composition, though targeting conceptually the same objective, will always be different. If the procedure is repeated frequently at different locations, we have to produce new compositions again and again. Another example are *user-centric systems*, whose operation evolves around the needs and constraints of a specific user. For instance, it could

*Correspondence: bucchiarone@fbk.eu
Fondazione Bruno Kessler, Via Sommarive, 18, 38123 Trento, Italy

be a mobile application that allows the user to integrate (compose) multiple mobile services (local phone services, Internet services, near-field communication services, etc..) and execute them consistently. In this case, the choice of services and composition objectives are determined by user's environment and personal preferences/constraints/goals.

It is quite clear that predefined solutions are not going to work in these IoS-based systems. Indeed, each composition heavily depends on the run-time parameters of the execution environment, namely, current execution context, set of available services, concrete user's needs, etc. Since these parameters are not predictable at design time (sometimes we may not even know which services will be available at the time of composition), it is impossible to produce reliable solutions a priori. In order to address this problem we need a *dynamic composition framework* that would automate the whole service composition life-cycle, from requirements derivation, to composition generation, to deployment and execution [1, 2].

Another important aspect that directly follows from system dynamicity is *context-aware composition and execution*. Services are often closely connected to the context in which they are executed (e.g., a parking web service execution may depend on the type of a car to be parked, on space availability, weather, etc.). In turn, the context tends to be volatile, i.e. exogenous events may change the context state and thus affect composition execution. In this setting, to be able to produce compositions that are consistent with the surrounding context it is important to have a context-aware service model that reflects contextual characteristics of services. This information has to be taken into account in service composition, thus enabling more robust solutions. It is worth to notice that the problem of context-awareness of service composition has not yet received enough attention from the scientific community and only very few works are currently available on the topic [3–5]. Many existing approaches to service composition suffer from over simplification, both for what concerns the service model (e.g., services are often considered as atomic synchronous operations) and composition requirements (e.g., requirements languages do not reflect real-world composition needs). As a result, these solutions can only be applied to very limited set of composition problems. At the same time, a few approaches demonstrate more maturity in addressing these aspects.

In this article, for the first time, we present a comprehensive framework, and its implementation, for automated service composition that is specifically designed to be used in dynamic execution environments and allows for context-aware service composition and execution.

In very general terms, the idea consists in organizing the composition life cycle in a such a way that most human activities can be accomplished at design time.

As a consequence, run-time composition management, from the derivation of composition requirements to the composition synthesis to the deployment of executable processes, is completely automated. Moreover, whenever human involvement is required at run-time (e.g., plugging-in a new service into the system), the change is automatically dealt by the framework, without affecting the system execution. In addition to that, our composition framework features explicit context model that is used to express various contextual characteristics of services. Later, these characteristics can be taken into account in automated reasoning so that context-aware service compositions are produced. The approach exploits AI planning techniques that can deal with realistic service models (asynchronous, stateful and nondeterministic services) and allows for rich control- and data-flow requirements[1]. This makes it powerful enough to be used in real service-based systems, including those mentioned above. The demonstration is given also by its usage, as a core component, in different previous works to support the incremental refinement and adaptation of context-aware service based systems [6–8].

In the article, as composable components we use *process fragments* (or simply fragments). Fragments [9] are a way to represent reusable process knowledge in service compositions and encode elementary subprocesses that can be used as constructing blocks for more complex processes. Process fragments are also a very effective mean to model stateful and asynchronous services [10].

The rest of the article is structured as follows. In Section 2, we present the Car Logistics scenario used as a reference throughout the article and explain the challenges it poses to service composition. In Section 3, we present our composition framework, formally defining all the concepts and models used for context-aware dynamic service composition and show how the composition problem is solved through AI planning techniques. The experimental validation of the approach can be found in Section 4 where we have used the implementation of the Car Logistics scenario to demonstrate our approach in action and evaluate its performance and scalability. Finally, we conclude the article with related work survey (Section 5) and conclusions (Section 7).

2 Motivating scenario and research challenges

In this Section we introduce the car logistics scenario that helps understanding the problem we want to solve and the research challenges that it poses.

2.1 Car logistics scenario

The motivating scenario (later referred to as Car Logistics Scenario or CLS) is inspired by the operation of the seaport of Bremerhaven (Bremen, Germany) [11]. Every year this port receives around 2 million cars transported by ships in order to further deliver them to retailers. The delivery process for each car (see Fig. 1) includes a number of steps to be accomplished. Cars arrive by ship and each ship is able to approach and leave a gate interacting with the landing manager, which is in charge of coordinating and controlling the landing procedure for all the ships in the port. Then cars are unloaded and unpacked at one of the terminals. Once a car is unpacked, it has to be moved to one of the storage areas: the chosen area depends on the car type/brand and on the availability of parking spaces; different storage areas have different parking procedures that need to be followed. The car remains at the storage area until it is ordered by a retailer. Once a car stored is ordered, it continues its way towards the delivery. In particular, the car is treated at dedicated treatment areas (e. g., washing, painting, equipment) according to the details of the order and the car brand/model. When a car is ready to be delivered it is moved to the assigned delivery gate, where it is loaded onto a truck and eventually delivered to the retailer. It is important that every step in the chain is customizable according to the car brand, model, retailer requirements, etc. This means different cars may utilize different procedures to accomplish the same task.

These procedures are partially automated and exploit digital services as well as sensors and smart manufacturing equipment [11]. We tried to move this scenario a little further to fully capture the opportunities offered by paradigms such as IoS and IoT, yet keeping its current needs, regulations and practices. Our goal was to develop a service-based system that supports the synergistic cooperation of the numerous actors (i. e., cars, ships, trucks, treatment areas, parking facilities, drivers, etc.) allowing them to follow their current procedures and business policies. The CLS scenario presents several example of dinamicity that we list in the following.

- *Customization.* The system should consider the customization of each car procedure. It means that different brands and models of cars in a similar but customizable way according to the specific order and context (e.g., facility in which they are treated).
- *Openness.* The system should be able to easily integrate new actors and services at run-time. This

happens, for example, when new car models, having specific requirements and procedures, is handled at the seaport, when a new truck/ship company comes into play, as well as whenever there is a new functionality provided by the sensors and machineries used in the different port facilities.
- *Flexibility.* The system needs to flexibly deal with changes in the procedures and business policies of all the actors such as ships (e.g., changes in approaching procedure), trucks (e.g., changes in delivery procedure), port facilities (e.g., update in a parking service or in a certain procedure supported by a machinery in a treatment facility).
- *Context-awareness.* The system needs to deal with situations where contextual changes invalidate some choices made before. For example, if a car books a space at some storage area and upon arrival realizes that the facility is not available, it needs to rearrange the things so that it can be stored at a different facility.

2.2   Research challenges

In the previous section, we gave an example of a system where dynamic composition techniques are strongly required. As a result, it is hardly affordable to involve human experts to participate in resolving composition problems on-line. This essentially means that all the composition steps, from abstract requirements' specification, to service discovery and composition, to service deployment, must be automated.

This challenge is hardly coped with by the existing composition techniques. In general, every automated composition engine follows the scheme shown in Fig. 2. As input, it takes specifications of *software components* and *composition requirements* and, as output, it produces an executable process.

The major problem of most existing composition tools is that they assume that the set of services to be composed is always known to the designer at the moment of specifying composition requirements. Consequently, it is assumed that composition requirements may include implementation-specific details of services that they are supposed to be used with. As such, requirements become linked to particular service implementation and cannot

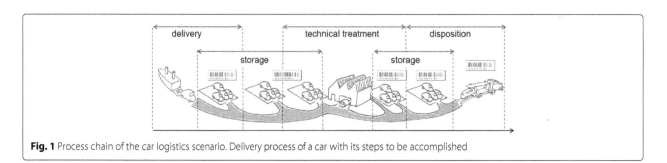

Fig. 1 Process chain of the car logistics scenario. Delivery process of a car with its steps to be accomplished

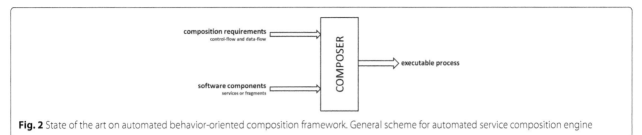

Fig. 2 State of the art on automated behavior-oriented composition framework. General scheme for automated service composition engine

further be used with conceptually similar services that are implemented differently (e.g., when we would like to use a new ticket booking service in place of the one for which the requirements were originally created). In dynamic systems this causes an important problem: while the list of available service is dynamic and can only be discovered at run time, the composition requirements are fixed at design time. Consequently, we need to understand *how to create a composition architecture that allows design-time requirements to be consistently used with an arbitrary set of services discovered at run time with no human intervention* (Challenge 1).

Another problem concerns *context-awareness*. In several cases, process execution is tightly connected to the context. When numerous services are available, *it is critical to select correct services and produce a composition that is valid for the given context model and for the current state of this model* (Challenge 2).

Finally, we need to recall that composable components may be quite complex and may feature 1) *statefulness* (complex protocol), 2) *non-determinism* and 3) *asynchronous* communication. As a result, *the composition architecture has to rely on a service model that reflects these properties of real services* (Challenge 3).

3 Dynamic service composition framework

In this section we present our framework for modeling dynamic context-aware systems such as the CLS scenario described in Section 2.

3.1 System model

The system operation is modeled through a set of *entities* (e.g., cars, ships, storage managers, etc..), each specifying its behavior through a *process*, as depicted in Fig. 3. Unlike traditional system specifications, where processes are static descriptions of the expected run-time operation,

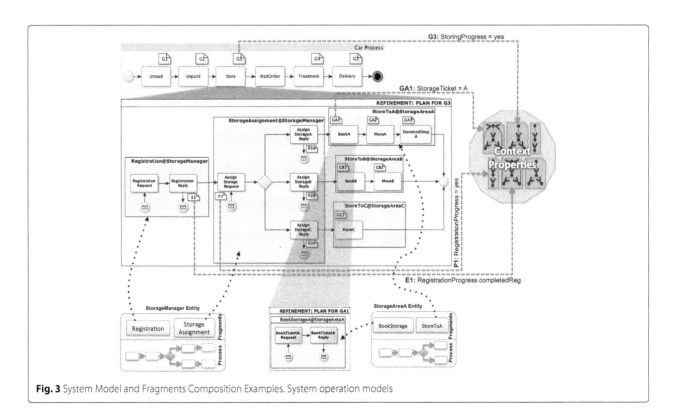

Fig. 3 System Model and Fragments Composition Examples. System operation models

our approach allows to define dynamic processes that are refined at run time according to the features offered by the system.

Processes are designed in Adaptable Pervasive Flows Language, (APFL) [12, 13], an extension of traditional workflow languages (e.g., BPEL [14][2]), which makes them suitable for adaptation and execution in dynamic environments. Unlike traditional processes, where their behaviors are completely specified, our approach allows the partial specification through *abstract activities* that can be specialized at run-time according to the services offered by the other entites in the system.

Abstract activities (e.g., *Store* of the *Car* entity process in Fig. 3) corresponds to tasks that are hard to implement at design time, since they strongly depend on the concrete run-time state (context configuration, availability of services provided by other entities etc.). In our approach, each abstract activity is dynamically replaced (refined) with a fragment composition realizing the corresponding task. As a result, a design-time specification of a process can be quite abstract, with many concrete details being refined only at run time, when the actual execution context is clear.

In addition to the classical workflow language constructs (e.g., input, output, data manipulation activities, complex control flow constructs), APFL adds the possibility to relate the process execution to the system context by annotating activities with preconditions and effects. Preconditions constrain the activity execution to specific context configurations, and in our framework are used to catch violations in the expected behavior and trigger run-time adaptation.

The underline idea is that entities can join the system dynamically, publish their functionalities through a set of *process fragments* that can be used by other entities to interoperate, discover fragments offered by the other entities, and use them to automatically refine their own processes.

For instance, within the CLS, whenever a *car* must be stored, it discovers the fragments provided by the *Storage Manager* and by the associated *Storage Area* (A, B, or C in Fig. 3). These fragments model the harbor-specific procedures and regulations that the car should execute for the storing. Different fragments may be provided by the storage manager and by the different storage areas to be used by certain types of car.

In our framework, we use a unified model for both fragments and fragment-based processes, and uniformly use the term of *fragment* for both of them. We model fragments as labelled transition systems (LTS) (as depicted in Figs. 5 and 6) where transitions are labelled with two different types of actions : *controllable* and *uncontrollable*. Controllable actions are used to model process activities that can be triggered by the process itself (e. g., variable

assignment, message send). Uncontrollable actions model activities whose execution depends on external actors (e. g., message receive, event notification). The distinction between controllable and uncontrollable actions is crucial for proper handling of the asynchronicity of fragment behaviour in composition. Here and later in the text we denote with '!' and '?' controllable and uncontrollable fragment actions respectively. The fragment LTS is formally defined as follows:

Definition 1 (Fragment) *A fragment is a deterministic state transition system* $f = \langle S, s^0, I, O, R \rangle$, *where*

- S *is the set of states and* $s^0 \subseteq S$ *is the initial state;*
- I *and* O *are sets of controllable and uncontrollable actions such that* $I \cap O = \emptyset$;
- $R \subseteq S \times \{I \cup O\} \times S$ *is a transition relation.*

Another important feature of the proposed framework is the possibility of leaving the handling of extraordinary/improbable situations to run time instead of analyzing all the extraordinary situations at design time and embedding the corresponding recovery activities in the process. This kind of modeling extremely simplifies the specification of processes that have to operate in dynamic environments, since the developer does not need to think about and specify all the possible alternatives to deal with specific situations (e.g., context changes, availability of functionalities, improbable events). These dynamic features offered by the framework rely on a shared *context model*, describing the operational environment of the system. The context is defined through a set of *context properties*, each describing a particular aspect of the system domain (e.g., current location of a car, status of a car, availability of a storage area). A context property may evolve as an effect of the execution of a fragment activity, which corresponds to the normal behavior of the domain (e.g., current location of car is storage area A), but also as a result of exogenous changes (e.g., car status is damaged, storage area unavailable).

The aim of context properties is to model those aspects of the context that are relevant for dynamic fragments' composition. Their intent is not to provide a comprehensive and detailed representation of the properties and state of the execution environment. Rather, they are an abstraction of the context, capturing only key domain concepts (e.g., car, ship, storage area) and their evolution. These information are used to reason on how fragments execution (preconditions/effects) is related to and affects the context state.

Context property behaviour is described by a labelled transition system that contains all possible states of the context property and transitions between them[3]. Each transition is labeled with a context event. Formally:

Definition 2 (Context Property) *A context property is a state transition system $p = \langle L, l^0, E, T \rangle$, where:*

- *L is a set of context states and $l^0 \in L$ is the initial state;*
- *E is a set of context property events;*
- *$T \subseteq L \times E \times L$ is a transition relation.*

Examples of context properties (of a car) are shown in Fig. 4. It includes a complex `Location` property reflecting current car location and, two of progress tracking properties (*RegistrationProgress, StoringProgress*).

Considering a context model containing more than one context property, we require that such context properties feature mutually disjoint sets of context events, so that evolutions of different context properties within the same context do not correlate explicitly. Formally, *context* is defined as follows:

Definition 3 (Context) *A context is a set of context properties $C = \{p_1, p_2, \ldots, p_n\}$ such that if $p_i = \langle L_i, l^0{}_i, E_i, T_i \rangle$ for all $i \in [1, n]$ then for any two constituent context properties $p_i, p_j \in C$ sets of events do not intersect (i.e., $E_i \cap E_j = \emptyset$). The set of all context states is defined as $L_C = \prod_{i=1}^{n} L_i$ and the initial context state is $l^0{}_C = \left(l^0{}_1, l^0{}_2, \ldots, l^0{}_n \right)$. We also denote a set of all context events as $E_C = \bigcup_{i=1}^{n} E_i$.*

In order to be able to succinctly specify groups of context states we use *context formulas* which are disjunctions of conjunctions over states of context properties:

Definition 4 (Context Formula) *Let $C = \{p_1, p_2, \ldots, p_n\}$ be a context such that $p_k = \langle L_k, l^0{}_k, E_k, T_k \rangle$ for all $k \in [1, n]$. A state formula for C is a propositional formula $\bigvee_i \bigwedge_j l_{ij}$, where $l_{ij} \in \bigcup_{k=1}^{n} L_k$ and for any two constituent context properties $p_i, p_j \in C$ sets of states do not intersect (i.e., $L_i \cap L_j = \emptyset$).*

The space of all context formulas of context C is denoted as R_C.

In order to make fragments context-aware, we introduce context annotations of actions in fragments. Annotations intensively exploit the notion of context formulas, and can be of three types:

- action *precondition* is a context formula indicating in which context states action execution is allowed (e.g., P1 in Fig. 5);
- action *effect* is a set of context events that are triggered as a result of action execution (e.g., E1 in Fig. 5);

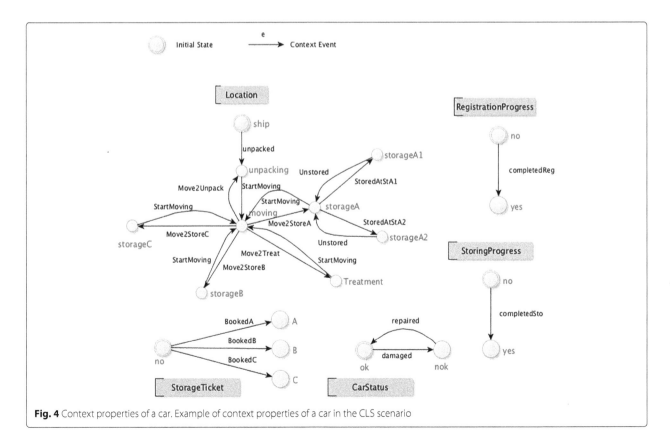

Fig. 4 Context properties of a car. Example of context properties of a car in the CLS scenario

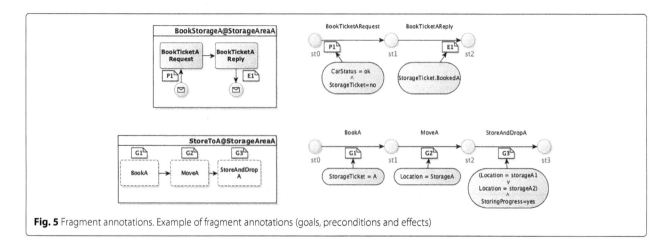

Fig. 5 Fragment annotations. Example of fragment annotations (goals, preconditions and effects)

- action *goal* is a context formula specifying the condition that must hold after the action is executed (e.g., G1, G2 and G3 in Fig. 5).

Any process action can be annotated with a precondition. Since both effects and goals express the contextual intention of an action, we explicitly require that an action can be annotated either with a goal (if it is an abstract activity) or with an effect (for all other activities). Formally, *fragment annotation* is defined as follows:

Definition 5 (Fragment Annotation) *Let* $f = \langle S, s^0, I, O, R \rangle$ *be a fragment and let C be a context. An annotation of fragment f over context C is a tuple* $\omega = \langle P, E, G \rangle$, *where:*

- $P : \{I \cup O\} \rightarrow R_C$ *is the precondition labeling function;*
- $E : \{I \cup O\} \rightarrow E_C$ *is the effect labeling function.*
- *Any action effect* $E(a)$ *may contain no more than one event per context property; For any context property* $p = \langle L, l^0, E, T \rangle \in C$ *the following holds:* $\nexists e_1, e_2 \in E(a) : e_1, e_2 \in E.$
- *If* $E(a) \neq \emptyset$ *then* $G(a) = \emptyset$ *(i.e., an action can be annotated either with a goal or with an effect);*
- $G : \{I \cup O\} \rightarrow R_C$ *is the goal labeling function, such that* $G(a) \neq \emptyset$ *only if* $E(a) = \emptyset$ *(i.e., an action can be annotated either with a goal or with an effect).*

In Fig. 5 we show two fragments (e.g., *BookStorageA* and *StoreToA*), both provided by *Storage Area A* entity. The examples include all types of annotations. The annotations, in turn, are related to the context property examples in Fig. 4. For instance, BookStorageA includes two activities (request and reply). The request activity is annotated with a precondition that guards that ticket booking is executed only in the absence of a ticket. The effect of the reply activity indicates that this fragment eventually brings a ticket object to state A, thus providing ticket booking. StoreToA fragment specifies the

storing procedure for storage area A. This includes three abstract activities annotated with goals in terms of context model.

In the following we present the synopsis of our APFL language with annotations and the details of how an annotated APFL process can be transformed into an annotated LTS as defined in Def. 5. Since both fragments and processes are defined in the same language, the translations below are valid for both of them. In Fig. 6 the translation for basic activities is shown. Specifically, SEND and CONCRETE are represented with a single controllable transition, while RECEIVE is a single uncontrollable transition.

ABSTRACT activities are way more complex since at the moment of creating a new process they are not refined to a concrete process and the only thing we know about them is their abstract goals. We treat an abstract activity as a "black box" that performs a task as defined by its goal. In this regard, an abstract activity combines the properties of controllable and uncontrollable actions. On the one hand, the initiation of an abstract activity is controllable (within a process we can decide if to execute it and when). On the other hand, it is not possible to predict a priori the terminal context configuration. In LTS, such behaviour can be modeled as a controllable action followed by a number of uncontrollable actions corresponding to all possible terminal context states. We actually reduce the number of terminal states to the number of conjunctive clauses in the goal formula[4].

3.2 Fragment composition model

The central idea of our framework for fragment composition can be captured from Fig. 7. The explicit model of the execution context in the center of the figure, is a collection of *context properties*.

In our approach, the context model is specifically used to reason on how a certain objective can be achieved through fragment execution, rather than for process modeling purposes.

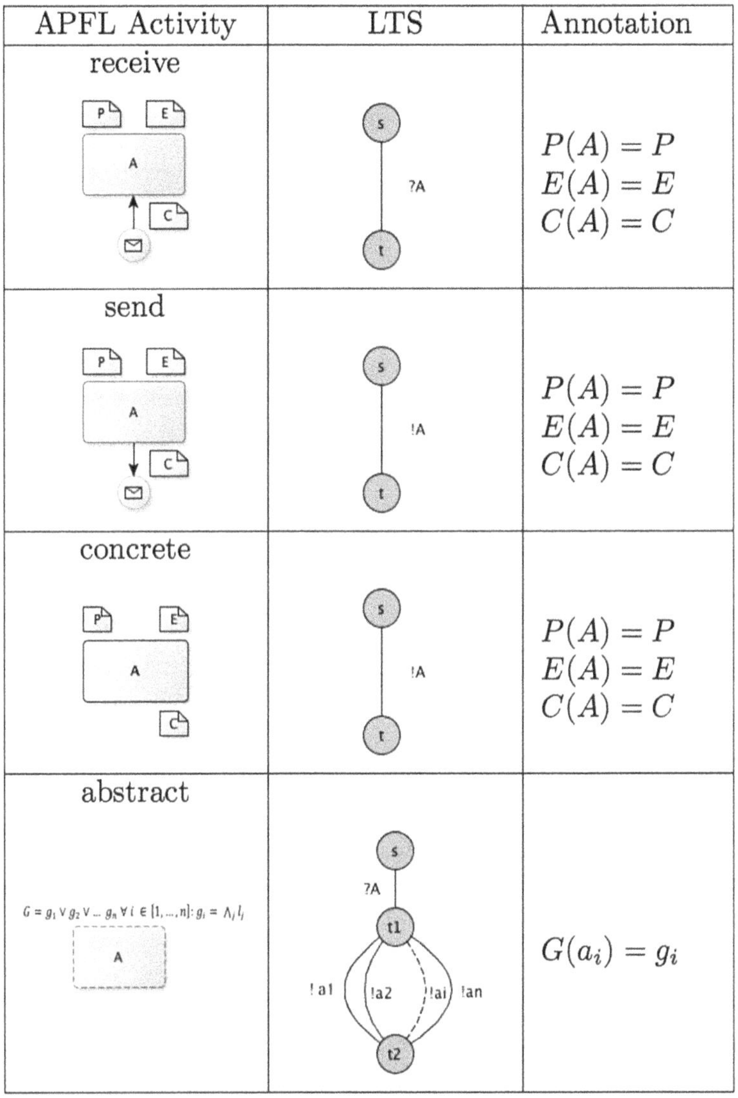

APFL Activity	LTS	Annotation
receive		$P(A) = P$ $E(A) = E$ $C(A) = C$
send		$P(A) = P$ $E(A) = E$ $C(A) = C$
concrete		$P(A) = P$ $E(A) = E$ $C(A) = C$
abstract		$G(a_i) = g_i$

Fig. 6 Translation of basic APFL activities into LTSs. Synopsis of our APFL language with annotations and the details of how an annotated APFL process can be transformed into an annotated LTS

To link fragments to context properties, we annotate the former with context-related information (as Defined in Def. 5 and depicted in Fig. 8). In this way, we explicitly connect the execution of fragment activities to states and transitions of context properties. In particular, a fragment activity may be annotated with *effect* and *precondition*. The effect shows which events this activity triggers once executed, while the precondition shows in which contextual states the execution of the activity is allowed.

Moreover, every abstract activity has a *goal* associated. Such goal specifies a context state(s) to be reached as a result of activity refinement and execution (e.g., if the *StorageTicket* is initially in state no, the goal of BookA activity in Fig. 3 may be to have this context property in state A).

One of the most important aspects of our approach is that *composition requirements* are expressed over context model, and not over fragments as done in most existing composition techniques. The core idea of our fragment composition model is that while fragment execution is closely related to context evolution, the modelling of the latter is solely determined by the application domain and does not depend on particular fragment implementations. As such, *by expressing composition requirements on the level of the context model on the one side, and by annotating fragments with context information on the other side, we create a composition framework in which composition requirements, though detached from fragment implementations, can always be automatically grounded on them.*

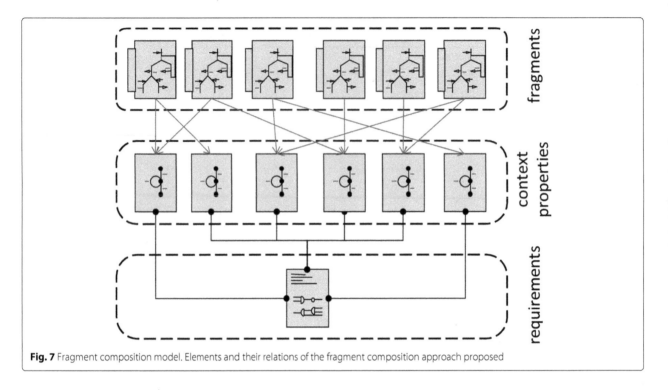

Fig. 7 Fragment composition model. Elements and their relations of the fragment composition approach proposed

The ability to specify composition requirements on context properties makes it possible to efficiently use our approach in extremely dynamic environments, where both the set of available fragments and the execution context are constantly changing. At design time, the requirements are defined only conceptually (with no adherence to any particular set of fragments). Despite we do not know a priori the set of fragment, through annotation-based grounding, the conceptual requirements can always be restated for the actual (dynamically discovered) set of fragments. As such, we automate one of the most critical steps in service composition: run-time derivation of composition requirements.

It is worth to notice that in this way it becomes much easier to introduce new fragments to a scenario at run time: it is enough that new fragments are properly annotated, while it is not necessary to change the context model

nor composition requirements[5]. As we will show in the next Section, once context properties and composition requirements are specified and component fragments are properly annotated, the whole set of specifications can be converted into a planning problem which is then resolved using planning algorithms. The obtained plan encodes a process that, if executed from the current context state, brings the system to one of the goal context configurations. The plan is further translated into an executable APFL process.

3.3 Fragment composition via planning

The overview of our fragment composition approach is given in Fig. 9. The composition engine accepts as input a context C represented by context properties $p_1, p_2, \ldots, p_m$, a set of fragments $F^+ = \{f_1^+, f_2^+, \ldots, f_n^+\}$ annotated over C (together C and F^+ form a context-

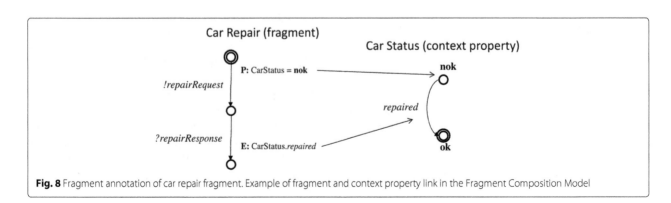

Fig. 8 Fragment annotation of car repair fragment. Example of fragment and context property link in the Fragment Composition Model

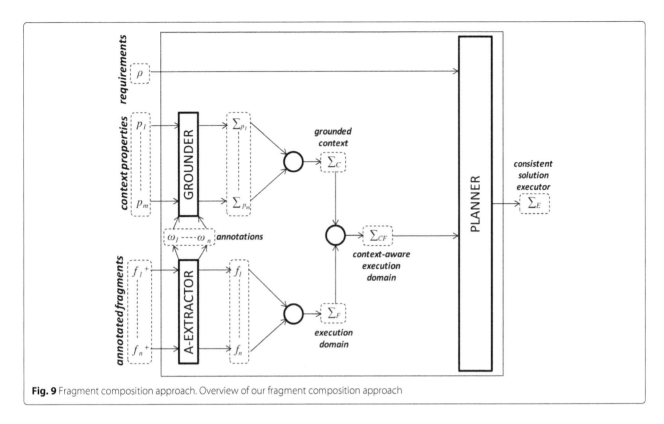

Fig. 9 Fragment composition approach. Overview of our fragment composition approach

aware system $\Psi = \langle F^+, C \rangle$) and composition requirements ρ expressed as a context formula over C. The output is an executor Σ_E that is a consistent solution executor for Ψ and ρ.

The focus of this article is to extensively present the service composition approach under the assumption that the set of eligible fragments for a specific composition problem has been already identified at the time of the composition. The selection of relevant fragments but also their reuse in similar composition problems is a very relevant aspect to make the composition approach more scalable.

Our implementation includes this optimization component and the complete formalization has been already presented in [8]. In it, we have defined a way to reduce the complexity of a planning problem (for a specific composition) by minimizing the search space according to the specific execution context, and reusing solutions (i.e., selected fragments) by learning from past executions. To select the relevant fragments in a specific context, QoS-aware service selection approaches as [15] can be also used. Another important aspect to highlight is that the composition approach proposed can be used not only

```
1   function plan(I,G)
2       OldSA := ⊥_SA
3       SA := ∅
4       while (OldSA ≠ SA ∧ I ∉ (G ∪ StatesOf(SA)))
5           Pr := StrongPreImage(G ∪ StatesOf(SA))
6           NewSA := PruneStates(Pr, G ∪ StatesOf(SA))
7           OldSA := SA
8           SA := SA ∪ NewSA
9       done
10      if (I ∈ (G ∪ StatesOf(SA)))
11          return SA
12      else
13          return ⊥_SA
14      fi
```

Fig. 10 (Backward) Planning Algorithm. Algorithm for strong planning in asynchronous domain

to reach a specific goal of a certain *abstract* activity but also to repair or recompose broken service compositions [16, 17], as a reaction to context changes (i.e., precondition violations or service unavailability).

The very general idea of the approach consists in building a planning domain Σ_{CF}, that together with goal ρ form a planing problem. While, the resolution of a specific planning problem is carried out by an existing algorithm planning [18], the novel part of this article is the definition and the formalization of a composition problem that takes into account the system context at a specific execution time. To make it possible, the *execution domain* Σ_F is built as asynchronous product of fragments F^+. We assume that fragments within a single context-aware system have uncorrelated actions, i.e., such fragments have mutually disjoint sets of actions. In order to encode all possible parallel executions of fragments for some context-aware system we introduce the notion of *execution domain*, which is a parallel (asynchronous) product of fragments:

Definition 6 (Execution Domain) *Let* $f_1 = \langle S_1, s^0{}_1, I_1,$ $O_1, R_1 \rangle$ *and* $f_2 = \langle S_2, s^0{}_2, I_2, O_2, R_2 \rangle$ *be two observable state transition systems such that* $(I_1 \cup O_1) \cap (I_2 \cup O_2) = \emptyset$. *An execution domain* Σ_F *for fragments* $F = \{f_1, f_2\}$ *is an asynchronous product of two fragments:*

$$\Sigma_F = \left\langle S_1 \times S_2, \left(s^0{}_1, s^0{}_2\right), I_1 \cup I_2, O_1 \cup O_2, R_F \right\rangle$$

where:

$$((s_1, s_2), a, (s'_1, s_2)) \in R_F, if (s_1, a, s'_1) \in R_1$$
$$((s_1, s_2), a, (s_1, s'_2)) \in R_F, if (s_2, a, s'_2) \in R_2$$
$$R_F = \{R_1 || R_2\}$$

Using fragment annotations $(\omega_1, \omega_2, \ldots, \omega_n)$ extracted by *A-EXTRACTOR*, context properties are grounded on fragment actions by *GROUNDER* so that the grounded context properties $\Sigma_{p_1}, \Sigma_{p_2}, \ldots, \Sigma_{p_m}$ are produced.

The grounding procedure, consists in replacing event-labeled transitions in context properties with action-labeled transition, which allows us to reflect the impact of fragment actions on the property state. Additionally, we use transition guards to reflect the executability of actions. As a result, the *grounded context property* features the same set of states as the orginal context property, but has different transition relation:

Definition 7 (Grounded Context Property) *Let* $\Psi = \langle F^+, C \rangle$ *be a context-aware system and let* R_C *be a space of context formulas of context* C. *A grounded context property for context property* $p = \langle L, l^0, E, T \rangle$ *is a tuple* $\Sigma_p = \langle L, l^0, A_F, T^g \rangle$, *where:*

- *L is a set of states and* $l^0 \in L$ *is the initial state;*
- A_F *is a set of all fragment actions of fragments* F^+;
- $T^g \subseteq L \times R_C \times A_F \times L$ *is a guarded transition relation.*

The grounding procedure consists in defining a grounded context property Σ_p on top of a context property p. While the sets of states in p and Σ_p are the same, in Σ_p the event-based transitions of p are replaced with action-based transitions as indicated by annotations. For each transition of p labelled with event e and for each action a whose effect contains e, we define a transition in Σ_p with the same initial and final state and labelled with a. For each goal-labeled action a_{abs}, if an action goal (which is a conjunctive clause) requires that this property has to be in a particular state l (i.e., a proposition corresponding to l appears in the conjunctive clause expressing the goal of a_{abs}), for every state in Σ_p we add a transition that starts in this state, terminates in l and is labelled with a_{abs}. Finally, for each action a_{less} that has no impact on the property and for each state in Σ_p we define a transition that starts and finishes in this state and is labelled with a_{less}. As such, we reflect the impact of all actions with respect to context property p. In order to take into account action preconditions, for each transition we introduce the guard, which is a precondition formula of its labelling action. A transition guard must be interpreted as a condition on the state of the whole context for which the transition is enabled. Formally:

Definition 8 (Grounding) *Let* $\Psi = \langle F^+, C \rangle$ *be a context-aware system. A grounding of a context property* $p = \langle L, l^0, E, T \rangle \in C$ *is a grounded context property* $\Sigma_p = \langle L, l^0, A_F, T^g \rangle$ *such that for every action* $a \in A_F$:

1. *if* $\exists e \in E(a) : e \in E$ *then for every transition* $(l, e, l') \in T$ *there exists transition* $(l, P(a), a, l') \in T^g$;
2. *if state* $l_g \in L$ *appears in conjunctive clause* $G(a)$ *then for every state* $l \in T$ *there exists transition* $(l, P(a), a, l_g) \in T^g$;
3. *if* $E(a) = \emptyset \wedge G(a) = \emptyset$ *or* $(E(a) \neq \emptyset) \wedge (E(a) \cap E = \emptyset)$ *or* $(G(a) \neq \emptyset) \wedge (\nexists l_g \in L : l_g \in G(a))$ *then for every state* $l \in L$ *there exists a transition* $(l, P(a), a, l) \in T^g$;
4. *no other states and transitions belong to* Σ_p.

Since action effect contains no more than one event per context property, and since a goal conjunctive clause cannot contain more than one state per context property, the grounded context property is a deterministic LTS (only one transition with the same label is possible from each state).

In order to reflect the impact and executabilty of fragment actions with respect to the whole context we introduce the notion of *grounded context*, which is a synchronous product of all constituent grounded context properties. We remark that the guards in the synchronous product can be removed. Indeed, for any guarded transition we can unambiguously figure out if the initial state of a transition satisfies the guard. Consequently, if the initial state satisfies the guard it is always 'unlocked' and we can replace it with the unguarded transition with the same properties, and if the initial state does not satisfy the guard it is always 'locked' and can be removed from the transition relation. Formally:

Definition 9 (Grounded Context) *Let* $\Psi = \langle F^+, C \rangle$ *be a context-aware system with context* $C = \{p_1, p_2, \ldots, p_n\}$ *and let* $\Sigma_{p_1}, \Sigma_{p_2}, \ldots, \Sigma_{p_n}$ *be the respective grounded context properties such that* $\Sigma_{p_i} = \langle L_i, l^0{}_i, A_F, T_i \rangle$ *for all* $i \in [1, n]$. *Grounded context for* Ψ *is an LTS* $\Sigma_C = \langle L_C, l^0{}_C, A_F, T_C \rangle$ *which is defined as follows:*

$$\Sigma_C = \langle L_1 \times \ldots \times L_n, \{l^0{}_1, \ldots l^0{}_n\}, A_F, T_C \rangle$$

where:

$$((l_1, \ldots, l_n), a, (l'_1, \ldots l'_n)) \in T_C, \qquad (1)$$
$$if \left(l_i, P(a), a, l'_i\right) \in T_i \text{ for all } i \in [1, n] \qquad (2)$$
$$and \ (l_1, \ldots, l_n) \models P(a) \qquad (3)$$

In turn, the context-aware execution domain can be constructed as a synchronous product of grounded context and execution domain.

Composition requirements ρ are compliant with the context-aware execution domain. By directly applying the planning algorithm to planning domain Σ_{CF} and planning goal ρ, we obtain the plan that is a consistent solution executor for a composition problem of Ψ and ρ. Moreover, if such plan is not found, then a consistent solution executor for a given composition problem does not exist.

3.3.1 Algorithm

For our convenience in this section we will omit the indices and denote the domain as follows: $D = \langle S, s^0, I, O, R \rangle$. The initial state of D becomes the initial state of the planning problem $I = s^0$, and the goal states are all states of the domain that satisfy ρ, that is $G = \{s \in S : s \models \rho\}$. As such, we obtain a conventional planning problem $\{D, I, G\}$.

Once a planning problem is obtained, a consistent solution executor is derived by the algorithm for strong planning in asynchronous domain presented in [18]. In the following, we briefly recap the description of this algorithm and definitions of theorems proving its termination, correctness and completeness.

The routine for searching a consistent solution executor is presented in Fig. 10. In this routine, we assume that the domain D is globally available, while we explicitly pass its initial states I and goal states G. The algorithm is a greatest fixed point iteration that incrementally constructs a

state-action table SA, which indicates which action has to be executed in certain state of D in order to reach a goal state. As such, SA encodes all transitions of the domain that can potentially be presented in the consistent solution executor. SA is initially empty and grows at each iteration by adding state-actions which unconditionally lead to the states that are already covered by SA or goal states (i.e., states STATESOF(SA) $\cup$ G). The termination of the algorithm is caused by either the situation when 1) no new states are included in the next iteration or 2) the current state-action table already contains all initial states I, which actually means that the solution for the initial states is already found.

The algorithm is defined such that it explicitly deals with the constraints imposed by a consistent solution executor. This logic is essentially realized by the key primitives STRONGPREIMAGE and PRUNESTATES.

STRONGPREIMAGE is the basis of the backward search. For a subset S of states of Σ_{CF}, STRONGPREIMAGE returns a set of state-action pairs $\{\langle s, a \rangle\}$ that encode all transitions of Σ_{CF} that immediately lead to S. It takes into account that uncontrollable actions can be neither controlled nor predicted. So the function guarantees that ones a state-action $\langle s, a \rangle$ is included in the table, states of S can always be reached from s despite non-determinism.

The primitive is defined as follows:

STRONGPREIMAGE(S) $=$

$$\{\langle s, a \rangle : (a \in I) \wedge (\exists (s, a, s') \in R : s' \in S) \wedge \qquad (4)$$
$$(\nexists (s, a', s'') \in R) : a \in O)\} \bigcup \qquad (5)$$
$$\{(s, a) : (a \in O) \wedge (\exists (s, a, s') \in R : s' \in S) \wedge \qquad (6)$$
$$\forall (s, a', s'') \in R : (a' \in O) \rightarrow (s'' \in S))\} \ . \qquad (7)$$

In order to properly reflect the requirements imposed by the definition of consistent solution executor, controllable and uncontrollable actions are treated differently. For example, when we include controllable state-action, not only do we check that it leads to the states that are already in the state-action table but also make sure that uncontrollable actions are not available from the same state. Similarly, the way we treat uncontrollable actions guarantees that none of the uncontrollable actions originating from the same state are disregarded. Consequently, the strong pre-imaging function significantly contributes to the satisfaction of condition 1 (executor is runnable) of of consistent solution executor. We remark that this planning algorithm is significantly different from the conventional strong planning algorithms (e.g., [19]) that treat all the actions of the planning domain uniformly.

PRUNESTATES function is responsible for removing from the current pre-image all the state for which the solution is already available (i.e., those that are already included in the state-action table). It is defined as follows:

$$\textsc{PruneStates}(\gamma, S) = \{\langle s, a \rangle \in \gamma : s \notin S\}.$$

We remark that the purpose of the pruning goes beyond avoiding the duplication of the same state-actions in the resulting table. The pruning ensures that for each state no more than one controllable state-action is included which closely relates to condition 1 of consistent solution executor. It also guarantees that the state-action table does not contain loops (conditions 3). Another property of the pruning that has nothing to do with the definition of consistent solution executor is that only the shortest solution from any state appears in the state-action table.

The resulting *state-action table* (a collection of state-action pairs) shows how the resulting executable process should behave in different states. Uncontrollable state-actions indicate which uncontrollable actions have to be expected in the respective state. Similarly, controllable state-actions indicate which controllable action has to be executed from the respective state. The consistent solution executor Σ_{SA} can be directly derived from the state-action table using forward analysis.

For the given algorithms the following theorems can be proved (the respective proofs can be found in [18]).

Theorem 1 (Termination) *Let* $D = \langle S, s^0, I, O, R \rangle$ *be a context-aware execution domain, let* $I = s^0$ *be its initial state and let* $G \subseteq S$ *be a set of goal states. The execution of* PLAN(I,G) *on D terminates.*

Theorem 2 (Correctness and Completeness) *If* PLAN(I,G) *returns state-action table SA, then* Σ_{SA} *is a consistent solution executor for the respective composition problem. If* PLAN(I,G) *returns* FAIL, *then no consistent solution executor to the respective composition problem exists.*

3.4 Framework implementation

The framework introduced in the previous sections has been implemented and is part of an extended version[6] of the ASTRO-CAptEvo framework [20, 21]. Its architecture is depicted in Fig. 11 and is composed by three layers, namely the Presentation, Execution and Adaptation layers.

The Adaptation layer is where the composition approach proposed in this paper has been implemented. The operation in this layer is regulated by the *Adaptation Manager*. It is notified about the need to refine an abstract activity with its respective goal, together with the information on the current context. All these information are passed to the *Domain Builder*. The *Domain Builder* builds an initial version of the composition problem, which is made of a context model, a set of available annotated fragments, the current context configuration (current states of context properties), and a set of goal context configurations. The *Domain*

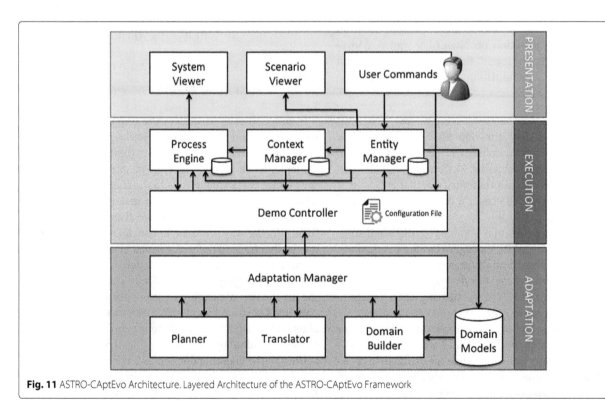

Fig. 11 ASTRO-CAptEvo Architecture. Layered Architecture of the ASTRO-CAptEvo Framework

Builder extracts all necessary specification from the repository of *Domain Models*. Taking into account the current context and the composition goal, the *Domain Builder* simplifies the context model by pruning all unreachable configurations and removing all fragments that are useless for the goal specified (see [8] for details on this pruning step). Thanks to this optimization phase, the size of the planning domain is reduced and the computation time for the planning phase is significantly reduced.

The *Translator* translates a composition problem into a planning problem such that it can be resolved by the *Planner*. It is also responsible for interpreting the results of the *Planner*. The back translation transforms a plan obtained into an executable process. Finally, the executable process is sent to the *Demo Controller* that injects it into the current process instance. All these steps are implemented in our framework and are graphically represented in the sequence diagram depicted in Fig. 12.

The Execution layer is in charge of 1) simulating the application domain, 2) executing process instances, 3) detecting when to call the Adaptation Layer to realize fragments composition, and 4) refining a process instance according to the solution received from the *Adaptation layer*.

The *Entity Manager* manages all active entities within the scenario (e.g., ships, cars, tracks, storage managers, etc.) and it simulates their behaviour. When the *Entity Manager* creates a new entity (either within the initialization phase, or in response to a user command), it deploys the entity process to the *Process Engine*, it adds the corresponding context properties to the context model in the *Context Manager* and it puts all the entity-related specifications (such as fragment models and the context property diagrams provided by the entity) to the *Domain*

Models Repository. When the entity "exits" the scenario, contrary actions are performed. In between, the *Entity Manager* simulates the entity behaviour, which is synchronized with the execution of the entity process, and updates the *Context Manager* and the *Scenario Viewer* with the current status. Finally, the *Entity Manager* processes all the user commands bringing changes to the domain (e.g., creation of new ships and orders, damage of a car, unavailability of fragments, etc..).

The *Context Manager* stores the system context (i.e., a set of context properties of all active entities) and it constantly synchronizes its current configuration with the application domain by monitoring the simulation going on in the *Entity Manager*.

The *Process Engine* executes the entity processes and suspends them every time that an abstract activity is reached and need to be refined. When it happens, the need is reported to the *Demo Controller*.

The *Demo Controller* aggregates all the data that is needed by the *Adaptation layer* to manage an abstract activity refinement (i.e., composition). This includes the current context provided by the *Context Manager* and the description of the need (process instance affected, its execution status, type of need) provided by the *Process Engine*. After the data is sent to the *Adaptation layer* and the solution is returned back, the *Demo Controller* adapts the process instance.

Finally, the adapted process instance is redeployed and restarted by the *Process Engine*.

The Presentation layer provides a detailed live view of the simulation taking place in the *Execution layer*. It also gives some control over the simulation and lets the user affect the application domain to model different situations.

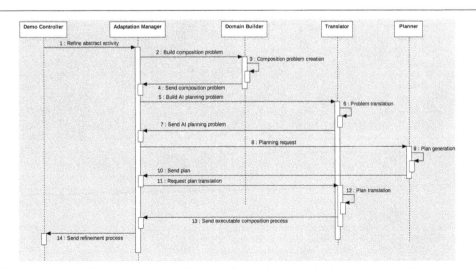

Fig. 12 ASTRO-CAptEvo: Fragments Composition approach. Sequence diagram that shows the dynamic part of the fragments composition approach

In particular, The *Scenario Viewer* provides a graphical representation of the application domain through a map containing all the facilities (landing gates, storage areas, roads etc.) and showing all the entities of the domain (cars, ships, managers, etc.) in action (see Fig. 13).

For each active entity, the *System Viewer* gives access to 1) the list of provided fragments and 2) the list of process instances. In turn, each process instance can be examined in a *Process Viewer* window (Fig. 14). Here the user can find:

- the process context information including all context properties and their current values;
- the process model with the execution progress;
- the execution history including all the applied compositions;

If the user is interested in how a certain abstract activity has been refined, the *Composition Inspector* (Fig. 15 provides full report from composition goals and fragments selection, to the details of the planning phase (planning domain, a resulting process, etc.).

The *User Commands* are used to control the simulation running in the *Execution layer* and bring changes to the running scenario. The user can affect the scenario by triggering exogenous events (e.g., unavailability of entities and fragments) and creating new entities. To replicate the usage of the framework, in other application domains it is enough to: (1) define all the scenario models (entities, processes, fragments and context properties) that will be saved in the *Domain Models* repository; (2) define a *configuration file* that includes the specification of which types of entity must be instantiated and executed at simulation time. While all the other components of Fig. 11 can be executed without domain-specific extensions, the *Scenario Viewer* must be implemented from scratch, since it should provide a graphical representation of the application domain (e.g., as the harbour map in the Car Logistics).

4 Experiments and results

To demonstrate our approach in action and evaluate its performance and scalability, we have used the implementation presented in Section 3.4 to model and run the Car Logistics scenario introduced in Section 2. In the following sections we present the outcome of the set of experiments done.

4.1 Experimental evaluation

We ran the ASTRO-CAptEvo framework in continuous mode for around an hour and collected information on 1060 compositions performed within this time. The run was performed on a Windows laptop with dual-core 2.8GHz CPU with 8Gb of RAM (we remark, however, that

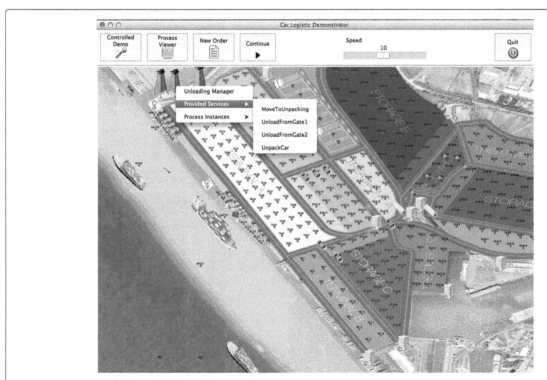

Fig. 13 Scenario Viewer. Scenario Viewer component of the ASTRO-CAptEvo framework

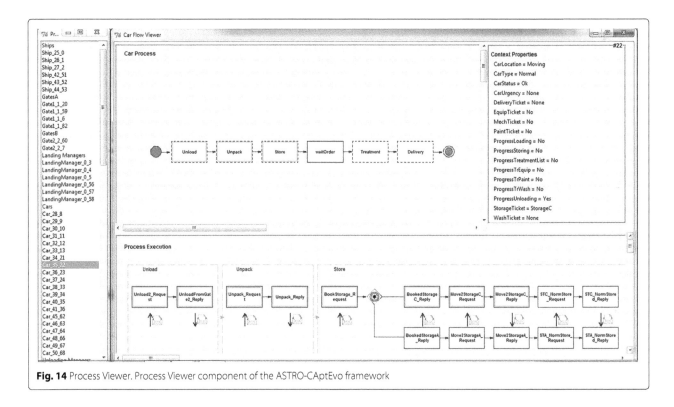

Fig. 14 Process Viewer. Process Viewer component of the ASTRO-CAptEvo framework

the planner implementation is single-threaded). For each composition, we measured a number of indicators that characterized the complexity of the problem and the timing. Then we tried to organize them into charts to make conclusion about the applicability of the approach.

While conducting the measurements, we took into account the general conclusion about the performance of the planning algorithm given in [18]. In particular the authors stated that "the performance of synthesis appears to degrade sub-exponentially with the size of the components; and in vast majority of cases, it degrades polynomially with the number of components".

However, when working with bigger domains the performance may degrade to exponential. The most reasonable explanation for that is based on the implementation details of the BDD (binary decision diagram) library used: big domains are much more memory demanding and for them the garbage collection and data re-arrangement mechanisms may take considerable time to keep the memory consumption within certain limits.

In the chart in Fig. 16 we show the dependency between the number of fragments passed to the planner and the time it takes to produce a plan (in logarithmic scale). It can be seen that it shows exponential scalability. In general, this result corresponds to that of [18]. The performance degradation to exponential even for small numbers of fragments (that was not present in [18]) can be explained by the fact that, in addition to fragments, the planning domain in context-aware composition also contains

context-related LTSs. As a result, even for small number of fragments, the domain becomes relatively large and results in exponential scalability.

Alternatively, we propose our own indicator of domain complexity that is the total number of transitions in fragments and context properties making up the domain:

$$Complexity = NumContextTrans + NumFragTrans.$$

We find this indicator more precise compared to the number of fragments. It also allows us to see a more fine-grained distribution of all composition problems with respect to complexity. The performance scalability with respect to composition complexity is represented by the chart in Fig. 17. It can be observed that it generally corresponds to the chart in Fig. 16 and features exponential growth. However, it makes sense to consider this chart along with the complexity distribution of all composition problems analyzed in Fig. 17. It can be observed that most composition cases reside in the region with low or moderate complexity, while the cases with high complexity are quite few. We remark that such distribution also affects the precision of the scalability chart in the region of high complexity (less experiments are carried out there).

Consequently, from the charts in Fig. 17 we can derive the following table showing the percentage of composition cases that are resolved in no more than n seconds:

n, sec	compositions resolved within n sec, %
0.1	19.07
1	91.12
3	96.51
10	99.62
30	100.00

From the table it can be observed that the vast majority of adaptation-related compositions actually take less than 10 seconds. This is the first evidence of practical applicability of our composition technique: although the performance of context-aware composition degrades exponentially with growing complexity of a composition problem, it is still enough to be used for the actual problem of process adaptation. This becomes especially true when we notice that in many application domain there are no severe restrictions on the performance of composition

related tasks. For example, in the CLS scenario, the typical life cycle of a car may have duration up to several weeks and usually it is affordable for a user-centric system to take up to half a minute to produce a solution.

The last important observation is that for each particular composition problem we build a planning domain that includes only the information that is relevant for this problem, namely: 1) the subset of context properties that are relevant for entities under consideration, which is normally a small portion of the overall context of the scenario and 2) the subset of all fragments that may be useful within the current composition problem, which is, again, only a small portion of all fragments currently available in the system. The idea of fragments and context pre-selection is quite natural: if the system resolves a problem for a particular car it needs only the part of context that are relevant for this car (and not for dozens of other cars and ships in the system), and fragments that

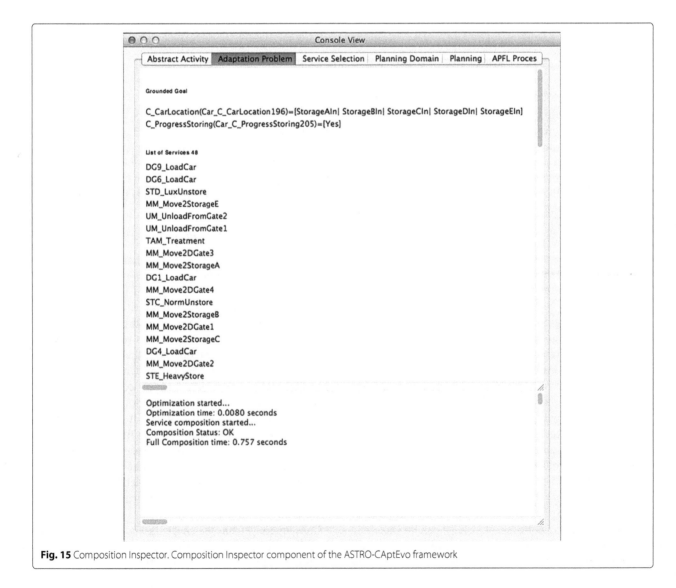

Fig. 15 Composition Inspector. Composition Inspector component of the ASTRO-CAptEvo framework

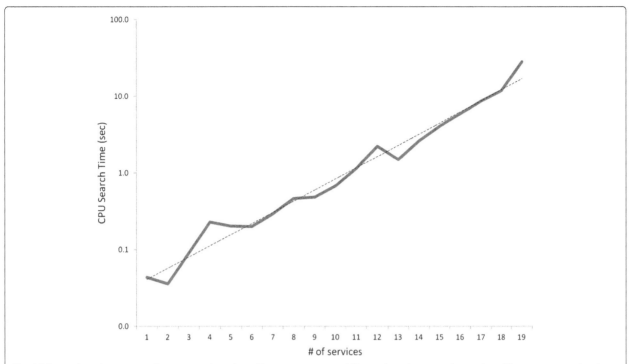

Fig. 16 Dependency between performance and number of fragments composed. Dependency between the number of fragments passed to the planner and the time it takes to produce a plan

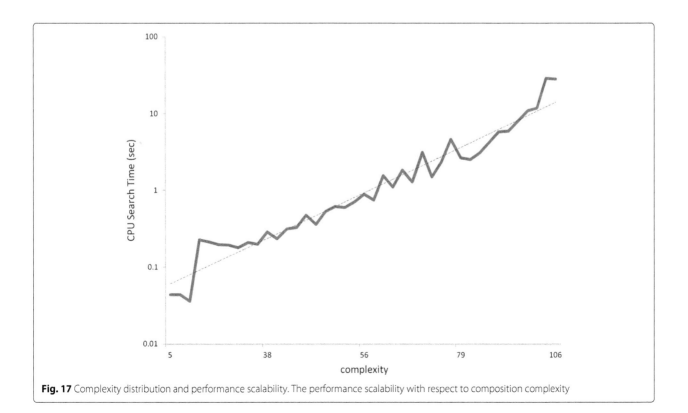

Fig. 17 Complexity distribution and performance scalability. The performance scalability with respect to composition complexity

are relevant for car only (e.g., it does not make sense to consider a fragment for ship landing). We expect this pre-selection to allow us to preserve the same average size of the planning problem even for much larger (with respect to the number of entities) domains. Indeed, if within the scenario we operate thousands of cars instead of dozens, the complexity of an average composition problem for a particular car would not grow and remain the same: the proper selection will always come up with more or less the same amount of relevant fragments and context. The increase in the amount of cars in the harbour does not functionally affect the way a car procedure should be planned and executed. As such, we expect our approach to be easily scalable in this regard.

5   Related work

In last years, different approaches have been proposed for the modeling of services in a suitable way for making efficient dynamic service composition. From the scenario and the challenges discussed in this paper, a specific need has emerged: being able to define services in such a way that they can dynamically be specialized to the context, when this is discovered or when it changes. Where the context is characterized by the state of the execution environment and by the available services at a specific time and location.

An approach targeting this problem is presented by Hull et al. [22] in their work about *Business Artifacts*. It consists in the definition of a formal/theoretical framework for defining conceptual entities, the artifacts, related to the execution of services whose operations influence the entities evolution, as they move through the business's operations. However, this approach mostly focuses on service modeling aspects and does not deal with dynamic service composition. Yu et al. propose MoDAR [23], an approach on how to design dynamically adaptive service-based systems. Essentially they propose a method to simplify business processes by using rules to abstract their complex structure and to capture their variable behavior. However, in dynamic context, revising rules to manage frequent and unpredictable changes might turn out to be very expensive and complex. In [24], the authors tackle the problem of unpredictable execution of service-based applications. In particular, they focused on how to evolve a running service composition and propose a way for modeling artifacts corresponding to composite services that can change at runtime. However, software engineer intervention is needed to manipulate the runtime model of services. Moreover, the adaptation and application logics are mixed making the model not very flexible. In [25] the authors present DAMASCo, a framework managing the discovery, composition, adaptation and monitoring of services in a context-aware fashion by taking into account semantic information rather than only the syntactic one.

Since they address the problem of making the reuse of software entities more agile and easy to model, they focus especially on the adaptation of pre-existing software entities that are used during the developing of service-based applications. Also the approach presented in [26] focuses on the need of explicitly manage the context in the composition of web services, to address the problem of semantic heterogeneities between services. The authors present a context-based mediation approach that allows services both to share a common meaning of exchanged data and to automatically resolve conflicts related to the semantic of the data, by using context-based annotations which offer an optimized handling of the data flow. It would be interesting to use the approaches [25, 26] in the management of the composition of fragments coming from the different entities and the definition of the data flow between them. In [27] the concepts of goals and plans are introduced in the business processes modeling with the purpose of extending the standard BPMN to make the BPM more flexible and responsive to change. However, even if plans are selected and executed at runtime, they are defined at design time together with the relations with the goals they can satisfy. Göser et al. [28] is a framework for, among other things, the management of the integration of services in the business processes implementation's process to speed the implementation and deployment phases. Services' integration is realized in a plug-and-play manner in which activities are selected from a repository and then dropped into a process. However, as regards the runtime adaptation of processes, in this approach only ad-hoc modifications are managed.

Hermosillo et al. [29] is a framework that combines complex event processing and dynamic business process adaptation, which allows to respond to the needs of the rapidity changing environment, and its adaptation language called SBPL, and extension to BPEL which adds flexibility to business processes. As in the previous framework, only ad-hoc adaptation processes are defined ad design-time together with the definition of specific adaptation points for the business process and the events that will trigger that adaptation.

In the context of Future Internet [30], some frameworks have been proposed to deploy and execute adaptable, QoS-aware service compositions. In [31], authors present an engine for the execution of service compositions based on a *unified model*. The unified model allows to execute service compositions that are specified by use of different languages with different underlying modeling paradigms, e.g. imperative and declarative service compositions by the same engine. Furthermore, the unified model and the presented engine enables the unification of the execution of service orchestrations and the enactment of service choreographies. CHOReOS project [32] proposes a dynamic development process, and associated methods, tools and middleware, to sustain the composition of services in the Future Internet. It proposes a synthesis approach able to automatically generate, out of a BPMN2 choreography specification, the needed adaptation and coordination logic, and distribute it between the participants so to enforce the choreography. Finally, in [16], authors propose service composition repair as an alternative solution that goes beyond the limits of service replacement while avoiding recomposition.

6 Discussion

We conclude this section with a discussion (summarized in Table 1) in which we try to point out the advantages of the proposed approach respect to related works. As regards to the standard approaches of service composition, such as those of orchestration and choreography, they have have some crucial limitations. A major problem of these approaches is that most of them are based on the assumption that during the specification of composition requirements, the application designer knows the services to be composed. Besides, some of them, such as [14, 33], remain focused on the syntax level without considering the semantic aspects of composition, which are, instead, necessary in context-based applications. Other approaches like [31, 34–38], have introduced the management of semantic knowledge in their models to drive the services' composition and interoperation but, despite this, they do not allow processes to be specialized at runtime, through dynamic service composition. Cubo and Pimentel [25], Mrissa et al. [26], Greenwood [27] allow for very efficient management of service compositions at runtime, while [16, 32] supports composition evolution through adaptation to possible changes in the discovered services. The adaptation strategies applied in these approaches in some cases are defined at design-time or are strongly

related to a prescribed coordination model (i.e., BPMN2 model in [32] does not open to runtime and context-aware refinements).

The approach proposed in this paper, instead, offers a lightweight-model, with respect to the existing languages for service composition. It is more flexible and able to define both orchestrations and choreographies thanks to its dynamic collaboration among entities. Moreover, the model explicitly handles the context by managing the dynamicity of services, which can enter or leave the system in any moment, with a flexible connection strategy between entities that exploit the *publish-subscribe paradigm*. Unlike specifications of traditional systems, where the behaviors are static descriptions of the expected run-time operation, our approach allows the application to define dynamic behaviors. This is realized thanks to the usage of *abstract activities* representing opening points in the definition of processes, which allow services being refined when the context is known or discovered. The *bottom-up approach* for the activities' refinement allows *fragments*, once they are selected for the composition, to climb the entities's relations to be embedded in the running process. Besides, the composition is defined at runtime, so that exactly the currently available services are considered for the composition. This feature, on the one hand enables a smooth exploitation of proximity services, and on the other hand makes the impact of run-time changes to services (modification of behavior, entrance or exit of services from the system) transparent to the system execution.

7 Conclusion

In this article, we presented a service composition framework that overcomes many limitations of the existing approaches. Our approach uses an AI planning algorithm as a reasoning mechanism, and can be used to solve composition problems of real-world complexity in dynamic

Table 1 Service composition approaches comparison

Approaches	Customization and context-awareness	Openness	Flexibility
Our approach	*Runtime* service composition in a dynamic context	Transparent handling of new services available at *runtime*	Structural changes in services functionalities and services unavailability
[22–29]	Context-aware selection of services using semantic information, or context events to identify adaptation situations	Not addressed	Adaptation plans defined at *design-time* together with the relations with the goals they can satisfy or predefined adaptation points.
[14, 33]	Not addressed	Syntax level service selection and composition at *design-time*	Not addressed
[16, 31, 32, 34–38],	Semantic Knowledge to drive the service composition	*Design-time* services selection, binding and composition	Service Choreography evolution through adaptation to possible changes in the discovered services

and pervasive setting like Logistics [8] or Smart Urban Mobility [7] domains.

The proposed framework uses an innovative service model in which services are considered to be stateful, non deterministic and asynchronous. The composition requirements model is based on the idea of abstracting composition requirements from implementation details of services. This allows for deep automation of the composition process. Even though in the article we only consider reachability goals as control-flow requirements, we emphasize that our approach can be easily adapted to use any advanced control-flow language used in planning (e.g., [39]). We also remark that our approach is compatible with data-flow requirements technique introduced in [40]. All this makes the new composition engine applicable to a wide range of real service composition problems.

Thanks to the abstraction of composition requirements from implementation of components we organized the composition life-cycle in such a way that almost all the human time-demanding operations can be accomplished at design time so that the composition run-time is fully automated. Moreover, the availability of a tool with such essential property brings new possibilities to composition dependent systems.

We generally consider two main future steps in the development of the ideas presented. One of them naturally consists in adopting the advanced compatible techniques for specifying complex control- and data-flow requirements. Another one concerns conducting experiments on using our approach in user-centric systems.

Endnotes

[1] In this article, we focus only on control-flow aspect of composition. Data-flow aspect can be handled using the technique presented in [40], which is compatible with the formal framework introduced.

[2] Although the proposed approach works with processes modeled using APFL, it can be also used extending other process-based languages like BPMN [41] or CMMN [42].

[3] We remark that in order to avoid state explosion and to keep a planning problem tractable, it is strictly required that the number of states of each context property is finite and reasonably small. One technique for dealing with context properties with large or infinite number of states in planning can be found in [43].

[4] In this article, as context formulas we use reachability goals over context states (i. e., a goal consists in achieving certain context states, known as goal states). At the same time, we emphasize that used AI planning

techniques support for more sophisticated constructs including procedural goals, reactive goals and goals with preferences (more details can be found in [39]).

[5] In our approach, the need to annotate newly created fragments to integrate them into the running system is the only human-dependent task that needs to be accomplished at run time. We do not see it as a significant limitation since 1) the annotation of new fragments is normally far less urgent task than resolving an ongoing failure and can hardly interrupt the normal operation of the system, and 2) the annotation effort can be distributed among multiple partners (each provider annotates its fragments).

[6] http://das.fbk.eu/astro-captevo

Authors' contributions

All authors are equal contributors. All authors read and approved the final manuscript.

Authors' information

Dr. Antonio Bucchiarone (PhD) is a senior researcher in the FBK-DAS research unit of FBK. He received his PhD in Computer Science and Engineering, from IMT of Lucca (Italy) in July 2008. His main research interests are: self-adaptive (collective) systems, applied formal methods, run-time service composition and adaptation, specification and verification of component-based systems, dynamic software architectures. He has been actively involved in various research projects in the context of self-adaptive systems.
Dr. Annapaola Marconi (PhD) is a senior researcher at FBK, where she directs the FBK-DAS research unit. She received her PhD in Computer Science in 2008, from the ICT International Doctoral School of the University of Trento. Her research interests include distributed systems, collective adaptive systems, and automated composition of service-based applications. She has been actively involved in various local and European research projects in the area of Smart Mobility.
Dr. Marco Pistore (PhD), is currently head of the FBK-SC unit. He received a PhD in Computer Science from the University of Pisa (Italy) in 1998. He has an h-index of 46 and more than 200 publications in international journals, conferences, and symposia. He has 12 years of experience in the management of research teams and projects: he has been responsible of research groups and project teams (up to more than 30 persons); he has been scientific coordinator and partner coordinator of regional, national and EU research and innovation projects; he has been responsible of technology transfer projects with National and International companies.
Dr. Heorhi Raik (PhD), is a junior researcher at FBK. He received his PhD in Computer Science in 2012, from the ICT International Doctoral School of the University of Trento, with a thesis titled: "Service Composition in Dynamic Environments: From Theory to Practice". His research interests include service composition, dynamic process adaptation, user-centric services, AI planning, collective adaptive systems.

References

1. Autili M, Tivoli M, Goldman A (2016) Thematic series on service composition for the future internet. J Internet Serv Appl 7(1):3–134
2. Issarny V, Georgantas N, Hachem S, Zarras A, Vassiliadist P, Autili M, Gerosa MA, Hamida AB (2011) Service-oriented middleware for the future internet: state of the art and research directions. J Internet Serv Appl 2(1):23–45

3. Zhou J, Gilman E, Palola J, Riekki J, Ylianttila M, Sun JZ (2011) Context-aware pervasive service composition and its implementation. Pers Ubiquit Comput 15(3):291–303

4. Tari K, Amirat Y, Chibani A, Yachir A, Mellouk A (2010) Context-aware dynamic service composition in ubiquitous environment. In: Proceedings of IEEE International Conference on Communications, ICC 2010. IEEE, Cape Town. pp 1–6

5. Truong HL, Dustdar S (2009) A survey on context-aware web service systems. IJWIS 5(1):5–31

6. Bucchiarone A, de Sanctis M, Marconi A, Pistore M, Traverso P (2015) Design for adaptation of distributed service-based systems. In: Service-Oriented Computing - 13th International Conference, ICSOC 2015, November 16-19, 2015, Proceedings. Springer, Goa. pp 383–393

7. Bucchiarone A, de Sanctis M, Marconi A, Pistore M, Traverso P (2016) Incremental composition for adaptive by-design service based systems. In: IEEE International Conference on Web Services, ICWS 2016, June 27 - July 2, 2016. IEEE, San Francisco. pp 236–243

8. Bucchiarone A, Marconi A, Mezzina CA, Pistore M, Raik H (2013) On-the-fly adaptation of dynamic service-based systems: Incrementality, reduction and reuse. In: Service-Oriented Computing - 11th International Conference, ICSOC 2013, December 2-5, 2013, Proceedings. Springer, Berlin. pp 146–161

9. Eberle H, Unger T, Leymann F (2009) Process fragments. In: On the Move to Meaningful Internet Systems: OTM 2009, Confederated International Conferences, CoopIS, DOA, IS, and ODBASE 2009, Vilamoura, Portugal, November 1-6, 2009, Proceedings, Part I. Springer. pp 398–405

10. Raik H (2012) Service Composition in Dynamic Environments: From Theory to Practice. PhD Dissertation. Available at http://eprints-phd.biblio.unitn.it/864/

11. Böse F, Piotrowski J (2009) Autonomously controlled storage management in vehicle logistics applications of rfid and mobile computing systems. Int J RT Technol Res Appl 1(1):57–76

12. Bucchiarone A, Lluch-Lafuente A, Marconi A, Pistore M (2009) A formalisation of adaptable pervasive flows. In: Web Services and Formal Methods, 6th International Workshop, WS-FM 2009, September 4-5, 2009, Revised Selected Papers. Springer, Bologna. pp 61–75

13. Herrmann K, Rothermel K, Kortuem G, Dulay N (2008) Adaptable pervasive flows - an emerging technology for pervasive adaptation. In: Workshop on Pervasive Adaptation (PerAda)

14. Committee OWT (2007) Web services business process execution language, version 2.0. Available at http://docs.oasis-open.org/wsbpel/2.0/wsbpel-v2.0

15. Haddad JE, Manouvrier M, Rukoz M (2010) Tqos: Transactional and qos-aware selection algorithm for automatic web service composition. IEEE Trans Serv Comput 3(1):73–85

16. Yan Y, Poizat P, Zhao L (2010) Repair vs. recomposition for broken service compositions. In: Service-Oriented Computing - 8th International Conference, ICSOC 2010, ecember 7-10, 2010. Proceedings. Springer, San Francisco. pp 152–166

17. Bucchiarone A, Marconi A, Pistore M, Raik H (2012) Dynamic adaptation of fragment-based and context-aware business processes. In: 2012 IEEE 19th International Conference on Web Services, June 24-29, 2012, Honolulu. pp 33–41

18. Bertoli P, Pistore M, Traverso P (2010) Automated composition of web services via planning in asynchronous domains. Artif Intell 174:316–361

19. Cimatti A, Pistore M, Roveri M, Traverso P (2003) Weak, strong, and strong cyclic planning via symbolic model checking. Artif Intell 1-2:35–84

20. Bucchiarone A, Marconi A, Pistore M, Raik H (2012) Dynamic adaptation of fragment-based and context-aware business processes. In: 2012 IEEE 19th International Conference on Web Services, June 24-29, 2012. IEEE, Honolulu. pp 33–41

21. Raik H, Bucchiarone A, Khurshid N, Marconi A, Pistore M (2012) Astro-captevo: Dynamic context-aware adaptation for service-based systems. In: Eighth IEEE World Congress on Services, SERVICES 2012, June 24-29, 2012, Honolulu. pp 385–392

22. Hull R, Damaggio E, De Masellis R, Fournier F, Gupta M, Heath III FT, Hobson S, Linehan MH, Maradugu S, Nigam A, Sukaviriya PN, Vaculín R (2011) Business artifacts with guard-stage-milestone lifecycles: managing artifact interactions with conditions and events. In: Proceedings of the Fifth ACM International Conference on Distributed Event-Based Systems, DEBS 2011, July 11-15, 2011. ACM, New York. pp 51–62

23. Yu J, Sheng QZ, Swee JKY (2010) Model-driven development of adaptive service-based systems with aspects and rules. In: WISE. Lecture Notes in Computer Science, vol. 6488. pp 548–563

24. Hussein M, Han J, Yu Y, Colman A (2013) Enabling runtime evolution of context-aware adaptive services. IEEE International Conference on Services Computing

25. Cubo J, Pimentel E (2011) Damasco: A framework for the automatic composition of component-based and service-oriented architectures. In: Software Architecture - 5th European Conference, ECSA 2011, September 13-16, 2011. Proceedings. Springer, Essen. pp 388–404

26. Mrissa M, Ghedira C, Benslimane D, Maamar Z, Rosenberg F, Dustdar S (2007) A context-based mediation approach to compose semantic web services. ACM Trans Internet Techn 8(1)

27. Greenwood DAP (2008) Goal-oriented autonomic business process modeling and execution: Engineering change management demonstration. In: Business Process Management, 6th International Conference, BPM 2008, September 2-4, 2008. Proceedings. Springer, Milan. pp 390–393

28. Göser K, Jurisch M, Acker H, Kreher U, Lauer M, Rinderle S, Reichert M, Dadam P (2007) Next-generation process management with ADEPT2. In: Proceedings of the BPM Demonstration Program at the Fifth International Conference on Business Process Management (BPM'07), 24-27 September 2007. Brisbane. Springer

29. Hermosillo G, Seinturier L, Duchien L (2010) Creating context-adaptive business processes. In: Service-Oriented Computing - 8th International Conference, ICSOC 2010, San Francisco, CA, USA, December 7-10, 2010. Proceedings. pp 228–242

30. Autili M, Goldman A, Tivoli M (2015) IEEE services visionary track on service composition for the future internet (SCFI 2015). In: 2015 IEEE World Congress on Services, SERVICES 2015, June 27 - July 2, 2015. IEEE, New York City. pp 327–328

31. Görlach K, Leymann F (2015) A flexible engine for the unified execution of service compositions. In: 2015 IEEE Symposium on Service-Oriented System Engineering, SOSE 2015, March 30 - April 3, 2015. San Francisco Bay. IEEE. pp 133–142

32. Autili M, Inverardi P, Tivoli M (2014) CHOREOS: large scale choreographies for the future internet. In: 2014 Software Evolution Week - IEEE Conference on Software Maintenance, Reengineering, and Reverse Engineering, CSMR-WCRE 2014, February 3-6, 2014. Antwerp. IEEE. pp 391–394

33. Kavantzas N, Burdett GRD (2004) Wscdl v1.0. Available at http://www.w3.org/TR/2004/WD-ws-cdl-10-20040427/

34. BPML.org (2002) Business process modeling language (bpml). Available at http://www.bpmi.org

35. Arkin A, Askary S, Fordin S, Jekeli W, Kawaguchi K, Orchard D, et al (2002) Web service choreography interface (wsci). Available at http://www.w3.org/TR/wsci

36. McGuinness DL, van Harmelen F (2004) Owl web ontology language overview [online]. Available at http://www.w3.org/TR/owl-features/

37. McIlraith SA, Son T, Zeng H (2001) Semantic web services. IEEE Int Syst 16(2):46–53

38. WSMO Wsmo working group. Available at http://www.wsmo.org

39. Traverso P, Pistore M (2004) Automated composition of semantic web services into executable processes. In: International Semantic Web Conference (ISWC). pp 380–394

40. Kazhamiakin R, Marconi A, Pistore M, Heorki R (2013) Data-flow requirements for dynamic service composition. In: Proceedings of the 20th International Conference on Web Services. pp 243–250

41. Group OM (2011) Business process model and notation - version 2.0. Available at http://www.omg.org/spec/BPMN/2.0/

42. Group OM (2016) Case management model and notation (cmmn) - version 1.1. Available at http://www.omg.org/spec/CMMN/1.1/

43. Pistore M, Marconi A, Bertoli P, Traverso P (2005) Automated composition of web services by planning at the knowledge level. In: IJCAI-05, Proceedings of the Nineteenth International Joint Conference on Artificial Intelligence, July 30 - August 5, 2005, Edinburgh. pp 1252–1259

Permissions

The contributors of this book come from diverse backgrounds, making this book a truly international effort. This book will bring forth new frontiers with its revolutionizing research information and detailed analysis of the nascent developments around the world.

We would like to thank all the contributing authors for lending their expertise to make the book truly unique. They have played a crucial role in the development of this book. Without their invaluable contributions this book wouldn't have been possible. They have made vital efforts to compile up to date information on the varied aspects of this subject to make this book a valuable addition to the collection of many professionals and students.

This book was conceptualized with the vision of imparting up-to-date information and advanced data in this field. To ensure the same, a matchless editorial board was set up. Every individual on the board went through rigorous rounds of assessment to prove their worth. After which they invested a large part of their time researching and compiling the most relevant data for our readers.

The editorial board has been involved in producing this book since its inception. They have spent rigorous hours researching and exploring the diverse topics which have resulted in the successful publishing of this book. They have passed on their knowledge of decades through this book. To expedite this challenging task, the publisher supported the team at every step. A small team of assistant editors was also appointed to further simplify the editing procedure and attain best results for the readers.

Apart from the editorial board, the designing team has also invested a significant amount of their time in understanding the subject and creating the most relevant covers. They scrutinized every image to scout for the most suitable representation of the subject and create an appropriate cover for the book.

The publishing team has been an ardent support to the editorial, designing and production team. Their endless efforts to recruit the best for this project, has resulted in the accomplishment of this book. They are a veteran in the field of academics and their pool of knowledge is as vast as their experience in printing. Their expertise and guidance has proved useful at every step. Their uncompromising quality standards have made this book an exceptional effort. Their encouragement from time to time has been an inspiration for everyone.

The publisher and the editorial board hope that this book will prove to be a valuable piece of knowledge for researchers, students, practitioners and scholars across the globe.

List of Contributors

Thomas Cerqueus, Antoine Boutet and Sonia Ben Mokhtar
Université de Lyon, CNRS, INSA-Lyon, LIRIS, UMR5205, F-69621 Lyon, France

Albin Petit
Université de Lyon, CNRS, INSA-Lyon, LIRIS, UMR5205, F-69621 Lyon, France
Universität Passau, Innstrasse 43, 94032 Passau, Germany

David Coquil and Harald Kosch
Universität Passau, Innstrasse 43, 94032 Passau, Germany

Salman Hooshmand, Gregor V. Bochmann and Guy-Vincent Jourdan
University of Ottawa, 800 King Edward Avenue, K1N 6N5 Ottawa, Canada

Russell Couturier
IBM Security, Rogers St, MA 02140 Cambridge, USA

Iosif-Viorel Onut
IBM Centre for Advanced Studies, Ottawa, Canada

Gunnar Wolf
Instituto de Investigaciones Económicas, Universidad Nacional Autónoma de México, Mexico City, Mexico

Víctor González Quiroga
Facultad de Ciencias, Universidad Nacional Autónoma de México, Mexico City, Mexico

Josemar A. Caetano, Hélder S. Lima, Mateus F. Santos and Humberto T. Marques-Neto
Department of Computer Science, Pontifical Catholic University of Minas Gerais (PUC Minas), Belo Horizonte, MG, Brazil

Karima Velasquez, David Perez Abreu, Nuno Laranjeiro, Marilia Curado, Marco Vieira and Edmundo Monteiro
Department of Informatics Engineering, University of Coimbra, Polo II – Pinhal de Marrocos, 3030-290, Coimbra, Portugal

Marcio R. M. Assis, Carlos Senna, Diego F. Aranha, Luiz F. Bittencourt and Edmundo Madeira
Institute of Computing - University of Campinas, Av. Albert Einstein, 1251, Campinas - São Paulo, Brazil

Marco Brambilla and Eric Umuhoza
Politecnico di Milano. Dipartimento di Elettronica, Informazione e Bioingegneria, Piazza L. Da Vinci 32, 20133 Milan, Italy

Roberto Acerbis
WebRatio s.r.l, Piazzale Cadorna, 10, 20123 Milan, Italy

Alexandre Lucchesi, André C. Drummond and George Teodoro
Department of Computer Science, University of Brasília, Brasília, Brazil

V. Kulathumani and M. Nakagawa
Department of Computer Science and Electrical Engineering, West Virginia University, Morgantown WV 26505, USA

A. Arora
The Samraksh Company, Dublin OH 43017, USA.

Daniel Woods, Ioannis Agrafiotis, Jason R. C. Nurse and Sadie Creese
Department of Computer Science, University of Oxford, Oxford, UK

Vincent Reniers, Ansar Rafique, Dimitri Van Landuyt and Wouter Joosen
Department of Computer Science, KU Leuven, Celestijnenlaan 200A, B-3001 Heverlee, Belgium

Elias P. Duarte Jr.
Department Informatics, Federal University of Parana, UFPR, Curitiba, Brazil

Rogério C. Turchetti
Department Informatics, Federal University of Parana, UFPR, Curitiba, Brazil
CTISM, Federal University of Santa Maria, UFSM, Santa Maria, Brazil

Luciana Arantes and Pierre Sens
Sorbonne Université, UPMC Univ. Paris 06, CNRS, Inria, LIP6, Paris, France

Gowri Sankar Ramachandran, Wilfried Daniels, Christophe Huygens, Wouter Joosen and Danny Hughes
iMinds-DistriNet, KU Leuven, 3001 Leuven, Belgium

José Proença
iMinds-DistriNet, KU Leuven, 3001 Leuven, Belgium
HASLab/INESC TEC, Universidade do Minho,Braga, Portugal

Mario Pickavet and Dimitri Staessens
iMinds-IBCN, Ghent University, 9000 Gent, Belgium

Pedro G. M. R. Alves and Diego F. Aranha
Institute of Computing, University of Campinas, Albert Einstein Ave. 1251, 13083-852 Campinas/ SP, Brazil

Antonio Bucchiarone, Annapaola Marconi, Marco Pistore and Heorhi Raik
Fondazione Bruno Kessler, Via Sommarive, 18, 38123 Trento, Italy

Index

Printed in the USA
CPSIA information can be obtained
at www.ICGtesting.com
JSHW051423221024
72173JS00006B/1394